What's New in This Edition

Over the last few years Java has been maturing and evolving into the latest Java release, 1.1—a much more robust programming language. This edition of the *Java Developer's Guide* has been updated to match this new release and show you the new maturity and capability of the language.

As well as reorganizing the material in the text to make it easier to understand, we have added some informational chapters to help you understand the Java paradigm by tying together some of the less obvious concepts. We also have added additional technical chapters, specifically coverage of the remote invocation package, the SQL package, printing, security, and many other new concepts.

When studying the trends in Java development, we found that the future of Java is dependent upon database architecture and the implementation of distributed applications. For this reason, we added two new sections with multiple chapters to help you understand these most important features in Java. At the same time we know that without enhanced security, any application is doomed; therefore, we've added coverage of the new security features of Java 1.1 also.

Although you'll see other new topics covered in the book, don't skip over Java's latest component technology. We've provided an in-depth coverage of JavaBeans and what it means to the application environment.

JAVA 1.1

Developer's Guide
Second Edition

Jamie Jaworski

201 West 103rd Street
Indianapolis, Indiana 46290

This book is dedicated to my parents, Stanley and Gloria.

President, Sams.net Publishing	*Richard K. Swadley*
Publishing Manager	*Greg Wiegand*
Director of Editorial Services	*Cindy Morrow*
Managing Editor	*Kitty Wilson Jarrett*
Director of Marketing	*Kelli Spencer*
Product Marketing Managers	*Wendy Gilbride*
	Kim Margolius
Associate Product Marketing Manager	*Jennifer Pock*
Marketing Coordinator	*Linda Beckwith*

Acquisitions Editor
Christopher Denny

Development Editor
Anthony Amico

Software Development Specialist
Brad Myers

Production Editor
Colleen Williams

Indexer
Christine Nelsen

Technical Reviewer
Craig Olague
Jeff Perkins

Editorial Coordinators
Mandie Rowell
Katie Wise

Technical Edit Coordinator
Lynette Quinn

Editorial Assistants
Carol Ackerman
Andi Richter
Rhonda Tinch-Mize
Karen Williams

Cover Designer
Alyssa Yesh

Book Designer
Anne Jones

Copy Writer
David Reichwein

Production Team Supervisors
Brad Chinn
Charlotte Clapp

Production
Mona Brown
Jeanne Clark
Jennifer Dierdorff
Lana Dominguez
Brad Lenser
Becky Stutzman

Overview

Contents

X Appendixes

Acknowledgments

I'd like to thank everyone who helped to see this book to completion. In particular, I'd like to thank George Stones for introducing me to Java and Margot Maley for making the book possible. I'd also like to thank Jeff Perkins and Craig Olague for their numerous suggestions that improved the book's overall technical quality. Special thanks go to Chris Denny, Tony Amico, and Colleen Williams of Sams.net for their great support. Finally, I'd like to thank Jason, Emily, and Lisa for their patience, love, and understanding.

About the Author

Jamie Jaworski develops advanced systems for the United States Department of Defense. He has used Java in several research and development projects, including a terrain analysis program and a genetic algorithm demonstration. He is also the author of *Mastering JavaScript* and *Do-It-Yourself Web Publishing with HoTMetaL*.

Tell Us What You Think!

As a reader, you are the most important critic and commentator of our books. We value your opinion and want to know what we're doing right, what we could do better, what areas you'd like to see us publish in, and any other words of wisdom you're willing to pass our way. You can help us make strong books that meet your needs and give you the computer guidance you require.

Do you have access to CompuServe or the World Wide Web? Then check out our CompuServe forum by typing `GO SAMS` at any prompt. If you prefer the World Wide Web, check out our site at `http://www.mcp.com`.

> **NOTE**
>
> If you have a technical question about this book, call the technical support line at 317-581-4669.

As the team leader of the group that created this book, I welcome your comments. You can fax, e-mail, or write me directly to let me know what you did or didn't like about this book—as well as what we can do to make our books stronger. Here's the information:

FAX: 317-581-4669

E-mail: `programming_mgr@sams.mcp.com`

Mail: Greg Wiegand
          Comments Department
          Sams.net Publishing
          201 W. 103rd Street
          Indianapolis, IN 46290

Introduction

Never before has a new programming language received so much attention and become so popular so quickly. In less than a year, Java evolved from experimental Alpha and Beta versions to its initial release. Along the way, it took the Web by storm and became its adopted programming language. The Java phenomenon has captivated the imaginations of Web programmers and content developers and is leading the way toward the next era of Internet application development.

Java's appeal lies in its simplicity, its familiarity, and the careful selection of programming features that it includes and excludes. Java was not designed by a government committee or by a clique of academics. It shares the spirit of its birth with C more than any syntactical similarities. It is a programming language that was designed by programmers for programmers.

This book shows you how to program in Java. It covers all the details of the Java language and the JDK 1.1 API. It provides you with plenty of programming examples, and most importantly, arms you with the mindset needed to write Java code in a manner that is simple, efficient, and true to the nature of the language.

Who Should Read This Book

If you want someone to teach you how to program in Java, this book is for you. You will learn how to develop both standalone Java programs and Java applets. You will learn how to program window GUI controls, work with TCP/IP sockets, use remote method invocation, develop JavaBeans, and connect to databases using JDBC. You will learn to develop object-oriented programs and explore the breadth and depth of the Java application program interface. If you want to become a Java programmer, this book will show you how.

This book is for programmers and those who aspire to become Java programmers. It consists of 60 chapters that are filled with programming examples. If you have written programs in other languages, you will have the necessary background to understand the material presented in this book. If you have programmed in C or C++, you will be able to quickly get up to speed with Java because its syntax is based on these languages. If you have never programmed before, you will have a difficult time using this book because it assumes familiarity with basic programming concepts such as variables, types, statements, and expressions. I suggest that you pick up an introductory programming book to help you learn this material.

Conventions Used in This Book

This book uses certain conventions that make it easier for you to use.

A `monospaced font` is used to identify program code. Anything that you type when using Java is displayed using a **`bold monospaced font`**. An *`italic monospaced font`* is used to identify placeholders used in Java syntax descriptions.

> **NOTE**
>
> Notes like this are used to call your attention to information that is important to understanding and using Java.

> **TIP**
>
> Tips like this are used to identify ways that you can use Java more efficiently or to take advantage of undocumented features in the Java Development Kit or Java-enabled browsers.

> **WARNING**
>
> Warnings like this are used to help you to avoid common problems encountered when using Java and to keep you clear of potential programming difficulties.

In order to help you understand where you are going and where you have been, each chapter begins with a short description of the information that will be presented and ends with a summary of the material that has been covered.

Getting Started

To use this book, you'll need a computer and operating system that support version 1.1 of the Java Development Kit. There are a wide variety of operating systems that support the JDK 1.1, including Windows 95, Windows NT, Linux, and Solaris. Ports of the JDK 1.1 to the Macintosh OS, OS/2, and other varieties of UNIX are also in the works. This book focuses on using Java under Windows 95, but all of the book's examples also run under other JDK 1.1 implementations.

To effectively use Java with Windows 95, you will need the following:

- A personal computer that is capable of running Windows 95
- At least 8MB of RAM
- At least 20MB of available hard disk space
- A VGA monitor
- A mouse

To effectively use this book, you will need access to a compact disk drive so that you can copy files from the enclosed CD. In addition, an Internet connection will be required to complete some of the networking examples, and a JDK 1.1–compatible browser, such as HotJava, will be needed to work with Java applets. A sound card and speakers will be needed to use audio-playing applets.

You can get started if you are able to run Windows 95 and have access to the Web. Chapter 2, "Java Overview," shows you how to obtain the Java Development Kit from JavaSoft's Web site. You can add additional hardware, as necessary, to complete the programming examples of each chapter.

The best way to use this book is to start with Chapter 1, "The Java Phenomenon," and proceed through each chapter, in succession, working through each programming example that is presented. You will learn to program in Java by compiling, running, analyzing, and understanding the sample programs. Additional hands-on learning can be acquired by tinkering with the sample programs, modifying them, and augmenting their capabilities.

I

Introduction to Java

1

The Java Phenomenon

In its brief existence, the World Wide Web has evolved into a truly global information space. Not only does it offer information on any subject, it provides its citizens with the power to globally publish information on any subject and at minimal cost. The massive international participation in the Web has resulted in the creation of many Web pages that are not only informative, but also entertaining. This entertainment value has further fueled the Web's growth and has led to browsing becoming an international pastime.

Browsing involves scanning Web pages for interesting information, following useful links to other pages, and repeating the process until we come across something that makes us temporarily stop and focus. Sometimes we mutter, "Hmm" or "That's interesting!" and create a bookmark. Then, eventually, we move on.

The tendency to move on and continue browsing is natural. We usually don't read the same book over and over. If we have a stack of magazines in front of us, we're likely to flip through them all. Web pages are like magazine pages, except that they are more available, usually free, and have more "next" pages to which to turn.

Computer programs are different. They are active, while books, magazines, and Web pages are static or passive. People do use programs over and over. I still use WordPerfect 5.1. Some people still use CP/M. I have a friend who played DOOM several hours a day for months.

This difference between active computer programs and passive Web pages is what makes Java an attractive addition to the Web. When we click on a Web page containing a Java applet, we don't just read it, listen to it, or watch it—we *interact* with it. Interactivity is the difference between a program and a page, and Java has brought dynamic, interactive content to the Web.

Java's rapidly growing popularity is due to the Web. But Java's inherent power does not come from the fact that it is a Web programming language. The talented software engineers at Sun, in bringing Java to the Web, have elegantly solved a much broader and more significant problem—how to develop network-capable windowing software that will run on almost any 32-bit computer and operating system.

The modern software developer faces enormous headaches and challenges when he tries to develop software that is portable to Microsoft Windows, X Window systems, Motif, MacOS, and OS/2 windowing and networking environments. The usual approach is to pick a target operating system (OS), write software for that OS, and eventually migrate it to the other OS platforms. This usually involves great expense in terms of labor and software development resources. It also results in the sacrifice of features that are difficult to support across multiple OS platforms.

Java fulfills the software developer's dream of being able to write software in a single language that will support windowing and networking on all major OS platforms, without specialized tailoring *or even recompilation.* But Java's attractiveness does not end here. Sun's engineers were thoughtful enough to develop in Java a language and runtime system that are simple, compact, object-oriented, extendible, and secure. And then they gave it away for free!

The objective of this book is to provide an introduction to using the gift of Java in its broader context—as a platform-independent software development language. Java's capabilities to provide interactive content to Web pages, in the form of applets, is covered within this broader context, but these capabilities do not limit the focus of the book's presentation.

What Is Java?

Forrest Gump might say that Java is as Java does. Java is a programming language, a runtime system, a set of development tools, and an application programming interface (API). The relationships between these elements are depicted in Figure 1.1.

FIGURE 1.1.
Java unveiled.

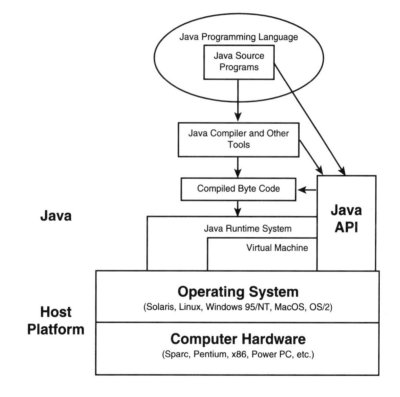

As illustrated in Figure 1.1, a software developer writes programs in the Java language that use predefined software packages of the Java API. The developer compiles his or her programs using the Java compiler. This results in what is known as compiled byte code. *Byte code* is in a form that can be executed on the Java virtual machine, the core of the Java runtime system. You can think of the virtual machine as a microprocessor that is implemented in software and runs using the capabilities provided by your operating system and computer hardware. Because the Java virtual machine is not a real microprocessor, the Java byte code is interpreted, rather than executed directly in the native machine instructions of the host computer. (Just-in-time compilers translate Java byte code into machine code on-the-fly.) The Java runtime system consists of the virtual machine plus additional software, such as dynamic link libraries, that are needed to implement the Java API on your operating system and hardware.

The Java API contains predefined software packages with numerous platform-independent "hooks" into the native windowing and networking capabilities of the host operating system. The Java API provides a single common API across all operating systems to which Java is ported.

The keys to Java's portability are its runtime system and its API. The runtime system is very compact, evolving from earlier Sun efforts to build a software platform for consumer electronics. Because this platform was not designed around any existing microprocessor, it was built from scratch to be simple and efficient. The fact that it was not tied to a given hardware architecture enabled it to be architecture neutral. The simple, efficient, compact, and architecture-neutral nature of the runtime system allows it to be highly portable and still provide effective performance.

The powerful windowing and networking features included in the Java API make it easier for programmers to develop software that is both attractive and platform independent. For example, Ada is a programming language that is highly standardized and supported on most operating systems. Yet Ada applications are not very portable. This is because Ada does not come with a common API that supports windowing and networking on all platforms. Java differs from Ada and all other programming languages in that there is one universal, but powerful, Java API for all operating system platforms. That is why Java is the most portable language.

The Origin of Java

At this point, you may wonder how Sun's engineers were able to develop such a powerful software development environment and surpass all known programming languages. The answer is they didn't—at least not directly. Java evolved from other research projects at Sun.

The development of Java wasn't as accidental or monumental as the discovery of penicillin, but it shares some of its characteristics. The origins of Java trace back to 1991, when Sun was investigating consumer electronics products. At this time, Mosaic and the World Wide Web were just interesting concepts.

James Gosling, the father of Java, was intent on building a low-cost, hardware-independent software platform using C++. For a number of technical reasons, C++ was dropped, and a new language, called Oak, was developed, based on C++, but eliminating its shortcomings. These shortcomings include problems associated with multiple inheritance, automatic type conversion, the use of pointers, and memory management.

Oak was used to develop a small electronics device called *7. This project resulted in the precursors of many of the components of Java: the development environment, runtime system, and API. The technology was explored in a number of consumer applications, but was a little ahead of its time.

By 1994 the Web emerged, Oak was renamed Java, and the proverbial lightbulb went on in the minds of the Java developers. Java was used by Sun as the basis for a Web browser called WebRunner. WebRunner was successfully demonstrated and led to the development of HotJava.

HotJava, Java, and the Java documentation and source code were made available over the Web, as an alpha version, in early 1995. Initially, Java was hosted on SPARC Solaris and then on Windows NT. In the summer of 1995, Java was ported to Windows 95 and Linux. In the fall of 1995, the Java Beta 1 version was released through Sun's Web site, and Java support was introduced in the Netscape Navigator 2.0 browser.

The Java Beta 1 release led scores of vendors to license Java technology, and Java porting efforts were initiated for all major operating systems.

In December 1995 the Java Beta 2 version was released, and JavaScript was announced by Sun and Netscape. Java's success became inevitable when, in early December, both Microsoft and IBM announced their intention to license Java technology.

On January 23, 1996, Java 1.0 was officially released and made available for download over the Internet. During 1996, Java 1.01 and Java 1.02 were released to correct security flaws and some minor bugs. Netscape and Microsoft Internet Explorer supported Java in both their browsers and Web servers.

Later in 1996, the Java 1.1 beta versions began to appear. Java 1.1 introduced minor changes to the language syntax, but added incredible capabilities to the Java API. These capabilities include support for remote method invocation, database connectivity, cryptographic security, signed applets, JavaBeans, and much more!

Java 1.1 was officially released in March 1997.

Why Program in Java?

So far we have only touched on two reasons to program in Java—it is platform independent and it supports interactive content on Web pages. Does this mean that Java is for everybody? Certainly not!

If you are developing highly complex, performance-critical number crunching algorithms for a Cray computer, Java is probably not the language for you. Try FORTRAN. If you are developing patches to legacy code from the 1970s, you might use COBOL. If you are developing software for the U.S. Department of Defense, you should probably use Ada.

So, for what types of software applications is Java well suited? The answer is almost everything else. Figure 1.2 summarizes the types of applications at which Java excels.

FIGURE 1.2.
Where Java excels.

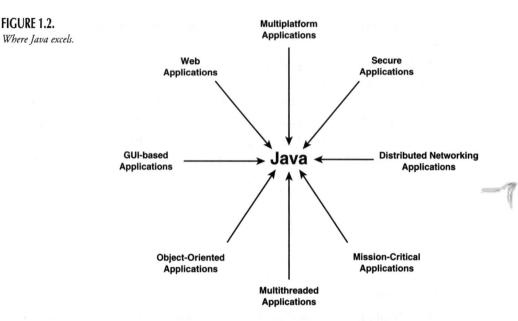

Because of its intended use on the Web, where even the smallest security vulnerability could potentially be exploited and cause global mayhem, Java was designed with multiple layers of security countermeasures embedded in the compiler, runtime system, and in browsers that support Java, known as Java-enabled browsers. These countermeasures make Java inherently more secure for developing any type of trusted application software. See Chapter 60, "Java Security," for more information.

Java is exceptionally well suited to distributed networking applications because of its built-in networking support and the runtime system's capability to dynamically load Java byte code across the network. Java also provides the capability to dynamically utilize new content-handling and protocol-handling software. The HotJava browser, written in Java, is an excellent example of these capabilities. Java's support for remote method invocation and remote database connectivity makes it the leading choice for developing distributed applications.

Java is a sound choice for developing software where reliability is of utmost concern, such as mission-critical applications. Java's object-oriented nature combined with numerous, compile-time and runtime integrity checks eliminate many difficult to find programming errors. The Java language has removed many of the dangerous programming capabilities, such as modifiable pointers, unchecked type conversion, and relaxed bounds checking, that are commonly found in other programming languages, such as C and C++.

The Java API provides full support of multithreaded programming. Multithreaded programs can be developed in a single, consistent manner, independent of the vagaries of the host operating system interface.

Java classes and objects directly support the object-oriented concepts of encapsulation, inheritance, messages and methods, and data hiding. Java interfaces provide support for multiple inheritance and polymorphism. The Java language retains all the benefits of object-oriented programming without the performance impacts associated with pure object languages, such as SmallTalk.

The Java API provides extensive support of windowing and graphical user interface development without the complexities associated with maintaining multiple window class libraries. Several visual programming tools have been developed for Java. Chapter 57, "Java Development Tools," describes some of these tools.

Java and HotJava

My first experience with Java was through an early version of HotJava. Java and HotJava are sometimes confused. Java is the language, development and runtime environments, and API. HotJava is a Web browser that is written in Java. HotJava highlights many of the Java features mentioned in the previous section.

HotJava is a Java-enabled browser. This means that HotJava can execute Java applets contained on Web pages. In order to accomplish this, HotJava calls the Java runtime system. The latest versions of Netscape Navigator and Microsoft Internet Explorer browsers, like HotJava, are also Java-enabled. They contain a copy of the Java runtime system embedded within them. Figure 1.3 illustrates the operation of HotJava and other Java-enabled browsers.

FIGURE 1.3.
How HotJava and Netscape Navigator support Java applets.

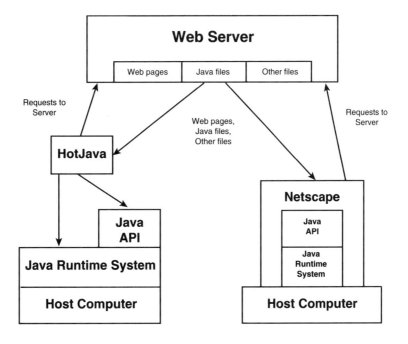

Both HotJava and Navigator request Web pages, written in HTML, from Web servers on the Internet. Because HotJava is written in Java, it uses the Java API and runtime system to display the Web pages to a user. Netscape, on the other hand, is written in C++ and uses C++ functions to display HTML documents.

When either browser encounters an APPLET tag in an HTML file, it requests the Java byte code file necessary to execute the Applet from the Web server. HotJava loads and executes the byte code file using the Java runtime system. Netscape executes the byte code file using an embedded version of the Java runtime system.

Summary

This chapter provides a brief description of Java's capabilities. It explains what Java is and why you should be interested in learning to use Java. It also summarizes the history of Java's development. In the next chapter, you will receive a more detailed overview of the Java language, development kit, and application programming interface.

2

Java Overview

This chapter lays the foundation for learning Java. It provides an overview of the Java Developer's Kit (JDK), the Java language, and the Java API from the perspective of a software developer.

You will download and install the JDK, and take a quick tour of its contents. You will then learn the features of the Java language that set it apart from its predecessors, C++ and C. You will be introduced to the Java API and learn how Java programs are built from and extend the API. So grab yourself a cup of you-know-what and let's begin.

Getting the JDK

Java is distributed as the JDK. It is available from Sun's Java home page at `http://java.sun.com` or `http://www.javasoft.com`. Figure 2.1 shows the Java home page at the time of this writing. From there, you can click on the Products and Services link to download a version of the JDK for your computer and operating system.

FIGURE 2.1.

The Java home page.

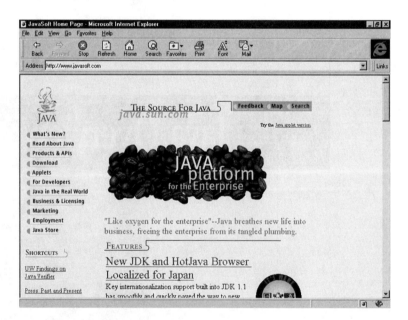

Figures 2.2 and 2.3 show some of the pages you are likely to encounter on the way to finding the JDK that is right for you. Sun makes earlier versions of the software available for download. Always download the latest version that is compatible with your hardware and operating system. The examples in this book use JDK 1.1.1. As long as you are using JDK 1.1, or later, you will be able to work through these examples. I will be running Java under Windows 95. If you are using another operating system, follow the installation instructions for that operating system.

FIGURE 2.2.

JavaSoft products and services.

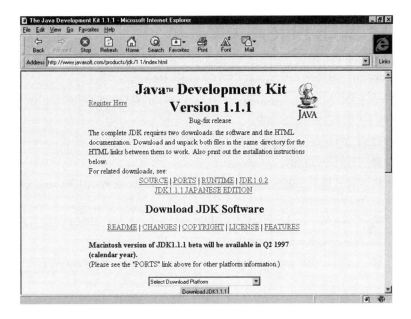

FIGURE 2.3.

The binary code license.

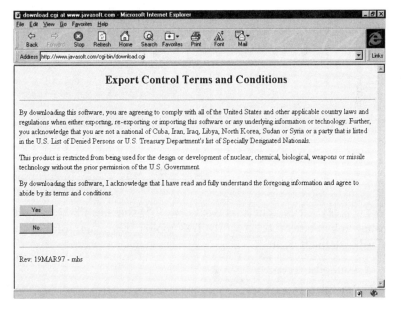

The JDK 1.1 for Windows 95/NT is distributed as a self-extracting, self-installing executable file. Move it to a temporary directory and then execute it. It will extract itself and set up its directory structure. I am using the JDK version 1.1.1. It is installed in the `c:\jdk1.1.1` directory. This is the default directory where the JDK is installed. I urge you to use the same directory in order to make it easier to follow the examples in this book.

A Quick Tour of the JDK

Now that you have the latest version of the JDK installed on your computer, you're probably wondering what's inside. Let's take a quick look.

Figure 2.4 shows the contents of the c:\jdk1.1.1 directory. It consists of four subdirectories and six files, which include

■ The Java copyright

■ The Java license agreement

■ An HTML file that contains information about your JDK and links to online documentation

■ A Readme file that provides additional information about your JDK release

■ A list of changes since the last JDK release

■ A zipped file containing the java source code for the Java API library files

FIGURE 2.4.

The c:\jdk1.1.1
directory.

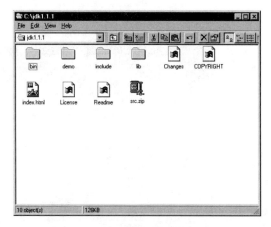

The c:\jdk1.1.1\bin directory (see Figure 2.5) contains all the executable programs and dynamic link libraries (DLLs) for the JDK toolset. The major software development tools provided with the JDK are

■ Compiler (javac)

■ Interpreter (java)

■ Debugger (jdb)

■ Disassembler (javap)

■ Documentation tool (javadoc)

■ Applet viewer (appletviewer)

■ C Header file tool (javah)

- Remote method invocation tools (`rmic`, `rmiregistry`, and `serialver`)
- Unicode converter (`native2ascii`)
- Archiver (`jar`)
- Digital signature tool (`javakey`)

We're going to examine these tools in Chapter 3, "Using the Java Development Kit." If you absolutely can't wait to get your hands on Java, go ahead to Chapter 3, but make sure you come back and browse through the rest of this overview.

FIGURE 2.5.

The Java toolset.

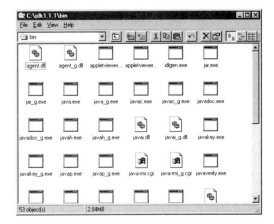

The `c:\jdk1.1.1\demo` directory, shown in Figure 2.6, contains lots of nifty demos that highlight Java's finer features. I'll show you how to run these demos in Chapter 3. If you can't control the urge to run some of the demos now, click on the HTML files in the demo folders. Be sure to use a Java-enabled browser, such as HotJava.

FIGURE 2.6.

Java demos.

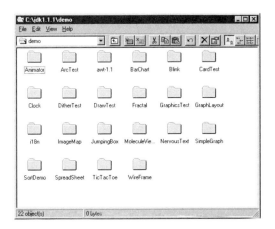

The c:\jdk1.1.1\include directory (see Figure 2.7) contains C header files that are used to write C programs, called native methods, that extend the Java API. We won't be getting involved with native methods until Chapter 59, "Creating Native Methods."

FIGURE 2.7.

*C header files for
writing native methods.*

Finally, the c:\jdk1.1.1\lib directory, shown in Figure 2.8, contains the class library files for the Java API. The file classes.zip contains all the compiled library files. The Java compiler and interpreter are able to work with the library files, in compressed form, which saves you some disk space and provides more efficient operation.

FIGURE 2.8.

Class library files.

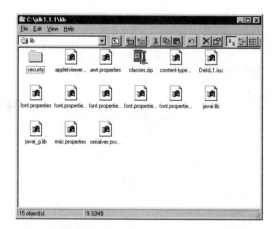

Now that you know a little bit about what's inside the JDK, let's quickly cover the Java language and application programming interface so we can get started using the JDK tools.

The Java Language

The Java language is a remarkable example of programming language evolution. Java builds on the familiar and useful features of C++ while removing its complex, dangerous, and superfluous elements. The result is a language that is safer, simpler, and easier to use. The following subsections describe Java in contrast to C++. Appendix A, "Differences Between Java and C++," provides a detailed identification of the differences between the two languages.

Java Is Familiar and Simple

If you have ever programmed in C++, you will find Java's appeal to be instantaneous. Because Java's syntax mirrors that of C++, you will be able to write Java programs within minutes. Your first programs will come quickly and easily, with a lot less programming overhead.

You will have the feeling that you have eliminated a lot of clutter from your programs—and you will have. All the cryptic header files and preprocessor statements of C and C++ are gone. All the arcane #define statements and typedefs have been taken away. You will no longer have to delve through several levels of header files to correctly reference API calls. And no one will have to suffer to figure out how to use your software.

Java programs simply import the software packages they need. These packages may be in another directory, on another drive, or on a machine on the other side of the Internet. The Java compiler and interpreter figure out what objects are referenced and supply the necessary linkage.

Java Is Object-Oriented

If you think C++ is an object-oriented programming language, you are in for a big surprise. After using Java to write a few programs, you'll get a better feeling for what object-oriented software is all about. I know I did.

Java deals with classes and objects, pure and simple. They aren't just more data structures that are available to the programmer—they are the basis for the entire programming language.

In C++, you can declare a class, but you don't have to. You can declare a structure or a union instead. You can declare a whole bunch of loosely associated variables and use them with C-style functions. In Java, classes and objects are at the center of the language. Everything else revolves around them. You can't declare functions and procedures. They don't exist. You can't use structures, unions, or typedefs. They're gone, too. You either use classes and objects or you don't use Java. It's that simple.

Java provides all the luxuries of object-oriented programming: class hierarchy, inheritance, encapsulation, and polymorphism—in a context that is truly useful and efficient. If you are new to object-oriented software, a complete introduction to these topics is in Chapter 5, "Classes and Objects." The main reason for developing object-oriented software, beside clarity and simplicity, is the desperate hope that somehow the objects you develop will be reused. Java not only encourages software reuse, it demands it. To write any sort of Java program, no matter how simple, you must build on the classes and methods of the Java API.

Once you have begun developing software in Java, you have two choices:

■ Build on the classes that you have developed, thereby reusing them.

■ Rewrite your software from scratch, copying and tailoring useful parts of existing software.

With Java, the temptation to start from scratch is no longer appealing. Java's object-oriented structure forces you to develop more useful, more tailorable, and much simpler software the first time around.

Java Is Safer and More Reliable

Java is safer to use than C++ because it keeps you from doing the things that you do badly, while making it easier to do the things that you do well.

Java won't automatically convert data types. You have to explicitly convert from one class to another. C++, under the most undesirable conditions, will automatically convert one type to another. It has all the flexibility of assembly code. Java doesn't assume that you know what you are doing. It makes sure that you do.

Pointers don't exist in Java. You can no longer access objects indirectly or by chance. You don't need to. You declare objects and reference those objects directly. Complex pointer arithmetic is avoided. If you need an indexed set of objects, you can use an array of objects. The concept of "the address of an object" is eliminated from the programming model, and another assembly language dinosaur is laid to rest. As a result, it becomes much easier to do things correctly in Java.

Java's reliability extends beyond the language level to the compiler and the runtime system. Compile-time checks identify many programming errors that go undetected in other programming languages. These checks go beyond syntactic checking to ensure that statements are semantically correct.

Runtime checks are also more extensive and effective. Remember your teacher or mom telling you to "Check your work twice to make sure it's right"? The Java linker understands class types and performs compiler-level type checking, adding redundancy to reliability. It also performs bounds checking and eliminates indirect object access, even under error conditions.

Java Is Secure

If you gave a skilled hacker a program written in C or C++ and told him to find any security flaws, there are half a dozen things that he would immediately look for: gaining access to the operating system, causing an unexpected return of control, overwriting critical memory areas, acquiring the ability to spoof or modify other programs, browsing for security information, and gaining unauthorized access to the file system.

Why is C or C++ more vulnerable? When a programmer develops software, he or she usually focuses on how to get the software to work correctly and efficiently. C and C++ do not constrain the programmer from meeting these goals and provide a number of flexible features that enable the programmer to meet his end. The hacker is also able to take advantage of these features and use them in ways that weren't originally intended, causing the undesirable consequences identified in the previous paragraph. In short, C and C++ provide a great offense, but no defense. Java, on the other hand, is defensive by nature. Every time a Java-enabled browser downloads a compiled Java class, such as an applet, it runs the risk of running Trojan horse code. Because of this ever-present threat, it subjects the code to a series of checks that ensure that it is correct and secure.

The Java runtime system is designed to enforce a security policy that prevents execution of malicious code. It does this by remembering how objects are stored in memory and enforcing correct and secure access to those objects according to its security rules. It performs byte code verification by passing compiled classes through a simple theorem prover that either proves that the code is secure or prevents the code from being loaded and executed. The class is Java's basic execution unit, and security is implemented at the class level.

The Java runtime system also segregates software according to its origin. Classes from the local system are processed separately from those of other systems. This prevents remote systems from replacing local system software with code that is less trustworthy.

Java-enabled browsers, such as HotJava, allow the user to control the accesses that Java software may make of the local system. When a Java applet needs permission to access local resources, such as files, a security dialog box is presented to the user, requesting explicit user permission. This "Mother may I" approach ensures that the user always has the final say in the security of his system.

Java security is covered in detail in Chapter 60, "Java Security."

Java Is Multithreaded

Java, like Ada, and unlike other languages, provides built-in language support for multithreading. Multithreading allows more than one thread of execution to take place within a single program. This allows your program to do many things at once: make the Duke dance, play his favorite tune, and interact with the user, seemingly all at the same time. Multithreading is an important asset because it allows the programmer to write programs as independent threads, rather than as a convoluted gaggle of intertwined activities. Multithreading also allows Java to use idle CPU time to perform necessary garbage collection and general system maintenance, enabling these functions to be performed with less impact on program performance.

Writing multithreaded programs is like dating several people concurrently. Everything works fine until the threads start to interact with each other in unexpected ways. Java provides the support necessary to make multithreading work safely and correctly. Java supports multithreading by providing synchronization capabilities that ensure that threads share information and execution time in a way that is *thread safe*. These capabilities are illustrated with several programming examples in Chapter 8, "Multithreading."

Java Is Interpreted and Portable

While it is true that compiled code will almost always run more quickly than interpreted code, it is also true that interpreted code can usually be developed and fielded more inexpensively, more quickly, and in a more flexible manner. It is also usually much more portable.

Java, in order to be a truly platform-independent programming language, must be interpreted. It does not run as fast as compiled native code, but it doesn't run much slower, either. For the cases where execution in native machine code is absolutely essential, just-in-time compilers translate Java byte code into machine code as it is loaded.

The advantages of being interpreted outweigh any performance impacts. Because Java is interpreted, it is much more portable. If an operating system can run the Java interpreter and support the Java API, it can faithfully run all Java programs.

Interpreted programs are much more easily kept up-to-date. You don't have to recompile them for every change. In Java, recompilation is automatic. The interpreter detects the fact that a program's byte code file is out-of-date with respect to its source code file and recompiles it as it is loaded.

Because of its interpreted nature, linking is also more powerful and flexible. Java's runtime system supports dynamic linking between local class files and those that are downloaded from across the Internet. This feature provides the basis for Web programming.

Java Is the Programming Language of the Web

Java has become the de facto programming language of the Web. It has been licensed by nearly every major software company. It has some offshoots and potential competition, such as JavaScript, ActiveX, and Lucent Technology's Inferno, but it remains the first Web programming language and the most powerful language for developing platform-independent software.

Java is also evolving beyond the Web and becoming a key component in distributed application development. Sun's release of the NEO and JOE products emphasizes Java's importance to distributed object-based software development. Several other vendors have introduced products that enable Java to be integrated into the Common Object Request Broker Architecture (CORBA), which is the framework for distributed object communication. The JDK 1.1 provides capabilities, such as remote method invocation and database connectivity, which form the basis for the development of distributed applications.

The Java API

The Java API is what makes Java attractive and useful. It consists of a set of packages that is distributed with the JDK as class libraries. These packages provide a common interface for developing Java programs on all Java platforms. The Java API furnishes all the capabilities needed to develop console programs, window programs, client and server networking software, applets, and distributed applications. It is the difference that takes Java from being a really good programming language to making it a very powerful and efficient programming environment.

The Java API consists of 12 major development packages, a supporting debug package (sun.tools.debug), and two packages that support JDK 1.02 JavaBeans compatibility (sunw.io and sunw.util), as shown in Figure 2.9. *Packages* are collections of related classes and interfaces. For example, there are separate packages for developing window programs, applets, and networking software.

FIGURE 2.9.
The organization of the Java API.

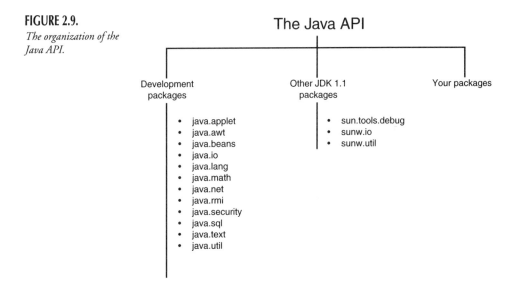

Java packages contain classes, interfaces, and exceptions, as illustrated in Figure 2.10.

Classes form the basis for object-oriented software development in Java. They declare variables and methods. Variables are data containers. Methods implement operations on the class and its variables. For example, there is a class in the java.awt package called Rectangle. It consists of variables that specify the position and dimensions of a rectangle, and methods, such as setLocation() and setSize(), that enable operations to be performed on rectangles. Chapter 5 provides an introduction to classes.

FIGURE 2.10.

How Java packages are organized.

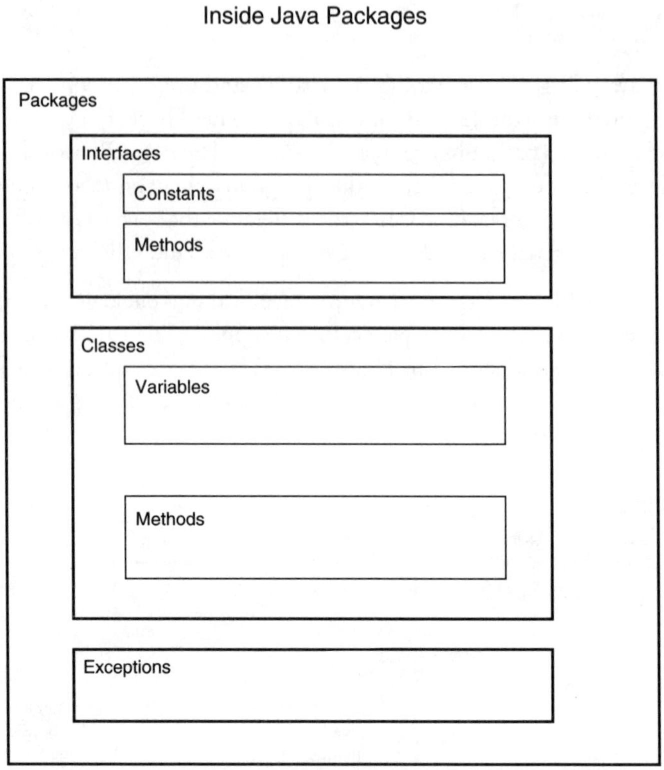

Inside Java Packages

> **NOTE**
>
> Variables are also referred to as *field variables* or *fields*.

Interfaces are collections of related constants and methods. An example of an interface is the DataInput interface of the java.io package. It specifies a collection of methods that must be defined for a class to implement the DataInput interface. Exceptions are events that alter the normal course of program execution. Chapter 6, "Interfaces," introduces interfaces, and Chapter 7, "Exceptions," covers exceptions.

The Java API is used to develop Java programs. Figure 2.11 summarizes this process.

You write your Java programs using the Java API as a template and building block. You use the API to construct objects that are instances of API classes, implement API interfaces, and respond to API exceptions. These objects are used by your application program, which is itself an instance of a Java API class. Think of your program as a collection of objects that work together to support a common set of operations.

FIGURE 2.11.
*Developing software
using the Java API.*

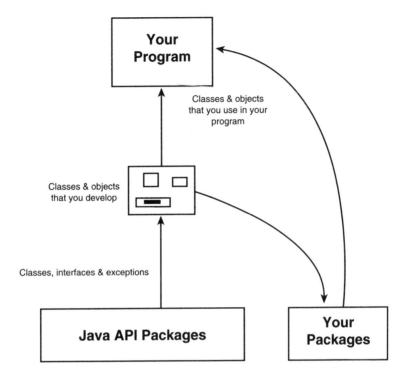

You can also create your own classes, interfaces, and exceptions, building on those that are defined in the API. You can collect them into custom packages that are integrated within and extend the Java API. These API extensions can then be used to develop other programs or even more sophisticated packages and API extensions.

This building-block approach to software development is the essence of object-oriented programming and software reuse. The Java API supports platform-independent software reuse by providing a powerful set of components from which to start.

Summary

In order to learn Java, you have to learn the Java language, learn to use the Java API, and learn how to use the JDK toolset. In this chapter, you have explored the JDK software and learned the tools it contains. The following chapter will show you how to operate those tools.

This chapter highlights the key features of the Java language. In Part II, "Programming in Java," you will focus on learning Java's syntax and application by developing a series of sample programs. These programs will also familiarize you with using the JDK tools and relevant parts of the Java API.

You have been introduced to the Java API and shown how it is used to construct Java programs. Part III, "Using the Java API," focuses on learning the Java API. You will do this by studying the components contained in the API packages and using these components to build Java programs.

By the time you have finished Part III, you will be a competent Java programmer. The rest of the book shows you how to extend your skills by focusing on specific areas of Java software development.

3

Using the Java Development Kit

This chapter provides an introduction to the software development tools contained in the Java Development Kit (JDK). It explains what each tool does and how it is used with the other tools in the toolkit, and shows you how to operate each tool and work with its command-line options.

This chapter has a dual purpose—it serves both as an initial introduction to the JDK and as a JDK reference manual. When reading this chapter for the first time, just try to understand how each of the JDK programs is used. Do not worry about learning all the options that are available to you. These options are illustrated via sample programs during the course of this book. Many of these options are useful only in special circumstances that you might never encounter. When you are working on later chapters, you can refer back here for a full description of the options used during the course of a programming example.

Overview

The purpose of the JDK is to provide a complete set of tools for the development, test, documentation, and execution of Java programs and applets. The JDK provides tools that support each of these activities and more. It consists of the following 13 programs:

Program Name	Description
javac	Compiler
java	Interpreter
jdb	Debugger
javap	Disassembler
appletviewer	Applet Viewer
javadoc	Documentation Generator
javah	C Header File Generator
rmic	Remote Method Invocation Stub Generator
rmiregistry	Remote Object Registry Tool
serialver	Serial Version Identification Tool
native2ascii	Unicode Converter
jar	Archiver
javakey	Digital Signature Tool

Usually, you will write Java programs by using a text editor to develop Java *source files*. These files consist of source code packages that declare Java classes and interfaces. Source files use the .java extension.

The Java compiler, javac, is used to convert the source files into files that can be executed using the Java interpreter. These files are referred to as *byte code files* and end with the .class extension.

The Java interpreter, `java`, executes classes from the byte code (`.class`) files. It verifies the integrity, correct operation, and security of each class, as it is loaded and executed, and interacts with the host operating system, windowing environment, and communication facilities to produce the desired program behavior.

The debugger, `jdb`, is like the interpreter in that it executes Java classes that have been compiled into byte code files, but it also provides special capabilities to stop program execution at selected breakpoints and display the values of class variables. These capabilities are very useful in finding programming errors.

The disassembler, `javap`, takes the byte code files and displays the classes, interfaces, variables, and methods that have been compiled into the byte codes. It also identifies the byte code instructions used to implement each method. The disassembler is a handy tool for recovering the source code design of those compiled Java classes for which no source code is available—for example, those that you would retrieve from the Web.

The applet viewer, `appletviewer`, displays Java applets contained within Web pages, located in your local file system or at accessible Web sites. It is used to test applets that you develop.

The automated documentation tool, `javadoc`, is used to convert portions of Java source files into *Hypertext Markup Language* (HTML) files. HTML is the language used to write Web pages. The HTML files generated by `javadoc` document the classes, variables, methods, interfaces, and exceptions contained in Java source files based on special comments inserted into these files.

The C header file tool, `javah`, is used to generate C-language header and source files from a Java byte code file. The files generated by `javah` are used to develop *native methods*—Java classes that are written in languages other than Java.

The RMI stub generator, `rmic`, generates skeleton and stub files for use with remote objects. The skeleton file contains code that is used to forward accesses to the remote object. The stub file is a local proxy for the remote object.

The RMI registry tool, `rmiregistry`, creates and starts a remote object registry on the local host using the specified port. The remote object registry associates names with remote objects.

The serial version identification tool, `serialver`, identifies the `serialVersionUID` for specified classes. The `serialVersionUID` is used to identify and access an object that has been serialized into a stream.

The Unicode converter, `native2ascii`, converts non-Unicode files to Unicode files.

The archiver tool, `jar`, compresses and archives Java byte code files for distribution over the Internet.

The digital signature tool, `javakey`, manages a database of certificates and keys, and creates/verifies digital signatures.

The Compiler

The Java compiler is used to translate Java source code files into byte code files for execution by the Java interpreter. The source code files must end with the `.java` extension. They are translated into files with the same name, but with the `.class` extension.

For example, suppose the file `test.java` is located in the `c:\myfiles\source` directory. To compile `test.java`, change directories to `c:\myfiles\source` and enter the command `javac test.java`. If your compilation is successful, `javac` will create a file named `test.class` that will contain the compiled byte codes for `test.java`. If your compile is unsuccessful, you will receive error messages that will help you to figure out what went wrong.

> ### TIP
>
> Set your PATH variable to the directory containing the JDK executable programs so your operating system shell can find them. If you installed Java as described in the previous chapter, add `c:\jdk1.1.1\bin` to your PATH.

In general, the Java compiler is executed as follows:

```
javac options java_source_files
```

Figure 3.1 illustrates the operation of the Java compiler. The compiler options are covered in the following sections. You get hands-on experience using `javac` to compile sample programs in Chapter 4, "First Programs: Hello World! to BlackJack."

FIGURE 3.1.
The operation of the Java compiler.

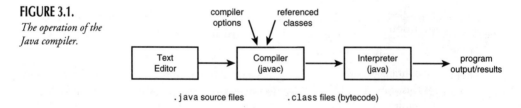

Using Classes from Other Packages

Every Java program uses classes that are defined outside of the program's source code file. Most often these *external classes* are contained in the Java API. However, you will also want to be able to reuse classes that you develop. The Java compiler must be able to locate these external classes in order to determine how to correctly compile code that references them. This section shows how the Java compiler and other programs in the JDK locate compiled classes. Understanding this information is important to using the JDK programs most effectively.

All Java declarations, such as classes, interfaces, and exceptions, are organized into logical units called *packages*. A class or interface must be identified as public to be used outside of its package. Only one public class or interface is allowed in a given source file. See Chapter 6, "Interfaces," for more information.

A compiled Java class is identified by its package name, followed by a period (.), and followed by its class name. For example, suppose you've developed and compiled a class called TestClass and it is contained in the TestAPI package. Your class would be identified by TestAPI.TestClass. The identifier, TestAPI.TestClass, is referred to as the *fully qualified* or *full name* of the class TestClass. Figure 3.2 shows how package names are combined with class names to produce full class names.

FIGURE 3.2.
How class names are formed.

The full name of a class is used to locate the class with respect to the CLASSPATH. The CLASSPATH is a system environment variable containing a list of directories where Java packages can be found. The full name is converted to a path offset by replacing any periods in the name with backslashes (\) for Windows 95/NT systems and slashes (/) for UNIX systems. This path offset is then combined with directories in the CLASSPATH to locate the byte code (.class) files containing Java classes.

> **NOTE**
>
> Windows 95 and NT use backslashes (\) to indicate and separate directories. UNIX uses slashes (/). Because this book is oriented toward Windows 95, it uses the Windows 95 convention. Any differences for UNIX systems are indicated as appropriate.

The package that contains a particular class is identified using the Java package statement. You'll learn how to use this statement in the next chapter. If no package is identified for a class, the class is put in a default package with no name. The full name for the class is then just the class name. Java assumes that the name of the byte code file containing a class is the name of the class concatenated with the .class extension, as illustrated in Figure 3.3.

Setting Your CLASSPATH

CLASSPATH tells the JDK programs where to find Java classes. You must set the CLASSPATH to identify the location of your classes. You set CLASSPATH differently depending on your operating system. For Windows 95 and Windows NT, enter

```
set CLASSPATH=path
```

at the console command line to set your CLASSPATH. A common CLASSPATH is .;c:\jdk1.1.1;c:\ jdk1.1.1\lib\classes.zip. This tells the Java compiler and other JDK tools to use the current directory (.), the c:\jdk1.1.1 directory, and the file c:\jdk1.1.1\lib\classes.zip as a base for finding Java class files. You would enter the following to set this CLASSPATH:

```
set CLASSPATH=.;c:\jdk1.1.1;c:\jdk1.1.1\lib\classes.zip
```

You can also put this statement in your AUTOEXEC.BAT file so that it will be set automatically each time you start a DOS shell. Windows NT users can use the System option in the Control Panel to set the CLASSPATH variable.

FIGURE 3.3.

The relationship between source code filenames, class names, and byte code filenames.

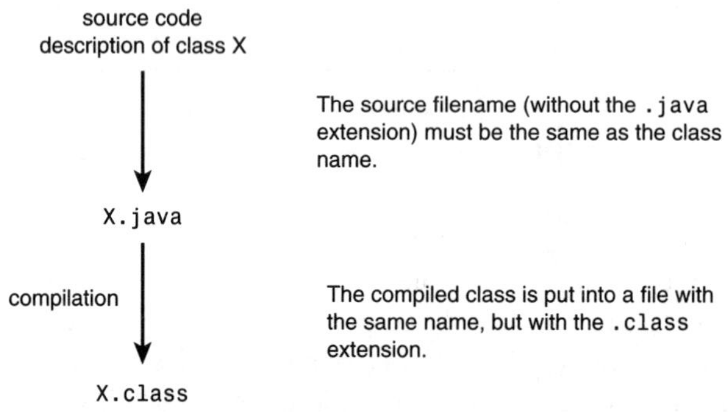

source code description of class X

↓

The source filename (without the .java extension) must be the same as the class name.

X.java

compilation ↓

The compiled class is put into a file with the same name, but with the .class extension.

X.class

On UNIX systems that use the C Shell, you set CLASSPATH using the setenv command. Java is typically installed under /usr/local on UNIX systems. Suppose that you want to set CLASSPATH to the current directory, your home directory, and the location of the JDK classes. You would enter the following at the shell prompt:

```
setenv CLASSPATH .:~:/usr/local/jdk1.1.1/lib/classes.zip
```

For systems that use the Bourne Again Shell (bash), you would enter the following at the shell prompt:

```
CLASSPATH=.:~:/usr/local/jdk1.1.1/lib/classes.zip
export CLASSPATH
```

NOTE

UNIX systems use the colon (:) to separate path elements. Windows 95 and NT use the semicolon (;).

The CLASSPATH can also be set from the javac command line using the -classpath option. For example, to compile test.java with the .;c:\otherclasses path, you would use the following command line:

```
javac test.java -classpath .;c:\otherclasses
```

The CLASSPATH set by the -classpath option is temporary and only applies to the current file being compiled.

Changing the Root Directory

Normally, javac will put the .class byte code file that it generates in the same directory as the .java source file that it compiles. You can change this using the -d option. For example, to put the test.class file generated by compiling test.java in the c:\classes directory, you would use the following command:

```
javac -d c:\classes test.java
```

The -d option does not affect the CLASSPATH.

Generating Debugging Tables

The Java debugger needs additional information to be placed in .class files in order to support enhanced debugging operations. Normally, only information about line numbers is inserted in .class files. Additional information about local variables is produced as the result of using the -g option. For example, the following produces the test.class file with additional debugging information included:

```
javac -g test.java
```

The javac_g program is a non-optimized version of javac that can be used with debuggers.

Code Optimization

The byte code files produced by Java are usually not optimized for execution speed. Optimized files are generally larger, and this is undesirable for some applications, such as Java applets, which may be downloaded over slow Internet connections.

Optimization for execution speed can be turned on using the -O option. This results in inline expansion of code, where possible, to reduce delays associated with loading and calling certain methods. Static, final, and private methods are optimized via inline expansion. For example, the following will optimize the test.class file for speedier execution:

```
javac -O test.java
```

Suppressing Warnings

Sometimes your .java files will contain code that could lead to potential errors. The compiler will warn you about these problem areas. If you do not want to see these warnings, you can turn them off using the -nowarn option. For example, the following command will suppress warnings from being generated when compiling test.java:

```
javac -nowarn test.java
```

Using Verbose Mode

If you want more detailed information about the compiler's operation, *verbose mode* is for you. When verbose mode is turned on, the compiler identifies the source files that it compiles and the .class files that it loads in order to compile these files. Verbose mode is turned on using the -verbose option. For example, the following will compile test.java and display information on what .class files are loaded during the compilation:

```
javac -verbose test.java
```

Other Compiler Options

The -nowrite option is used to run the compiler without producing a .class output file. This allows you to perform syntax checking without code generation.

The -depend option instructs the compiler to recompile other files that the current file being compiled depends on.

The -J option is used to pass a string to the Java interpreter (which runs the compiler) as an argument. The option must not contain any embedded spaces. It is used as follows:

```
javac -Joption source_code_file
```

The -J option would be typically used to adjust the memory that is available to the compiler. However, the use of this option is rarely needed.

The Interpreter

The Java interpreter executes the byte code files produced by the Java compiler. It is invoked using the java command, as follows:

```
java options class arguments
```

The class is the full name of the compiled Java class generated by the Java compiler. In order for the compiler to locate and execute the class, the class must meet the following requirements:

- It must have a valid main() method. The main() method is analogous to the main() function in C and C++ programs. You'll learn how to construct a main() method in the next chapter.
- It must be contained in a byte code file with the same name as the class followed by the .class extension.
- The location of the class must be determined using the CLASSPATH and the full name of the class, as discussed in the "Using Classes from Other Packages" section earlier in this chapter.

The program arguments are optional parameters that are passed to the main() method of the class that is executed. They are analogous to command-line arguments that are passed to C and C++ programs. The arguments are processed by the class's main() method and not by the Java interpreter. For example, suppose that you developed a Java class called TestClass with a main() method that merely displayed the arguments passed to it. Also, assume that TestClass is in the TestAPI package. The following command would merely print the numbers 1, 2, and 3:

```
java TestAPI.TestClass 1 2 3
```

Interpreter options are used to control different aspects of the interpreter's operation. These options are covered in the following subsections.

Help and Version Information

The -help option prints out a list of available compiler options. An example of using the -help option follows:

```
C:\jdk1.1.1\jdg>java -help
usage: java [-options] class

where options include:
    -help               print out this message
    -version            print out the build version
    -v -verbose         turn on verbose mode
    -debug              enable remote JAVA debugging
    -noasyncgc          don't allow asynchronous garbage collection
    -verbosegc          print a message when garbage collection occurs
    -noclassgc          disable class garbage collection
    -cs -checksource    check if source is newer when loading classes
    -ss<number>         set the maximum native stack size for any thread
    -oss<number>        set the maximum Java stack size for any thread
    -ms<number>         set the initial Java heap size
    -mx<number>         set the maximum Java heap size
    -classpath <directories separated by semicolons>
                        list directories in which to look for classes
    -prof[:<file>]      output profiling data to .\java.prof or .\<file>
    -verify             verify all classes when read in
    -verifyremote       verify classes read in over the network [default]
    -noverify           do not verify any classC:\jdk1.1.1\jdg>
```

The -version option prints out the version of the Java interpreter. The following is an example of using the -version option:

```
C:\jdk1.1.1\jdg>java -version
java version "1.1.1"
C:\jdk1.1.1\jdg>
```

Changing the CLASSPATH

The Java interpreter has a -classpath option that is identical to that of the compiler. It is used to temporarily change the CLASSPATH for the duration of the class being executed. For example, the following will result in the execution of the `main()` method of the compiled `TestClass` located in the file `c:\other\TestAPI.TestClass.class`:

```
java -classpath c:\other TestAPI.TestClass
```

NOTE

The `CLASSPATH` environment variable is written in uppercase. The `-classpath` option is written in lowercase.

Checking for Source Code Changes

The Java interpreter has a useful option that checks to see if the source code file of the class to be executed has been modified since the last time that it was compiled. This option is the `checksource` option and is identified with `-cs` or `-checksource`. If the date/time of modification of the source code file is more recent than that of the byte code file, the source code file is recompiled before the specified class is executed.

For example, suppose you developed and compiled the `TestClass` class, and then later in the day made modifications to the `TestClass.java` file from which `TestClass` was compiled. You have the choice of recompiling `TestClass.java` and executing it using `java` or using the `checksource` option to accomplish compilation and execution with a single command. In the latter case, you could use the following to perform both recompilation and execution:

```
java -cs TestAPI.TestClass
```

Verifying Your Code

The Java interpreter has three options to control the byte code verification of class files that it loads and executes:

- `-verify`—Causes the interpreter to verify all code that it loads.
- `-noverify`—Causes the interpreter to skip all code verification.
- `-verifyremote`—Causes the interpreter to verify all code that is loaded via a classloader. This is the default operation of the interpreter.

Byte code verification is performed by the Java interpreter to ensure the security, integrity, and correctness of the code that it executes. It consists of a series of tests that verify that the code can be safely executed. The advantage of verification is that it promotes security, safety, and reliability. The disadvantage is that it takes time to perform and, therefore, slows down overall program execution.

The default `-verifyremote` option only applies verification to code that is loaded by a classloader. A *classloader* is a Java method that loads classes from remote systems into the local file system.

The `-verifyremote` option assumes that local classes are trustworthy and do not need to be verified, but remotely loaded classes are suspect and subject to verification.

Examples of using the verify options are

```
java -verify TestAPI.TestClass
java -noverify TestAPI.TestClass
java -verifyremote TestAPI.TestClass
```

In the first case, all classes are verified as they are loaded. In the second case, no classes are verified. In the last case, only classes that are remotely loaded are verified.

Controlling the Garbage Collector

The Java interpreter automatically allocates and deallocates memory resources as they are needed by Java programs. Memory is allocated as program objects are created and deallocated as the result of the Java *garbage collector*. The Java runtime system keeps track of objects that are created, monitors references to objects, and uses the garbage collector to free the memory associated with objects when no more references to the objects exist.

The garbage collector runs as a separate, low-priority background thread that executes when no other threads are active. It checks object references and frees those objects that are no longer in use. The garbage collector is not explicitly called by executing programs, but operates during periods of low activity. It is said to operate *asynchronously* with respect to program execution.

The `-noasyncgc` option turns off asynchronous garbage collection. This prevents the garbage collector from being run except when a program calls it or the runtime system is out of memory. The `-noasyncgc` option is generally used when a program calls the garbage collector directly. This only occurs in memory-intensive programs that require more direct control over memory resources. The `-noclassgc` option is used to turn off garbage collection for Java classes.

The Java interpreter provides the `-verbosegc` option for monitoring the operation of the garbage collector. This option instructs the garbage collector to display a message to the console window when it frees a previously allocated object. It is used to monitor the operation of the garbage collector and is generally limited to program testing and debugging.

Changing Properties

The Java interpreter allows you to change the values of predefined system parameters, referred to as *system properties*. These properties are used to specify the default values of variables that control the overall behavior of the Java runtime system.

You change or add a property using the `-D` option. If a property specified by the `-D` option does not currently exist in the system properties, it will be added to the list of defined properties. For example, the following will change the predefined os.name property from Windows 95 to Windows 97:

```
java -Dos.name="Windows 97" TestAPI.TestClass
```

The following example adds the `myProperty` property to the list of system properties and gives it the value `1234`:

```
java -DmyProperty=1234 TestAPI.TestClass
```

You will learn to use properties in Chapter 12, "Portable Software and the `java.lang` Packages," when you explore the `java.lang.System` class.

Setting Memory and Stack Limits

The Java interpreter uses three major memory data structures to execute Java classes. These are the memory allocation pool, the Java code stack, and the C-code stack.

The *memory allocation pool* is used to create objects for use in Java programs. It is controlled by the Java runtime system and the garbage collector. It is initially 1MB in size and has a maximum size of 16MB. The `-ms` and `-mx` options can be used to change the startup size and maximum size of the memory allocation pool. The memory size may be specified in bytes (default), kilobytes (using the `k` suffix), or megabytes (using the `m` suffix). For example, each of the following set the startup size of the memory allocation pool to 2MB and the maximum size to 8MB for the execution of `TestClass`:

```
java -ms 2097152 -mx 8388608 TestAPI.TestClass
java -ms 2048k -mx 8192k TestAPI.TestClass
java -ms 2m -mx 8m TestAPI.TestClass
```

In general, you should not attempt to change the default memory allocation pool values unless you have a memory-intensive program or a computer with a less-than-average amount of RAM. The memory allocation pool must be larger than 1,000 bytes; the default size is 3MB.

A *Java code stack* is created for every thread of a Java program. It is used to execute the byte codes that comprise the Java thread. By increasing the size of the Java code stack, you provide more room for program instructions. By decreasing its size, you lower the memory requirements for your program. The default maximum size of the stack is 400KB. It can be changed using the `-oss` option. It specifies the stack size in bytes, kilobytes, and megabytes as previously described for the memory allocation pool. For example, the following command will execute `TestClass` with only 250KB of Java code stack by program thread:

```
java -oss 250k TestAPI.TestClass
```

The Java code stack size should be changed only if you have a program with an unusually large number of Java byte code instructions or a computer with significantly limited RAM.

The *C-code stack* is similar to the Java code stack. It is used to execute C-code for a given thread. Its default size is 128KB and can be changed using the `-ss` option. Its size must be greater than 1,000 bytes. For example, the following command will execute `TestClass` with 256KB of C-code stack per program thread:

```
java -ss 256k TestAPI.TestClass
```

The code stack is used to pass parameters to methods and to return the results of a method's calculations. It is similar to the memory functions used in calculators. Unless you plan to use a large amount of C-language native methods in your Java programs, you should never have to change the C-code stack size.

Debugging Options

The Java interpreter provides a number of options that support the debugging and testing of Java classes. First and foremost, java lets you attach the Java debugger to an executing Java program. The -debug option tells the interpreter that you may want to attach the debugger to a java session. The interpreter responds by displaying an *agent password* to the console window. This password must be entered when you attach the debugger to the active session. Use of the Java debugger is covered in the next section.

The -verbose option for the Java interpreter is similar to that used with the compiler. This option causes the interpreter to identify all classes that are loaded during a program's execution. The -verbose option can also be identified using -v. For example, the following command will display all classes that are loaded during the execution of TestClass:

```
java -verbose TestAPI.TestClass
```

There is a special version of the Java interpreter, java_g, that is oriented toward debugging. It includes the -t option for tracing the instructions executed during the course of a program's execution. Even for very short programs, the amount of data generated by this option can be overwhelming. For example, if you enter

```
java_g -t TestAPI.TestClass
```

you will receive a seemingly endless stream of information concerning the methods and instructions executed.

The Debugger

The Java debugger is used to monitor the execution of Java programs in support of debugging and test activities. It supports debugging of both locally executing and remotely executing Java programs.

The debugger can be started in two ways. In the first way, the debugger is started with a fully qualified class name. The debugger then calls the interpreter with the name of the class to be debugged. For example, the following command line starts the debugger with TestAPI.TestClass. The debugger then invokes the interpreter to load TestAPI.TestClass. The interpreter returns control to the debugger before executing any instructions of TestClass:

```
jdb TestAPI.TestClass
```

The -debug option runs jdb to test and debug the applets contained in the selected HTML document. The -J option is similar to the -J option of the compiler. It is used to pass an argument to the Java interpreter.

The following section shows how to run the applet viewer.

Running the Demo Programs

The JDK comes with more than 30 sample applets that demonstrate the capabilities of the Java language and API. These applets are located in the jdk1.1.1\demo directory of the JDK. If you installed the JDK under your C: drive, the applets will be located under c:\jdk1.1.1\demo. The demo directory has 22 subdirectories, each containing one or more sample applets. To execute any of the applets, open an MS-DOS window and change to the subdirectory of c:\jdk1.1.1\demo where the applet is located. In the subdirectory are files named example1.html, example2.html, and so on that are the HTML files containing links to the demo applets. Most of the subdirectories only contain a single sample file. To execute the applet, just run appletviewer with the name of the HTML file as a command-line argument.

I'll walk you through the execution of an applet so that you can get the hang of it. First, open an MS-DOS window and change directories to c:\jdk1.1.1\demo\Animator. If you do a directory listing, you will see that it contains the following files:

```
C:\jdk1.1.1\demo\Animator>dir

 Volume in drive C has no label
 Volume Serial Number is 0DE2-1446
 Directory of C:\jdk1.1.1\demo\Animator

.               <DIR>        04-06-97   3:30p .
..              <DIR>        04-06-97   3:30p ..
EXAMPL~1 HTM          710    03-10-97   4:09p example1.html
EXAMPL~2 HTM          675    03-10-97   4:09p example2.html
EXAMPL~3 HTM          760    03-10-97   4:09p example3.html
EXAMPL~4 HTM          698    03-10-97   4:09p example4.html
INDEX~1  HTM        7,938    02-18-97  11:19a index.html
10~1     2    <DIR>        04-06-97   3:30p 1.0.2
1        1    <DIR>        04-06-97   3:30p 1.1
         5 file(s)         10,781 bytes
         4 dir(s)     773,390,336 bytes free
C:\jdk1.1.1\demo\Animator>
```

Entering the command appletviewer example1.html results in the appletviewer being launched with the example1.html file. The applet viewer will then load and display any applets pointed to by the HTML file. The first time that you use the applet viewer, you will need to indicate your acceptance of Sun's license agreement. The animation applet referenced by example1.html produces the animation shown in Figure 3.4.

FIGURE 3.4.
The applet viewer.

This applet displays an animation of coffee beans that move about to form the word Java. An audio file is played in the background.

Automating Software Documentation

The Java documentation generator, `javadoc`, is the tool that created the excellent Java API documentation. This documentation can (and should) be obtained from Sun's Java Web site. Make sure that you get the documentation that is applicable to your Java release. You can find it by pointing your browser at `http://java.sun.com` and then clicking on the documentation link.

The documentation generator is executed using either the name of a Java source code file or a package name. If it is executed with a package name, it will automatically load the source code associated with all the classes in the package. If it is executed with a source code file, it will generate documentation for all classes and interfaces defined in the file.

The `javadoc` command line is as follows:

```
javadoc options package
javadoc options source_file
```

The `-classpath` option is the same as with the compiler and interpreter. The `-sourcepath` option tells the tool where to look for source files. The `-d` option is used to specify the directory to which the generated HTML files are to be stored. It is similar to the `-d` option used with the compiler.

The `-version` and `-author` options cause `@version` and `@author` tags to be included in the documentation output. The `-nodeprecated` option causes deprecated language elements to be omitted from the documentation. The `-noindex` and `-notree` options cause the package index and class hierarchy documentation to be eliminated.

The `-J` option is used in the same way as with the compiler.

The `-verbose` option results in a comprehensive display of the files that are loaded during the documentation-generation process.

Chapter 10, "Automating Software Documentation," shows how to use `javadoc` to automatically generate Java software documentation.

Header File Generation

The header file generation tool, `javah`, is used to produce the C files required to develop native methods. It produces both header and source files. The header files contain C-language definitions that map to Java class definitions. The source files contain the stubs for C functions that map to class methods.

The command line used to invoke `javah` is

```
javah options classes
```

where *classes* refers to the full class names of the classes for which header files are to be generated. The `javah` options control the way the header files are generated:

- The `-o` option combines all the files generated into a single file.
- The `-d` option identifies the directory where `javah` is to put the header and source files that it generates.
- The `-td` option specifies where `javah` is to store temporary files used in the header file generation process. The default directory is the `\tmp` directory.
- The `-stubs` option causes `javah` to generate C function stubs for class methods.
- The `-verbose` option is used to display status information concerning the files generated.
- The `-jni` option generates an output file with Java native interface (JNI) function prototypes.
- The `-classpath` option is used in the same way as it is used with the compiler and interpreter.

See Chapter 59, "Creating Native Methods," for more information on this process.

Other Tools

The RMI stub generator, RMI registry tool, and serial version identification tool are used with the new Java API remote method invocation packages to develop distributed applications using Java. These tools are covered in Chapter 18, "Building Distributed Applications with the `java.rmi` Packages."

The Unicode converter, `native2ascii`, is used to convert files to Unicode format. It is covered in Chapter 21, "Internationalization and the `java.text` Package," where Java's internationalization features are discussed. The Java archive tool is used to compress and archive related byte code and other files. It is covered in Chapter 42, "Using `.jar` Files and Signed Applets." The digital signature tool is covered in Chapter 20, "Security and the `java.security` Packages." It is used to manage keys and certificates.

Summary

You have covered a lot of information in this lesson. You studied the tools of the Java Development Kit and learned what each tool does and how it is used with the other tools in the JDK. You learned how to operate these tools and work with their command-line arguments. In Chapter 4 you will start programming. You'll code, compile, and execute four simple programs that illustrate the basic elements of the Java language.

II

Programming in Java

4

First Programs: Hello World! to BlackJack

This chapter will quickly get you up to speed writing Java programs. If you have previously programmed in C++, this chapter will be a breeze. If you have programmed in some other language, the examples presented here will be familiar; you will just be learning a new syntax. If you have never programmed before, you will face the task of debugging your first programs. It will be easy or difficult depending on the mistakes you make and your ability to find programming errors. You may want to ask for help from someone who has programmed before.

In order to carry out the examples in this chapter and in the rest of the book, you need access to a computer that supports the JDK 1.1 or later. The type of computer and operating system that you use to write your programs won't matter. After all, that's the beauty of Java. The examples in this book have been developed using Java running under Windows 95. If you use Windows 95, I strongly recommend that you use a text editor other than Notepad or WordPad. These editors do not allow you to save files easily with the .java extension and will drive you crazy during program development. I use the shareware program, TextPad, from Helios Software Solutions. It works well with both Windows 95 and NT, and is both convenient and affordable. It can be found in most Windows 95 FTP archives. If you are using Solaris, Linux, or any other Java port, use a text editor that is native to your system.

Hello World!

Since Brian Kernighan and Dennis Ritchie released The C Programming Language in 1978, the traditional first program has been to display Hello World! on the console display. Who are we to break with tradition?

Fire up your computer and change to the directory where you have the JDK installed. On my computer, it is located in the c:\jdk1.1.1 directory. Create a subdirectory called jdg under your JDK directory (that is, c:\jdk1.1.1\jdg). If you are using a system, such as UNIX or Windows NT, where you may not have write access to the jdk1.1.1 directory, create a jdg directory under your home directory.

You will store all the files that you develop under the jdg directory. Separate subdirectories will be created for each chapter, as shown in Figure 4.1. Go ahead and create a directory ch04 for this lesson.

The CD-ROM that accompanies this book has an analogous directory structure to the one that you'll create. It contains the source and byte code files for each example in the book. If you don't want to type in any of the sample programs, you can simply copy them from the CD-ROM. The CD-ROM also contains images, audio and video files, and other files used in the examples.

FIGURE 4.1.

Files contained on the CD-ROM mirror the ones you'll create.

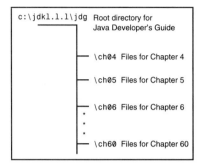
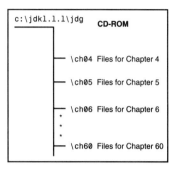

I recommend that you type in the first few programs. By doing so you will quickly get a feel for the Java syntax.

Now start your favorite text editor and key in the Java program in Listing 4.1.

Listing 4.1. The source code of the Hello World! program.

```
package jdg.ch04;
/* HelloWorldApp.java */
import java.lang.System;
class HelloWorldApp {
 /**
 * Traditional "Hello World!" program.
 */
 public static void main (String args[]) {
  // Write to stdout.
  System.out.println("Hello World!");
 }
}
```

Save this program as `HelloWorldApp.java` in the `c:\jdk1.1.1\jdg\ch04` directory.

While in the `c:\jdk1.1.1\jdg\ch04` directory, enter `javac HelloWorldApp.java`. This invokes the Java compiler and compiles the `HelloWorldApp.java` source file creating the `HelloWorldApp.class` binary file. A listing of your directory should look similar to this:

```
C:\jdk1.1.1\jdg\ch04>dir
 Volume in drive C has no label
 Volume Serial Number is 1621-15F9
 Directory of C:\jdk1.1.1\jdg\ch04
 .               <DIR>        02-14-97  9:59a .
 ..              <DIR>        02-14-97  9:59a ..
```

```
HELLOW~1 JAV           264   02-14-97 10:02a HelloWorldApp.java
HELLOW~1 CLA           487   02-14-97 10:05a HelloWorldApp.class
        2 file(s)             751 bytes
        2 dir(s)      271,532,032 bytes free
C:\jdk1.1.1\jdg\ch04>
```

If you receive any compiler errors, go back to your editor and make sure that you typed the program correctly. Then recompile your program using javac. Make sure you set your PATH and CLASSPATH environment variables as discussed in Chapter 3, "Using the Java Development Kit." PATH tells your operating system shell where to find your Java Development Kit programs. CLASSPATH tells the Java runtime system where to find Java classes.

When you're ready to run HelloWorldApp, using the Java interpreter, enter java jdg.ch04.HelloWorldApp from your shell command prompt. You should get the following output:

```
C:\jdk1.1.1\jdg\ch04>java jdg.ch04.HelloWorldApp
Hello World!
```

> **NOTE**
>
> If you get an error message saying that Java can't find the HelloWorldApp class, make sure that your CLASSPATH is correctly set.

At this point, you are probably not impressed with the power of Java, but you soon will be. Let's walk through the program source code and learn some Java syntax.

Comments

Java allows three kinds of comments. You can use any of these comment styles to document your Java programs. An example of each kind is provided in the HelloWorldApp.java source code. The C-style comments begin with /* and end with */. Here is an example:

```
/* HelloWorldApp.java */
```

The C++-style comments begin with // and continue to the end of a line:

```
// Write to stdout.
```

The Java automated documentation support comments begin with /** and end with */. They are found immediately before or after a Java declaration:

```
/**
 * Traditional "Hello World!" program.
 */
```

These comments are used by javadoc to automate documentation. See Chapter 10, "Automating Software Documentation," for more information about this Java feature.

Java Program Structure

Java programs are built from classes and interfaces. A *class* defines a set of data structures, called *variables*, and the operations, referred to as *methods*, that are permitted on the variables. An *interface* defines a collection of methods that are to be implemented by a class. Your `HelloWorldApp` program was built from the `HelloWorldApp` class. It also uses the `System` class. Figure 4.2 summarizes the Java program structure.

FIGURE 4.2.

The Java program structure.

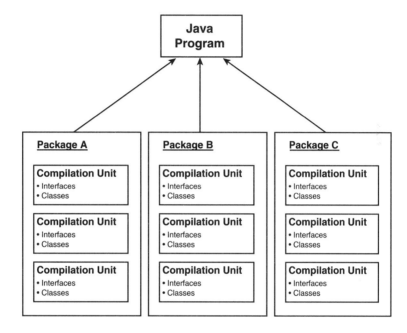

Classes and interfaces are organized into `.java` files that are separately compiled. These `.java` files are called *compilation units*. The `HelloWorldApp.java` file that you created with your text editor and compiled using `javac` is an example of a compilation unit.

The classes and interfaces contained in compilation units are organized into *packages*. Packages are used to group related classes and interfaces and to avoid naming conflicts. Your `HelloWorldApp` class is in the `jdg.ch04` package. The `System` class, referenced by your program, is in the `java.lang` package.

Package Statement

The *package statement* identifies which package a compilation unit is in. The package statement must be the first statement in a compilation unit. Its syntax is

```
package packageName;
```

For example, the following package statement was used to identify the package containing the `HelloWorldApp` as `jdg.ch04`:

```
package jdg.ch04;
```

If a compilation unit does not contain a package statement, the classes and interfaces contained in the compilation unit are put into a default package—the package with no name. This default package is the same for all classes within a particular directory.

The `import` Statement

The `java.lang.System` class is used to display `Hello World!`. The `System` class is in the `java.lang` package. In order to tell the compiler to use the `System` class in the `java.lang` package (as opposed to the `System` class in another package), import the `System` class using the `import` statement. *Importing* a class tells the compiler to use that class when it compiles your source code file.

The syntax of the `import` statement is

```
import fullClassName;
```

or

```
import classWithWildcard;
```

The class name supplied with the `import` statement must be a fully qualified class name, as described in Chapter 3. This means that the name of the package containing the class must be prepended to the name of the class.

For example, the following `import` statement imports the `System` class from `java.lang`:

```
import java.lang.System;
```

The * wildcard character can be used instead of the class name in the `import` statement. It indicates that all classes in the package should be imported. For example, the following `import` statement imports all classes in the `java.lang` package:

```
import java.lang.*;
```

An alternative to using the `import` statement is to prefix the name of a class with its package name. For example, the command

```
java.lang.System.out.println("Hello World!");
```

could have been used in place of

```
import java.lang.System;
    .
    .
    .
System.out.println("Hello World!");
```

The last statement above would be replaced by the sample prefix statement.

It is generally easier to use the `import` statement than to spell out package names. In the case where two or more classes of the same name are imported into a compilation unit, you must prepend the package name when referencing one of the ambiguous classes.

Classes and Methods

The `HelloWorldApp` program was built upon the `HelloWorldApp` class. This class is declared beginning with

```
class HelloWorldApp {
```

The class declaration ends with the last brace (}) of the file. `HelloWorldApp` declares and implements one method—the `main()` method:

```
public static void main (String args[]) {
  // Write to stdout.
  System.out.println("Hello World!");
 }
```

The `main()` method is the method that is executed when a class is run from the command line using the Java interpreter. For example, the following statement causes the `main()` method of the `jdg.ch04.HelloWorldApp` class to be executed:

```
java jdg.ch04.HelloWorldApp
```

The `main()` method is always defined as `public` (that is, publicly accessible), `static` (applying to the class as a whole), and in the case of `HelloWorldApp`, `void` (no return value). The `args[]` parameter of `main()` is defined as an array of class `String`. The `args[]` parameter is used to pass command-line arguments to the `main()` method. Don't worry if you don't understand these terms—they will all be defined by the end of Chapter 5, "Classes and Objects."

The implementation of the `main()` method consists of the following statement:

```
System.out.println("Hello World!");
```

This statement executes the `println()` method of the object referred to by the `out` variable of the `System` class. The `println()` method is executed using the `"Hello World!"` parameter. This is what causes `Hello World!` to be displayed on your console window.

The System Class

The `System` class provides an interface to a number of useful system resources. Among these are the `System.in` and `System.out` input and output streams. The `System.out` stream was used in this example. The following example illustrates the use of `System.in`.

I Can Read!

This program builds on what you learned from HelloWorldApp. HelloWorldApp just displayed a message to your console window. The ICanReadApp program will read your name from the keyboard characters you type and display it on the console window. It introduces the concepts of identifiers, variable declarations, Java keywords, and object constructors.

Use your text editor to create a file called ICanReadApp.java with the program in Listing 4.2.

Listing 4.2. The source code of the I Can Read! program.

```
// ICanReadApp.java
import java.lang.System;
import java.io.InputStreamReader;
import java.io.BufferedReader;
import java.io.IOException;
class ICanReadApp {
 public static void main (String args[]) throws IOException {
  System.out.print("Enter your name: ");
  System.out.flush();
  String name;
  BufferedReader keyboardInput =
   new BufferedReader(new InputStreamReader(System.in));
  name=keyboardInput.readLine();
  System.out.println("Your name is: "+name);
 }
}
```

Save the file in your c:\jdk1.1.1\jdg\ch04 directory. Compile it with the following command line:

```
javac ICanReadApp.java
```

This will produce a file named ICanReadApp.class that contains the binary compiled code for your program. Run the program with the following command line:

```
java ICanReadApp
```

Make sure that your CLASSPATH is correctly set so that Java can find the ICanReadApp class.

The program will prompt you to enter your name. When you enter your name, it will display it to you. Here is a sample program run:

```
C:\jdk1.1.1\jdg\ch04>java ICanReadApp
Enter your name: Jamie
Your name is: Jamie
```

It may seem that you're going nowhere fast, but this little program illustrates some more basic Java syntax. Hang in there—by the time you get to the end of the chapter, you'll be having fun at Java console programming.

Overview of `ICanReadApp`

One of the first things that you probably noticed about this program is that it doesn't contain a package statement. That was done deliberately to show you what happens when a package statement is omitted. The package name of the `ICanReadApp` class is set to the no name (blank) package, by default. This means that you don't have to prepend the package name to the class name in order to execute it using the interpreter. Although not using a package name might seem like a benefit, it also limits the extent to which the classes you develop can be accessed by other Java programs. Because the package name is blank, and your `CLASSPATH` variable is `.;c:\jdk1.1.1;c:\jdk1.1.1\lib\classes.zip`, the `ICanReadApp` class can only be accessed from within the `c:\jdk1.1.1\jdg\ch04` directory. However, you can change your `CLASSPATH` to include this directory, as discussed in Chapter 2, "Java Overview."

The first line of the `ICanReadApp` program is a comment that identifies the name of the source file. Four import statements are used to import the classes `java.lang.System`, `java.io.InputStreamReader`, `java.io.BufferedReader`, and `java.io.IOException` into the compilation unit:

```
import java.lang.System;
import java.io.InputStreamReader;
import java.io.BufferedReader;
import java.io.IOException;
```

The `ICanReadApp` class is then declared. It consists of a single method called `main()`. The `main()` method contains a throws clause that identifies the fact that an `IOException` may be thrown during the course of its execution. When an exception is thrown, program control immediately transfers to an exception handler. This issue is covered in Chapter 7, "Exceptions."

The `main()` method consists of the following six statements. These statements are summarized and then explained in the following subsections. Note that the fourth statement is continued over two lines:

```
System.out.print("Enter your name: ");
System.out.flush();
String name;
BufferedReader keyboardInput =
 new BufferedReader(new InputStreamReader(System.in));
name=keyboardInput.readLine();
System.out.println("Your name is: "+name);
```

The first statement displays the prompt `Enter your name:` on the console window.

The second statement flushes the output to the console to make sure that the data is displayed, even though a line termination was not sent to the console.

The third statement declares a variable called `name` of class `String`.

The fourth statement declares a variable named `keyboardInput` of class `BufferedReader`. It then creates an object of class `BufferedReader` that is constructed from the `System.in` object. This new object is then assigned to keyboardInput. The System.in object is converted to an object of class InputStreamReader before it is used to construct the BufferedReader object.

The fifth statement reads a line of data from the keyboardInput object and assigns it to the name variable.

The last statement displays the string Your name is: followed by the value of the object referred to by the name variable.

Declaring Variables and Creating Objects

Statements three and four of the main() method declare two variables: name and keyboardInput. Variables are used to refer to data of a predefined Java type, an array of values, an object of a particular Java class, or an object that implements a particular Java interface. Variables are given names, called *identifiers*. The type of data that the variable refers to is specified in the variable declaration. The name variable is declared to refer to an object of class String. The keyboardInput variable is declared to refer to an object of class BufferedReader.

Notice the difference between statements three and four. In statement three, the name variable is declared—nothing more. No objects are created or referred to by name. It is like a blank street sign. We know it is a street sign, but we don't know on which street it will be posted.

In statement four, after keyboardInput is declared, it is assigned a new object of class BufferedReader that is created using two new operators and the System.in parameter. The innermost (right-most) new operator is used to create an object of the InputStreamReader class from the System.in variable. This intermediate object is then used to create an object of the BufferedReader class.

The new operator is used to create an object that is an instance of a particular class. You'll learn all about classes in Chapter 5. The keyboardInput variable refers to the object that is created.

The name variable is assigned an object in line five. When the readLine() method is applied to the object referred to by keyboardInput, an object of class String is created. This object is created and initialized with the keyboard data that you type in response to the Enter your name: prompt. The assignment statement causes name to refer to this newly created String object.

Identifiers and Keywords

Identifiers are used to name variables, classes, interfaces, methods, and other Java language elements. An identifier is a sequence of characters that starts with an underscore (_), dollar sign ($), or a letter (ASCII or Unicode). Subsequent characters may contain these characters plus the digits 0 through 9. Unicode letters come from the Unicode character set and are covered in Chapter 11, "Language Summary." Java reserves certain identifiers as keywords. Their use is restricted by Java and cannot be used in any other way. The reserved Java keywords are also listed in Chapter 11.

The following are valid identifiers:

```
myID
_score
$money
$$99__
```

These are not valid identifiers:

```
2time
dog#
spaced out
```

The problem with `2time` is that it begins with a digit. The `dog#` contains a pound (#) character that is not allowed in identifiers. The last example fails because it contains a space character.

Using `System.in`

Console (that is, non-Windows) programs process user keyboard inputs and display data to the console window. The console window is an MS-DOS window in Windows 95 and NT implementations of Java and a shell, or `xterm` window, in UNIX-based Java implementations. In the `HelloWorldApp` program, you learned how to write to the console window. The `ICanReadApp` program shows how to read from the keyboard.

You might compare `System.in` with `System.out` and wonder why I had to create an object of class `InputStreamReader` and then `BufferedReader`. The `System.out` variable refers to an object of class `PrintStream`. The `PrintStream` class provides the `println()` method for writing to objects of this class. The `System.in` variable refers to an object of the `InputStream` class. The methods provided by the `InputStream` class aren't all that great for reading a line of text entered at the keyboard and returning that data as a string. The `InputStream` methods are fairly primitive. The `BufferedReader` class is a subclass of the `Reader` class, which is a subclass of `Object`. Subclasses are classes that are built upon another class as a foundation. The methods of `BufferedReader` build upon the methods of `Reader` and `Object`. The `readLine()` method is one such method. The example used the `BufferedReader` class because it provides an easier method of reading keyboard input.

> **NOTE**
>
> Don't worry about learning all the new classes that are used in this chapter. They are all covered in Part III, "Using the Java API."

In statement four, when the new `BufferedReader` object is created, it uses the object referred to by `System.in` as a foundation.

Type This!

In the ICanReadApp program, you were introduced to variable declarations and the construction and assignment of objects to variables. Variables may refer to objects of a particular class, objects of one of the predefined Java types, to arrays, or to objects that implement a particular interface. You have already encountered the first case. The TypeThisApp program introduces the primitive Java types. Arrays are presented in the last example of this chapter. Interfaces are covered in Chapter 6, "Interfaces."

Start up your text editor and enter the program code shown in Listing 4.3. Then save it as TypeThisApp.java in your ch04 directory.

Listing 4.3. Type this!

```java
// TypeThisApp.java
import java.lang.System;
class TypeThisApp {
 public static void main (String args[]) {
  // Integer types
  byte oneByte = 57;
  short twoBytes = 1024;
  int fourBytes = 1234567;
  long eightBytes = 0x123456789ABCDEF1;
  // Floating point types
  float thirtyTwoBits = 1234.56f;
  double sixtyFourBits = 6.282E123;
  // Boolean type
  boolean ownSelf = true;
  // Character type
  char malcolm = 'X';
  System.out.println(oneByte);
  System.out.println(twoBytes);
  System.out.println(fourBytes);
  System.out.println(eightBytes);
  System.out.println(thirtyTwoBits);
  System.out.println(sixtyFourBits);
  System.out.println(ownSelf);
  System.out.println(malcolm);
 }
}
```

Compile the program using the following command line:

```
javac TypeThisApp.java
```

This will produce the TypeThisApp.class file that you can execute using the following:

```
java TypeThisApp
```

The following output should be displayed on your console window:

```
C:\jdk1.1.1\jdg\ch04>java TypeThisApp
57
1024
1234567
81985529216486895
1234.56
6.282E+123
true
X
```

Overview of TypeThisApp

TypeThisApp, like HelloWorldApp and ICanReadApp, declares only one class with a single method—main(). The main() method consists of eight variable declarations and assignments followed by eight invocations of the println() method for the System.out object.

The eight variable declarations declare variables of the primitive data types byte, short, int, long, float, double, boolean, and char. Each of the declarations is combined with an assignment of a literal value to the declared variable.

The Primitive Java Data Types

Java supports three major primitive data types: integer, floating point, and boolean. The integer type has five subtypes: byte, short, char, int, and long. These correspond to 1-byte (byte), 2-byte (short and char), 4-byte (int), and 8-byte (long) integer values. The floating point type consists of a 4-byte float subtype and an 8-byte double subtype. The floating point type follows IEEE 754, a recognized standard for floating-point arithmetic developed by the Institute of Electrical and Electronics Engineers.

The boolean type consists of the literal values true and false. boolean types are not automatically converted into integer types because they are not defined in terms of integers as they are in C and C++. Explicit conversion is required.

The char subtype uses the standard Unicode character set and is a 16-bit unsigned integer. Variables of the char type store single characters. The java.lang.String class is used to store strings of characters.

Literal Values

TypeThisApp illustrates the use of literal values with the primitive types. Integer literals can be expressed as decimal, hexadecimal, or octal values, using the conventions established by C and C++. An integer literal that begins with a 0 is assumed to represent an octal value. An integer literal beginning with 0x or 0X is assumed to be a hexadecimal value. An l or L appended to an integer literal indicates that the literal is of type long.

Floating-point literals use the standard exponential notation described in Chapter 11. Floating-point literals are of type `double`, by default. An `f` or `F` appended to a floating point literal indicates that the literal is of type `float`.

Boolean types simply use the values `true` and `false`.

Character types use standard Unicode, which is a superset of ASCII. Unicode is covered in Chapters 11 and 21. The C and C++ conventions for representing character literals are used by Java.

BlackJack

The programs that you've written so far in this chapter have been deliberately kept short and simple. Their purpose was to quickly get you started in Java programming and to cover some of the basic elements of the Java language. The next example allows you to spread your wings and have a little fun at the same time. The `BlackJackApp` program that you will develop in this section is a simplified, character-based version of the popular blackjack card game. This example, while entertaining, illustrates the use of Java arrays and provides many examples of Java statements and expressions.

The `BlackJackApp` program is rather long, compared to the previous examples. You have the option of copying the source code from the CD-ROM or typing it in yourself. I recommend typing it in. By doing so you will be sure to cover every statement in the program and increase your knowledge of Java syntax. Depending on how accurately you type, you might be called upon to develop some Java debugging skills.

Listing 4.4 is the program source code. Either type it into a file and save it as `c:\jdk1.1.1\jdg\ch04\BlackJackApp.java`, or copy the file `\jdk1.1.1\jdg\ch04\BlackJackApp.java` from the CD-ROM drive to your `ch04` directory.

Listing 4.4. The source code of the BlackJack program.

```
// BlackJackApp.java
// Import all the Java API classes needed by this program.
import java.lang.System;
import java.lang.Integer;
import java.lang.NumberFormatException;
import java.io.InputStreamReader;
import java.io.BufferedReader;
import java.io.IOException;
import java.util.Random;
class BlackJackApp {
 public static void main (String args[]) throws IOException {
  // Create a BlackJackGame object ...
  BlackJackGame game = new BlackJackGame();
```

```
  // and play it!
  game.play();
 }
}
class BlackJackGame {
 // Variable declarations
 int bet;
 int money;
 Deck deck;
 Hand playersHand;
 Hand dealersHand;
 BufferedReader keyboardInput;
 // Method declarations
 public BlackJackGame() { // Constructor
  bet = 0;
  money = 1000;
  deck = new Deck();
  keyboardInput =
   new BufferedReader(new InputStreamReader(System.in));
 }
 void play() throws IOException {
  System.out.println("Welcome to Blackjack!");
  System.out.println("You have $"+Integer.toString(money)+".");
  do {
   placeBet();
   if(bet>0) {
    initialDeal();
    if(playersHand.blackjack()) playerWins();
    else{
     while(playersHand.under(22) && playerTakesAHit()) {
      playersHand.addCard(deck.deal());
      playersHand.show(false,false);
     }
     while(dealersHand.mustHit())
      dealersHand.addCard(deck.deal());
     dealersHand.show(true,false);
     showResults();
    }
   }
  } while (bet>0);
 }
 void placeBet() throws IOException, NumberFormatException {
  do{
   System.out.print("Enter bet: ");
   System.out.flush();
   bet = Integer.parseInt(keyboardInput.readLine());
  } while(bet<0 || bet>money);
 }
 void initialDeal() {
  System.out.println("New hand...");
  playersHand = new Hand();
  dealersHand = new Hand();
  for(int i = 0;i<2;++i) {
   playersHand.addCard(deck.deal());
   dealersHand.addCard(deck.deal());
  }
```

continues

Listing 4.4. continued

```java
  dealersHand.show(true,true);
  playersHand.show(false,false);
 }
 void playerWins() {
  money += bet;
  System.out.println("Player wins $"+Integer.toString(bet)+".");
  System.out.println("Player has $"+Integer.toString(money)+".");
 }
 void dealerWins() {
  money -= bet;
  System.out.println("Player loses $"+Integer.toString(bet)+".");
  System.out.println("Player has $"+Integer.toString(money)+".");
 }
 void tie() {
  System.out.println("Tie.");
  System.out.println("Player has $"+Integer.toString(money)+".");
 }
 boolean playerTakesAHit() throws IOException {
  char ch = ' ';
  do{
   System.out.print("Hit or Stay: ");
   System.out.flush();
   String playersDecision = keyboardInput.readLine();
   try{
    ch = playersDecision.charAt(0);
   }catch (StringIndexOutOfBoundsException exception){
   }
   if(ch == 'H' || ch == 'h') return true;
   if(ch == 'S' || ch == 's') return false;
  } while(true);
 }
 void showResults() {
  if(playersHand.busted() && dealersHand.busted()) tie();
  else if(playersHand.busted()) dealerWins();
  else if(dealersHand.busted()) playerWins();
  else if(playersHand.bestScore() > dealersHand.bestScore()) playerWins();
  else if(playersHand.bestScore() < dealersHand.bestScore()) dealerWins();
  else tie();
 }
} // End of BlackJackGame class
class Deck {
// Variable declarations
 int cards[];     // Array of 52 cards
 int topCard;     // 0-51 (index of card in deck)
 Random random;
 // Method declarations
 public Deck() { // Constructor
  cards = new int[52];
  for(int i = 0;i<52;++i) cards[i] = i;
  topCard = 0;
  random = new Random();
  shuffle();
 }
```

```
public void shuffle() {
 // Repeat 52 times
 for(int i = 0;i<52;++i) {
  // Randomly exchange two cards in the deck.
  int j = randomCard();
  int k = randomCard();
  int temp = cards[j];
  cards[j] = cards[k];
  cards[k] = temp;
 }
}
int randomCard() {
 int r = random.nextInt();
 if(r<0) r = 0-r;
 return r%52;
}
Card deal() {
 if(topCard>51) {
  shuffle();
  topCard = 0;
 }
 Card card = new Card(cards[topCard]);
 ++topCard;
 return card;
}
} // End of Deck class
class Hand {
 // Variable declarations
 int numCards;
 Card cards[];
 static int MaxCards = 12;
 //Method declarations
 public Hand() { // Constructor
  numCards = 0;
  cards = new Card[MaxCards];
 }
 void addCard(Card c) {
  cards[numCards] = c;
  ++numCards;
 }
 void show(boolean isDealer,boolean hideFirstCard) {
  if(isDealer) System.out.println("Dealer:");
  else System.out.println("Player:");
  for(int i = 0;i<numCards;++i) {
   if(i == 0 && hideFirstCard) System.out.println("  Hidden");
   else System.out.println("  "+cards[i].value+" of "+cards[i].suit);
  }
 }
boolean blackjack() {
 if(numCards == 2) {
  if(cards[0].iValue == 1 && cards[1].iValue == 10) return true;
  if(cards[1].iValue == 1 && cards[0].iValue == 10) return true;
 }
 return false;
}
```

continues

Listing 4.4. continued

```java
boolean under(int n) {
 int points = 0;
 for(int i = 0;i<numCards;++i) points += cards[i].iValue;
 if(points<n) return true;
 else return false;
}
int bestScore() {
 int points = 0;
 boolean haveAce = false;
 for(int i = 0;i<numCards;++i) {
  points += cards[i].iValue;
  if(cards[i].iValue == 1) haveAce = true;
 }
 if(haveAce) {
  if(points+10 < 22) points += 10;
 }
 return points;
}
boolean mustHit() {
 if(bestScore()<17) return true;
 else return false;
}
 boolean busted() {
  if(!under(22)) return true;
  else return false;
 }
} // End of Hand class
class Card {
 // Variable declarations
 int iValue;   // Numeric value corresponding to card.
 String value; // "A" "2" through "9" "T" "J" "Q" "K"
 String suit; // "S" "H" "C" "D"
 // Method declarations
 public Card(int n) { // Constructor
  int iSuit = n/13;
  iValue = n%13+1;
  switch(iSuit) {
   case 0:
    suit = "Spades";
    break;
   case 1:
    suit = "Hearts";
    break;
   case 2:
    suit = "Clubs";
    break;
   default:
    suit = "Diamonds";
  }
  if(iValue == 1) value = "Ace";
  else if(iValue == 10) value = "Ten";
  else if(iValue == 11) value = "Jack";
  else if(iValue == 12) value = "Queen";
  else if(iValue == 13) value = "King";
  else value = Integer.toString(iValue);
  if(iValue>10) iValue = 10;
```

```
  }
  int getValue() {
    return iValue;
  }
} // End of Card class
```

Having produced `BlackJackApp.java`, in one way or another, compile it using the command line:

`javac BlackJackApp.java`

This will produce the `BlackJackApp.class` file. If your file does not compile, fix any typing errors and try again. Once you have a successful compile, execute the program using

`java BlackJackApp`

This will result in the following display:

```
C:\jdk1.1.1\jdg\ch04>java BlackJackApp
Welcome to Blackjack!
You have $1000.
Enter bet:
```

The `BlackJackApp` program will provide you with $1000 with which to play blackjack. You use this money to bet. You place a bet between 0 and the amount of money you have. Then, the computer, acting as dealer, will deal two cards to you and two to itself. For example, upon entering a bet of `10`, I received the following program output:

```
C:\jdk1.1.1\jdg\ch04>java BlackJackApp
Welcome to Blackjack!
You have $1000.
Enter bet: 10
New hand...
Dealer:
  Hidden
  2 of Hearts
Player:
  Queen of Clubs
  3 of Spades
Hit or Stay:
```

I, being the player, was dealt a queen of clubs and a three of spades. This gives me a total of 13 points. Points are calculated as follows:

Card Point	Value
Ace	1 or 11 (whichever is better)
2 through 10	Face value of card (that is, 2 through 10)
Jack, Queen, King	10

The objective of the game is to get as close to 21 as you can, without going over. Whoever gets the closest wins. If you go over 21, you lose, unless the dealer does also, in which case you tie.

When you are dealt your initial two cards, you are shown one of the dealer's cards. This helps you to determine whether you should take another card, referred to as *hitting*, or *stay* with the cards that you have. You can enter h or s to inform the dealer of your decision. If you enter h, you will be dealt another card. If you enter s, the dealer will begin to play its hand.

> **NOTE**
>
> If the point total of your first two cards is 21, you are said to have *blackjack* and immediately win.

The dealer must take a hit until the total points in its hand is 17 or over, at which point it must stay. When both you and the dealer have finished playing your hands, the total number of points acquired by each is used to determine the winner. Play is repeated until you enter a 0 bet.

The following program output shows a game played between myself and the BlackJackApp program:

```
C:\jdk1.1.1\jdg\ch04>java BlackJackApp
Welcome to Blackjack!
You have $1000.
Enter bet: 10
New hand...
Dealer:
  Hidden
  2 of Hearts
Player:
  Queen of Clubs
  3 of Spades
Hit or Stay: h
Player:
  Queen of Clubs
  3 of Spades
  7 of Spades
Hit or Stay: s
Dealer:
  Queen of Spades
  2 of Hearts
  5 of Spades
Player wins $10.
Player has $1010.
Enter bet: 20
New hand...
Dealer:
  Hidden
  7 of Clubs
```

```
Player:
  King of Clubs
  9 of Spades
Hit or Stay: s
Dealer:
  2 of Clubs
  7 of Clubs
  9 of Clubs
Player wins $20.
Player has $1030.
Enter bet: 0
C:\jdk1.1.1\jdg\ch04>
```

On the initial deal, I bet 10 bucks. I was given a queen of clubs and a three of spades, for a total of 13 points. The dealer was given a two of hearts and another (hidden) card. I elected to take a hit and was dealt a seven of spades, bringing the total in my hand up to 20 points—beginner's luck! The dealer turned over the hidden card to reveal a queen of spades. He then drew a five of spades for a total of 17 points. Because the dealer reached 17, he was forced to stay, and I had won $10. Feeling a little lightheaded, I proceeded to double my bet to $20. I was dealt a king of clubs and a nine of spades for a total of 19 points. I decided to stay with that hand. The dealer's hand was revealed to be a two of clubs and a seven of clubs. The dealer drew a nine of clubs for a total of 18 points. I had won again! At that point I elected to take the money and continue writing this book. I entered a 0 bet to end the game.

The point of the example is not to turn you into a blackjack gambler, but to serve as a more interesting example from which to discuss Java arrays, statements, and expressions.

Overview of BlackJackApp

The BlackJackApp.java file is long, but don't let that daunt you. I'm going to break it down, class by class, and method by method, to explain its operation.

The program begins with a comment identifying the name of the program:

```
// BlackJackApp.java
```

It then imports all the Java API classes that it needs to perform its processing:

```
// Import all the Java API classes needed by this program.
import java.lang.System;
import java.lang.Integer;
import java.lang.NumberFormatException;
import java.io.InputStreamReader;
import java.io.BufferedReader;
import java.io.IOException;
import java.util.Random;
```

Next, it declares the BlackJackApp class, the class that implements your blackjack application. This class has a single main() method, like all the other programs that you've developed so far.

The `main()` method consists of two Java statements. The first declares the game variable as having class type `BlackJackGame` and assigns it a new object of class `BlackJackGame`. The second statement invokes the `play()` method of the object referenced by game, as shown in the following code:

```
class BlackJackApp {
 public static void main (String args[]) throws IOException {
  // Create a BlackJackGame object ...
  BlackJackGame game = new BlackJackGame();
  // and play it!
  game.play();
 }
}
```

The `BlackJackGame` Class

The `BlackJackGame` class is not defined as part of the Java API. I wonder why they left it out? Because it doesn't exist anywhere else, it is a class that must be declared as part of the program. The `BlackJackGame` class and other classes could have been defined and compiled, separately, but they were combined into a single compilation unit to keep this example somewhat compact.

The `BlackJackGame` class is rather long. It declares six variables and nine methods. The variables are data structures that represent the state of a blackjack game. The `bet` variable identifies the amount bet by the player. The `money` variable identifies how much money the player has left. The `deck` variable references an object of class `Deck` that is used to represent a deck of cards. Two `Hand` variables are declared, representing the player's hand and the dealer's hand. Finally, our old friend, `keyboardInput`, has returned for a repeat performance:

```
class BlackJackGame {
 // Variable declarations
 int bet;
 int money;
 Deck deck;
 Hand playersHand;
 Hand dealersHand;
 BufferedReader keyboardInput;
   .
   .
   .
}
```

The first method declared for `BlackJackGame` is its *constructor*. A constructor is used to initialize objects that are new instances of a class. In the `main()` method of the `BlackJackApp` class, the `BlackJackGame()` constructor is invoked to initialize the newly created `BlackJackGame` object that is assigned to game:

```
BlackJackGame game = new BlackJackGame();
```

The `BlackJackGame()` constructor initializes four of the six variables of the `BlackJackGame` class. The player's bet is set to 0, and the player is given $1000. The `playersHand` and `dealersHand` variables are not initialized until the cards are dealt.

A new `Deck` object is created and assigned to the `deck` variable. The new object is initialized using the `Deck()` constructor for the `Deck` class. If you typed in the program, you probably know where to find it in the source code listing.

Finally, the `keyboardInput` variable is assigned a new object of class `BufferedReader`. This object is created using the `BufferedReader()` and `InputStreamReader()` constructors with the `System.in` variable as an argument:

```
// Method declarations public BlackJackGame() { // Constructor
  bet = 0;
  money = 1000;
  deck = new Deck();
  keyboardInput =
   new BufferedReader(new InputStreamReader(System.in));
 }
```

NOTE

An *argument* is a value that is provided as an input to a method invocation. It does not denote disagreement.

The second method defined for `BlackJackGame` is the `play()` method. This method is invoked in the `main()` method of `BlackJackApp` to cause the `BlackJackGame` object, referenced by `game`, to be played:

```
game.play();
```

The `play()` method begins with the `void` keyword to indicate that it does not return any value. It also identifies the fact that `IOException` may be thrown during its processing. Exceptions are covered in Chapter 7. The general structure of the `play()` method is as follows:

```
void play() throws IOException {
  .
  .
  .
}
```

The `play()` method begins by displaying the `Welcome to Blackjack!` text and the amount of money available to the player. The second `println()` method takes three arguments. First it displays `You have $`, then it displays the contents of the `money` variable, and then it displays a period (.). It converts the integer value of money to a String value before printing it. String is a class defined in the Java API that represents strings of characters. These statements are as follows:

```
System.out.println("Welcome to Blackjack!");
System.out.println("You have $"+Integer.toString(money)+".");
```

The rest of statements of the play() method are surrounded by

```
do {
    .
    .
    .
} while (bet>0);
```

This is a do statement, and it causes the statements between the braces to be repeatedly executed while the value of bet is greater than 0.

The block of statements within the do statement begins with an invocation of the placeBet() method. Because no object is identified with the placeBet() method, it is invoked using the current object—that which is invoked with the play() method:

```
placeBet();
```

The placeBet() method, as you'll see shortly, is used to prompt the player to enter his bet. After the placeBet() method is invoked, the next statement is an if statement that checks to see whether the bet is greater than 0. If the bet is greater than 0, the statements between its braces are executed.

If the bet is not greater than 0, execution continues after the if statement. In this case, the end of the do statement is encountered, the do statement terminates, the play() procedure returns, and the BlackJackApp main() method finishes its processing. In other words, the game is over.

The following code tests whether bet is greater than 0:

```
if(bet>0) {
    .
    .
    .
}
```

If bet is greater than 0, the initialDeal() method is invoked. This method is used to deal a new hand to the player and to the dealer. It causes the playersHand and dealersHand variables to each be initialized with an object of class Hand. The initialDeal() method is invoked using the following code:

```
initialDeal();
```

Another if statement is then executed. This if statement checks to see if the player was dealt blackjack (21 points). It does this by invoking the blackjack() method for the object referenced by the playersHand variable. In the case that the blackjack() method returns the boolean value true, the player wins the bet and the playerWins() method is invoked. If the player was not fortunate enough to be dealt blackjack, the statements within the else part of the if statement are executed, as shown in the following code:

```
if(playersHand.blackjack()) playerWins();
else{
  .
  .
  .
}
```

The else part begins with a while statement. A while statement is similar to a do statement in that it repeatedly executes the block of statements enclosed by braces. It differs from the do statement in that it checks to see if it is finished *before* executing the statement block. The while statement checks to see if the player has 21 points or less in his hand and whether he wants to take a another card. It does this by invoking the under()method for the object referenced by the playersHand variable, passing it the integer 22 as an argument. If the under() method returns the boolean value true, the playerTakesAHit() method is invoked to prompt the player to hit or stay. If the user elects to take a hit, playerTakesAHit()returns a boolean true and the statements enclosed by the while statement are executed. If either under() or playerTakesAHit() returns false, the next statement after the while statement is executed.

The statements enclosed within the while statement invoke methods for the Hand object referenced by the playersHand variable. The first method causes a card to be added to the player's hand by dealing it from the deck. The second method determines if and how the player's hand should be displayed. The code that performs this processing follows:

```
while(playersHand.under(22) && playerTakesAHit()) {
 playersHand.addCard(deck.deal());
 playersHand.show(false,false);
}
```

The previous while statement is followed by another while statement. This while statement does not enclose a block of statements within braces. It only applies to a single statement:

```
while(dealersHand.mustHit())
 dealersHand.addCard(deck.deal());
```

The while statement is used to play the dealer's hand. It invokes the mustHit() method with the object referenced by the dealersHand variable to determine whether the dealer has less than 17 points in his hand and, therefore, must take a hit. If the dealer must take a hit, the addCard() method is invoked to deal a card to the dealer.

After the dealer's hand is played, the show()method is invoked to display it to the console. The showResults()method is then invoked to show the results of the hand. This concludes the description of the play() method. It's a good idea to review the source code of the play() method to make sure that you know how it works before going on. The following statements invoke the show() and showResults() methods:

```
dealersHand.show(true,false);
showResults();
```

The `placeBet()`method is invoked by the `play()` method to prompt the player to enter a bet. It declares two potential exceptions in its `throw` clause.

The `placeBet()` method uses a `do` statement to repeatedly prompt the user to enter a bet that is at least 0 and at most is the amount of money that he has left. The statement block enclosed by the `do` statement displays the prompt, reads the line entered by the user, converts it to an integer, and then assigns it to the `bet` variable. The source code of the `placeBet()` method follows:

```
void placeBet() throws IOException, NumberFormatException {
 do{
  System.out.print("Enter bet: ");
  System.out.flush();
  bet = Integer.parseInt(keyboardInput.readLine());
 } while(bet<0 ¦¦ bet>money);
}
```

The `initialDeal()` method is invoked by the `play()` method to deal a new hand to the player and the dealer. It displays the `New hand...` text to the console window to inform the player that a new hand is being dealt. It then creates two new objects of class `Hand`, initializes them with the `Hand()` constructor, and assigns them to the `playersHand` and `dealersHand` variables. The source code of the `initialDeal()` method follows:

```
void initialDeal() {
 System.out.println("New hand...");
 playersHand = new Hand();
 dealersHand = new Hand();
     .
     .
     .
}
```

After creating the two new hands, the `initialDeal()` method executes a `for` statement. The `for` statement iterates the execution of the block of statements enclosed by braces, based upon the conditions identified immediately before the statement block. In this case a variable, `i`, of type `int`, is created for the duration of the `for` statement's execution and assigned a value of 0. The statement block is then executed while `i` is less than 2. Each time the statement block is executed, the value of `i` is incremented by 1. The expression, `++i`, causes `i` to be incremented by 1.

The `for` statement is used to sequentially deal two cards to the player and two to the dealer by invoking the `addCard()` method. Note that the value returned by the `deal()` method is used as an argument to the `addCard()`method, in both instances. The source code of the `for` statement follows:

```
for(int i = 0;i<2;++i) {
 playersHand.addCard(deck.deal());
 dealersHand.addCard(deck.deal());
}
```

After the player and dealer have been dealt their hands, the mysterious `show()`method is invoked, as shown in the following code, to display the new hands (you'll find out what the `boolean` values are used for when you study the `show()` method):

```
dealersHand.show(true,true);
playersHand.show(false,false);
```

The next three methods—`playerWins()`, `dealerWins()`, and `tie()`—are used to update the `money` variable based on the `bet` variable and the outcome of the hand:

```
void playerWins() {
 money += bet;
 System.out.println("Player wins $"+Integer.toString(bet)+".");
 System.out.println("Player has $"+Integer.toString(money)+".");
}
void dealerWins() {
 money -= bet;
 System.out.println("Player loses $"+Integer.toString(bet)+".");
 System.out.println("Player has $"+Integer.toString(money)+".");
}
void tie() {
 System.out.println("Tie.");
 System.out.println("Player has $"+Integer.toString(money)+".");
}
```

These methods also display the results to the player by converting the values of `bet` and `money` to `String` objects. The `+=` operator causes the value of `bet` to be added to the value of `money` and assigned to the `money` variable. Similarly, the `-=` operator causes the value of `bet` to be subtracted from the value of `money` before it is assigned to the `money` variable.

The `playerTakesAHit()` method is an example of a method that returns a result. The `boolean` keyword at the beginning of the method declaration specifies that the method should return a result of type `boolean`. Any valid primitive type, array type, class type, or interface type can be used to specify the return type of a method. For example, the return type could be `long`, `String`, or an array of `double` values.

The method begins by declaring a variable of type `char` and assigning it a space character. It then executes an infinite `do` statement. The statement is infinite because the `while` condition at the end of the `do` statement is literally always `true`. This doesn't mean that the statement will execute forever, however. Return statements within the block of the `do` statement will cause statement execution to return to the method that invoked `playerTakesAHit()`.

The `do` block begins by displaying the `Hit or Stay:` prompt to the player and reads the player's input from the keyboard. A `try` statement is then executed. The `try` statement executes a block of statements and, if an exception is thrown, uses a `catch` clause to process the exception. This `try` statement sets the variable `ch` to the first character of the `playersDecision` variable. The `playersDecision` variable references a `String` object that is created when the player's input is read from the keyboard. The `charAt()` method is defined in the `String` class of the Java API. If the player enters a blank line, the `StringIndexOutOfBoundsException` will be thrown. The `catch` clause is used to prevent the exception from terminating program execution.

If the character assigned to ch, via playersDecision, is H or h, the value of true is returned as the result of the playerTakesAHit() method. If ch equals S or s, false is returned. Otherwise, the do statement causes the player to be repeatedly prompted until he hits or stays. The playerTakesAHit() method follows:

```java
boolean playerTakesAHit() throws IOException {
 char ch = ' ';
 do{
  System.out.print("Hit or Stay: ");
  System.out.flush();
  String playersDecision = keyboardInput.readLine();
  try{
   ch = playersDecision.charAt(0);
  }catch (StringIndexOutOfBoundsException exception){
  }
  if(ch == 'H' || ch == 'h') return true;
  if(ch == 'S' || ch == 's') return false;
 } while(true);
}
```

The showResults() method is the last method declared for the BlackJackGame class. This method illustrates the use of nested if statements. The first if statement checks to see if the player's hand and the dealer's hand are both busted (over 21 points). If so, the tie() method is invoked to display the results to the player. If not, the statement following the else is executed. This turns out to be another if statement.

The second if statement checks to see if the player's hand is busted. Because the else part of the first if statement was executed, it is impossible for both the player and the dealer to be busted. So, if the player is busted, the dealer wins.

The third if statement is executed in the else parts of the first and second if statements. It uses the same logic as the second if statement to determine whether the dealer busted and the player wins.

The fourth if statement is only executed if neither the player nor the dealer busted. It checks the points in both of their hands to see if the player is higher than the dealer and, therefore, is the victor.

The fifth if statement is only executed if neither busts and the player is not higher than the dealer. If the dealer is higher than the player, the dealer wins. If the dealer is not higher than the player, the final else part is executed. At this point, neither has busted, but neither is higher than the other, so both must have the same number of points and a tie is declared. The showResults() method follows:

```java
void showResults() {
 if(playersHand.busted() && dealersHand.busted()) tie();
 else if(playersHand.busted()) dealerWins();
 else if(dealersHand.busted()) playerWins();
 else if(playersHand.bestScore() > dealersHand.bestScore()) playerWins();
 else if(playersHand.bestScore() < dealersHand.bestScore()) dealerWins();
 else tie();
}
```

The Deck Class

The third class declared within `BlackJackApp.java` is the `Deck` class. It is used to simulate a deck of cards.

The `Deck` class declares three variables and four methods. The `cards[]` variable is an example of an *array*. Arrays are objects that contain a number of variables of the same type. The variables contained in an array are referred to as the *component variables* of the array and are referenced using the integer indices $0,\ldots,n-1$, where n is the number of components contained within the array. The `cards[]` array is declared to contain components of type `int`. The brackets (`[]`) indicate the declaration of an array.

The `topCard` variable is an integer that identifies the next card to be dealt from the deck. The `random` variable is used to generate random numbers. It references objects that are of class `java.util.Random`, a class defined within the Java API. The variable declarations of the `Deck` class follow:

```
class Deck {
  // Variable declarations
  int cards[];     // Array of 52 cards
  int topCard;     // 0-51 (index of card in deck)
  Random random;
     .
     .
     .
}
```

The constructor for the `Deck` class allocates an array of 52 integers and assigns it to `cards[]`. The `cards[]` array simulates the 52 cards found in a normal deck of playing cards.

A `for` statement is used to assign 0 to `cards[0]`, 1 to `cards[1]`, 2 to `cards[2]`, and so on, until 51 is assigned to `cards[51]`. This creates a deck of cards in which all the cards are ordered by suit and by value. The integers 0 through 51 are logically mapped to playing cards, as follows:

> 0 through 12 are mapped to the ace of spades through the king of spades
>
> 13 through 25 are mapped to the ace of hearts through the king of hearts
>
> 26 through 38 are mapped to the ace of clubs through the king of clubs
>
> 39 through 51 are mapped to the ace of diamonds through the king of diamonds

The `topCard` of the deck is set to 0. It is used as an index into the `cards[]` array. The `random` variable is assigned a new object of class `Random`. Finally, the `shuffle()` method is invoked to shuffle the new deck of cards. The constructor of the `Deck` class follows:

```
// Method declarations
public Deck() { // Constructor
  cards = new int[52];
  for(int i = 0;i<52;++i) cards[i] = i;
  topCard = 0;
  random = new Random();
  shuffle();
}
```

The shuffle() method shuffles the deck of cards by randomly switching two cards in the deck 52 times. It does this by invoking the randomCard() method to generate a random integer between 0 and 51. These random integers are used to randomly select components of cards and exchange their values. The shuffle() method follows:

```
public void shuffle() {
 // Repeat 52 times
 for(int i = 0;i<52;++i) {
 // Randomly exchange two cards in the deck.
 int j = randomCard();
 int k = randomCard();
 int temp = cards[j];
 cards[j] = cards[k];
 cards[k] = temp;
 }
}
```

The randomCard() method returns an integer between 0 and 51 inclusive. It identifies the int return value in its method declaration. It begins by declaring a variable r and assigning it a random integer value generated by applying the nextInt() method to the random variable. The nextInt() method is defined in the java.util.Random class. If the value assigned to r is less than 0, it is changed to a positive integer. The randomCard() method then returns an integer between 0 and 51 by returning the random integer modulus 52. The randomCard() method follows:

```
int randomCard() {
 int r = random.nextInt();
 if(r<0) r = 0-r;
 return r%52;
}
```

The deal() method is used to deal a card off the top of the deck. It does this by using the topCard variable as an index into the cards[] array. It starts at 0 and is incremented until it is greater than 51, indicating that all the cards in the deck have been dealt. In this case, the deck is reshuffled and topCard is set to 0 once again. This creates the effect of another deck being used because the player and dealer are not required to throw back any cards that are currently in their hands before the deck is shuffled.

The Card class is used to translate the integer card values to String values that can be displayed on the console. A card is dealt by constructing a new instance of Card using the value of cards[] indexed by topCard as an argument. The topCard is then incremented to move to the next card in the deck. Note that deal() returns the object of class Card that was created using the Card() constructor. The deal() method follows:

```
Card deal() {
 if(topCard>51) {
  shuffle();
  topCard = 0;
 }
```

```
Card card = new Card(cards[topCard]);
++topCard;
return card;
}
```

The Hand Class

The Hand class is used to implement a hand of cards as played by both the player and the dealer. It declares three variables and eight methods.

The numCards variable identifies the number of cards contained in the hand. The cards[] array has the same name as the cards[] array declared in the Deck class, but it is logically and physically distinct. Because it is declared in a separate class, it is contained in objects that are instances of the Hand class and not of the Deck class. The MaxCards variable is declared to be static. This means that it is used with the class, as a whole, and not with individual objects that are instances of the class. You'll learn more about class and instance variables in Chapter 5. MaxCards is used to identify the number of components to be allocated within cards[]. The Hand class is structured as follows:

```
class Hand {
 // Variable declarations
 int numCards;
 Card cards[];
 static int MaxCards = 12;
   .
   .
   .
}
```

The constructor for the Hand class sets numCards to 0 to indicate an empty hand, and then creates a MaxCards size array of Card objects and assigns it to cards. The constructor for the Hand class follows:

```
//Method declarations
public Hand() { // Constructor
 numCards = 0;
 cards = new Card[MaxCards];
}
```

Cards are added to a hand using the addCard() method. This method takes an object of class Card as an argument and adds it to the first available position within the cards[] array. It then increments numCards so that it will index the next available position within cards[]. The addCard() method follows:

```
void addCard(Card c) {
  cards[numCards] = c;
  ++numCards;
 }
```

The show() method displays either the dealer's or the player's hand. It takes two boolean arguments that specify whether the hand belongs to the dealer, and if so, whether the first card should be hidden when the hand is displayed. The isDealer parameter is used in the initial if statement to determine whether a dealer or a player heading should be displayed. A for statement is then used to iterate numCards times in order to display each card of the hand. The statement block enclosed by the for statement uses the hideFirstCard parameter to determine whether the first card should be hidden or displayed. The show() method follows:

```java
void show(boolean isDealer,boolean hideFirstCard) {
  if(isDealer) System.out.println("Dealer:");
  else System.out.println("Player:");
  for(int i = 0;i<numCards;++i) {
   if(i == 0 && hideFirstCard) System.out.println("  Hidden");
   else System.out.println("  "+cards[i].value+" of "+cards[i].suit);
  }
}
```

The blackjack() method returns a boolean value indicating whether the hand is blackjack. It uses an if statement to make sure that there are only two cards in the hand. If there are not two cards, false is returned to indicate that the hand is not blackjack. If the number of cards is exactly two, it uses the iValue variable of the Card objects contained in the cards[] array to determine whether the current hand is blackjack. The iValue variable is discussed with the Card class. It identifies the number of points associated with a card. A card with iValue = 1 is an ace. Aces can be either 1 or 11 points. The blackjack() method follows:

```java
boolean blackjack() {
 if(numCards == 2) {
  if(cards[0].iValue == 1 && cards[1].iValue == 10) return true;
  if(cards[1].iValue == 1 && cards[0].iValue == 10) return true;
 }
 return false;
}
```

The under() method returns a boolean value indicating whether the number of points in a hand is less than the argument passed via the n parameter. It declares a points variable of type int and uses a for statement to sum the points for all cards in the hand. It then checks to see if the number of points in the hand is less than n and returns an appropriate value of true or false. The under() method follows:

```java
boolean under(int n) {
 int points = 0;
 for(int i = 0;i<numCards;++i) points += cards[i].iValue;
 if(points<n) return true;
 else return false;
}
```

The bestScore() method returns an integer value identifying the best possible point score for the hand. It adjusts the value associated with aces to either 1 or 11, depending upon whether it causes the hand to go over 21 points. It uses a variable, haveAce, of type boolean, to identify whether the hand contains an ace. It uses a for statement to calculate the minimum number of points in the hand and to determine whether any aces are present. If an ace is found, it determines whether it is better to use the 11- or 1-point value of the ace. The bestScore() method follows:

```
int bestScore() {
 int points = 0;
 boolean haveAce = false;
 for(int i = 0;i<numCards;++i) {
  points += cards[i].iValue;
  if(cards[i].iValue == 1) haveAce = true;
 }
 if(haveAce) {
  if(points+10 < 22) points += 10;
 }
 return points;
}
```

The mustHit() method is used to play out the dealer's hand. If the bestScore of the dealer's hand is lower than 17, the dealer must take a hit. If it is 17 or higher, the dealer must stay. The mustHit() method follows:

```
boolean mustHit() {
 if(bestScore()<17) return true;
 else return false;
}
```

The busted() method uses an if statement to determine whether the number of points in a hand is under 22. If it is not under, the hand is busted and true is returned. Otherwise, false is returned. The busted() method follows:

```
boolean busted() {
  if(!under(22)) return true;
  else return false;
 }
```

The Card Class

The Card class is used to translate the integer value of cards, maintained by objects of the Deck class, into objects of type String. It declares three variables and two methods.

The iValue variable is used to keep track of the number of points associated with a card. It is an abbreviation for integer value and is used to differentiate it from the value variable. The value variable references a text string that is used to describe the face value of a playing card. The suit variable is used to identify the suit of a playing card. The variables declared for the Card class are shown:

```
class Card {
 // Variable declarations
 int iValue;   // Numeric value corresponding to card.
 String value; // "A" "2" through "9" "T" "J" "Q" "K"
 String suit; // "S" "H" "C" "D"
    .
    .
    .
}
```

The Card() constructor is the heart of the Card class and is an example of a constructor that takes an argument. It expects a value of 0 through 51 of a card value from the Deck class. The Card class constructor follows:

```
// Method declarations
 public Card(int n) { // Constructor
    .
    .
    .
 }
```

Card() first determines the suit of the card identified by the n parameter. It does this by dividing n by 13 and assigning the result to an integer variable named iSuit. It determines the point value of the card by calculating n modulus 13 and adding 1. It adjusts this value later in the method. This is shown in the following code:

```
int iSuit = n/13;
  iValue = n%13+1;
```

Card() then uses a switch statement to assign the correct text string to the suit variable. The switch statement takes the iSuit variable and compares it to the values identified in each of the case labels. If a case label matches the value of iSuit, control of execution is passed to the statement after the case label. These statements consist of assignment statements that set suit to the correct text string. The default label is used if no other label matches iSuit. The break statement is used to "jump out" of the execution of the switch statement to the statement immediately following the switch statement. It is also used with other statements, such as the for, while, and do statements. The switch statement follows:

```
switch(iSuit) {
    case 0:
     suit = "Spades";
     break;
    case 1:
     suit = "Hearts";
     break;
    case 2:
     suit = "Clubs";
     break;
    default:
     suit = "Diamonds";
   }
```

The statements following the switch statement show how a switch statement can be coded using a series of nested if statements:

```
if(iValue == 1) value = "Ace";
else if(iValue == 10) value = "Ten";
else if(iValue == 11) value = "Jack";
else if(iValue == 12) value = "Queen";
else if(iValue == 13) value = "King";
else value = Integer.toString(iValue);
if(iValue>10) iValue = 10;
```

These statements are equivalent to the following `switch` statement:

```
value=Integer.toString(iValue);
switch(iValue) {
case 1:
    value = "Ace";
    break;
case 10:
    value = "Ten";
    break;
case 11:
    value = "Jack";
    iValue = 10;
    break;
case 12:
    value = "Queen";
    iValue = 10;
    break;
case 13:
    value = "King";
    iValue = 10;
    break;
}
```

Finally, the `getValue()` method is used to return the value of `iValue`, the point value of the card. It is fairly simple, as far as methods go, but it shows how the values of an object's variables can be made available without having to provide access to the variable itself. The `getValue()` method follows:

```
int getValue() {
  return iValue;
 }
```

Arrays

Arrays are objects that contain a number of variables of the same type. These component variables are referenced using the integer indices $0,\ldots,n-1$, where n is the length of the array. The type of the array is identified by appending `[]` to the type of its components. For example, `int[]` identifies an array of type `int`, `Object[]` identifies an array of type `Object`, and `char[][]` identifies an array of an array of type `char`.

> **NOTE**
>
> Java only supports single-dimensional arrays. Multidimensional array capabilities can be achieved by using arrays of arrays.

Arrays are declared by declaring a variable to be of an array type. For example, the following declares `nums` to be an array of type `int`:

```
int[] nums;
```

The declaration can also be written as follows:

```
int nums[];
```

You can place the brackets after either the type or the variable name.

Array Allocation

When a variable of an array type is declared, the size of the array is not identified, and the array object is not allocated. To allocate storage for an array, you can use the new operator to create an array object of a specific size. For example, the following creates a char array of length 24, the individual component variables of which can be referenced by ch[0], ch[2], ..., ch[23]:

```
char ch[] = new char[24];
```

The following statement creates an array of type Dice[] of length 6:

```
Dice[] d = new Dice[6];
```

Arrays can also be allocated by specifying their initial values. For example, the following allocates a String array of length 7 that contains abbreviations for the days of the week:

```
String days[] = {"sun", "mon", "tue", "wed", "thu", "fri", "sat"};
```

The length of an array can always be found by appending .length to the name of the array. For example, days.length returns the integer 7 as the length of days[].

Statements

The BlackJackApp example introduces a number of Java statements. These statements implement the bodies of the various methods used in the example. The following subsections describe the types of statements that are used in the BlackJackApp example. A complete description of Java statements is provided in Chapter 11. When you read through the following sections and learn about a particular statement, go back through the BlackJackApp program and see how many examples of the statement you can find. This will help you to associate the statement's syntax with the different contexts in which it can be used and elevate your understanding from the syntactic to the semantic level.

> **NOTE**
>
> Java statements, like C and C++ statements, are separated by semicolons.

Statement Blocks

Java statements are organized into statement *blocks*. Blocks begin with an opening brace ({) and end with a closing brace (}). They are used to indicate a group of statements and variable declarations that are to be considered as a single syntactical unit. Blocks are used to define the scope of execution of statements in which they are enclosed. For example, the body of a method can be considered to be a single block. Blocks are used in other statements, such as the `if` and `do` statements, to identify groups of statements that are to be executed as if they were a single statement.

> **NOTE**
>
> Statement blocks can be considered to be syntactically equivalent to a single statement.

An example of a statement block is taken from the `BlackJackGame()` constructor:

```
... {
bet = 0;
money = 1000;
deck = new Deck();
keyboardInput =
    new BufferedReader(new InputStreamReader(System.in));
}
```

The `if` Statement

The `if` statement is used to decide whether a particular statement should be executed. Its syntax is as follows:

```
if ( BooleanExpression ) Statement1
else Statement2
```

The `else` part of the statement is optional. If the `boolean` expression, referred to as the `if` condition, evaluates to `true`, *Statement1* is executed; otherwise *Statement2* is executed. Program execution then continues with the next statement following the `if` statement. If the `else` part is omitted, execution proceeds immediately to the next statement when the `if` condition is false. Either *Statement1* or *Statement2* can be a statement block.

An example of an `if` statement is taken from the `show()` method of the `Hand` class:

```
if(isDealer) System.out.println("Dealer:");
else System.out.println("Player:");
```

If the value of `isDealer` is `true`, the text `Dealer:` is displayed; otherwise the text `Player:` is displayed.

The switch Statement

The switch statement is like a sequence of embedded if statements. It is used to transfer control to the first labeled statement within a block of statements that matches the value of the expression in the switch expression. The syntax of the switch statement is

```
switch ( SwitchExpression ) StatementBlock;
```

where statements within the statement block are labeled by preceding them with prefixes of the form

```
case ConstantExpression :
```

or

```
default :
```

The switch expression must evaluate to a value of type char, byte, short, or int. The same is true of the constant expressions in the case labels. The switch statement evaluates the switch expression and transfers program execution to the first labeled statement whose constant expression has the same value as the switch expression. If no case-labeled expression matches the switch expression, control is transferred to the first statement with a default label. Otherwise, control is transferred to the next statement following the switch statement.

An example of a switch statement is taken from the Card() constructor:

```
switch(iSuit) {
  case 0:
   suit = "Spades";
   break;
  case 1:
   suit = "Hearts";
   break;
  case 2:
   suit = "Clubs";
   break;
  default:
   suit = "Diamonds";
}
```

The value of iSuit is compared to the values 0, 1, and 2 of the case labels. If it matches any of these values, program execution is transferred to the labeled statement. Otherwise, program execution is transferred to the statement labeled as default. The break statements are used to transfer control to the first statement following the switch statement, as you'll learn in the following section.

The break Statement

The break statement is used to terminate execution of a statement block and transfer control to the first statement following the statement in which the block is enclosed. The syntax of the break statement is

```
break;
```

or

```
break label;
```

where *label* is an optional label that can be attached to the statement enclosing the statement block. Refer to Chapter 11 for a discussion of the use of labels with the break statement.

The break statement is used with the case, do, while, and for statements to exit the enclosed statement block and transfer control to the first statement following the enclosing statement.

The sample switch statement, shown in the previous section, contains several break statements that cause program execution to be transferred to the first statement following the switch statement.

The for Statement

The for statement is used to iterate the execution of a statement or statement block. Its syntax is as follows:

```
for (InitializationClause; ForExpression; IncrementClause) EnclosedStatement
```

The initialization clause consists of a statement that is executed once at the beginning of the for statement. The for expression is then checked. If it is false, the for statement ends and program execution continues with the next statement following the for statement. If the for expression is true, the enclosed statement is executed. The enclosed statement can be a statement block.

When the execution of the enclosed statement is completed, the statement contained in the increment clause is executed. The for expression is then reevaluated to determine whether the enclosed statement should be executed again. The enclosed statement, increment statement, and evaluation of the for expression repeat their execution until the for expression evaluates to false, at which point execution of the for statement is complete and program execution continues with the statement following the for statement.

NOTE

The increment clause does not end with a semicolon (;).

A sample `for` statement is taken from the `under()` method of the `Hand` class:

```
for(int i = 0;i<numCards;++i) points += cards[i].iValue;
```

This statement begins by setting the variable `i` to `0`. It then checks to see if `i` is less than `numCards`. If it is not, the `for` statement terminates. If `i` is less than `numCards`, the following statement is executed:

```
points += cards[i].iValue;
```

This statement is used to add the `iValue` variable of the `i`th `card[]` array element to the `points` variable. When execution of this statement is completed, the `++i` statement is executed to increment `i` by 1. The `for` expression, `i<numCards`, is reevaluated, and the `for` statement's execution continues.

> **NOTE**
>
> The operators used by Java are similar to those of C and C++.

The `do` Statement

The `do` statement is used to repeatedly execute a statement until a specified condition becomes `false`. The syntax of the `do` statement is

```
do EnclosedStatement while (BooleanExpression) ;
```

The `do` statement repeatedly executes the enclosed statement until the `boolean` expression becomes `false`. The enclosed statement will be executed at least once because the `boolean` expression is evaluated after its execution. The enclosed statement can be a statement block.

An example of a do statement is taken from the `placeBet()` method of the `BlackJackGame` class:

```
do{
 System.out.print("Enter bet: ");
 System.out.flush();
 bet = Integer.parseInt(keyboardInput.readLine());
} while(bet<0 ¦¦ bet>money);
```

The `do` statement executes the statement block until a bet between 0 and the value of `money` is entered by the player.

The `while` Statement

The `while` statement is similar to the `do` statement, except that the `boolean` expression is evaluated before execution of the enclosed statement. If the `boolean` expression evaluates to `false`, the while statement is terminated and execution continues with the next statement following the while statement. The while statement syntax is as follows:

```
while (BooleanExpression) EnclosedStatement
```

A sample while statement is taken from the play() method of the BlackJackGame class:

```
while(dealersHand.mustHit())
 dealersHand.addCard(deck.deal());
```

The while statement checks to see if the dealer must take a hit and, if so, adds a card to the dealer's hand. The while statement repeats this processing until the dealer is no longer required to take a hit.

The return Statement

The return statement is used to terminate execution of a method and return a value of the type specified in the method's declaration. Its syntax is

```
return Expression;
```

Expression must evaluate to a value that is compatible with the result type of the method in which it is used.

A sample return statement is taken from the getValue() method of the Card class:

```
int getValue() {
 return iValue;
}
```

This simple method returns the value iValue and completes the execution of the getValue() method.

Summary

In this chapter, you toured the elements of the Java language by writing four sample programs. You learned about the structure of Java programs, how to compile and execute them, and about many Java language elements. You should now be up and running with Java and capable of experimenting with it by writing your own programs. Although this chapter covers many elements of the Java syntax, use Chapter 11 as a complete reference for the Java language. Chapter 5 supplements the information you learned in this chapter with a solid background in Java's support of object-oriented programming.

5

Classes and Objects

In this chapter you'll learn all about Java and object-oriented programming. You'll first cover general object-oriented programming concepts and then learn how to use Java classes to build object-oriented software. You'll use the information you learn to develop a sample Java program that illustrates the benefits of object-oriented programming.

Object-Oriented Programming Concepts

Over the many years since the dawn of computing, people have studied software-development approaches to figure out which approaches are quickest, cheapest, most reliable, and produce the best software. And over the years, many approaches and technologies have reigned as the best. As time goes on, we learn more about software development and are able to modify and adapt our approaches based on what we learn. The type of software that we develop also changes over time as a result of improvements in computer hardware, innovations in computer science, and changes in user expectations. These improvements affect our development approaches as well.

Of all the known approaches to developing software, one approach, called the *object-oriented* approach, has repeatedly proven itself to be the best approach for a large class of common software applications. It's likely that the object-oriented approach will undergo further evolution and that a new, improved software-development paradigm will take its place. But for right now and the foreseeable future, it is recognized as the best approach for the majority of software that we develop today.

Object-oriented programming focuses on the development of self-contained software components, called *objects*. These objects are modeled after things, such as files, forms, buttons, and windows, that appear in the real world. Objects are defined in terms of the information they contain and the operations they provide for using and manipulating this information.

It's an Object-Oriented World

This book is an object. It contains a lot of information. (If you don't believe me, try retyping it.) It also has methods for accessing the information it contains. For example, you can open the book, turn a page, read a paragraph, search the table of contents, and so on. The information contained in the book, together with the methods for accessing it, are what comprise the object known as this book.

In order to read this book, you need some sort of light source. You could be reading it in the open sunshine or by moonlight, but let's assume that you are using a lamp of some kind. A lamp is also an object. It is an example of an object that contains information about its state. The *state* of an object is the particular condition that it is in. For example, a lamp can be on or off. The lamp's methods—turn lamp on and turn lamp off—are used to access the state of the lamp.

Getting back to this book, it also has state information. For example, it can be open or closed. If it is open, it can be opened to a particular page. The pages are objects in their own right. They contain information and can be accessed through the read page method. The book object can be viewed as being composed of page objects. The book's methods provide access to pages, and the page methods provide access to the information contained on a particular page.

The information contained in an object, whether it is state-specific or not, is referred to as the object's *data*. The object's methods are said to *access* the data. Some methods return information about the object's data and are said to support *read access*. Other methods cause the data to be modified and are said to provide *write access* to the data. Finally, as you'll learn in later sections, some methods, called *constructors*, are used to create objects.

Composition and Reuse

The fact that one object can be composed of, or built from, other objects is the heart of object-oriented programming. This allows more complex objects to be constructed from simple object components. Just as you would not write a book as one continuous stream of text (unless you are Jack Kerouac), you wouldn't write a program as a single sequence of source code instructions. You design your program as an application object and construct it from other objects that are built or borrowed.

For example, suppose that you are developing a drawing program. Your draw application would consist of objects such as windows, menus, a drawing canvas, a tool palette, a color palette, and so on. Some of these objects would be available in object libraries and others would be built from more primitive components. You would develop your drawing application by gathering and building its component objects and assembling them into an integrated whole.

Object composition not only allows you to simplify the organization of your programs, it also lets you reuse the software you develop. For example, you could develop drawing objects as part of your draw program and then reuse those objects in a paint program and a desktop publishing program. You could also package up your drawing objects and give or sell them to others so that they can use them as a foundation for building their own custom objects.

Object reuse provides you with the capability to build or acquire a library of objects from which you can more quickly and easily piece together your programs. Without this capability, you are forced to start from scratch with every program that you develop.

Object reuse is not limited to object composition. It also exploits a powerful capability of object-oriented programming known as *inheritance*. Inheritance not only allows objects to be used as is, but also allows new objects to be created by extending and tailoring existing objects. Before you learn about inheritance, however, the concept of an object's class must be explained.

Classes

At this point, you might be wondering just how you go about developing objects. The answer, of course, depends on the language that you are using. Java, C++, SmallTalk, and some other object-oriented languages follow a class-based approach. This approach allows you to declare *classes* that serve as templates from which objects are created.

As you would expect, a *class* defines the type of data that is contained in an object and the methods that are used to access this data. A class also defines one or more methods to be used to create objects that are *instances* of the class. An instance of a class is a concrete manifestation of the class in your computer's memory.

For example, consider a job application form as an object. It contains data—the different form fields that must be filled out. There are also methods for accessing the data—for example, fill in form and read form. Now suppose that you develop an application form for a company that will use it for new job applicants. When a job is advertised, 100 potential applicants show up. In order for these applicants to use your form, they must all be given a unique instance of the form. These form instances are created by using the form you developed as a master copy and then duplicating the master copy as many times as needed to create each instance. The job applicants then fill in their instances of the form, using the fill-in-form method.

In the preceding example, the master form is analogous to a class. The master form defines the data to be contained in each of its instances and implicitly provides methods by which the data can be accessed. In the same way, a class defines the data that can be contained in an object as well as the methods that can be used to access this data.

Classification and Inheritance

Classification is a common way that we organize knowledge. When we encounter a new object in our daily experience, we try to fit that object in our hierarchical classification scheme. If it fits in an existing category, we know what kind of object it is. If it doesn't fit, we add a new category. Figure 5.1 illustrates how we use classification to represent knowledge.

When we classify objects in this hierarchical fashion, the object categories at the top of the classification tree include all the object categories below them. If an object category appears in the classification tree, it satisfies the properties of all object categories above it in the tree. Figure 5.2 presents a classification tree for vehicles. All categories in the tree below the category automobile, for example, share the common characteristics of being four-wheeled, self-powered, and designed for passenger transportation.

FIGURE 5.1.

Hierarchical classification of knowledge.

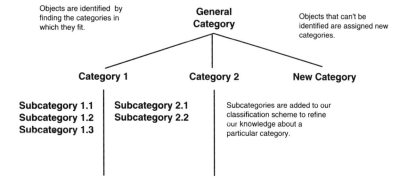

FIGURE 5.2.

The vehicle classification tree.

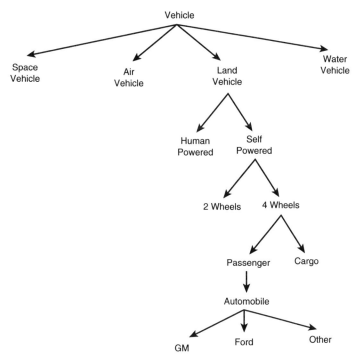

The fact that a lower-level category shares the characteristics of the categories above it on the classification tree is known as *inheritance*. The lower-level categories are said to inherit the characteristics of the categories above them on the tree.

At this point, you're probably wondering what any of this has to do with object-oriented programming in general, and Java software development in particular. We're almost there.

The classes you learned about in the previous section can also be organized in a hierarchical fashion. A class X is said to *extend* another class Y if it contains all the data contained in class Y and implements all the methods implemented by class Y. Class X is said to be a *subclass* of class Y, and class Y is said to be a *superclass,* or *parent class,* of class X.

Classes form a hierarchical classification tree under the subclass relationship. If a class X is a subclass of a class Y, it inherits the properties of Y. This means that all the data and methods defined for class Y are available to class X.

Most object-oriented programming languages, and Java in particular, allow you to easily define subclasses that automatically inherit the data and methods of the classes they extend. This is a very powerful feature for software reuse. Not only can you reuse classes as they are defined, but you can easily extend and tailor their definitions by adding additional data and access methods to their subclasses.

There are many times that you may have a class definition you can use in your program, but it would be better if it supported additional state information or access methods. Java's support of subclassing enables you to easily extend such classes by supplying only the additional data and methods that are unique to the subclass. This allows you to take advantage of all the features of the superclass without having to implement any of them.

Multiple Inheritance

When a class extends another class, it inherits the data and methods of the class it extends. This is known as *single inheritance.* It is also possible for a class to extend classes on more than one branch of the class hierarchy tree, as shown in Figure 5.3. This is known as *multiple inheritance.*

FIGURE 5.3.

Multiple inheritance.

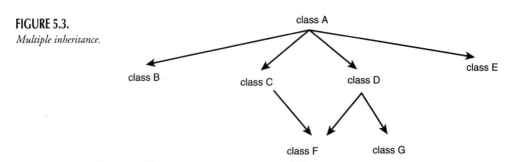

Class F inherits data and methods
from both classes C and D.

Multiple inheritance poses some difficulties for object-oriented programming. Most of these difficulties stem from the problem of determining which parent of a class to use under certain conditions. Numerous ambiguities arise when a class may have more than one immediate parent. For example, suppose a class X extends both a class Y and a class Z. Both class Y and class Z implement a unique print method. How does the compiler determine which method should be used to print objects of class X? What if the ambiguity arises during runtime for an object that inherits methods over several widely spaced branches of the class hierarchy? What's a poor compiler to do?

It is possible to design compilers and runtime systems that solve the ambiguities resulting from multiple inheritance, but these solutions tend to introduce a significant amount of processing overhead, adversely affecting program size and performance. The developers of Java have opted to support only single inheritance. This greatly simplifies the Java language, compiler, and runtime system. Java uses the interface construct to provide the benefits of multiple inheritance without the drawbacks resulting from parent ambiguity. You learn more about this construct in Chapter 6, "Interfaces."

Messages, Methods, and Object Interaction

In a pure object-oriented programming model, such as that used by SmallTalk, objects interact by sending messages to each other. When an object receives a message, the object invokes a method to process the message. The method may change the state of the object, return information contained in the object, or cause objects to be created or deleted.

The object model used by Java is consistent with the concept of message passing, but does not emphasize it. In the Java model, objects interact by invoking each other's methods. *Methods* provide access to the information contained in an object. The type of access varies depending on the method.

Encapsulation

One characteristic of object-oriented programming that is often touted is *encapsulation*. The term carries the connotation of an object being enclosed in some sort of container—and that is exactly what it means. Encapsulation is the combining of data and the code that manipulates that data into a single component—that is, an object. Encapsulation also refers to the control of access to the details of an object's implementation. Object access is limited to a well-defined, controlled interface. This allows objects to be self-contained and protects them from accidental misuse, both of which are important to reliable software design. Encapsulation provides the basis for developing security-rich objects.

Polymorphism

Polymorphism is the capability to assume different forms. In object-oriented programming, this refers to the capability of objects to have many methods of the same name, but with different forms. The compiler and runtime system support polymorphism by matching each method invocation to the correct method, class, and object. The capability to figure out which method to use in complex situations is the essence of polymorphism.

Luckily for us, polymorphism is implemented in the compiler and runtime system—we don't need to do anything to make it happen. We just need to know that it works.

Dynamic Binding

Sometimes a program might need to interface with objects of many different classes. For example, consider a program that has the responsibility of sending out objects over a communication link. The program may not know what class an object belongs to until it is time to send it. The capability to defer until runtime decisions about what class an object belongs to and the methods for accessing the object is known as *dynamic binding*.

Dynamic binding is important to object-oriented programming because it eliminates many potentially constraining assumptions about the classes that an object belongs to and enables objects to be designed in a more general and open manner.

Dynamic binding also provides capabilities that are necessary for the advanced network programming capabilities of Java applets. When a browser executes a Java applet, the applet could require the loading of classes located on other sites across the Internet. Furthermore, these classes could be in a continual state of modification and upgrade. Dynamic binding allows new and modified objects to be used by executing software without requiring recompilation. The compiler and interpreter work together to provide executable code with the capabilities needed to dynamically interface with unknown objects during program execution.

Java Classes

In this section, you will develop a Java program, CDrawApp, that illustrates the concepts of encapsulation, composition and reuse, classification and inheritance, polymorphism, and dynamic binding. CDrawApp will allow you to draw points, boxes, and text strings on a character-based grid that is displayed using the Java console window.

The program will be introduced as a series of Java classes that cover different aspects of class and object syntax. Each new class will make use of the capabilities provided by previous classes and will provide additional building blocks required for the program's development. It is important that you understand each class that is presented before moving on to subsequent classes.

You should create a ch05 directory, under c:\jdk1.1.1\jdg, to store the Java source and byte code files for this lesson. All classes will be developed in the jdg.ch05 package.

Class Syntax

The Java language is class and object oriented. Classes are templates for the creation of objects. They define the data contained in an object together with methods for accessing that data.

Classes are declared as follows:

```
ClassModifiers class ClassName ExtendsClause ImplementsClause ClassBody
```

The *ClassModifiers*, *ExtendsClause*, and *ImplementsClause* are optional. Interfaces and the *ImplementsClause* are covered in the next chapter. The *ClassBody* is enclosed by braces, and contains zero or more class body declarations.

An example of a simple class declaration is

```
class SimpleClass {
}
```

It declares a class, named SimpleClass, that is a subclass of Object, the highest-level class in the Java class hierarchy. SimpleClass declares no variables or methods of its own; it has only those that it inherits from Object.

The Point Class

The first class that you'll define for the CDrawApp program is the Point class. This class is used to identify a point on a grid by its x and y coordinates. The source code for the class declaration is shown in Listing 5.1. You should enter the code in a file named Point.java and store it in your c:\jdk1.1.1\jdg\ch05 directory. Then compile it using the command javac Point.java.

Listing 5.1. The Point class source code.

```
package jdg.ch05;
// Point.java
public class Point {
 // Variable declarations
 private int x;
 private int y;
 //Method declarations
 public Point() {
  x = 0;
  y = 0;
 }
 public Point(int xValue, int yValue) {
  x = xValue;
  y = yValue;
 }
```

continues

Listing 5.1. continued

```
public Point(Point p) {
 x = p.x();
 y = p.y();
}
public int x() {
 return x;
}
public int y() {
 return y;
}
public void xSet(int xValue) {
 x = xValue;
}
public void ySet(int yValue) {
 y = yValue;
}
public Point add(Point p) {
 return new Point(x+p.x(), y+p.y());
}
public Point add(int i,int j) {
 return new Point(x+i,y+j);
}
public String toString() {
 return new String("("+String.valueOf(x)+","+String.valueOf(y)+")");
}
}
```

Class Modifiers

The `Point` class is declared using the `public` class modifier. *Class modifiers* are keywords that are used to specify the properties of a class. Three class modifiers are supported: `public`, `final`, and `abstract`. If a class is declared as `public`, it can be accessed outside of its package; otherwise it cannot. Because `Point` is declared as `public`, it can be accessed outside its package. Only one `public` class or interface is allowed in a compilation unit. `Point` is the only class in `Point.java` and, therefore, follows this rule.

If a class is declared as `final`, it cannot be extended. `final` classes form the leaves of the class hierarchy tree.

An `abstract` class is used to define the general behavior for an intended set of subclasses. `abstract` classes are used to set the stage for subsequent subclass development. They are, by definition, incomplete and cannot be instantiated in terms of objects. `abstract` classes describe the behavior expected of their subclasses through the declaration of `abstract` methods. `abstract` methods must be redefined, or *overridden*, before they can be used. Only `abstract` classes are allowed to declare or inherit `abstract` methods. The `CGObject` class is an example of an abstract class. It is presented in the section "The `CGObject` class," later in this chapter.

Extending Superclasses

When a class declaration does not contain an `extends` clause, the class is automatically made a subclass of the `Object` class. The `Point` class does not contain an `extends` clause and, therefore, is a subclass of `Object`. The `Object` class is at the top of the Java class hierarchy, being the *superclass* of all Java classes.

You can change a class's position in the class hierarchy by identifying its immediate superclass in the class declaration. The *immediate superclass* is the parent class directly above it in the class hierarchy. You identify the immediate superclass of a class using the `extends` clause in the class declaration. For example, you can place `SimpleClass` under `ExampleClass` in the class hierarchy as follows:

```
class SimpleClass extends ExampleClass {
}
```

`SimpleClass` does not have any unique variables or methods of its own, but it inherits those of `ExampleClass` and all superclasses of `ExampleClass`.

Adding Body to Classes

The body of the `Point` class consists of all declarations between the opening and closing braces. If a class is to add any features to its superclass, it does so in its class body. It is here that additional variables and methods (including constructors) are declared and static initializers are included. These additional declarations are referred to as *class body declarations*. Static initializers are covered in Chapter 11, "Language Summary."

The class body declarations are identified within the opening and closing braces (`{` and `}`) of the class body. You need to supply the braces even if you don't intend to declare any fields, as you saw in the `SimpleClass` example.

Variable Declarations

Variables are the components of an object that store data and state information. They are declared as follows:

VariableModifiers Type VariableDeclarators

The *VariableModifiers* are keywords that identify special properties of the variables being declared. The *Type* is the Java type of the declared variables. It may be a primitive type, a class type, an interface type, or an array type. The *VariableDeclarators* identify the names of the declared variables and can be used to specify the initial values of these variables.

The `Point` class declares two integer variables: `x` and `y`. They are used to store the location of a point on a two-dimensional grid. These variables are declared with the `private` modifier. This modifier restricts access to the x and y variables to within the Point class. The Point class illustrates the principles of encapsulation. Data and methods are combined with a well-defined interface to provide maximum modularity. Access to the internal operation of the class is controlled.

Constructor Declarations

Constructors are special methods that are used to initialize newly created objects. They are used together with the new operator to create and initialize objects that are instances of a class.

Constructors are declared in a slightly different manner than other methods. Their syntax is as follows:

AccessSpecifier ConstructorDeclarator ThrowsClause ConstructorBody

The *AccessSpecifier* identifies the type of access allowed to the constructor. The *ConstructorDeclarator* identifies a method with the same name as the class and specifies its parameter list. The parameter list is a comma-separated list of parameter declarations where each parameter declaration identifies the type and name of a parameter that is passed to the constructor upon invocation.

The *ThrowsClause* is used to identify any exceptions that can be thrown by the constructor. Exceptions are covered in Chapter 7, "Exceptions."

The *ConstructorBody* contains the code that implements the constructor.

The Point class has three constructors:

```
public Point() {
  x = 0;
  y = 0;
}
public Point(int xValue, int yValue) {
  x = xValue;
  y = yValue;
}
public Point(Point p) {
  x = p.x();
  y = p.y();
}
```

All three constructors are identified as public. This allows them to be accessed outside their package. The first constructor does not have any parameters. It simply initializes the x and y variables to 0. The second constructor has two parameters, xValue and yValue, of integer type. They are used to set the value of x and y. The third constructor takes an object of class Point as its parameter. It sets the values of x and y based upon the values of the parameter point p. It is an example of a *copy constructor* because it creates a new point that is a copy of the point that is passed as its parameter.

The declaration of the three `Point` constructors is an example of *overloading*. Overloading occurs when two or more methods with the same name are declared within a class. The overloaded methods must differ in their parameter lists. The `add()` methods of the `Point` class are also overloaded.

Overloading is an example of polymorphism. When an overloaded method is to be invoked during program execution, the number and type of method arguments used in the invocation determine which method is used.

Access Method Declarations

Methods are executable units of code that provide access to the data stored in variables. Methods that are not constructors are referred to as *non-constructor* methods, or *access* methods. Access methods are declared within the body of a class as follows:

```
MethodModifiers ResultType MethodDeclarator ThrowsClause MethodBody
```

The `MethodModifiers` identify special properties of a method. All the methods of class `Point` are `public`, allowing them to be accessed outside their package.

The `ResultType` of a method identifies the type of value that is returned by the method. If an access method does not return a value, it must use the `void` return type. Constructors do not have a return type. The access methods of class `Point` have return values of type `int`, `void`, `Point`, and `String`.

The `MethodDeclarator` identifies the method, by name, and specifies its parameter list. The parameter list of access methods is specified in the same manner as with constructors.

The `MethodBody` contains the code that implements the Java method.

The `Point` class has seven access methods. The `x()` and `y()` methods return the x and y coordinates of a point. The `xSet()` and `ySet()` methods set the values of these coordinates based on the values of the `xValue` and `yValue` parameters. The two `add()` methods are used to create a new `Point` object by adding to the coordinates of the point being accessed. The `new` operator creates new instances of a class. It is always followed by a constructor that initializes the newly created instance. The `toString()` method returns an object of class `String` that describes the point as an ordered pair.

The `CGrid` Class

The `CGrid` class is used to define a grid of characters of specified dimensions. It provides a basic set of grid methods and is extended by other classes that add to these methods. Its source code is shown in Listing 5.2. It should be entered into the `CGrid.java` file and compiled using `javac`.

Listing 5.2. The CGrid class source code.

```
package jdg.ch05;
// CGrid.java
public class CGrid {
 // Variable declarations
 protected int width;
 protected int depth;
 protected char grid[][];
 // Method declarations
 public CGrid(int widthValue,int depthValue) {
  width = widthValue;
  depth = depthValue;
  grid = new char[depth][width];
  blankGrid();
 }
 public void blankGrid() {
  fillGrid(' ');
 }
 public void fillGrid(char ch) {
  for(int j=0; j<depth; ++j)
   for(int i=0; i<width; ++i)
    grid[j][i]= ch;
 }
 public void putCharAt(char ch,Point p){
  grid[p.y()][p.x()] = ch;
 }
 public char getCharFrom(Point p) {
  return grid[p.y()][p.x()];
 }
}
```

CGrid declares three variables: width, depth, and grid[][]. The width and depth variables are used to specify the horizontal and vertical dimensions of grid[][], an array of character arrays that holds the characters of the grid. The grid[][] array is used as a two-dimensional array of characters, although Java technically does not have multidimensional arrays.

The CGrid variables are declared as protected. This specifies that they can only be accessed in the package jdg.ch05, in which they are declared, and in any subclasses of CGrid.

CGrid has a single constructor that sets the values of width and depth, allocates the grid[][] array, and then invokes blankGrid() to fill grid[][] with spaces.

CGrid has four access methods. The fillGrid() method sets each element of the grid[][] array to the ch parameter. The blankGrid() method simply calls fillGrid() with a space character. The putCharAt() and getCharFrom() methods are used to set a point in the grid to a particular character and to find out what character is at a given location in the grid.

Note that the putCharAt() and getCharFrom() methods use the Point class to define their parameters. Because Point is in the same package as CGrid, it does not need to be imported.

The CGObject Class

The CGObject class is an example of an abstract class. abstract classes are used to constrain the behavior of their subclasses by defining abstract methods. The abstract methods must be implemented by any non-abstract subclasses. Listing 5.3 shows the source code of the CGObject class.

Listing 5.3. The CGObject class source code.

```
package jdg.ch05;
// CGObject.java
public abstract class CGObject {
 // Variable declarations
 public Point location;
 public char drawCharacter;
 // Method declarations
 public void addToGrid(PrintCGrid grid) {
  grid.addCGObject(this);
 }
 public abstract void display(PrintCGrid grid);
 public abstract void describe();
}
```

The CGObject class is used to define the general behavior of objects that may be displayed on a grid. It declares two variables: location and drawCharacter. The location variable is of type Point and is used to specify the point on a grid where an object is located. The drawCharacter variable identifies the character that should be used to draw the object.

CGObject has three methods and no constructors. abstract classes cannot have constructors because they are incompletely defined and, therefore, cannot have object instances.

The first method, addToGrid(), is not abstract. It takes an object of class PrintCGrid as a parameter and invokes the addCGObject() method of PrintCGrid to add this to the grid. The this keyword is used to refer to the current object. Whatever object of a subclass of CGObject that is invoked with the addToGrid() method is added to an object of class PrintCGrid.

CGObject's other two methods are declared with the abstract keyword. This signifies that they must be overridden before they can be used by any non-abstract subclasses of CGObject. The overridden methods must have the same names, parameters, and return values as the abstract methods. The display() method will be used to display an object on a grid of class PrintCGrid. The describe() method will be used to display a description of a grid object.

Enter the source code for CGObject before going on to the PrintCGrid class. In case you forgot, it should be entered into a file of the same name, with the .java extension—that is, CGObject.java. However, don't compile CGObject.java yet—you'll need to enter the code for PrintCGrid first.

The `PrintCGrid` Class

The `PrintCGrid` class is a subclass of the `CGrid` class. It defines additional variables and methods that allow objects to be added to a grid. It also provides methods for displaying the grid. The source code of the `PrintCGrid` class is shown in Listing 5.4.

Listing 5.4. The `PrintCGrid` class source code.

```
package jdg.ch05;
import java.lang.System;
// PrintCGrid.java
public class PrintCGrid extends CGrid {
 // Variable declarations
 protected CGObject displayList[];
 protected static final int maxObjects = 100;
 protected int numObjects;
 // Method declarations
 public PrintCGrid(int x,int y) {
  super(x,y);
  numObjects = 0;
  displayList = new CGObject[maxObjects];
 }
 public void addCGObject(CGObject obj) {
  if(numObjects < maxObjects) {
   displayList[numObjects] = obj;
   ++numObjects;
  }
 }
 public void deleteCGObject(int index) {
  if(index < numObjects && numObjects > 0) {
   for(int i = index; i < numObjects -1 ; ++i)
    displayList[i] = displayList[i+1];
   --numObjects;
  }
 }
 public void deleteLastObject() {
   if(numObjects > 0) --numObjects;
 }
 public int getNumObjects() {
  return numObjects;
 }
 public CGObject getObject(int index) {
  return displayList[index];
 }
 public void clearGrid() {
  numObjects = 0;
 }
 public void drawGrid() {
  blankGrid();
  for(int i = 0; i < numObjects ; ++i)
   displayList[i].display(this);
 }
```

```
public void displayGrid() {
  for(int i=0;i<depth;++i)
    System.out.println(String.valueOf(grid[i]));
 }
 public void displayRow(int row) {
  System.out.print(String.valueOf(grid[row]));
 }
 public void show() {
  drawGrid();
  displayGrid();
 }
}
```

Once you've entered the code of PrintCGrid into PrintCGrid.java, go ahead and compile CGObject.java, using the command

```
javac CGObject.java
```

Because CGObject depends on the definition of PrintCGrid, the Java compiler will automatically compile PrintCGrid.java. You can verify this by looking for PrintCGrid.class in the c:\jdk1.1.1\jdg\ch05 directory.

PrintCGrid is identified as a subclass of CGrid by the extends clause in the PrintCGrid class declaration. This means that all of the variables and methods defined in CGrid are available to PrintCGrid. You should now begin to get a feel for the power of inheritance. PrintCGrid uses CGrid as a base from which other grid display variables and methods are added.

PrintCGrid declares three variables: displayList[], maxObjects, and numObjects. These variables are declared as protected, thereby limiting their access to the jdg.ch05 package and subclasses of PrintCGrid.

The displayList[] variable is an array of class CGObject. This does not mean that it will contain objects that are instances of this class. That would be impossible because CGObject is abstract. Declaring displayList[] to be an array of class CGObject allows it to hold objects of any class that is a subclass of CGObject. In general, if a variable is declared to be of class X, then the variable can be assigned any object of a class that is a subclass of X.

The maxObjects variable is declared as both static and final. Variables that are declared using the static modifier are common to all objects that are instances of a class and are not replicated for each instance. Static variables are referred to as *class* variables. Variables that aren't declared as static are *instance* variables and are replicated for each object that is an instance of a class.

The final modifier is used to identify a variable as a constant. A variable that is declared with the final modifier must be initialized and cannot be assigned a value anywhere else outside of its declaration. The maxObjects constant is initialized to 100. It is used to identify the maximum number of objects that can be added to displayList[].

The numObjects variable is used to count the actual number of objects that have been added to the grid's displayList[].

PrintCGrid has a single constructor. This constructor has two parameters, x and y, that represent the horizontal and vertical dimensions of the grid. The constructor invokes the super() method, passing these variables as arguments. The super() method is an example of a *constructor call statement*. It invokes the constructor of PrintCGrid's superclass, that is, CGrid, with the arguments x and y. CGrid's constructor initializes its width and depth variables, allocates the grid[][] array, and fills it with spaces. When CGrid's constructor is finished, PrintCGrid's constructor continues by setting numObjects to 0 and allocating the displayList[] array.

PrintCGrid provides 10 access methods. The addCGObject() method adds an object to the displayList[] array. The deleteCGObject() method deletes the object at the specified index. All subsequent objects in the array are moved to fill the hole left by the deleted object. The deleteLastObject()method deletes the last object by merely decrementing numObjects.

The getNumObjects() method returns the number of objects in displayList[]. The getObject() method returns the object at the specified position within displayList[]. The clearGrid() method clears all objects by setting numObjects to 0.

The drawGrid() method is an interesting example of dynamic binding and the use of abstract classes. It blanks the grid, using the method that it inherits from CGrid, and then invokes the display() method of each object in displayList[]. It does not know what kind of objects are contained in displayList[]. It only knows that they are of some subclass of CGObject, and therefore must implement the display() method. Dynamic binding enables the display() method to be invoked for the correct object class.

The displayGrid()method displays each row of the grid to the console window. It is an example of inheritance. The grid[][] array was defined in the CGrid class and inherited by PrintCGrid. It is updated by drawGrid() and the display() methods of all subclasses of CGObject. It is used by PrintCGrid to print characters to the console window.

The valueOf() method used in displayGrid() is a static method of the String class. It converts an array of characters into a String object. A static method is similar to a static variable in that it applies to the class as a whole rather than to objects that are instances of the class. Because of this class orientation, a static method can access only static variables. final methods are methods that cannot be overridden.

The displayRow() method displays a single row of the grid to the console window and the show() method combines the drawGrid() and displayGrid() methods into a single method.

The BorderedPrintCGrid Class

The BorderedPrintCGrid class further extends the CGrid class by subclassing PrintCGrid. It adds additional variables and methods for creating a border around objects of class PrintCGrid. Listing 5.5 contains the source code of the BorderedPrintCGrid class.

Listing 5.5. The `BorderedPrintCGrid` class source code.

```java
package jdg.ch05;
// BorderedPrintCGrid.java
public class BorderedPrintCGrid extends PrintCGrid {
 // Variable declarations
 private boolean useBorder;
 private char borderCharacter;
 private String horizEdge;
 private String vertEdge;
 // Method declarations
 public BorderedPrintCGrid() {
  super(75,20);
  setBorderDefaults('*');
 }
 public BorderedPrintCGrid(int x,int y,char ch) {
  super(x,y);
  setBorderDefaults(ch);
 }
 private void setBorderDefaults(char ch) {
  useBorder = true;
  setBorderCharacter(ch);
 }
 public void enableBorder(boolean toggle) {
  useBorder = toggle;
 }
 public void setBorderCharacter(char ch) {
  borderCharacter = ch;
  char border[] = new char[width+2];
  for(int i=0;i<width+2;++i) border[i] = borderCharacter;
  horizEdge = new String(border);
  vertEdge = String.valueOf(borderCharacter);
 }
 public void displayGrid() {
  if(useBorder) {
   System.out.println(horizEdge);
   for(int i=0;i<depth;++i) {
    System.out.print(vertEdge);
    displayRow(i);
    System.out.println(vertEdge);
   }
   System.out.println(horizEdge);
  }else super.displayGrid();
 }
}
```

`BorderedPrintCGrid` declares four private variables: `useBorder`, `borderCharacter`, `horizEdge`, and `vertEdge`. The `useBorder` variable is of type `boolean` and determines whether a border should be displayed. The `borderCharacter` variable contains the character to be used to display the border. The `horizEdge` and `vertEdge` variables contain the `String` objects to be displayed for the horizontal and vertical edges of the border. These objects are computed from the `borderEdge` character based on the `grid[][]` dimensions.

BorderedPrintCGrid has two constructors. The first does not take any parameters. It constructs a grid 75 characters wide and 20 rows in height by calling the constructor of PrintCGrid. Note that PrintCGrid's constructor passes the call farther up the class hierarchy to CGrid's constructor. This is an example of how classification and inheritance work together to simplify the development of new classes and methods. The setBorderDefaults() method is used to initialize the variables of BorderedPrintCGrid. The second constructor is similar to the first, but provides the capability for the grid's dimensions to be specified directly.

BorderedPrintCGrid provides four access methods. The setBorderDefaults()method initializes the variables of the BorderedPrintCGrid class using the enableBorder() and setBorderCharacter() methods. The enableBorder() method allows the useBorder variable to be set to true or false. The setBorderCharacter() method sets the borderCharacter, horizEdge, and vertEdge variables for use by the displayGrid() method.

The displayGrid()method overrides the displayGrid() method of the PrintCGrid class. By doing so, it redefines the method to suit its own needs. It checks to see if the useBorder variable is true. If it is true, a bordered grid is displayed using the displayRow() method of PrintCGrid. If it is false, it invokes the displayGrid() method of its superclass, PrintCGrid, to display the grid. The super keyword is used to identify the fact that a superclass method should be used instead of the one defined for the current class. The name of the superclass can also be used to indicate which method should be used. The method invocation could have used PrintCGrid.displayGrid() instead of super.displayGrid().

The CGPoint Class

The CGPoint class shows how a non-abstract class extends an abstract class. The CGPoint class extends CGObject. It does not add any new variables to those that it inherits, and the only methods that it declares are constructors and the abstract methods that it is required to implement. Listing 5.6 shows the source code of the CGPoint class.

Listing 5.6. The CGPoint class source code.

```
package jdg.ch05;
// CGPoint.java
public class CGPoint extends CGObject {
 // Method declarations
 public CGPoint(int x, int y,char ch) {
  location = new Point(x,y);
  drawCharacter = ch;
 }
 public CGPoint(int x, int y) {
  this(x,y,'+');
 }
 public CGPoint(Point p) {
  this(p.x(),p.y(),'+');
 }
```

```
public CGPoint(Point p,char ch) {
  this(p.x(),p.y(),ch);
}
public void display(PrintCGrid grid) {
  grid.putCharAt(drawCharacter,location);
}
public void describe() {
  System.out.print("CGPoint "+String.valueOf(drawCharacter)+" ");
  System.out.println(location.toString());
}
}
```

CGPoint has four constructors. The first takes the x and y coordinates of a point and the character to be displayed, and initializes the location and drawCharacter variables declared in CGObject. The remaining constructors invoke the this() constructor. The this() constructor invokes a constructor for the current class that has a matching argument list. The matching constructor is the first constructor, in all three cases. The second, third, and fourth constructors provide a variety of parameter lists by which objects of CGPoint can be constructed. The second and third constructors supply default values for the drawCharacter.

The this() constructor call statement is similar to the super() constructor call statement used with the PrintCGrid and BorderedPrintCGrid classes. Each allows part of the construction details to be handed off to other constructors in the same and parent classes. If no constructor call statement is used, a default super() constructor is used. This ensures that when an object is created, constructors from all of its superclasses are called to initialize all variables inherited by the object.

CGPoint overrides the display() and describe() abstract methods defined by CGObject. The display() method uses the putCharAt() method defined for class CGrid to draw a character in the grid[][] array. The describe() method prints a description of the point to the console window. It uses the toString() method of the Point class.

The CGBox Class

The CGBox class also extends CGObject. It provides an additional variable to allow a rectangle to be displayed on a grid. Listing 5.7 contains the CGBox class source code.

Listing 5.7. The CGBox class source code.

```
package jdg.ch05;
// CGBox.java
public class CGBox extends CGObject {
  // Variable declarations
  protected Point lr; // Lower right corner of a box
  // Method declarations
```

continues

Listing 5.7. continued

```
public CGBox(Point ulCorner, Point lrCorner,char ch) {
  location = ulCorner;
  lr = lrCorner;
  drawCharacter = ch;
}
public CGBox(Point ulCorner, Point lrCorner) {
  this(ulCorner,lrCorner,'#');
}
public void display(PrintCGrid grid) {
  int width = lr.x() - location.x() + 1;
  int height = lr.y() - location.y() + 1;
  Point topRow = new Point(location);
  Point bottomRow = new Point(location.x(),lr.y());
  for(int i=0; i<width; ++i) {
    grid.putCharAt(drawCharacter,topRow);
    grid.putCharAt(drawCharacter,bottomRow);
    topRow = topRow.add(1,0);
    bottomRow = bottomRow.add(1,0);
  }
  Point leftCol = new Point(location);
  Point rightCol = new Point(lr.x(),location.y());
  for(int i=0;i<height;++i){
    grid.putCharAt(drawCharacter,leftCol);
    grid.putCharAt(drawCharacter,rightCol);
    leftCol = leftCol.add(0,1);
    rightCol = rightCol.add(0,1);
  }
}
public void describe() {
  System.out.print("CGBox "+String.valueOf(drawCharacter)+" ");
  System.out.println(location.toString()+" "+lr.toString());
}
}
```

The location variable defined in CGObject is used as the upper-left corner of the rectangle. The lr variable defined by CGBox is the lower-right corner of the rectangle.

CGBox provides two constructors. The first takes arguments for the upper-left and lower-right corners of the rectangle and a character to be used as the drawCharacter. The second constructor provides for a default box drawCharacter and uses a call to the first constructor to accomplish its initialization.

The display() method displays a box on an object of class PrintCGrid. It is a good example of object composition because it uses objects of several different classes to accomplish this purpose. It begins by calculating the box's width and height dimensions from the location and lr variables. The location variable is the upper-left corner of the box, and the lr variable is the lower-right corner. It then creates two points, topRow and bottomRow, that will be used to step through the top and bottom rows of the box's display. The first for statement is used to display the box's top and bottom rows. The putCharAt() method of CGrid is used to display the drawCharacter at the locations specified by topRow and bottomRow. The putCharAt() method is inherited by objects of class PrintCGrid. The x-coordinates of the topRow and bottomRow variables are incremented by 1 to step through the rows' display using the add() method of the Point class.

The display() method creates the leftCol and rightCol points to be used to step through the display of the box's left and right columns. The second for statement displays these columns in a manner similar to the first for statement. The y-coordinates of the leftCol and rightCol variables are incremented by 1 to step through the columns' display.

The describe() method displays a description of a box's parameters to the console window. This description identifies the drawCharacter and upper-left and lower-right corners of the box.

The CGText Class

The CGText class is the third and final subclass of CGObject that is declared in this chapter. (See Listing 5.8.) The CGObject class hierarchy is extended further in Chapter 6.

Listing 5.8. The CGText class source code.

```
package jdg.ch05;
// CGText.java
public class CGText extends CGObject {
 // Variable declarations
 String text;
 // Method declarations
 public CGText(Point p,String s) {
  location = p;
  drawCharacter = ' ';
  text = s;
 }
 public void display(PrintCGrid grid) {
  Point p = new Point(location);
  for(int i=0;i<text.length();++i){
   grid.putCharAt(text.charAt(i),p);
   p = p.add(1,0);
  }
 }
 public void describe() {
  System.out.println("CGText "+location.toString()+" "+text);
 }
}
```

CGText declares one variable, text, that is used to store a string of text to be displayed on the grid. It has a single constructor that takes two arguments: a Point value that identifies the point on the grid where the text is to be displayed and a String value that specifies this text. Because the `drawCharacter` is not displayed, it is initialized to a space. `CGText` implements the two abstract methods required of it. The `display()` method displays the text variable at the location specified by the `location` variable. The `describe()` method displays the location of the point and its text to the console window.

The `KeyboardInput` Class

The `KeyboardInput` class (declared in `KeyboardInput.java`) extends the `BufferedReader` class of the Java API to provide a set of common simple methods for getting keyboard input from the user. (See Listing 5.9.)

Listing 5.9. The `KeyboardInput` class source code.

```java
package jdg.ch05;
import java.lang.System;
import java.io.InputStreamReader;
import java.io.BufferedReader;
import java.io.InputStream;
import java.io.IOException;
public class KeyboardInput extends BufferedReader {
 public KeyboardInput(InputStream inStream) {
  super(new InputStreamReader(System.in));
 }
 public char getChar() throws IOException {
  String line = readLine();
  if(line.length()==0) return ' ';
  return line.charAt(0);
 }
 public String getText() throws IOException {
  String line = readLine();
  return line;
 }
 public int getInt() throws IOException {
  String line = readLine();
  Integer i = new Integer(line);
  return i.intValue();
 }
 public Point getPoint() throws IOException {
  System.out.print("  x-coordinate: ");
  System.out.flush();
  int x = getInt();
  System.out.print("  y-coordinate: ");
  System.out.flush();
  int y = getInt();
  return new Point(x,y);
 }
}
```

`KeyboardInput` has a single constructor that takes an object of class `InputStream` as a parameter. This object should be `java.lang.System.in`, but may be mapped to other input streams if necessary. The `KeyboardInput` constructor passes the `InputStream` object to `BufferedReader`'s constructor using the `super()` constructor call.

`KeyboardInput` defines four access methods that get objects of type, `char`, `String`, `int`, and `Point` from the user. The `getChar()` method uses the `readLine()` method of `BufferedReader` to read a line of data entered by the user. If the line is blank, it returns the space character; otherwise it returns the first character in the input line. The `getText()` method simply returns the entire line entered by the user, whether it is blank or not. The `getInt()` method works the same way as `getChar()` except that it uses a constructor of the `Integer` class to construct an object of class `Integer` directly from the input line. It then converts the `Integer` object to an object of type `int` before it returns it using the `return` statement. The `Integer` class is an example of a class that wraps the primitive type `int`. Class wrappers are covered in Chapter 12, "Portable Software and the `java.lang` Packages."

The `getPoint()` method interacts with the user to get the x- and y-coordinates of a point. It then constructs an object of class `Point` that it uses as its return value. The `getPoint()` method uses the `getInt()` method to get the values of the x- and y-coordinates.

The `CDrawApp` Program

You're finally ready to use all the classes that you've developed in this chapter to build the `CDrawApp` program. Make sure that you've compiled all the classes that have been introduced. Your `c:\jdk1.1.1\jdg\ch05` directory should have compiled classes for `Point.java`, `CGrid.java`, `CGObject.java`, `PrintCGrid.java`, `BorderedPrintCGrid.java`, `CGPoint.java`, `CGBox.java`, `CGText.java`, and `KeyboardInput.java`. The `CDrawApp.java` file is shown in Listing 5.10.

Listing 5.10. The `CDrawApp` and `CDraw` classes.

```
package jdg.ch05;
import java.lang.System;
import java.io.IOException;
class CDrawApp {
 public static void main(String args[]) throws IOException {
  CDraw program = new CDraw();
  program.run();
 }
}
class CDraw {
 // Variable declarations
 static KeyboardInput kbd = new KeyboardInput(System.in);
 BorderedPrintCGrid grid;
 // Method declarations
 CDraw() {
  grid = new BorderedPrintCGrid();
 }
```

continues

Listing 5.10. continued

```java
void run() throws IOException {
 boolean finished = false;
 do {
  char command = getCommand();
  switch(command){
   case 'P':
    addPoint();
    System.out.println();
    break;
   case 'B':
    addBox();
    System.out.println();
    break;
   case 'T':
    addText();
    System.out.println();
    break;
   case 'U':
    grid.deleteLastObject();
    System.out.println();
    break;
   case 'C':
    grid.clearGrid();
    System.out.println();
    break;
   case 'S':
    grid.show();
    break;
   case 'X':
    finished = true;
   default:
    System.out.println();
  }
 } while (!finished);
}
char getCommand() throws IOException {
 System.out.println("CDrawApp    P - Add a Point   U - Undo Last Add");
 System.out.print("Main Menu   B - Add a Box    C - Clear Grid");
 System.out.println("       X - Exit CDrawApp");
 System.out.print("            T - Add Text     S - Show Grid");
 System.out.print("        Enter command: ");
 System.out.flush();
 return Character.toUpperCase(kbd.getChar());
}
void addPoint() throws IOException {
 System.out.println("Add Point Menu");
 System.out.println(" Location:");
 Point p = kbd.getPoint();
 System.out.print(" Character: ");
 System.out.flush();
 char ch = kbd.getChar();
 if(ch==' ') ch = '+';
 CGPoint cgp = new CGPoint(p,ch);
 cgp.addToGrid(grid);
}
```

```
void addBox() throws IOException {
 System.out.println("Add Box Menu");
 System.out.println(" Upper Left Corner:");
 Point ul = kbd.getPoint();
 System.out.println(" Lower Right Corner:");
 Point lr = kbd.getPoint();
 System.out.print(" Character: ");
 System.out.flush();
 char ch = kbd.getChar();
 if(ch==' ') ch = '#';
 CGBox box = new CGBox(ul,lr,ch);
 box.addToGrid(grid);
}
void addText() throws IOException {
 System.out.println("Add Text Menu");
 System.out.println(" Location:");
 Point p = kbd.getPoint();
 System.out.print(" Text: ");
 System.out.flush();
 String text = kbd.getText();
 CGText cgt = new CGText(p,text);
 cgt.addToGrid(grid);
 }
}
```

The declaration of the CDrawApp class is very small. It consists of a main() method that creates an object of class CDraw and then invokes the run() method for that object. The reason that a separate CDraw object is created has to do with the fact that the main() method is static. static methods are like static variables. They apply to the class as a whole and not to objects that are individual instances of a class. static methods can only access variables that they create or that are static variables of the class. By creating the CDraw class, you are able to avoid any limitations posed by static's main() method.

The CDraw class declares two variables: kbd and grid. The kbd variable is used to get input from the user. The grid variable is used to display objects such as points, boxes, and text. The kbd variable is created as a static variable of class KeyboardInput. It is initialized using the KeyboardInput() constructor and the predefined java.lang.System.in input stream. A variable initializer is used to create and initialize the value of kbd. Other initializers, called *static initializers*, are also supported by Java. Static initializers allow blocks of statements to be executed during class initialization. They are covered in Chapter 11.

CDraw has a single constructor that creates an object that is a new instance of BorderedPrintCGrid and assigns it to the grid variable. The BorderedPrintCGrid() constructor creates a default grid 75 characters wide and 20 characters high. The default border character is an asterisk (*).

CDraw has five access methods. The run() method implements the core processing of the CDrawApp program. It uses a do statement that repeatedly processes user keyboard commands. It invokes the getCommand() method to display a menu to the user and retrieve the user's command selection. It then uses a switch statement to process the command. It invokes the addPoint(), addBox(), and addText()methods to add points, boxes, and text to the grid. It invokes the deleteLastObject() and clearGrid() methods of the PrintCGrid class to remove the last object added to the grid or to completely clear the grid of all objects. The show() method of PrintCGrid is used to draw and display the grid. If the user enters a command line beginning with X or x, the boolean variable finished is set to true, the do statement finishes, and the CDrawApp program terminates.

The getCommand()method displays a menu to the user and uses the getChar() method of the KeyboardInput class to get a character command from the user. The static toUpperCase() method of the Character class is used to convert the character returned by getChar() to uppercase.

The addPoint()method queries the user to enter the location of a point and the character to be displayed at that location. It uses the getPoint() and getChar() methods of the KeyboardInput class. If a user enters a space for the display character, addPoint() uses the plus (+) character as a default. It uses the data obtained from the user to construct an object of class CGPoint and adds the object to grid using the addToGrid() method of class CGObject that is inherited by class CGPoint.

The addBox()method is similar to the addPoint() method except that it must obtain two points from the user—the upper-left and lower-right corners of a rectangle. It also obtains a box display character from the user, the default value of which is the pound (#) sign. An object of class CGBox is constructed from the user-supplied information and added to the grid using the CGObject addToGrid() method.

The final method of CDraw, addText(), retrieves a location and a text string from the user and uses this information to create an object of class CGText. The new object is then added to the grid in the same manner as the CGPoint and CGBox objects.

Running CDrawApp

Assuming that you have compiled all the classes introduced in this chapter, go ahead and compile CDrawApp. You can then run CDrawApp using the following command line:

```
C:\jdk1.1.1\jdg\ch05>java jdg.ch05.CDrawApp
```

CDrawApp begins by displaying the following menu:

```
CDrawApp    P - Add a Point   U - Undo Last Add
Main Menu   B - Add a Box     C - Clear Grid      X - Exit CDrawApp
            T - Add Text      S - Show Grid       Enter command:
```

This menu provides you with seven command options: P, B, T, U, C, S, and X. Entering X will cause CDrawApp to terminate. You don't want to do this yet. Entering S will cause CDrawApp to display the character grid. Go ahead and enter S. Your screen should look like this:

```
*************************************************************************
*                                                                       *
*                                                                       *
*                                                                       *
*                                                                       *
*                                                                       *
*                                                                       *
*                                                                       *
*                                                                       *
*                                                                       *
*                                                                       *
*                                                                       *
*                                                                       *
*                                                                       *
*                                                                       *
*                                                                       *
*                                                                       *
*                                                                       *
*                                                                       *
*************************************************************************
CDrawApp    P - Add a Point    U - Undo Last Add
Main Menu   B - Add a Box      C - Clear Grid      X - Exit CDrawApp
            T - Add Text       S - Show Grid       Enter command:
```

CDrawApp displays a blank bordered grid using the show() method of the PrintCGrid class. You should be able to trace program execution up to this point by examining the source code files of the classes used in this chapter. The CDraw run() and getCommand() methods perform most of the user interface processing.

You can add a point to the grid by entering a P command. You will get the following display:

```
Add Point Menu
 Location:
  x-coordinate:
```

The Add Point Menu prompt is displayed by the addPoint() method of the CDraw class. It prompts you to enter the x-coordinate of a grid point. The upper-left corner of the grid is (0,0) and the lower-right corner of the grid is (74,19) where 74 is the maximum x-coordinate and 19 is the maximum y-coordinate. Enter 35 for the x-coordinate. The Add Point Menu then prompts you to enter the y-coordinate:

```
Add Point Menu
 Location:
  x-coordinate: 35
  y-coordinate:
```

Enter 10 for the y-coordinate. You are prompted to enter the character to be displayed at location 35,10. Enter x to finish adding a point:

```
Add Point Menu
 Location:
  x-coordinate: 35
  y-coordinate: 10
 Character: x
CDrawApp    P - Add a Point  U - Undo Last Add
Main Menu   B - Add a Box    C - Clear Grid    X - Exit CDrawApp
            T - Add Text     S - Show Grid     Enter command:
```

The CDrawApp main menu is displayed again. To verify that the point you just entered was, in fact, added to the grid, redisplay the grid by entering S. You will see the x in the middle of the grid:

```
******************************************************************************
*                                                                            *
*                                                                            *
*                                                                            *
*                                                                            *
*                                                                            *
*                                                                            *
*                                                                            *
*                                                                            *
*                                                                            *
*                                                                            *
*                                    x                                       *
*                                                                            *
*                                                                            *
*                                                                            *
*                                                                            *
*                                                                            *
*                                                                            *
*                                                                            *
*                                                                            *
******************************************************************************
CDrawApp    P - Add a Point  U - Undo Last Add
Main Menu   B - Add a Box    C - Clear Grid    X - Exit CDrawApp
            T - Add Text     S - Show Grid     Enter command:
```

Now use the B command to enter a box:

```
CDrawApp    P - Add a Point  U - Undo Last Add
Main Menu   B - Add a Box    C - Clear Grid    X - Exit CDrawApp
            T - Add Text     S - Show Grid     Enter command: b
Add Box Menu
 Upper Left Corner:
  x-coordinate:
```

You will have to enter two points and a character to specify a box. Enter 5 for the x-coordinate of the upper-left corner and 1 for its y-coordinate:

```
Add Box Menu
 Upper Left Corner:
  x-coordinate: 5
```

```
 y-coordinate: 1
Lower Right Corner:
 x-coordinate:
```

Enter 70 for the x-coordinate of the lower-right corner and 18 for its y-coordinate:

```
Add Box Menu
 Upper Left Corner:
  x-coordinate: 5
  y-coordinate: 1
 Lower Right Corner:
  x-coordinate: 70
  y-coordinate: 18
 Character:
```

Finally, set the box character to the equals sign (=):

```
Add Box Menu
 Upper Left Corner:
  x-coordinate: 5
  y-coordinate: 1
 Lower Right Corner:
  x-coordinate: 70
  y-coordinate: 18
 Character: =
CDrawApp    P - Add a Point   U - Undo Last Add
Main Menu   B - Add a Box     C - Clear Grid      X - Exit CDrawApp
            T - Add Text      S - Show Grid       Enter command:
```

Go ahead and redisplay the grid using the Show Grid command:

```
***********************************************************************
*                                                                     *
*      =============================================================  *
*      =                                                           =  *
*      =                                                           =  *
*      =                                                           =  *
*      =                                                           =  *
*      =                                                           =  *
*      =                                                           =  *
*      =                                                           =  *
*      =                                                           =  *
*      =                                                           =  *
*      =                              X                            =  *
*      =                                                           =  *
*      =                                                           =  *
*      =                                                           =  *
*      =                                                           =  *
*      =                                                           =  *
*      =                                                           =  *
*      =============================================================  *
*                                                                     *
***********************************************************************
CDrawApp    P - Add a Point   U - Undo Last Add
Main Menu   B - Add a Box     C - Clear Grid      X - Exit CDrawApp
            T - Add Text      S - Show Grid       Enter command:
```

Notice how the box was added to the grid. Now, let's add text to the grid. Enter T to bring up the Add Text Menu prompt:

```
Add Text Menu
 Location:
  x-coordinate:
```

Set the x-coordinate to 36 and the y-coordinate to 11:

```
Add Text Menu
 Location:
  x-coordinate: 36
  y-coordinate: 11
 Text:
```

Enter I love Java. at the Text: prompt:

```
Add Text Menu
 Location:
  x-coordinate: 36
  y-coordinate: 11
 Text: I love Java.
```

The CDrawApp main menu is displayed. Use the Show Grid command to redisplay the grid:

```
**************************************************************************
*                                                                        *
*     ================================================================   *
*     =                                                             =    *
*     =                                                             =    *
*     =                                                             =    *
*     =                                                             =    *
*     =                                                             =    *
*     =                                                             =    *
*     =                                                             =    *
*     =                                                             =    *
*     =                            X                                =    *
*     =                         I love Java.                        =    *
*     =                                                             =    *
*     =                                                             =    *
*     =                                                             =    *
*     =                                                             =    *
*     =                                                             =    *
*     =                                                             =    *
*     ================================================================   *
*                                                                        *
**************************************************************************
CDrawApp     P - Add a Point   U - Undo Last Add
Main Menu    B - Add a Box     C - Clear Grid     X - Exit CDrawApp
             T - Add Text      S - Show Grid      Enter command:
```

Enter U to invoke the Undo Last Add command. This results in the text being deleted from the display. Verify this by redisplaying the grid. Then clear the grid by entering C. Once again, use the Show Grid command to verify that the command worked correctly.

You have now covered all the commands of CDrawApp. Enter X to exit the program.

CDrawApp's Implementation of Object-Oriented Concepts

The purpose of CDrawApp isn't to bolster your graphics production capabilities. It is used as a comprehensive example of how Java classes, objects, and methods can be used to implement the object-oriented programming concepts studied earlier in the chapter.

In building CDrawApp, you created 11 classes, six of which extended classes other than Object. The class hierarchy for the CDrawApp program is shown in Figure 5.4.

FIGURE 5.4.
The CDrawApp *class hierarchy.*

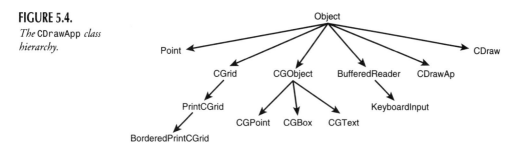

The development of the CGrid, PrintCGrid, and BorderedPrintCGrid classes shows how sub-classes extend the data and methods inherited from their parents to successively add more features to their branch of the class hierarchy. CGrid provides the basic data and methods to implement character grid objects. PrintCGrid adds the capability to add and remove objects from the grid, and to display these objects on the console window. BorderedPrintCGrid uses the methods provided by CGrid and PrintCGrid to develop additional capabilities for display-ing a bordered grid.

The CGObject, CGPoint, CGBox, and CGText classes are examples of how abstract classes are used to specify the behavior of their subclasses. CGObject provides the addToGrid() method, which is inherited by all of its subclasses. It defines the display() and describe() methods as abstract, requiring all subclasses to implement these methods in a manner that is applicable to the sub-class. CGPoint, CGBox, and CGText define specific types of graphical objects that fit within the framework established by CGObject.

The drawGrid() method of PrintCGrid utilizes the CGObject class as an abstraction for dealing with objects in the displayList[]. The dynamic binding and polymorphic capabilities of the Java compiler and runtime system enable drawGrid() to interact with objects of subclasses of CGObject without specific knowledge of their class type.

The grid object of class BorderedPrintCGrid that is used in the CDraw class provides an example of advanced polymorphic behavior. When grid's show() method is invoked, the show() method of the PrintCGrid class is used. The show() method invokes the PrintCGrid drawGrid() method to cause each object in the displayList[] to display itself on the grid. It then invokes the displayGrid() method to display the grid. BorderedPrintCGrid overrides the displayGrid() method of PrintCGrid. Which displayGrid() method does show() invoke—that of PrintCGrid or BorderedPrintCGrid? The show() method is able to discern from runtime information that it is being invoked for an object of class BorderedPrintCGrid so it uses the BorderedPrintCGrid displayGrid() method. This method checks to see if the useBorder variable is true, and if so, displays a grid with a border. However, if useBorder is false, it invokes the displayGrid() method of PrintCGrid.

The Point class is an example of encapsulation. It has a modular, well-defined interface and hides the details of its implementation from other classes. The x- and y-coordinates of a point are inaccessible to methods outside the Point class. Even the methods within Point use the x() and y() methods to access these values. The Point class, because of this encapsulation, can be reused in many other applications that use two-dimensional grids.

The KeyboardInput class shows how classes from the Java API may be extended by user-defined subclasses. It uses the readLine() method from BufferedReader, the charAt() method from the String class, and the intValue() method of the Integer class to provide convenient methods for accessing user input lines.

The CDraw and CDrawApp classes illustrate the principle of object composition. They assemble the other classes defined in this chapter into a short, two-page program that uses all of the features provided by these classes.

Summary

In this chapter you also learned some general object-oriented programming concepts and how these concepts apply to Java programs. You also learned how to use classes to develop a sample Java program that illustrates the fundamental elements of Java object-oriented programming.

The classes you developed in this chapter will be reused in Chapters 6 and 7. In Chapter 6, you'll learn how to use interfaces to support features of multiple inheritance. In Chapter 7, you'll learn how to use exceptions to respond to errors and other anomalies during program execution.

6

Interfaces

In this chapter you'll learn how to use Java interfaces to provide a common set of methods by which a group of classes can be accessed and to implement features of multiple inheritance. You'll cover the use of interface constants and learn how to declare objects using interface types. You will also learn how to extend and combine interfaces. When you finish this chapter, you'll be able to use interfaces with your Java classes.

The Purpose of Java Interfaces

The Java interface construct is borrowed from the Objective-C protocol. It is used to identify a common set of methods for the group of classes that implement the interface. It is also used to share constants between classes. Interfaces are used to provide the benefits of multiple inheritance without its implementation difficulties. They allow several classes to share a standard set of methods and constants without requiring these methods and constants to be implemented by a common superclass.

Interfaces provide a standard framework for accessing classes. They are analogous to the interfaces that we encounter in everyday life. Any large class of real-world objects that you regularly manipulate usually has a standard interface. Radios and televisions provide a common set of controls for tuning channels and adjusting audio volume. Cars come with a standard interface for steering, throttling, and braking. Automated bank tellers provide the same general interface for performing bank transactions.

To realize the potential use of Java interfaces, consider the diversity of objects that are manipulated by GUI-building programs. Such programs provide the capability to generate graphical user interfaces by clicking on interface controls and dragging them to appropriate places on the windows and dialog boxes being developed. The objects implementing these controls may support many different sets of methods. For example, one subset of the controls may be required to support cut, copy, and paste operations. These methods might be grouped into an `EditObject` interface. Another subset of the interface controls may be required to support click and double-click operations. These objects might implement a `Clickable` interface. Another subset may support drag-and-drop operations and implement the `Draggable` interface. Other groups of objects may implement multiple interfaces. For example, there might be objects that are both `Clickable` and `Draggable`.

The Benefits of Interfaces

Interfaces provide many advantages to the Java programmer. One is that they allow standard sets of methods to be used across the class hierarchy. For example, you can define the `Editable` interface to support cut, copy, and paste operations. The `Editable` interface can then be implemented by relevant classes and establish a uniform approach to implementing these common operations.

Interface types allow objects to be referenced by the methods they support without considering their location in the class hierarchy. They make maximal use of dynamic binding, allowing objects to be accessed independent of their implementation details. For example, parameters can be defined as interface types and used by methods. These methods can invoke the interface methods of their arguments without having to determine the classes to which the arguments belong.

Interfaces also support *selective* multiple inheritance. They allow various subsets of the features supported by different classes to be shared without mandating that all features of these classes be uniformly imposed as the result of inheritance.

Finally, because interfaces are declared independent of classes, they are unaffected by changes to specific classes or to the class hierarchy as a whole.

Declaring Interfaces

Interfaces, like classes, are not objects, but type definitions that can be used to declare an object. Interfaces are declared as follows:

`InterfaceModifiers interface InterfaceName ExtendsClause InterfaceBody`

The allowed interface modifiers are `abstract` and `public`. By default, all interfaces are `abstract`, and the `abstract` keyword need not be used. The `public` access specifier allows interfaces to be accessed outside of the package in which they are declared, in the same manner as with classes. Only one class or interface may be declared `public` in a given compilation unit. The compilation unit must have the same name as its `public` interface or class. The `extends` clause is similar to the class `extends` clause and is covered later in this chapter.

The body of an interface begins with an opening brace ({), consists of zero or more variable or method declarations, and ends with a closing brace (}).

All variables declared in an interface body that are assumed to be `public`, `static`, and `final` must have an initializer, and are implemented as constant class variables.

All methods declared in an interface body are assumed to be `abstract` and do not have method bodies. A semicolon (;) replaces the method body in the method declaration. Only access methods can be declared within an interface; constructors are not allowed. The access specifier of a method is that of the interface in which it is declared.

An example of a simple interface declaration is as follows:

```
public interface Clickable {
 void click();
 void doubleClick();
}
```

This Clickable interface is declared as public so that it can be accessed outside its package. It contains two method declarations, click() and doubleClick(). These methods must be supported by all classes that implement the Clickable interface.

Implementing Interfaces

The interfaces implemented by a class are identified in the implements clause of the class declaration. For example, the following class implements the Scrollable and Clickable interfaces:

```
class ExampleClass implements Scrollable, Clickable {
}
```

A non-abstract class must implement all interface methods that are not implemented by its superclasses. abstract classes are not required to implement interface methods. They can defer interface implementation to their non-abstract subclasses.

The CDrawApp Interface Example

To provide a concrete example of the use of interfaces, we'll extend the CDrawApp program, introduced in Chapter 5, "Classes and Objects," to include support for editable objects. Editable objects are objects that display text on the grid and can be edited using the CGTextEdit interface. The CGText class will be modified to support this interface. The CGPoint and CGBox classes will be extended by the subclasses, CGTextPoint and CGTextBox, both of which provide the capability to display text on the grid. The CGText, CGTextPoint, and CGTextBox classes will implement the CGTextEdit interface. Figure 6.1 shows the extensions to the Chapter 5 class hierarchy that were made to support this example.

FIGURE 6.1.

Extensions to the CDrawApp class hierarchy.

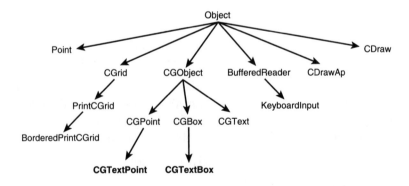

Before going on to edit and compile the source code files for this example, be sure to create a ch06 subdirectory under c:\jdk1.1.1\jdg. This subdirectory should be used to store all of the source Java files that you develop in this chapter.

The CGTextEdit Interface

The CGTextEdit interface is quite simple. Its source code is shown in Listing 6.1.

Listing 6.1. The CGTextEdit interface source code.

```
package jdg.ch06;
public interface CGTextEdit {
 public void replaceText(String s);
 public void upperCase();
 public void lowerCase();
}
```

It declares three methods: replaceText(), upperCase(), and lowerCase(). These methods must be provided by all classes that implement the CGTextEdit interface. The replaceString() method is used to replace the text associated with an object with the text contained in the String's parameter. The upperCase() and lowerCase() methods are used to convert the text associated with an object to upper- and lowercase, respectively. CGTextEdit and all of its interfaces are declared as public, allowing them to be accessed outside of the jdg.ch06 package. The public modifiers used with the method declarations are redundant. Any method declared in a public interface is public, by default.

After you have entered the CGTextEdit interface into the file, CGTextEdit.java, use javac to compile CGTextEdit.java. Do this from within the ch06 directory.

Updating the CGText Class

The CGText class, shown in Chapter 5, will be updated to implement the CGTextEdit interface. The easiest way to do this is to copy CGText.java from the c:\jdk1.1.1\jdg\ch05 directory to the c:\jdk1.1.1\jdg\ch06 directory and then edit it. Its source code is shown in Listing 6.2.

Listing 6.2. The CGText class source code.

```
package jdg.ch06;
import jdg.ch05.CGObject;
import jdg.ch05.Point;
import jdg.ch05.PrintCGrid;
import java.lang.System;
```

continues

Listing 6.2. continued

```java
// CGText.java
public class CGText extends CGObject implements CGTextEdit {
 // Variable declarations
 String text;
 // Method declarations
 public CGText(Point p,String s) {
  location = p;
  drawCharacter = ' ';
  text = s;
 }
 public void display(PrintCGrid grid) {
  Point p = new Point(location);
  for(int i=0;i<text.length();++i){
   grid.putCharAt(text.charAt(i),p);
   p = p.add(1,0);
  }
 }
 public void describe() {
  System.out.println("CGText "+location.toString()+" "+text);
 }
 public void replaceText(String s) {
  text=s;
 }
 public void upperCase() {
  text = text.toUpperCase();
 }
 public void lowerCase() {
  text = text.toLowerCase();
 }
}
```

All you need to do is to change the package statement, add the import statements, edit the class declaration, and add the last three methods that implement the CGTextEdit interface.

Because this class is contained in the jdg.ch06 package, you need to import the CGObject, Point, and PrintCGrid classes from the jdg.ch05 package.

The class declaration is changed to add the implements clause with the CGTextEdit interface.

The three new methods are all very simple. The replaceText() method assigns text to the new value passed by the s parameter. The upperCase() and lowerCase() methods use the toUpperCase() and toLowerCase() methods of the String class to perform their conversions.

You should compile the new CGText.java before moving on to the next class.

The CGTextPoint Class

The CGTextPoint class extends the CGPoint class to add the capability to display text along with the character point. (See Listing 6.3.)

Listing 6.3. The CGTextPoint class source code.

```
package jdg.ch06;
import jdg.ch05.Point;
import jdg.ch05.CGPoint;
import jdg.ch05.PrintCGrid;
import java.lang.System;
// CGTextPoint.java
public class CGTextPoint extends CGPoint implements CGTextEdit {
 // Variable declarations
 String text;
 // Method declarations
 public CGTextPoint(Point p,char ch,String s) {
  super(p,ch);
  text = s;
 }
 public CGTextPoint(Point p,String s) {
  super(p);
  text = s;
 }
 public CGTextPoint(Point p,char ch) {
  super(p,ch);
  text = "";
 }
 public CGTextPoint(Point p) {
  super(p);
  text = "";
 }
 public void display(PrintCGrid grid) {
  super.display(grid);
  Point p = location.add(1,0);
  for(int i=0;i<text.length();++i){
   grid.putCharAt(text.charAt(i),p);
   p = p.add(1,0);
  }
 }
 public void describe() {
  System.out.print("CGTextPoint "+String.valueOf(drawCharacter)+" ");
  System.out.println(location.toString()+" "+text);
 }
 public void replaceText(String s) {
  text=s;
 }
 public void upperCase() {
  text = text.toUpperCase();
 }
 public void lowerCase() {
  text = text.toLowerCase();
 }
}
```

CGTextPoint declares the variable text. This variable is used to store the text associated with the point. It provides four constructors; each uses the super() constructor call statement to invoke the constructors of the CGPoint class. The four constructors allow CGTextPoint to be constructed using different combinations of parameters.

The `display()` method invokes the `display()` method of its superclass to display the point at its location on the grid. It then displays the value of the text variable to the immediate right of this point. The `describe()` method displays a description of the text point on the console window. The `replaceText()`, `upperCase()`, and `lowerCase()` methods are the same as those of the new `CGText` class.

The `CGTextBox` Class

The `CGTextBox` class extends the `CGBox` class to add the capability to display text within a box. (See Listing 6.4.) The size of the box is automatically fitted to the size of the text to be displayed.

Listing 6.4. The `CGTextBox` class source code.

```
package jdg.ch06;
import jdg.ch05.Point;
import jdg.ch05.CGBox;
import jdg.ch05.PrintCGrid;
import java.lang.System;
// CGTextBox.java
public class CGTextBox extends CGBox implements CGTextEdit {
 // Variable declarations
 String text;
 // Method declarations
 public CGTextBox(Point ulCorner, char ch, String s) {
  super(ulCorner,ulCorner.add(s.length()+1,2),ch);
  text = s;
 }
 public CGTextBox(Point ulCorner, String s) {
  super(ulCorner,ulCorner.add(s.length()+1,2));
  text = s;
 }
 public void display(PrintCGrid grid) {
  super.display(grid);
  Point p = location.add(1,1);
  for(int i=0;i<text.length();++i){
   grid.putCharAt(text.charAt(i),p);
   p = p.add(1,0);
  }
 }
 public void describe() {
  System.out.print("CGTextBox "+String.valueOf(drawCharacter)+" ");
  System.out.println(location.toString()+" "+lr.toString()+" "+text);
 }
 public void replaceText(String s) {
  text=s;
  lr=location.add(text.length()+1,2);
 }
 public void upperCase() {
  text = text.toUpperCase();
 }
```

```
public void lowerCase() {
  text = text.toLowerCase();
 }
}
```

The CGTextBox class defines the text variable in the same manner as the CGTextPoint class and provides two constructors for initializing objects of its class. Both constructors use calls to the CGBox class to support the initialization. The parameters to these calls calculate the lower-right corner of the box using the upper-left corner as a reference point and adding horizontal and vertical offsets that size the box based on the length of the text it contains.

The display() method displays a box using the display() method of its parent. It then displays the text within the box. The describe() method prints a box's parameters on the console window.

The upperCase() and lowerCase() methods are the same as those of the CGTextPoint class, but the replaceText() method is different. It updates the lr variable to correctly resize the box based on changes to the length of the text variable.

Updating the CDraw Class

The CDraw class is updated to support the Edit Text command. This requires changes to all of its access methods except the addText() method. The source code of the CDrawApp and CDraw classes is shown in Listing 6.5.

Listing 6.5. The CDrawApp and CDraw classes.

```
package jdg.ch06;
import jdg.ch05.Point;
import jdg.ch05.CGrid;
import jdg.ch05.PrintCGrid;
import jdg.ch05.BorderedPrintCGrid;
import jdg.ch05.CGObject;
import jdg.ch05.CGPoint;
import jdg.ch05.CGBox;
import jdg.ch05.KeyboardInput;
import java.lang.System;
import java.lang.ClassCastException;
import java.io.IOException;
class CDrawApp {
 public static void main(String args[]) throws IOException {
  CDraw program = new CDraw();
  program.run();
 }
}
class CDraw {
 // Variable declarations
```

continues

Listing 6.5. continued

```
static KeyboardInput kbd = new KeyboardInput(System.in);
BorderedPrintCGrid grid;
// Method declarations
CDraw() {
 grid = new BorderedPrintCGrid();
}
void run() throws IOException {
 boolean finished = false;
 do {
  char command = getCommand();
  switch(command){
   case 'P':
    addPoint();
    System.out.println();
    break;
   case 'B':
    addBox();
    System.out.println();
    break;
   case 'T':
    addText();
    System.out.println();
    break;
   case 'U':
    grid.deleteLastObject();
    System.out.println();
    break;
   case 'C':
    grid.clearGrid();
    System.out.println();
    break;
   case 'S':
    grid.show();
    break;
  case 'E':
   editText();
   break;
  case 'X':
   finished = true;
   default:
    System.out.println();
  }
 } while (!finished);
}
char getCommand() throws IOException {
 System.out.print("CDrawApp     P - Add a Point   U - Undo Last Add");
 System.out.println("   E - Edit Text");
 System.out.print("Main Menu   B - Add a Box      C - Clear Grid");
 System.out.println("     X - Exit CDrawApp");
 System.out.print("            T - Add Text     S - Show Grid");
 System.out.print("         Enter command: ");
 System.out.flush();
 return Character.toUpperCase(kbd.getChar());
}
```

```
void addPoint() throws IOException {
 System.out.println("Add Point Menu");
 System.out.println(" Location:");
 Point p = kbd.getPoint();
 System.out.print(" Character: ");
 System.out.flush();
 char ch = kbd.getChar();
 if(ch==' ') ch = '+';
 System.out.print(" Add text (y/n): ");
 System.out.flush();
 if('Y'==Character.toUpperCase(kbd.getChar())) {
  System.out.print("  Text: ");
  System.out.flush();
  String s = kbd.getText();
  CGTextPoint cgtp = new CGTextPoint(p,ch,s);
  cgtp.addToGrid(grid);
 }else{
  CGPoint cgp = new CGPoint(p,ch);
  cgp.addToGrid(grid);
 }
}
void addBox() throws IOException {
 System.out.println("Add Box Menu");
 System.out.println(" Upper Left Corner:");
 Point ul = kbd.getPoint();
 System.out.print(" Add text (y/n): ");
 System.out.flush();
 if('Y'==Character.toUpperCase(kbd.getChar())) {
  System.out.print("  Text: ");
  System.out.flush();
  String s = kbd.getText();
  System.out.print(" Character: ");
  System.out.flush();
  char ch = kbd.getChar();
  if(ch==' ') ch = '#';
  CGTextBox cgtb = new CGTextBox(ul,ch,s);
  cgtb.addToGrid(grid);
 }else{
  System.out.println(" Lower Right Corner:");
  Point lr = kbd.getPoint();
  System.out.print(" Character: ");
  System.out.flush();
  char ch = kbd.getChar();
  if(ch==' ') ch = '#';
  CGBox box = new CGBox(ul,lr,ch);
  box.addToGrid(grid);
 }
}
void addText() throws IOException {
 System.out.println("Add Text Menu");
 System.out.println(" Location:");
 Point p = kbd.getPoint();
 System.out.print(" Text: ");
 System.out.flush();
 String text = kbd.getText();
```

continues

Listing 6.5. continued

```java
    CGText cgt = new CGText(p,text);
    cgt.addToGrid(grid);
  }
  void editText() throws IOException {
   System.out.println("Current Objects:");
   int numObjects = grid.getNumObjects();
   for(int i=0;i<numObjects;++i){
    System.out.print(" "+String.valueOf(i)+" ");
    grid.getObject(i).describe();
   }
   if(numObjects > 0){
    System.out.print("Select an object to edit: ");
    System.out.flush();
    int objIndex = kbd.getInt();
    CGObject obj = grid.getObject(objIndex);
    try {
     editText((CGTextEdit) obj);
    }catch (ClassCastException ex){
     System.out.println("Object is not editable.");
    }
   }else System.out.println("(none)");
   System.out.println();
  }
  void editText(CGTextEdit obj) throws IOException {
   System.out.println("Text Edit Menu");
   System.out.println(" R - Replace Text");
   System.out.println(" L - Lower Case");
   System.out.println(" U - Upper Case");
   System.out.print("Enter command: ");
   System.out.flush();
   char ch = kbd.getChar();
   ch = Character.toUpperCase(ch);
   switch(ch) {
    case 'R':
     System.out.print("Enter new text: ");
     System.out.flush();
     String s = kbd.getText();
     obj.replaceText(s);
     break;
    case 'L':
     obj.lowerCase();
     break;
    case 'U':
     obj.upperCase();
     break;
   }
  }
}
```

The `run()`, `getCommand()`, `addPoint()`, and `addBox()` methods are updated to support the Edit Text command. The two overloaded `editText()` methods are added to process this command.

The `switch` statement of the `run()` method adds the `'E'` case to its list of command options, calling the `editText()` method to process the Edit Text command. The `getCommand()` method adds the Edit Text command to its menu display.

The `addPoint()` and `addBox()` methods query the user to determine whether text should be added to the point or box. If the user declines to add text, a `CGPoint` or `CGBox` object is created and added to the grid. If the user indicates that he or she wants to add text to the point or box, the user is prompted to enter the text. In this case, `CGTextPoint` and `CGTextBox` objects are created and added to the grid.

The two `editText()` methods share the same name but provide completely different processing. The first `editText()` method is invoked when the user enters the Edit Text command. It displays a list of the objects that are currently added to the grid. It does this by using the `getNumObjects()` method of the `PrintCGrid` class to find out how many objects there are and then retrieving those objects using the `getObject()` method of the `PrintCGrid` class. The following line of code concatenates two method invocations:

```
grid.getObject(i).describe();
```

It retrieves an object of class `CGObject` by invoking the `getObject()` method of the `PrintCGrid` class. It then invokes the object's `describe()` method so that it will display its description on the console window. If there are no objects currently added to the grid, the `editText()` method indicates this fact by displaying `(none)` to the console window. Otherwise, the user is prompted to enter the number of the object to edit. This number is the number listed in the current object display. The number entered by the user is used to retrieve the object to be edited using the `getObject()` method. After the object is retrieved, the `editText()` method tries to edit the text associated with the object by invoking the second `editText()` method. If the object does not implement the `CGTextEdit` interface, a `ClassCastException` is thrown during the invocation of the second `editText()` method. The first `editText()` method catches this exception and reports the selected object as not being editable.

The second `editText()` method displays a Text Edit Menu prompt to the user and invokes the `replaceText()`, `lowerCase()`, and `upperCase()` methods to process the commands entered by the user.

Running the Example

The `CDrawApp` program is compiled and executed in the same manner as its Chapter 5 predecessor:

```
C:\jdk1.1.1\jdg\ch06>java jdg.ch06.CDrawApp
```

You should notice the additional Edit Text command provided in the CDrawApp main menu:

```
CDrawApp      P - Add a Point    U - Undo Last Add    E - Edit Text
Main Menu     B - Add a Box      C - Clear Grid       X - Exit CDrawApp
              T - Add Text       S - Show Grid        Enter command:
```

We'll add a few objects to the grid, display them, and then edit their text. After you learn how to use the new program, we'll discuss its features as they relate to interfaces.

Enter P to add a point to the grid. Set its x-coordinate to 60, its y-coordinate to 10, and its draw character to @:

```
Add Point Menu
 Location:
  x-coordinate: 60
  y-coordinate: 10
 Character: @
 Add text (y/n):
```

You are asked whether you want to add text to the point. Press Y to add text. You are then prompted to add your text. Enter at sign as your text, as shown in the following display output:

```
Add Point Menu
 Location:
  x-coordinate: 60
  y-coordinate: 10
 Character: @
 Add text (y/n): y
  Text:  at sign
```

The CDrawApp main menu is then redisplayed. Enter B to add a box. Set the box's upper-left corner as follows:

```
Add Box Menu
 Upper Left Corner:
  x-coordinate: 4
  y-coordinate: 4
 Add text (y/n):
```

Enter Y to add text to the box. You are prompted to enter your text. Enter the text Java's interfaces support multiple inheritance.. Then set the box's draw character to +. Your display output should look like the following:

```
Add Box Menu
 Upper Left Corner:
  x-coordinate: 4
  y-coordinate: 4
 Add text (y/n): y
  Text: Java's interfaces support multiple inheritance.
 Character: +
```

Enter B to enter another box. This box will not contain any text. Enter the coordinates for the box's corners, as follows:

```
Add Box Menu
 Upper Left Corner:
  x-coordinate: 65
  y-coordinate: 15
 Add text (y/n): n
 Lower Right Corner:
  x-coordinate: 72
  y-coordinate: 18
```

Then set its draw character to a hyphen:

```
Character: -
```

You should have noticed that when a box contains text, its lower-right corner is not specified. That's because the program computes the corner based on the length of the text to be displayed with the box.

You're almost done adding objects to the grid. Enter T to add text to the grid. Set the text's location and value as follows:

```
Add Text Menu
 Location:
  x-coordinate: 1
  y-coordinate: 18
 Text: UPPER CASE Or lower case
```

You now have enough objects to work with. Enter S to display the grid. It should look like this:

```
**************************************************************************
*                                                                        *
*                                                                        *
*                                                                        *
*                                                                        *
*      +++++++++++++++++++++++++++++++++++++++++++++++++++                *
*      +Java's interfaces support multiple inheritance.+                  *
*      +++++++++++++++++++++++++++++++++++++++++++++++++++                *
*                                                                        *
*                                                                        *
*                                                                        *
*                                                  @ at sign             *
*                                                                        *
*                                                                        *
*                                                                        *
*                                                                        *
*                                                       _ _ _ _          *
*                                                       .       .        *
*                                                       .       .        *
* UPPER CASE Or lower case                              _ _ _ _          *
*                                                                        *
**************************************************************************
```

Let's start editing these objects. Enter E to select an object to edit:

```
CDrawApp    P - Add a Point    U - Undo Last Add    E - Edit Text
Main Menu   B - Add a Box      C - Clear Grid       X - Exit CDrawApp
            T - Add Text       S - Show Grid         Enter command: e
Current Objects:
 0 CGTextPoint @ (60,10)  at sign
 1 CGTextBox + (4,4) (52,6) Java's interfaces support multiple inheritance.
 2 CGBox - (65,15) (72,18)
 3 CGText (1,18) UPPER CASE Or lower case
Select an object to edit:
```

A list of the grid's current objects is displayed. Enter 2 to select the object of class CGBox. Because this object does not implement the CGTextEdit interface, it is identified as not being editable, as shown in the following console output:

```
Object is not editable.
```

See if you can find where this processing was performed within the CDraw class. Enter E again to edit another object. The list of current objects is displayed again. Enter 1 to select the object of class CGTextBox. The Text Edit Menu prompt is displayed as follows:

```
Text Edit Menu
 R - Replace Text
 L - Lower Case
 U - Upper Case
Enter command:
```

This menu allows you to use the methods of the CGTextEdit interface to edit the objects that implement the interface. Enter R to replace the text associated with the CGTextBox object. You are then prompted to enter the new text for this object. Enter interfaces to complete the editing. Your display should contain the following output:

```
Enter command: r
Enter new text: interfaces
```

Enter S to see how the grid was updated. Notice how the size of the CGTextBox was changed to fit the size of the text it contains:

```
++++++++++++
+interfaces+
++++++++++++
```

Enter E and then 0 to edit the object of class CGTextPoint. Then type U to change it to uppercase. Use the show command to verify that the text has been changed to uppercase.

Enter E, 3, and L in succession to change the case of the text contained in the CGText object. Use the Show Grid command to redisplay the grid:

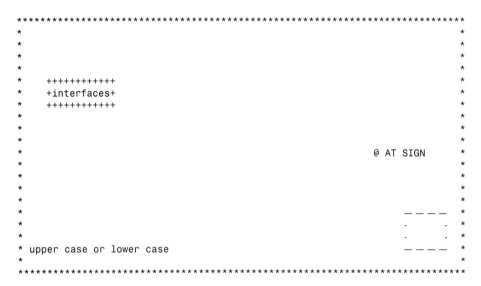

```
*************************************************************************
*                                                                       *
*                                                                       *
*                                                                       *
*                                                                       *
*    +++++++++++                                                        *
*    +interfaces+                                                       *
*    +++++++++++                                                        *
*                                                                       *
*                                                                       *
*                                                                       *
*                                                      @ AT SIGN        *
*                                                                       *
*                                                                       *
*                                                                       *
*                                                           _ _ _ _    *
*                                                          .        .  *
*                                                          .        .  *
* upper case or lower case                                 _ _ _ _    *
*                                                                       *
*************************************************************************
```

Now type X to exit the CDrawApp program.

Example Summary

The CDrawApp program illustrates the use of a simple interface. The CGTextEdit interface, used in this example, provides a common set of access methods to three classes on different branches of the CDrawApp class hierarchy, as shown in Figure 6.2.

FIGURE 6.2.

The CGTextEdit *interface.*

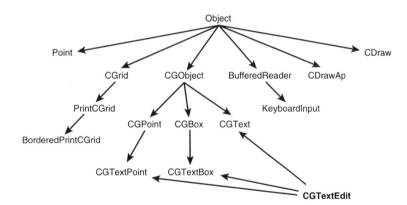

Providing a standard interface to the CGText, CGTextPoint, and CGTextBox classes makes it possible to manipulate objects of these classes as if they belong to a single type. This is illustrated in the second editText() method of the CDraw class. This method takes an object of the CGTextEdit interface type as an argument and edits that object without having to know to which class the object belongs. Although the methods of the CGTextEdit interface are very simple, the capability provided by the interface is not. The second editText() method is able to manipulate any object that implements the CGTextEdit interface, even those that may be defined in the future.

The first editText() method of the CDraw class also provides an interesting example of the use of interfaces. The first part of the method displays the list of current objects, one of which is selected by the user. The try statement tests to see if the selected object implements the CGTextEdit interface by trying to cast it to an object of interface type CGTextEdit. The casting is performed when the object is used as an argument to the second editText() method:

```
try {
 editText((CGTextEdit) obj);
}catch (ClassCastException ex){
 System.out.println("Object is not editable.");
}
```

Casting is the process of changing the type by which an object is accessed. It is covered in Chapter 11, "Language Summary." An object can be cast to an interface type if the object implements the interface; otherwise a ClassCastException is thrown.

The editText() method uses casting to determine whether an object implements the CGTextEdit interface. If the object implements the CGTextEdit interface, the casting is allowed and the second editText() method is invoked to edit the object. If the object does not implement the CGTextEdit interface, an exception is thrown. This exception is caught by the catch part of the try statement, and the object is identified as not editable.

Using Interfaces as Abstract Types

The preceding example shows how interfaces can be used to declare method parameters. Such declarations require only that the objects passed as arguments during a method invocation implement the identified interface.

In the following example, the restart() method of ExampleClass declares the currentSelection parameter to be of type ExampleInterface. The restart() method has no idea what class of object is passed to it via currentSelection. It only requires it to implement the ExampleInterface. The fact that the correct methods are called for the object identified by currentSelection is an example of *polymorphism*. The code for ExampleInterface follows:

```
interface ExampleInterface {
    void rewind();
    void play();
    void stop();
}
```

```
class ExampleClass {
    void restart(ExampleInterface currentSelection) {
        currentSelection.stop();
        currentSelection.rewind();
        currentSelection.play();
    }
}
```

The `restart()` method uses the `ExampleInterface` methods of the `currentSelection` object to perform its processing. Note that `ExampleClass` does not need to implement `ExampleInterface`. The interface only needs to be implemented by the object passed via the `currentSelection` parameter.

Interface Constants

The variables declared in an interface body are available as constants to classes that implement the interface. This enables pools of related constants to be defined and made available to classes that require use of these constants. Common constant pools are color constants, mathematical constants, and formatting constants. Variables declared in an interface are implicitly `public`, `static`, and `final` and must be initialized in their declaration.

The following example shows how interface variables are used to define a constant pool. Create a file in your `ch06` directory called `ColorConstants.java` and enter the code shown in Listing 6.6.

Listing 6.6. The `ColorConstants` interface defines red, blue, and green constants.

```
package jdg.ch06;
public interface ColorConstants {
 int red = 0xff0000;
 int green = 0xff00;
 int blue = 0xff;
}
```

Compile this code using `javac`. Then create another file called `ColorTestApp.java`, as shown in Listing 6.7.

Listing 6.7. The `ColorTestApp` class source code.

```
package jdg.ch06;
import java.lang.System;
class ColorTestApp implements ColorConstants {
 public static void main(String args[]) {
  System.out.println(red);
  System.out.println(green);
  System.out.println(blue);
 }
}
```

Compile `ColorTestApp.java` and execute it using `java`. Your console window should display the following output:

```
C:\jdk1.1.1\jdg\ch06>java jdg.ch06.ColorTestApp
16711680
65280
255
```

The `main()` method of the `ColorTestApp` class is able to access the constants defined in the `ColorConstants` interface as if they were inherited variables. The `main()` function displays these hexadecimal constants as decimal integers.

Extending Interfaces

The interface `extends` clause is similar to the `extends` clause used with classes. An interface is allowed to extend more than one interface, but a class can extend only a single class. The extending interface inherits all the methods and constants defined in the interfaces that it extends. When a class implements an interface X, it must implement all methods of all interfaces that X extends.

The following example declares the `MoreTextEdit` interface as extending the `CGTextEdit` interface. All classes that implement the `MoreTextEdit` interface must implement the methods of both `CGTextEdit` and `MoreTextEdit`:

```
interface MoreTextEdit extends CGTextEdit {
 void insertText(int pos, String s);
 void appendText(String s);
}
```

Combining Interfaces

Two or more interfaces may be combined into a single interface through extension. The following example shows how interfaces are combined:

```
interface TV {
 void changeChannel(int channelNumber);
 void changeVolume(int volumeSetting);
}
interface VCR {
 void play();
 void rewind();
 void record();
}
interface TVCR extends TV, VCR {
}
```

Any non-abstract class that implements the `TVCR` interface is required to implement the methods of the `TV` interface and the `VCR` interface.

Summary

In this chapter you learned how to use Java interfaces to provide a common set of methods by which a group of classes can be accessed. You added the `CGTextEdit` interface to the `CDrawApp` example from Chapter 5 and learned how to declare objects using interface types. You also learned how to use interface constants. In Chapter 7, "Exceptions," you'll learn how to use Java exceptions to perform error processing.

7

Exceptions

In this chapter you'll learn how to use exceptions to implement error-handling capabilities in your Java programs. You'll learn how to declare exceptions and identify methods that use them. You'll also learn how to throw exceptions in response to error conditions and how to catch exceptions in support of error processing. When you finish this chapter, you'll be able to use exceptions to handle all sorts of errors in your programs.

Eliminating Software Errors

Programs are reliable, in part, because they are able to cope with errors and exceptions that occur during their execution. The development of reliable, error-tolerant software is a multiphase effort that spans program design, coding, compilation, loading, and execution.

The most serious errors are those that are designed into a program. Many design errors can be eliminated by following a sound development approach, using modern software engineering methods, and making a firm commitment to software quality. The use of an object-oriented approach to software development helps to simplify software design, reduce errors, and promote software reliability.

Programming errors initially occur when a software design is translated into source code. Program verification, validation, analysis, and test activities help to eliminate design and programming errors. The implementation of coding standards and code walk-throughs also reduces the likelihood of undetected programming errors.

The Java language eliminates whole classes of errors that result from the use of dangerous programming constructs such as pointers and automatic type conversions. The simplicity and familiarity of the language also reduce the occurrence of programming errors.

The Java compiler and runtime environment help to keep errors from being introduced into executable Java code. The compiler performs extensive type checking to ensure that objects are correctly referenced and updated and that methods are properly invoked. The runtime system duplicates compile-time checks and implements additional checks to verify that executable code follows established rules for program correctness.

With all the error checking that takes place before a program is executed, you might think that it would be unlikely that errors could still creep into a program. They can and always do, in accordance with Murphy's Law. Runtime error and exception handling is used to identify error conditions and perform processing that minimizes their impact.

Error Processing and Exceptions

Java provides superior support for runtime error and exception handling, allowing programs to check for anomalous conditions and respond to them with minimal impact on the normal flow of program execution. This allows error- and exception-handling code to be added easily to existing methods.

Exceptions are generated by the Java runtime system in response to errors that are detected as classes are loaded and their methods are executed. The runtime system is said to *throw* these *runtime exceptions*. Runtime exceptions are objects of the class java.lang.RuntimeException or of its subclasses.

Exceptions may also be thrown directly by Java code using the throw statement. These exceptions are thrown when code detects a condition that could potentially lead to a program malfunction. The exceptions thrown by user programs are generally not objects of a subclass of RuntimeException. These non-runtime exceptions are referred to as *program* exceptions.

NOTE

It is possible for user programs to throw runtime exceptions, but it is almost always a bad programming practice.

Both program and runtime exceptions must be caught in order for them to be processed by exception-handling code. If a thrown exception is not caught, its thread of execution is terminated and an error message is displayed on the Java console window.

The approach used by Java to catch and handle exceptions is to surround blocks of statements for which exception processing is to be performed by a try statement. The try statement contains a catch clause that identifies what processing is to be performed for different types of exceptions. When an exception occurs, the Java runtime system matches the exception to the appropriate catch clause. The catch clause then handles the exception in an appropriate manner.

Throwing Exceptions

Exceptions are thrown using the throw statement. Its syntax is as follows:

```
throw Expression;
```

Expression must evaluate to an object that is an instance of a subclass of the java.lang.Throwable class. The Throwable class is defined in the Java API. When an exception is thrown, execution does not continue after the throw statement. Instead, it continues with any code that catches the exception. If an exception is not caught, the current thread of execution is terminated and an error is displayed on the console window.

For example, the following statement will throw an exception, using an object of class ExampleException:

```
throw new ExampleException();
```

The new operator is invoked with the ExampleException() constructor to allocate and initialize an object of class ExampleException. This object is then thrown by the throw statement.

> **NOTE**
>
> A `throw` statement can throw an object of any class that is a subclass of
> `java.lang.Throwable`; however, it is wise to stick with the standard convention of only
> throwing objects that are a subclass of class `Exception`.

Declaring Exceptions

A method's `throws` clause lists the types of exceptions that can be thrown during a method's execution. The `throws` clause appears immediately before a method's body in the method declaration. For example, the following method throws the `ExampleException`:

```
public void exampleMethod() throws ExampleException {
 throw new ExampleException();
}
```

When more than one exception may be thrown during the execution of a method, the exceptions are separated by commas in the `throws` clause. For example, the following method can throw either the `Test1Exception` or the `Test2Exception`:

```
public void testMethod(int i) throws Test1Exception, Test2Exception {
 if(i==1) throw new Test1Exception();
 if(i==2) throw new Test2Exception();
}
```

The types identified in the `throws` clause must be capable of being legally assigned to the exceptions that may be thrown.

Declare or Catch?

If a program exception can be thrown during the execution of a method, the method must either catch the expression or declare it in the `throws` clause of its method declaration. If an exception is not caught, it must be declared, even if it is thrown in other methods that are invoked during the method's execution.

For example, suppose that method A of object X invokes method B of object Y, which invokes method C of object Z. If method C throws an exception, it must be caught by method C or declared in method C's `throws` clause. If it is not caught by method C, it must be caught by method B or declared in method B's `throws` clause. Similarly, if the exception is not caught by method B, it must be caught by method A or declared in method A's `throws` clause. The handling of exceptions is a hierarchical process that mirrors the method invocation hierarchy (or call tree). Either an exception is caught by a method and removed from the hierarchy or it must be declared and propagated back through the method invocation hierarchy.

> **NOTE**
>
> Because runtime exceptions can occur almost anywhere in a program's execution, the catch or declare requirement only applies to program exceptions.

The CDrawApp programs of Chapters 5, "Classes and Objects," and 6, "Interfaces," provide an extended example of the declaration of uncaught exceptions. The jdg.ch05.KeyboardInput class contains three access methods that use the readLine() method: getChar(), getText(), and getInt(). The readLine() method is inherited from the BufferedReader class. It throws an exception of class IOException. Because the getChar(), getText(), and getInt() methods invoke the readLine() method, they must either catch the exception or declare it in their throws clauses. None of these methods catches IOException; therefore, all declare it in their throws clauses. The getCommand() method of class CDraw invokes the getChar() method of an object of class KeyboardInput. It does not catch IOException, so it also must declare it. Because the run() method of class CDraw invokes the getCommand() method, it too is faced with catching or declaring IOException. Because run() declares IOException and the main() method of CDrawApp invokes the run() method for a CDraw object, it also must declare IOException in its throws clause.

At this point you are probably coming to the conclusion that it is a lot easier to catch and handle an exception than to declare it throughout the class hierarchy. If so, you have discovered a key benefit of Java's exception-handling approach. Java makes it easier to develop more reliable software and harder to develop less reliable software. If you are a lazy programmer like me, Java will exploit your tendency to do things the easy way to encourage you to do things the right way.

Using the try Statement

Statements for which exception processing is to be performed are surrounded by a try statement with a valid catch or finally clause. The syntax of the try statement is as follows:

```
try TryBlock CatchClauses FinallyClause;
```

At least one catch clause or finally clause must be defined. More than one catch clause may be used, but no more than one finally clause may be identified.

The try block is a sequence of Java statements that are preceded by an opening brace ({) and followed by a closing brace (}).

The catch clauses are a sequence of clauses of the form:

```
catch (Parameter) {
/*
* Exception handling statements
*/
}
```

The *Parameter* is a variable that is declared to be a class or interface. The statements within the catch clause are used to process the exceptions that they "catch," as I'll explain shortly.

The finally clause identifies a block of code that is to be executed at the conclusion of the try statement and after any catch clauses. Its syntax is as follows:

```
finally {
/*
* Statements in finally clause
*/
}
```

The finally clause is always executed, no matter whether an exception is thrown.

Catching Exceptions

The try statement executes a statement block. If an exception is thrown during the block's execution, it terminates execution of the statement block and checks the catch clauses to determine which, if any, of the catch clauses can catch the thrown exception. If none of the catch clauses can catch the exception, the exception is propagated to the next higher level try statement. This process is repeated until the exception is caught or no more try statements remain.

A catch clause can catch an exception if its argument may be legally assigned the object thrown in the throw statement. If the argument of a catch clause is a class, the catch clause can catch any object whose class is a subclass of this class. If the argument to a catch clause is an interface, the catch clause can catch any object that implements that interface.

The try statement tries each catch clause, in order, and selects the first one that can catch the exception that was thrown. It then executes the statements in the catch clause. If a finally clause occurs in the try statement, the statements in the finally clause are executed after execution of the catch clause has been completed. Execution then continues with the statement following the try statement.

The following example shows how catch clauses are used to process exceptions that are thrown within the try statement. Create a directory ch07 under c:\jdk1.1.1\jdg and enter the source code in the file ExceptionTest.java. Compile it using the command javac ExceptionTest.java. The source code for the ExceptionTest program is shown in Listing 7.1.

Listing 7.1. The source code of the ExceptionTest program.

```
import jdg.ch05.KeyboardInput;
import java.lang.System;
import java.lang.Exception;
import java.io.IOException;
class VowelException extends Exception {}
class BlankException extends Exception {}
class ExitException extends Exception {}
```

```
class ExceptionTest {
 static KeyboardInput kbd = new KeyboardInput(System.in);
 public static void main(String args[]) {
  boolean finished = false;
  do {
    try {
     processUserInput();
    }catch (VowelException x) {
     System.out.println("A vowel exception occurred.");
    }catch (BlankException x) {
     System.out.println("A blank exception occurred.");
    }catch (ExitException x) {
     System.out.println("An exit exception occurred.");
     finished = true;
    }finally {
     System.out.println("This is the finally clause.\n");
    }
  } while(!finished);
 }
 static void processUserInput() throws VowelException, BlankException,
  ExitException {
  System.out.print("Enter a character: ");
  System.out.flush();
  char ch;
  try {
   ch=Character.toUpperCase(kbd.getChar());
  } catch (IOException x) {
   System.out.println("An IOException occurred.");
   return;
  }
  switch(ch) {
   case 'A':
   case 'E':
   case 'I':
   case 'O':
   case 'U':
    throw new VowelException();
   case ' ':
    throw new BlankException();
   case 'X':
    throw new ExitException();
  }
 }
}
```

The ExceptionTest program uses the jdg.ch05.KeyboardInput class to retrieve a character entered by the user. It then throws and catches a VowelException, BlankException, or ExitException based on the user's input.

The ExceptionTest class consists of a single class variable, kbd, that is statically initialized to an object of class KeyboardInput, with System.in as an argument to its constructor.

ExceptionTest provides two static methods, main() and processUserInput(). The main() method consists of a simple do statement that repeatedly tries to invoke processUserInput(). The try statement has three catch clauses and a finally clause. The three catch clauses notify the user of the type of exception they catch. The catch clause with an ExitException parameter causes the do statement and the program to terminate by setting finished to true. The finally clause just displays the fact that it has been executed.

The processUserInput() method prompts the user to enter a character. The actual reading of the character occurs within a try statement. IOException is caught by the try statement, eliminating the need to declare the exception in the processUserInput() throws clause. The IOException is handled by notifying the user that the exception occurred and continuing with program execution.

The processUserInput() method throws one of three exceptions based upon the character entered by the user. If the user enters a vowel, VowelException is thrown. If the user enters a line beginning with a non-printable character, BlankException is thrown. If the user enters x or X, ExitException is thrown.

To run ExceptionTest, type java ExceptionTest. The program outputs the following:

```
C:\jdk1.1.1\jdg\ch07>java ExceptionTest
Enter a character:
```

The program prompts you to enter a character. Enter a blank line, and the following output is displayed:

```
A blank exception occurred.
This is the finally clause.
Enter a character:
```

The program notifies you that a blank exception has occurred and displays the fact that the finally clause of the main() try statement was executed. The processUserInput() method, upon encountering a space character returned by getChar(), throws the BlankException, which is caught by the main() method. The finally clause always executes no matter whether processUserInput() throws an exception or not.

Enter a at the program prompt, and the following output appears:

```
Enter a character: a
A vowel exception occurred.
This is the finally clause.
Enter a character:
```

Here the program notifies you that a vowel exception has occurred. The processing of the vowel exception is similar to the blank exception. See if you can trace the program flow of control involved in this processing.

Enter j, and the following is displayed:

```
Enter a character: j
This is the finally clause.
Enter a character:
```

No exceptions are thrown for the j character, but the `finally` clause is executed. The `finally` clause is always executed, no matter what happens during the execution of a `try` statement. Type x to exit the `ExceptionTest` program. The program displays the following output:

```
Enter a character: x
An exit exception occurred.
This is the finally clause.
```

The exception then returns you to the command prompt.

The output acknowledges the fact that the exit exception was thrown by `processUserInput()` and caught by `main()`.

The `ExceptionTest` program provides a simple example of exception throwing and catching. The example in the following section illustrates more complex exception handling.

Nested Exception Handling

`try` statements can be nested to provide multiple levels of exception-handling capabilities. This is accomplished by enclosing a method or block of statements containing a lower-level `try` statement within the `try` block of a higher-level `try` statement. When an exception is thrown in the `try` block of the lower-level `try` statement that cannot be caught, it continues to be thrown until it reaches the higher-level `try` statement. The higher-level `try` statement can then determine whether the exception can be caught and processed by any of its `catch` clauses. Any number of `try` statements can be nested. Figure 7.1 illustrates this concept.

FIGURE 7.1.

Nested exception handling: An exception generated within the lower-level `try` *statement is first passed to its catch clause(s). If it is not handled, it is propagated to the higher-level* catch *clause(s). If it is not handled by the higher-level* catch *clause(s), it is propagated further up the exception-handling hierarchy.*

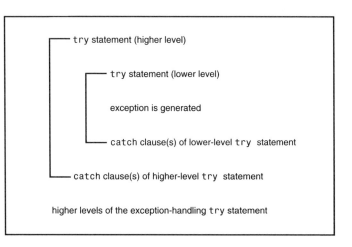

Rethrowing Exceptions

When an exception is caught in the catch clause of a try statement, that exception may be rethrown. When an exception is rethrown, it can then be caught and processed by the catch clause of a higher-level try statement. A higher-level catch clause can then perform any secondary clean-up processing.

The following example illustrates nested exception handling and the rethrowing of exceptions. Enter the source code shown in Listing 7.2 into NestedExceptionTest.java and compile it.

Listing 7.2. The source code of the NestedExceptionTest program.

```
import jdg.ch05.KeyboardInput;
import java.lang.System;
import java.lang.Exception;
import java.io.IOException;
class VowelException extends Exception {}
class BlankException extends Exception {}
class ExitException extends Exception {}
class NestedExceptionTest {
 static KeyboardInput kbd = new KeyboardInput(System.in);
 public static void main(String args[]) {
  do{} while(!exitExceptionTest());
 }
 static boolean exitExceptionTest() {
  try {
   vowelExceptionTest();
   System.out.println("Acceptable.\n");
  }catch (ExitException x) {
   try {
    System.out.print("Exit (y/n): ");
    System.out.flush();
    char ch = Character.toUpperCase(kbd.getChar());
    System.out.println();
    if(ch=='Y') return true;
    else return false;
   }catch (IOException iox) {
    return false;
   }
  }catch (Exception x) {
   System.out.println("Not acceptable. Try again.\n");
  }
  return false;
 }
 static void vowelExceptionTest() throws VowelException, ExitException {
  try {
   blankExceptionTest();
  }catch (BlankException x) {
   System.out.println("Next time type a printable character.\n");
   vowelExceptionTest();
  }catch (VowelException x) {
   System.out.println("You typed a vowel.");
   throw x;
  }
```

```
}
static void blankExceptionTest() throws VowelException, BlankException,
 ExitException {
 try {
  processUserInput();
 }catch (BlankException x) {
  System.out.println("You entered a blank line. Try again.");
  throw x;
 }
}
static void processUserInput() throws VowelException, BlankException,
 ExitException {
 System.out.print("Enter a character: ");
 System.out.flush();
 char ch;
 try {
  ch=Character.toUpperCase(kbd.getChar());
 } catch (IOException x) {
  System.out.println("An IOException occurred.");
  return;
 }
 switch(ch) {
  case 'A':
  case 'E':
  case 'I':
  case 'O':
  case 'U':
   throw new VowelException();
  case ' ':
   throw new BlankException();
  case 'X':
   throw new ExitException();
 }
 }
}
```

This example is based on the previous example, but it is significantly more complex. The exception handling has been removed from the main() method and distributed among three nested exception handlers: exitExceptionTest(), vowelExceptionTest(), and blankExceptionTest().

The main() method invokes exitExceptionTest()at each iteration of the do statement. The exitExceptionTest() method returns a boolean value indicating whether the do statement should terminate. The normal (non-exception) processing performed by exitExceptionTest() consists of the following three statements:

```
vowelExceptionTest();
System.out.println("Acceptable.\n");
return false;
```

All other exitExceptionTest()processing is error handling. The first two statements are executed within the try statement and are subject to error processing. The last statement executes upon completion of the try statement, assuming that no transfer of control occurs as the result of exception handling involving the catch clauses.

The try statement has two catch clauses. The first catch clause handles ExitException processing. It consists of a try statement with a catch clause that catches the pesky IOException. The try statement contains a block of statements that asks the user for a confirmation before exiting the program.

The second catch clause catches all other objects that are instances of a subclass of Exception. It displays a short warning to the user.

The vowelExceptionTest() method consists of a try statement that invokes blankExceptionTest(). The rest of the processing performed by vowelExceptionTest() is exception handling. It catches two exceptions: BlankException and VowelException. It handles BlankException by warning the user to type a printable character and reinvoking itself. It handles the vowel exception by notifying the user that he typed a vowel and rethrowing the VowelException. By rethrowing the exception, it allows exitExceptionTest() to perform additional exception handling. Because vowelExceptionTest() rethrows the VowelException, it must declare it in its throws clause. It also must declare the ExitException because the ExitException is declared in the throws clause of blankExceptionTest() and is not caught by vowelExceptionTest().

The blankExceptionTest() simply invokes processUserInput() as part of its normal processing. It handles one exception thrown by processUserInput(): the BlankException. It handles the BlankException by informing the user that he typed a blank line and that he should try again. It then rethrows the BlankException so that it can be rehandled by vowelExceptionTest().

The processUserInput() method performs in the same manner as described in the previous example.

Analysis of NestedExceptionTest

If NestedExceptionTest seems overly complex, don't worry—it was meant to be. Its purpose is to give you a good understanding of the complex ways that exception handlers can be nested and how exceptions are rethrown. Go ahead and run NestedExceptionTest using the command java NestedExceptionTest:

```
C:\jdk1.1.1\jdg\ch07>java NestedExceptionTest
Enter a character:
```

When you run NestedExceptionTest, the main() method invokes exitExceptionTest(), which invokes vowelExceptionTest(), which invokes blankExceptionTest(), which invokes processUserInput(). The processUserInput() method prompts you to enter a character and then does one of four things depending on the character you enter. If you enter a vowel, it throws a VowelException. If you enter a nonprintable character or blank line, it throws a BlankException. If you enter x or X, it throws an ExitException. Finally, as a default, if you enter any other printable character, it will simply return control to the blankExceptionTest() method.

Let's work through all four scenarios. First, enter j to cause normal program processing to occur:

```
Enter a character: j
Acceptable.
Enter a character:
```

The processUserInput() method returns control to blankExceptionTest(), which in turn returns control to vowelExceptionTest(), which returns control to exitExceptionTest(). The exitExceptionTest() method informs the user that he has entered an acceptable character and returns control to the main() method, which starts another character-input cycle.

Now let's go through the case when the user enters a blank line. Just enter a blank line at the prompt:

```
Enter a character:
You entered a blank line. Try again.
Next time type a printable character.
Enter a character:
```

A blank line causes processUserInput() to throw the BlankException. This exception is caught by blankExceptionTest(). The blankExceptionTest() method handles the exception by informing the user that he has entered a blank line and that he should try again. It then rethrows the exception; the rethrown exception is caught by vowelExceptionTest(). The vowelExceptionTest() method handles the rethrown BlankException by telling the user that he should enter a printable character the next time he is prompted. It then invokes itself, starting the character-input cycle all over.

Let's go through the case where the user enters a vowel. Enter a at the prompt:

```
Enter a character: a
You typed a vowel.
Not acceptable. Try again.
Enter a character:
```

When a vowel is entered, processUserInput() throws the VowelException. The VowelException is not caught by blankExceptionTest() and continues to be thrown until it is caught by vowelExceptionTest(). The vowelExceptionTest() method handles the exception by informing the user that he has typed a vowel and then rethrows the exception. The rethrown exception is caught by exitExceptionTest(), and exitExceptionTest() handles it by informing the user that his input is not acceptable. Execution control returns to the main() method, which starts another character-input cycle.

This last case examines what happens when the user types x at the character prompt. Enter x to see what happens:

```
Enter a character: x
Exit (y/n):
```

The processUserInput() method throws an ExitException, which is not caught by blankExceptionTest() nor vowelExceptionTest(). The exception continues to be thrown until it is caught by exitExceptionTest(). The exitExceptionTest() method prompts the user to enter a y to exit the application or an n to not exit the application. If the user enters an n or any other character besides y, control returns to the main() method and another character-input cycle is initiated. If the user enters a y, control is returned to the main() method, but the true return value is passed, causing the do statement and the program to terminate.

Go ahead and type y to terminate the NestedExceptionTest program.

Summary

In this chapter you learned how to use Java exceptions to implement error-handling capabilities in your Java programs. You also learned how to throw exceptions in response to error conditions and how to catch exceptions to perform error processing. You learned how to implement nested exception handling and how to rethrow exceptions. In Chapter 8, "Multithreading," you will learn how to use Java's multithreading capabilities to write programs that use multiple threads of execution.

8

Multithreading

This chapter introduces you to multithreaded programs and describes how multithreading is supported by Java. You'll learn how to create, run, and synchronize multiple threads in your programs. You'll also learn about thread scheduling and how a thread's priority determines when it is scheduled. When you finish this chapter you will be able to develop multithreaded programs using Java.

Understanding Multithreading

All the sample programs you developed in the preceding chapters have had only a single thread of execution. Each program proceeded sequentially, one instruction after another, until it completed its processing and terminated.

Multithreaded programs are similar to the single-threaded programs that you have been studying. They differ only in the fact that they support more than one *concurrent* thread of execution—that is, they are able to simultaneously execute multiple sequences of instructions. Each instruction sequence has its own unique flow of control that is independent of all others. These independently executed instruction sequences are known as *threads*.

If your computer has only a single CPU, you might be wondering how it can execute more than one thread at the same time. In single-processor systems, only a single thread of execution occurs at a given instant. The CPU quickly switches back and forth between several threads to create the illusion that the threads are executing at the same time. Single-processor systems support *logical concurrency*, not *physical concurrency*. Logical concurrency is the characteristic exhibited when multiple threads execute with separate, independent flows of control. On multiprocessor systems, several threads do, in fact, execute at the same time, and physical concurrency is achieved. The important feature of multithreaded programs is that they support logical concurrency, not whether physical concurrency is actually achieved.

Many programming languages support *multiprogramming*. Multiprogramming is the logically concurrent execution of multiple programs. For example, a program can request that the operating system execute programs A, B, and C by having it spawn a separate process for each program. These programs can run in parallel, depending upon the multiprogramming features supported by the underlying operating system. Multithreading differs from multiprogramming in that multithreading provides concurrency within the context of a single process and multiprogramming provides concurrency between processes. Threads are not complete processes in and of themselves. They are a separate flow of control that occurs within a process. Figure 8.1 illustrates the difference between multithreading and multiprogramming.

An executing program is generally associated with a single process. The advantage of multithreading is that concurrency can be used within a process to provide multiple simultaneous services to the user. Multithreading also requires less processing overhead than multiprogramming because concurrent threads are able to share common resources more easily. Multiple executing programs tend to duplicate resources and share data as the result of more time-consuming interprocess communication.

FIGURE 8.1.

Multithreading versus multiprogramming.

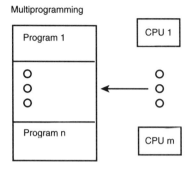

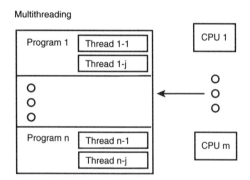

How Java Supports Multithreading

Java provides extensive support for both multithreading and multiprogramming. Multithreading is covered in this chapter. Java's support for multiprogramming is covered in Chapter 12, "Portable Software and the java.lang Packages."

Java's multithreading support is centered around the java.lang.Thread class. The Thread class provides the capability to create objects of class Thread, each with their own separate flow of control. The Thread class encapsulates the data and methods associated with separate threads of execution and allows multithreading to be integrated within the object-oriented framework.

Java provides two approaches to creating threads. In the first approach, you create a subclass of class Thread and override the run() method to provide an entry point into the thread's execution. When you create an instance of your Thread subclass, you invoke its start() method to cause the thread to execute as an independent sequence of instructions. The start() method is inherited from the Thread class. It initializes the Thread object using your operating system's multithreading capabilities and invokes the run() method. In the next section you will learn how to create threads using this approach.

NOTE

This chapter makes heavy use of the Java API methods defined for class `Thread` and related classes. If you haven't obtained and installed a copy of the Java API documentation, now is a good time to do so. The API documentation is available at JavaSoft's Web site, `http://www.javasoft.com`.

The approach to creating threads identified in the previous paragraph is very simple and straight-forward. However, it has the drawback of requiring your `Thread` objects to be under the `Thread` class in the class hierarchy. In some cases, as you'll see when you study applets in Part VI, "Web Programming," this requirement can be somewhat limiting.

Java's other approach to creating threads does not limit the location of your `Thread` objects within the class hierarchy. In this approach, your class implements the `java.lang.Runnable` interface. The `Runnable` interface consists of a single method, the `run()` method, which must be overridden by your class. The `run()` method provides an entry point into your thread's execution. In order to run an object of your class as an independent thread, you pass it as an argument to a constructor of class `Thread`. You learn how to create threads using this approach later in this chapter in the section titled "Implementing `Runnable`."

Creating Subclasses of Thread

In this section, you create your first multithreaded program by creating a subclass of `Thread` and then creating, initializing, and starting two `Thread` objects from your class. The threads will execute concurrently and display `Java is hot, aromatic, and invigorating.` to the console window.

Create a `ch08` directory under `c:\jdk1.1.1\jdg` and enter source code from Listing 8.1 into `ThreadTest1.java`. Then compile it using the command `javac ThreadTest1.java`.

Listing 8.1. The source code of the `ThreadTest1` program.

```
import java.lang.Thread;
import java.lang.System;
import java.lang.Math;
import java.lang.InterruptedException;
class ThreadTest1 {
 public static void main(String args[]) {
  MyThread thread1 = new MyThread("thread1: ");
  MyThread thread2 = new MyThread("thread2: ");
  thread1.start();
  thread2.start();
  boolean thread1IsAlive = true;
  boolean thread2IsAlive = true;
  do {
   if(thread1IsAlive && !thread1.isAlive()){
    thread1IsAlive = false;
    System.out.println("Thread 1 is dead.");
```

```
  }
  if(thread2IsAlive && !thread2.isAlive()){
    thread2IsAlive = false;
    System.out.println("Thread 2 is dead.");
  }
 }while(thread1IsAlive || thread2IsAlive);
 }
}
class MyThread extends Thread {
 static String message[] = {"Java","is","hot,","aromatic,","and",
 "invigorating."};
 public MyThread(String id) {
  super(id);
 }
 public void run() {
  String name = getName();
  for(int i=0;i<message.length;++i) {
   randomWait();
   System.out.println(name+message[i]);
  }
 }
 void randomWait(){
  try {
   sleep((long)(3000*Math.random()));
  }catch (InterruptedException x){
   System.out.println("Interrupted!");
  }
 }
}
```

This program creates two threads of execution, `thread1` and `thread2`, from the `MyThread` class. It then starts both threads and executes a do statement that waits for the threads to die. The threads display the `Java is hot, aromatic, and invgorating.` message word by word, while waiting a short, random amount of time between each word. Because both threads share the console window, the program's output identifies which threads were able to write to the console at various times during the program's execution.

> **NOTE**
>
> The Java documentation refers to threads that have completed their execution as being *dead.* The term is descriptive, but somewhat morose.

Run `ThreadTest1` to get an idea of the output that it produces. Each time you run the program you might get a different program display. This is because the program uses a random number generator to determine how long each thread should wait before displaying its output. Look at the following output:

```
C:\jdk1.1.1\jdg\ch08>java ThreadTest1
thread1: Java
thread2: Java
thread2: is
```

```
thread2: hot,
thread2: aromatic,
thread1: is
thread1: hot,
thread2: and
thread1: aromatic,
thread1: and
thread2: invigorating.
Thread 2 is dead.
thread1: invigorating.
Thread 1 is dead.
```

This output shows that thread1 executed first and displayed Java to the console window. It then waited to execute while thread2 displayed Java, is, hot, and aromatic,. After that, thread2 waited while thread1 continued its execution. thread1 displayed is and then hot,. At this point, thread2 took over again. thread2 displayed and and then went back into waiting. thread1 then displayed aromatic, and and. thread2 finished its execution by displaying invigorating.. Having completed its execution, thread2 died, leaving thread1 as the only executing task. thread1 displayed invigorating. and then completed its execution.

The ThreadTest1 class consists of a single main() method. This method begins by creating thread1 and thread2 as new objects of class MyThread. It then starts both threads using the start() method. At this point, main() enters a do loop that continues until both thread1 and thread2 are no longer alive. The loop monitors the execution of the two threads and displays a message when it has detected the death of each thread. It uses the isAlive() method of the Thread class to tell when a thread has died. The thread1IsAlive and thread2IsAlive variables are used to ensure that a thread's obituary is only displayed once.

The MyThread class extends class Thread. It declares a statically initialized array, named message[], that contains the message to be displayed by each thread. It has a single constructor that invokes the Thread class constructor via super(). It contains two access methods: run() and randomWait(). The run() method is required. It uses the getName() method of class Thread to get the name of the currently executing thread. It then prints each word of the output display message while waiting a random length of time between each print. The randomWait() method invokes the sleep() method within a try statement. The sleep() method is another method inherited from class Thread. It causes the currently executing task to "go to sleep" or wait until a randomly specified number of milliseconds has transpired. Because the sleep() method throws the InterruptedException when its sleep is interrupted (how grouchy!), the exception is caught and handled by the randomWait() method. The exception is handled by displaying the fact that an interruption has occurred to the console window.

Implementing Runnable

In the previous section, you created a multithreaded program by creating the MyThread subclass of Thread. In this section, you create a program with similar behavior, but you create your threads as objects of the class MyClass, which is not a subclass of Thread. MyClass will implement the Runnable interface, and objects of MyClass will be executed as threads by passing them as arguments to the Thread constructor.

The ThreadTest2 program's source code is shown in Listing 8.2. Enter it into the ThreadTest2.java file and compile it.

Listing 8.2. The source code of the ThreadTest2 program.

```
import java.lang.Thread;
import java.lang.System;
import java.lang.Math;
import java.lang.InterruptedException;
import java.lang.Runnable;
class ThreadTest2 {
 public static void main(String args[]) {
  Thread thread1 = new Thread(new MyClass("thread1: "));
  Thread thread2 = new Thread(new MyClass("thread2: "));
  thread1.start();
  thread2.start();
  boolean thread1IsAlive = true;
  boolean thread2IsAlive = true;
  do {
   if(thread1IsAlive && !thread1.isAlive()){
    thread1IsAlive = false;
    System.out.println("Thread 1 is dead.");
   }
   if(thread2IsAlive && !thread2.isAlive()){
    thread2IsAlive = false;
    System.out.println("Thread 2 is dead.");
   }
  }while(thread1IsAlive || thread2IsAlive);
 }
}
class MyClass implements Runnable {
 static String message[] = {"Java","is","hot,","aromatic,","and",
  "invigorating."};
 String name;
 public MyClass(String id) {
  name = id;
 }
 public void run() {
  for(int i=0;i<message.length;++i) {
   randomWait();
   System.out.println(name+message[i]);
  }
 }
 void randomWait(){
  try {
   Thread.currentThread().sleep((long)(3000*Math.random()));
  }catch (InterruptedException x){
   System.out.println("Interrupted!");
  }
 }
}
```

The `ThreadTest2` program is very similar to `ThreadTest1`. It differs only in the way that the threads are created. You should run `ThreadTest2` a few times to examine its output. Here are the results of a sample run I made on my computer:

```
C:\jdk1.1.1\jdg\ch08>java ThreadTest2
thread2: Java
thread1: Java
thread2: is
thread2: hot,
thread1: is
thread2: aromatic,
thread1: hot,
thread1: aromatic,
thread1: and
thread2: and
thread1: invigorating.
Thread 1 is dead.
thread2: invigorating.
Thread 2 is dead.
```

These results show `thread2` beginning its output before `thread1`. It does not mean that `thread2` began executing before `thread1`. `thread1` executed first, but went to sleep before generating any output. `thread2` then executed and started its output display before going to sleep. You can follow these results on your own to analyze how `thread1` and `thread2` switched back and forth during their execution to display their results to the console window.

The `main()` method of `ThreadTest2` differs from that of `ThreadTest1` in the way that it creates `thread1` and `thread2`. `ThreadTest1` created the threads as new instances of the `MyThread` class. `ThreadTest2` was not able to create the threads directly, because `MyClass` is not a subclass of `Thread`. Instead, `ThreadTest2` first created instances of `MyClass` and then passed them to the `Thread()` constructor, creating instances of class `Thread`. The `Thread()` constructor used by `ThreadTest2` takes as its argument any class that implements the `Runnable` interface. This is an example of the flexibility and multiple-inheritance features provided by Java interfaces. The rest of the `ThreadTest2` `main()` method is the same as that of `ThreadTest1`.

`MyClass` is declared as implementing the `Runnable` interface. This is a simple interface to implement; it only requires that you implement the `run()` method. `MyClass` declares the `name` variable to hold the name of `MyClass` objects that are created. In the first example, the `MyThread` class did not need to do this because a thread-naming capability was provided by `Thread` and inherited by `MyThread`. `MyClass` contains a simple constructor that initializes the `name` variable.

The `run()` methods of `ThreadTest2` and `ThreadTest1` are nearly identical, differing only with respect to the name issue. This is also true of the `randomWait()` method. In `ThreadTest2`, the `randomWait()` method must use the `currentThread()` method of class `Thread` to acquire a reference to an instance of the current thread in order to invoke its `sleep()` method.

Because these two examples are so similar, you might be wondering why you would pick one approach to creating a class over another. The advantage of using the `Runnable` interface is that your class does not need to extend the `Thread` class. This will be a helpful feature when you start using multithreading in applets in Part VI of this book. The only disadvantages to this approach are ones of convenience. You have to do a little more work to create your threads and to access their methods.

Thread States

You have now learned how to declare, create, initialize, start, and run Java threads. The ThreadTest1 and ThreadTest2 programs also introduced you to the concept of a thread's death. Threads transition through several states from the time they are created until the time of their death. This section reviews these states.

A thread is created by producing a new object of class Thread or one of its subclasses. When a thread is first created, it does not exist as an independently executing set of instructions. Instead, it is a template from which an executing thread will be created. It first executes as a thread when it is started using the start() method and run via the run() method. Before a thread is started it is said to be in the *new thread* state. After a thread is started, it is in the *runnable* state. When a thread is in the runnable state, it may be executing or temporarily waiting to share processing resources with other threads. A runnable thread enters an extended wait state when one of its methods are invoked that causes it to drop from the runnable state into a not runnable state. In the *not runnable* state, a thread is not just waiting for its share of processing resources, but is blocked waiting for the occurrence of an event that will send it back to the runnable state.

For example, the sleep() method was invoked in the ThreadTest1 and ThreadTest2 programs to cause a thread to wait for a short period of time so that the other thread could execute. The sleep() method causes a thread to enter the not runnable state until the specified time has expired. A thread may also enter the not runnable state while it is waiting for I/O to be completed, or as the result of the invocation of other methods. Chapter 12 provides a detailed description of the methods of the Thread class that are inherited by all threads.

> **NOTE**
>
> There is no connection between a thread's runnable state and a class's Runnable interface.

A thread leaves the not runnable state and returns to the runnable state when the event that it is waiting for has occurred. For example, a sleeping thread must wait for its specified sleep time to occur. A thread that is waiting on I/O must wait for the I/O operation to be completed.

A thread may transition from the new thread, runnable, or not runnable state to the *dead* state when its stop() method is invoked or the thread's execution is completed. When a thread enters the dead state, it's a goner. It can't be revived and returned to any other state.

Thread Priority and Scheduling

From an abstract or a logical perspective, multiple threads execute as concurrent sequences of instructions. This may be physically true for multiprocessor systems, under certain conditions. However, in the general case, multiple threads do not always physically execute at the same time. Instead, the threads share execution time with each other based on the availability of the system's CPU (or CPUs).

The approach used to determining which threads should execute at a given time is referred to as *scheduling*. Scheduling is performed by the Java runtime system. It schedules threads based on their *priority*. The highest-priority thread that is in the runnable state is the thread that is run at any given instant. The highest-priority thread continues to run until it enters the dead state, enters the not runnable state, or has its priority lowered, or when a higher-priority thread becomes runnable.

A thread's priority is an integer value between MIN_PRIORITY and MAX_PRIORITY. These constants are defined in the Thread class. In the JDK 1.1, MIN_PRIORITY is 1 and MAX_PRIORITY is 10. A thread's priority is set when it is created. It is set to the same priority as the thread that created it. The default priority of a thread is NORM_PRIORITY and is equal to 5. The priority of a thread can be changed using the setPriority() method.

Java's approach to scheduling is referred to as *preemptive scheduling*. When a thread of higher priority becomes runnable, it preempts threads of lower priority and is immediately executed in their place. If two or more higher-priority threads become runnable, the Java scheduler alternates between them when allocating execution time.

Synchronization

There are many situations in which multiple threads must share access to common objects. For example, all of the programs in this chapter have illustrated the effects of multithreading by having multiple executing threads write to the Java console, a common shared object. These examples have not required any coordination or synchronization in the way the threads access the console window: Whatever thread was currently executing was able to write to the console window. No coordination between concurrent threads was required.

There are times when you might want to coordinate access to shared resources. For example, in a database system, you might not want one thread to be updating a database record while another thread is trying to read it. Java enables you to coordinate the actions of multiple threads using *synchronized methods* and *synchronized statements*.

An object for which access is to be coordinated is accessed through the use of synchronized methods. (Synchronized statements are covered in Chapter 11, "Language Summary.") These methods are declared with the synchronized keyword. Only one synchronized method can be invoked for an object at a given point in time. This keeps synchronized methods in multiple threads from conflicting with each other.

All classes and objects are associated with a unique *monitor*. The monitor is used to control the way in which synchronized methods are allowed to access the class or object. When a synchronized method is invoked for a given object, it is said to *acquire* the monitor for that object. No other synchronized method may be invoked for that object until the monitor is released. A monitor is automatically released when the method completes its execution and returns. A monitor may also be released when a synchronized method executes certain methods, such as wait(). The thread associated with the currently executing synchronized method becomes not runnable until the wait condition is satisfied and no other method has acquired the object's monitor.

The following example shows how synchronized methods and object monitors are used to coordinate access to a common object by multiple threads. This example adapts the ThreadTest1 program for use with synchronized methods, as shown in Listing 8.3.

Listing 8.3. The source code of the ThreadSynchronization program.

```
import java.lang.Thread;
import java.lang.System;
import java.lang.Math;
import java.lang.InterruptedException;
class ThreadSynchronization {
 public static void main(String args[]) {
  MyThread thread1 = new MyThread("thread1: ");
  MyThread thread2 = new MyThread("thread2: ");
  thread1.start();
  thread2.start();
  boolean thread1IsAlive = true;
  boolean thread2IsAlive = true;
  do {
   if(thread1IsAlive && !thread1.isAlive()){
    thread1IsAlive = false;
    System.out.println("Thread 1 is dead.");
   }
   if(thread2IsAlive && !thread2.isAlive()){
    thread2IsAlive = false;
    System.out.println("Thread 2 is dead.");
   }
  }while(thread1IsAlive || thread2IsAlive);
 }
}
class MyThread extends Thread {
 static String message[] = {"Java","is","hot,","aromatic,",
  "and","invigorating."};
 public MyThread(String id) {
  super(id);
 }
 public void run() {
  SynchronizedOutput.displayList(getName(),message);
 }
```

continues

Listing 8.3. continued

```
void randomWait(){
  try {
   sleep((long)(3000*Math.random()));
  }catch (InterruptedException x){
   System.out.println("Interrupted!");
  }
 }
}
class SynchronizedOutput {
 public static synchronized void displayList(String name,String list[]) {
  for(int i=0;i<list.length;++i) {
   MyThread t = (MyThread) Thread.currentThread();
   t.randomWait();
   System.out.println(name+list[i]);
  }
 }
}
```

Compile and run the program before going on with its analysis. You might be surprised at the results that you've obtained. Here are the results of an example run on my system:

```
C:\jdk1.1.1\jdg\ch08>java ThreadSynchronization
thread1: Java
thread1: is
thread1: hot,
thread1: aromatic,
thread1: and
thread1: invigorating.
Thread 1 is dead.
thread2: Java
thread2: is
thread2: hot,
thread2: aromatic,
thread2: and
thread2: invigorating.
Thread 2 is dead.
```

Now edit ThreadSynchronization.java and delete the synchronized keyword in the declaration of the displayList() method of class SynchronizedOutput. It should look like this when you are finished:

```
class SynchronizedOutput {
 public static void displayList(String name,String list[]) {
```

Save ThreadSynchronization.java, recompile it, and rerun it with the new change in place. You may now get output similar to this:

```
C:\jdk1.1.1\jdg\ch08>java ThreadSynchronization
thread2: Java
thread1: Java
thread1: is
thread2: is
thread2: hot,
thread2: aromatic,
thread1: hot,
```

```
thread2: and
thread2: invigorating.
Thread 2 is dead.
thread1: aromatic,
thread1: and
thread1: invigorating.
Thread 1 is dead.
```

The difference in the program's output should give you a feel for the effects of synchronization upon multithreaded program execution. Let's analyze the program and explain these results.

The ThreadSynchronization class is essentially the same as the ThreadTest1 class. The only difference is the class name.

The MyThread class was modified slightly to allow for the use of the SynchronizedOutput class. Instead of the output being displayed in the run() method, as in ThreadTest1, the run() method simply invokes the displayList() method of the SynchronizedOutput class. It is important to understand that the displayList() method is static and applies to the SynchronizedOutput class as a whole, not to any particular instance of the class. The method displays the Java is hot, aromatic, and invigorating. message in the same manner as it was displayed in the previous examples of this chapter. It invokes randomWait() to wait a random amount of time before displaying each word in the message. The displayList() method uses the currentThread() method of class Thread to reference the current thread in order to invoke randomWait().

What difference, then, does the fact that displayList() is synchronized have on the program's execution? When displayList() is not synchronized, it may be invoked by one thread, say thread1, display some output, and wait while thread2 executes. When thread2 executes, it too invokes displayList() to display some output. Two separate invocations of displayList(), one for thread1 and the other for thread2, execute concurrently. This explains the mixed output display.

When the synchronized keyword is used, thread1 invokes displayList(), acquires a monitor for the SynchronizedOutput class (because displayList() is a static method), and displayList() proceeds with the output display for thread1. Because thread1 acquired a monitor for the SynchronizedOutput class, thread2 must wait until the monitor is released before it is able to invoke displayList() to display its output. This explains why one task's output is completed before the other's.

Daemon Threads

Java borrows the notion of a daemon thread from the UNIX daemon process. A *daemon thread* is a thread that executes in the background and provides services to other threads. It typically executes a continuous loop of instructions that wait for a service request, perform the service, and wait for the next service request. Daemon threads continue to execute until there are no more threads for which services can be provided. At this time, the daemon threads die and the Java interpreter terminates its execution. Any thread can be changed to a daemon thread using the setDaemon() method.

Thread Groups

Thread groups are objects that consist of a collection of threads. All threads are a member of a unique thread group. Thread groups are used to invoke methods that apply to all threads in the group. For example, a thread group can be used to start or stop all threads in a group, to change their priorities, or to change them to daemon threads.

A thread is entered into a thread group when it is created. After the thread enters a thread group, it remains a member of the group throughout its existence. A thread can never become a member of another group.

Threads are entered into a group using `Thread` constructors that take a `ThreadGroup` parameter. These constructors are described in the `Thread` class API documentation. If a thread's group is not specified in its constructor, as is the usual case, the thread is entered into the same group as the thread that created it. The default thread group for a newly executing Java application is the `main` group. All of the threads created in this chapter's examples have been members of the default `main` thread group. The `ThreadGroup` class is covered in Chapter 12.

Summary

In this chapter you learned how to develop multithreaded programs using Java threads. You learned how to synchronize multiple threads in order to share common resources. You also learned how to use thread priorities to control thread scheduling. You now covered the main features of the Java language. A complete language summary is provided in Chapter 11. In Chapter 9, "Using the Debugger," you'll learn how to use the Java debugger to help debug the programs you develop.

9

Using the Debugger

In this chapter, you'll learn to use the Java debugger to trace and debug the Java programs you develop. You'll learn how to invoke the debugger, load class files, and examine classes as they are executed. You'll also explore the commands provided by the debugger and learn to use them through a hands-on tutorial. When you have finished this chapter, you will know how to use the debugger to analyze, test, and debug your Java programs.

Overview of the Debugger

The Java debugger enables Java programmers to debug their programs without having to insert special debugging instructions into their code. The debugger has a number of features, including support for multithreaded programs and remote applications. You can use the debugger to step through your programs and examine how they work. You can also use the debugger to test your programs and look for any coding errors.

NOTE

The Java debugger has a few bugs of its own. To get the debugger to run properly, you may have to establish an active Internet connection.

The debugger is invoked with the `jdb` command. To get a quick summary of the commands provided by the debugger, enter the debugger command as follows:

```
C:\jdk1.1.1\jdg>jdb
Initializing jdb...
>
```

The debugger takes a few seconds to initialize and then provides you with the debugger prompt. At the debugger prompt, type `help` to get a description of the commands it supports:

```
C:\jdk1.1.1\jdg>jdb
Initializing jdb...
> help
** command list **
threads [threadgroup]        — list threads
thread <thread id>           — set default thread
suspend [thread id(s)]       — suspend threads (default: all)
resume [thread id(s)]        — resume threads (default: all)
where [thread id] ¦ all      — dump a thread's stack
threadgroups                 — list threadgroups
threadgroup <name>           — set current threadgroup
print <id> [id(s)]           — print object or field
dump <id> [id(s)]            — print all object information
locals                       — print all local variables in current stack frame
classes                      — list currently known classes
methods <class id>           — list a class's methods
stop in <class id>.<method>  — set a breakpoint in a method
stop at <class id>:<line>    — set a breakpoint at a line
up [n frames]                — move up a thread's stack
```

```
down [n frames]              — move down a thread's stack
clear <class id>:<line>      — clear a breakpoint
step                         — execute current line
cont                         — continue execution from breakpoint
catch <class id>             — break for the specified exception
ignore <class id>            — ignore when the specified exception
list [line number¦method]    — print source code
use [source file path]       — display or change the source path
memory                       — report memory usage
gc                           — free unused objects
load classname               — load Java class to be debugged
run <class> [args]           — start execution of a loaded Java class
!!                           — repeat last command
help (or ?)                  — list commands
exit (or quit)               — exit debugger
>
```

Learning the debugger involves learning how to use each of these commands. Enter exit to exit the debugger.

An Extended Example

In order to get you quickly up to speed on the operation of the debugger, let's use it to analyze a program that you've already developed. Change directories to the ch06 directory and recompile the ch06 source files using the -g option. This will result in additional debugging information being inserted into the compiled byte code files:

```
C:\jdk1.1.1\jdg\ch06>javac -g CGTextEdit.java
C:\jdk1.1.1\jdg\ch06>javac -g CGText.java
C:\jdk1.1.1\jdg\ch06>javac -g CGTextPoint.java
C:\jdk1.1.1\jdg\ch06>javac -g CGTextBox.java
C:\jdk1.1.1\jdg\ch06>javac -g CDrawApp.java
```

When you have finished compiling the source files, run the debugger by entering the jdb command:

```
C:\jdk1.1.1\jdg\ch06>jdb
Initializing jdb...
>
```

At the debugger prompt, type load jdg.ch06.CDrawApp:

```
> load jdg.ch06.CDrawApp
0xe89cd8:class(jdg.ch06.CDrawApp)
>
```

The debugger responds by loading the CDrawApp class. The hexadecimal number preceding the class name is a Java runtime identifier for the CDrawApp class. Load the CDraw class by typing load jdg.ch06.CDraw:

```
> load jdg.ch06.CDraw
0xe89fe8:class(jdg.ch06.CDraw)
>
```

Now that you've loaded these two classes, you want to set a breakpoint in the main() method of CDrawApp. A *breakpoint* is a place in your program where the debugger stops execution to allow you to enter debugging commands. You set a breakpoint using the stop in command:

```
> stop in CDrawApp.main
Breakpoint set in jdg.ch06.CDrawApp.main
>
```

This tells the debugger to stop execution when it encounters the main() method of CDrawApp. Because the main() method is the first method executed in the CDrawApp program, the debugger will stop just as it starts to execute CDrawApp. Run the debugger for CDrawApp to see how the breakpoint works:

```
> run CDrawApp
running ...
main[1]
Breakpoint hit: jdg.ch06.CDrawApp.main (CDrawApp:17)
main[1]
```

> **NOTE**
>
> The debugger's output may vary slightly when you run CDrawApp.

The debugger runs CDrawApp and stops at the breakpoint. It changes its prompt to main[1] to let you know that it is suspended in the number 1 stack frame of the main thread. A *stack frame* represents the state of the stack of the Java virtual machine as a result of a method invocation. Now that you've stopped the debugger with your breakpoint, use the list command to see where you are in the program's flow of control:

```
main[1] list
13          import java.io.IOException;
14
15          class CDrawApp {
16           public static void main(String args[]) throws IOException {
17      =>    CDraw program = new CDraw();
18            program.run();
19           }
20          }
21
main[1]
```

The arrow indicates that the debugger has stopped at the point where the program instance of CDrawApp is about to be created. Now step into the CDraw() constructor using the step command. This command allows you to control a program's execution one instruction at a time, and it is used to produce the following debugger output:

```
main[1] step
main[1]
Breakpoint hit: jdg.ch06.CDraw.<init> (CDraw:28)
main[1]
```

The debugger informs you that it has stopped at a breakpoint in the CDraw constructor. The <init> identifier is used to indicate a constructor. Enter another list command to see where you are:

```
main[1] list
24          static KeyboardInput kbd = new KeyboardInput(System.in);
25          BorderedPrintCGrid grid;
26
27          // Method declarations
28      =>  CDraw() {
29            grid = new BorderedPrintCGrid();
30          }
31          void run() throws IOException {
32            boolean finished = false;
main[1]
```

The debugger indicates that you're about to execute the CDraw() constructor. Let's skip forward in the program's execution until you reach the run() method of CDraw. First, set a breakpoint at the run() method:

```
main[1] stop in CDraw.run
Breakpoint set in jdg.ch06.CDraw.run
main[1]
```

Now continue running the debugger with the cont (continue) command:

```
main[1] cont
main[1]
Breakpoint hit: jdg.ch06.CDraw.run (CDraw:32)
main[1]
```

The debugger indicates that it stopped at your breakpoint. Use the list command to see where the debugger stopped:

```
main[1] list
28          CDraw() {
29            grid = new BorderedPrintCGrid();
30          }
31          void run() throws IOException {
32      =>    boolean finished = false;
33            do {
34              char command = getCommand();
35              switch(command){
36                case 'P':
main[1]
```

You're at the first instruction in the run() method. Let's take a little break here and look around a bit. First, use the methods command to list the methods that are available to the CDraw class:

```
main[1] methods CDraw
void <init>()
void run()
char getCommand()
void addPoint()
void addBox()
void addText()
void editText()
```

```
void editText(CGTextEdit)
void <clinit>()
main[1]
```

The debugger responds by listing all methods declared for CDraw, including its constructors, <init> and <clinit>. These constructors are internal methods generated by the Java virtual machine.

The classes command lists all classes that are currently known (loaded) by the debugger. Let's take a look at them:

```
main[1] classes
** classes list **
0xe60000:class(java.lang.Thread)
0xe60010:class(java.lang.Object)
0xe60020:class(java.lang.Class)
0xe60028:class(java.lang.String)
0xe60038:interface(java.io.Serializable)
0xe60048:class(java.lang.ThreadDeath)
0xe60058:class(java.lang.Error)
0xe60068:class(java.lang.Throwable)
0xe60078:class(java.lang.Exception)
0xe60088:class(java.lang.RuntimeException)
0xe60098:interface(java.lang.Cloneable)
0xe60140:interface(java.lang.Runnable)
0xe60158:class(java.lang.ThreadGroup)
0xe60188:class(java.lang.StringBuffer)
0xe601b8:class(java.lang.System)
0xe601c8:class(java.lang.Integer)
0xe601d8:class(java.lang.Number)
0xe60208:class(java.lang.Character)
0xe60268:class(java.lang.NoClassDefFoundError)
0xe60278:class(java.lang.LinkageError)
0xe60288:class(java.lang.OutOfMemoryError)
0xe60298:class(java.lang.VirtualMachineError)
0xe602b0:class(java.util.Properties)
0xe602c0:class(java.util.Hashtable)
0xe602d0:class(java.util.Dictionary)
0xe602e8:class(java.util.HashtableEntry)
0xe60798:class(java.io.FileInputStream)
0xe607a8:class(java.io.InputStream)
0xe607c0:class(java.io.FileDescriptor)
0xe607e8:class(java.io.FileOutputStream)
0xe607f8:class(java.io.OutputStream)
0xe60818:class(java.io.BufferedInputStream)
0xe60828:class(java.io.FilterInputStream)
0xe60848:class(java.io.PrintStream)
0xe60858:class(java.io.FilterOutputStream)
0xe60870:class(java.io.BufferedOutputStream)
0xe60890:class(java.io.OutputStreamWriter)
0xe608a0:class(java.io.Writer)
0xe608b8:class(sun.io.CharToByteConverter)
0xe608f8:class(sun.io.CharacterEncoding)
0xe62f40:class(sun.io.CharToByte8859_1)
0xe62f68:class(java.io.BufferedWriter)
0xe64fd8:class(java.util.zip.ZipEntry)
0xe63020:class(sun.tools.debug.Agent)
0xe63030:interface(sun.tools.debug.AgentConstants)
```

```
0xe63050:interface(sun.tools.java.Constants)
0xe630c0:interface(sun.tools.java.RuntimeConstants)
0xe63e90:class(sun.tools.java.Identifier)
0xe649c0:class(java.lang.Runtime)
0xe64a30:class(java.net.ServerSocket)
0xe64a48:class(java.net.PlainSocketImpl)
0xe64a88:class(java.net.SocketImpl)
0xe64a98:interface(java.net.SocketOptions)
0xe64ae0:class(java.net.InetAddress)
0xe64b60:class(java.net.InetAddressImpl)
0xe6be98:class(sun.tools.debug.EmptyApp)
0xe64c18:class([Ljava.net.InetAddress;)
0xe64cb8:class(java.lang.Math)
0xe64cc8:class(java.util.Random)
0xe64dd8:class(sun.tools.java.ClassPath)
0xe64de8:class(java.io.File)
0xe64e20:class(sun.tools.java.ClassPathEntry)
0xe64ef8:class(java.util.zip.ZipFile)
0xe64f08:interface(java.util.zip.ZipConstants)
0xe64f20:class(java.io.RandomAccessFile)
0xe64f30:interface(java.io.DataOutput)
0xe64f40:interface(java.io.DataInput)
0xe87a98:class(sun.tools.debug.BreakpointHandler)
0xe87ac8:class(sun.tools.debug.BreakpointQueue)
0xe87b00:class(java.util.Vector)
0xe87cc0:class(java.net.Socket)
0xe87e80:class(java.io.DataInputStream)
0xe87ea0:class(java.net.SocketInputStream)
0xe87ec8:class(sun.tools.debug.ResponseStream)
0xe87ee0:class(java.net.SocketOutputStream)
0xe87f08:class(java.io.DataOutputStream)
0xe87f68:class(sun.tools.debug.AgentOutputStream)
0xe88038:class(java.util.HashtableEnumerator)
0xe88048:interface(java.util.Enumeration)
0xe88070:class(java.util.VectorEnumerator)
0xe89cd8:class(jdg.ch06.CDrawApp)
0xe89fe8:class(jdg.ch06.CDraw)
0xe89ff8:class(jdg.ch05.KeyboardInput)
0xe8a008:class(java.io.BufferedReader)
0xe8a018:class(java.io.Reader)
0xe8a030:class(java.io.InputStreamReader)
0xe8a048:class(sun.io.ByteToCharConverter)
0xe8a088:class(sun.io.ByteToChar8859_1)
0xe8a5d0:class(java.lang.ClassNotFoundException)
0xe8a918:class(sun.tools.debug.Field)
0xe8aa40:class(sun.tools.debug.BreakpointSet)
0xe8add0:class(sun.tools.debug.MainThread)
0xe8af60:class(sun.tools.debug.StackFrame)
0xe8afb0:class(sun.tools.debug.LocalVariable)
0xe8b210:class(sun.tools.java.Package)
0xe8b2a8:class([Ljava.lang.String;)
0xe8b568:class(sun.tools.java.ClassFile)
0xe8b6c8:class(sun.tools.debug.LineNumber)
0xe8c9a8:class(jdg.ch05.BorderedPrintCGrid)
0xe8c9b8:class(jdg.ch05.PrintCGrid)
0xe8c9c8:class(jdg.ch05.CGrid)
0xe8c9e0:class([[C)
0xe8c9f0:class([C)
0xe8caa8:class(jdg.ch05.CGObject)
main[1]
```

That's quite a number of classes! Look through this list to see if there are any that you recognize. You should be able to identify some classes that are used by the CDrawApp program.

The threadgroups command lists the threadgroups that are currently defined by the program:

```
main[1] threadgroups
1. (java.lang.ThreadGroup)0xe60168 system
2. (java.lang.ThreadGroup)0xe64da0 main
3. (java.lang.ThreadGroup)0xe8ad88 jdg.ch06.CDrawApp.main
main[1]
```

The three threadgroups are the system threadgroup (used by the Java runtime system), the default main threadgroup, and the threadgroup associated with the CDrawApp program.

The threads command tells you what threads are in a threadgroup:

```
main[1] threads system
Group system:
 1. (java.lang.Thread)0xe60180              Finalizer thread    suspended
 2. (java.lang.Thread)0xe64d20              Debugger agent      running
 3. (sun.tools.debug.BreakpointHandler)0xe87aa8 Breakpoint handler cond. waitin
Group main:
 4. (java.lang.Thread)0xe60150 main suspended
Group jdg.ch06.CDrawApp.main:
 5. (sun.tools.debug.MainThread)0xe8ade0 main at breakpoint
main[1]
```

When you list the threads in the system threadgroup, you get a list of all threads maintained by the Java runtime system.

The memory command tells you how much memory is available to the Java runtime system:

```
main[1] memory
Free: 200496, total: 1662968
main[1]
```

The available memory on your computer may differ from mine. For your information, I'm currently running Java on a Pentium 133MHz notebook computer with 16MB of RAM.

The where command dumps the stack used by the Java virtual machine. It displays the current list of methods that have been invoked to get you to your breakpoint. An example of the where command follows:

```
main[1] where
  [1] jdg.ch06.CDraw.run (CDraw:32)
  [2] jdg.ch06.CDrawApp.main (CDrawApp:18)
  [3] sun.tools.debug.MainThread.run (MainThread:55)
main[1]
```

The where command comes in handy when you are deep in the inner layers of several nested method invocations. It shows you how you got to where you are within the program.

You can use the up and down commands to move up and down the stack. The up command moves you to a higher stack frame within the stack:

```
main[1] up
main[2]
```

Do a `list` command to see the results of the up command:

```
main[2] list
14
15        class CDrawApp {
16          public static void main(String args[]) throws IOException {
17            CDraw program = new CDraw();
18      =>     program.run();
19          }
20        }
21
22        class CDraw {
main[2]
```

Now use the `down` command to go back down the stack to where you were before:

```
main[2] down
main[1]
```

Type another `list` command to verify that you have returned to where you were before you entered the up command:

```
main[1] list
28          CDraw() {
29            grid = new BorderedPrintCGrid();
30          }
31          void run() throws IOException {
32      =>    boolean finished = false;
33          do {
34            char command = getCommand();
35            switch(command){
36              case 'P':
main[1]
```

Now let's look at some variables. Enter the `locals` command to get a list of local variables of the `run()` method:

```
main[1] locals
Method arguments:
  this = jdg.ch06.CDraw@1d16f5
Local variables:
  finished is not in scope.
  command is not in scope.
main[1]
```

The `finished` and `command` variables are not in the current scope because they have not yet been declared. Step over to the next statement:

```
main[1] step
main[1]
Breakpoint hit: jdg.ch06.CDraw.run (CDraw:34)
main[1]
```

Enter the `list` command to see where you have stepped:

```
main[1] list
30          }
31          void run() throws IOException {
32            boolean finished = false;
```

```
33              do {
34       =>      char command = getCommand();
35              switch(command){
36               case 'P':
37                 addPoint();
38                 System.out.println();
main[1]
```

Type another `locals` command. The finished variable should now be in scope:

```
main[1] locals
Method arguments:
  this = jdg.ch06.CDraw@1d16f5
Local variables:
  finished = false
  command is not in scope.
main[1]
```

You have now covered most of the debugger commands. Now let's go on to debugging multithreaded programs. Type `exit` to exit the debugger.

Debugging Multithreaded Programs

The Java debugger supports the debugging of multithreaded programs. In fact, it provides a great tool for understanding how multithreaded programs work. In this section, you use the debugger to debug the `ThreadTest1` program that you developed in Chapter 8, "Multithreading."

Change directories to the `ch08` directory and enter `javac -g ThreadTest1.java` to add additional debugging information to the `ThreadTest1.class` byte code file:

```
C:\jdk1.1.1\jdg\ch08>javac -g ThreadTest1.java
C:\jdk1.1.1\jdg\ch08>
```

Now start `jdb` and load `ThreadTest1` with the command `jdb ThreadTest1`:

```
C:\jdk1.1.1\jdg\ch08>jdb ThreadTest1
Initializing jdb...
0xe89cd8:class(ThreadTest1)
>
```

Set a breakpoint at the `main()` method of `ThreadTest1`:

```
> stop in ThreadTest1.main
Breakpoint set in ThreadTest1.main
>
```

Run `ThreadTest1`:

```
> run ThreadTest1
running ...
main[1]
Breakpoint hit: ThreadTest1.main (ThreadTest1:8)
main[1]
```

The debugger runs ThreadTest1 and stops at your breakpoint. Do a list command to see where the debugger stopped:

```
main[1] list
4          import java.lang.InterruptedException;
5
6          class ThreadTest1 {
7           public static void main(String args[]) {
8     =>    MyThread thread1 = new MyThread("thread1: ");
9           MyThread thread2 = new MyThread("thread2: ");
10          thread1.start();
11          thread2.start();
12          boolean thread1IsAlive = true;
main[1]
```

The debugger is at the beginning of the main() method. It has not created any new threads at this time. Use the threads command to verify this:

```
main[1] threads
Group ThreadTest1.main:
 1. (sun.tools.debug.MainThread)0xe8a788 main at breakpoint
main[1]
```

The only thread is the current main thread of execution. Set a breakpoint to line 10 of ThreadTest1, the point where both thread1 and thread2 will be declared:

```
main[1] stop at ThreadTest1:10
Breakpoint set at ThreadTest1:10
main[1]
```

Now jump to that point in the program:

```
main[1] cont
main[1]
Breakpoint hit: ThreadTest1.main (ThreadTest1:10)
main[1]
```

Use the threads command again to see the effect of the thread1 and thread2 declarations:

```
main[1] threads
Group ThreadTest1.main:
 1. (sun.tools.debug.MainThread)0xe8a788 main      at breakpoint
 2. (MyThread)0xe8b558                   thread1:  zombie
 3. (MyThread)0xe8b578                   thread2:  zombie
main[1]
```

Both thread1 and thread2 are in the New Thread state. The debugger refers to them as *zombies*. That's a curious term considering that the threads have neither started nor died at this point in the program's execution.

Now jump ahead in the program to line 12, where both threads are started. First, set the breakpoint:

```
main[1] stop at ThreadTest1:12
Breakpoint set at ThreadTest1:12
main[1]
```

Now jump ahead to the breakpoint:

```
main[1] cont
main[1]
Breakpoint hit: ThreadTest1.main (ThreadTest1:12)
main[1]
```

Let's take a quick look around to make sure you are where you want to be:

```
main[1] list
8            MyThread thread1 = new MyThread("thread1: ");
9            MyThread thread2 = new MyThread("thread2: ");
10           thread1.start();
11           thread2.start();
12    =>     boolean thread1IsAlive = true;
13           boolean thread2IsAlive = true;
14           do {
15            if(thread1IsAlive && !thread1.isAlive()){
16              thread1IsAlive = false;
main[1]
```

Now execute the `threads` command:

```
main[1] threads
Group ThreadTest1.main:
 1. (sun.tools.debug.MainThread)0xe8a788 main      at breakpoint
 2. (MyThread)0xe8b558                   thread1:  suspended
 3. (MyThread)0xe8b578                   thread2:  suspended
main[1]
```

> **NOTE**
>
> Depending on the machine on which you run the jdb, you may find that both threads are suspended or that one thread is suspended and the other is running when you execute the threads command.

The debugger tells us that both threads are suspended. The `suspend` command is used to suspend the execution of a running thread. It takes the number of the thread identified by the `threads` command as its argument.

Now switch threads to thread1 using the `thread` command:

```
main[1] thread 2
thread1: [1]
```

Notice how the prompt changed to indicate that you switched to thread1. When you enter thread 1, you get the main[1] prompt, thread 2 returns the thread1: prompt, and thread 3 returns the thread2: prompt. There are only three program threads—main, thread1, and thread2. Switch to thread2 by entering thread 3:

```
thread1: [1] thread 3
thread2: [1]
```

Set a breakpoint for `thread1` and `thread2`:

```
thread2: [1] stop at MyThread:35
Breakpoint set at MyThread:35
thread2: [1] thread 2
thread1: [1] stop at MyThread:35
Breakpoint set at MyThread:35
thread1: [1]
```

Now continue the execution of `thread1`:

```
thread1: [1] cont
thread1: [1]
Breakpoint hit: MyThread.run (MyThread:35)
thread1: [1]
```

Use the `list` command to verify that `thread1` stopped at the breakpoint:

```
thread1: [1] list
31            }
32          public void run() {
33            String name = getName();
34            for(int i=0;i<message.length;++i) {
35      =>      randomWait();
36              System.out.println(name+message[i]);
37            }
38          }
39          void randomWait(){
thread1: [1]
```

The thread executed up to the breakpoint. You can also verify this by running the `threads` command:

```
thread1: [1] threads
Group ThreadTest1.main:
  1. (sun.tools.debug.MainThread)0xe8a788 main        suspended
  2. (MyThread)0xe8b558                   thread1:    at breakpoint
  3. (MyThread)0xe8b578                   thread2:    suspended
thread1: [1]
```

If you use the `step` command, `thread1` becomes suspended and `thread2` reaches the breakpoint:

```
thread1: [1] step
thread1: [1]
Breakpoint hit: MyThread.run (MyThread:35)
thread2: [1] threads
Group ThreadTest1.main:
  1. (sun.tools.debug.MainThread)0xe8a788 main        suspended
  2. (MyThread)0xe8b558                   thread1:    suspended
  3. (MyThread)0xe8b578                   thread2:    at breakpoint
thread2: [1]
```

You can use the `print` and `dump` commands to display the values of the message field of `MyThread`.

These commands are somewhat buggy. They may complain that the fields are not valid, but display the values of the fields anyway.

At this point, you've covered all the important features of the Java debugger. You can experiment with the debugger to see how the two threads continue their execution. When you are finished, use the `exit` command to terminate the debugger.

Summary

In this chapter, you learned how to use the Java debugger to step through the execution of a Java program. You learned how to invoke the debugger, load class files, and examine classes as they are executed. In Chapter 10, "Automating Software Documentation," you will learn how to use another program contained in the Java toolkit—the Java documentation tool. You'll see how this tool can help you to quickly and easily develop documentation for your Java programs.

10

Automating Software Documentation

In this chapter you'll learn how to use the Java documentation tool, `javadoc`, to automate the documentation of your software. This is the tool that is used to create the superb Java API documentation. It translates your source code into *Hypertext Markup Language* (HTML) files that can be displayed by a Web browser. When you finish this chapter, you'll be able to quickly and easily document your software using `javadoc`.

How `javadoc` Works

The `javadoc` program examines your source code and generates HTML files that provide a fully integrated set of documentation for your Java software. The HTML files generated by `javadoc` document the classes, interfaces, variables, methods, and exceptions that you declare and use in your programs. These files describe your software at the package and class level. The linking capabilities of HTML are used to provide extensive cross-referencing between related software components. These links allow you to quickly access all of the documentation that is relevant to a particular topic.

`javadoc` differs from other documentation generators in that it goes beyond simple comment-scanning and actually parses your source code in order to generate documentation that describes the structure and behavior of your programs. It makes judicious use of HTML links to generate documentation that allows you to easily traverse the structure of your software.

`javadoc` recognizes special types of comments that you insert in your source code. When it parses your source code, it combines these comments with the structural information it generates. Your comments then are integrated into your software's HTML description. The special comments recognized by `javadoc` consist of doc comments, `javadoc` tags, and HTML tags.

Doc comments are based on the traditional C `/*` and `*/` comment delimiters. They are distinguished from ordinary C comments in that they begin with `/**` instead of `/*`. They are used to identify comments that are to be automatically added to the HTML documentation produced by `javadoc`.

The `javadoc` tags are special tags that are embedded in doc comments. These tags allow you to include reference information in your software. For example, you can include a `javadoc` comment that says, `See also: class X`. Some references result in links being automatically inserted into your software's documentation.

`javadoc` also allows you to insert HTML tags directly in your source code. However, `javadoc` recommends that you limit your HTML to small, simple, and correctly formatted HTML elements so as not to conflict with the HTML that it generates. Your HTML tags are combined with those produced by `javadoc` to create an integrated set of HTML pages.

Using `javadoc`

The best way to understand how `javadoc` works is by using it and then exploring the documentation that it produces. `javadoc` is so simple to use that it only requires a single command line to generate integrated software documentation for multiple software packages.

To use `javadoc`, create a separate `ch10` directory under your `c:\jdk1.1.1\jdg` path. This directory will be used to store the HTML files that `javadoc` produces. You could store these files in the same directory in which you store your Java API documentation, but it's not a good idea to clutter up your API directory with other documentation. Because you will not be storing your documentation in your API directory, you will have to copy the `images` subdirectory from your API directory to `ch10`. The images are needed by your documentation so that Web browsers can display all the fancy icons, images, and bullets that are characteristic of the API documentation. With these images, your documentation looks outstanding. Without the images, your browser will substitute its missing icon images for the Java images, and your documentation will look horrendous.

After you have copied the `images` subdirectory to your `ch10` directory, launch a DOS shell and enter the following DOS command line:

```
C:\jdk1.1.1\jdg\ch10>javadoc jdg.ch05 jdg.ch06
Loading source files for jdg.ch05
Loading source files for jdg.ch06
Generating package.html
generating documentation for class jdg.ch05.BorderedPrintCGrid
generating documentation for class jdg.ch05.CGBox
generating documentation for class jdg.ch05.CGObject
generating documentation for class jdg.ch05.CGPoint
generating documentation for class jdg.ch05.CGText
generating documentation for class jdg.ch05.CGrid
generating documentation for class jdg.ch05.KeyboardInput
generating documentation for class jdg.ch05.Point
generating documentation for class jdg.ch05.PrintCGrid
generating documentation for interface jdg.ch06.CGTextEdit
generating documentation for interface jdg.ch06.ColorConstants
generating documentation for class jdg.ch06.CGText
generating documentation for class jdg.ch06.CGTextBox
generating documentation for class jdg.ch06.CGTextPoint
Generating index
Sorting 90 items…done
Generating tree
C:\jdk1.1.1\jdg\ch10>
```

As the result of that single command line, `javadoc` generates a complete set of HTML documentation for the software you produced in Chapters 5, "Classes and Objects," and 6, "Interfaces." This documentation will have the same look and feel as the Java API documentation.

When `javadoc` has finished producing the documentation, use your browser to view it. I'll be using Netscape Navigator 4.0. It is my favorite browser, and it's Java-compatible.

Launch your browser and use its local file open feature to open the file `packages.html`, located in the `ch10` directory. Your browser will display a Sun-style Package Index page, as shown in Figure 10.1.

FIGURE 10.1

The Package Index page.

This page looks great, but has a defect owing to the fact that it was not created in the same directory as your Java API—the link to the API User's Guide doesn't work. That's a small price to pay in order to avoid messing up your Java API directory. The rest of the links work fine.

With you browser open to the Package Index, click on the Class Hierarchy link. A Web page showing all the classes in the jdg.ch05 and jdg.ch06 packages is presented to you. The page shows how your classes fit within the rest of the Java class hierarchy. It also identifies the interfaces that are implemented by your classes. The information presented in the Class Hierarchy page is extremely useful in understanding the structure of Java programs. (See Figure 10.2.)

While you have the Class Hierarchy page loaded, click on the Index link. Another great Web page is displayed that contains an alphabetized index of all the fields (variables) and methods declared in the jdg.ch05 and jdg.ch06 packages. When I first saw this page, my immediate reaction was, "Where did all this come from?" Go ahead and click around this page to see some of the items that you've used in your programs. When you have finished, click on the All Packages link to go back to the Package Index (see Figure 10.3).

From the Package Index, click on the jdg.ch05 link. This will bring you into the Class Index for the jdg.ch05 package. This page documents the classes that are declared in this package (see Figure 10.4).

FIGURE 10.2.

The Class Hierarchy description page.

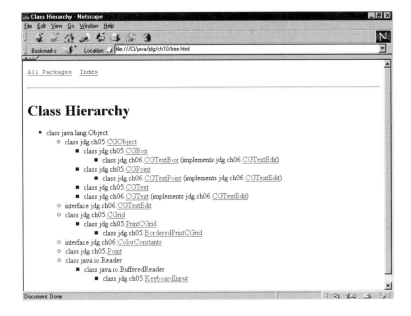

FIGURE 10.3.

The Index of all Fields and Methods page.

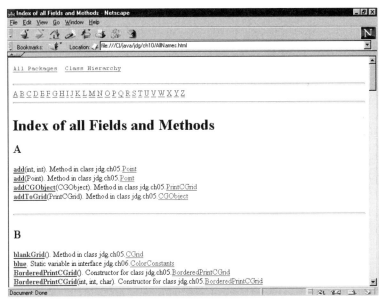

FIGURE 10.4.

The jdg.ch05 *Class Index page.*

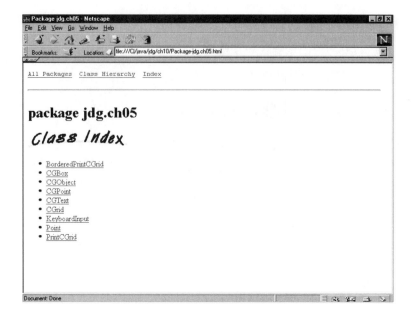

From here, click on the BorderedPrintCGrid link. The class's description is displayed. Notice how it identifies the branch of the class hierarchy leading to the BorderedPrintCGrid class. You can click on the links in the class hierarchy branch to find out information about the variables and methods that are inherited by a class. A list of constructors appears under the class hierarchy diagram. Click on any of the constructor links to find a more detailed description of the constructors (see Figure 10.5).

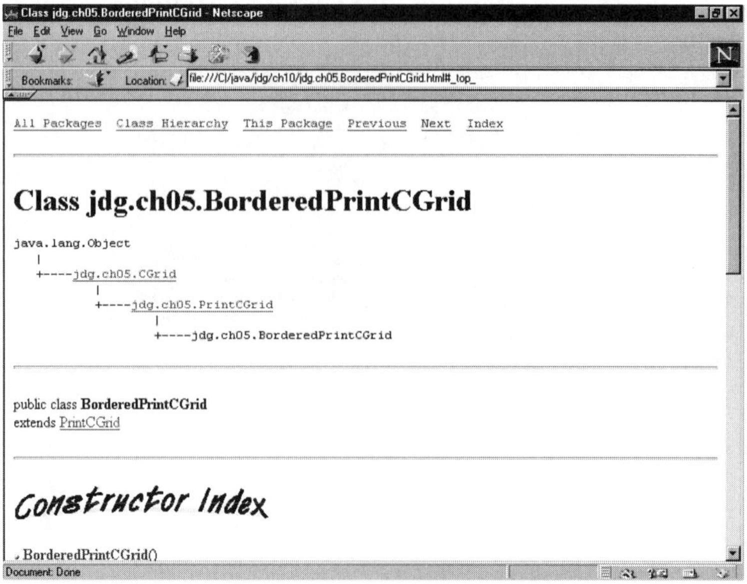

FIGURE 10.5.

The BorderedPrintCGrid *class page.*

Under the constructor list is a list of access methods that are declared for the `BorderedPrintCGrid` class. The class-specific Web pages only document the public and protected variables, constructors, and methods of a class. To see a description of class variables, click on the link to the `CGrid` class at the top of the `BorderedPrintCGrid` Web page (see Figure 10.6).

FIGURE 10.6.

The `CGrid` *class page.*

The `CGrid` class defines three protected variables: `depth`, `grid`, and `width`. You can click on the link to the `depth` variable to see how these variables are documented (see Figure 10.7).

You should now have a pretty good idea of the kind of documentation that can be produced using `javadoc`. The most remarkable fact about the documentation produced in this section is that you did not have to write a single comment in your source code. It was generated automatically and is far more effective than any traditional program comments. However, if this level of documentation is not enough to satisfy your requirements, you can insert additional comments in your source code that will be integrated with the documentation produced by `javadoc`.

FIGURE 10.7.
How javadoc *describes variables.*

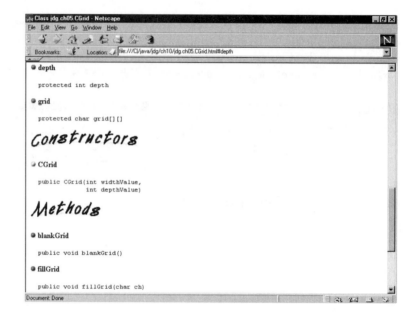

Placing Doc Comments

Doc comments, as discussed in the beginning of this chapter, are normal C comments that begin with an extra asterisk. They are easy to insert into your Java programs, and they add implementation-specific information to your documentation. To show how they are used, I've added doc comments to the CGBox.java source code. These comments can be easily identified in the new program listing for CGBox. (See Listing 10.1.) I haven't included the whole listing, just the part where I've added doc comments. If you want to duplicate what I have done, you have to copy and paste the doc comments into the CGBox.java file and then regenerate its documentation using javadoc.

Listing 10.1. The new CGBox.java.

```
package jdg.ch05;
// CGBox.java
/**
 * The CGBox class describes box objects that
 * are displayed on a PrintCGrid.
 */
public class CGBox extends CGObject {
// Variable declarations
/**
 * The lr is used to identify the lower right-hand
 * corner of a box.
 */
protected Point lr; // Lower right corner of a box
// Method declarations
/**
```

```
 * A CGBox object is constructed using an upper
 * left-hand corner point, a lower right-hand corner
 * point, and a box drawing character.
 */
public CGBox(Point ulCorner, Point lrCorner,char ch) {
 location = ulCorner;
 lr = lrCorner;
 drawCharacter = ch;
}
```

You can see how these doc comments were integrated into the appropriate class, variable, and constructor descriptions by looking for them in my browser's display (see Figure 10.8).

FIGURE 10.8.

Doc comments as displayed by a browser.

Using javadoc **Tags**

javadoc tags are special tags that are inserted in doc comments. They are used to identify specific references in your code. Special javadoc tags are provided for documenting classes, variables, and methods.

javadoc tags consist of an "at" sign (@) followed by a tag type and then a specific comment reference. Their syntax is as follows:

`@tagType commentReference`

Java classes and interfaces are allowed to use the see, version, author, and deprecated tag types. Variables can only use the see and deprecated tag types. Methods are allowed to use the see, param, return, exception, and deprecated tag types.

The see tag type has the following syntax:

```
@see HTMLlink
@see className
@see fullClassName
@see fullClassName#methodName
```

The see tag is used to reference other classes and methods that are related to the class, interface, variable, or method being documented.

The version and author tag types are used like this:

```
@version versionID
@author authorNames
```

The version tag is used to associate a software version identifier with a class or interface. The author tag is used to identify the author of the class or interface.

The param, return, and exception tags are used as follows:

```
@param parameterName description
@return description
@exception fullClassName description
```

The param tag is used to document a method parameter. The return tag is used to describe the value returned by a method. The exception tag is used to document the exceptions that are thrown by a method.

The deprecated tag is a new tag introduced with the JDK 1.1. It is used to mark old API classes, interfaces, variables, and methods as superseded and about to be phased out. It is used as follows:

```
@deprecated comment
```

The optional comment is used to provide instructions on how to replace the superseded API element. For a good example of the deprecated tag, check out the JDK 1.1 API description of the readLine() method of the java.io.DataInputStream class. If you used the JDK 1.0, you probably used readLine() to read console input. This method has been replaced by the readLine() method of the java.io.BufferedReader class.

In order to demonstrate the use of these tags, I have modified the jdg.ch05.CGText.java file to include param tags (see Listing 10.2).

Listing 10.2. The new CGText.

```
/**
 * @param p Text location
 * @param s Text string
 */
public CGText(Point p,String s) {
  location = p;
  drawCharacter = ' ';
  text = s;
}
```

Figure 10.9 shows how the javadoc tags are integrated by javadoc and displayed by my browser.

FIGURE 10.9.

The browser's display of the javadoc *tags.*

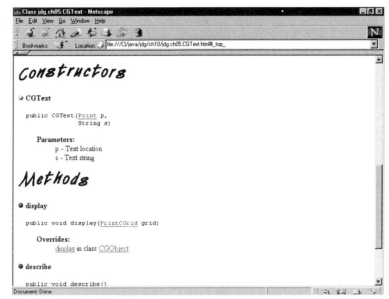

Embedding Standard HTML

If the doc comments and javadoc tags still aren't enough to meet your documentation requirements, you can always insert your own HTML markup into a doc comment. However, using HTML is a little bit dangerous because your HTML tags might conflict with the HTML tags inserted by javadoc. If you're going to use HTML in your documentation, try to keep it as simple as possible.

I've modified the source code in CGPoint.java to include HTML address tags so that I can put my e-mail address in the doc comment. (See Listing 10.3.)

Listing 10.3. The new CGPoint.

```
// CGPoint.java
/**
 * Send your bug reports to:
 * <ADDRESS>jamie@jaworski.com</ADDRESS>
 */
public class CGPoint extends CGObject {
 // Method declarations
 public CGPoint(int x, int y,char ch) {
  location = new Point(x,y);
  drawCharacter = ch;
 }
```

Figure 10.10 shows how the HTML tags are integrated by javadoc and displayed by my browser.

FIGURE 10.10.

How a browser displays javadoc *tags.*

Summary

In this chapter you learned how to use the Java documentation tool javadoc to automate the documentation of your software. You used it to document the software you developed in Chapters 5 and 6. You also learned how to use doc comments, javadoc tags, and HTML elements with javadoc. You have now covered most of the elements of the Java language and have learned how to use the compiler, interpreter, debugger, and documentation generator. Chapter 11, "Language Summary," provides a complete description of the Java language. It is a good idea to browse Chapter 11 before you move out of this part of the book and go on to the details of the Java API.

11

Language Summary

In the previous chapters you've covered most of the elements of the Java language and learned to use those elements through programming examples. This chapter provides a summary of the Java language syntax. You can use it to review what you've learned so far, and also as a quick reference guide when you need to look up a particular aspect of the language.

The `package` Statement

Java programs are organized into *packages*. Packages contain the source code declarations of Java classes and interfaces. Packages are identified by the `package` statement. It is the first statement in a source code file:

```
package packageName;
```

If a `package` statement is omitted, the classes and interfaces declared within the package are put into the default package—the package with no name.

The package name and the `CLASSPATH` are used to find a class. Only one class or interface may be declared as `public` for a given source code file.

The `import` Statement

The `import` statement is used to reference classes and interfaces that are declared in other packages. There are two forms of the `import` statement:

```
import packageName.className;
import packageName.*;
```

The first form allows the identified classes and interfaces to be referenced without specifying the name of their package. The second form allows all classes and interfaces in the specified package to be referenced without specifying the name of their package.

Comments

Java provides three styles of comments: .

```
/* This is a comment. */
// This is a comment.
/** This is a javadoc comment */
```

The first comment style supports traditional C-language comments. All text appearing between `/*` and `*/` is treated as a comment. Comments of this style can span multiple lines.

The second comment style supports C++ comments. All text following the `//` until the end of the line is treated as a comment. Comments of this style do not span multiple lines.

The third comment style is used by the `javadoc` documentation generation tool. All text between the `/**` and `*/` is treated as a `javadoc` comment. `javadoc` comments may span multiple lines.

Comments cannot be nested and cannot appear within string and character literals.

Identifiers

Identifiers are used to name Java language entities. They begin with a letter, underscore character (_), or dollar sign ($). Subsequent characters consist of these characters and digits. Identifiers are case sensitive and cannot be the same as a reserved word. Avoid using the dollar sign character; it is used for compiler-generated identifiers.

Reserved Words

The following words are reserved by the Java language; they cannot be used as identifiers:

abstract	do	import	return	void
boolean	double	instanceof	short	volatile
break	else	int	static	while
byte	extends	interface	super	
case	final	long	switch	
catch	finally	native	synchronized	
char	float	new	this	
class	for	package	throw	
const	goto	private	throws	
continue	if	protected	transient	
default	implements	public	try	

> **NOTE**
>
> Some of the reserved words have not yet been implemented.

Primitive Data Types and Literal Values

Java defines eight primitive types. Variables that are declared as a primitive type are not objects. They are only placeholders to store primitive values. The eight primitive types are `byte`, `short`, `int`, `long`, `float`, `double`, `char`, and `boolean`.

The byte, short, int, and long types represent 8-, 16-, 32-, and 64-bit integer values. The literal values of these types are written using positive or negative decimal, hexadecimal, or octal integers. Hexadecimal values are preceded by 0x or 0X and use the letters a through f (upper- or lowercase) to represent the digits 10 through 15. Octal numbers are preceded by 0. Long decimal values have an l or L appended to the end of the number.

The float and double types represent 32- and 64-bit IEEE 754 floating-point numbers. Float numbers have the f or F suffix. Double numbers have d or D. If no suffix is provided, the default double type is assumed. Floating-point numbers may be written in any of the following four forms:

```
digits . optionalDigits optionalExponentPart suffix
. digits optionalExponentPart suffix
digits exponentPart suffix
NaN
```

suffix is optional. It consists of f, F, d, or D, as described previously.

exponentPart is optional in the first two forms and required in the third form. It consists of an e or E followed by a signed integer. It is used to identify the exponent of 10 of the number written in scientific notation. For example, 1000000.0 could be represented as 1.0E6.

The special value NaN is used to represent the value "not a number" that occurs as the result of undefined mathematical operations such as division by zero.

The char type represents 16-bit Unicode characters. Unicode is a 16-bit superset of the ASCII character set that provides many foreign-language characters. A single character is specified by putting the character within single quotes ('). There are three exceptions: single quote ('), double quote ("), and backslash (\). The backslash character (\) is used as an escape code to represent special character values. The character escape codes are shown in Table 11.1.

Table 11.1. Character escape codes.

Escape Code	Character
\b	Backspace
\t	Tab
\n	Linefeed
\f	Form feed
\r	Carriage return
\"	Double quote
\'	Single quote
\\	Backslash

The backslash can also be followed by an 8-bit octal value or by a u or U followed by a four-digit hexadecimal value. The four-digit value is used to specify the value of Unicode characters.

The `boolean` type represents the logical values `true` and `false`.

String literals are also provided by Java although strings are not primitive values. Strings consist of characters enclosed by double quotes (`"`). The character escape codes may be used within strings.

The literal value `null` is used to identify the fact that an object is not assigned to a value. It may be used with any variable that is not of a primitive data type.

With the JDK 1.1, Java introduces class literals. A class literal is formed by appending `.class` to the name of a primitive or reference type. It evaluates to an object of type `Class`, which is the `Class` object for the identified type. `void.class` evaluates to void. You use class literals to directly refer to the class of a variable. For example, suppose `Test` is a class that you've declared. The following statement prints out the name of the `Test` class:

```
System.out.println(Test.class);
```

Class Declarations

Class declarations allow new classes to be defined for use in Java programs. Classes are declared as follows:

```
classModifiers class className extendsClause implementsClause classBody
```

The class modifiers, `extends` clause, and `implements` clause are optional.

The class modifiers are `abstract`, `public`, and `final`. An `abstract` class provides an abstract class declaration that cannot be instantiated. `abstract` classes are used as building blocks for the declaration of subclasses. A class that is declared as `public` can be referenced outside its package. If a class is not declared as `public`, it can be referenced only within its package. A `final` class cannot be subclassed. A class cannot be declared as both `final` and `abstract`.

The `extends` clause is used to identify the immediate superclass of a class and thereby position the class within the overall class hierarchy. It is written as follows:

```
extends immediateSuperclass
```

The `implements` clause identifies the interfaces that are implemented by a class. It is written as follows:

```
implements interfaceNames
```

The *interfaceNames* consists of one or more interface names separated by commas.

The class body declares the variables, constructors, and access methods of a class. It is written as follows:

```
{ classBodyDeclarations }
```

The `classBodyDeclarations` consists of zero or more variable, constructor, or access method declarations or static initializers.

Beginning with Java 1.1, a class body declaration may also consist of nested classes, referred to as *inner classes.* Inner classes may also be declared local to a statement block. They are used to declare classes for use within a limited local scope.

Java 1.1 also allows inner classes to be declared anonymously within an expression. These classes are referred to as *anonymous classes.* You'll see examples of these classes and other inner classes in Part III, "Using the Java API."

Variable Declarations

Variables are used to refer to objects and primitive data types. They are declared as follows:

```
variableModifiers type extendedVariableName variableInitialization ;
```

The `variableModifiers` and `variableInitialization` are optional. A variable's *type* may be a primitive data type, class type, or interface type. The `extendedVariableName` is a variable name followed by zero or more bracket sets (`[ ]`) indicating that the variable is an array.

The `variableInitialization` consists of an equal sign (=) followed by a variable initialization.

A *variable initialization* is an expression yielding a value of the variable's type. If the variable being declared is an array, it can be assigned to an array initializer. Array initializers are written as follows:

```
{elementInitializers}
```

The `elementInitializers` are expressions that yield values that are consistent with the element type of the array.

There are seven variable modifiers: `public`, `protected`, `private`, `static`, `final`, `transient`, and `volatile`.

The `public`, `protected`, and `private` modifiers are used to designate the specific manner in which a variable can be accessed. Variables that are declared as `public` can be accessed anywhere that the class in which they are defined can be accessed. Variables that are declared as `protected` can be accessed within the package in which they are declared and in subclasses of the class in which they are defined. Variables that are declared as `private` are only accessible in the class in which they are defined and not in any of its subclasses. If a variable is declared as neither `public`, `protected`, nor `private`, it can be accessed only within the package in which it is declared.

A variable that is declared as `static` is associated with its class and is shared by objects that are instances of its class. A `static` variable is also known as a *class variable*.

A variable that is declared as `final` is a constant and cannot be modified. `final` variables must be initialized before they are used. Java 1.1 allows the initialization of a `final` variable to be separated from its declaration.

A variable that is declared as `transient` refers to objects and primitive values within the Java virtual machine. `transient` variables have not been implemented within Java 1.1.

A variable that is declared as `volatile` refers to objects and primitive values that can be modified asynchronously. They are treated in a special manner by the compiler to control the manner in which they can be updated.

Constructor Declarations

Constructors are methods that are used to initialize newly created objects of a class. They are declared as follows:

```
constructorModifiers constructorNameAndParameters throwsClause constructorBody
```

The constructor modifiers are `public`, `protected`, and `private`. They control access to the constructor and are used in the same manner as they are for variables.

The constructor name is the same as the class name in which it is declared. It is followed by a parameter list, written as follows:

```
(parameterDeclarations)
```

The parameter list consists of an opening parenthesis followed by zero or more parameter declarations followed by a closing parenthesis. The parameter declarations are separated by commas. Parameter declarations are written as follows:

```
type parameterName
```

Each parameter declaration consists of a type followed by a parameter name. A parameter name may be followed by sets of matched brackets (`[]`) to indicate that it is an array.

The `throws` clause identifies all uncaught exceptions that are thrown within the constructor. It is written as follows:

```
throws uncaughtExceptions
```

The exceptions are separated by whitespace characters.

The body of a constructor specifies the manner in which an object of the constructor's class is to be initialized. It is written as follows:

```
{constructorCallStatement blockBody}
```

The `constructorCallStatement` and `blockBody` are optional, but the opening and closing braces must be supplied.

The constructor call statement allows another constructor of the class or its superclass to be invoked before the constructor's block body. It is written as follows:

```
this(argumentList);
super(argumentList);
```

The first form results in a constructor for the current class being invoked with the specified arguments. The second form results in the constructor of the class's superclass being invoked. The argument list consists of expressions that evaluate to the allowed values of a particular constructor.

If no constructor call statement is specified, a default `super()` constructor is invoked before the constructor block body.

Access Method Declarations

Access methods are methods used to perform operations on the data contained in an object or on `static` class variables. They are written as follows:

```
methodModifiers returnType methodNameAndParameters throwsClause methodBody
```

The `methodNameAndParameters` is the same as for constructor declarations. Access method names are different from their class names.

The `throws` clause is also the same as for constructor declarations.

The method body differs from the constructor body in that it does not allow a constructor call statement.

The modifiers allowed for a method include the `public`, `protected`, and `private` modifiers defined for constructors as well as the `final`, `static`, `abstract`, `native`, and `synchronized` modifiers.

The `final` modifier identifies a method that cannot be overridden.

The `static` modifier identifies a class method. Class methods are allowed to access `static` class variables only. `static` methods are `final`.

An `abstract` method is used to identify a method that cannot be invoked and must be overridden by any non-abstract subclasses of the class in which it is declared. An `abstract` method does not have a method body. Instead, it has a semicolon (;).

A `native` method is a method written in a language other than Java. It is like an `abstract` method in that its body is replaced by a semicolon.

A `synchronized` method is a method that must acquire a lock on an object or on a class before it can be executed.

Static and Instance Initializers

A *static initializer* is a block of code that is used to initialize the static variables of a class. It is written as follows:

```
static block
```

Static initializers can only access `static` class variables. They are executed in the order in which they appear in a class declaration.

Java 1.1 introduces non-static initializers, referred to as instance initializers. Instance initializers do not have the static keyword. They are used to initialize each instance of a class and are executed immediately after a class's superclass constructor is invoked.

Interfaces

An *interface* specifies a collection of abstract methods that must be overridden by classes that implement the interface. Interfaces are declared as follows:

```
interfaceModifiers interface interfaceName extendsClause interfaceBody
```

The interface modifiers are `public` and `abstract`. `public` interfaces can be accessed in other packages. All interfaces are `abstract`. The `abstract` modifier is superfluous.

The optional `extends` clause is used to identify any interfaces that are extended by an interface. It is written as follows:

```
extends interfaceNames
```

The interface names are separated by commas. An interface includes all the methods of all interfaces that it extends.

The interface body consists of zero or more variable and abstract method declarations. They are enclosed within braces ({ and }).

Variables declared within an interface must be `static` and `final`. The `static` and `final` modifiers need not be displayed. Variables declared in a `public` interface are `public`. The `public` keyword need not be specified.

Methods declared within an interface are `abstract`. The `abstract` keyword need not be specified.

Blocks and Block Bodies

Blocks consist of sequences of local variable declarations and statements. They are written as follows:

```
{ blockBody }
```

The *blockBody* is a sequence of local variable declarations or statements.

A block can also consist of a single statement without the enclosing braces.

Local Variable Declarations

Local variables are declared in the same manner as field declarations are declared except that local variables do not include modifiers. They are accessible within the block in which they are declared. The this and super variables are predefined. They refer to the current object for which a method is invoked and the superclass of the current object being invoked.

Statements

The programming statements provided by Java are described in the following subsections.

Empty Statement

The *empty statement* performs no processing. It consists of a single semicolon (;).

Block Statement

A *block statement* consists of a sequence of statements and local variable declarations that are treated as a single statement block. The statements are enclosed within braces ({ and }).

Method Invocation

A *method invocation* invokes a method for an object or class. Method invocations may be used within an expression or as a separate statement. To be used as a separate statement, the method being invoked must be declared with a void return value. Method invocation statements take the following forms:

```
objectName.methodName(argumentList);
className.methodName(argumentList);
```

The argumentList consists of a comma-separated list of zero or more expressions that are consistent with the method's parameters.

Allocation Statements

When an object is *allocated*, it is typically assigned to a variable. However, it is not required to be assigned when it is allocated. An allocation statement is of the following form:

```
new constructor(argumentList);
```

The new operator is used to allocate an object of the class specified by the constructor. The constructor is then invoked to initialize the object using the arguments specified in the argument list.

Assignment Statements

The *assignment statement* assigns an object or value to a variable. Its general form is

```
variableName = expression;
```

where the expression yields a value that is consistent with the variable's type.

Other assignment operators may be used in addition to the = operator. See the section titled "Operators," later in this chapter.

The if Statement

The if statement is used to select among alternative paths of execution. It is written in the following two forms:

```
if ( booleanExpression ) statement
if ( booleanExpression ) statement1 else statement2
```

In the first form, statement is executed only if the boolean expression is true. In the second form, statement1 is executed if the boolean expression is true and statement2 is executed if the boolean expression is false.

Statement Labels

A statement can be *labeled* by prefixing an identifier to the statement as follows:

```
label: statement
```

The label can be a name or integer.

The switch Statement

The switch statement is similar to the if statement in that it enables a selection from alternative paths of execution. It is written as follows:

```
switch (expression) caseBlock
```

The expression must evaluate to a byte, char, short, or int value. Control is transferred to the next statement in the block that is labeled with a value that matches the expression.

The *caseBlock* contains a sequence of case-labeled statements. These statements are written as follows:

```
case value: statement
```

An optional default-value statement may also appear in the case block. It is written as follows:

```
default: statement
```

If no value matches the expression and a default-valued statement is provided, control is transferred to this statement. If there is no default-value statement, the next statement following the `switch` statement is executed.

The `break` Statement

The `break` statement is used to transfer control to a labeled statement or out-of-statement block. It takes the following forms:

```
break;
break label;
```

The first form transfers control to the first statement following the current statement block. The second form transfers control to the statement with the identified label.

The `for` Statement

The `for` statement is used to iteratively execute a statement. It takes the following form:

```
for (initializationStatement ; booleanExpression ; incrementStatement)
    iteratedStatement
```

The initialization statement is executed at the beginning of the `for` statement, and then the `boolean` expression is tested. If the expression is `true`, the iterated statement is executed. The increment statement is executed after the iterated statement and then the `boolean` expression is retested. The iterated statement–increment statement loop continues until the `boolean` expression evaluates to `false`. The increment statement does not end with a semicolon (;).

The `while` Statement

The `while` statement is used to execute a statement while a `boolean` expression is `true`. It is written as follows:

```
while (booleanExpression) iteratedStatement
```

The `boolean` expression is evaluated; if it is `true`, the iterated statement is executed. It continues to execute until the `boolean` expression is `false`.

The `do` Statement

The `do` statement, like the `while` statement, is used to execute a statement until a `boolean` expression becomes `false`. The only difference is that the expression is tested after the statement is executed. The `do` statement is written as follows:

```
do iteratedStatement while (booleanExpression);
```

The `continue` Statement

The `continue` statement is used to continue execution of a loop (`for`, `do`, or `while`) without completing execution of the iterated statement. The `continue` statement may take an optional label. It is written as follows:

```
continue label;
```

If a label is supplied, the loop continues at the labeled loop.

The `synchronized` Statement

The `synchronized` statement is used to execute a statement after acquiring a lock on an object. It is written as follows:

```
synchronized ( expression ) statement
```

The expression yields the object for which the lock must be acquired.

The `try` Statement

The `try` statement executes a block of statements while setting up exception handlers. If an exception occurs, the appropriate handler, if any, is executed to handle the exception. A `finally` clause may also be specified to perform absolutely required processing.

The `try` statement is written as follows:

```
try block catchClauses finallyClause
```

At least one `catch` clause or a `finally` clause must be provided. The format of the `catch` clause is as follows:

```
catch (exceptionDeclaration) block
```

If an exception is thrown within the block executed by the `try` statement and it can be assigned to the type of exception declared in the `catch` clause, the block of the `catch` clause is executed.

The `finally` clause, if it is provided, is always executed regardless of whether an exception is generated.

The `return` Statement

The `return` statement is used to return an object or value as the result of a method's invocation. It is written as follows:

```
return expression;
```

The value of the expression must match the return value identified in the method's declaration.

Operators

Java defines arithmetic, relational, logical, bit-manipulation, caste, class, selection, and assignment operators. Table 11.2 summarizes these operators.

Table 11.2. Java operators.

Operator Type	Operator	Description	Example
Arithmetic	+	Addition	a + b
	-	Subtraction	a - b
	*	Multiplication	a * b
	/	Division	a / b
	%	Modulus	a % b
Relational	>	Greater than	a > b
	<	Less than	a < b
	>=	Greater than or equal	a >= b
	<=	Less than or equal	a <= b
	!=	Not equal	a != b
	==	Equal	a == b
Logical	!	Not	!a
	&&	And	a && b
	¦¦	Or	a ¦¦ b
Bit-manipulation	~	Complement	~a
	&	And	a & b
	¦	Or	a ¦ b
	^	Exclusive or	a ^ b
	<<	Left shift	a << b
	>>	Right shift	a >> B
	>>>	Zero-filled right shift	a >>> b
Assignment	=	Assignment	a = b
	++	Increment and assign	a++
	--	Decrement and assign	a--
	+=	Add and assign	a += b
	-=	Subtract and assign	a -= b

Operator Type	Operator	Description	Example
	*=	Multiply and assign	a *= b
	/=	Divide and assign	a /= b
	%=	Take modulus and assign	a %= b
	¦=	OR and assign	a ¦= b
	&=	AND and assign	a &= b
	^=	XOR and assign	a ^= b
	<<=	Left shift and assign	a <<= b
	>>=	Right shift and assign	a >>= b
	>>>=	Zero-filled left shift and assign	a >>>= b
Caste	(type)	Convert to type	(char) b
Instance	instanceof	Is instance of class?	a instanceof b
Allocation	new	Create a new object of a class	new A()
Selection	? :	If...Then selection	a ? b : c

Summary

This chapter provides a summary of the Java language. It reviews the language-specific material covered in Chapters 4 through 10. Part III introduces the Java API.

III

Using the Java API

12

Portable Software and the java.lang Packages

In this chapter you'll learn how to use the `java.lang` package. This package contains the core API classes of the JDK. It includes the `Object` class, which is the top class in the Java class hierarchy, and the `Class` class, which provides runtime class information for all Java objects. You learn about classes that control the operation of the Java runtime system and about the all-important `System` class. You'll also learn how "wrapped" classes are used to convert primitive data types into usable objects. By the time you have completed this chapter, you will have been introduced to all of the classes contained in the `java.lang` package.

> **NOTE**
>
> The objective of this part of the book is to familiarize you with each of the packages of the Java API. In order to make best use of these chapters, you should browse through the pages of the API documentation that discuss each of the classes as they are covered here.

The `Object` and `Class` Classes

`Object` and `Class` are two of the most important classes in the Java API. The `Object` class is at the top of the Java class hierarchy. All classes are subclasses of `Object` and therefore inherit its methods. The `Class` class is used to provide class descriptors for all objects created during Java program execution.

Object

The `Object` class does not have any variables and has only one constructor. However, it provides 11 methods that are inherited by all Java classes and support general operations used by all objects. For example, the `equals()` and `hashCode()` methods are used to construct hash tables of Java objects. *Hash tables* are like arrays, but they are indexed by key values and dynamically grow in size. They make use of *hash functions* to quickly access the data that they contain. The `hashCode()`method creates a *hashcode* for an object. Hashcodes are used to quickly determine whether two objects are different. You'll learn more about hash tables in Chapter 14, "Useful Tools in the `java.util` and `java.math` Packages."

The `clone()` method creates an identical copy of an object. The object must implement the `Cloneable` interface. This interface is defined within the `java.lang` package. It contains no methods and is used only to differentiate clonable from nonclonable classes.

The `getClass()` method identifies the class of an object by returning an object of `Class`. You'll learn how to use this method in the next programming example. (See the "A Touch of Class" section later in this chapter.)

The toString() method creates a String representation of the value of an object. This method is handy for quickly displaying the contents of an object. When an object is displayed, using print() or println(), the toString() method of its class is automatically called to convert the object into a string before printing. Classes that override the toString() method can easily provide a custom display for their objects.

The finalize() method of an object is executed when an object is garbage-collected. The method performs no action, by default, and needs to be overridden by any class that requires specialized finalization processing.

The Object class provides three wait() and two notify() methods that support thread control. These methods are implemented by the Object class so that they can be made available to threads that are not created from subclasses of class Thread. The wait() methods cause a thread to wait until it is notified or until a specified amount of time has elapsed. The notify() methods are used to notify waiting threads that their wait is over.

Class

The Class class provides 32 methods that support the runtime processing of an object's class and interface information. This class does not have a constructor. Objects of this class, referred to as *class descriptors*, are automatically created and associated with the objects to which they refer. Despite their name, class descriptors are used for interfaces as well as classes.

The getName() and toString() methods return the String containing the name of a class or interface. The toString() method differs in that it prepends the string class or interface, depending on whether the class descriptor is a class or an interface. The static forName() method loads the class specified by a String object and returns a class descriptor for that class.

The getSuperclass() method returns the class descriptor of the superclass of a class. The isInterface() method identifies whether a class descriptor applies to a class or an interface. The getInterfaces() method returns an array of Class objects that specify the interfaces of a class, if any.

The newInstance() method creates an object that is a new instance of the specified class. It can be used in lieu of a class's constructor, although it is generally safer and clearer to use a constructor rather than newInstance().

The getClassLoader() method returns the class loader of a class, if one exists. Classes are not usually loaded by a class loader. However, in the case when a class is loaded from outside the CLASSPATH, such as over a network, a class loader is used to convert the class byte stream into a class descriptor. The ClassLoader class is covered later in this chapter in the "ClassLoader" section.

The `Class` class contains a number of other methods that begin with `get` and `is`. These methods are as follows:

- `getClasses()`—Returns an array of all classes and interfaces that are members of the class.
- `getComponentType()`—Returns the component type of an array.
- `getConstructor()` and `getConstructors()`—Return `Constructor` objects for the class.
- `getDeclaredClasses()`, `getDeclaredConstructor()`, `getDeclaredConstructors()`, `getDeclaredField()`, `getDeclaredFields()`, `getDeclaredMethod()`, and `getDeclaredMethods()`—Return the classes, constructors, fields, and methods that are declared for a class or interface.
- `getDeclaringClass()`—Returns the class in which the referenced class is declared (if any).
- `getField()` and `getFields()`—Returns a specific `Field` object or all `Field` objects of a class or interface.
- `getMethod()` and `getMethods()`—Returns a specific `Method` object or all `Method` objects of a class or interface.
- `getModifiers()`—Returns the class or interface modifiers as a coded integer.
- `getResource()` and `getResourceAsStream()`—Locates system resources. *System resources* are objects that are used by the runtime system or local Java implementation.
- `getSigners()`—Returns the signers of a class. See Chapter 20, "Security and the `java.security` Packages," for more information about class signing.
- `isArray()`—Returns `true` if the `Class` object represents an array.
- `isAssignableFrom()`—Used to determine whether an object of one class can be assigned to an object of another class.
- `isInstance()`—Equivalent to the `isinstanceof` operator.
- `isPrimitive()`—Returns `true` if the object represents a primitive type.

A Touch of Class

In order to give you a feel for how the `Object` and `Class` methods can be used, let's create and run a small program called `ClassApp`. If you have not already done so, create a `ch12` directory to be used for this lesson. The program's source code is shown in Listing 12.1.

Listing 12.1. The source code of the `ClassApp` program.

```
import java.lang.System;
import java.lang.Class;
import jdg.ch05.Point;
import jdg.ch06.CGTextPoint;
public class ClassApp {
```

```
public static void main(String args[]) {
 CGTextPoint p = new CGTextPoint(new Point(7,11));
 Object obj = new Object();
 Class cl = p.getClass();
 Class objcl = obj.getClass();
 do {
  describeClass(cl);
  cl = cl.getSuperclass();
 } while(cl!=objcl);
}
public static void describeClass(Class classDesc){
 System.out.println("Class: "+classDesc.getName());
 System.out.println("Superclass: "+classDesc.getSuperclass().getName());
 Class interfaces[] = classDesc.getInterfaces();
 for(int i=0;i<interfaces.length;++i)
  System.out.println("has interface: "+interfaces[i].getName());
 System.out.println();
 }
}
```

The program shows how the Object and Class methods can be used to generate runtime class and interface information about an arbitrary object. It creates an instance of class CGTextPoint by importing the classes developed in Chapters 5, "Classes and Objects," and 6, "Interfaces." It also creates a generic instance of class Object in order to obtain the class descriptor of that class. The following lines of code use the Object getClass() method to obtain the class descriptors of the CGTextPoint and Object classes:

```
Class cl = p.getClass();
Class objcl = obj.getClass();
```

These class descriptors are instances of Class. They are used in a simple do loop. The loop invokes the describeClass() method for the class identified by cl and then assigns cl to its superclass. The loop repeats until cl becomes the class descriptor for Object.

The describeClass() method uses the getName() method to get the name of the class and its superclass. The describeClass() method displays this information to the console. It uses the getInterfaces() method to get all interfaces implemented by a class and the getName() method to get and display the name of each interface.

Go ahead and compile and run the ClassApp program. Its output is as follows:

```
Class: jdg.ch06.CGTextPoint
Superclass: jdg.ch05.CGPoint
has interface: jdg.ch06.CGTextEdit
Class: jdg.ch05.CGPoint
Superclass: jdg.ch05.CGObject
Class: jdg.ch05.CGObject
Superclass: java.lang.Object
```

It steps up the class hierarchy from CGTextPoint to CGObject to display information about each class. See if you can modify the program to work with objects of other classes. You can do this by assigning the class of these objects to the cl variable in the main() method.

The `ClassLoader`, `SecurityManager`, and `Runtime` **Classes**

The `ClassLoader`, `SecurityManager`, and `Runtime` classes provide a fine level of control over the operation of the Java runtime system. However, most of the time you will not need or want to exercise this control because Java is set up to perform optimally for a variety of applications. The `ClassLoader` class allows you to define custom loaders for classes that you load outside of your `CLASSPATH`—for example, over a network. The `SecurityManager` class allows you to define a variety of security policies that govern the accesses that classes may make to threads, executable programs, your network, and your file system. The `Runtime` class provides you with the capability to control and monitor the Java runtime system. It also allows you to execute external programs.

ClassLoader

Classes that are loaded from outside the `CLASSPATH` require a class loader to convert the class byte stream into a class descriptor. `ClassLoader` is an abstract class that is used to define class loaders. It uses the `defineClass()` method to convert an array of bytes into a class descriptor. The `loadClass()` method is used to load a class from its source, usually a network. The `resolveClass()` method resolves all the classes referenced by a particular class by loading and defining those classes. The `findSystemClass()` method is used to load classes that are located within the `CLASSPATH` and, therefore, do not require a class loader. The `findLoadedClass()` method is used to access a class that has been loaded.

The methods of `getResource()`, `getResourceAsStream()`, `getSystemResource()`, and `getSystemResourceAsStream()` are used to access application- or system-specific resources. Resources are additional files or other objects that are associated with an application or the runtime system.

The `setSigners()` method is used to set the signers of a loaded class.

SecurityManager

The `SecurityManager` class is an abstract class that works with class loaders to implement a security policy. It contains several methods that can be overridden to implement customized security policies. This class is covered in Chapter 60, "Java Security." For right now, just be aware that it is in `java.lang`.

Runtime

The `Runtime` class provides access to the Java runtime system. It consists of a number of methods that implement system-level services.

The `getRuntime()` method is a static method that is used to obtain access to an object of class `Runtime`. The `exec()` methods are used to execute external programs from the Java runtime system. The `exec()` methods provide a number of alternatives for passing parameters to the executed program. These alternatives are similar to the standard C methods for passing command-line and environment information. The `exec()` methods are subject to security checking to ensure that they are executed by trusted code. See Chapter 39 for more information about runtime security checking.

The `exit()` method is used to exit the Java runtime system with an error code. It is similar to the `exit` function found in standard C libraries.

The `totalMemory()`, `freeMemory()`, and `gc()` methods are used to obtain information about and control the memory used by the runtime system. The `totalMemory()` method identifies the total memory available to the runtime system. The `freeMemory()` method identifies the amount of free (unused) memory. The `gc()` method is used to run the garbage collector to free up memory allocated to objects that are no longer being used. In general, you should not use the `gc()` method, but rather let Java perform its own automated garbage collection.

The `getLocalizedInputStream()` and `getLocalizedOutputStream()` methods are used to convert local (usually ASCII) input and output streams to Unicode-based streams.

The `load()` and `loadLibrary()` methods are used to load dynamic link libraries. This is usually performed in conjunction with native methods, which are described in Chapter 59, "Creating Native Methods."

The `runFinalization()` method causes the `finalize()` method of each object awaiting finalization to be invoked. The `runFinalizersOnExit()` method can toggle on or off whether finalization occurs when the runtime system exits. The `traceInstructions()` and `traceMethodCalls()` methods are used to enable or disable instruction and method tracing. You will most likely never need to use any of these methods in your programs. They are used in programs, such as the debugger, to trace through the execution of Java methods and instructions.

Using `Runtime`

Most of the methods provided by `Runtime` are not typically used in application programs. However, some methods are pretty useful. The program in Listing 12.2 shows how the `Runtime` methods can be used to display memory status information.

Listing 12.2. The source code of the `RuntimeMemApp` program.

```
import java.lang.System;
import java.lang.Runtime;
import java.io.IOException;
public class RuntimeMemApp {
```

continues

Listing 12.2. continued

```
public static void main(String args[]) throws IOException {
  Runtime r = Runtime.getRuntime();
  System.out.println(r.totalMemory());
  System.out.println(r.freeMemory());
 }
}
```

This program uses the static getRuntime() method to get an instance of Runtime that represents the current Java runtime system. The totalMemory() method is used to display the total number of bytes of runtime system memory. The freeMemory() method is used to display the number of bytes of memory that are unallocated and currently available.

When you run the program, you should get results that are similar to the following:

```
1048568
932528
```

Listing 12.3 demonstrates how to use the Runtime exec() method to execute external programs. This example assumes that you are using Windows 95. It may not work with other Java implementations. However, it can be easily tailored to launch application programs on other operating-system platforms.

Listing 12.3. The source code of the RuntimeExecApp program.

```
import java.lang.System;
import java.lang.Runtime;
import java.io.IOException;
public class RuntimeExecApp {
 public static void main(String args[]) throws IOException {
  Runtime r = Runtime.getRuntime();
  r.exec("C:\\Windows\\Explorer.exe");
 }
}
```

This program uses getRuntime() to get the current instance of the runtime system and then uses exec() to execute the Windows Explorer. The double backslashes (\\) are Java escape codes for a single backslash (\). When you run this program, it should launch a copy of the Windows Explorer. Under Windows 95, the exec() function works with true Win32 programs. It cannot be used to execute built-in DOS commands.

The System Class

You are no stranger to the System class because you have used it in several previous programming examples. It is one of the most important and useful classes provided by java.lang.

It provides a standard interface to common system resources and functions. It implements the standard input, output, and error streams, and supplies a set of methods that provide control over the Java runtime system. Some of these methods duplicate those provided by the `Runtime` class.

Standard Streams

The `in`, `out`, and `err` variables are, by default, assigned to the standard input, output, and error streams. The `setIn()`, `setOut()`, and `setErr()` methods can be used to reassign these variables to other streams.

Property-Related Methods

The `System` class provides three properties-related methods. *Properties* are extensions of the `Dictionary` and `Hashtable` classes and are defined in the `java.util` package. A set of system properties is available through the `System` class that describe the general characteristics of the operating system and runtime system that you are using. The `getProperties()` method gets all of the system properties and stores them in an object of class `Properties`. The `getProperty()` method gets a single property, as specified by a key. The `setProperties()` method sets the system properties to the values of a `Properties` object. The `identityHashCode()` method returns the hash code associated with an object. The sample program presented in Listing 12.4 introduces you to these system properties.

Security Manager–Related Methods

The `getSecurityManager()` and `setSecurityManager()` methods provide access to the Security Manager that is currently in effect. The Security Manager is discussed in Chapter 60.

Runtime-Related Methods

Several of the methods defined for the `Runtime` class are made available through the `System` class. These methods are `exit()`, `gc()`, `load()`, `loadLibrary()`, `runFinalizersOnExit()`, and `runFinalization()`.

Odds and Ends

The `arraycopy()` method is used to copy data from one array to another. This function provides the opportunity for system-specific memory copy operations to optimize memory-to-memory copies.

The `currentTimeMillis()` method returns the current time in milliseconds since January 1, 1970. If you want more capable date and time methods, check out the `Date` class in `java.util`.

The getenv() method is used to obtain the value of an environment variable. This method, however, is identified as obsolete in the Java API documentation and can no longer be used.

Time and Properties

The short program in Listing 12.4 illustrates a few of the methods provided by the System class. If your heyday was in the 1960s, it will allow you to keep track of the number of milliseconds that have elapsed since the good old days. It also gets and displays the System properties. Take a look through these properties to get a feel for the type of information that is provided. Finally, the exit() method is used to terminate the program, returning a status code of 13.

Listing 12.4. The source code of the SystemApp program.

```
import java.lang.System;
import java.util.Properties;
public class SystemApp {
 public static void main(String args[]) {
  long time = System.currentTimeMillis();
  System.out.print("Milliseconds elapsed since January 1, 1970: ");
  System.out.println(time);
  Properties p=System.getProperties();
  p.list(System.out);
  System.exit(13);
 }
}
```

The program generated the following output on my computer:

```
Milliseconds elapsed since January 1, 1970: 864952931970
-- listing properties --
user.language=en
java.home=C:\jdk1.1.1
awt.toolkit=sun.awt.windows.WToolkit
file.encoding.pkg=sun.io
java.version=1.1.1
file.separator=\
line.separator=

user.region=US
file.encoding=8859_1
java.vendor=Sun Microsystems Inc.
user.timezone=PST
user.name=Jamie
os.arch=x86
os.name=Windows 95
java.vendor.url=http://www.sun.com/
user.dir=c:\jdk1.1.1\jdg\ch12
java.class.path=.;C:\JDK1.1.1\LIB\CLASSES.ZIP;C:\jdk1...
java.class.version=45.3
os.version=4.0
path.separator=;
user.home=\home\jamie
```

Wrapped Classes

Variables that are declared using the primitive Java types are not objects and cannot be created and accessed using methods. Primitive types also cannot be subclassed. To get around the limitations of primitive types, the java.lang package defines class *wrappers* for these types. These class wrappers furnish methods that provide basic capabilities such as class conversion, value testing, hash codes, and equality checks. The constructors for the wrapped classes allow objects to be created and converted from primitive values and strings. Be sure to browse the API pages for each of these classes to familiarize yourself with the methods they provide.

The Boolean Class

The Boolean class is a wrapper for the boolean primitive type. It provides the getBoolean(), toString(), valueOf(), and booleanValue() methods to support type and class conversion. The toString(), equals(), and hashCode() methods override those of the Object class.

The Character Class

The Character class is a wrapper for the char primitive type. It provides several methods that support case, type, and class testing and conversion. Check out the API pages on these methods. We'll use some of them in the upcoming example.

The Byte, Short, Integer, and Long Classes

These classes wrap the byte, short, int, and long primitive types. They provide the MIN_VALUE and MAX_VALUE constants, as well as a number of type and class testing and conversion methods. The parseInt() and parseLong() methods are used to parse String objects and convert them to Byte, Short, Integer, and Long objects.

The Double and Float Classes

The Double and Float classes wrap the double and float primitive types. They provide the MIN_VALUE, MAX_VALUE, POSITIVE_INFINITY, and NEGATIVE_INFINITY constants, as well as the NaN (not-a-number) constant. NaN is used as a value that is not equal to any value, including itself. These classes provide a number of type and class testing and conversion methods, including methods that support conversion to and from integer bit representations.

The Number Class

The Number class is an abstract numeric class that is subclassed by Byte, Short, Integer, Long, Float, and Double. It provides six methods that support conversion of objects from one class to another.

All Wrapped Up

The program in Listing 12.5 shows some of the methods that can be used with the primitive types when they are wrapped as objects. Look up these methods in the API pages for each class and try to figure out how they work before moving on to their explanations.

Listing 12.5. The source code of the WrappedClassApp program.

```
import java.lang.System;
import java.lang.Boolean;
import java.lang.Character;
import java.lang.Integer;
import java.lang.Long;
import java.lang.Float;
import java.lang.Double;
public class WrappedClassApp {
 public static void main(String args[]) {
  Boolean b1 = new Boolean("TRUE");
  Boolean b2 = new Boolean("FALSE");
  System.out.println(b1.toString()+" or "+b2.toString());
  for(int j=0;j<16;++j)
   System.out.print(Character.forDigit(j,16));
  System.out.println();
  Integer i = new Integer(Integer.parseInt("ef",16));
  Long l = new Long(Long.parseLong("abcd",16));
  long m=l.longValue()*i.longValue();
  System.out.println(Long.toString(m,8));
  System.out.println(Float.MIN_VALUE);
  System.out.println(Double.MAX_VALUE);
 }
}
```

The program examines some of the more useful methods provided by the wrapped classes. It creates two objects of class Boolean from string arguments passed to their constructors. It assigns these objects to b1 and b2 and then converts them back to String objects, when it displays them. They are displayed in lowercase, as boolean values are traditionally represented.

The program then executes a for loop that prints out the character corresponding to each of the hexadecimal digits. The static forDigit() method of the Character class is used to generate the character values of digits in a number system of a different radix.

The static parseInt() and parseLong()methods are used to parse strings according to different radices. In the example, they are used to convert strings representing hexadecimal numbers into Integer and Long values. These values are then multiplied together and converted to a string that represents the resulting value in base 8. This is accomplished using an overloaded version of the toString() method.

The sample program concludes by displaying the minimum float value and the maximum double value using the predefined class constants of the Float and Double classes.

The program's output is as follows:

```
true or false
0123456789abcdef
50062143
1.4E-45
1.7976931348623157E308
```

The Math Class

The `Math` class provides an extensive set of mathematical methods in the form of a static class library. It also defines the mathematical constants `E` and `PI`. The supported methods include arithmetic, trigonometric, exponential, logarithmic, random number, and conversion routines. You should browse the API page of this class to get a feel for the methods it provides. The example in Listing 12.6 only touches on a few of these methods.

Listing 12.6. The source code of the MathApp program.

```
import java.lang.System;
import java.lang.Math;
public class MathApp {
 public static void main(String args[]) {
  System.out.println(Math.E);
  System.out.println(Math.PI);
  System.out.println(Math.abs(-1234));
  System.out.println(Math.cos(Math.PI/4));
  System.out.println(Math.sin(Math.PI/2));
  System.out.println(Math.tan(Math.PI/4));
  System.out.println(Math.log(1));
  System.out.println(Math.exp(Math.PI));
  for(int i=0;i<3;++i)
   System.out.print(Math.random()+" ");
  System.out.println();
 }
}
```

This program prints the constants e and π, |-1234|, $\cos(\pi/4)$, $\sin(\pi/2)$, $\tan(\pi/4)$, $\ln(1)$, e^{π}, and then three random double numbers between 0.0 and 1.1. Its output is as follows:

```
2.718281828459045
3.141592653589793
1234
0.7071067811865476
1.0
0.9999999999999999
0.0
23.14069263277926
0.5214844573332809 0.7036104523989761 0.15555052349418896
```

The random numbers you generate will almost certainly differ from those shown here.

The `String` and `StringBuffer` Classes

The `String` and `StringBuffer` classes are used to support operations on strings of characters. The `String` class supports constant (unchanging) strings, whereas the `StringBuffer` class supports growable, modifiable strings. `String` objects are more compact than `StringBuffer` objects, but `StringBuffer` objects are more flexible.

`String` Literals

`String` literals are strings that are specified using double quotes. `"This is a string"` and `"xyz"` are examples of string literals. `String` literals are different than the literal values used with primitive types. When the `javac` compiler encounters a `String` literal, it converts it to a `String` constructor. For example, the following

```
String str = "text";
```

is equivalent to this:

```
String str = new String("text");
```

The fact that the compiler automatically supplies `String` constructors allows you to use `String` literals everywhere that you could use objects of the `String` class.

The + Operator and `StringBuffer`

If `String` objects are constant, how can they be concatenated with the + operator and be assigned to existing `String` objects? In the following example, the code will result in the string `"ab"` being assigned to the s object:

```
String s = "";
s = s + "a" + "b";
```

How can this be possible if `String`s are constant? The answer lies in the fact that the Java compiler uses `StringBuffer` objects to accomplish the string manipulations. This code would be rendered as something similar to the following by the Java compiler:

```
String s = "";
s = new StringBuffer("").append("a").append("b").toString();
```

A new object of class `StringBuffer` is created with the `""` argument. The `StringBuffer` `append()` method is used to append the strings `"a"` and `"b"` to the new object, and then the object is converted to an object of class `String` via the `toString()` method. The `toString()` method creates a new object of class `String` before it is assigned to the s variable. In this way, the s variable always refers to a constant (although new) `String` object.

String **Constructors**

The String class provides 11 constructors for the creation and initialization of String objects. These constructors allow strings to be created from other strings, string literals, arrays of characters, arrays of bytes, and StringBuffer objects. Browse through the API page for the String class to become familiar with these constructors.

String **Access Methods**

The String class provides a very powerful set of methods for working with String objects. These methods allow you to access individual characters and substrings; test and compare strings; copy, concatenate, and replace parts of strings; convert and create strings; and perform other useful string operations.

The most important String methods are the length() method, which returns an integer value identifying the length of a string; the charAt() method, which allows the individual characters of a string to be accessed; the substring() method, which allows substrings of a string to be accessed; and the valueOf() method, which allows primitive data types to be converted into strings.

In addition to these methods, the Object class provides a toString() method for converting other objects to String objects. This method is often overridden by subclasses to provide a more appropriate object-to-String conversion.

Character and Substring Methods

Several String methods allow you to access individual characters and substrings of a string. These include charAt(), getBytes(), getChars(), indexOf(), lastIndexOf(), and substring(). Whenever you need to perform string manipulations, check the API documentation to make sure that you don't overlook an easy-to-use, predefined String method.

String Comparison and Test Methods

Several String methods allow you to compare strings, substrings, byte arrays, and other objects with a given string. Some of these methods are compareTo(), endsWith(), equals(), equalsIgnoreCase(), regionMatches(), and startsWith().

Copy, Concatenation, and Replace Methods

The following methods are useful for copying, concatenating, and manipulating strings: concat(), copyValueOf(), replace(), and trim().

String Conversion and Generation

A number of string methods support String conversion. These are intern(), toCharArray(), toLowerCase(), toString(), toUpperCase(), and valueOf(). You explore the use of some of these methods in the following example.

Stringing Along

The program in Listing 12.7 provides a glimpse at the operation of some of the methods identified in the previous subsections. Because strings are frequently used in application programs, learning to use the available methods is essential to being able to use the String class most effectively.

Listing 12.7. The source code of the StringApp program.

```
import java.lang.System;
import java.lang.String;
public class StringApp {
 public static void main(String args[]) {
  String s = "  Java Developer's Guide  ";
  System.out.println(s);
  System.out.println(s.toUpperCase());
  System.out.println(s.toLowerCase());
  System.out.println("["+s+"]");
  s=s.trim();
  System.out.println("["+s+"]");
  s=s.replace('J','X');
  s=s.replace('D','Y');
  s=s.replace('G','Z');
  System.out.println(s);
  int i1 = s.indexOf('X');
  int i2 = s.indexOf('Y');
  int i3 = s.indexOf('Z');
  char ch[] = s.toCharArray();
  ch[i1]='J';
  ch[i2]='D';
  ch[i3]='G';
  s = new String(ch);
  System.out.println(s);
 }
}
```

This program performs several manipulations of a string s that is initially set to " Java Developer's Guide ". It prints the original string and then prints upper- and lowercase versions of it, illustrating the use of the toUpperCase() and toLowerCase() methods. It prints the string enclosed between two braces to show that it contains leading and trailing spaces. It then trims away these spaces using the trim() method and reprints the string to show that these spaces were removed.

The program uses the replace() method to replace the letters 'J', 'D', and 'G' with 'X', 'Y', and 'Z' and prints out the string to show the changes. The replace() method is case sensitive. It uses the indexOf() method to get the indices of 'X', 'Y', and 'Z' within s. It uses the toCharArray() to convert the string to a char array. It then uses the indices to put 'J', 'D', and 'G' back in their proper locations within the character array. The String() constructor is used to construct a new string from the character array. The new string is assigned to s and is printed.

The program's output is as follows:

```
  Java Developer's Guide
  JAVA DEVELOPER'S GUIDE
  java developer's guide
[   Java Developer's Guide   ]
[Java Developer's Guide]
Xava Yeveloper's Zuide
Java Developer's Guide
```

The StringBuffer Class

The StringBuffer class is the force behind the scene for most complex string manipulations. The compiler automatically declares and manipulates objects of this class to implement common string operations.

The StringBuffer class provides three constructors: an empty constructor, a constructor with a specified initial buffer length, and a constructor that creates a StringBuffer object from a String object. In general, you will find yourself constructing StringBuffer objects from String objects, and the last constructor will be the one you use most often.

The StringBuffer class provides several versions of the append() method to convert and append other objects and primitive data types to StringBuffer objects. It provides a similar set of insert() methods for inserting objects and primitive data types into StringBuffer objects. It also provides methods to access the character-buffering capacity of StringBuffer and methods for accessing the characters contained in a string. It is well worth a visit to the StringBuffer API pages to take a look at the methods that it has to offer.

Strung Out

The program in Listing 12.8 shows how StringBuffer objects can be manipulated using the append(), insert(), and setCharAt() methods.

Listing 12.8. The source code of the StringBufferApp program.

```
import java.lang.System;
import java.lang.String;
import java.lang.StringBuffer;
public class StringBufferApp {
```

continues

Listing 12.8. continued

```
public static void main(String args[]) {
  StringBuffer sb = new StringBuffer(" is ");
  sb.append("Hot");
  sb.append('!');
  sb.insert(0,"Java");
  sb.append('\n');
  sb.append("This is ");
  sb.append(true);
  sb.setCharAt(21,'T');
  sb.append('\n');
  sb.append("Java is #");
  sb.append(1);
  String s = sb.toString();
  System.out.println(s);
 }
}
```

The program creates a StringBuffer object using the string " is ". It appends the string "Hot" using the append() method and the character '!' using an overloaded version of the same method. The insert() method is used to insert the string "Java" at the beginning of the string buffer.

Three appends are used to tack on a newline character (\n), the string "This is ", and the boolean value true. The append() method is overloaded to support the appending of the primitive data types as well as arbitrary Java objects.

The setCharAt() method is used to replace the letter 't' at index 21 with the letter 'T'. The charAt() and setCharAt() methods allow StringBuffer objects to be treated as arrays of characters.

Finally, another newline character is appended to sb, followed by the string "Java is #" and the int value 1. The StringBuffer object is then converted to a string and displayed to the console window.

The output of the program is as follows:

```
Java is Hot!
This is True
Java is #1
```

Threads and Processes

Chapter 8, "Multithreading," provides a detailed description of multithreading in Java. This section briefly describes the classes of java.lang that support multithreading. It also covers the Process class, which is used to manipulate processes that are executed using the System.exec() methods.

Runnable

The `Runnable` interface provides a common approach to identifying the code to be executed as part of an active thread. It consists of a single method, `run()`, which is executed when a thread is activated. The `Runnable` interface is implemented by the `Thread` class and by other classes that support threaded execution.

Thread

The `Thread` class is used to construct and access individual threads of execution that are executed as part of a multithreaded program. It defines the priority constants, `MIN_PRIORITY`, `MAX_PRIORITY`, and `NORM_PRIORITY`, that are used to control task scheduling. It provides seven constructors for creating instances of class `Thread`. The four constructors with the `Runnable` parameters are used to construct threads for classes that do not subclass the `Thread` class. The other constructors are used for the construction of `Thread` objects from `Thread` subclasses.

`Thread` supports many methods for accessing `Thread` objects. These methods provide the capabilities to work with a thread's group; obtain detailed information about a thread's activities; set and test a thread's properties; and cause a thread to wait, be interrupted, or be destroyed.

ThreadGroup

The `ThreadGroup` class is used to encapsulate a group of threads as a single object so that they can be accessed as a single unit. A number of access methods are provided for manipulating `ThreadGroup` objects. These methods keep track of the threads and thread groups contained in a thread group and perform global operations on all threads in the group. The global operations are group versions of the operations that are provided by the `Thread` class.

Process

The `Process` class is used to encapsulate processes that are executed with the `System.exec()` methods. An instance of class `Process` is returned by the `Runtime` class `exec()` method when it executes a process that is external to the Java runtime system. This `Process` object can be destroyed using the `destroy()` method and waited on using the `waitFor()` method. The `exitValue()` method returns the system exit value of the process. The `getInputStream()`, `getOutputStream()`, and `getErrorStream()` methods are used to access the standard input, output, and error streams of the process.

Hello Again

The simple program in Listing 12.9 actually performs some pretty complex processing. It is provided as an example of some of the powerful things that can be accomplished using the `Process` class.

Listing 12.9. The source code of the ProcessApp program.

```
import java.lang.System;
import java.lang.Runtime;
import java.lang.Process;
import java.io.InputStreamReader;
import java.io.BufferedReader;
import java.io.IOException;
public class ProcessApp {
 public static void main(String args[]) throws IOException {
  Runtime r = Runtime.getRuntime();
  Process p = r.exec("java jdg.ch04.HelloWorldApp");
  BufferedReader kbdInput =
   new BufferedReader(new InputStreamReader(p.getInputStream()));
  String line = kbdInput.readLine();
  System.out.println(line);
 }
}
```

The program uses the static getRuntime() method to get the current instance of the Java runtime system. It then uses the exec() method to execute another separate copy of the Java interpreter with the HelloWorldApp program that was developed in Chapter 4, "First Programs: Hello World! to BlackJack." It creates a BufferedReader object, kbdInput, that is connected to the output stream of the HelloWorldApp program. It then uses kbdInput to read the output of the HelloWorldApp program and display it on the console window as follows:

Hello World!

The exec() methods combined with the Process class provide a powerful set of tools by which Java programs can be used to launch and control the execution of other programs.

The Compiler Class

The Compiler class consists of five static methods that are used to compile Java classes in the rare event that you want to compile classes directly from a program or applet. These methods allow you to build your own customized Java development environment.

Exceptions and Errors

The java.lang package establishes the Java exception hierarchy and declares numerous exceptions and errors. Errors are used to indicate the occurrence of abnormal and fatal events that should not be handled within application programs. (See Chapter 7, "Exceptions.")

The Throwable Class

The Throwable class is at the top of the Java error-and-exception hierarchy. It is extended by the Error and Exception classes and provides methods that are common to both classes. These methods consist of stack tracing methods, the getMessage() method, and the toString() method, which is an override of the method inherited from the Object class. The getMessage() method is used to retrieve any messages that are supplied in the creation of Throwable objects.

The fillInStackTrace() and printStackTrace() methods are used to add information to supply and print information that is used to trace the propagation of exceptions and errors throughout a program's execution.

The Error Class

The Error class is used to provide a common superclass to define abnormal and fatal events that should not occur. It provides two constructors and no other methods. Four major classes of errors extend the Error class: AWTError, LinkageError, ThreadDeath, and VirtualMachineError.

The AWTError class identifies fatal errors that occur in the Abstract Window Toolkit packages. It is a single identifier for all AWT errors and is not subclassed.

The LinkageError class is used to define errors that occur as the result of incompatibilities between dependent classes. These incompatibilities result when a class X that another class Y depends on is changed before class Y can be recompiled. The LinkageError class is extensively subclassed to identify specific manifestations of this type of error.

The ThreadDeath error class is used to indicate that a thread has been stopped. Instances of this class can be caught and then rethrown to ensure that a thread is gracefully terminated, although this is not recommended. The ThreadDeath class is not subclassed.

The VirtualMachineError class is used to identify fatal errors occurring in the operation of the Java virtual machine. It has four subclasses: InternalError, OutOfMemoryError, StackOverflowError, and UnknownError.

The Exception Class

The Exception class provides a common superclass for the exceptions that can be defined for Java programs and applets.

The Void Class

The Void class is used to reference the Class object representing the void type. It is provided for completeness. It has no constructors or methods.

Reflection and the `java.lang.reflect` Package

The `java.lang.reflect` package is a new package provided with the JDK 1.1. It allows classes, interfaces, and objects to be examined and their public fields, constructors, and methods to be discovered and used at runtime. These capabilities are used by JavaBeans, object inspection tools, Java runtime tools (such as the debugger), and other Java applications and applets.

The `java.lang.reflect` package consists of the `Member` interface and five classes: `Array`, `Constructor`, `Field`, `Method`, and `Modifier`.

The `Member` Interface

The `Member` interface is used to provide information about a `Field`, `Constructor`, or `Method`. It defines two constant variables and three methods. The `DECLARED` constant identifies the class members (fields, constructors, and methods) that are declared for a class. The `PUBLIC` constant identifies all members of a class or interface, including those that are inherited. The `getName()` method returns the name of the referenced `Member`. The `getModifiers()` method returns the modifiers of the referenced `Member` encoded as an integer. The `Modifier` class is used to decode this integer. The `getDeclaringClass()` method returns the class in which the `Member` is declared.

The `Array` Class

The `Array` class is used to obtain information about, create, and manipulate arrays. It consists of 21 `static` methods. The `getLength()` method is used to access the length of an array.

The `get()` method is used to access an indexed element of an array. The `getBoolean()`, `getByte()`, `getChar()`, `getDouble()`, `getFloat()`, `getInt()`, `getLong()`, and `getShort()` methods are used to access an indexed element of an array as a particular primitive type.

The `set()` method is used to set an indexed element of an array. The `setBoolean()`, `setByte()`, `setChar()`, `setDouble()`, `setFloat()`, `setInt()`, `setLong()`, and `setShort()` methods are used to set an indexed element of an array to a value of a particular primitive type.

The `newInstance()` method is used to create new arrays of a specified size.

The `Constructor` Class

The `Constructor` class is used to obtain information about and access the constructors of a class. It consists of nine methods.

The `getName()` method returns the name of the constructor. The `getDeclaringClass()` method identifies the class to which the constructor applies.

The `newInstance()` method is used to create a new instance of the class to which the constructor applies. The `getParameterTypes()` method provides access to the parameters used by the constructor. The `getModifiers()` method encodes the constructor's modifiers as an integer that can be decoded by the `Modifier` class. The `getExceptionTypes()` method identifies the exceptions that are thrown by the constructor.

The `equals()`, `hashCode()`, and `toString()` methods override those of the `Object` class.

The `Field` Class

The `Field` class is used to obtain information about and access the field variables of a class. It consists of 25 methods.

The `getName()` method returns the name of the variable. The `getDeclaringClass()` method identifies the class in which the variable is declared. The `getType()` method provides access to the data type of the variable. The `getModifiers()` method encodes the variable's modifiers as integers that can be decoded by the `Modifier` class.

The `get()` method is used to access the value of the variable. The `getBoolean()`, `getByte()`, `getChar()`, `getDouble()`, `getFloat()`, `getInt()`, `getLong()`, and `getShort()` methods are used to access the value as a particular primitive type.

The `set()` method is used to set the value of the variable. The `setBoolean()`, `setByte()`, `setChar()`, `setDouble()`, `setFloat()`, `setInt()`, `setLong()`, and `setShort()` methods are used to set the value to a particular primitive type.

The `equals()`, `hashCode()`, and `toString()` methods override those of the `Object` class.

The `Method` Class

The `Method` class is used to obtain information about and access the methods of a class. It consists of 10 methods.

The `getName()` method returns the name of the method. The `getDeclaringClass()` method identifies the class in which the method is declared.

The `invoke()` method is used to invoke the method for a particular object and list of parameters. The `getParameterTypes()` method provides access to the parameters used by the method. The `getModifiers()` method encodes the method's modifiers as an integer that can be decoded by the `Modifier` class. The `getExceptionTypes()` method identifies the exceptions that are thrown by the method. The `getReturnType()` method identifies the type of object returned by the method.

The `equals()`, `hashCode()`, and `toString()` methods override those of the `Object` class.

The Modifier Class

The Modifier class is used to decode integers that represent the modifiers of classes, interfaces, field variables, constructors, and methods. It consists of 11 constants, a single parameterless constructor, and 12 static access methods.

The eleven constants are used to represent all possible modifiers. They are ABSTRACT, FINAL, INTERFACE, NATIVE, PRIVATE, PROTECTED, PUBLIC, STATIC, SYNCHRONIZED, TRANSIENT, and VOLATILE.

The toString() method returns a string containing the modifiers encoded in an integer. The isAbstract(), isFinal(), isInterface(), isNative(), isPrivate(), isProtected(), isPublic(), isStatic(), isSynchronized(), isTransient(), and isVolatile() methods return a boolean value indicating whether the respective modifier is encoded in an integer.

A Reflection Example

The java.lang.reflect provides a number of useful methods for discovering information about the members of a class or interface. In most cases, you will use it with the Class class of java.lang. The example shown in Listing 12.10 shows how Class and the classes of java.lang.reflect can be used together to create a program that discovers and displays information about classes and interfaces.

Listing 12.10. The source code of the ReflectApp program.

```
import java.lang.reflect.*;
public class ReflectApp {
 public static void main(String args[]) {
  String parm = args[0];
  Class className = void.class;
  try {
   className= Class.forName(parm);
  }catch (ClassNotFoundException ex){
   System.out.println("Not a class or interface.");
   System.exit(0);
  }
  describeClassOrInterface(className,parm);
 }
 static void describeClassOrInterface(Class className,String name){
  if(className.isInterface()){
   System.out.println("Interface: "+name);
   displayModifiers(className.getModifiers());
   displayFields(className.getDeclaredFields());
   displayMethods(className.getDeclaredMethods());
  }else{
   System.out.println("Class: "+name);
   displayModifiers(className.getModifiers());
   displayInterfaces(className.getInterfaces());
   displayFields(className.getDeclaredFields());
   displayConstructors(className.getDeclaredConstructors());
   displayMethods(className.getDeclaredMethods());
```

```
  }
}
static void displayModifiers(int m){
 System.out.println("Modifiers: "+Modifier.toString(m));
}
static void displayInterfaces(Class[] interfaces){
 if(interfaces.length>0){
  System.out.println("Interfaces: ");
  for(int i=0;i<interfaces.length;++i)
   System.out.println(interfaces[i].getName());
 }
}
static void displayFields(Field[] fields){
 if(fields.length>0){
  System.out.println("Fields: ");
  for(int i=0;i<fields.length;++i)
   System.out.println(fields[i].toString());
 }
}
static void displayConstructors(Constructor[] constructors){
 if(constructors.length>0){
  System.out.println("Constructors: ");
  for(int i=0;i<constructors.length;++i)
   System.out.println(constructors[i].toString());
 }
}
static void displayMethods(Method[] methods){
 if(methods.length>0){
  System.out.println("Methods: ");
  for(int i=0;i<methods.length;++i)
   System.out.println(methods[i].toString());
 }
}
}
```

Compile the program and run it as follows. It takes the fully qualified name of a class or interface as a command line argument. The following output shows the information that it generates when the `jdg.ch06.CGText` class is used as an argument. It identifies the class modifiers as `public` and `synchronized` and identifies `CGTextEdit` as an implemented interface. The `text` variable is identified as a field of `CGText`. A single constructor that takes a `Point` and `String` parameter is displayed along with five access methods: `display()`, `describe()`, `replaceText()`, `upperCase()`, and `lowerCase()`:

```
C:\jdk1.1.1\jdg\Ch12>java ReflectApp jdg.ch06.CGText
Class: jdg.ch06.CGText
Modifiers: public synchronized
Interfaces:
jdg.ch06.CGTextEdit
Fields:
java.lang.String jdg.ch06.CGText.text
Constructors:
public jdg.ch06.CGText(jdg.ch05.Point,java.lang.String)
Methods:
public void jdg.ch06.CGText.display(jdg.ch05.PrintCGrid)
```

```
public void jdg.ch06.CGText.describe()
public void jdg.ch06.CGText.replaceText(java.lang.String)
public void jdg.ch06.CGText.upperCase()
public void jdg.ch06.CGText.lowerCase()
```

Try running it with other classes and interfaces. The following output is generated when you use the `jdg.ch06.CGTextEdit` interface as an argument. The interface's modifiers and methods are displayed:

```
C:\jdk1.1.1\jdg\Ch12>java ReflectApp jdg.ch06.CGTextEdit
Interface: jdg.ch06.CGTextEdit
Modifiers: public abstract synchronized interface
Methods:
public abstract void jdg.ch06.CGTextEdit.replaceText(java.lang.String)
public abstract void jdg.ch06.CGTextEdit.upperCase()
public abstract void jdg.ch06.CGTextEdit.lowerCase()
```

`ReflectApp` takes the first command line argument and uses the `forName()` method of `Class` to create a `Class` object representing the class or interface identified by the argument. This `Class` object is assigned to the `className` variable. The `describeClassOrInterface()` method is invoked to display information about the class or interface.

The `describeClassOrInterface()` method uses the `isInterface()` method of `Class` to determine whether the `Class` object refers to an interface or class. It uses `getInterfaces()` to retrieve all of the interfaces of a class and invokes `displayInterfaces()` to display those interfaces.

The `describeClassOrInterface()` method uses `getModifiers()`, `getDeclaredFields()`, `getDeclaredConstructors()`, and `getDeclaredMethods()` to retrieve the `Modifier`, `Field`, `Constructor`, and `Method` objects associated with a class or interface. It invokes `displayModifiers()`, `displayFields()`, `displayConstructors()`, and `displayMethods()` to display information about these objects. These display methods use the `toString()` method to convert the objects into a useful display string.

Summary

In this chapter you learned how to use the `java.lang` package. You took a tour of its classes and their methods and wrote some sample programs that illustrate their use. You also learned to use the reflection classes of the `java.lang.reflect` class. In the next chapter you'll learn to use the `java.io` package to perform stream-based I/O to files, memory buffers, and the console window.

13

Stream-Based Input/ Output and the `java.io` Package

In this chapter you'll learn to use Java streams to perform sophisticated input and output using standard I/O, memory buffers, and files. You'll cover all the classes of the java.io package and learn about the new Reader and Writer classes introduced by Java 1.1. You'll explore the input and output stream class hierarchy and learn to use stream filters to simplify I/O processing. You'll also learn how to perform random-access I/O and how to use the StreamTokenizer class to construct input parsers. When you finish this chapter, you'll be able to add sophisticated I/O processing to your Java programs.

Streams

Java input and output is based on the use of streams. *Streams* are sequences of bytes that travel from a source to a destination over a communication path. If your program is writing to a stream, it is the stream's *source*. If it is reading from a stream, it is the stream's *destination*. The communication path is dependent on the type of I/O being performed. It can consist of memory-to-memory transfers, file system, network, and other forms of I/O.

Streams are not complicated. They are powerful because they abstract away the details of the communication path from input and output operations. This allows all I/O to be performed using a common set of methods. These methods can be tailored and extended to provide higher-level custom I/O capabilities.

Java defines two major classes of byte streams: InputStream and OutputStream. These streams are subclassed to provide a variety of I/O capabilities. Java 1.1 introduced the Reader and Writer classes to provide the foundation for 16-bit Unicode character-oriented I/O. These classes support internationalization of Java I/O. The Reader and Writer classes, such as InputStream and OutputStream, are subclassed to support additional capabilities.

The java.io Class Hierarchy

Figure 13.1 identifies the java.io class hierarchy. As described in the previous section, the InputStream, OutputStream, Reader, and Writer classes are the major components of this hierarchy. Other high-level classes include the File, FileDescriptor, RandomAccessFile, ObjectStreamClass, and StreamTokenizer classes.

The InputStream and OutputStream classes have complementary subclasses. For example, both have subclasses for performing I/O via memory buffers, files, and pipes. The InputStream subclasses perform the input and the OutputStream classes perform the output.

FIGURE 13.1.
The classes of the
`java.io` *hierarchy.*

```
java.io
        InputStream
                FilterInputStream
                        BufferedInputStream
                        DataInputStream
                        LineNumberInputStream
                        PushbackInputStream
                ByteArrayInputStream
                FileInputStream
                ObjectInputStream
                PipedInputStream
                SequenceInputStream
                StringBufferInputStream
        OutputStream
                FilterOutputStream
                        BufferedOutputStream
                        DataOutputStream
                        PrintStream
                ByteArrayOutputStream
                FileOutputStream
                ObjectOutputStream
                PipedOutputStream
        Reader
                BufferedReader
                        LineNumberReader
                CharArrayReader
                FilterReader
                        PushbackReader
                InputStreamReader
                        FileReader
                PipedReader
                StringReader
        Writer
                BufferedWriter
                CharArrayWriter
                FilterWriter
                OutputStreamWriter
                        FileWriter
                PipedWriter
                PrintWriter
                StringWriter
        File
        RandomAccessFile
        FileDescriptor
        ObjectStreamClass
        StreamTokenizer
```

The `InputStream` class has seven direct subclasses. The `ByteArrayInputStream` class is used to convert an array into an input stream. The `StreamBufferInputStream` class uses a `StreamBuffer` as an input stream. The `FileInputStream` class allows files to be used as input streams. The `ObjectInputStream` class is used to read primitive types and objects that have been previously written to a stream. The `PipedInputStream` class allows a pipe to be constructed between two threads and supports input through the pipe. The `SequenceInputStream` class allows two or more streams to be concatenated into a single stream. The `FilterInputStream` class is an abstract class from which other input-filtering classes are constructed.

Filters are objects that read from one stream and write to another, usually altering the data in some way as they pass it from one stream to another. Filters can be used to buffer data, read and write objects, keep track of line numbers, and perform other operations on the data they move. Filters can be combined, with one filter using the output of another as its input. You can create custom filters by combining existing filters.

FilterInputStream has four filtering subclasses. The BufferedInputStream class maintains a buffer of the input data that it receives. This eliminates the need to read from the stream's source every time an input byte is needed. The DataInputStream class implements the DataInput interface, a set of methods that allow objects and primitive data types to be read from a stream. The LineNumberInputStream is used to keep track of input line numbers. The PushbackInputStream provides the capability to push back data onto the stream that it is read from so that it can be read again.

> **NOTE**
>
> Other Java API packages, such as java.util, contain classes and interfaces that extend those of java.io. In particular, the java.util package defines input and output stream classes that can be used to support file and stream compression.

The OutputStream class hierarchy consists of five direct subclasses. The ByteArrayOutputStream, FileOutputStream, ObjectOutputStream, and PipedOutputStream classes are the output complements to the ByteArrayInputStream, FileInputStream, ObjectInputStream, and PipedInputStream classes. The FilterOutputStream class provides subclasses that complement the FilterInputStream classes.

The BufferedOutputStream class is the output analog to the BufferedInputStream class. It buffers output so that output bytes can be written to devices in larger groups. The DataOutputStream class implements the DataOutput interface. This interface complements the DataInput interface. It provides methods that write objects and primitive data types to streams so that they can be read by the DataInput interface methods. The PrintStream class provides the familiar print() and println() methods used in most of the sample programs that you've developed so far in this book. It provides a number of overloaded methods that simplify data output.

The Reader class is similar to the InputStream class in that it is the root of an input class hierarchy. Reader supports 16-bit Unicode character input, while InputStream supports 8-bit byte input. The Reader class has six direct subclasses:

- The BufferedReader class supports buffered character input. Its LineNumberReader subclass supports buffered input and keeps track of line numbers.

- The CharArrayReader class provides the capability to read a character input stream from a character buffer.

- The `FilterReader` class is an abstract class that provides the basis for filtering character input streams. Its `PushbackReader` subclass provides a filter that allows characters to be pushed back onto the input stream.
- The `InputStreamReader` class is used to convert byte input streams to character input streams. Its `FileReader` subclass is used to read character files.
- The `PipedReader` class is used to read characters from a pipe.
- The `StringReader` class is used to read characters from a `String`.

The `Writer` class is the output analog of the `Reader` class. It supports 16-bit Unicode character output. It has seven direct subclasses:

- The `BufferedWriter` class supports buffered character output.
- The `CharArrayWriter` class supports output to a character array.
- The `FilterWriter` class is an abstract class that supports character output filtering.
- The `OutputStreamWriter` class allows a character stream to be converted to a byte stream. Its `FileWriter` subclass is used to perform character output to files.
- The `PipedWriter` class supports character output to pipes.
- The `PrintWriter` class supports platform-independent character printing.
- The `StringWriter` class supports character output to `String` objects.

The `File` class is used to access the files and directories of the local file system. The `FileDescriptor` class is an encapsulation of the information used by the host system to track files that are being accessed. The `RandomAccessFile` class provides the capabilities needed to directly access data contained in a file. The `ObjectStreamClass` class is used to describe classes whose objects can be written (serialized) to a stream. The `StreamTokenizer` class is used to create parsers that operate on stream data.

> **NOTE**
>
> Other packages, such as `java.util.zip`, provide classes that extend the `java.io` class hierarchy shown in Figure 13.1.

The `java.io` Interfaces

The `java.io` package declares eight interfaces. The `DataInput` and `DataOutput` interfaces provide methods that support machine-independent I/O. The `ObjectInput` and `ObjectOutput` interfaces extend `DataInput` and `DataOutput` to work with objects. The `ObjectInputValidation` interface supports the validation of objects that are read from a stream. The `Serializable` and `Externalizable` interfaces support the serialized writing of objects to streams. The `FilenameFilter` interface is used to select filenames from a list.

The `InputStream` Class

The `InputStream` class is an abstract class that lays the foundation for the Java `Input` class hierarchy. As such, it provides methods that are inherited by all `InputStream` classes.

The `read()` Method

The `read()` method is the most important method of the `InputStream` class hierarchy. It reads a byte of data from an input stream and blocks if no data is available. When a method *blocks*, it causes the thread in which it is executing to wait until data becomes available. This is not a problem in multithreaded programs. The `read()` method takes on several overloaded forms. It can read a single byte or an array of bytes, depending upon what form is used. It returns the number of bytes read or -1 if an end of file is encountered with no bytes read.

The `read()` method is overridden and overloaded by subclasses to provide custom read capabilities.

The `available()` Method

The `available()` method returns the number of bytes that are available to be read without blocking. It is used to peek into the input stream to see how much data is available. However, depending on the input stream, it might not be accurate or useful. Some input streams on some operating systems may always report `zero` available bytes. In general, it is not a good idea to blindly rely on this method to perform input processing.

The `close()` Method

The `close()` method closes an input stream and releases resources associated with the stream. It is always a good idea to close a stream to ensure that the stream processing is correctly terminated.

Markable Streams

Java supports *markable streams*. These are streams that provide the capability to mark a position in the stream and then later reset the stream so that it can be reread from the marked position. If a stream can be marked, it must contain some memory associated with it to keep track of the data between the mark and the current position of the stream. When this buffering capability is exceeded, the mark becomes invalidated.

The `markSupported()` method returns a `boolean` value that identifies whether a stream supports mark and reset capabilities. The `mark()` method marks a position in the stream. It takes an integer parameter that identifies the number of bytes that can be read before the mark becomes invalid. This is used to set the buffering capacity of the stream. The `reset()` method simply repositions the stream to its last marked position.

The `skip()` Method

The `skip()` method skips over a specified number of input bytes. It takes a `long` value as a parameter.

The `OutputStream` Class

The `OutputStream` class is an abstract class that lays the foundation for the output stream hierarchy. It provides a set of methods that is the output analog to the `InputStream` methods.

The `write()` Method

The `write()` method allows bytes to be written to the output stream. It provides three overloaded forms to write a single byte, an array of bytes, or a segment of an array. The `write()` method, like the `read()` method, may block when it tries to write to a stream. The blocking causes the thread executing the `write()` method to wait until the write operation has been completed.

> **NOTE**
>
> The `OutputStream` class defines three overloaded forms for the `write()` method. These forms allow you to write an integer, an array of bytes, or a subarray of bytes to an `OutputStream` object. You will often see several overloaded forms for methods that perform the same operation using different types of data.

The `flush()` Method

The `flush()` method causes any buffered data to be immediately written to the output stream. Some subclasses of `OutputStream` support buffering and override this method to "clean out" their buffers and write all buffered data to the output stream. They must override the `OutputStream` `flush()` method because, by default, it does not perform any operations and is used as a placeholder.

The `close()` Method

It is generally more important to close output streams than input streams, so that any data written to the stream is stored before the stream is deallocated and lost. The `close()` method of `OutputStream` is used in the same manner as that of `InputStream`.

Byte Array I/O

Java supports byte array input and output via the `ByteArrayInputStream` and `ByteArrayOutputStream` classes. These classes use memory buffers as the source and destination of the input and output streams. These streams do not have to be used together. They are covered in the same section here because they provide similar and complementary methods. The `StringBufferInputStream` class is similar to the `ByteArrayInput` class and is also covered in this section.

The `CharArrayReader`, `CharArrayWriter`, `StringReader`, and `StringWriter` classes support character-based I/O in a similar manner to the `ByteArrayInputStream`, `ByteArrayOutputStream`, and `StringBufferInputStream` classes. They are covered later in this chapter.

The `ByteArrayInputStream` Class

The `ByteArrayInputStream` class creates an input stream from a memory buffer. The buffer is an array of bytes. It provides two constructors that use a byte array argument to create the input stream. The class does not support any new methods, but overrides the `read()`, `skip()`, `available()`, and `reset()` methods of `InputStream`.

The `read()` and `skip()` methods are implemented as specified for `InputStream`. The `available()` method is reliable and can be used to check on the number of available bytes in the buffer. The `reset()` method resets the stream to the marked position.

The `ByteArrayOutputStream` Class

The `ByteArrayOutputStream` class is a little more sophisticated than its input complement. It creates an output stream on a byte array, but provides additional capabilities to allow the output array to accommodate new data that is written to it. It also provides the `toByteArray()` and `toString()` methods for converting the stream to a byte array or `String` object.

`ByteArrayOutputStream` provides two constructors. One takes an integer argument that is used to set the output byte array to an initial size. The other constructor does not take an argument and sets the output buffer to a default size.

`ByteArrayOutputStream` provides some additional methods not declared for `OutputStream`. The `reset()` method resets the output buffer to allow writing to restart at the beginning of the buffer. The `size()` method returns the current number of bytes that has been written to the buffer. The `writeTo()` method is new. It takes an object of class `OutputStream` as an argument and writes the contents of the output buffer to the specified output stream. The `write()` methods override those of `OutputStream` to support array output.

The `ByteArrayIOApp` Program

Having learned about both sides of the byte array I/O classes, you now have a base from which to create a sample program. Remember to create a `ch13` directory under `\jdk1.1.1\jdg` from which to store the files created in this chapter. The source code of the `ByteArrayIOApp` program is provided in Listing 13.1.

Listing 13.1. The source code of the `ByteArrayIOApp` program.

```java
import java.lang.System;
import java.io.ByteArrayInputStream;
import java.io.ByteArrayOutputStream;
import java.io.IOException;

public class ByteArrayIOApp {
 public static void main(String args[]) throws IOException {
  ByteArrayOutputStream outStream = new ByteArrayOutputStream();
  String s = "This is a test.";
  for(int i=0;i<s.length();++i)
   outStream.write(s.charAt(i));
  System.out.println("outstream: "+outStream);
  System.out.println("size: "+outStream.size());
  ByteArrayInputStream inStream;
  inStream = new ByteArrayInputStream(outStream.toByteArray());
  int inBytes = inStream.available();
  System.out.println("inStream has "+inBytes+" available bytes");
  byte inBuf[] = new byte[inBytes];
  int bytesRead = inStream.read(inBuf,0,inBytes);
  System.out.println(bytesRead+" bytes were read");
  System.out.println("They are: "+new String(inBuf));
 }
}
```

The program creates a `ByteArrayOutputStream` object, `outStream`, and an array, s, that contains the text `"This is a test."` to be written to the stream. Each character of s is written, one at a time, to `outStream`. The contents of `outStream` are then printed, along with the number of bytes written.

A `ByteArrayInputStream` object, `inStream`, is created by invoking the `toByteArray()` method of `outStream` to create a byte array that is used as an argument to the `ByteArrayInputStream` constructor. The `available()` method is used to determine the number of available input bytes stored in the buffer. This number is stored as `inBytes` and is used to allocate a byte array to store the data that is read. The `read()` method is invoked for `inStream` to read `inBytes` worth of data. The actual number of bytes read is stored in `bytesRead`. This number is displayed, followed on the next line by the bytes that were read from `inStream`, as follows:

```
outStream: This is a test.
size: 15
inStream has 15 available bytes
15 bytes were read
They are: This is a test.
```

The `StringBufferInputStream` Class

`StringBufferInputStream` is similar to `ByteArrayInputStream` except that it uses a `StringBuffer` to store input data. The input stream is constructed using a `String` argument. Its methods are identical to those provided by `ByteArrayInputStream`. The `StringBufferInputStream` is deprecated in Java 1.1. This means that it has been superceded. The `StringReader` class is now the preferred class for `String`-based input.

File I/O

Java supports stream-based file input and output through the `File`, `FileDescriptor`, `FileInputStream`, and `FileOutputStream` classes. It supports direct or random access I/O using the `File`, `FileDescriptor`, and `RandomAccessFile` classes. Random access I/O is covered later in this chapter. The `FileReader` and `FileWriter` classes support Unicode-based file I/O. These classes are also covered later in this chapter.

The `File` class provides access to file and directory objects, and supports a number of operations on files and directories. The `FileDescriptor` class encapsulates the information used by the host system to track files that are being accessed. The `FileInputStream` and `FileOutputStream` classes provide the capability to read and write to file streams.

The `File` Class

The `File` class is used to access file and directory objects. It uses the file-naming conventions of the host operating system. The `File` class encapsulates these conventions using the `File` class constants.

`File` provides constructors for creating files and directories. These constructors take absolute and relative file paths, and file and directory names.

The `File` class provides numerous access methods that can be used to perform all common file and directory operations. It is important for you to review the API page for this class because file I/O, and file and directory operations are common to most programs.

File methods allow files to be created, deleted, and renamed. They provide access to a file's path name and determine whether a `File` object is a file or directory. These methods also check read and write access permissions.

Directory methods allow directories to be created, deleted, renamed, and listed. Directory methods also allow directory trees to be traversed by providing access to the parent and sibling directories.

The `FileDescriptor` Class

The `FileDescriptor` class provides access to the file descriptors maintained by operating systems when files and directories are being accessed. This class is *opaque* in that it does not provide visibility into the specific information maintained by the operating system. It provides only one method, the `valid()` method, which is used to determine whether a file descriptor object is currently valid.

The `FileInputStream` Class

The `FileInputStream` class allows input to be read from a file in the form of a stream. Objects of class `FileInputStream` are created using a filename string or a `File` or `FileDescriptor` object as an argument. `FileInputStream` overrides the methods of the `InputStream` class and provides two new methods, `finalize()` and `getFD()`. The `finalize()` method is used to close a stream when it is processed by the Java garbage collector. The `getFD()` method is used to obtain access to the `FileDescriptor` associated with the input stream.

The `FileOutputStream` Class

The `FileOutputStream` class allows output to be written to a file stream. Objects of class `FileOutputStream` are created in the same way as those of class `FileInputStream`, using a filename string, `File` object, or `FileDescriptor` object as an argument. `FileOutputStream` overrides the methods of the `OutputStream` class and supports the `finalize()` and `getFD()` methods described for the `FileInputStream` class.

The `FileIOApp` Program

The program in Listing 13.2 illustrates the use of the `FileInputStream`, `FileOutputStream`, and `File` classes. It writes a string to an output file and then reads the file to verify that the output was written correctly. The file used for the I/O is then deleted.

Listing 13.2. The source code of the `FileIOApp` program.

```
import java.lang.System;
import java.io.FileInputStream;
import java.io.FileOutputStream;
import java.io.File;
import java.io.IOException;

public class FileIOApp {
 public static void main(String args[]) throws IOException {
  FileOutputStream outStream = new FileOutputStream("test.txt");
  String s = "This is a test.";
  for(int i=0;i<s.length();++i)
```

continues

Listing 13.2. continued

```
  outStream.write(s.charAt(i));
outStream.close();
FileInputStream inStream = new FileInputStream("test.txt");
int inBytes = inStream.available();
System.out.println("inStream has "+inBytes+" available bytes");
byte inBuf[] = new byte[inBytes];
int bytesRead = inStream.read(inBuf,0,inBytes);
System.out.println(bytesRead+" bytes were read");
System.out.println("They are: "+new String(inBuf));
inStream.close();
File f = new File("test.txt");
f.delete();
 }
}
```

The `FileOutputStream` constructor creates an output stream on the file `test.txt`. The file is automatically created in the current working directory. It then writes the string `"This is a test."` to the output file stream. Note the similarity between this program and the previous one. The power of streams is that the same methods can be used no matter what type of stream is being used.

The output stream is closed to make sure that all the data is written to the file. The file is then reopened as an input file by creating an object of class `FileInputStream`. The same methods used in the `ByteArrayIOApp` program are used to determine the number of available bytes in the file and read these bytes into a byte array. The number of bytes read is displayed along with the characters corresponding to those bytes.

The input stream is closed and then a `File` object is created to provide access to the file. The `File` object is used to delete the file using the `delete()` method. The program's output follows:

```
inStream has 15 available bytes
15 bytes were read
They are: This is a test.
```

The `SequenceInputStream` Class

The `SequenceInputStream` class is used to combine two or more input streams into a single input stream. The input streams are concatenated, which allows the individual streams to be treated as a single, logical stream. The `SequenceInputStream` class does not introduce any new access methods. Its power is derived from the two constructors that it provides. One constructor takes two `InputStream` objects as arguments. The other takes an `Enumeration` of `InputStream` objects. The `Enumeration` interface is described in Chapter 14, "Useful Tools in the `java.util` and `java.math` Packages." It provides methods for dealing with a sequence of related objects.

The SequenceIOApp Program

The program in Listing 13.3 reads the two Java source files, ByteArrayIOApp.java and FileIOApp.java, as a single file courtesy of the SequenceInputStream class.

Listing 13.3. The source code of the SequenceIOApp program.

```
import java.lang.System;
import java.io.FileInputStream;
import java.io.SequenceInputStream;
import java.io.IOException;

public class SequenceIOApp {
 public static void main(String args[]) throws IOException {
  SequenceInputStream inStream;
  FileInputStream f1 = new FileInputStream("ByteArrayIOApp.java");
  FileInputStream f2 = new FileInputStream("FileIOApp.java");
  inStream = new SequenceInputStream(f1,f2);
  boolean eof = false;
  int byteCount = 0;
  while (!eof) {
   int c = inStream.read();
   if(c == -1) eof = true;
   else{
    System.out.print((char) c);
    ++byteCount;
   }
  }
  System.out.println(byteCount+" bytes were read");
  inStream.close();
  f1.close();
  f2.close();
 }
}
```

The program creates two objects of class FileInputStream for the files ByteArrayIOApp.java and FileIOApp.java. These files should be in the jdg\ch13 directory, which is the same directory from which you execute SequenceIOApp. The SequenceInputClass constructor is used to construct a single input stream from the two FileInputStream objects. The program then uses a while loop to read all bytes in the combined file and display them to the console window. The loop stops when the end of the combined file is encountered. This is signaled when the read() method returns -1. The streams are closed after the combined files have been read. The program's output is as follows:

```
import java.lang.System;
import java.io.ByteArrayInputStream;
import java.io.ByteArrayOutputStream;
import java.io.IOException;
```

```
public class ByteArrayIOApp {
 public static void main(String args[]) throws IOException {
  ByteArrayOutputStream outStream = new ByteArrayOutputStream();
  String s = "This is a test.";
  for(int i=0;i<s.length();++i)
   outStream.write(s.charAt(i));
  System.out.println("outstream: "+outStream);
  System.out.println("size: "+outStream.size());
  ByteArrayInputStream inStream;
  inStream = new ByteArrayInputStream(outStream.toByteArray());
  int inBytes = inStream.available();
  System.out.println("inStream has "+inBytes+" available bytes");
  byte inBuf[] = new byte[inBytes];
  int bytesRead = inStream.read(inBuf,0,inBytes);
  System.out.println(bytesRead+" bytes were read");
  System.out.println("They are: "+new String(inBuf));
 }
}

import java.lang.System;
import java.io.FileInputStream;
import java.io.FileOutputStream;
import java.io.File;
import java.io.IOException;

public class FileIOApp {
 public static void main(String args[]) throws IOException {
  FileOutputStream outStream = new FileOutputStream("test.txt");
  String s = "This is a test.";
  for(int i=0;i<s.length();++i)
   outStream.write(s.charAt(i));
  outStream.close();
  FileInputStream inStream = new FileInputStream("test.txt");
  int inBytes = inStream.available();
  System.out.println("inStream has "+inBytes+" available bytes");
  byte inBuf[] = new byte[inBytes];
  int bytesRead = inStream.read(inBuf,0,inBytes);
  System.out.println(bytesRead+" bytes were read");
  System.out.println("They are: "+new String(inBuf));
  inStream.close();
  File f = new File("test.txt");
  f.delete();
 }
}
1763 bytes were read
```

The SequenceIOApp program displays the combined contents of the two source files followed by a line identifying the number of bytes that were read.

Filtered I/O

The filtered input and output stream classes provide the capability to filter I/O in a number of useful ways. I/O filters are used to adapt streams to specific program needs. These filters sit between an input stream and an output stream, and perform special processing on the bytes they transfer from input to output. You can combine filters to perform a sequence of filtering operations where one filter acts on the output of another, as shown in Figure 13.2.

FIGURE 13.2.
Combining filters.

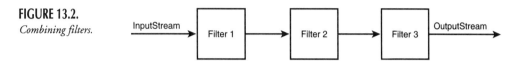

The `FilterInputStream` Class

The `FilterInputStream` class is an abstract class that is the parent of all filtered input stream classes. The `FilterInputStream` class provides the basic capability to create one stream from another. It allows one stream to be read and provided as output as another stream. This is accomplished through the use of the `in` variable, which is used to maintain a separate object of class `InputStream`. The design of the `FilterInputStream` class allows multiple chained filters to be created using several layers of nesting. Each subsequent class accesses the output of the previous class through the `in` variable. Because the `in` variable is an object of class `InputStream`, arbitrary `InputStream` objects can be filtered.

The `FilterOutputStream` Class

The `FilterOutputStream` class is the complement of the `FilterInputStream` class. It is an abstract class that is the parent of all filtered output stream classes. It is similar to the `FilterInputStream` class in that it maintains an object of class `OutputStream` as an `out` variable. Data written to an object of `FilterOutputStream` can be modified as needed to perform filtering operations and then forwarded to the `out` `OutputStream` object. Because `out` is declared to be of class `OutputStream`, arbitrary output streams can be filtered. Multiple `FilterOutputStream` objects can be combined in a manner that is analogous to `FilterInputStream` objects. The input of subsequent `FilterOutputStream` objects is linked to the output of preceding objects.

Buffered I/O

Buffered input and output is used to temporarily cache data that is read from or written to a stream. This allows programs to read and write small amounts of data without adversely affecting system performance. When buffered input is performed, a large number of bytes is read at a single time and stored in an input buffer. When a program reads from the input stream, the input bytes are read from the input buffer. Several reads may be performed before the buffer needs to refilled. Input buffering is used to speed up overall stream input processing.

Output buffering is performed in a similar manner to input buffering. When a program writes to a stream, the output data is stored in an output buffer until the buffer becomes full or the output stream is flushed. Only then is the buffered output actually forwarded to the output stream's destination.

Java implements buffered I/O as filters. The filters maintain and operate the buffer that sits between the program and the source or destination of a buffered stream.

The BufferedInputStream Class

The BufferedInputStream class supports input buffering by automatically creating and maintaining a buffer for a designated input stream. This allows programs to read data from the stream one byte at a time without degrading system performance. Because the BufferedInputStream class is a filter, it can be applied to arbitrary objects of class InputStream and combined with other input filters.

The BufferedInputStream class uses several variables to implement input buffering. These variables are described in the Java API page for this class. However, because these variables are declared as protected, they cannot be directly accessed by your program.

BufferedInputStream defines two constructors. One allows the size of an input buffer to be specified and the other does not. Both constructors take an object of class InputStream as an argument. It is usually better to let BufferedInputStream select the best size for the input buffer than to specify one yourself unless you have specific knowledge that one buffer size is better than another.

BufferedInputStream overrides the access methods provided by InputStream and does not introduce any new methods of its own.

The BufferedOutputStream Class

The BufferedOutputStream class performs output buffering in a manner that is analogous to BufferedInputStream. It allows the size of the output buffer to be specified in a constructor as well as providing for a default buffer size. It overrides the methods of the OutputStream class and does not introduce any new methods of its own.

The BufferedIOApp Program

The BufferedIOApp program (see Listing 13.4) builds on the SequenceIOApp example that was previously presented. It performs buffering on the SequenceInputStream object used to combine the input from two separate files. It also performs buffering on program output so that characters do not need to be displayed to the console window a single character at a time.

Listing 13.4. The source code of the BufferedIOApp program.

```
import java.lang.System;
import java.io.BufferedInputStream;
import java.io.BufferedOutputStream;
import java.io.FileInputStream;
import java.io.SequenceInputStream;
import java.io.IOException;
```

```
public class BufferedIOApp {
 public static void main(String args[]) throws IOException {
  SequenceInputStream f3;
  FileInputStream f1 = new FileInputStream("ByteArrayIOApp.java");
  FileInputStream f2 = new FileInputStream("FileIOApp.java");
  f3 = new SequenceInputStream(f1,f2);
  BufferedInputStream inStream = new BufferedInputStream(f3);
  BufferedOutputStream outStream = new BufferedOutputStream(System.out);
  inStream.skip(500);
  boolean eof = false;
  int byteCount = 0;
  while (!eof) {
   int c = inStream.read();
   if(c == -1) eof = true;
   else{
    outStream.write((char) c);
    ++byteCount;
   }
  }
  String bytesRead = String.valueOf(byteCount);
  bytesRead+=" bytes were read\n";
  outStream.write(bytesRead.getBytes(),0,bytesRead.length());
  inStream.close();
  outStream.close();
  f1.close();
  f2.close();
 }
}
```

The program begins by creating two objects of `FileInputStream` and combining them into a single input stream using the `SequenceInputStream` constructor. It then uses this stream to create an object of `BufferedInputStream` using the default buffer size.

A `BufferedOutputStream` object is created using the `System.out` output stream and a default buffer size. The `skip()` method is used to skip over 500 bytes of the input stream. This is done for two reasons: to illustrate the use of the `skip()` method and to cut down on the size of the program output. The rest of the input is read and printed as in the previous example.

The program output is similar to that of the preceding example. You should execute `BufferedIOApp` from the `jdg\ch13` directory. The `skip()` method was used to skip more than 500 bytes of input. These bytes are also absent from the program's output. The program's output is as follows:

```
rrayInputStream inStream;
  inStream = new ByteArrayInputStream(outStream.toByteArray());
  int inBytes = inStream.available();
  System.out.println("inStream has "+inBytes+" available bytes");
  byte inBuf[] = new byte[inBytes];
  int bytesRead = inStream.read(inBuf,0,inBytes);
  System.out.println(bytesRead+" bytes were read");
  System.out.println("They are: "+new String(inBuf));
 }
}
```

```
import java.lang.System;
import java.io.FileInputStream;
import java.io.FileOutputStream;
import java.io.File;
import java.io.IOException;

public class FileIOApp {
 public static void main(String args[]) throws IOException {
  FileOutputStream outStream = new FileOutputStream("test.txt");
  String s = "This is a test.";
  for(int i=0;i<s.length();++i)
   outStream.write(s.charAt(i));
  outStream.close();
  FileInputStream inStream = new FileInputStream("test.txt");
  int inBytes = inStream.available();
  System.out.println("inStream has "+inBytes+" available bytes");
  byte inBuf[] = new byte[inBytes];
  int bytesRead = inStream.read(inBuf,0,inBytes);
  System.out.println(bytesRead+" bytes were read");
  System.out.println("They are: "+new String(inBuf));
  inStream.close();
  File f = new File("test.txt");
  f.delete();
 }
}
1263 bytes were read
```

PushbackInputStream

PushbackInputStream is a filter that lets you push a byte that was previously read back onto the input stream so that it can be reread. This type of filter is commonly used with parsers. When a character indicating a new input token is read, it is pushed back onto the input stream, until the current input token is processed. It is then reread when processing of the next input token is initiated. PushbackInputStream allows only a single byte to be pushed back. This is generally enough for most applications.

The pushback character is stored in a variable named pushBack.

The unread() method is the only new method introduced by this class. It is used to push a specified character back onto the input stream.

The PushbackIOApp Program

The PushbackIOApp program illustrates the use of the PushbackInputStream class (see Listing 13.5.) It adds a pushback filter to the ByteArrayIOApp program studied earlier in this chapter.

Listing 13.5. The source code of the PushbackIOApp program.

```
import java.lang.System;
import java.io.PushbackInputStream;
import java.io.ByteArrayInputStream;
```

```
import java.io.ByteArrayOutputStream;
import java.io.IOException;

public class PushbackIOApp {
 public static void main(String args[]) throws IOException {
  ByteArrayOutputStream outStream = new ByteArrayOutputStream();
  String s = "This is a test.";
  for(int i=0;i<s.length();++i)
   outStream.write(s.charAt(i));
  System.out.println("outstream: "+outStream);
  System.out.println("size: "+outStream.size());
  ByteArrayInputStream inByteArray;
  inByteArray = new ByteArrayInputStream(outStream.toByteArray());
  PushbackInputStream inStream;
  inStream = new PushbackInputStream(inByteArray);
  char ch = (char) inStream.read();
  System.out.println("First character of inStream is "+ch);
  inStream.unread((int) 't');
  int inBytes = inStream.available();
  System.out.println("inStream has "+inBytes+" available bytes");
  byte inBuf[] = new byte[inBytes];
  for(int i=0;i<inBytes;++i) inBuf[i]=(byte) inStream.read();
  System.out.println("They are: "+new String(inBuf));
 }
}
```

`PushbackIOApp` creates a stream to be used for byte array input using the code of the `ByteArrayIOApp` program. It applies a pushback filter to this stream by using the `PushbackInputStream` filter to create an object of class `PushbackInputStream`. It reads the first character of the input stream and displays it. It then pushes back a t onto the input stream. Note that any character could have been pushed back upon the input stream. The new input stream is then read and displayed.

The program output shows how the pushback filter was used to change the first character of the input stream from an uppercase T to a lowercase t. The program output consists of the following:

```
outstream: This is a test.
size: 15
First character of inStream is T
inStream has 15 available bytes
They are: this is a test.
```

The `LineNumberInputStream` Class

The `LineNumberInputStream` class provides a handy capability for keeping track of input line numbers. It is also a subclass of `FilterInputStream`. This class provides two new methods to support line number processing. The `setLineNumber()` method is used to set the current line number to a particular value. The `getLineNumber()` method is used to obtain the value of the current line number.

Up until Java 1.1, the `LineNumberInputStream` class was the preferred class for tracking input line numbers. In Java 1.1, significant support was added for internationalization. As a result, the `LineNumberInputStream` class has been deprecated. The `LineNumberReader` class (covered later in this chapter) is now the preferred class for tracking input line numbers.

Data I/O

The `DataInputStream` and `DataOutputStream` classes implement the `DataInput` and `DataOutput` interfaces. These interfaces identify methods that allow primitive data types to be read from and written to a stream. By implementing these interfaces, the `DataInputStream` and `DataOutputStream` classes provide the basis for implementing portable input and output streams.

The `DataInputStream` Class

The `DataInputStream` class provides the capability to read arbitrary objects and primitive types from an input stream. It implements the methods of the `DataInput` interface. These methods provide a full range of input capabilities:

- `readBoolean()`—Reads a `boolean` value
- `readByte()`—Reads a byte as an 8-bit signed value
- `readChar()`—Reads a Unicode character
- `readDouble()`—Reads a `double` value
- `readFloat()`—Reads a `float` value
- `readFully()`—Reads an array of bytes
- `readInt()`—Reads an `int` value
- `readLine()`—Reads a line of text (deprecated)
- `readLong()`—Reads a `long` value
- `readShort()`—Reads a `short` value
- `readUnsignedByte()`—Reads a byte as an 8-bit unsigned value
- `readUnsignedShort()`—Reads an unsigned 16-bit value
- `readUTF()`—Reads a string that is in the UTF-8 format
- `skipBytes()`—Skips over a specified amount of input bytes

Note that most, but not all, of these methods raise the `EOFException` when an end of file is encountered. The `readLine()` method returns a null value to signify a read past the end of a file. This method is deprecated in Java 1.1. The `readLine()` method of the `BufferedReader` class should be used instead. `BufferedReader` provides better support for internationalization. Its `readLine()` method corrects errors that exist in the `readLine()` method of `DataInputStream`.

The DataOutputStream Class

The DataOutputStream class provides an output complement to DataInputStream. It allows arbitrary objects and primitive data types to be written to an output stream. It also keeps track of the number of bytes written to the output stream. It is an output filter and can be combined with any output-filtering streams.

The DataIOApp Program

The program in Listing 13.6 shows how DataInputStream and DataOutputStream can be used to easily read and write a variety of values using streams.

Listing 13.6. The source code of the DataIOApp program.

```
import java.lang.System;
import java.io.DataInputStream;
import java.io.DataOutputStream;
import java.io.FileInputStream;
import java.io.FileOutputStream;
import java.io.File;
import java.io.IOException;

public class DataIOApp {
 public static void main(String args[]) throws IOException {
  File file = new File("test.txt");
  FileOutputStream outFile = new FileOutputStream(file);
  DataOutputStream outStream = new DataOutputStream(outFile);
  outStream.writeBoolean(true);
  outStream.writeInt(123456);
  outStream.writeChar('j');
  outStream.writeDouble(1234.56);
  System.out.println(outStream.size()+" bytes were written");
  outStream.close();
  outFile.close();
  FileInputStream inFile = new FileInputStream(file);
  DataInputStream inStream = new DataInputStream(inFile);
  System.out.println(inStream.readBoolean());
  System.out.println(inStream.readInt());
  System.out.println(inStream.readChar());
  System.out.println(inStream.readDouble());
  inStream.close();
  inFile.close();
  file.delete();
 }
}
```

The program creates an object of class File that is used to access the test.txt file. This object is used to create an instance of class FileOutputStream that is assigned to the outFile variable. An object of class DataOutputStream is then constructed as a filter for the FileOutputStream object.

The `writeBoolean()`, `writeChar()`, `writeInt()`, and `writeDouble()` methods of `DataOutputStream` are used to write examples of primitive data types to the filtered output stream. The number of bytes written to the output stream is determined from the `size()` method and displayed to the console window. The output streams are then closed.

The `File` object, created at the beginning of the program, is then used to create an object of class `FileInputStream`. The output stream is then filtered by creating an object of `DataInputStream`.

The primitive data types that were written to the output file in the beginning of the program are now read from the filtered input stream and displayed to the console window.

The program's output shows that the data values were successfully written and read using the data I/O filters:

```
15 bytes were written
true
123456
j
1234.56
```

The `PrintStream` Class

The `PrintStream` class should be no stranger to you. The `System.out` object that you have been using for most of the sample programs is an instance of the `PrintStream` class. It is used to write output to the Java console window.

`PrintStream`'s power lies in the fact that it provides two methods, `print()` and `println()`, that are overloaded to print any primitive data type or object. Objects are printed by first converting them to strings using their `toString()` method inherited from the `Object` class. To provide custom printing for any class, all you have to do is override the `toString()` method for that class.

`PrintStream` provides the capability to automatically flush all output bytes in the stream when a newline character is written to the stream. This feature can be enabled or disabled when the stream is created.

Because `PrintStream` is a filter, it takes an instance of `OutputStream` as an argument to its constructor. A second constructor adds the capability to use the autoflushing feature.

`PrintStream` introduces only one new method beside the extensively overloaded `print()` and `println()` methods. The `checkError()`method is used to flush stream output and determine whether an error occurred on the output stream. This capability is useful for printing output to devices, such as printers, where error status is needed to notify the user of any changes to the device state.

> **NOTE**
>
> The `PrintStream` class is on the way out. While the class itself has not yet been depre-cated, its constructors have. Existing Java applications still work with `PrintStream`; however, the move is on to transfer from `PrintStream` to the preferred `PrintWriter` class. The `PrintWriter` class supports platform-independent printing while `PrintStream` does not.

Pipe I/O

Piped I/O provides the capability for threads to communicate via streams. A thread sends data to another thread by creating an object of `PipedOutputStream` that it connects to an object of `PipedInputStream`. The output data written by one thread is read by another thread using the `PipedInputStream` object.

The process of connecting piped input and output threads is symmetric. An object of class `PipedInputThread` can also be connected to an existing object of class `PipedOutputThread`.

Java automatically performs synchronization with respect to piped input and output streams. The thread that reads from an input pipe does not have to worry about any conflicts with tasks that are writing to the corresponding output stream thread.

Both `PipedInputStream` and `PipedOutputStream` override the standard I/O methods of `InputStream` and `OutputStream`. The only new method provided by these classes is the `connect()` method. Both classes provide the capability to connect a piped stream when it is constructed by passing the argument of the piped stream to which it is to be connected as an argument to the constructor.

The `PipedIOApp` Program

The `PipedIOApp` program creates two threads of execution, named `Producer` and `Consumer`, that communicate using connected objects of classes `PipedOutputStream` and `PipedInputStream`. `Producer` sends the message `This is a test.` to `Consumer` one character at a time, and `Consumer` reads the message in the same manner. `Producer` displays its name and any characters that it writes to the console window. `Consumer` reads the message and displays its name and the characters it reads to the console window. The source code for the `PipedIOApp` program is shown in Listing 13.7.

Listing 13.7. The source code of the `PipedIOApp` program.

```java
import java.lang.Thread;
import java.lang.System;
import java.lang.InterruptedException;
import java.lang.Runnable;
import java.io.PipedInputStream;
import java.io.PipedOutputStream;
import java.io.IOException;

class PipedIOApp {
 public static void main(String args[]) {
  Thread thread1 = new Thread(new PipeOutput("Producer"));
  Thread thread2 = new Thread(new PipeInput("Consumer"));
  thread1.start();
  thread2.start();
  boolean thread1IsAlive = true;
  boolean thread2IsAlive = true;
  do {
   if(thread1IsAlive && !thread1.isAlive()){
    thread1IsAlive = false;
    System.out.println("Thread 1 is dead.");
   }
   if(thread2IsAlive && !thread2.isAlive()){
    thread2IsAlive = false;
    System.out.println("Thread 2 is dead.");
   }
  }while(thread1IsAlive || thread2IsAlive);
 }
}
class PipeIO {
 static PipedOutputStream outputPipe = new PipedOutputStream();
 static PipedInputStream inputPipe = new PipedInputStream();
 static {
  try {
   outputPipe.connect(inputPipe);
  }catch (IOException ex) {
   System.out.println("IOException in static initializer");
  }
 }
 String name;
 public PipeIO(String id) {
  name = id;
 }
}
class PipeOutput extends PipeIO implements Runnable {
 public PipeOutput(String id) {
  super(id);
 }
 public void run() {
  String s = "This is a test.";
  try {
   for(int i=0;i<s.length();++i){
    outputPipe.write(s.charAt(i));
    System.out.println(name+" wrote "+s.charAt(i));
   }
   outputPipe.write('!');
  } catch(IOException ex) {
```

```
    System.out.println("IOException in PipeOutput");
   }
 }
}
class PipeInput extends PipeIO implements Runnable {
 public PipeInput(String id) {
  super(id);
 }
 public void run() {
  boolean eof = false;
  try {
   while (!eof) {
    int inChar = inputPipe.read();
    if(inChar != -1) {
     char ch = (char) inChar;
     if(ch=='!'){
      eof=true;
      break;
     }else System.out.println(name+" read "+ch);
    }
   }
  } catch(IOException ex) {
   System.out.println("IOException in PipeOutput");
  }
 }
}
```

This program is somewhat longer than the other examples in this chapter due to the overhead needed to set up the threading. The main() method creates the two Producer and Consumer threads as objects of classes PipeOutput and PipeInput. These classes are subclasses of PipeIO that implement the Runnable interface. The main() method starts both threads and then loops, checking for their death.

The PipeIO class is the superclass of the PipeOutput and PipeInput classes. It contains the static variables, outputPipe and inputPipe, that are used for interthread communication. These variables are assigned objects of classes PipedOutputStream and PipeInputStream. The static initializer is used to connect outputPipe with inputPipe using the connect() method. The PipeIO constructor provides the capability to maintain the name of its instances. This is used by the PipeInput and PipeOutput classes to store thread names.

The PipeOutput class extends PipeIO and implements the Runnable interface, making it eligible to be executed as a separate thread. The required run() method performs all thread processing. It loops to write the test message one character at a time to the outputPipe. It also displays its name and the characters that it writes to the console window. The ! character is used to signal the end of the message transmission. Notice that IOException is handled within the thread rather than being identified in the throws clause of the run() method. In order for run() to properly implement the Runnable interface, it cannot throw any exceptions.

The PipeInput class also extends PipeIO and implements the Runnable interface. It simply loops and reads a character at a time from inputPipe, displaying its name and the characters that it reads to the console window. It also handles IOException in order to avoid having to identify the exception in its throws clause.

The output of PipeIOApp shows the time sequencing of the thread input and output taking place using the connected pipe I/O streams. The output generated by running the program on your computer will probably differ because of differences in your computer's execution speed and I/O performance. The output generated when I ran the program is as follows:

```
Producer wrote T
Producer wrote h
Producer wrote i
Producer wrote s
Producer wrote
Consumer read T
Consumer read h
Consumer read i
Producer wrote i
Producer wrote s
Producer wrote
Consumer read s
Consumer read
Producer wrote a
Producer wrote
Producer wrote t
Consumer read i
Consumer read s
Consumer read
Producer wrote e
Producer wrote s
Consumer read a
Consumer read
Consumer read t
Producer wrote t
Producer wrote .
Thread 1 is dead.
Consumer read e
Consumer read s
Consumer read t
Consumer read .
Thread 2 is dead.
```

Object I/O

The ObjectOutputStream and ObjectInputStream classes allow objects and values of primitive types to be written to and read from streams. These classes implement the ObjectOutput and ObjectInput interfaces. Of the methods specified by ObjectOutput, the writeObject() method is the most interesting; it writes objects which implement the Serializable interface to a stream. The ObjectInput interface provides the readObject() method to read the objects written to a stream by the writeObject() method.

The `Serializable` interfaces are used to identify objects that can be written to a stream. It does not define any constants or methods, but it does place some constraints on which classes are serializable. Chapter 53, "Using Object Serialization," covers the `Serialization` interface and object I/O in detail.

The `ObjectIOApp` Program

The `ObjectIOApp` program, shown in Listing 13.8, shows how the `ObjectOutputStream` and `ObjectInputStream` classes can be used to write and read objects from streams.

Listing 13.8. The source code of the `ObjectIOApp` program.

```
import java.io.ObjectInputStream;
import java.io.ObjectOutputStream;
import java.io.Serializable;
import java.io.FileInputStream;
import java.io.FileOutputStream;
import java.io.File;
import java.io.IOException;
import java.util.Date;

public class ObjectIOApp {
 public static void main(String args[]) throws IOException,
   ClassNotFoundException {
  File file = new File("test.txt");
  FileOutputStream outFile = new FileOutputStream(file);
  ObjectOutputStream outStream = new ObjectOutputStream(outFile);
  TestClass1 t1 = new TestClass1(true,9,'A',0.0001,"java");
  TestClass2 t2 = new TestClass2();
  String t3 = "This is a test.";
  Date t4 = new Date();
  outStream.writeObject(t1);
  outStream.writeObject(t2);
  outStream.writeObject(t3);
  outStream.writeObject(t4);
  outStream.close();
  outFile.close();
  FileInputStream inFile = new FileInputStream(file);
  ObjectInputStream inStream = new ObjectInputStream(inFile);
  System.out.println(inStream.readObject());
  System.out.println(inStream.readObject());
  System.out.println(inStream.readObject());
  System.out.println(inStream.readObject());
  inStream.close();
  inFile.close();
  file.delete();
 }
}
```

continues

Listing 13.8. continued

```
class TestClass1 implements Serializable {
 boolean b;
 int i;
 char c;
 double d;
 String s;
 TestClass1(boolean b,int i,char c,double d,String s){
  this.b = b;
  this.i = i;
  this.c = c;
  this.d = d;
  this.s = s;
 }
 public String toString(){
  String r = String.valueOf(b)+" ";
  r += String.valueOf(i)+" ";
  r += String.valueOf(c)+" ";
  r += String.valueOf(d)+" ";
  r += String.valueOf(s);
  return r;
 }
}

class TestClass2 implements Serializable {
 int i;
 TestClass1 tc1;
 TestClass1 tc2;
 TestClass2(){
  i=0;
  tc1 = new TestClass1(true,2,'j',1.234,"Java");
  tc2 = new TestClass1(false,7,'J',2.468,"JAVA");
 }
 public String toString(){
  String r = String.valueOf(i)+" ";
  r += tc1.toString()+" ";
  r += tc2.toString();
  return r;
 }
}
```

ObjectIOApp is similar in design to the DataIOApp program of Listing 13.6. It creates a File object to support I/O to the test.txt file. The File object is used to create an object of class FileOutputStream. This object is then used to create an object of class ObjectOutputStream which is assigned to the outStream variable.

Four objects are created and assigned to the t1 through t4 variables. An object of class TestClass1 is assigned to the t1 variable and an object of class TestClass2 is assigned to the t2 variable. The TestClass1 and TestClass2 classes are declared at the end of Listing 13.8. A String object is assigned to t3 and a Date object is assigned to t4. You'll cover the Date class in Chapter 14.

The objects referenced by the t1 through t4 variables are written to outStream using the writeObject() method. The stream and file are then closed. The test.txt file is then reopened as a FileInputStream object. This object is then converted to an ObjectInputStream object and assigned to the inStream variable. Four objects are then read from inStream, using the readObject() method, and then written to standard output. The program's output is as follows:

```
true 9 A 1.0E-4 java
0 true 2 j 1.234 Java false 7 J 2.468 JAVA
This is a test.
Sun Feb 23 00:07:35 PST 1997
```

Note that you'll receive a different date value from the one shown above. TestClass1 and TestClass2 are dummy test classes that are used to make the example work. Their toString() methods are automatically invoked by the println() method to convert objects to string values for printing.

The Reader and Writer Classes

The Reader and Writer classes are abstract classes at the top of a class hierarchy that supports the reading and writing of Unicode character streams. These classes are new additions, being introduced with Java 1.1.

The Reader Class

The Reader class supports the standard read(), reset(), skip(), mark(), markSupported(), and close() methods. In addition to these, the ready() method returns a boolean value that indicates whether the next read operation will succeed without blocking.

The direct subclasses of the Reader class are BufferedReader, CharArrayReader, FilterReader, InputStreamReader, PipedReader, and StringReader.

The Writer Class

The Writer class is the output complement of the Reader class. It declares the write(), flush(), and close() methods. Its direct subclasses are BufferedWriter, CharArrayWriter, FilterWriter, OutputStreamWriter, PipedWriter, StringWriter, and PrintWriter. Each of these subclasses, except PrintWriter, is an output complement to a Reader subclass.

Character Array and String I/O

The CharArrayReader and CharArrayWriter classes are similar to the ByteArrayInputStream and ByteArrayOutputStream classes in that they support I/O from memory buffers. The difference between these classes is that `CharArrayReader` and `CharArrayWriter` support 16-bit character I/O, and `ByteArrayInputStream` and `ByteArrayOutputStream` support 8-bit byte array I/O.

The `CharArrayReader` class does not add any new methods to those provided by `Reader`. The `CharArrayWriter` class adds the following methods to those provided by `Writer`:

- `reset()`—Resets the buffer so that it can be read
- `size()`—Returns the current size of the buffer
- `toCharArray()`—Returns a character array copy of the output buffer
- `toString()`—Copies and converts the output buffer to a `String` object
- `writeTo()`—Writes the buffer to another output stream (`Writer` object)

These methods are similar to those provided by the `ByteArrayOutputStream` class.

The `StringReader` class provides the capability to read character input from a string. Like `CharArrayReader`, it does not add any additional methods to those provided by `Reader`. The `StringWriter` class is used to write character output to a `StringBuffer` object. It adds the `getBuffer()` and `toString()` methods. The `getBuffer()` method returns the `StringBuffer` object corresponding to the output buffer. The `toString()` method returns a `String` copy of the output buffer.

The `CharArrayIOApp` and `StringIOApp` Programs

The `CharArrayIOApp` program (see Listing 13.9) is based on the `ByteArrayIOApp` program (see Listing 13.1) introduced at the beginning of this chapter. It writes the string `"This is a test."` one character at a time to a `CharArrayWriter` object. It then converts the output buffer to a `CharArrayReader` object. Each character of the input buffer is read and appended to a `StringBuffer` object. The `StringBuffer` object is then converted to a `String` object. The number of characters read and the `String` object are then displayed. The program output follows:

```
outstream: This is a test.
size: 15
15 characters were read
They are: This is a test.
```

The `StringIOApp` program (see Listing 13.10) is similar to `CharArrayIOApp`. It writes output to a `StringBuffer` instead of a character array. It produces the same output as `CharArrayIOApp`.

Listing 13.9. The source code of the `CharArrayIOApp` program.

```
import java.lang.System;
import java.io.CharArrayReader;
import java.io.CharArrayWriter;
import java.io.IOException;
```

```
public class CharArrayIOApp {
 public static void main(String args[]) throws IOException {
  CharArrayWriter outStream = new CharArrayWriter();
  String s = "This is a test.";
  for(int i=0;i<s.length();++i)
   outStream.write(s.charAt(i));
  System.out.println("outstream: "+outStream);
  System.out.println("size: "+outStream.size());
  CharArrayReader inStream;
  inStream = new CharArrayReader(outStream.toCharArray());
  int ch=0;
  StringBuffer sb = new StringBuffer("");
  while((ch = inStream.read()) != -1)
   sb.append((char) ch);
  s = sb.toString();
  System.out.println(s.length()+" characters were read");
  System.out.println("They are: "+s);
 }
}
```

Listing 13.10. The source code of the StringIOApp program.

```
import java.lang.System;
import java.io.StringReader;
import java.io.StringWriter;
import java.io.IOException;

public class StringIOApp {
 public static void main(String args[]) throws IOException {
  StringWriter outStream = new StringWriter();
  String s = "This is a test.";
  for(int i=0;i<s.length();++i)
   outStream.write(s.charAt(i));
  System.out.println("outstream: "+outStream);
  System.out.println("size: "+outStream.toString().length());
  StringReader inStream;
  inStream = new StringReader(outStream.toString());
  int ch=0;
  StringBuffer sb = new StringBuffer("");
  while((ch = inStream.read()) != -1)
   sb.append((char) ch);
  s = sb.toString();
  System.out.println(s.length()+" characters were read");
  System.out.println("They are: "+s);
 }
}
```

The InputStreamReader and OutputStreamWriter Classes

The InputStreamReader and OutputStreamWriter classes are used to convert between byte streams and character streams. The InputStreamReader class converts an object of an InputStream subclass into a character-oriented stream. The OutputStreamWriter class converts a character output stream to a byte output stream.

The InputStreamReader Class

The InputStreamReader() constructor takes an InputStream object as a parameter and creates an InputStreamReader object. This provides a bridge between byte-oriented input streams and character-oriented input streams. A second InputStreamReader constructor also takes a String parameter that identifies the character encoding to be used in byte-to-character conversion. The getEncoding() method may be used to retrieve the encoding that is in effect. The ready() method is used to determine whether a character can be read without blocking.

The InputConversionApp Program

The InputConversionApp program, shown in Listing 13.11, converts the standard input stream (System.in) from a byte stream to a character stream. The input characters are echoed to standard output. It also prints out the encoding that is in effect on your system. The following is an example of the output generated when the program is run on my computer:

```
Encoding: 8859_1
>This is a test.
This is a test.
>
```

The 8859_1 encoding is the International Standard Organization (ISO) Latin-1 character encoding. Chapter 21, "Internationalization and the java.text Package," identifies other encodings.

Listing 13.11. The source code of the InputConversionApp program.

```
import java.lang.System;
import java.io.InputStreamReader;
import java.io.BufferedReader;
import java.io.IOException;

public class InputConversionApp {
 public static void main(String args[]) throws IOException {
  InputStreamReader in = new InputStreamReader(System.in);
  BufferedReader inStream = new BufferedReader(in);
  System.out.println("Encoding: "+in.getEncoding());
```

```
  String inputLine;
  do {
   System.out.print(">");
   System.out.flush();
   inputLine=inStream.readLine();
   System.out.println(inputLine);
  } while (inputLine.length() != 0);
 }
}
```

The OutputStreamWriter Class

The OutputStreamWriter class allows a character stream to be converted to a byte stream. Its constructor takes the name of an object of an OutputStream subclass as a parameter. The characters written to an OutputStreamWriter object are translated and written to the OutputStream object specified in the OutputStreamWriter object's constructor. The translation is performed according to the encoding specified in the System property file.encoding. A different encoding scheme may be specified by supplying the name of the encoding scheme in the OutputStreamWriter constructor. The getEncoding()method may be used to retrieve the current character encoding that is in effect.

The FileReader and FileWriter Classes

The FileReader and FileWriter classes are subclasses of InputStreamReader and OutputStreamWriter that are used to perform character-based file I/O. These classes do not provide any additional access methods; however, their constructors provide the capability to create input and output character streams using String objects that represent filenames, File objects, and FileDescriptor objects.

The CharFileIOApp Program

The following example (see Listing 13.12) demonstrates the use of the FileReader and FileWriter classes. It converts the FileIOApp program (see Listing 13.2) that was introduced earlier in the chapter to character-oriented I/O and produces the following output:

```
15 characters were read
They are: This is a test.
```

The main difference between CharFileIOApp and FileIOApp is that FileReader and FileWriter classes are used instead of the FileInputStream and FileOutputStream classes. The other difference is the use of a StringBuffer object (instead of a byte array) to capture the characters read from the input file stream.

Listing 13.12. The source code of the `CharFileIOApp` program.

```
import java.lang.System;
import java.io.FileReader;
import java.io.FileWriter;
import java.io.File;
import java.io.IOException;

public class CharFileIOApp {
 public static void main(String args[]) throws IOException {
  FileWriter outStream = new FileWriter("test.txt");
  String s = "This is a test.";
  for(int i=0;i<s.length();++i)
   outStream.write(s.charAt(i));
  outStream.close();
  FileReader inStream = new FileReader("test.txt");
  StringBuffer sb = new StringBuffer("");
  int ch=0;
  while((ch = inStream.read()) != -1)
   sb.append((char) ch);
  s = sb.toString();
  System.out.println(s.length()+" characters were read");
  System.out.println("They are: "+s);
  inStream.close();
  File f = new File("test.txt");
  f.delete();
 }
}
```

Buffered Character I/O

Buffered character I/O is supported by the `BufferedReader` and `BufferedWriter` classes. These classes are character-based analogs to the `BufferedInputStream` and `BufferedOutputStream` classes. In Java 1.1, the `readLine()` method of the `BufferedReader` class replaces the `readLine()` method of the `DataInputStream` class for reading lines of text from the console, a file, or other character-oriented input streams. You have already used this method in some of the sample programs of Part II, "Programming in Java."

The `BufferedWriter` class provides the capability to write buffered data to character-based output streams. It adds the `newLine()` method to the methods that it inherits (and overrides) from the `Writer` class. The `newLine()` method allows new line characters to be written in a system-independent manner. It is preferred to simply writing a \n character to the output stream. The `line.separator` system property defines the system-specific new line character.

The `LineNumberReader` Class

The `LineNumberReader` class is a subclass of the `BufferedReader` class that is used to associate line numbers with each line of text that is read from a stream. Lines are terminated by a new line character (\n), a carriage return (\r), or a carriage return-new line combination (\r\n).

In addition to the methods that it inherits from BufferedReader, the LineNumberReader class declares the getLineNumber() and setLineNumber() methods. The getLineNumber() method returns the current line number. The setLineNumber() method sets the current line number to an integer value.

The LineNumberIOApp Program

The LineNumberIOApp program (see Listing 13.13) illustrates the use of the LineNumberReader class. It creates a FileReader on the LineNumberIOApp.java source file and then uses the FileReader object to create a LineNumberReader object. The character file is read, one line at a time, and its contents are displayed using line numbers obtained via the getLineNumber() method. The output of this program follows:

```
1. import java.lang.System;
2. import java.io.LineNumberReader;
3. import java.io.FileReader;
4. import java.io.BufferedWriter;
5. import java.io.IOException;
6.
7. public class LineNumberIOApp {
8.   public static void main(String args[]) throws IOException {
9.    FileReader inFile = new FileReader("LineNumberIOApp.java");
10.    LineNumberReader inLines = new LineNumberReader(inFile);
11.    String inputLine;
12.    while ((inputLine=inLines.readLine()) != null) {
13.     System.out.println(inLines.getLineNumber()+". "+inputLine);
14.    }
15.  }
16. }
```

Listing 13.13. The source code of the LineNumberIOApp program.

```
import java.lang.System;
import java.io.LineNumberReader;
import java.io.FileReader;
import java.io.BufferedWriter;
import java.io.IOException;

public class LineNumberIOApp {
 public static void main(String args[]) throws IOException {
  FileReader inFile = new FileReader("LineNumberIOApp.java");
  LineNumberReader inLines = new LineNumberReader(inFile);
  String inputLine;
  while ((inputLine=inLines.readLine()) != null) {
   System.out.println(inLines.getLineNumber()+". "+inputLine);
  }
 }
}
```

Filtered Character I/O

The FilterReader and FilterWriter classes are character-oriented analogs of the FilterInputStream and FilterOutputStream classes. The FilterReader class uses the in variable for input filtering, and FilterWriter class uses the out variable for output filtering. Consult the "Filtered I/O" section earlier in this chapter for a description of I/O filtering.

The PushbackReader Class

The PushbackReader class is a subclass of FilterReader that provides the capability to push a character that was previously read back onto the input stream so that it can be read again. It is the character-oriented analog of the PushbackInputStream class that you studied earlier in the chapter.

The PipedReader and PipedWriter Classes

The PipedReader and PipedWriter classes support character-oriented piped I/O in the same way as PipedInputStream and PipedOutputStream support byte-oriented piped I/O. Consult the section, "Piped I/O," earlier in this chapter for a description of piped input and output.

The PrintWriter Class

The PrintWriter class is the character-oriented replacement for the PrintStream class. As of Java 1.1, the PrintStream constructors have been deprecated. PrintWriter is now the preferred class for character printing. The PrintWriter class improves PrintStream by using a platform-dependent line separator to print lines instead of the new line (\n) character. The System line.separator property identifies the system unique line separator. PrintWriter also provides better support for Unicode characters than PrintStream. The checkError() method is used to flush printed output and test for an error condition. The setError() method is used to set an error condition. PrintWriter provides support for printing primitive data types, character arrays, strings, and general objects. Objects are converted to a string (via the inherited or overridden toString() method) before being printed.

The RandomAccessFile Class

The RandomAccessFile class provides the capability to perform I/O directly to specific locations within a file. The name *random access* comes from the fact that data can be read from or written to random locations within a file rather than as a continuous stream of information. Random access is supported through the seek() method, which allows the pointer corresponding to the current file position to be set to arbitrary locations within the file.

RandomAccessFile implements both the DataInput and DataOuput interfaces. This provides the capability to perform I/O using primitive data types.

RandomAccessFile also supports basic file read/write permissions, allowing files to be accessed in read-only or read-write modes. A mode stream argument is passed to the RandomAccessFile constructor as r or rw, indicating read-only and read-write file access. The read-only access attribute may be used to prevent a file from being inadvertently modified.

RandomAccessFile introduces several new methods besides those inherited from Object and implemented from DataInput and DataOutput. These methods include seek(), getFilePointer(), and length(). The seek()method sets the file pointer to a particular location within the file. The getFilePointer()method returns the current location of the file pointer. The length()method returns the length of the file in bytes.

The RandomIOApp Program

The RandomIOApp program provides a simple demonstration of the capabilities of random-access I/O. It writes a boolean, int, char, and double value to a file and then uses the seek() method to seek offsetting location 1 within the file. This is the position after the first byte in the file. It then reads the int, char, and double values from the file and displays them to the console window. Next, it moves the file pointer to the beginning of the file and reads the boolean value that was first written to the file. This value is also written to the console window. The source code of the RandomIOApp program is shown in Listing 13.14.

Listing 13.14. The source code of the RandomIOApp program.

```
import java.lang.System;
import java.io.RandomAccessFile;
import java.io.IOException;

public class RandomIOApp {
 public static void main(String args[]) throws IOException {
  RandomAccessFile file = new RandomAccessFile("test.txt","rw");
  file.writeBoolean(true);
  file.writeInt(123456);
  file.writeChar('j');
  file.writeDouble(1234.56);
  file.seek(1);
  System.out.println(file.readInt());
  System.out.println(file.readChar());
  System.out.println(file.readDouble());
  file.seek(0);
  System.out.println(file.readBoolean());
  file.close();
 }
}
```

Although the processing performed by RandomIOApp is quite simple, it illustrates how random I/O allows you to move the file pointer to various locations within a file to directly access values and objects contained within the file.

The program's output is as follows:

```
123456
j
1234.56
true
```

The StreamTokenizer Class

The StreamTokenizer class is used by parsers to convert an input character stream into a stream of lexical tokens. It uses special methods to identify parser parameters such as ordinary, whitespace, quote, and comment characters. These methods also enable and disable number and end-of-line parsing.

Seven variables are defined for the StreamTokenizer class, four of which are constant class variables. The TT_EOF, TT_EOL, TT_NUMBER, and TT_WORD constants are used to identify the type of input token encountered when parsing the input stream. The ttype variable is set either to one of these constants or to a single character based on the kind of token that is read from the input stream. The TT_ constants are used to indicate a number, word, end of line, or end of file. When a word token is read, the actual word is stored in the sval variable and ttype is set to TT_WORD. When a number token is read, its value is stored in the nval variable and ttype is set to TT_NUMBER. When other special characters, such as @ or *, are read from the input stream, they are assigned directly to the ttype variable.

The StreamTokenizer constructor takes a Reader object as an argument and generates a StreamTokenizer object. The StreamTokenizer access methods can be divided into two groups: parser parameter–definition methods and stream-processing methods.

The parser parameter–definition methods are used to control the operation of the parser. The commentChar(), slashSlashComments(), and slashStarComments() methods are used to define comments. Comments are ignored by the parser. The whitespaceChars(), wordChars(), quoteChar(), ordinaryChar(), and ordinaryChars() methods are used to set the parser's token-generation parameters. The parseNumbers() and eolIsSignificant() methods toggle number and end-of-line parsing. The lowerCaseMode() method controls whether input words are converted to lowercase, and the resetSyntax() method is used to reset the syntax table, causing all characters to be treated as special characters.

The stream-processing methods are used to read tokens from the input stream, push tokens back out onto the input stream, and return the current line number associated with the input stream. The nextToken() method is used to get the next token from the input stream. The pushBack() method pushes the current token back out onto the input stream. The lineno() method returns the current line number associated with the input stream.

The toString() method of class Object is overwritten to allow printing of the current token.

The StreamTokenApp Program

The StreamTokenApp program, shown in Listing 13.15, demonstrates the ease with which StreamTokenizer can be used to create a parser. This program reads input from the standard input stream, parses input tokens, and displays the token type and value to the console window.

Listing 13.15. The source code of the StreamTokenApp program.

```
import java.lang.System;
import java.io.StreamTokenizer;
import java.io.InputStreamReader;
import java.io.BufferedReader;
import java.io.IOException;

public class StreamTokenApp {
 public static void main(String args[]) throws IOException {
  BufferedReader inData =
   new BufferedReader(new InputStreamReader(System.in));
  StreamTokenizer inStream = new StreamTokenizer(inData);
  inStream.commentChar('#');
  boolean eof = false;
  do {
   int token=inStream.nextToken();
   switch(token){
   case inStream.TT_EOF:
    System.out.println("EOF encountered.");
    eof = true;
    break;
   case inStream.TT_EOL:
    System.out.println("EOL encountered.");
    break;
   case inStream.TT_WORD:
    System.out.println("Word: "+inStream.sval);
    break;
   case inStream.TT_NUMBER:
    System.out.println("Number: "+inStream.nval);
    break;
   default:
    System.out.println((char) token+" encountered.");
    if(token=='!') eof=true;
   }
  } while(!eof);
 }
}
```

The program creates a new object of class BufferedReader using System.in as an argument. It converts the BufferedReader object into a StreamTokenizer object and assigns it to the inStream variable. It then sets the comment-line character to #.

Having set up the parser, StreamTokenApp reads tokens from inStream until the end of file is encountered. It uses a switch statement to identify the type and value of each token read.

The following is an example of the output produced by StreamTokenizer. Try running it with different input lines. An exclamation point (!) is used to terminate the program's execution:

```
This is a test.
Word: This
Word: is
Word: a
Word: test.
123 456
Number: 123.0
Number: 456.0
12.34 56.78
Number: 12.34
Number: 56.78
@ $ % ^
@ encountered.
$ encountered.
% encountered.
^ encountered.
#This is a comment
This is #a comment
Word: This
Word: is
!
! encountered.
```

Summary

In this chapter you learned to work with Java input and output streams to perform input and output using standard I/O, memory buffers, and files. You explored the input and output stream class hierarchy and learned to use stream filters to simplify I/O processing. You learned how the new Reader and Writer classes support character-oriented I/O. You also learned how to perform random-access I/O and how to use the StreamTokenizer class to construct an input parser. In Chapter 14 you will learn how to use the utility classes provided in the java.util packages.

14

Useful Tools in the
java.util and
java.math Packages

In this chapter you'll learn how to work with all the useful utility classes contained in the java.util and java.math packages. You'll learn to use the date-related classes, to generate random numbers using the Random class, and to work with data structures such as dictionaries, stacks, hash tables, vectors, and bit sets. You'll also learn about the data compression and checksum classes of java.util and the large number classes of java.math. When you finish this chapter you'll be able to make productive use of these classes in your own programs.

Date-Related Classes

The JDK 1.0 provided the Date class to encapsulate date and time as an object. In JDK 1.1, many of the functions of the Date class have been deprecated in favor of more international handling of date and time. The Calendar, GregorianCalendar, SimpleTimeZone, and TimeZone classes have been added to provide more comprehensive and international support of date and time. The DateFormat class of the java.text package has also been added to support international date formatting.

> **NOTE**
>
> A *deprecated* API element is one that has been replaced by an improved alternative. In most cases, the deprecated element may still be used. However, compiler warnings are generated to inform you that an improved alternative exists.

Date

The Date class encapsulates date and time information and allows date objects to be accessed in a system-independent manner.

Four of the six Date JDK 1.0 constructors have been deprecated. Only the default constructor, which creates a Date object with the current system date and time, and a constructor that creates a Date object from a long value are not deprecated in JDK 1.1.

The access methods defined by the Date class support comparisons between dates and provide access to specific date information, including the time zone offset. However, many of the JDK 1.0 methods have been deprecated in favor of methods provided by the Calendar, DateFormat, and TimeZone classes.

Calendar

The Calendar class provides support for date conversions that were previously implemented by the Date class. The support provided by Calendar is more comprehensive and international. The Calendar class is an abstract class that can be extended to provide conversions for specific calendar systems. The GregorianCalendar subclass supports the predominant calendar system used by many countries.

The Calendar class provides two constructors—a default parameterless constructor that constructs a calendar with the default TimeZone and Locale objects and a constructor that allows the TimeZone and Locale objects to be specified. It supplies many constants for accessing the days of the week, the months of the year, hours, minutes, seconds, milliseconds, and other values.

The Calendar class provides a number of methods for performing data comparisons, arithmetic, and conversions. The getInstance() method returns a locale-specific calendar that is a GregorianCalendar object, by default.

GregorianCalendar

The GregorianCalendar class is a subset of the Calendar class that supports calendar operations for most of the world. It supports the eras B.C. and A.D. by defining them as class constants. It provides seven constructors that allow GregorianCalendar objects to be created using a combination of different date, time, time zone, and locale values. Its methods override those provided by the Calendar class.

TimeZone

The TimeZone class is used to encapsulate the notion of a time zone. It allows you to work in the local time zone as well as time zones that are selected by a time zone ID. The TimeZone class keeps track of daylight savings time.

The TimeZone class provides a single parameterless constructor that creates a TimeZone object corresponding to the local time zone. The TimeZone class does not define any field variables.

The access methods of TimeZone allow you to get a list of available time zone IDs, to retrieve the local time zone (from the operating system), to get the local time zone offset (and adjust it for daylight savings time), and to create TimeZone objects for other time zone IDs.

SimpleTimeZone

The SimpleTimeZone class extends TimeZone to provide support for GregorianCalendar objects. It creates SimpleTimeZone objects using the time zone IDs and offsets defined in the TimeZone class. It provides methods for changing the way daylight savings time is calculated.

DateApp

The DateApp program illustrates the use of the date-related classes covered in the previous sections. It shows how Date, GregorianCalendar, and TimeZone objects are created and how to use their methods to access date/time information. The DateApp program is presented in Listing 14.1.

Listing 14.1. The source code of the DateApp program.

```java
import java.lang.System;
import java.util.Date;
import java.util.Calendar;
import java.util.GregorianCalendar;
import java.util.TimeZone;

public class DateApp {
 public static void main(String args[]){
  Date today = new Date();
  GregorianCalendar cal = new GregorianCalendar();
  cal.setTime(today);
  System.out.println("Today: ");
  displayDateInfo(cal);
  cal.clear();
  cal.set(2000,0,0);
  System.out.println("\nNew Years Day 2000: ");
  displayDateInfo(cal);
 }
 static void displayDateInfo(GregorianCalendar cal){
  String days[] = {"","Sun","Mon","Tue","Wed","Thu","Fri","Sat"};
  String months[] = {"January","February","March","April","May",
    "June","July","August","September","October","November",
    "December"};
  String am_pm[] = {"AM","PM"};
  System.out.println("Year: "+cal.get(Calendar.YEAR));
  System.out.println("Month: "+months[cal.get(Calendar.MONTH)]);
  System.out.println("Date: "+cal.get(Calendar.DATE));
  System.out.println("Day: "+days[cal.get(Calendar.DAY_OF_WEEK)]);
  System.out.println("Hour: "+(cal.get(Calendar.HOUR)+12)%13);
  System.out.println("Minute: "+cal.get(Calendar.MINUTE));
  System.out.println("Second: "+cal.get(Calendar.SECOND));
  System.out.println(am_pm[cal.get(Calendar.AM_PM)]);
  TimeZone tz=cal.getTimeZone();
  System.out.println("Time Zone: "+tz.getID());
 }
}
```

The program creates a Date object and a GregorianCalendar object using the default Date() and GregorianCalendar() constructors. The Date object is assigned to the today variable, and the GregorianCalendar object is assigned to the cal variable. The cal variable is updated with the current date by invoking its setTime() method with the Date object stored in today. The displayDateInfo() method is then invoked to display date and time information about the cal variable.

The clear() method of the Calendar class is invoked to reset the date of the GregorianCalendar object stored in cal. The set() method is used to set its date to New Year's 2000. There are several versions of the set() method, each of which takes a different set of parameters. The version used in DateApp takes the year, month, and date as parameters. Note that the month value ranges from 0 to 12, where the year and date values begin at 1. The displayDateInfo() method is invoked again to display information about the new calendar date.

The `displayDateInfo()` method creates the `days`, `months`, and `am_pm` arrays to define string values corresponding to the days of the week, months of the year, and a.m./p.m. It then prints a line corresponding to date and time values. These values are retrieved using the `get()` method of the `Calendar` class and the `Calendar` constants corresponding to date/time values. The `getTimeZone()` method of `Calendar` is invoked to retrieve the local `TimeZone` object. The `getID()` method of the `TimeZone` class is used to retrieve the local time zone ID string.

The output of the `DateApp` program follows. When you run the program, you will obviously get a different date for the first part of the program's processing. The following are the results that were displayed when I ran the program:

```
Today:
Year: 1997
Month: May
Date: 29
Day: Thu
Hour: 5
Minute: 13
Second: 27
PM
Time Zone: PST

New Years Day 2000:
Year: 2000
Month: January
Date: 1
Day:
Hour: 12
Minute: 0
Second: 0
AM
Time Zone: PST
```

The Random Class

The `Random` class provides a template for the creation of random number generators. It differs from the `random()` method of the `java.lang.Math` class in that it allows any number of random number generators to be created as separate objects. The `Math.random()` method provides a `static` function for the generation of random `double` values. This `static` method is shared by all program code.

Objects of the `Random` class generate random numbers using a linear congruential formula. Two constructors are provided for creating `Random` objects. The default constructor initializes the seed of the random number generator using the current system time. The other constructor allows the seed to be set to an initial `long` value.

The `Random` class provides eight access methods; seven of which are used to generate random values. The `next()`, `nextInt()`, `nextLong()`, `nextFloat()`, and `nextDouble()` methods generate values for the numeric data types. The values generated by `nextFloat()` and `nextDouble()` are between 0.0 and 1.0. The `nextGaussian()` method generates a Gaussian distribution of double values with mean 0.0 and standard deviation 1.0. The `nextBytes()` method generates a random byte array.

The `setSeed()` method is used to reset the seed of the random number generator.

RandomApp

The `RandomApp` program demonstrates the use of the `Random` class (see Listing 14.2). It creates an object of class `Random` using the default constructor and assigns it to `r`. This causes the random number generator to be seeded using the current system time. Three `for` loops are used to print random `int`, `double`, and Gaussian-distributed `double` values. Each loop prints four values.

Listing 14.2. The source code of the `RandomApp` program.

```
import java.lang.System;
import java.util.Random;

public class RandomApp {
 public static void main(String args[]){
  Random r = new Random();
  for(int i=0;i<4;++i) System.out.print(r.nextInt()+" ");
  System.out.println();
  r = new Random(123456789);
  for(int i=0;i<4;++i) System.out.print(r.nextDouble()+" ");
  System.out.println();
  r.setSeed(234567890);
  for(int i=0;i<4;++i) System.out.print(r.nextGaussian()+" ");
  System.out.println();
 }
}
```

The following is the output generated by the program when it was run on my computer:

```
-854287801 -2056322098 1372478715 1217144804
0.664038103272266 0.45695178590520646 0.39050647939140426 0.8933411602003871
0.11378145160284903 0.4122962630933344 -1.5726230841498485 0.07568285309772235
```

It will produce different results when it is run on your computer because the first line that is printed uses the `Random()` constructor to generate the output data.

The Enumeration Interface

The `Enumeration` interface provides two methods for stepping through an indexed set of objects or values: `hasMoreElements()` and `nextElement()`. The `hasMoreElements()` method enables you to determine whether more elements are contained in an `Enumeration` object. The `nextElement()` method returns the `nextElement()` contained by an object.

Enumeration-implementing objects are said to be *consumed* by their use. This means that the `Enumeration` objects cannot be restarted to reaccess through the elements they contain. Their elements may be accessed only once.

The `Enumeration` interface is implemented by the `StringTokenizer` class, as discussed later in the section "The `StringTokenizer` Class." It is also used to obtain a list of elements contained in a vector, as shown in the programming example of the next section.

The `Vector` Class

The `Vector` class provides the capability to implement a growable array. The array grows larger as more elements are added to it. The array may also be reduced in size, after some of its elements have been deleted. This is accomplished using the `trimToSize()` method.

`Vector` operates by creating an initial storage capacity and then adding to this capacity as needed. It grows by an increment defined by the `capacityIncrement` variable. The initial storage capacity and `capacityIncrement` can be specified in `Vector`'s constructor. A second constructor is used when you want to specify only the initial storage capacity. A third, default constructor specifies neither the initial capacity nor the `capacityIncrement`. This constructor lets Java figure out the best parameters to use for `Vector` objects.

The access methods provided by the `Vector` class support array-like operations and operations related to the size of `Vector` objects. The array-like operations allow elements to be added, deleted, and inserted into vectors. They also allow tests to be performed on the contents of vectors and specific elements to be retrieved. The size-related operations allow the byte size and number of elements of the vector to be determined and the vector size to be increased to a certain capacity or trimmed to the minimum capacity needed. Consult the `Vector` API page for a complete description of these methods.

VectorApp

The `VectorApp` program illustrates the use of vectors and the `Enumeration` interface. (See Listing 14.3.)

Listing 14.3. The source code of the `VectorApp` program.

```
import java.lang.System;
import java.util.Vector;
import java.util.Enumeration;

public class VectorApp {
 public static void main(String args[]){
  Vector v = new Vector();
  v.addElement("one");
  v.addElement("two");
  v.addElement("three");
```

continues

Listing 14.3. continued

```
    v.insertElementAt("zero",0);
    v.insertElementAt("oops",3);
    v.insertElementAt("four",5);
    System.out.println("Size: "+v.size());
    Enumeration enum = v.elements();
    while (enum.hasMoreElements())
      System.out.print(enum.nextElement()+" ");
    System.out.println();
    v.removeElement("oops");
    System.out.println("Size: "+v.size());
    for(int i=0;i<v.size();++i)
      System.out.print(v.elementAt(i)+" ");
    System.out.println();
  }
}
```

The program creates a `Vector` object using the default constructor and uses the `addElement()` method to add the strings `"one"`, `"two"`, and `"three"` to the vector. It then uses the `insertElementAt()` method to insert the strings `"zero"`, `"oops"`, and `"four"` at locations 0, 3, and 5 within the vector. The `size()` method is used to retrieve the vector size for display to the console window.

The `elements()` method of the `Vector` class is used to retrieve an enumeration of the elements that were added to the vector. A `while` loop is then used to cycle through and print the elements contained in the enumeration. The `hasMoreElements()` method is used to determine whether the enumeration contains more elements. If it does, the `nextElement()` method is used to retrieve the object for printing.

The `removeElement()` of the `Vector` class is used to remove the vector element containing the string `"oops"`. The new size of the vector is displayed and the elements of the vector are redisplayed. The `for` loop indexes each element in the vector using the `elementAt()` method.

The output of the `VectorApp` program is as follows:

```
Size: 6
zero one two oops three four
Size: 5
zero one two three four
```

The Stack Class

The `Stack` class provides the capability to create and use stacks within your Java programs. *Stacks* are storage objects that store information by pushing it onto a stack and remove and retrieve information by popping it off the stack. Stacks implement a last-in-first-out storage capability. The last object pushed on a stack is the first object that can be retrieved from the stack. The `Stack` class extends the `Vector` class.

The Stack class provides a single default constructor, Stack(), that is used to create an empty stack.

Objects are placed on the stack using the push() method and retrieved from the stack using the pop() method. The search() method allows you to search through a stack to see whether a particular object is contained on the stack. The peek() method returns the top element of the stack without popping it off. The empty() method is used to determine whether a stack is empty. The pop() and peek() methods both throw the EmptyStackException if the stack is empty. Use of the empty() method can help to avoid the generation of this exception.

StackApp

The StackApp program demonstrates the operation of a stack (see Listing 14.4). It creates a Stack object and then uses the push() method to push the strings "one", "two", and "three" onto the stack. Because the stack operates in last-in-first-out fashion, the top of the stack is the string "three". This is verified by using the peek() method. The contents of the stack are then popped off and printed using a while loop. The empty() method is used to determine when the loop should terminate. The pop() method is used to pop objects off the top of the stack.

Listing 14.4. The source code of the StackApp program.

```
import java.lang.System;
import java.util.Stack;

public class StackApp {
 public static void main(String args[]){
  Stack s = new Stack();
  s.push("one");
  s.push("two");
  s.push("three");
  System.out.println("Top of stack: "+s.peek());
  while (!s.empty())
   System.out.println(s.pop());
 }
}
```

The output of the StackApp program is as follows:

```
Top of stack: three
three
two
one
```

The BitSet Class

The BitSet class is used to create objects that maintain a set of bits. The bits are maintained as a growable set. The capacity of the bit set is increased, as needed. Bit sets are used to maintain a list of *flags* that indicate the state of each element of a set of conditions. Flags are `boolean` values that are used to represent the state of an object.

Two `BitSet` constructors are provided. One allows the initial capacity of a `BitSet` object to be specified. The other is a default constructor that initializes a `BitSet` to a default size.

The `BitSet` access methods provide and, or, and exclusive or logical operations on bit sets, enable specific bits to be set and cleared, and override general methods declared for the `Object` class.

BitSetApp

The `BitSetApp` program demonstrates the operation of bit sets. (See Listing 14.5.)

Listing 14.5. The source code of the `BitSetApp` program.

```
import java.lang.System;
import java.util.BitSet;

public class BitSetApp {
 public static void main(String args[]){
   int size = 8;
   BitSet b1 = new BitSet(size);
   for(int i=0;i<size;++i) b1.set(i);
   BitSet b2 = (BitSet) b1.clone();
   for(int i=0;i<size;i=i+2) b2.clear(i);
   System.out.print("b1: ");
   for(int i=0;i<size;++i) System.out.print(b1.get(i)+" ");
   System.out.print("\nb2: ");
   for(int i=0;i<size;++i) System.out.print(b2.get(i)+" ");
   System.out.println();
   System.out.println("b1: "+b1);
   System.out.println("b2: "+b2);
   b1.xor(b2);
   System.out.println("b1 xor b2 = "+b1);
   b1.and(b2);
   System.out.println("b1 and b2 = "+b1);
   b1.or(b2);
   System.out.println("b1 or b2 = "+b1);
 }
}
```

The program begins by creating a `BitSet` object, b1, of size 8. It executes a `for` statement to index through b1 and set each bit in the bit set. It then uses the `clone()` method to create an identical copy of b1 and assign it to b2. Another `for` statement is executed to clear every even-numbered bit in b2. The values of the b1 and b2 bit sets are then printed. This results in the display of two lists of `boolean` values. The bit sets are printed as objects, resulting in a set-oriented display. Only the bits with `true` `boolean` values are identified as members of the displayed bit sets.

The `xor()` method is used to compute the exclusive or of b1 and b2, updating b1 with the result. The new value of b1 is then displayed.

The `and()` method is used to calculate the logical and of b1 and b2, again, updating b1 with the result and displaying b1's new value.

Finally, the logical or of b1 and b2 is computed, using the `or()` method. The result is used to update b1, and b1's value is displayed.

The output of `BitSetApp` is as follows:

```
b1: true true true true true true true true
b2: false true false true false true false true
b1: {0, 1, 2, 3, 4, 5, 6, 7}
b2: {1, 3, 5, 7}
b1 xor b2 = {0, 2, 4, 6}
b1 and b2 = {}
b1 or b2 = {1, 3, 5, 7}
```

The `Dictionary`, `Hashtable`, and `Properties` Classes

The `Dictionary`, `Hashtable`, and `Properties` classes are three generations of classes that implement the capability to provide key-based data storage and retrieval. The `Dictionary` class is the abstract superclass of `Hashtable`, which is, in turn, the superclass of `Properties`.

Dictionary

`Dictionary` provides the abstract functions used to store and retrieve objects by key–value associations. The class allows any object to be used as a key or value. This provides great flexibility in the design of key-based storage and retrieval classes. `Hashtable` and `Properties` are two examples of these classes.

The `Dictionary` class can be understood using its namesake abstraction. A real-world hardcopy dictionary maps words to their definitions. The words can be considered the keys of the dictionary and the definitions can be considered the values of the keys. Java dictionaries operate in the same fashion. One object is used as the key to access another object. This abstraction will become clearer as you investigate the `Hashtable` and `Properties` classes.

The `Dictionary` class defines several methods that are inherited by its subclasses. The `elements()` method is used to return an `Enumeration` object containing the values of the key–value pairs stored within the dictionary. The `keys()` method returns an enumeration of the dictionary keys. The `get()` method is used to retrieve an object from the dictionary based on its key. The `put()` method puts a `Value` object in the dictionary and indexes it using a `Key` object. The `isEmpty()` method determines whether a dictionary contains any elements, and the `size()`method identifies the dictionary's size in terms of the number of elements it contains. The `remove()`method deletes a key–value pair from the dictionary, based on the object's key.

Hashtable

The `Hashtable` class implements a hash table data structure. A *hash table* indexes and stores objects in a dictionary using hash codes as the objects' keys. *Hash codes* are integer values that identify objects. They are computed in such a manner that different objects are very likely to have different hash values and, therefore, different dictionary keys.

The `Object` class implements the `hashCode()` method. This method allows the hash code of an arbitrary Java object to be calculated. All Java classes and objects inherit this method from `Object`. The `hashCode()` method is used to compute the hash code key for storing objects within a hash table. `Object` also implements the `equals()` method. This method is used to determine whether two objects with the same hash code are, in fact, equal.

The Java `Hashtable` class is very similar to the `Dictionary` class from which it is derived. Objects are added to a hash table as key–value pairs. The object used as the key is hashed, using its `hashCode()` method, and the hash code is used as the actual key for the value object. When an object is to be retrieved from a hash table, using a key, the key's hash code is computed and used to find the object.

The `Hashtable` class provides three constructors. The first constructor allows a hash table to be created with a specific initial capacity and load factor. The *load factor* is a `float` value between 0.0 and 1.0 that identifies the percentage of hash table usage that causes the hash table to be rehashed into a larger table. For example, suppose a hash table is created with a capacity of 100 entries and a 0.70 load factor. When the hash table is 70 percent full, a new, larger hash table will be created, and the current `Hashtable` entries will have their hash values recalculated for the larger table.

The second `Hashtable` constructor just specifies the table's initial capacity and ignores the load factor. The default hash table constructor does not specify either hash table parameter.

The access methods defined for the `Hashtable` class allow key–value pairs to be added to and removed from a `Hashtable`, search the hash table for a particular key or object value, create an enumeration of the table's keys and values, determine the size of the hash table, and recalculate the hash table, as needed. Many of these methods are inherited or overridden from the `Dictionary` class.

HashApp

The `HashApp` program illustrates the operation and use of hash tables. (See Listing 14.6.)

Listing 14.6. The source code of the HashApp program.

```
import java.lang.System;
import java.util.Hashtable;
import java.util.Enumeration;

public class HashApp {
 public static void main(String args[]){
  Hashtable h = new Hashtable();
  h.put("height","6 feet");
  h.put("weight","200 pounds");
  h.put("eye color","blue");
  h.put("hair color","brown");
  System.out.println("h: "+h);
  Enumeration enum = h.keys();
  System.out.print("keys: ");
  while (enum.hasMoreElements()) System.out.print(enum.nextElement()+", ");
  System.out.print("\nelements: ");
  enum = h.elements();
  while (enum.hasMoreElements()) System.out.print(enum.nextElement()+", ");
  System.out.println();
  System.out.println("height: "+h.get("height"));
  System.out.println("weight: "+h.get("weight"));
  System.out.println("eyes: "+h.get("eye color"));
  System.out.println("hair: "+h.get("hair color"));
  h.remove("weight");
  System.out.println("h: "+h);
 }
}
```

The program begins by creating a Hashtable object using the default constructor. It then adds four key–value pairs to the hash table using the put() method. The hash table is then printed using the default print method for objects of class Hashtable.

The keys() method is used to create an enumeration of the hash table's keys. These keys are then printed one at a time by indexing through the enumeration object.

The elements() method is used to create an enumeration of the hash table's values. This enumeration is printed in the same way as the key enumeration.

The values of the hash table are again displayed by using the get() method to get the values corresponding to specific key values.

Finally, the remove() method is used to remove the key–value pair associated with the weight key, and the hash table is reprinted using the default print convention.

The program output is as follows:

```
h: {height=6 feet, weight=200 pounds, eye color=blue, hair color=brown}
keys: height, weight, eye color, hair color,
elements: 6 feet, 200 pounds, blue, brown,
height: 6 feet
weight: 200 pounds
eyes: blue
```

```
hair: brown
h: {height=6 feet, eye color=blue, hair color=brown}
```

The Properties Class

The Properties class is a subclass of Hashtable that can be read from or written to a stream. It also provides the capability to specify a set of default values to be used if a specified key is not found in the table. The default values themselves are specified as an object of class Properties. This allows an object of class Properties to have a default Properties object, which, in turn, has its own default properties and so on.

Properties supports two constructors: a default constructor with no parameters and a constructor that accepts the default properties to be associated with the Properties object being constructed.

The Properties class declares several new access methods. The getProperty() methods allows a property to be retrieved using a String object as a key. A second overloaded getProperty() method allows a value string to be used as the default in case the key is not contained in the Properties object.

The load() and save() methods are used to load a Properties object from an input stream and save it to an output stream. The save() method allows an optional header comment to be saved at the beginning of the saved object's position in the output stream.

The propertyNames() method provides an enumeration of all the property keys, and the list() method provides a convenient way to print a Properties object on a PrintStream object.

PropApp

The PropApp program illustrates the use of the Properties class by retrieving the System properties and displaying them to the console. (See Listing 14.7.)

Listing 14.7. The source code of the PropApp program.

```
import java.lang.System;
import java.util.Properties;

public class PropApp {
 public static void main(String args[]){
  Properties sysProp = System.getProperties();
  sysProp.list(System.out);
 }
}
```

The program uses the getProperties() method of the System class to retrieve the system properties and assign them to the sysProp variable. The system properties are then listed on the console window using the list() method.

The program's output will vary from machine to machine. Its output, when run from my computer, is as follows:

```
-- listing properties --
user.language=en
java.home=C:\jdk1.1.1
awt.toolkit=sun.awt.windows.WToolkit
file.encoding.pkg=sun.io
java.version=1.1.1
file.separator=\
line.separator=

user.region=US
file.encoding=8859_1
java.vendor=Sun Microsystems Inc.
user.timezone=PST
user.name=Jamie
os.arch=x86
os.name=Windows 95
java.vendor.url=http://www.sun.com/
user.dir=c:\jdk1.1.1\jdg\ch14
java.class.path=.;C:\JDK1.1.1\LIB\CLASSES.ZIP;C:\jdk1...
java.class.version=45.3
os.version=4.0
path.separator=;
user.home=\home\jamie
```

The `Locale` Class

The `Locale` class supports internationalization by describing geographic, political, or cultural regions. `Locale` objects are used to tailor program output to the conventions of that region. They are created using the `Locale()` constructors, which take `language` and `country` arguments and an optional `variant` argument. The `variant` argument is used to specify software-specific characteristics, such as operating system or browser. The `Locale` class defines constants for the most popular languages and countries. The access methods of `Locale` support the setting and retrieving of language, country, and variant-related values. Examples of using the `Locale` class are provided in Chapter 21, "Internationalization and the `java.text` Package."

The `ResourceBundle` Class

The `ResourceBundle` class also supports internationalization. `ResourceBundle` subclasses are used to store locale-specific resources that can be loaded by a program to tailor the program's appearance to the particular locale in which it is being run. Resource bundles provide the capability to isolate a program's locale-specific resources in a standard and modular manner.

The `ResourceBundle` class provides a single parameterless constructor. The `parent` field variable is used to identify the `ResourceBundle` class that is the parent of a particular class. This parent can be set using the `setParent()` method. The parent is used to find resources that are not available in a particular class.

The `ResourceBundle` access methods are used to retrieve the resources that are specific to a particular locale. The `ResourceBundle` class and its subclasses are covered in Chapter 21.

The `ListResourceBundle` Class

The `ListResourceBundle` class extends the `ResourceBundle` class to simplify access to locale-specific resources. It organizes resources in terms of an array of object pairs, where the first object is a `String` key and the second object is the key's value. The `getContents()` method returns the key-value array.

The `PropertyResourceBundle` Class

The `PropertyResourceBundle` class extends the `ResourceBundle` class to organize locale-specific resources using a property file. An `InputStream` object is supplied to the `PropertyResourceBundle()` constructor to enable reading of the property file.

The `StringTokenizer` Class

The `StringTokenizer` class is used to create a parser for `String` objects. It parses strings according to a set of delimiter characters. It implements the `Enumeration` interface in order to provide access to the tokens contained within a string. The `StringTokenizer` class is similar to the `StreamTokenizer` class covered in Chapter 13, "Stream-Based Input/Output and the `java.io` Package."

`StringTokenizer` provides three constructors. All three have the input string as a parameter. The first constructor includes two other parameters: a set of delimiters to be used in the string parsing and a `boolean` value used to specify whether the delimiter characters should be returned as tokens. The second constructor accepts the delimiter string but not the return token's toggle. The last constructor uses the default delimiter set consisting of the space, tab, newline, and carriage-return characters.

The access methods provided by `StringTokenizer` include the `Enumeration` methods, `hasMoreElements()` and `nextElement()`, `hasMoreTokens()` and `nextToken()`, and `countTokens()`. The `countTokens()` method returns the number of tokens in the string being parsed.

TokenApp

The `TokenApp` program prompts the user to enter a line of keyboard input and then parses the line, identifying the number and value of the tokens that it found. (See Listing 14.8.)

Listing 14.8. The source code of the TokenApp program.

```
import java.lang.System;
import java.io.*;
import java.util.StringTokenizer;

public class TokenApp {
 public static void main(String args[]) throws IOException {
  BufferedReader keyboardInput = new BufferedReader(
   new InputStreamReader(System.in));
  int numTokens;
  do {
   System.out.print("=> ");
   System.out.flush();
   StringTokenizer st = new StringTokenizer(keyboardInput.readLine());
   numTokens = st.countTokens();
   System.out.println(numTokens+" tokens");
   while (st.hasMoreTokens())
    System.out.println(" "+st.nextToken());
  } while(numTokens!=0);
 }
}
```

The program begins by creating a BufferedReader object using the System.in stream as an argument to its constructor. A do loop is used to read a line of input from the user, construct a StringTokenizer object on the input line, display the number of tokens in the line, and display each token as parsed using the standard delimiter set. The loop continues until a line with no tokens is entered.

The program's output is as follows:

```
=> this is a test
4 tokens
 this
 is
 a
 test
=> 1 2 3 4.5 6
5 tokens
 1
 2
 3
 4.5
 6
=> @ # $ % ^
5 tokens
 @
 #
 $
 %
 ^
=>
0 tokens
```

Observer **and** Observable

The Observer interface and Observable class are used to implement an abstract system by which observable objects can be observed by objects that implement the Observer interface. *Observable* objects are objects that subclass the abstract Observable class. These objects maintain a list of observers. When an observable object is updated, it invokes the update() method of its observers to notify the observers that it has changed state.

The update() method is the only method that is specified in the Observer interface. The update() method is used to notify an observer that an observable has changed. The method takes the observable object and a second notification message Object as its parameters.

Observable

The Observable class is an abstract class that must be subclassed by observable objects. It provides several methods for adding, deleting, and notifying observers and for manipulating change status. These methods are described in the class's API page.

The EventObject Class and the EventListener Interface

The EventObject class is the top-level class of the Java event hierarchy. *Events* represent actions that occur during the course of program execution. Most events are generated as the result of user actions such as mouse clicks and keyboard actions. The java.awt.event package declares event classes that are subclasses of EventObject. The EventObject class contains a single constructor that identifies the object that is the source of the event. This object is accessible through the source field variable. The EventObject class also provides the getSource() method for accessing the event source.

Events are *handled* by responding to their occurrence and providing feedback to the user. Java 1.1 provides the capability to deliver events to specific objects—a capability that was lacking in Java 1.0.

It makes use of special classes, called *adapter classes,* whose objects *listen* for the occurrence of events on behalf of objects of other classes. These classes implement event listener interfaces that specify methods for identifying and responding to the occurrence of related events. The EventListener interface is the top-level interface that all listener interfaces must implement. It is an empty interface and does not declare any methods.

You'll learn more about events, event listeners, and event handling in Part IV, "Window Programming," (Chapters 23 through 33) where you'll create event handlers for handling window-related events.

The `java.util.zip` Package

The `java.util.zip` package provides one interface and fourteen classes to support the compression and decompression of files and streams and to support checksum calculation. These classes are described in the following sections.

Checksum

The `Checksum` interface provides four methods that support checksum calculation. The `getValue()` method returns the current value of a checksum. The `reset()` method resets a checksum to its initial value. The two `update()` methods update a checksum based on a single byte or an array of bytes.

Adler32

The `Adler32` class implements the `Checksum` interface to compute an `Adler32` checksum. The `Adler32` checksum is computed quickly, but is less reliable than the `CRC32` checksum.

CRC32

The `CRC32` class implements the `Checksum` interface to calculate a standard 32-bit cyclic redundancy code.

CheckedInputStream

The `CheckedInputStream` class extends the `FilterInputStream` class of `java.io` to include a checksum calculation for data read from the stream. The checksum is used to verify the integrity of the stream's data. The `CheckedInputStream()` constructor creates a `CheckedInputStream` object from an `InputStream` object and an object that implements the `Checksum` interface. The `getChecksum()` method returns the `Checksum` object associated with the stream. Other methods support low-level input.

CheckedOutputStream

The `CheckedOutputStream` class extends the `FilterOutputStream` class of `java.io` to include a checksum calculation for data written to the stream. The checksum is used to verify the integrity of the stream's data. The `CheckedOutputStream()` constructor creates a `CheckedOutputStream` object from an `OutputStream` object and an object that implements the `Checksum` interface. The `getChecksum()` method returns the `Checksum` object associated with the stream. Other methods support low-level output.

Deflater

The `Deflater` class supports compression using the compression approaches described in Request For Comments (RFCs) 1950, 1951, and 1952. RFCs are publicly available Internet standards that can be found at `ftp://ds.internic.net/rfc/`. The `Deflater` class supports the following compression levels and strategies, as defined by its field constants:

■ `BEST_COMPRESSION`—Most compression

■ `BEST_SPEED`—Fastest compression

■ `DEFAULT_COMPRESSION`—Default trade-off between compression and speed

■ `DEFAULT_STRATEGY`—Default compression strategy

■ `DEFLATED`—Simple deflation

■ `FILTERED`—Emphasizes Huffman coding over string matching

■ `HUFFMAN_ONLY`—Uses Huffman coding and not string matching

■ `NO_COMPRESSION`—Turns compression off

The compression level can be selected when constructing a `Deflater` object.

The methods of the `Deflater` class support data compression, the selection of a compression level and strategy, and the use of preset data dictionaries. These methods perform block-oriented compression on byte arrays.

Inflater

The `Inflater` class is used to decompress data that is compressed by the `Deflater` class. This decompression is also covered in RFCs 1950, 1951, and 1952. The `Inflater()` constructor provides the `nowrap` parameter to support GZIP- and PKZIP-compatible compression. GZIP compression is the Gnu public version of the commercial PKZIP compression algorithm developed by Phil Katz.

The methods of the `Inflater` class support decompression and the use of preset data dictionaries. These methods perform block-oriented decompression on byte arrays.

DeflaterOutputStream

The `DeflaterOutputStream` class extends the `FilterOutputStream` class to provide support for stream-oriented compression. Its two field variables, `buf` and `def`, identify the output buffer used to write compressed data and the type of compressor in use. The `DeflaterOutputStream()` constructors allow the `OutputStream` and `Deflater` objects to be specified, as well as the output buffer size.

The `deflate()` method writes the next block of compressed data to the output stream. The `finish()` method completes the compression of the output stream by writing all compressed data to the stream. Other methods support low-level data output.

InflaterInputStream

The `InflaterInputStream` class is the input analog of the `DeflaterOutputStream` class. `InflaterInputStream` reads and decompresses data that is written to a compressed output stream using a `DeflaterOutputStream` object. It extends the `FilterInputStream` class of `java.io`.

`InflaterInputStream` defines three field variables: `buf`, `inf`, and `len`. These variables identify the input buffer used for decompression, the type of decompressor to be used, and the length of the input buffer. The `InflaterInputStream()` constructors allow `InputStream` and `Inflater` objects to be specified, as well as the input buffer size.

The `fill()` method is used to fill the input buffer with compressed data. Other methods are used to read uncompressed data from the stream.

GZIPOutputStream

The `GZIPOutputStream` class extends `DeflaterOutputStream` to support GZIP compression. It adds the `crc` field variable to calculate a `CRC32` checksum on the compressed data. The `GZIPOutputStream()` constructors allow the `OutputStream` object and the output buffer size to be specified.

GZIPInputStream

The `GZIPInputStream` class is the input analog of the `GZIPOutputStream` class. It extends `InflaterInputStream` and defines two additional variables and a constant. The `crc` variable identifies the `CRC32` checksum of the compressed data. The `eos` variable identifies the end of the output stream. The `GZIP_MAGIC` constant identifies the *magic number* of the GZIP header. Magic numbers are used to uniquely identify files of a given format. The `GZIPInputStream()` constructors allow the `InputStream` object and the input buffer size to be specified.

ZipFile

The `ZipFile` class is used to read `.ZIP` compressed files. The `ZipFile()` constructor opens a `.ZIP` file for reading. A `File` object or a `String` object containing a filename may be provided to the `ZipFile()` constructor.

The methods of the `ZipFile` class support the reading and examination of `.ZIP` files. They are as follows:

- ■ `entries()`—Returns an `Enumeration` object containing the `.ZIP` file entries.
- ■ `getEntry()`—Returns a `ZipEntry` object corresponding to the pathname passed as a string argument.
- ■ `getInputStream()`—Returns an `InputStream` object corresponding to the `ZipEntry` object passed as an argument to the method. The `InputStream` object is used to read the contents of the `ZipEntry` object.

- `getName()`—Returns the pathname of the .ZIP file.
- `close()`—Closes the .ZIP file.

ZipEntry

The `ZipEntry` class encapsulates a .ZIP file entry. It represents a compressed file that is stored within the .ZIP file. The DEFLATED and STORED constants are used to identify whether a .ZIP entry is compressed or merely stored as uncompressed data within the .ZIP file. The `ZipEntry()` constructor is used to create a named .ZIP file entry. Several methods are provided to read the following aspects of a `ZipEntry` object:

- Name of the entry
- Comment string
- Size of the compressed and uncompressed data
- CRC32 checksum of the compressed data
- Extra field data
- Compression method
- Modification time of the entry
- Whether the entry is a directory

Other methods are provided to set the comment string, CRC, extra field data, entry size, and time of modification. The `toString()` method is overridden to convert a `ZipEntry` object to a `String` object.

ZipOutputStream

The `ZipOutputStream` class extends the `DeflaterOutputStream` class to support the writing of file streams that are compressed in the .ZIP file format. The DEFLATED and STORED constants are used to identify whether data should be compressed (DEFLATED) or stored as uncompressed data (STORED). The `ZipOutputStream()` constructor creates a `ZipOutputStream` object from an `OutputStream` object.

In addition to low-level output methods, the `ZipOutputStream` class provides the following methods:

- `putNextEntry()`—Starts the writing of a new ZIP entry
- `closeEntry()`—Closes the current entry and positions the stream for writing the next entry
- `setMethod()`—Sets the compression method
- `setLevel()`—Sets the compression level
- `setComment()`—Sets the .ZIP file comment
- `finish()`—Completes the writing of the zipped output stream

ZipInputStream

The `ZipInputStream` class is the input analog to the `ZipOutputStream` class. It is used to read a compressed `.ZIP` format file. The `ZipInputStream` class extends the `InflaterInputStream` class.

The `ZipInputStream()` constructor creates a `ZipInputStream` object from an `InputStream` object. In addition to low-level input methods, it provides the `getNextEntry()` method for reading the next `.ZIP` file entry and the `closeEntry()` method for closing a `.ZIP` file entry.

The `UnzipApp` Program

The `UnzipApp` program, shown in Listing 14.9, illustrates the power of the `java.util.zip` in working with compressed files. This program can be used to unzip files in the `.ZIP` format.

Listing 14.9. The source code of the `UnzipApp` program.

```
import java.lang.System;
import java.util.*;
import java.util.zip.*;
import java.io.*;

public class UnzipApp {
 public static void main(String args[]) throws IOException {
  if(args.length==0) System.exit(0);
  ZipFile f = new ZipFile(args[0]);
  Enumeration entries = f.entries();
  System.out.println("Decompressing "+args[0]+" ...");
  while(entries.hasMoreElements()){
   ZipEntry entry = (ZipEntry) entries.nextElement();
   System.out.println("  "+entry.getName());
   InputStream in = f.getInputStream(entry);
   FileOutputStream out = new FileOutputStream(entry.getName());
   for(int ch=in.read();ch!=-1;ch=in.read()) out.write(ch);
   out.close();
   in.close();
  }
  f.close();
 }
}
```

To show how the program works, I've included the file `rfcs.zip` on the CD-ROM included with this book. This file contains the files `rfc1950.txt`, `rfc1951.txt`, and `rfc1952.txt` in compressed form. These files document the conventions and formats used for ZLIB, DEFLATE, and GZIP.

The `UnzipApp` program takes a single argument—the name of the file that you want to unzip. To unzip `rfcs.zip`, use:

```
java UnzipApp rfcs.zip
```

The program's output is as follows:

```
Decompressing rfcs.zip ...
   rfc1950.txt
   rfc1952.txt
   rfc1951.txt
```

The files `rfc1950.txt`, `rfc1951.txt`, and `rfc1952.txt` are created and placed in your current working directory.

The program makes use of the `ZipFile` and `ZipEntry` classes of `java.util.zip` and the `Enumeration` interface of `java.util`. It creates a new `ZipFile` object from the filename that you pass to the program as a command line argument. It then invokes the `entries()` method of `ZipFile` to create an `Enumeration` object of `ZipEntry` objects corresponding to the entries into the `ZipFile` object.

A `while` statement is used to loop through the `Enumeration` object and process each entry. The `hasMoreElements()` method of the `Enumeration` interface is used to determine whether all entries have been processed. The individual `ZipEntry` objects are extracted from the `Enumeration` object via the `nextElement()` method and assigned to the entry variable. The `getName()` method of the `ZipEntry` class is used to retrieve the filename associated with each `ZipEntry` object.

The `ZipEntry` objects are extracted to individual files by using the `getInputStream()` method of `ZipFile` to read the contents of the `ZipEntry` object and write this data to files that are created using the `FileOutputStream` class of `java.io`.

The `java.math` Package

The `java.math` package includes two classes, `BigDecimal` and `BigNumber`, that can be used to perform arbitrary precision mathematical calculations. The `BigDecimal` class supports decimal arithmetic, and the `BigInteger` class supports integer arithmetic. Both of these classes extend the `Number` class.

BigDecimal

The `BigDecimal` class is implemented as an arbitrary precision integer number and a non-negative scale value that identifies the number of digits to the right of the decimal point. `BigDecimal` provides eight modes for rounding support. These modes are defined using class constants:

- ■ `ROUND_CEILING`—Use `ROUND_UP` for positive numbers and `ROUND_DOWN` for negative numbers.
- ■ `ROUND_DOWN`—Round toward zero.
- ■ `ROUND_FLOOR`—Use `ROUND_DOWN` for positive numbers and `ROUND_UP` for negative numbers.

- ROUND_HALF_DOWN—Use ROUND_UP if the discarded fraction is greater than .5. Use ROUND_DOWN otherwise.

- ROUND_HALF_EVEN—Use ROUND_HALF_UP if the digit to the left of the discarded fraction is odd. Use ROUND_HALF_DOWN if the digit to the left of the discarded fraction is even.

- ROUND_HALF_UP—Use ROUND_UP if the discarded fraction is greater than or equal to .5. Otherwise, use ROUND_DOWN.

- ROUND_UNNECESSARY—An exception is thrown if rounding is required.

- ROUND_UP—Round away from zero.

These modes provide a great deal of flexibility in the rounding policy used by the BigDecimal class.

The BigDecimal class provides constructors that allow BigDecimal objects to be created from String, double, and BigInteger objects. The methods of BigDecimal support arithmetic operations, comparisons, rounding and scaling, and conversions to other types and classes.

BigInteger

The BigInteger class is similar to BigDecimal, but it is limited to integer operations. It does not have any public field values, like BigDecimal, because it does not deal with rounding. Its constructors allow BigInteger objects to be constructed from strings, byte arrays, and randomly within a specified range. Its methods support arithmetic, logical, bitwise, and comparison operations. Its methods also support modular arithmetic, greatest common divisor calculation, and prime number generation and testing.

The BigNumApp Program

The BigNumApp program illustrates the ease by which large number computations can be performed. It calculates the first number greater than a trillion (10 to the 12 power) that is probably prime. Listing 14.10 contains the source code of the BigNumApp program.

Listing 14.10. The source code of the BigNumApp program.

```
import java.lang.System;
import java.math.BigInteger;

public class BigNumApp {
 public static void main(String args[]){
  BigInteger n=new BigInteger("1000000000000");
  BigInteger one=new BigInteger("1");
  while(!n.isProbablePrime(7)) n=n.add(one);
  System.out.println(n.toString(10)+" is probably prime.");
  System.out.println("It is "+n.bitLength()+" bits in length.");
 }
}
```

The `BigNumApp` program creates a `BigInteger` equal to one trillion and assigns it to `n`. It then creates a `BigInteger` equal to 1 and assigns it to the one variable. It uses a `while` loop to test numbers greater than a trillion until it finds one that is probably prime with a certainty of 7. This certainty value means that the probability of the number being prime is (1 - (1/2**7)), which is greater than 99%. The `bitLength()` method is to determine the length of the prime number in bits.

The program's output is as follows:

```
1000000000039 is probably prime.
It is 40 bits in length.
```

Summary

In this chapter you learned how to work with all the useful utility classes contained in the `java.util` package. You learned to use date-related classes, to generate random numbers, and to work with a range of data structures, such as dictionaries, stacks, hash tables, vectors, and bit sets. You also learned how to use the data compression and checksum classes of `java.util` and the large number classes of `java.math`. In Chapter 15, "Windows Programming with the `java.awt` Packages," you'll preview the Java Abstract Windows Toolkit (AWT) and learn what window components are available to develop window-based programs using Java.

15

Window Programming with the `java.awt` Packages

This chapter introduces the classes and interfaces of the java.awt packages. These classes and interfaces provide the foundation for Java window programming. You'll learn how the java.awt package is organized and cover each of the classes that it contains. You'll also cover the java.awt.datatransfer, java.awt.event, and java.awt.image packages. This chapter, unlike others in Part III, "Using the Java API," does not provide programming examples. Part IV, "Window Programming," provides a detailed tutorial of Java window programming, including numerous programming examples.

Window Programming Classes

The Java *Abstract Windowing Toolkit* (AWT) provides numerous classes that support window program development. These classes are used to create and organize windows, implement GUI components, handle events, draw text and graphics, support clipboard operations and printing, perform image processing, and obtain access to the native windows implementation.

This chapter covers these classes in sections consisting of logically related classes. The "Components and Containers" section introduces the GUI components supported by the AWT and the windows classes that contain these components. The "Constructing Menus" section describes the classes that are used to implement menu bars and pull-down menus. The "Organizing Windows" section describes the classes that are used to organize windows and lay out the components they contain. The "Printing" section covers JDK 1.1 printing enhancements. The "Handling Events" section introduces the java.awt.event package and describes the process of Java event handling. The "Using the Clipboard" section introduces the java.awt.datatransfer package and covers clipboard operations. The "Working with Images" section introduces the Image class and the image-processing classes of the java.awt.image package. The "Geometrical Objects" section covers the Java classes that are used to represent points, rectangles, polygons, and dimensions. The "Using Fonts" section introduces the Font and FontMetrics classes and shows how to use these classes to control the display of text. The "Using the Toolkit" section describes the interface between the platform-independent AWT classes and their native platform-dependent implementations.

Components and Containers

The Component class is the superclass of the set of AWT classes that implement graphical user interface controls. These components include windows, dialog boxes, buttons, labels, text fields, and other common GUI components. The Component class provides a common set of methods that are used by all these subclasses. These include methods for working with event handlers, images, fonts, and colors. More than 100 methods are implemented by this class. It is a good idea to browse the API pages of the Component class to get a feel for the kinds of methods that are available. You don't have to worry about learning them now. The important methods are covered in Part IV.

Although Component contains many GUI-related subclasses, its Container subclass is the class used to define window objects that contain other objects. As such, it defines classes for working with application windows, dialog boxes, panels, and applets. The Container class and subclasses are covered in the next section. The classes for GUI controls are covered in later parts of that section.

The Container Class

The Container class is a subclass of the Component class that is used to define components that have the capability to contain other components. It provides methods for adding, retrieving, displaying, counting, and removing the components that it contains. The Container class also provides methods for working with layouts. The layout classes control the layout of components within a container.

The Container class has three major subclasses: Window, Panel, and ScrollPane. Window provides a common superclass for application main windows (Frame objects) and Dialog windows. The Panel class is a generic container that can be displayed within a window. It is subclassed by the java.applet.Applet class as the base class for all Java applets. The ScrollPane class was introduced with the JDK 1.1 in order to simplify the development of scrollable applications. The ScrollPane class is like a combination of a Panel and vertical and horizontal scrollbars.

The Window Class

The Window class provides an encapsulation of a generic Window object. It is subclassed by Frame and Dialog to provide the capabilities needed to support application main windows and dialog box support.

The Window class contains a single constructor that creates a window that has a frame window as its parent. The parent frame window is necessary because only objects of the Frame class or its subclasses contain the functionality needed to implement an independent application window.

The Window class implements important methods that are used by its Frame and Dialog subclasses. The pack() method is used to arrange the components contained in the window according to the window layout style. Layout classes are covered later in this chapter in the "Organizing Windows" section. The show() method is used to display a window. Windows are hidden (invisible), by default, and are only displayed as a result of invoking their show() method. The toFront() and toBack() methods are used to position windows relative to their frame window. The dispose() method is used to release the resources associated with a window and delete the Window object. The getWarningString() method is used to retrieve the warning message associated with untrusted windows. Warning messages are associated with windows that are created by applets.

A Window object does not have a border or a menu bar when it is created. In this state it may be used to implement a pop-up window. The default layout for a Window object is BorderLayout. You'll learn more about layouts in the "Organizing Windows" section later in this chapter.

Frame

The Frame class is used to provide the main window of an application. It is a subclass of Window that supports the capabilities to specify the icon, cursor, menu bar, and title. Because it implements the MenuContainer interface, it is capable of working with MenuBar objects.

The Frame class defines 14 constants that are used to specify different types of cursors to be used within the frame. As of JDK 1.1, a separate Cursor class is available for working with cursors.

Frame provides two constructors: a default parameterless constructor that creates an untitled frame window and a constructor that accepts a String argument to be used as the frame window's title. The second constructor is typically used.

Frame extends the set of access methods that it inherits from Window by adding methods to get and set the window title, icon image, and menu bar. Methods for removing the menu bar and specifying whether the window is resizable are also provided.

Dialog

The Dialog class is a subclass of the Window class that is used to implement dialog box windows. A dialog box is a window that takes input from the user. The Dialog class allows dialog boxes to be constructed that are modal. *Modal* dialog boxes must be closed before control returns to the window that launched them. The Dialog class also provides the capability to construct non-modal dialog boxes. *Non-modal* dialog boxes do not need to be closed before other program windows can be accessed.

The Dialog class provides four constructors. These constructors allow the Window object containing the dialog box to be specified as well as the modal flag and the dialog box's title.

The Dialog class provides only a handful of access methods. These methods are used to get and set its title, determine whether it is modal, and get and set the dialog box's resizable properties.

FileDialog

The FileDialog class is used to construct dialog boxes that support the selection of files for input and output operations. It is a subset of the Dialog class and provides three constructors. These constructors take as arguments the Frame window that contains the dialog box, the title to be used at the top of the dialog box, and a mode parameter that can be set to the LOAD or SAVE constants defined by FileDialog.

FileDialog provides methods that are used to access the directory and filename of the user-selected file and to specify an object that implements the FileNameFilter interface. The TextEditApp program of Chapter 23, "Opening Windows," shows how to use the FileDialog class.

Panel

The Panel class is a subclass of the Container class that is used to organize GUI components within other container objects. The methods used with Panel objects are inherited from the Component and Container classes. The Applet class of the java.applet package is a subclass of the Panel class. The default layout for a Panel object is FlowLayout.

ScrollPane

The ScrollPane class is a subclass of the Container class that is similar to a Panel with horizontal and vertical scrollbars. It provides constants that can be used to specify the scrollbar display policy. The methods of the ScrollPane class are used to control how a ScrollPane object is laid out and to get and set the position of the scrollbars. You'll learn more about the ScrollPane class in Chapter 29, "Scrollbars."

The Label Class

The Label class is used to display read-only text labels within a window or other GUI container. It has three constructors. The first constructor takes no parameters and is used to construct a blank label. The second constructor takes a String object as its parameter that is used to specify the label's text. The third constructor has an alignment parameter in addition to the text string. This parameter specifies how the label should be aligned within its container. The Label class defines the LEFT, CENTER, and RIGHT constants for use as alignment values.

The Label class provides methods to get and set the displayed label and its alignment value.

The Button Class

The Button class implements a clickable button GUI control. The button is capable of displaying a text label. Two Button constructors are provided. The first constructor takes no parameters and creates a button with a blank label. The second constructor accepts a String object that is displayed as the button's label. The Button class provides methods for getting and setting its label and for identifying event-handling code to handle button-related events.

The Checkbox Class

The Checkbox class is used to implement checkbox and radio button GUI controls. The checkbox or radio button is associated with a label. If a Checkbox object is not associated with a CheckboxGroup object, it is implemented as a traditional checkbox. If a Checkbox object is associated with a CheckboxGroup object, it is implemented as a radio button.

The Checkbox class provides five constructors that allow the checkbox label, initial state, and CheckboxGroup object to be specified. The Checkbox class provides methods for getting and setting the label and state of the checkbox and its CheckboxGroup object, if any. The state of the checkbox is boolean. The Checkbox class also provides methods for identifying event-handling code.

CheckboxGroup

The CheckboxGroup class is used with the Checkbox class to implement radio buttons. All Checkbox objects that are associated with a CheckboxGroup object are treated as a single set of radio buttons. Only one button in the group may be set or on at a given point in time. The CheckboxGroup provides a single, parameterless constructor. It also provides methods for getting and setting the Checkbox object.

The Choice Class

The Choice class is used to implement pull-down lists that can be placed in the main area of a window. These lists are known as *option menus* or a *pop-up menu of choices* and allow the user to select a single menu value. The Choice class provides a single, parameterless constructor. It also provides access methods that are used to add items to the list, count the number of items contained in the list, select a list item, handle events, and determine which list item is selected.

The List Class

The List class implements single- and multiple-selection list GUI controls. The lists provided by the List class are more sophisticated than those provided by the Choice class: The List class provides the capability to specify the size of the scrollable window in which the list items are displayed and to select multiple items from the list. The List class has three constructors. The first one takes no parameters and constructs a generic List object. The second one allows the number of rows of the visible window to be specified. The third constructor allows the number of rows to be specified and whether or not multiple selections are allowed.

The List class provides several access methods that are used to add, delete, and replace list items, count the number of items in the list, determine which items are selected, handle events, and select items within the list.

The TextComponent Class

The TextComponent class is the superclass of all text-based classes. It provides a common set of methods used by its TextField and TextArea subclasses. It does not provide any constructors and cannot be instantiated. It provides methods for getting and setting the text that is displayed in a text object, setting the text object to an editable or read-only state, handling text editing events, and selecting text that is contained within an object.

TextField

The `TextField` class implements a one-line text entry field. It provides four constructors that are used to specify the width of the text field in character columns and the default text to be displayed within the field. It provides several methods for accessing the field's size and for specifying whether the characters typed by the user should be displayed. The `setEchoCharacter()` method is used to specify a character that is to be displayed in lieu of text typed by the user. This method is used to implement password-like fields.

TextArea

The `TextArea` class implements scrollable text entry objects that span multiple lines and columns. It provides five constructors that allow the number of rows and columns and the default text display to be specified. It provides several methods that return the dimensions of the text area and insert, append, and replace the text that is contained in the text area. It also provides the capability to set the text to read-only or edit mode.

The `Canvas` Class

The `Canvas` class implements a GUI object that supports drawing. Drawing is not implemented on the canvas itself, but on the `Graphics` object provided by the canvas. The `Canvas` class is usually subclassed to implement a custom graphics object. It provides a single, parameterless constructor and one useful method—the `paint()` method, which specifies how its `Graphics` object is to be updated.

Graphics

The `Graphics` class supports the drawing of graphical objects and text within a window. It is used with all graphical applications. The `Graphics` class is an abstract class that is created through methods of other classes. A `Graphics` object is typically provided as an argument to the `paint()` method of a `Canvas` object.

The `Graphics` class provides numerous methods for drawing lines, ovals, rectangles, polygons, text, images, and other objects that can be displayed within a window. It also provides methods for setting the foreground and background colors and the current text font. You should browse through the API description of this class to get a feel for all the methods it provides.

The `Scrollbar` Class

The `Scrollbar` class is used to implement vertical and horizontal scrollbars. It provides three constructors that allow the orientation of the scrollbar to be specified, as well as parameters that control the scrollbar's operation. It provides several methods that allow the scrollbar's parameters and current value to be read and set. See Chapter 29 for more information.

The `Adjustable` Interface

The `Adjustable` interface defines methods that are implemented by user-adjustable window components. This interface is implemented by the `Scrollbar` and `ScrollPane` classes. The methods specified by the `Adjustable` interface support the reading and writing of the value of the adjusted object and the identification of event-handling code.

The `ItemSelectable` Interface

The `ItemSelectable` interface is implemented by GUI components that support the selection of items from a list. The methods of this interface are used to determine what item is selected and to handle item-selection events.

Constructing Menus

Java provides several classes that allow menu bars to be constructed and attached to a `Frame` window. These classes are directly descended from the `Object` class and are not subclasses of the component class.

The `MenuComponent` class is the superclass of the menu-related classes and provides a common set of methods that are used by its subclasses. The `MenuComponent` class provides a default parameterless constructor, although objects of this class should not be directly created. The `getFont()` and `setFont()` methods are used to specify the font to be used with a `MenuComponent` object. The `getParent()` method is used to retrieve an object that implements the `MenuContainer` interface and contains a specified `MenuComponent` object. The `getName()` and `setName()` methods are used to access the name of a `MenuComponent` object. Other methods are provided to support menu-related event handling.

The `MenuBar` Class

The `MenuBar` class implements a menu bar that is attached to a `Frame` window. It provides a default parameterless constructor and several access methods for adding and removing `Menu` objects from the menu bar. It also provides methods that are used to return the current number of menus, work with menu shortcuts, and to get and set a special help menu.

The `MenuItem` Class

The `MenuItem` class is used to implement items that may be selected from a pull-down menu. It is extended by the `Menu` and `CheckboxMenuItem` classes. The `MenuItem` class implements items that can be selected from a pull-down menu. Because it is subclassed by the `Menu` and `CheckboxMenuItem` classes, it provides the capability for objects of these classes to be selected from a pull-down menu. This allows multiple levels of menus to be implemented.

The MenuItem class provides three constructors that take a String object and a MenuShortcut object as parameters. The String object is used as the label of the menu item. The MenuShortcut object is used to assign a keyboard accelerator to the MenuItem object.

The MenuItem class provides methods for enabling and disabling a menu item and for getting and setting its label.

The Menu Class

The Menu class implements a single pull-down menu that is attached to a menu bar or other menu. It provides three constructors that allow the menu's label to be specified and determine whether it is to be implemented as a tear-off menu. It also provides methods that are used to add or remove menu items, add menu separators, count the number of items in the menu, and determine what menu item is currently selected.

The CheckboxMenuItem Class

The CheckboxMenuItem class is used to implement menu items that may be checked on or off. It provides three constructors that take as arguments the label to be used with the checkbox menu item and the initial state of the checkbox menu item. The setState()and getState() methods are used to determine the checked state of the menu item. Other methods are provided to support event processing.

The PopupMenu Class

The PopupMenu class was introduced with the JDK 1.1. It allows context-specific menus to be popped up in response to mouse events. In Windows 95, this event is the clicking of the right mouse button. The PopupMenu class is a subclass of the Menu class and inherits the Menu class methods. It provides a single constructor that takes the name of the menu as an argument. The show()method is used to display a PopupMenu object at a specific position relative to a Container object.

The MenuShortcut Class

The MenuShortcut class is a new class introduced with the JDK 1.1. It allows keyboard inputs to be associated with menu items. Its two constructors take the integer value of the keyboard input as an argument. A boolean value indicating whether the Shift key needs to be pressed can also be supplied. The integer keyboard value is defined by the keyCode field of the KeyEvent class of java.awt.event.

The MenuContainer **Interface**

The MenuContainer interface provides a set of methods that are implemented by classes that contain menus. These methods are getFont(), postEvent(), and remove(). The getFont() method returns the current font associated with a menu object. The postEvent() method is used to generate a menu-related event. The remove() method is used to remove a MenuComponent object.

Organizing Windows

The method by which the components of a Container object are organized is determined by an object that implements the LayoutManager interface. The layout of a Container is specified using the setLayout() method of the Container class. It passes an object that implements the LayoutManager interface as a parameter.

The LayoutManager **and** LayoutManager2 **Interfaces**

The LayoutManager interface provides a set of methods that are implemented by classes that control the layout of a container. These methods include those that add or remove components from a layout, specify the size of the container, and lay out the components of the container. The LayoutManager2 interface extends the LayoutManager interface to deal with constraint-based layouts.

The BorderLayout **Class**

The BorderLayout class is used to lay out the GUI components contained in a Container object. It lays out components along the North, South, East, and West borders of the container and in the center of the container. The center component gets any space left over from the North, South, East, and West border components. It is the default layout for the Window, Frame, and Dialog classes. It provides the capability to specify the horizontal and vertical gap between the laid out components and the container.

The CardLayout **Class**

The CardLayout class is used to lay out the components of a Container object in the form of a deck of cards where only one card is visible at a time. The class provides methods that are used to specify the first, last, next, and previous components in the container.

The FlowLayout **Class**

The FlowLayout class is used to lay out the components of a Container object in a left-to-right, top-to-bottom fashion. It is the default layout used with the Panel class. It allows the alignment of the components it lays out to be specified by the LEFT, CENTER, and RIGHT constants.

The `GridLayout` Class

The `GridLayout` class is used to lay out the components of a `Container` object in a grid where all components are the same size. The `GridLayout` constructor is used to specify the number of rows and columns of the grid.

The `GridBagLayout` Class

The `GridBagLayout` class lays out the components of a `Container` object in a grid-like fashion, where some components may occupy more than one row or column. The `GridBagConstraints` class is used to identify the positioning parameters of a component that is contained within an object laid out using a `GridBagLayout`. The `Insets` class is used to specify the margins associated with an object that is laid out using a `GridBagLayout` object. Refer to the API description of the `GridBagLayout` class for more information on how to use this layout.

> **NOTE**
>
> The `LayoutApp` program of Chapter 24, "Organizing Window Programs," provides examples of the use of each of the layout classes.

Printing

Support for printing was introduced with the JDK 1.1. The `PrintJob` class provides an encapsulation of a system-dependent print request. A single parameterless `PrintJob()` constructor is provided. However, `PrintJob` objects are created via the `getPrintJob()` method of the `Toolkit` class. The `PrintJob` class provides the following six access methods:

- `getGraphics()`—Returns a `Graphics` object that is drawn on to accomplish printing. The `Graphics` object is sent to the printer when its `disposed()` method is invoked.
- `getPageDimension()`—Returns a `Dimension` object that identifies the width and height of the page to be printed in pixels.
- `getPageResolution()`—Identifies the page resolution in pixels per inch.
- `lastPageFirst()`—Returns a `boolean` value indicating whether the pages of a print job are printed in reverse order.
- `end()`—Completes the printing of the print job.
- `finalize()`—Invoked by the garbage collector when the `PrintJob` is completed.

The `PrintGraphics` interface is used to distinguish between a `Graphics` object that is used for printing and one that is used for screen display. It consists of a single method, `getPrintJob()`, which returns the `PrintJob` associated with a `Graphics` object.

Handling Events

The user communicates with window programs by performing actions such as clicking a mouse button or pressing a key on the keyboard. These actions result in the generation of events. The process of responding to the occurrence of an event is known as *event handling.* Window programs are said to be *event driven* because they operate by performing actions in response to events.

The JDK 1.02 supported an approach to event handling referred to as an *inheritance model.* In this approach, events are handled by subclassing window components and overriding their action() and handleEvent() methods. These methods return true or false to indicate whether they have successfully handled an event. If a true value is returned, the event processing is complete. Otherwise, the event is sent to the object's container for further processing.

The JDK 1.02 approach to event handling is replaced by an *event delegation model* in JDK 1.1; however, the old inheritance event model is still supported. JDK 1.1 provides the capability to deliver events to specific objects—a capability that was lacking in JDK 1.02. This new approach to event handling is less complex and more efficient. It makes use of special classes, called *adapter classes,* whose objects *listen* for the occurrence of events on behalf of objects of other classes.

In the event delegation model, event handling is delegated to specific event-handling adapter classes. In this model, a source object generates events that are listened for by a listener object. The source object is usually a window GUI component, like a button or menu item. The listener object is an adapter class that implements an event-listener interface. The source object provides methods that allow listener objects to register themselves to listen for its events.

The JDK 1.1 event model is a significant improvement over that of Java 1.02. The JDK 1.02 model required GUI components to be subclassed in order to handle events. While it is still possible to do so in JDK 1.1, it is no longer necessary. Events can be handled by adapter classes that are separate from the component from which the event is generated.

The following sections describe the classes and interfaces used for JDK 1.02 event handling, followed by those used for JDK 1.1 event handling.

JDK 1.02 Event Handling

In the JDK 1.02 inheritance model, the Event class encapsulates all Windows event processing. The Event class defines the entire list of events handled by window programs using *class constants.* These constants are used to identify the events that are passed to event-handling methods. You can review the Java API description of the Event class to familiarize yourself with these constants.

The Event class provides three constructors for creating events, but you probably won't need to use these constructors because events are internally generated by the Java runtime system in response to user interface actions. The Event class also provides methods for determining whether the Control, Shift, or Meta (Alt) keys were pressed during the generation of an event.

JDK 1.1 Event Handling

In the JDK 1.1 event delegation model, the java.util.EventObject class is the top-level class of an event hierarchy. This class provides a source field variable to identify the object that is the source of an event, the getSource() method to retrieve this object, and a toString() method for converting an event into a String representation. It provides a single constructor that takes the object that is the source of the event as an argument.

The java.awt.AWTEvent class extends the java.util.EventObject class to support AWT events. It provides several variables, constants, and methods that are used to identify events and determine whether they are consumed. The AWTEvent class is extended by the following classes of java.awt.event:

- ActionEvent—Generated as the result of user interface actions such as clicking on a button or selecting a menu item
- AdjustmentEvent—Generated as the result of scrolling actions
- ComponentEvent—Generated as the result of changes to the position, focus, or sizing of a window component or as the result of a keyboard input or other mouse action
- ItemEvent—Generated as the result of a component state change, such as selecting an item from a list
- TextEvent—Generated as the result of text-related events, such as changing the value of a text field

The ComponentEvent class is further extended by the following classes:

- FocusEvent—Generated as the result of the change in the status of a component's input focus
- InputEvent—Subclassed by KeyEvent and MouseEvent to cover events generated by keyboard actions and low-level mouse events
- ContainerEvent—Generated by events associated with adding and removing components from a container
- PaintEvent—Generated by the painting/repainting of a window
- WindowEvent—Generated by events such as the opening, closing, and minimizing of a window

The AWTEvent class and its subclasses allow window-related events to be directed to specific objects that listen for those events. These objects implement EventListener interfaces. The java.util.EventListener interface is the top-level interface of the event listener hierarchy. It is an interface in name only because it does not define any constants or methods. It is extended by the following interfaces of `java.awt.event`:

- `ActionListener`—Implemented by objects that handle `ActionEvent` events
- `AdjustmentListener`—Implemented by objects that handle `AdjustmentEvent` events
- `ComponentListener`—Implemented by objects that handle `ComponentEvent` events
- `ContainerListener`—Implemented by objects that handle `ContainerEvent` events
- `FocusListener`—Implemented by objects that handle `FocusEvent` events
- `ItemListener`—Implemented by objects that handle `ItemEvent` events
- `KeyListener`—Implemented by objects that handle `KeyEvent` events
- `MouseListener`—Implemented by objects that handle clicking-related `MouseEvent` events
- `MouseMotionListener`—Implemented by objects that handle movement-related `MouseEvent` events
- `TextListener`—Implemented by objects that handle `TextEvent` events
- `WindowListener`—Implemented by objects that handle `WindowEvent` events

As a convenience, the `java.awt.event` package provides adapter classes to implement the event listener interfaces. These classes may be subclassed to override specific event handling methods of interest. The adapter classes of `java.awt.event` are as follows:

- `ComponentAdapter`—Implements the `ComponentListener` interface and handles `ComponentEvent` events
- `ContainerAdapter`—Implements the `ContainerListener` interface and handles `ContainerEvent` events
- `FocusAdapter`—Implements the `FocusListener` interface and handles `FocusEvent` events
- `KeyAdapter`—Implements the `KeyListener` interface and handles `KeyEvent` events
- `MouseAdapter`—Implements the `MouseListener` interface and handles clicking-related `MouseEvent` events
- `MouseMotionAdapter`—Implements the `MouseListener` interface and handles movement-related `MouseEvent` events
- `WindowAdapter`—Implements the `WindowListener` interface and handles `WindowEvent` events

The preceding adapter classes are convenience classes in that they provide stubs for the methods of the interfaces that you don't wish to implement yourself.

The `java.awt.EventQueue` class supports the queuing of events. It allows event listeners to monitor the queue and retrieve specific events for processing.

The java.awt.AWTEventMulticaster class provides the capability to listen for multiple events and then forward them to multiple event listeners. It provides a thread-safe mechanism by which event listeners can be added and removed from its event listening destination list.

Using the Clipboard

JDK 1.1 provides the capability to support clipboard cut, copy, and paste operations. The java.awt.datatransfer package contains the classes that implement this support:

- ■ Clipboard—The Clipboard class provides access to the system clipboard and to Java-internal clipboard objects. A system Clipboard object is returned by the getSystemClipboard() method of the Toolkit class. The three Clipboard access methods—getName(), getContents(), and setContents()—are used to identify a Clipboard object, get the contents of the clipboard, and put new data on the clipboard.

- ■ Transferable—The data copied to and pasted from a Clipboard object (via setContents() and getContents()) must implement the Transferable interface. This interface provides methods to support the reading of clipboard data.

- ■ DataFlavor—Clipboard data that implements the Transferable interface identifies the formatting options that it supports through data flavors. The DataFlavor class encapsulates data flavors in terms of the human-readable name of the data format, its MIME type, and the Java class by which the data can be accessed.

- ■ StringSelection—The StringSelection class implements both the Transferable and ClipboardOwner interfaces to support the transfer of String objects to and from the clipboard.

- ■ ClipboardOwner—The ClipboardOwner interface provides a callback method, lostOwnership(), that notifies the current clipboard owner that it has lost ownership of the clipboard.

Working with Images

The Image class is an abstract class that provides a content-independent mechanism for implementing graphical images. Images are created by invoking methods of other classes that create images. The createImage() methods of the Component and Applet classes and the getImage() methods of the Toolkit and Applet classes allow images to be created. Image objects are usually displayed on a Graphics object using the drawImage() method of the Graphics class. The Image class provides several constants for specifying how images are to be scaled and methods for accessing the properties of an image.

The Color and SystemColor Classes

The Color class provides a system-independent color implementation and defines several color constants. It provides three constructors that allow a color to be constructed from its red, green, and blue (RGB) color components. Its access methods provide access to the RGB values of a color; brighten and darken a color; and convert colors to a hue, saturation, and brightness (HSB) representation.

The SystemColor class was introduced with the JDK 1.1 as a means of specifying the colors to be used with GUI components. It provides numerous field variables and constants that can be used to access the standard colors to be used with these components.

The java.awt.image Package

The java.awt.image package defines interfaces and classes that support image generation, storage, and processing. These classes are based on the concept of an image producer and an image consumer. The *image producer* provides the data associated with an image, and the *image consumer* uses the data produced by the image producer to process or display an image.

The ImageProducer interface provides a set of methods for classes that produce images. These methods are used to reconstruct or modify an image being produced. The ImageConsumer interface provides a set of constants and methods for accessing image data provided by classes that implement the ImageConsumer interface. The ImageObserver interface provides a set of constants and methods by which objects are notified about an image that is being constructed.

ColorModel

The ColorModel class is an abstract class that provides a general framework for representing colors and maps this framework to the RGB color model. It is extended by the DirectColorModel and IndexColorModel classes.

The DirectColorModel class is used to directly access the color values of a pixel. It specifies a method for directly translating pixel values to their RGB values. The IndexColorModel class translates fixed colormap pixel values to their RGB component colors using pixel values as an index into a color map.

FilteredImageSource

The FilteredImageSource class provides the capability to filter an image using an object of class ImageFilter. FilterImageSource implements the ImageProducer interface. Its objects are used as intermediate image producers by filtering the image data produced by an image's original image producer using an object of the ImageFilter class. The FilterImageSource constructor takes the original image's ImageProducer and an ImageFilter object as its parameters. Its access methods provide the capability to add and remove image consumers and control the generation of image data.

ImageFilter

The `ImageFilter` class provides a common set of methods for implementing image filters. It does not implement any filtering of its own and it must be subclassed to provide a specific filtering mechanism. It is extended by the `CropImageFilter`, `RGBImageFilter`, and `ReplicateScaleFilter` classes.

CropImageFilter

The `CropImageFilter` class is an image filter that is used to crop images to a specific area. Its constructor takes the upper-left coordinate of the location of the cropping rectangle and the rectangle's height and width. Its access methods provide the capability to work with subsets of the pixels of the cropped area.

RGBImageFilter

The `RGBImageFilter` class is an abstract class that is used to create image filters that modify the pixels of the default RGB color model. In order to create a color filter based on this class, you subclass it and override the `filterRGB()` method. This method provides the x- and y-coordinates and RGB value of the pixel at the specified coordinates and returns the filtered color value. Setting the `canFilterIndexColorModel` flag to `true` enables filtering to be performed on the color model instead of the image. This greatly speeds up the filtering process and should be used when the filter is position independent.

ReplicateScaleFilter

The `ReplicateScaleFilter` class is used to scale images up or down in size. It scales images down by dropping rows and columns of the original image. It scales images up by adding duplicate rows and columns. Its field variables, constructor, and access methods support the identification of the source and destination image sizes.

AreaAveragingScaleFilter

The `AreaAveragingScaleFilter` class extends the `ReplicateScaleFilter` class to support more sophisticated image scaling. It scales images by averaging the values of the source image to determine what the value of the pixels should be in the destination image (whether scaled up or scaled down).

PixelGrabber

The `PixelGrabber` class is used to capture the pixels of an image and store them in an array. It provides three constructors that specify the area to be captured and the array where the captured pixels are to be stored. The access methods provided by `PixelGrabber` are used to control the image capture process.

MemoryImageSource

The MemoryImageSource class is used to create an image using an array of pixel values. It implements the ImageProducer interface and provides six constructors for the creation of ImageProducer objects based on in-memory descriptions of the image's pixel values.

The MediaTracker Class

The MediaTracker class of java.awt provides a set of methods for managing images used to implement multimedia objects. It provides the capability to load a specified set of images, wait on the loading of the images in the set, and maintain the load status of the images. It defines the COMPLETE, ABORTED, LOADING, and ERRORED constants to indicate the load status of an image. It provides a single constructor that identifies the Component object for which the images are to be loaded. Its access methods are used to manage the image-loading process.

Geometrical Objects

Java provides several classes for working with standard geometrical objects: Point, Rectangle, Polygon, and Dimension. The Shape interface defines the getBounds() method for classes that represent geometric shapes. It returns the bounding box of the object.

The Point Class

The Point class is used to represent general two-dimensional x,y-coordinates. One constructor takes the x- and y-coordinates of the point to be created. Another constructor allows a Point object to be constructed from another Point object. The x and y field variables are declared as public, providing access to individual coordinates. Methods to perform movement and translation of points are provided.

The Rectangle Class

The Rectangle class represents a rectangle using the x,y-coordinates of its upper-left corner, its width, and its height. Several constructors are provided to allow rectangles to be created using a variety of approaches. Methods are provided that allow a rectangle's parameters to be accessed, to support movement and translation operations, and to perform other geometrical operations.

The Polygon Class

The Polygon class represents a polygon as a list of x,y-coordinates that identify the polygon's vertices. It provides a default parameterless constructor and a constructor that identifies the polygon's vertices. The Polygon class provides several access methods that are used to access the polygon's vertices, add vertices, test whether a point is contained in a polygon, and get the minimum bounding box containing a polygon.

The `Dimension` Class

The `Dimension` class is used to represent the width and height of a two-dimensional object. It provides three constructors: a default parameterless constructor, a constructor that creates a `Dimension` object using another `Dimension` object, and a constructor that takes width and height parameters. The access methods provided by the `Dimension` class allow the height and width of a dimension to be accessed.

Using Fonts

The `Font` class implements a system-independent set of fonts that control text display. Java font names are mapped to system-supported fonts. Fonts can be specified in terms of font name, style, and point size. The supported styles are defined by the `PLAIN`, `BOLD`, and `ITALIC` constants of the `Font` class. Font styles can be combined by adding these constants. Font sizes can be any integer size supported by the system. The `Font` class provides a single constructor that takes the font name, style constants, and point size as its parameters.

The `Font` class provides several methods for querying the parameters of a font. The `getName()` method returns the Java name for the font. The `getFamily()` method returns the system-dependent font name. The `getStyle()` and `getSize()` methods return the font's style and size parameters. The `isBold()`, `isItalic()`, and `isPlain()` methods provide the capability to test the style parameter.

The `FontMetrics` Class

The `FontMetrics` class is used to access the specific display parameters of a `Font` object. A `FontMetrics` object is usually constructed using the `getFontMetrics()` method of the `Component` class. It provides several methods for determining a font's display parameters, as described in Chapter 27, "Text and Fonts."

The `getHeight()`, `getLeading()`, `getAscent()`, and `getDescent()` methods are used to determine the vertical size properties of a font. The `stringWidth()`, `getWidths()`, `charWidth()`, `charsWidth()`, and `bytesWidth()` methods are used to determine a font's horizontal size properties.

Using the Toolkit

The `Toolkit` class provides the linkage between the platform-independent classes of the AWT and their platform-dependent implementation. It provides the capability to access the platform-dependent peer classes of the subclasses of the `Component` class. These classes can be used to obtain direct access to a component's local implementation. The use of peer classes is discouraged because it limits the portability of any software that utilizes these methods.

The `Toolkit` class also provides several methods that provide access to implementation-dependent characteristics that can be safely used in Java programs. The `getFontList()` method provides a list of the fonts that are supported by the windowing environment. The `getImage()` method allows an image to be retrieved from an URL or the local file system. The `getScreenSize()` and `getScreenResolution()` methods return useful characteristics of the screen display. You should read the API description of this class to familiarize yourself with the methods that it provides.

Summary

This chapter introduces you to the classes of the `java.awt` packages, which provide the foundation for Java window programming. You learned how the `java.awt` package is organized and covered the classes that it contains. You also covered the `java.awt.datatransfer`, `java.awt.event`, and `java.awt.image` packages. Part IV provides a detailed tutorial of Java window programming with numerous programming examples that will further help you understand the concepts.

16

Web Programming with the java.applet Package

This chapter introduces the classes of the `java.applet` package and explains how applets are integrated within Web documents. It includes a short introduction to HTML and explains how to use the HTML `<APPLET>` tag. It describes how applets use window components and identifies the major phases in an applet's life cycle. Applet audio capabilities are also covered. When you finish this chapter, you will have a good understanding of how applets work.

Applets and the World Wide Web

Applets are Java programs that are integrated in Web pages. When a Web page containing an applet is displayed by a Web browser, the applet is loaded and executed. The applet's output is displayed within a subset of the browser's display area. Figure 16.1 illustrates this concept.

FIGURE 16.1.

How an applet is displayed by a Web browser.

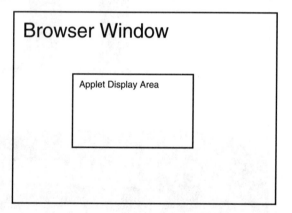

The `Applet` class is a subclass of the `Panel` class, and applets are implemented as a panel within a Web document. You'll learn more about the `Panel` class when you study window programming in Part IV, "Window Programming." Because the `Applet` class is a subclass of the `Panel` class, it inherits all the methods of the `Panel` class and is capable of using most window GUI components. In addition, applet events are handled in the same manner as in standalone Java window programs.

The `Applet` Class

The `java.applet` package is the smallest package in the Java API. It consists of a single class—the `Applet` class—and three interfaces: `AppletContext`, `AppletStub`, and `AudioClip`.

The `Applet` class contains a single default parameterless constructor, which is generally not used. Applets are constructed by the runtime environment when they are loaded and do not have to be explicitly constructed.

The `Applet` class contains 22 access methods that are used to display images, play audio files, respond to events, and obtain information about an applet's execution environment, referred to as the applet's *context*.

The `getImage()` and `getAudioClip()` methods are used to retrieve an `Image` or `AudioClip` object that is identified by an URL. The `play()` methods are used to play audio files at specified URLs.

The `init()`, `start()`, `stop()`, and `destroy()` methods are used to implement each of the four life cycle stages of an applet. The `init()` method is invoked by the runtime environment when an applet is initially loaded. It is invoked to perform any required initialization processing. The `start()` method is invoked by the runtime system when an applet is initially started or restarted as a result of a user switching between Web pages. The `stop()` method is invoked by the runtime system when the user switches from the Web page containing the applet to another Web page or another program. The `destroy()` method is invoked when an applet's execution is terminated, usually as the result of the user exiting the browser. The `isActive()` method is used to determine whether an applet is currently active.

The `getAppletContext()` method is used to obtain the `AppletContext` object associated with an applet. The `AppletContext` interface defines methods by which an applet can access its execution environment. The `getAppletInfo()` method returns a `String` object that provides information about an applet. This information can include version, copyright, and authorship data as well as applet-specific data. The `getAppletInfo()` method is overridden by `Applet` subclasses to provide this information. The `getCodeBase()` method returns the base URL specifying the applet's location. The `getDocumentBase()` returns the URL of the document in which the applet is contained. The `getParameter()` method is used to obtain parameter data that is passed to an applet in an HTML file. The `getParameterInfo()` method returns an array that describes all the parameters used by an object. It is overridden by `Applet` subclasses in the same manner as the `getAppletInfo()` method.

The `resize()` methods are used to resize an applet. The `setStub()` method is used to set the `AppletStub` associated with the applet. It should not be used unless you are constructing your own custom applet viewer. The `showStatus()` method is used to display a status message using the applet's context. The `getLocale()` method returns the `Locale` object associated with the applet. It is used to support language-independent applet programming.

The `AppletContext` interface defines methods that allow an applet to access the context in which it is being run. This is typically a Web browser, such as Netscape Navigator or Microsoft Internet Explorer, but could also be the applet viewer. The `AppletContext` interface of an applet is accessed using the `getAppletContext()` method of the `Applet` class. `AppletContext` provides seven methods that allow an applet to obtain information about and manipulate its environment. The `getApplets()` method returns an `Enumeration` object that contains all applets which are accessible in the applet's context. The `getApplet()` method returns an `Applet` object whose name matches a `String` parameter. The `getAudioClip()` method returns an `AudioClip` object that is referenced using an URL. The `getImage()` method returns an `Image` object that is identified by an URL. The two `showDocument()` methods are used to instruct a Web browser to display the Web document located at a particular URL. The `showStatus()` method is used to display a status message via the Web browser executing the applet.

The `AppletStub` interface is used to implement an applet viewer. It is not generally used by applets. It provides six methods that are used to retrieve applet information that can be used to support applet viewing.

The `AudioClip` interface defines three methods: `play()`, `stop()`, and `loop()`. The `play()` method plays an audio clip. The `stop()` method terminates the playing of an audio clip. The `loop()` method starts and plays an audio clip in a continuous loop.

Applets and HTML

Web documents are written in Hypertext Markup Language (HTML). HTML uses *tags* to describe the structure of Web documents. Tags are used to identify headings, paragraphs, and lists, as well as other elements of Web pages such as links, images, forms, and applets. In order to use applets in your Web documents, you need to learn about a few basic HTML tags. While a complete introduction to HTML is beyond the scope of this book, this section provides a quick summary of the basic HTML tags that you will need to work the examples in this book.

> **NOTE**
>
> For more information on HTML, point your Web browser at the URL `http://www.jaworski.com/htmlbook/`. Here you'll find links to introductory tutorials on HTML as well as links to more advanced HTML topics.

Using HTML Tags

HTML tags begin with a < and end with a >. The name of the tag is placed between the opening < and closing >. The tag name may be written using any combination of upper- or lowercase characters. I use the convention of writing tags in uppercase to set them apart from the text to which they apply. For example, the title tag is written `<TITLE>`, the head tag is written `<HEAD>`, and the body tag is written `<BODY>`.

HTML supports two types of tags—separating tags and surrounding tags. Separating tags are placed between the text elements to which they apply. For example, the break tag, written `<BR>`, is used to insert a line break within a line of text. It is placed at the point in the line where the break is desired, as shown in the following HTML:

```
This line ends at the break tag.<BR>This text is displayed on the next line.
```

Surrounding tags consist of pairs of tags that surround the text to which they apply. The first tag in the pair is referred to as the *opening tag* and the second tag is referred to as the *closing tag*. The closing tag contains a / between the opening < and the tag's name. Examples of surrounding tags are <HTML> and </HTML>, <HEAD> and </HEAD>, and <BODY> and </BODY>. You'll learn about these tags in subsequent sections.

Some HTML tags are allowed to specify *attributes*. Attributes are used to identify properties of the tag and are included in the tag between the tag name and the closing >. When attributes are used with surrounding tags, they are included in the opening tag but not in the closing tag. For example, the applet tag uses attributes to identify the name of the class to be loaded, the dimensions of the applet display region within the browser window, and other properties of the applet. The following HTML is an example of an applet tag that uses attributes:

```
<APPLET CODE="TestApplet.class" WIDTH=300 HEIGHT=300>
[alternate text to be displayed]
</APPLET>
```

The opening applet tag has three attributes: CODE, WIDTH, and HEIGHT. The CODE attribute has the value of "TestApplet.class" and identifies the name of the applet's bytecode file. The WIDTH and HEIGHT attributes both have the value 300 and specify a 300×300 pixel applet display region within the browser window. The text [alternate text to be displayed] appearing between the opening and closing applet tags identifies text that a browser should display if it does not support Java applets.

The HTML, Head, and Body Tags

HTML documents are written in ASCII text. The <HTML> and </HTML> tags mark the beginning and end of an HTML document. HTML documents consist of a single head and a single body. The head is used to identify information about an HTML document, such as its title, while the body contains the information displayed by the HTML document. The head and body are identified using the <HEAD> and </HEAD>, and <BODY> and </BODY> tags. The following HTML illustrates the use of these tags:

```
<HTML>
<HEAD>
The document title appears here.
</HEAD>
<BODY>
The information displayed by the HTML document appears here.
</BODY>
</HTML>
```

The Title Tag

The title of an HTML document is typically displayed at the top of the browser window, as shown in Figure 16.2. The title is placed in the head of a Web document and is surrounded by the <TITLE> and </TITLE> tags.

FIGURE 16.2.

The title of a Web document.

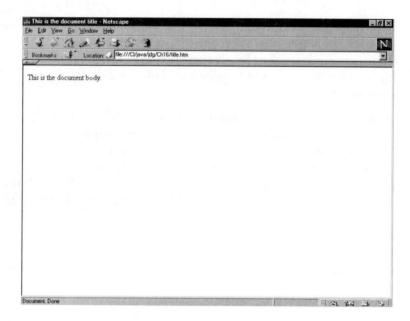

The HTML used to create the Web page is shown in Listing 16.1.

Listing 16.1. Using the title tag.

```
<HTML>
<HEAD>
<TITLE>This is the document title</TITLE>
</HEAD>
<BODY>
This is the document body.
</BODY>
</HTML>
```

The Heading and Paragraph Tags

The heading and paragraph tags are the most common tags found within the body of a Web document. The heading tags are used to specify document headings. These headings are used to organize Web documents into sections and subsections in the same manner in which the chapters of this book are organized into sections and subsections. HTML supports six heading levels. First-level headings are identified by the <H1> and </H1> tags, second-level headings are identified by the <H2> and </H2> tags, and so on. Sixth-level headings are identified by the <H6> and </H6> tags. The HTML in Listing 16.2 shows how all six heading levels are displayed.

Listing 16.2 Using heading tags.

```
<HTML>
<HEAD>
<TITLE>HTML Headings</TITLE>
</HEAD>
<BODY>
<H1>Heading Level 1</H1>
<H2>Heading Level 2</H2>
<H3>Heading Level 3</H3>
<H4>Heading Level 4</H4>
<H5>Heading Level 5</H5>
<H6>Heading Level 6</H6>
</BODY>
</HTML>
```

Figure 16.3 shows how this HTML file is displayed by my Web browser.

FIGURE 16.3.

HTML heading levels.

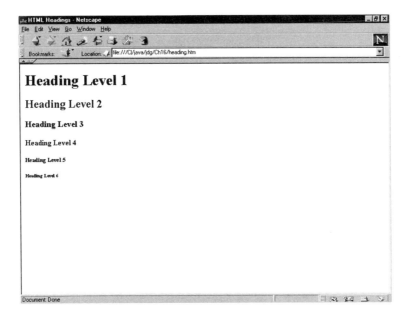

Paragraph tags are used to mark paragraphs within HTML documents. Spaces, tabs, carriage returns, and line feeds are referred to as *whitespace* characters in HTML. One or more whitespace characters are normally displayed as a single space by Web browsers. In order to mark the beginning and end of a paragraph, the HTML paragraph tags, `<P>` and `</P>`, must be used. For example, the HTML shown in Listing 16.3 illustrates the use of paragraph tags. Figure 16.4 shows how this HTML is displayed by a Web browser.

Listing 16.3. Using paragraph tags.

```
<HTML>
<HEAD>
<TITLE>HTML Paragraphs</TITLE>
</HEAD>
<BODY>
<H1>How paragraphs are marked in HTML</H1>
<P>This is paragraph 1.</P><P>This is paragraph 2.</P>
<P>This is paragraph 3.
This text also belongs to paragraph 3.
Notice that carriage returns and      multiple spaces      do
not affect the way paragraphs are formatted.</P>
</BODY>
</HTML>
```

FIGURE 16.4.

HTML paragraphs.

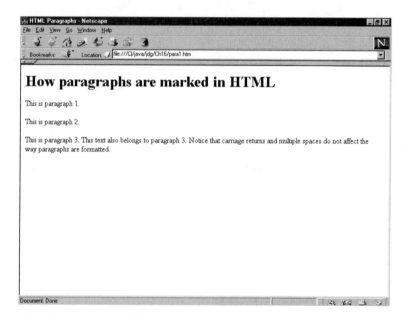

The paragraph tag may also be written as a single separating tag, <P>, although this is considered bad practice. The previous example could also have been written, as shown in Listing 16.4, using separating paragraph tags rather than surrounding paragraph tags. Figure 16.5 shows how it is displayed by my Web browser.

Listing 16.4. Using paragraph tags as separating tags.

```
<HTML>
<HEAD>
<TITLE>HTML Paragraphs using separating tags</TITLE>
</HEAD>
<BODY>
```

```
<H1>How paragraphs are marked in HTML</H1>
This is paragraph 1.<P>This is paragraph 2.
<P>This is paragraph 3.
This text also belongs to paragraph 3.
Notice that carriage returns and      multiple spaces      do
not affect the way paragraphs are formatted.
</BODY>
</HTML>
```

FIGURE 16.5.

Marking HTML paragraphs with separating tags.

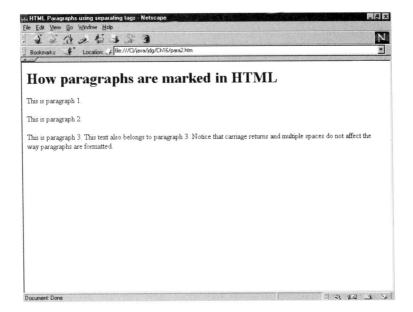

The Applet and Parameter Tags

While there are a number of different HTML tags that you can learn, the applet and parameter tags are the primary tags of interest for Web programmers.

The applet tag is a surrounding tag. It may surround zero or more parameter tags. It may also surround *alternative text.* Alternative text is text that appears between the <APPLET> and </APPLET> tags that is not included in a parameter tag. It is displayed by browsers that are not Java enabled as an alternative to the applet's display.

The parameter tag is used to pass named parameters to a Java applet. It is a separating tag that has two attributes: NAME and VALUE. The NAME attribute identifies the name of a parameter and the VALUE attribute identifies its value. The following are examples of the use of parameter tags:

```
<PARAM NAME="speed" VALUE="slow">
<PARAM NAME="duration" VALUE="long">
<PARAM NAME="delay" VALUE="short">
```

An applet uses the getParameter() method of the Applet class to retrieve the value of a parameter. The parameter tag may appear only between the <APPLET> and </APPLET> tags.

The applet tag supports eleven attributes: ALIGN, ALT, ARCHIVES, CODE, CODEBASE, HEIGHT, HSPACE, NAME, OBJECT, VSPACE, and WIDTH.

The ALIGN attribute specifies the alignment of an applet's display region with respect to the rest of the line being displayed by a browser. This line may consist of text, images, or other HTML elements. Values for this attribute are TOP, TEXTTOP, BOTTOM, ABSBOTTOM, BASELINE, MIDDLE, ABSMIDDLE, LEFT, and RIGHT. The TOP attribute value causes the top of an applet to be aligned with the top of the line being displayed by a browser. The TEXTTOP attribute causes the top of an applet to be aligned with the top of the text being displayed in the current line. The BASELINE and BOTTOM attributes cause the bottom of the applet to be aligned with the baseline of the text in the line being displayed. The ABSBOTTOM attribute causes the bottom of an applet to be aligned with the bottom of the current line being displayed. The MIDDLE attribute causes the middle of the applet to be aligned with the middle of the text displayed in the current line. The ABSMIDDLE attribute causes the middle of the applet to be aligned with the middle of the line being displayed. The LEFT and RIGHT attributes cause the applet to be aligned at the left and right margins of the browser window.

The ALT attribute identifies text that should be displayed by a browser if it understands the applet tags, but does not support Java applets or has applet processing disabled.

The ARCHIVES attribute identifies class archives that are preloaded to support applet execution.

The CODE attribute is a relative URL that identifies the name of the bytecode file of the applet.

Normally, the URL of the Web document displaying the applet is used as the base URL for locating the bytecode file referenced by the CODE attribute. The CODEBASE attribute is used to change the base URL to another location.

The HEIGHT attribute identifies the height of the display area required by the applet.

The HSPACE attribute specifies the number of pixels to be used as the left and right margins surrounding an applet.

The NAME attribute is used to assign a name to an applet. This name is used to support inter-applet communication.

The OBJECT attribute identifies a file that contains a serialized representation of an applet.

The VSPACE attribute specifies the number of pixels to be used as the top and bottom margins surrounding an applet.

The WIDTH attribute identifies the width of the display area required by the applet.

Of the eleven applet attributes, only the CODE, HEIGHT, and WIDTH attributes are required.

The HTML file sample.htm, which is shown in Listing 16.5, shows how an applet may be specified in a Web document.

Listing 16.5. The sample.htm file.

```
<HTML>
<HEAD>
<TITLE>Using the Applet Tag</TITLE>
</HEAD>
<BODY>
<H1>An Applet that Displays Text at a Designated Location</H1>
<APPLET CODE="SampleApplet.class" HEIGHT=300 WIDTH=300>
<PARAM NAME="text" VALUE="Applets are fun!">
<PARAM NAME="x" VALUE="50">
<PARAM NAME="y" VALUE="50">
Text displayed by browsers that are not Java-enabled.
</APPLET>
</BODY>
</HTML>
```

The applet specified in the applet tag displays the text Applets are fun! at the coordinates 50,50 within the 300×300 pixel applet display area, as shown in Figure 16.6.

FIGURE 16.6.

The display of SampleApplet.

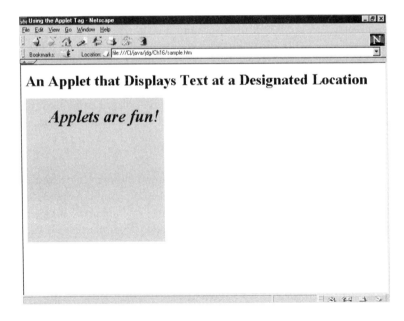

The source code of the `SampleApplet` applet is provided in Listing 16.6.

Listing 16.6. The `SampleApplet.java` source code file.

```java
import java.applet.*;
import java.awt.*;
public class SampleApplet extends Applet {
 String text = "error";
 int x = 0;
 int y = 20;
 public void init() {
  text = getParameter("text");
  try {
   x = Integer.parseInt(getParameter("x"));
   y = Integer.parseInt(getParameter("y"));
  }catch(NumberFormatException ex){
  }
 }
 public void paint(Graphics g) {
  g.setFont(new Font("TimesRoman",Font.BOLD+Font.ITALIC,36));
  g.drawString(text,x,y);
 }
}
```

You can compile `SampleApp.java` using the command `javac SampleApplet.java`. Create the `sample.htm` file shown in Listing 16.5 and store it in your `\jdk1.1.1\jdg\ch16` directory. Then open the `sample.htm` file using your Web browser. This should result in a display similar to that shown in Figure 16.6.

The `SampleApplet` class extends the `Applet` class. It declares three field variables: `text`, `x`, and `y`. The `text` variable is used to hold the text that is displayed in the `Applet` display area. The `x` and `y` variables specify the location where the text is to be displayed. The default value of the `text` variable is set to `"error"`. The default value of the `x` variable is set to `0`. The default value of the `y` variable is set to `20`.

The `init()` method is invoked by the Java runtime system to perform any required initialization. The `init()` method uses the `getParameter()` method of the `Applet` class to get the value of the `text`, `x`, and `y` parameters. The `parseInt()` method of the `Integer` class is used to convert the `String` value returned by the `getParameter()` method to an `int` value.

The `paint()` method is invoked by the Java runtime system to update the Java display area. It is automatically passed a `Graphics` object as a parameter. This object is used to draw on the applet's display area. The `paint()` method uses the `setFont()` method of the `Graphics` class to set the current font to a 36-point bold italic Times Roman font. The `drawString()` method of the `Graphics` class is used to display the value of the `text` variable at the x,y-coordinate.

Other HTML Tags

The HTML tags covered in the preceding sections are the minimum needed to get you started using applets with HTML documents. There are many more HTML tags that you can use with your Web pages. The URL `http://www.jaworski.com/jdg` contains links to Web documents that describe these other HTML tags.

The Life Cycle of an Applet

An applet has a well-defined life cycle, as shown in Figure 16.7. Applets do not need to be explicitly constructed. They are automatically constructed by the runtime environment associated with their applet context—a Web browser or the applet viewer. The `init()` method provides the capability to load applet parameters and perform any necessary initialization processing. The `start()` method serves as the execution entry point for an applet when it is initially executed and restarted as the result of a user returning to the Web page that contains the applet. The `stop()` method provides the capability to `stop()` an applet's execution when the Web page containing the applet is no longer active. The `destroy()` method is used at the end of an applet's life cycle to perform any termination processing.

FIGURE 16.7.
The stages of an applet's life cycle.

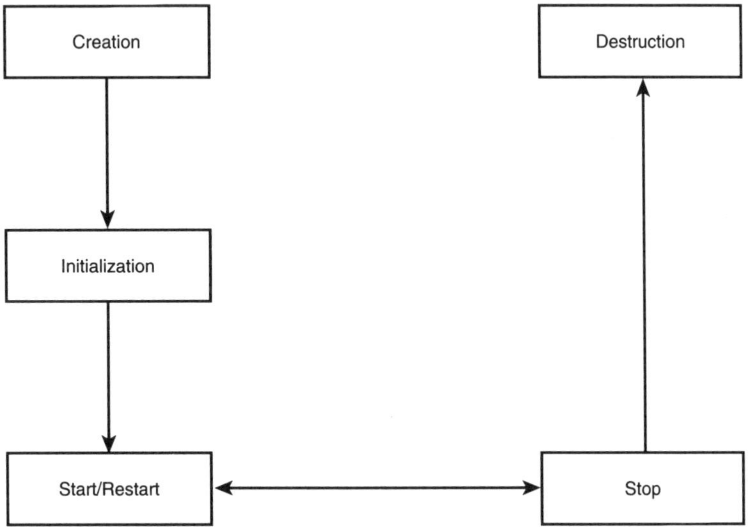

Responding to Events

Because the `Applet` class is a subclass of the `Panel` class and therefore part of the window class hierarchy, applets handle events in the same manner as other window components. All the window event handling approaches that you will learn in Part IV will also apply to `Applet` event handling. The `init()`, `start()`, `stop()`, and `destroy()` methods that you covered in the previous section are used to handle events that are generated by the Java runtime system. These methods are specific to applets and do not apply to other window components.

Using Window Components

Because the `Applet` class is a subclass of the `Panel` class, it can use most of the GUI components that are used by standalone window programs. This includes labels, buttons, checkboxes, radio buttons, lists, text components, canvases, and scrollbars. You will learn to use these components in Part IV. The only major GUI components that cannot be used within an applet are menu components. Menu components are attached to `Frame` objects, which are associated with an application window. It is possible for an applet to create and open a separate application window in the form of a `Frame` object; however, such an application window would be trusted only to the extent allowed by the applet security policy. This prevents the window from masquerading as other programs running on the user's system.

Adding Audio and Animation

The `Applet` class provides the capability to play audio files. These files must be in the Sun audio format and usually end with the `.au` extension. The `play()` method of the `Applet` class can be used to play an audio file that is identified by an URL. A more flexible approach is to load an object that implements the `AudioClip` interface and then invoke the object's `play()`, `loop()`, and `stop()` methods. The `getAudioClip()` method can be used to load an audio file by identifying its URL.

Java also supports the capability to include animation in standalone window programs and applets. Chapter 32, "Using Animation," covers this topic.

Summary

This chapter introduces the classes of the `java.applet` package and explains how applets are integrated within Web documents. It includes a short introduction to HTML and explains how to use the HTML `<APPLET>` tag. It describes how applets use window components and identifies the major phases in an applet's life cycle. Applet audio capabilities are also covered. Part VI, "Web Programming," provides a detailed tutorial on applet programming.

17

Network Programming with the java.net Package

In this chapter you'll learn about Java's support of network programming. You'll learn the basics of client/server computing and TCP/IP socket programming. You'll then examine the classes of the java.net package and learn how to use them to develop client/server applications. This chapter provides an introduction to the java.net package. Part V, "Network Programming," explores the information presented here in greater detail.

The Internet Protocol Suite

The java.net package provides a set of classes that support network programming using the communication protocols employed by the Internet. These protocols are known as the *Internet protocol suite* and include the *Internet Protocol* (IP), the *Transport Control Protocol* (TCP), and the *User Datagram Protocol* (UDP) as well as other, less-prominent supporting protocols. Although this section cannot provide a full description of the Internet protocols, it gives you the basic information that you need to get started with Java network programming. In order to take full advantage of this chapter, you will need an Internet connection.

What Is the Internet and How Does It Work?

Asking the question "What is the Internet?" may bring about a heated discussion in some circles. In this book, the *Internet* is defined as the collection of all computers that are able to communicate, using the Internet protocol suite, with the computers and networks registered with the *Internet Network Information Center* (InterNIC). This definition includes all computers to which you can directly (or indirectly through a firewall) send Internet Protocol packets.

Computers on the Internet communicate by exchanging packets of data, known as Internet Protocol (IP) packets. IP is the network protocol used to send information from one computer to another over the Internet. All computers on the Internet (by our definition in this book) communicate using IP. IP moves information contained in IP packets. The IP packets are routed via special routing algorithms from a source computer that sends the packets to a destination computer that receives them. The routing algorithms figure out the best way to send the packets from source to destination.

In order for IP to send packets from a source computer to a destination computer, it must have some way of identifying these computers. All computers on the Internet are identified using one or more IP addresses. A computer may have more than one IP address if it has more than one interface to computers that are connected to the Internet.

IP addresses are 32-bit numbers. They may be written in decimal, hexadecimal, or other formats, but the most common format is dotted decimal notation. This format breaks the 32-bit address up into four bytes and writes each byte of the address as unsigned decimal integers separated by dots. For example, one of my IP addresses is 0xCCD499C1. Because 0xCC = 204, 0xD4 = 212, 0x99 = 153, and 0xC1 = 193, my address in dotted decimal form is 204.212.153.193.

IP addresses are not easy to remember, even using dotted decimal notation. The Internet has adopted a mechanism, referred to as the *Domain Name System* (DNS), whereby computer names can be associated with IP addresses. These computer names are referred to as *domain names*. The DNS has several rules that determine how domain names are constructed and how they relate to one another. For the purposes of this chapter, it is sufficient to know that domain names are computer names and that they are mapped to IP addresses.

The mapping of domain names to IP addresses is maintained by a system of *domain name servers*. These servers are able to look up the IP address corresponding to a domain name. They also provide the capability to look up the domain name associated with a particular IP address, if one exists.

As I mentioned, IP enables communication between computers on the Internet by routing data from a source computer to a destination computer. However, computer-to-computer communication only solves half of the network communication problem. In order for an application program, such as a mail program, to communicate with another application, such as a mail server, there needs to be a way to send data to specific programs within a computer.

Ports are used to enable communication between programs. A *port* is an address within a computer. Port addresses are 16-bit addresses that are usually associated with a particular application protocol. An application server, such as a Web server or an FTP server, listens on a particular port for service requests, performs whatever service is requested of it, and returns information to the port used by the application program requesting the service.

Popular Internet application protocols are associated with *well-known ports*. The server programs implementing these protocols listen on these ports for service requests. The well-known ports for some common Internet application protocols are

Port	Protocol
21	File Transfer Protocol
23	Telnet Protocol
25	Simple Mail Transfer Protocol
80	Hypertext Transfer Protocol

The well-known ports are used to standardize the location of Internet services.

Connection-Oriented Versus Connectionless Communication

Transport protocols are used to deliver information from one port to another and thereby enable communication between application programs. They use either a connection-oriented or connectionless method of communication. TCP is a connection-oriented protocol, and UDP is a connectionless transport protocol.

The TCP connection-oriented protocol establishes a communication link between a source port/IP address and a destination port/IP address. The ports are bound together via this link until the connection is terminated and the link is broken. An example of a connection-oriented protocol is a telephone conversation. A telephone connection is established, communication takes place, and then the connection is terminated.

The reliability of the communication between the source and destination programs is ensured through error-detection and error-correction mechanisms that are implemented within TCP. TCP implements the connection as a stream of bytes from source to destination. This feature allows the use of the stream I/O classes provided by `java.io`.

The UDP connectionless protocol differs from the TCP connection-oriented protocol in that it does not establish a link for the duration of the connection. An example of a connectionless protocol is postal mail. To mail something, you just write down a destination address (and an optional return address) on the envelope of the item you're sending and drop it in a mailbox. When using UDP, an application program writes the destination port and IP address on a datagram and then sends the datagram to its destination. UDP is less reliable than TCP because there are no delivery-assurance or error-detection and -correction mechanisms built into the protocol.

Application protocols such as FTP, SMTP, and HTTP use TCP to provide reliable, stream-based communication between client and server programs. Other protocols, such as the Time Protocol, use UDP because speed of delivery is more important than end-to-end reliability.

Multicast Addressing

Most TCP/IP communication is *unicast*. Packets are sent from a source host to a destination host in a point-to-point fashion. Unicast communication is used by the majority of Internet services. However, there are some applications where it is desirable for a host to be able to simultaneously send IP packets to multiple destination hosts—for example, to transmit an audio or video stream. This form of communication is known as *multicast*. Multicast communication enables a host to transmit IP packets to multiple hosts, referred to as a host group, using a single destination IP address.

Host groups may be permanent or temporary. Permanent groups are assigned fixed IP addresses. Temporary groups are dynamically assigned IP address. Hosts may join or leave a host group in a dynamic fashion—even permanent groups. The existence of a host group is independent of its members. Multicast routers are used to send IP multicast packets to the members of host groups.

Client/Server Computing and the Internet

The Internet provides a variety of services that contribute to its appeal. These services include e-mail, newsgroups, file transfer, remote login, and the Web. Internet services are organized according to a client/server architecture. Client programs, such as Web browsers and file transfer programs, create connections to servers, such as Web and FTP servers. The clients make requests of the server, and the server responds to the requests by providing the service requested by the client.

The Web provides a good example of client/server computing. Web browsers are the clients and Web servers are the servers. Browsers request HTML files from Web servers on your behalf by establishing a connection with a Web server and submitting file requests to the server. The server receives the file requests, retrieves the files, and sends them to the browser over the established connection. The browser receives the files and displays them to your browser window.

Sockets and Client/Server Communication

Clients and servers establish connections and communicate via *sockets*. Connections are communication links that are created over the Internet using TCP. Some client/server applications are also built around the connectionless UDP. These applications also use sockets to communicate.

Sockets are the endpoints of Internet communication. Clients create client sockets and connect them to server sockets. Sockets are associated with a host address and a port address. The host address is the IP address of the host where the client or server program is located. The port address is the communication port used by the client or server program. Server programs use the well-known port number associated with their application protocol.

A client communicates with a server by establishing a connection to the socket of the server. The client and server then exchange data over the connection. Connection-oriented communication is more reliable than connectionless communication because the underlying TCP provides message-acknowledgment, error-detection, and error-recovery services.

When a connectionless protocol is used, the client and server communicate by sending datagrams to each other's socket. The UDP is used for connectionless protocols. It does not support reliable communication like TCP.

Overview of java.net

The java.net package provides several classes that support socket-based client/server communication.

The InetAddress class encapsulates Internet IP addresses and supports conversion between dotted decimal addresses and host names.

The Socket, ServerSocket, DatagramSocket, and MulticastSocket classes implement client and server sockets for connection-oriented and connectionless communication. The DatagramPacket class is used to construct UDP datagram packets. The `SocketImpl` and `DatagramSocketImpl` classes and the `SocketImplFactory` interface provide hooks for implementing custom sockets.

The `URL`, `URLConnection`, `HttpURLConnection`, and `URLEncoder` classes implement high-level browser–server Web connections. The `ContentHandler` and `URLStreamHandler` classes are abstract classes that provided the basis for the implementation of Web content and stream handlers. They are supported by the `ContentHandlerFactory` and `URLStreamHandlerFactory` interfaces.

The `FileNameMap` interface is used to map filenames to MIME types. You'll learn about MIME types later in this chapter in the section "`ContentHandler`, `ContentHandlerFactory`, and `FileNameMap`."

The `InetAddress` Class

The `InetAddress` class encapsulates Internet addresses. It supports both numeric IP addresses and host names.

The `InetAddress` class has no public variables or constructors. It provides 10 access methods that support common operations on Internet addresses. Three of these methods are `static`.

The `getLocalHost()` method is a `static` method that returns an `InetAddress` object that represents the Internet address of the local host computer. The `static` `getByName()` method returns an `InetAddress` object for a specified host. The `static` `getAllByName()` method returns an array of all Internet addresses associated with a particular host.

The `getAddress()` method gets the numeric IP address of the host identified by the `InetAddress` object, and the `getHostName()` method gets its domain name. The `getHostAddress()` method returns the numeric IP address of an `InetAddress` object as a dotted decimal string. The `isMulticastAddress()` method returns a `boolean` value that indicates whether an `InetAddress` object represents a multicast address.

The `equals()`, `hashCode()`, and `toString()` methods override those of the `Object` class.

The `NSLookupApp` program illustrates the use of the `InetAddress` class. It takes a host name as a parameter and identifies the primary IP address associated with that host. (See Listing 17.1.)

Listing 17.1. The source code of the NSLookupApp program.

```
import java.net.InetAddress;
import java.net.UnknownHostException;
import java.lang.System;

public class NSLookupApp {
 public static void main(String args[]) {
  try {
   if(args.length!=1){
```

```
   System.out.println("Usage: java NSLookupApp hostName");
   return;
  }
  InetAddress host = InetAddress.getByName(args[0]);
  String hostName = host.getHostName();
  System.out.println("Host name: "+hostName);
  System.out.println("IP address: "+host.getHostAddress());
 }catch(UnknownHostException ex) {
  System.out.println("Unknown host");
  return;
  }
 }
}
```

Compile NSLookupApp and run it as follows:

```
C:\jdk1.1.1\jdg\ch17>java NSLookupApp sun.com
Host name: sun.com
IP address: 192.9.9.1
```

This code example uses NSLookupApp to look up the primary IP address associated with the sun.com host. Try it with other Internet host names to look up their IP addresses.

NSLookupApp consists of a single main() method. A try statement surrounds most of the program's statements. It is used to catch the UnknownHostException, which is generated when an invalid host name is entered by the user or when a host name cannot be looked up from a DNS server.

NSLookupApp first checks the number of arguments supplied in the program invocation to make sure that a host name argument is provided by the user. It then uses the host name string of the first user argument with the static getByName() method of the InetAddress class to create an InetAddress object based on the user-supplied host name. This InetAddress object is assigned to the host variable. The getHostName() method gets the host's name from the host variable and assigns it to the hostName variable. The getHostAddress() method returns the four bytes of the host's IP address as a dotted decimal string. The host name and IP address then are printed.

The Socket Class

The Socket class implements client connection-based sockets. These sockets are used to develop applications that utilize services provided by connection-oriented server applications.

The Socket class provides eight constructors that create sockets and optionally connect them to a destination host and port. Two of these constructors have been deprecated in the JDK 1.1. The DatagramSocket constructor is the preferred constructor for creating UDP sockets.

The access methods of the Socket class are used to access the I/O streams and connection parameters associated with a connected socket. The getInetAddress() and getPort() methods get the IP address of the destination host and the destination host port number to which the socket is connected. The `getLocalPort()` method returns the source host local port associated with the socket. The `getLocalAddress()` method returns the local IP address associated with the socket. The `getInputStream()` and `getOutputStream()` methods are used to access the input and output streams associated with a socket. The `close()` method is used to close a socket.

The `getSoLinger()` and `setSoLinger()` methods are used to get and set a socket's `SO_LINGER` option. The `SO_LINGER` option identifies how long a socket is to remain open after a `close()` method has been invoked and data remains to be sent over the socket.

The `getSoTimeout()` and `setSoTimeout()` methods are used to get and set a socket's `SO_TIMEOUT` option. The `SO_TIMEOUT` option is used to identify how long a read operation on the socket is to block before it times out and the blocking ends.

The `getTcpNoDelay()` and `setTcpNoDelay()` methods are used to get and set a socket's `TCP_NODELAY` option. The `TCP_NODELAY` option is used to specify whether Nagle's algorithm should be used to buffer data that is sent over a socket connection. When `TCP_NODELAY` is true, Nagle's algorithm is disabled.

The `setSocketImplFactory()` class method is used to switch from the default Java socket implementation to a custom socket implementation. The `toString()` method returns a string representation of the socket.

The `PortTalkApp` program is used to talk to a particular port on a given host on a line-by-line basis. It provides the option of sending a line to the specified port, receiving a line from the other host, or terminating the connection. Its source code is shown in Listing 17.2.

Listing 17.2. The source code of the `PortTalkApp` program.

```
import java.lang.System;
import java.net.Socket;
import java.net.InetAddress;
import java.net.UnknownHostException;
import java.io.*;

public class PortTalkApp {
 public static void main(String args[]){
  PortTalk portTalk = new PortTalk(args);
  portTalk.displayDestinationParameters();
  portTalk.displayLocalParameters();
  portTalk.chat();
  portTalk.shutdown();
 }
}

class PortTalk {
 Socket connection;
 DataOutputStream outStream;
 BufferedReader inStream;
 public PortTalk(String args[]){
  if(args.length!=2) error("Usage: java PortTalkApp host port");
  String destination = args[0];
```

```
 int port = 0;
 try {
  port = Integer.valueOf(args[1]).intValue();
 }catch (NumberFormatException ex){
  error("Invalid port number");
 }
 try{
  connection = new Socket(destination,port);
 }catch (UnknownHostException ex){
  error("Unknown host");
 }
 catch (IOException ex){
  error("IO error creating socket");
 }
 try{
  inStream = new BufferedReader(
   new InputStreamReader(connection.getInputStream()));
  outStream = new DataOutputStream(connection.getOutputStream());
 }catch (IOException ex){
  error("IO error getting streams");
 }
 System.out.println("Connected to "+destination+" at port "+port+".");
}
public void displayDestinationParameters(){
 InetAddress destAddress = connection.getInetAddress();
 String name = destAddress.getHostName();
 byte ipAddress[] = destAddress.getAddress();
 int port = connection.getPort();
 displayParameters("Destination ",name,ipAddress,port);
}
public void displayLocalParameters(){
 InetAddress localAddress = null;
 try{
  localAddress = InetAddress.getLocalHost();
 }catch (UnknownHostException ex){
  error("Error getting local host information");
 }
 String name = localAddress.getHostName();
 byte ipAddress[] = localAddress.getAddress();
 int port = connection.getLocalPort();
 displayParameters("Local ",name,ipAddress,port);
}
public void displayParameters(String s,String name,byte ipAddress[],int port){
 System.out.println(s+"host is "+name+".");
 System.out.print(s+"IP address is ");
 for(int i=0;i<ipAddress.length;++i)
  System.out.print((ipAddress[i]+256)%256+".");
 System.out.println();
 System.out.println(s+"port number is "+port+".");
}
public void chat(){
 BufferedReader keyboardInput = new BufferedReader(
  new InputStreamReader(System.in));
 boolean finished = false;
 do {
  try{
```

continues

Listing 17.2. continued

```java
    System.out.print("Send, receive, or quit (S/R/Q): ");
    System.out.flush();
    String line = keyboardInput.readLine();
    if(line.length()>0){
     line=line.toUpperCase();
     switch (line.charAt(0)){
     case 'S':
      String sendLine = keyboardInput.readLine();
      outStream.writeBytes(sendLine);
      outStream.write(13);
      outStream.write(10);
      outStream.flush();
      break;
     case 'R':
      int inByte;
      System.out.print("***");
      while ((inByte = inStream.read()) != '\n')
      System.out.write(inByte);
      System.out.println();
      break;
     case 'Q':
      finished=true;
      break;
     default:
      break;
     }
    }
   }catch (IOException ex){
    error("Error reading from keyboard or socket");
   }
 } while(!finished);
}
 public void shutdown(){
  try{
   connection.close();
  }catch (IOException ex){
   error("IO error closing socket");
  }
 }
 public void error(String s){
  System.out.println(s);
  System.exit(1);
 }
}
```

To see how `PortTalkApp` works, run it using the following command line:

```
C:\jdk1.1.1\jdg\Ch17>java PortTalkApp jaworski.com 7
Connected to jaworski.com at port 7.
Destination host is jaworski.com.
Destination IP address is 204.212.153.193.
Destination port number is 7.
Local host is biscuit.jaworski.com.
Local IP address is 204.212.153.198.
Local port number is 1237.
Send, receive, or quit (S/R/Q):
```

`PortTalkApp` connects to my server at port 7. This is the port number for the `echo` server application. It is used to test Internet communication between hosts. It identifies my host's name, IP address, and destination port number. In this example, I am connecting from another computer on my local area network. Its name is `biscuit.jaworski.com` and has the `204.212.153.198` IP address. When you run the program, your host name and IP address will be displayed. The local port number that I am connecting from is port 1237.

`PortTalkApp` asks you whether you want to send a line, receive a line, or quit the program. Whether you elect to send or receive is important. If you decide to receive a line and the host is not sending any data, your program will block while it waits to receive information from a socket-based stream.

Enter an `S` to send a line and then enter `This is a test!` on the following line, like this:

```
Send, receive, or quit (S/R/Q): s
This is a test!
Send, receive, or quit (S/R/Q):
```

`PortTalkApp` will send your line to port 7 on my host and then prompt you for your next command. Enter `R` to receive a line of text from my server:

```
Send, receive, or quit (S/R/Q): r
***This is a test!
Send, receive, or quit (S/R/Q):
```

`PortTalkApp` reads a line of text from the socket stream and displays it prefixed with three asterisks. Now enter `Q` to close the connection and terminate the program. You can also use `PortTalkApp` to talk to other ports. For example, you can use it to talk to port 25 of hosts that support the Simple Mail Transport Protocol to send e-mail to someone who is served by that host.

`PortTalkApp` consists of a simple `main()` function that creates an object of class `PortTalk`, passing it the user-supplied host and port arguments. It invokes the `displayDestinationHostParameters()` and `displayLocalParameters()` methods of the `PortTalk` class to provide the initial connection-status information. The `chat()` method is used to send and receive lines of text over an established connection. The `shutdown()` method terminates the connection.

The `PortTalk` class implements the bulk of the processing performed by the program. It declares three field variables. The `connection` variable keeps track of the socket used with the connection. The `inStream` and `outStream` variables maintain the input and output streams derived from the socket.

The `PortTalk` constructor checks the arguments supplied by the user to make sure that a host and port number were supplied and converts the user-supplied port number to an integer. The `error()` method is used to display any errors to the console window. A new `Socket` object is created using the specified destination host name and port number and is assigned to the connection variable. The getInputStream() and getOutputStream() methods of the Socket class are used to attach input and output streams to the socket identified by the connection variable. These streams are then filtered as BufferedReader and DataOutputStream objects and assigned to the inStream and outStream variables. The constructor ends by displaying a connection status message to the console window.

The displayDestinationParameters() method uses the getInetAdress() method of the Socket class to get the InetAddress object associated with the destination host of the connection. It uses the getHostName() and getAddress() methods of the InetAddress class to obtain the name and IP address of the destination host. The getPort() method of the Socket class is used to get the destination port number. These parameters are displayed using the displayParameters() method.

The displayLocalParameters() method uses the getLocalHost(), getHostName(), and getAddress() methods of the InetAddress class to obtain the InetAddress object, name, and IP address of the local host. The getLocalPort() method of the Socket class is used to get the local port number. These parameters are displayed using the displayParameters() method.

The displayParameters() method displays the host name, IP address, and port number of an end of a socket connection. The s string parameter is used to differentiate between a local and destination host.

The chat() method implements the heart of the PortTalkApp program. It displays the Send, receive, or quit (S/R/Q): prompt to the user and then reads an input line from the user's keyboard.

If the user enters s for send, another line is read from the user's keyboard. This line is then written to the output stream associated with the socket connection. A carriage return and a line-feed character are then written to the output stream to signal an end of line. The carriage return–linefeed combination is the standard end-of-line identifier used with Internet application protocols.

If the user enters r for receive, three asterisks (***) are written to the console window to indicate input from the destination host. A byte at a time is then read from the input stream associated with the socket and displayed to the console window until a newline (\n) character is encountered.

If the user enters q for quit, the do loop of the chat() method is terminated.

The shutdown() method closes the Socket object referenced by the connection variable.

The error() method prints an error message to the console window and then terminates the program using the exit() method of the System class.

The ServerSocket Class

The ServerSocket class implements a TCP server socket. It provides three constructors that specify the port to which the server socket is to listen for incoming connection requests, an optional maximum connection request queue length, and an optional Internet address. The Internet address argument allows *multihomed* hosts (that is, hosts with more than one Internet address) to limit connections to a specific interface.

The accept() method is used to cause the server socket to listen and wait until an incoming connection is established. It returns an object of class Socket once a connection is made. This Socket object is then used to carry out a service for a single client. The getInetAddress() method returns the address of the host to which the socket is connected. The getLocalPort() method returns the port on which the server socket listens for an incoming connection. The toString() method returns the socket's address and port number as a string in preparation for printing.

The getSoTimeout() and setSoTimeout() methods set the socket's SO_TIMEOUT parameter. The close() method closes the server socket.

The static setSocketFactory() method is used to change the default ServerSocket implementation to a custom implementation. The implAccept() method is used by subclasses of ServerSocket to override the accept() method.

The ReverServerApp program is a simple server that listens on port 1234 for incoming connections from client programs. When ReverServerApp connects to a client, it reads one line of text at a time from the client, reverses the characters in the text line, and sends them back to the client. The source code of ReverServerApp is shown in Listing 17.3.

Listing 17.3. The source code of the ReverServerApp program.

```
import java.lang.System;
import java.net.ServerSocket;
import java.net.Socket;
import java.io.*;

public class ReverServerApp {
 public static void main(String args[]){
  try{
   ServerSocket server = new ServerSocket(1234);
   int localPort = server.getLocalPort();
   System.out.println("Reverse Server is listening on port "+localPort+".");
   Socket client = server.accept();
   String destName = client.getInetAddress().getHostName();
   int destPort = client.getPort();
   System.out.println("Accepted connection to "+destName+" on port "+
    destPort+".");
   BufferedReader inStream = new BufferedReader(
    new InputStreamReader(client.getInputStream()));
   DataOutputStream outStream = new DataOutputStream(client.getOutputStream());
```

continues

Listing 17.3. continued

```
     boolean finished = false;
     do {
      String inLine = inStream.readLine();
      System.out.println("Received: "+inLine);
      if(inLine.equalsIgnoreCase("quit")) finished=true;
      String outLine=new ReverseString(inLine.trim()).getString();
      for(int i=0;i<outLine.length();++i)
       outStream.write((byte)outLine.charAt(i));
      outStream.write(13);
      outStream.write(10);
      outStream.flush();
      System.out.println("Sent: "+outLine);
     } while(!finished);
     inStream.close();
     outStream.close();
     client.close();
     server.close();
    }catch (IOException ex){
     System.out.println("IOException occurred.");
    }
   }
 }
class ReverseString {
 String s;
 public ReverseString(String in){
  int len = in.length();
  char outChars[] = new char[len];
  for(int i=0;i<len;++i)
   outChars[len-1-i]=in.charAt(i);
  s = String.valueOf(outChars);
 }
 public String getString(){
  return s;
 }
}
```

To see how ReverServerApp works, you need to run it in a separate window and then use PortTalkApp to feed it lines of text. First, run ReverServerApp using the following command line:

```
C:\jdk1.1.1\jdg\ch17>java ReverServerApp
Reverse Server is listening on port 1234.
```

ReverServerApp notifies you that it is up and running. Now, in a separate window run PortTalkApp as follows, supplying your host name instead of athome.jaworski.com:

```
C:\jdk1.1.1\jdg\ch17>java PortTalkApp athome.jaworski.com 1234
Connected to athome.jaworski.com at port 1234.
Destination host is athome.jaworski.com.
Destination IP address is 204.212.153.194.
Destination port number is 1234.
Local host is athome.jaworski.com.
Local IP address is 204.212.153.194.
Local port number is 1302.
Send, receive, or quit (S/R/Q):
```

PortTalkApp displays all of the parameters of both end points of the connection. If you look in the window where ReverServerApp is running, you will see a message similar to the following:

```
Accepted connection to athome.jaworski.com on port 1302.
```

The port number reported by ReverServer is consistent with that reported by PortTalkApp. Now switch back to the PortTalkApp window and enter s to send a line of text, followed by the line of text This is a test!, as shown in the following output:

```
Send, receive, or quit (S/R/Q): s
This is a test!
```

The ReverServerApp window reports the following:

```
Received: This is a test!
Sent: !tset a si sihT
```

Enter an r in the PortTalkApp window, as shown in the following output:

```
Send, receive, or quit (S/R/Q): r
***!tset a si sihT
Send, receive, or quit (S/R/Q):
```

PortTalkApp displays the text that it received from ReverServerApp. Enter the s command followed by a quit text line:

```
Send, receive, or quit (S/R/Q): s
quit
```

The quit line is read by ReverServerApp, causing it to terminate the connection and exit. It displays the following:

```
Received: quit
Sent: tiuq

C:\jdk1.1.1\jdg\ch17>
```

In the PortTalkApp window, type q to terminate PortTalkApp, as shown in the following output:

```
Send, receive, or quit (S/R/Q): q

C:\jdk1.1.1\jdg\ch17>
```

The ReverServerApp program is smaller in size than PortTalkApp. It consists of a single main() method. The ReverseString class is also declared.

The `main()` method begins by creating a `ServerSocket` object on port 1234. It then uses the `getLocalPort()` method to get the local port number associated with the socket. This is to verify that it is indeed using port 1234. It then displays the fact that it is up and running and the number of the port on which it is listening for connections.

The `accept()` method is used to accept an incoming client connection and return the `Socket` object associated with the connection. The `getHostName()` and `getPort()` methods are used to get the host name and port number associated with the client program. These parameters are displayed to the console window. Input and output streams are then associated with the socket.

The `main()` method enters a loop where it reads a line of text from the input stream and then checks to see if it is the `quit` termination signal. The `ReverseString()` constructor and `getString()` method are used to reverse the line read from the input stream. The reversed line is then written to the output stream. If the `quit` line was received from the client, the loop is terminated and the input stream, output stream, client socket, and server socket are closed.

The `ReverseString` class provides a constructor that reverses a string and a `getString()` method for retrieving the reversed string.

The `DatagramSocket` Class

The `DatagramSocket` class implements client and server sockets using the UDP protocol. UDP is a connectionless protocol that allows application programs (both clients and servers) to exchange information using chunks of data known as *datagrams*.

`DatagramSocket` provides three constructors. The default constructor creates a datagram socket for use by client applications. No port number is specified. The second constructor allows a datagram socket to be created using a specified port. This constructor is typically used with server applications. The third constructor allows an Internet address to be specified in addition to the port. This is used to restrict service to a specific host interface.

The `send()` and `receive()` methods are used to send and receive datagrams using the socket. The datagrams are objects of class `DatagramPacket`. The `getLocalPort()` and `getLocalAddress()` methods return the local port and Internet address of the socket. The `close()` method closes this socket. The `getSoTimeout()` and `setSoTimeout()` methods get and set the socket's `SO_TIMEOUT` parameter.

The `DatagramPacket` Class

The `DatagramPacket` class encapsulates the actual datagrams that are sent and received using objects of class `DatagramSocket`. Two different constructors are provided: one for datagrams that are received from a datagram socket and one for creating datagrams that are sent over a datagram socket. The arguments to the received datagram constructor are a byte array used as a buffer for the received data and an integer that identifies the number of bytes received and stored in the buffer. The sending datagram constructor adds two additional parameters: the IP address and port where the datagram is to be sent.

Eight access methods are provided. The getAddress() and getPort()methods are used to read the destination IP address and port of the datagram. The getLength()and getData()methods are used to get the number of bytes of data contained in the datagram and to read the data into a byte array buffer. The setAddress(), setPort(), setLength(), and setData() methods allow the datagram's IP address, port, length, and data values to be set.

The TimeServerApp and GetTimeApp programs illustrate the use of client/server computing using datagrams. TimeServerApp listens on a UDP socket on port 2345 for incoming datagrams. When a datagram is received, it displays the data contained in the datagram to the console window and returns a datagram with the current date and time to the sending client program. It terminates its operation when it receives a datagram with the text quit as its data.

The GetTimeApp program sends five datagrams with the text time in each datagram to local port 2345. After sending each datagram, it waits for a return datagram from TimeServerApp. It displays the datagrams that it sends and receives to the console window. It then sends a quit datagram to TimeServerApp and terminates its operation.

The TimeServerApp program listing is shown in Listing 17.4. The code for GetTimeApp is in Listing 17.5.

Listing 17.4. The source code of the TimeServerApp program.

```
import java.lang.System;
import java.net.DatagramSocket;
import java.net.DatagramPacket;
import java.net.InetAddress;
import java.io.IOException;
import java.util.Date;

public class TimeServerApp {
 public static void main(String args[]){
  try{
   DatagramSocket socket = new DatagramSocket(2345);
   String localAddress = InetAddress.getLocalHost().getHostName().trim();
   int localPort = socket.getLocalPort();
   System.out.print(localAddress+": ");
   System.out.println("Time Server is listening on port "+localPort+".");
   int bufferLength = 256;
   byte outBuffer[];
   byte inBuffer[] = new byte[bufferLength];
   DatagramPacket outDatagram;
   DatagramPacket inDatagram = new DatagramPacket(inBuffer,inBuffer.length);
   boolean finished = false;
   do {
```

continues

Listing 17.4. continued

```
    socket.receive(inDatagram);
    InetAddress destAddress = inDatagram.getAddress();
    String destHost = destAddress.getHostName().trim();
    int destPort = inDatagram.getPort();
    System.out.println("\nReceived a datagram from "+destHost+" at port "+
     destPort+".");
    String data = new String(inDatagram.getData()).trim();
    System.out.println("It contained the data: "+data);
    if(data.equalsIgnoreCase("quit")) finished=true;
    String time = new Date().toString();
    outBuffer=time.getBytes();
    outDatagram = new DatagramPacket(outBuffer,outBuffer.length,destAddress,
     destPort);
    socket.send(outDatagram);
    System.out.println("Sent "+time+" to "+destHost+" at port "+destPort+".");
   } while(!finished);
  }catch (IOException ex){
   System.out.println("IOException occurred.");
  }
 }
}
```

Listing 17.5. The source code of the `GetTimeApp` program.

```
import java.lang.System;
import java.net.DatagramSocket;
import java.net.DatagramPacket;
import java.net.InetAddress;
import java.io.IOException;

public class GetTimeApp {
 public static void main(String args[]){
  try{
   DatagramSocket socket = new DatagramSocket();
   InetAddress localAddress = InetAddress.getLocalHost();
   String localHost = localAddress.getHostName();
   int bufferLength = 256;
   byte outBuffer[];
   byte inBuffer[] = new byte[bufferLength];
   DatagramPacket outDatagram;
   DatagramPacket inDatagram = new DatagramPacket(inBuffer,inBuffer.length);
   for(int i=0;i<5;++i){
    outBuffer = new byte[bufferLength];
    outBuffer = "time".getBytes();
    outDatagram = new DatagramPacket(outBuffer,outBuffer.length,
     localAddress,2345);
    socket.send(outDatagram);
    System.out.println("\nSent time request to "+localHost+" at port 2345.");
    socket.receive(inDatagram);
    InetAddress destAddress = inDatagram.getAddress();
```

```
      String destHost = destAddress.getHostName().trim();
      int destPort = inDatagram.getPort();
      System.out.println("Received a datagram from "+destHost+" at port "+
       destPort+".");
      String data = new String(inDatagram.getData());
      data=data.trim();
      System.out.println("It contained the following data: "+data);
     }
     outBuffer = new byte[bufferLength];
     outBuffer = "quit".getBytes();
     outDatagram = new DatagramPacket(outBuffer,outBuffer.length,
      localAddress,2345);
     socket.send(outDatagram);
    }catch (IOException ex){
     System.out.println("IOException occurred.");
    }
  }
}
```

TimeServerApp and GetTimeApp should be run in separate windows. First, start TimeServerApp using the following command line:

```
C:\jdk1.1.1\jdg\Ch17>java TimeServerApp
biscuit.jaworski.com: Time Server is listening on port 2345.
```

TimeServerApp will respond by letting you know that it is up and running and listening on port 2345.

Next, start GetTimeApp in a different window, as follows:

```
C:\jdk1.1.1\jdg\Ch17>java GetTimeApp

Sent time request to biscuit.jaworski.com at port 2345.
Received a datagram from 204.212.153.198 at port 2345.
It contained the following data: Mon Feb 24 21:10:53 PST 1997

Sent time request to biscuit.jaworski.com at port 2345.
Received a datagram from 204.212.153.198 at port 2345.
It contained the following data: Mon Feb 24 21:11:04 PST 1997

Sent time request to biscuit.jaworski.com at port 2345.
Received a datagram from 204.212.153.198 at port 2345.
It contained the following data: Mon Feb 24 21:11:13 PST 1997

Sent time request to biscuit.jaworski.com at port 2345.
Received a datagram from 204.212.153.198 at port 2345.
It contained the following data: Mon Feb 24 21:11:23 PST 1997

Sent time request to biscuit.jaworski.com at port 2345.
Received a datagram from 204.212.153.198 at port 2345.
It contained the following data: Mon Feb 24 21:11:33 PST 1997

C:\jdk1.1.1\jdg\Ch17>
```

GetTimeApp reports the packets it sends to and receives from TimeServerApp and then terminates. TimeServerApp provides a similar display in its window, as shown in the following output:

```
Received a datagram from 204.212.153.198 at port 1325.
It contained the data: time
Sent Mon Feb 24 21:10:53 PST 1997 to 204.212.153.198 at port 1325.

Received a datagram from 204.212.153.198 at port 1325.
It contained the data: time
Sent Mon Feb 24 21:11:04 PST 1997 to 204.212.153.198 at port 1325.

Received a datagram from 204.212.153.198 at port 1325.
It contained the data: time
Sent Mon Feb 24 21:11:13 PST 1997 to 204.212.153.198 at port 1325.

Received a datagram from 204.212.153.198 at port 1325.
It contained the data: time
Sent Mon Feb 24 21:11:23 PST 1997 to 204.212.153.198 at port 1325.

Received a datagram from 204.212.153.198 at port 1325.
It contained the data: time
Sent Mon Feb 24 21:11:33 PST 1997 to 204.212.153.198 at port 1325.

Received a datagram from 204.212.153.198 at port 1325.
It contained the data: quit
Sent Mon Feb 24 21:11:43 PST 1997 to 204.212.153.198 at port 1325.
```

```
C:\jdk1.1.1\jdg\Ch17>
```

These two simple programs illustrate the basic mechanics of datagram-based client/server applications. A UDP client sends a datagram to a UDP server at the server's port address. The UDP server listens on its port for a datagram, processes the datagram, and sends back information to the UDP client.

TimeServerApp

TimeServerApp begins by creating a DatagramSocket object on port 2345 and assigning it to the socket variable. It then obtains the host name and local port number using the getHostName() and getLocalPort() methods and displays this information to the console window.

TimeServerApp creates two byte buffers—outBuffer and inBuffer. outBuffer is an empty buffer that is used to send data in outgoing datagrams. inBuffer is initialized to a blank 256-byte buffer. TimeServerApp then declares two variables of the DatagramPacket class—a non-initialized outDatagram variable and an inDatagram that is initialized using the inBuffer[] array.

TimeServerApp executes a loop where it receives and processes datagrams received from client programs. It receives datagrams using the receive() method of the DatagramSocket class. It uses the getAddress() and getPort() methods of the DatagramPacket class to get the host address and port of the client program that sent the socket. It displays this information to the console window. It uses the getData() method of the DatagramPacket class to retrieve the data sent by the client program. It converts this data to a string and displays it on the console window. If the received data contains the quit string, it sets the finished flag to true. TimeServerApp processes the client time request by using the Date() constructor of the java.util package to construct a new Date object, converting the Date object to a byte array, and storing the data in outBuffer. It then creates a new DatagramPacket object, using outBuffer, with the destination address and port number of the sending client program. It sends the datagram to the client using the send() method of the DatagramSocket class. The console display is then updated with the data that was sent to the client program.

GetTimeApp

The GetTimeApp client program creates a DatagramSocket object and assigns it to the socket variable. It then creates a DatagramPacket object in the same manner as the TimeServerApp program. GetTimeApp uses a for statement to loop five times, sending five datagrams to port 2345 of the local host. After each datagram is sent, it waits to receive a return datagram from TimeServerApp. It uses the getAddress(), getPort(), and getData() methods of the DatagramPacket class to report this information to the console window.

After sending and receiving five datagrams, GetTimeApp sends a datagram with the quit text to tell TimeServerApp that it should terminate its processing.

The MulticastSocket Class

The MulticastSocket class is used for developing clients and servers for IP multicasting. It provides the capability for hosts to join and leave multicast groups. All hosts in a multicast group receive UDP datagrams that are sent to the IP address of the group. Each host in the group listens on a common UDP port for the datagrams of the multicast application.

The MulticastSocket class has two constructors—a default parameterless constructor and a constructor that specifies the port number on which to listen for multicast datagrams. The MulticastSocket class has seven access methods: joinGroup(), leaveGroup(), setInterface(), getInterface(), setTTL(), getTTL(), and send(). The joinGroup() and leaveGroup() methods are used to join and leave a multicast group at a specified Internet address. The getInterface() and setInterface() methods are used to get and set the IP address of the host interface that is used for multicasting. The getTTL() and setTTL() methods are used to get and set the time-to-live for multicast packets that are sent on the multicast socket. Time-to-live specifies the number of times that a packet is forwarded before it expires. The send() method is used to send a datagram to a multicast IP address.

The `SocketImpl` and `DataSocketImpl` Classes and the `SocketImplFactory` Interface

The `SocketImpl` and `DataSocketImpl` classes are abstract classes that are used as a basis for defining custom socket implementations. The `SocketImplFactory` interface must be implemented by new socket implementations.

NOTE

The `setSocketImplFactory()` method of the `Socket` class can be used to set the system `SocketImplFactory`. Once it is set, it cannot be changed.

The `SocketImpl` class provides four variables that are used to define a socket: the destination IP address and port, the local port, and a file descriptor used to create streams. The local IP address of the host need not be specified. The `DatagramSocketImpl` class uses only the local port and file descriptor because no connection with a destination IP address and port is required for UDP sockets.

Some of the access methods defined by `SocketImpl` are used to perform lower-level socket operations. These include listening for connections, accepting connections, binding a socket to a port, and implementing the actual connection. Other access methods are used to support stream-based I/O and to provide access to the IP address and port parameters of a socket. The `DatagramSocketImpl` class provides a similar set of methods that are oriented to the processing of UDP datagrams.

Web-Related Classes

In addition to providing the basic TCP- and UDP-based sockets used by almost all Internet client/server applications, the `java.net` package provides a useful set of classes that support higher-level, Web-specific applications. These classes are centered around the URL class, which encapsulates an object on the Web, typically a Web page, by its URL address.

URL stands for *uniform resource locator* and, as its name states, provides a uniform way to locate resources on the Web. Different types of URLs are used with different application protocols, the most common of which are the Hypertext Transfer Protocol (HTTP) and the File Transfer Protocol (FTP). URLs for these types of protocols are mainly used to identify the location of files, such as Web pages, supporting images, multimedia files, text files, and downloadable programs. HTTP URLs also refer to executable programs, such as CGI scripts, which perform Web-related services. *CGI scripts* are programs, usually written in a scripting language, that receive input and generate output in accordance with the common gateway interface (CGI) specification.

The URL Class

The URL class encapsulates Web objects by their URL address. It provides a set of constructors that allow URL objects to be easily constructed and a set of access methods that allow high-level read and write operations to be performed using URLs.

Most, but not all URLs typically consist of a protocol, host name, and the path and name of a file on the host. For example, the URL http://www.jaworski.com/jdg/index.htm refers to a Web page on my Web server. It specifies the HTTP protocol as the protocol used to access the Web page. It identifies my host name as www.jaworski.com, and it names the file as /jdg/ index.htm where /jdg/ is the directory path to the file (relative to my Web server's directory root) and index.htm is the file's name. In HTTP URLs, the path/filename is optional. For example, the URL http://www.jaworski.com/jdg/ is equivalent to the previous URL. My Web server uses the filename index.htm as the default name for a file. The path name can also be omitted. The URL http://www.jaworski.com would use the index.htm file in the Web server's root directory.

The four URL constructors allow URL objects to be created using a variety of URL parameters such as protocol type, host name, port, and file path. These parameters may be supplied separately or in text form as part of an URL string. The URL class treats a file's path and name as a single entity to provide a more convenient way of working with URL components.

URLs can be constructed using their absolute address or using an address that is relative to another URL. Up to now we have been working with the full, complete, or *absolute* address of a URL. A *relative address* is a path/filename or file offset that is specified relative to an absolute URL. For example, the absolute URL http://www.jaworski.com can be combined with the relative URL /jdg/index.htm to produce the URL to http://www.jaworski.com/jdg/index.htm.

The URL access methods provide a full set of URL processing capabilities. The getProtocol(), getHost(), getPort(), getFile(), and getRef() methods allow the individual address components of the URL to be determined. The getContent() and openStream() methods allow reading of the Web object pointed to by the URL. The toExternalForm() and toString() methods enable URLs to be converted into strings to support display and printing. The equals() method compares URLs, and the sameFile() method compares the Web objects pointed to by the URLs. The openConnection() method creates an object of class URLConnection to the Web object pointed to be the URL. This class is discussed after the "URLConnection" section of this chapter.

The GetURLApp program illustrates the power provided by the URL class. This small program implements a primitive Web browser. Just run the program with the name of an URL and it makes a connection to the destination Web server and downloads the referenced document. The program's source code is shown in Listing 17.6.

Listing 17.6. The source code of the GetURLApp program.

```
import java.lang.System;
import java.net.URL;
import java.net.MalformedURLException;
import java.io.*;

public class GetURLApp {
 public static void main(String args[]){
  try{
   if(args.length!=1) error("Usage: java GetURLApp URL");
   System.out.println("Fetching URL: "+args[0]);
   URL url = new URL(args[0]);
   BufferedReader inStream = new BufferedReader(
    new InputStreamReader(url.openStream()));
   String line;
   while ((line = inStream.readLine())!= null){
    System.out.println(line);
   }
   inStream.close();
  }catch (MalformedURLException ex){
   error("Bad URL");
  }catch (IOException ex){
   error("IOException occurred.");
  }
 }
 public static void error(String s){
  System.out.println(s);
  System.exit(1);
 }
}
```

After compiling the program, try running it with http://www.jaworski.com/java/GetURLApp.htm, as follows. Make sure that you use the correct uppercase and lowercase characters:

```
C:\jdk1.1.1\jdg\ch17>java GetURLApp http://www.jaworski.com/java/GetURLApp.htm
```

The program will respond by displaying the following Web document from my Web server:

```
C:\jdk1.1.1\jdg\ch17>java GetURLApp http://www.jaworski.com/java/GetURLApp.htm
Fetching URL: http://www.jaworski.com/java/GetURLApp.htm
<!DOCTYPE HTML PUBLIC "-//SQ//DTD HTML 2.0 HoTMetaL + extensions//EN">
<HTML><HEAD><TITLE>GetURLApp Test Results</TITLE></HEAD>
<BODY><H1>GetURLApp Test Results</H1>
<P>Congratulations! You were able to successfully compile and run GetURLApp.
</P>
</BODY></HTML>

C:\jdk1.1.1\jdg\ch17>
```

Try running the program with other URLs to see how they are displayed.

GetURLApp consists of a short main() method and the error() method, used to display error messages to the console window.

The `main()` method checks the arguments supplied by the user to make sure that the correct number of arguments are present. It then displays a message to the console window identifying the URL that it is trying to fetch. It creates an `URL` object using the URL name supplied by the user and assigns it to the `url` variable. It then uses the `openStream()` method of the `URL` class to create an input stream from the URL. The input stream is filtered as a `BufferedReader` object and is assigned to the `inStream` variable. The `inStream` variable is used to read and display the input stream one line at a time.

URLConnection **and** HttpURLConnection

The `URLConnnection` class is an `abstract` class that encapsulates an active HTTP connection to a Web object represented by an URL. It provides a number of methods for getting information about the Web object, about the connection to the Web object, and for interacting with the Web object.

`URLConnection` defines several class variables that specify the connection state and associated parameters. It also supplies numerous methods that provide access to the HTTP-specific fields of the connection. This class is studied in detail in Part V, "Network Programming," of this book. The next programming example covers a few aspects of its use.

The `HttpURLConnection` class is a subclass of `URLConnection` that provides direct access to the Hypertext Transfer Protocol parameters involved in a client/server HTTP connection. `HttpURLConnection` is also covered in Part V of this book.

URLEncoder

The `URLEncoder` class is a simple class that provides a single `static` method, `encode()`, for converting text strings to a form that is suitable for use as part of an URL. This format is known as `x-www-form-urlencoded` and is typically used to encode form data that is sent to a CGI script.

The `encode()` method converts spaces to plus signs (+) and uses the percent character (%) as an escape code to encode special characters. The two characters that immediately follow a percent sign are interpreted as hexadecimal digits that are combined to produce an eight-bit value.

Listing 17.7 illustrates the use of the `encode()` method and the `URLConnection` class. The `QueryURLApp` program accesses the echo-query CGI program on my Web server, passing it the `"/this/is/extra/path/information"` query string and the `"Query string with some special characters: @#$%?&+"` query string. The query string is encoded using the `encode()` method of the `URLEncoder` class. The echo-query CGI program creates an HTML file that describes the parameters passed to it by my Web server and returns this file to the `QueryURLApp` program. This file shows how the query string was encoded by the `encode()` method.

Listing 17.7. The source code of the `QueryURLApp` program.

```
import java.lang.System;
import java.net.URL;
import java.net.URLConnection;
import java.net.URLEncoder;
import java.net.MalformedURLException;
import java.net.UnknownServiceException;
import java.io.*;

public class QueryURLApp {
 public static void main(String args[]){
  try{
   String urlString = "http://www.jaworski.com/cgi-bin/echo-query";
   String extraPathInfo = "/this/is/extra/path/information";
   String queryString =
    URLEncoder.encode("Query string with some special characters: @#$%?&+");
   URL url = new URL(urlString+extraPathInfo+"?"+queryString);
   URLConnection connection = url.openConnection();
   BufferedReader fromURL = new BufferedReader(
    new InputStreamReader(url.openStream()));
   String line;
   while ((line = fromURL.readLine())!= null){
    System.out.println(line);
   }
   fromURL.close();
  }catch (MalformedURLException ex){
   error("Bad URL");
  }catch (UnknownServiceException ex){
   error("UnknownServiceException occurred.");
  }catch (IOException ex){
   error("IOException occurred.");
  }
 }
 public static void error(String s){
  System.out.println(s);
  System.exit(1);
 }
}
```

To run `QueryURLApp`, just type the following command line:

```
C:\jdk1.1.1\jdg\ch17>java QueryURLApp
```

`QueryURLApp` queries the echo-query program on my Web server and displays the HTML file generated by the echo-query program. Notice how the query string was encoded:

```
<HTML>
<HEAD>
<TITLE>Echo CGI Request</TITLE>
</HEAD>
<BODY>
<H1>CGI Request</H1>
<H2>Command Line Arguments</H2>
<P>Number of command line arguments: 7</P>
<P>Command line arguments: Query string with some special characters:
```

```
➥ @#\$%\?\&+
</P>
<H2>Environment Variables</H2>
<PRE>
AUTH_TYPE =
CONTENT_LENGTH =
CONTENT_TYPE =
GATEWAY_INTERFACE = CGI/1.1
HTTP_ACCEPT = text/html, image/gif, image/jpeg, *; q=.2, */*; q=.2
HTTP_USER_AGENT = Javainternal_build
PATH_INFO = /this/is/extra/path/information
PATH_TRANSLATED = /usr/local/etc/httpd/htdocs/this/is/extra/path/information
QUERY_STRING =
➥   Query+string+with+some+special+characters%3a+%40%23%24%25%3f%26%2b
REMOTE_ADDR = 204.212.153.194
REMOTE_HOST = athome.jaworski.com
REMOTE_IDENT =
REMOTE_USER =
REQUEST_METHOD = GET
SCRIPT_NAME = /cgi-bin/echo-query
SERVER_NAME = www.jaworski.com
SERVER_PORT = 80
SERVER_PROTOCOL = HTTP/1.0
SERVER_SOFTWARE = NCSA/1.4.2
</PRE>
<H2>Standard Input</H2>
</BODY>
</HTML>

C:\jdk1.1.1\jdg\ch17>
```

QueryURLApp creates an URL by concatenating the URL for the echo-query program, the extra path information, and the encoded query string. It then uses the openConnection() method of the URL class to create an URLConnection object, which it assigns to the connection variable. The connection is then read and displayed in the same manner as the GetURLApp program.

ContentHandler, ContentHandlerFactory, and FileNameMap

The ContentHandler class is an abstract class that is used to develop specialized objects that are able to extract and process data associated with new MIME types.

MIME, or *Multipurpose Internet Mail Extension,* is a general method by which the content of different types of Internet objects can be identified. MIME was originally developed to include different types of objects, such as sounds, images, and videos in Internet e-mail messages. It was also adopted and popularized by the Web and is used to identify multimedia and other types of Web objects so that appropriate external viewers or plug-in modules can be used to process and display these objects.

The ContentHandler class provides the basis for developing new viewers for processing MIME types that are not currently supported by Java. It consists of a single method, getContent(), that extracts an object of a particular MIME type from an URL connection.

The ContentHandlerFactory interface provides a standard method of associating a content handler with a MIME type. The FileNameMap interface provides the capability to associate a filename with a MIME type.

Chapter 36, "Content Handlers," provides a detailed description of how content handlers are developed.

The URLStreamHandler Class and the URLStreamHandlerFactory Interface

The URLStreamHandler class is an abstract class that is used to develop specialized objects that are able to communicate with Web resources using protocols that are currently not supported by Java. For example, suppose you develop a new protocol for a custom client/server application and you want that protocol to be accessible to Web browsers. You would develop an URLStreamHandler for that protocol. The URLStreamHandlerFactory interface is used to associate a stream handler with a particular protocol. Chapter 37, "Protocol Handlers," provides a detailed description of how protocol stream handlers are developed.

Summary

In this chapter you learned about Java's support of network programming and covered the basics of client/server computing and TCP/IP socket programming. You toured the classes of the java.net package and learned how to use them to develop client/server applications. You also covered the URL-centric classes that support Web-based applications. The next chapter covers the java.rmi packages used to build applications that are distributed over TCP/IP networks.

18

Building Distributed Applications with the `java.rmi` Packages

The Remote Method Invocation (RMI) API of JDK 1.1 adds the capability to develop fully distributed applications to Java's overwhelming list of credentials. This capability is provided by a set of intuitive and easy-to-use packages that make distributed application development a natural extension to single host programming. The RMI API, while only in its first release, outclasses all currently available distributed application programming frameworks, including Common Object Request Broker Architecture (CORBA) and Distributed Computing Environment (DCE).

In this chapter, you'll be introduced to distributed applications and learn why the RMI API provides a superior development approach for distributed programming in Java. You'll cover the packages of the RMI API and then use them to develop a simple distributed application. When you finish this chapter, you'll be thoroughly introduced to the java.rmi packages. Part VIII, "Developing Distributed Applications," is dedicated to distributed applications using RMI.

RMI and Distributed Applications

Distributed applications are applications that execute across multiple host systems. Objects executing on one host invoke methods of objects on other hosts to help them perform their processing. These methods execute on the remote hosts—hence the name remote method invocation. The remotely invoked objects perform computations and may return values that are used by the local objects. Figure 18.1 illustrates this concept.

A number of approaches to implementing distributed systems have been developed. The Internet and the Web are examples of distributed systems that have been developed using the client/server approach. Clients and servers communicate via TCP sockets. While the Internet and the Web are remarkably successful, the use of TCP sockets requires separate application-level protocols for client/server communication. The overhead associated with these protocols prohibits the fine grain parallel operation that is possible through other approaches.

The Distributed Computing Environment (DCE) makes use of remote procedure calls to allow processes executing on one system to spawn execution threads on other systems. DCE provides an excellent framework for developing distributed systems; however, its major shortcoming is a reliance on a procedural approach that lacks an object orientation.

The Common Object Request Broker Architecture (CORBA) supports an object-oriented framework for developing distributed systems. CORBA's strong point is that it supports a language-independent model. However, this advantage is a disadvantage when it comes to Java because it forces Java applications to use an external, albeit neutral, object model.

FIGURE 18.1.
A distributed application.

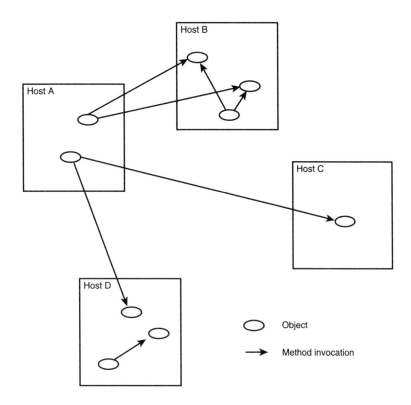

The Remote Method Invocation (RMI) API of Java is a Java-specific approach to developing distributed systems. RMI's major advantage is that it is fully integrated with the Java object model, highly intuitive, and easy to use.

RMI Terminology

Before describing the RMI API, let's cover some of the terminology it uses.

RMI is built upon the fundamental notion of local and remote objects. This concept is relative. *Local objects* are objects that execute on a particular host. *Remote objects* are objects that execute on all other hosts. Objects on remote hosts are *exported* so that they can be invoked remotely. An object exports itself by registering itself with a *remote registry server.* The remote registry server helps objects on other hosts to remotely access its registered objects. It does this by maintaining a database of names and the objects that are associated with these names (see Figure 18.2).

FIGURE 18.2.

Remote objects register themselves for remote access.

Objects that export themselves for remote access must implement the `Remote` interface. This interface identifies the object as being capable of being accessed remotely. Any methods that are to be invoked remotely must throw the `RemoteException`. This exception is used to indicate errors that may occur during an RMI.

Java's RMI approach is organized into a client/server framework. A local object that invokes a remote object's method is referred to as a *client object*, or simply a *client*. A remote object whose methods are invoked by a local object is referred to as a *server object*, or a *server*.

Java's RMI approach makes use of stubs and skeletons. A *stub* is a local object that acts as a proxy for the remote object. The stub provides the same methods of the remote object. Local objects invoke the methods of the stub as if they were the methods of the remote object. The stub then communicates these method invocations to the remote object via a skeleton that is implemented on the remote host. The skeleton is a proxy for the remote object that is located on the same host as the remote object. The skeleton communicates with the local stub and propagates method invocations on the stub to the actual remote object. It then receives the value returned (if any) by the remote method invocation and passes this value back to the stub. The stub, in turn, sends the return value on to the local object that initiated the remote method invocation.

Stubs and skeletons communicate through a remote reference layer. This layer provides stubs with the capability to communicate with skeletons via a transport protocol. RMI currently uses TCP for information transport, although it is flexible enough to use other protocols. Figure 18.3 shows how stubs and skeletons are used in Java RMI.

NOTE

This chapter provides a summary of how RMI works and covers the RMI API. Part VIII of this book shows you how to create distributed applications that use RMI.

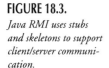

FIGURE 18.3.
Java RMI uses stubs and skeletons to support client/server communication.

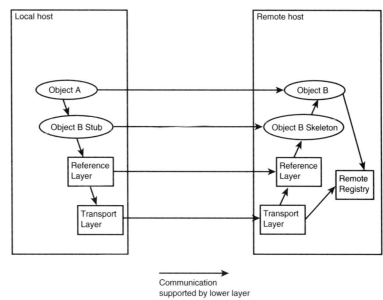

The `java.rmi` Packages

The RMI API is implemented by the following four packages:

- `java.rmi`—Provides the `Remote` interface, a class for accessing remote names, and a security manager for RMI.

- `java.rmi.registry`—Provides classes and interfaces that are used by the remote registry.

- `java.rmi.server`—Provides the classes and interfaces used to implement remote objects, stubs, and skeletons, and to support RMI communication. This package implements the bulk of the RMI API.

- `java.rmi.dgc`—Provides classes and interfaces that are used by the RMI distributed garbage collector.

The following sections describe each of these packages. Don't worry if it seems like there's a lot of material to learn. When you actually use RMI, you'll only use a small fraction of the RMI API. When you read over the description of the RMI packages, just try to get a feel for the classes and interfaces that are available to you.

The `java.rmi` **Package**

The `java.rmi` package declares the `Remote` interface, the `Naming` and `RMISecurityManager` classes, and a number of exceptions that are used with remote method invocation.

The `Remote` interface must be implemented by all remote objects. This interface has no methods. It is used for identification purposes.

The `Naming` class provides static methods for accessing remote objects via RMI URLs. The `bind()` and `rebind()` methods bind a remote object name to a specific RMI URL. The `unbind()` method removes the binding between an object name and an RMI URL. The `lookup()` method returns the remote object specified by an RMI URL. The `list()` method returns the list of URLs that are currently known to the RMI registry.

The syntax for RMI URLs is as follows:

```
rmi://host:port/remoteObjectName
```

The `host` and TCP `port` are optional. If the `host` is omitted, the local host is assumed. The default TCP port is 1099. For example, the following URL names the `MyObject` remote object that is located on the host `atwork.jaworski.com` and is accessible via TCP port 1234:

```
rmi://atwork.jaworski.com:1234/MyObject
```

The `RMISecurityManager` class defines the default security policy used for remote object stubs. It only applies to applications. Applets use the `AppletSecurityManager` class even if they perform RMI. You can extend `RMISecurityManager` and override its methods to implement your own RMI security policies. Use the `setSecurityManager()` method of the `System` class to set an `RMISecurityManager` object as the current security manager to be used for RMI stubs.

The `java.rmi` package defines a number of exceptions. The `RemoteException` class is the parent of all exceptions that are generated during RMI. It must be thrown by all methods of a remote object that can be accessed remotely.

> **NOTE**
>
> A remote object is allowed to have local methods that can be invoked locally. These methods do not need to throw `RemoteException`.

The `java.rmi.registry` **Package**

The `java.rmi.registry` package provides the `Registry` and `RegistryHandler` interfaces and the `LocateRegistry` class. These interfaces and classes are used to register and access remote objects by name. Remote objects are registered when they are identified to a host's registry process. The registry process is created when the `rmiregistry` program is executed.

The Registry interface defines the bind(), rebind(), unbind(), list(), and lookup() methods that are used by the Naming class to associate object names and RMI URLs. The registry interface also defines the REGISTRY_PORT constant that identifies the default TCP port used by the registry service.

The RegistryHandler interface provides methods for accessing objects that implement the Registry interface. The registryStub() method returns the local stub of a remote object that implements the Registry interface. The registryImpl() method constructs a Registry object and exports it via a specified TCP port.

The LocateRegistry class provides the static getRegistry() method for retrieving Registry objects on the local host or a remote host. It also provides the createRegistry() method to construct a Registry object and export it via a specified TCP port.

The java.rmi.server Package

The java.rmi.server package implements several interfaces and classes that support both client and server aspects of RMI.

The RemoteObject class implements the Remote interface and provides a remote implementation of the Object class. All classes that implement remote objects, both client and server, extend RemoteObject.

The RemoteServer class extends RemoteObject and is a common class that is subclassed by specific types of remote object implementations. It provides the static setLog() and getLog() methods for setting and retrieving an output stream used to log information about RMI accesses. It also provides the getClientHost() method that is used to retrieve the host name of the client performing the remote method invocation.

The UnicastRemoteObject class extends RemoteServer and provides the default remote object implementation. Classes that implement remote objects usually subclass UnicastRemoteObject. Objects of the UnicastRemoteObject class are accessed via TCP connections on port 1099, exist only for the duration of the process that creates them, and rely on a stream-based protocol for client/server communication.

The RemoteStub class extends RemoteObject and provides an abstract implementation of client-side stubs. A *client stub* is a local representation of a remote object that implements all remote methods of the remote object. The static setRef() method is used to associate a client stub with its corresponding remote object.

The RemoteCall interface provides methods that are used by stubs and skeletons to implement remote method invocations.

The RemoteRef interface is used by RemoteStub objects to reference remote objects. It provides methods for comparing and invoking remote objects and for working with objects that implement the RemoteCall interface.

The ServerRef interface extends the RemoteRef interface and is implemented by remote objects to gain access to their associated RemoteStub objects.

The Skeleton interface is implemented by remote skeletons. It provides methods that are used by the skeleton to access the methods being requested of the remote object and for working with method arguments and return values.

The Unreferenced interface is implemented by a remote object to enable it to determine when it is no longer referenced by a client.

The RMIClassLoader class supports the loading of remote classes. The location of a remote class is specified by either an URL or the java.rmi.server.codebase system property. The static loadClass() method loads a remote class and the static getSecurityContext() returns the security context in which the class loader operates. The LoaderHandler interface defines methods that are used by RMIClassClassLoader to load classes.

The Operation class is used to store a reference to a method. The getOperation() method returns the name of the method. The toString() method returns a String representation of the method's signature.

The ObjID class is used to create objects that serve as unique identifiers for objects that are exported as remote by a particular host. It provides methods for reading the object ID from and writing it to a stream. The UID class is an abstract class for creating unique object identifiers.

The LogStream class extends the PrintStream class to support the logging of errors that occur during RMI processing.

The RMISocketFactory class provides a default socket implementation for transporting information between clients and servers involved in RMI. This class provides three alternative approaches to establishing RMI connections that can be used with firewalls. The static setSocketFactory() method can be used to specify a custom socket implementation. The RMIFailureHandler interface defines methods that handle the failure of a server socket creation.

The java.rmi.dgc Package

The java.rmi.dgc package contains classes and interfaces that are used by the distributed garbage collector. The DGC interface is implemented by the server side of the distributed garbage collector. It defines two methods: dirty() and clean(). The dirty() method is used to indicate that a remote object is being referenced by a client. The clean() method is used to indicate that a remote reference has been completed.

The Lease class creates objects that are used to keep track of object references. The VMID class is used to create an ID that uniquely identifies a Java virtual machine on a particular host.

Implementing RMI

Now that you've been introduced to the RMI API and covered each of its packages, you're probably wondering how you go about implementing a remote method invocation. I'll summarize this process in this section and then explain it in detail in Part VIII. I'll organize the discussion according to the steps performed on the remote host (server) and local host (client).

Implementing the RMI Server on the Remote Host

Because a remote object must exist before it can be invoked, we'll first cover the steps involved in creating the remote object and registering it with the remote registry. In the following section, we'll look at what it takes for a local object to access a remote object and invoke its methods.

Create the Remote Interface

Remote objects are referenced via interfaces. In order to implement a remote object, you must first create an interface for that object. This interface must be `public` and must extend the `Remote` interface. Define the remote methods that you want to invoke within this interface. These methods must throw `RemoteException`.

Listing 18.1 provides an example of a remote interface. The `MyServer.java` file is defined in the `jdg.ch18.server` package. This file is located in the `ch18\server` directory. The reason that I put it in a named package is so that it can be found relative to your CLASSPATH. Your CLASSPATH should include `c:\jdk1.1.1`, and the `jdg` directory should be right under `c:\jdk1.1.1`. By doing so, the `jdg.ch18.server` package will be accessible from your CLASSPATH.

`MyServer` defines two methods: `getDataNum()` and `getData()`. The `getDataNum()` method returns an integer indicating the total number of data strings that are available on the server. The `getData()` method returns the nth data string.

Compile `MyServer.java` before going on to the next section.

Listing 18.1. The `MyServer` class.

```
package jdg.ch18.server;

import java.rmi.*;

public interface MyServer extends Remote {
 int getDataNum() throws RemoteException;
 String getData(int n) throws RemoteException;
}
```

Create a Class that Implements the Remote Interface

Having created the remote interface, next you must create a class that implements the remote interface. This class typically extends the `UnicastRemoteObject` class. However, it could also extend other subclasses of the `RemoteServer` class.

The implementation class should have a constructor that creates and initializes the remote object. It should also implement all of the methods defined in the remote interface. It should have a `main()` method so that it can be executed as a remote class. The `main()` method should use the `setSecurityManager()` method of the `System` class to set an object to be used as the remote object's security manager. It should register a name by which it can be remotely referenced with the remote registry.

Listing 18.2 provides the implementation class for the `MyServer` interface. The `MyServerImpl` class is also in the `jdg.ch18.server` package. You should change the `hostName` value to the name of the host where the remote object is to be located.

The `data` array contains five strings that are retrieved by the client object via the `getDataNum()` and `getData()` methods. The `getDataNum()` method returns the length of `data`, and the `getData()` method returns the nth element of the data array.

The `main()` method sets the security manager to an object of the `RMISecurityManager` class. It creates an instance of the `MyServerImpl` class and invokes the `rebind()` method of `Naming` to register the new object with remote registry. It registers the object with the name `MyServer`. It then informs you that it has successfully completed the registration process.

Compile `MyServerImpl.java` before going on to the next section.

Listing 18.2. The `MyServerImpl` class.

```
package jdg.ch18.server;

import java.rmi.*;
import java.rmi.server.*;

public class MyServerImpl extends UnicastRemoteObject
 implements MyServer {
 static String hostName="atwork.jaworski.com";
 static String data[] = {"Remote","Method","Invocation","Is","Great!"};
 public MyServerImpl() throws RemoteException {
  super();
 }
 public int getDataNum() throws RemoteException {
  return data.length;
 }
 public String getData(int n) throws RemoteException {
  return data[n%data.length];
 }
```

```
public static void main(String args[]){
 System.setSecurityManager(new RMISecurityManager());
 try {
  MyServerImpl instance = new MyServerImpl();
  Naming.rebind("//"+hostName+"/MyServer", instance);
  System.out.println("I'm registered!");
 } catch (Exception ex) {
  System.out.println(ex);
 }
 }
}
```

Create Stub and Skeleton Classes

Once you have created the class that implements the remote interface, use the rmic compiler to create the stub and skeleton classes:

```
C:\jdk1.1.1\jdg\ch18\server>rmic jdg.ch18.server.MyServerImpl
```

The rmic compiler creates the files MyServerImpl_Stub.class and MyServerImpl_Skel.class.

> **NOTE**
>
> You must supply the fully qualified package name of the class that you compile with rmic.

Copy the Remote Interface and Stub File to the Client Host

You'll need the MyServer.class interface file to compile your client software, and you'll need MyServer.class and MyServerImpl_Stub.class to run your client. Before going any further, you should copy these files to an appropriate location on your client host. They must be in a path jdg\ch18\server that is accessible via the client's CLASSPATH. I suggest putting them in c:\jdk1.1.1\jdg\ch18\server and putting c:\jdk1.1.1 in your CLASSPATH. If you run both the client and server on the same computer, the directory structure and files will already be in position.

> **NOTE**
>
> In Part VIII, I'll show you how to use applets and a Web server to automatically distribute client files.

Start Up the Remote Registry

Now you must start your remote registry server. This program listens on the default port 1099 for incoming requests to access named objects. The named objects must register themselves with the remote registry program in order to be made available to requestors. You start up the remote registry server as follows:

```
C:\jdk1.1.1\jdg\ch18\server>start rmiregistry
```

Under Windows 95, this command creates a new DOS window and runs the remote registry program as a background task.

Create and Register the Remote Object

You're almost done with the remote server. The last thing to do is execute the MyServerImpl program to create an object of the MyServerImpl class that registers itself with the remote registry. You do this as follows:

```
C:\jdk1.1.1\jdg\ch18\server>java jdg.ch18.server.MyServerImpl
I'm registered!
```

The program displays the I'm registered! string to let you know that it has successfully registered itself. Leave the server running while you start the client. If you run the client and server on the same computer, you'll need to open up a separate command line window for the client.

Implementing the RMI Client on the Local Host

Now that you have the remote server up and running, let's create a client program to remotely invoke the methods of the MyServer object and display the results it returns.

Listing 18.3 contains the MyClient program. You must change the hostName variable to the name of the remote server host where the remote object is registered. Compile this program and copy it to a jdg\ch18\client directory that is accessible from the CLASSPATH of the client host. Once you have compiled it, you can run it as follows:

```
C:\jdk1.1.1\jdg\ch18\client>java jdg.ch18.client.MyClient
Remote
Method
Invocation
Is
Great!
```

The MyClient program remotely invokes the methods of the server object and displays the data returned to the console window.

MyClient consists of a single main() method that invokes the lookup() method of the Naming class to retrieve a reference to the object named MyServer on the specified host. It casts this object to the MyServer interface. It then invokes the getDataNum() method of the remote object to retrieve the number of available data items and the getData() method to retrieve each specific data item. The retrieved data items are displayed in the console window.

You can shut down the client and server by terminating the programs and closing their command line windows.

Listing 18.3. The MyClient program.

```
package jdg.ch18.client;

import jdg.ch18.server.*;
import java.rmi.*;

public class MyClient {
 static String hostName="atwork.jaworski.com";
 public static void main(String args[]) {
  try {
   MyServer server = (MyServer) Naming.lookup("//"+hostName+"/MyServer");
   int n = server.getDataNum();
   for(int i=0;i<n;++i) {
    System.out.println(server.getData(i));
   }
  } catch (Exception ex) {
   System.out.println(ex);
  }
 }
}
```

Summary

This chapter introduces you to distributed applications. You learned why the RMI API provides a superior development approach for distributed programming in Java. You covered the packages of the RMI API and then used them to develop a simple distributed application. Part VIII of this book is dedicated to distributed applications using RMI. In the next chapter, you'll learn how to use the java.sql package to access remote databases from within Java applications.

19

Connecting to Databases with the java.sql Package

One of the most exciting developments in Java between the JDK 1.02 and JDK 1.1 is the JDBC API. The JDBC is an Application Programming Interface (API) for connecting Java applications and applets to databases. It was originally developed as a separate package from the JDK 1.02, but is now an integral part of the JDK 1.1 and is contained in the `java.sql` package.

> **NOTE**
>
> Many people associate JDBC with Java Database Connectivity. However, according to JavaSoft, JDBC is not an acronym.

The JDBC is a powerful tool for Java development. By providing database connectivity to applications and applets, it enables these programs to tap into company (internal), commercial, government, university, and other databases. This results in information-rich Java applications that can be used to replace and enhance current legacy information systems.

In this chapter, you'll learn the basics of the JDBC. You'll cover the classes of the `java.sql` package and learn to work with JDBC drivers. You'll also learn how to connect to databases, execute SQL statements, and work with result sets. This chapter provides a quick introduction to the `java.sql` package. If you are familiar with databases and SQL, this chapter will quickly get you up to speed with the database capabilities of JDBC. If you are not familiar with these concepts, don't worry; Part VII of this book, "Database Programming," provides a comprehensive introduction to Java database programming.

Setting Up a Database Connection

In order to use JDBC, you'll need a database server and a database driver. Because this book is geared to Windows 95 users, I'll be using Microsoft Access as my database server. You can choose to use Access or some other server. After you learn how to connect to your database, the type of server that you're using won't matter—JDBC provides a server-independent approach to database access. That's one of JDBC's major benefits!

You'll also need a database driver. The database driver provides the linkage between the JDBC and your database. The JDBC comes with a JDBC-ODBC bridge. This bridge allows you to access databases via Microsoft's Open Database Connectivity API. However, the JDBC-ODBC bridge is a temporary solution to database connectivity and has some significant drawbacks, such as requiring the bridge to be installed on your database users' computers. Chapter 48, "Database Fundamentals," covers database drivers in more detail. I will use the JDBC driver of IDS Software (http://www.idssoftware.com). The IDS JDBC driver is a pure Java driver that supports *zero installation* for applets. This means that you can provide database access via applets without requiring software to be preinstalled on the computers of applet users.

While you may use a JDBC driver of your choice to work through the examples in this book, I recommend the IDS driver because of its ease of use, great documentation, and zero installation features. If you are interested in using the IDS JDBC driver, check the IDS Web page for the availability of an evaluation copy. If you intend to develop Java-based database applications, it will be well worth obtaining a licensed version of the IDS software.

The `DriverManager` Class

The `DriverManager` class of `java.sql` is used to manage the JDBC drivers that are installed on your system. These drivers may be installed by setting the `jdbc.drivers` system property or by loading the driver class using the `forName()` method of the `Class` class. The `DriverApp` program, presented later in this chapter, shows how to load a JDBC driver using the `forName()` method.

The `DriverManager` class is static. It does not provide a constructor, and all of its methods are static. The `getDrivers()` method returns an enumeration of all the JDBC drivers that are installed on your system. The `getConnection()` method is used to establish a connection to a database. This method is provided in the following three forms:

■ `getConnection(String url)`

■ `getConnection(String url,String userID,String password)`

■ `getConnection(String url,Properties arguments)`

The first form takes a `String` argument that specifies the URL of the database. You'll learn about database URLs shortly. The second form takes two additional strings: the user ID and password required to access a database. The third form takes an additional `Properties` argument that specifies a list of connection arguments, such as user ID, password, database name, and so on. Consult your JDBC driver documentation for more information on which method to use with those drivers.

The URLs used to establish database connections vary with the JDBC drivers that you use. They, however, are of the following form:

`jdbc:subprotocol:subname`

All JDBC database protocols begin with `jdbc:`. The subprotocol is used to identify the connection mechanism or the JDBC driver. For example, the JDBC-ODBC bridge uses protocols of the form `jdbc:odbc:subname` and the IDS JDBC driver uses protocols of the form `jdbc:ids:subname`.

The subname of a database protocol identifies the database and provides other parameters that depend on the subprotocol and JDBC driver. For example, I use the following URL to establish a database connection to the Microsoft Access database named `DataSetName` on the host `atwork.jaworski.com` on protocol port 80:

```
jdbc:ids://atwork.jaworski.com:80/conn?dbtype=odbc&dsn=DataSetName
```

(The IDS Server supports Web service and database access via the same protocol port.) I use the Windows 95 32-bit ODBC Control Panel applet to associate an ODBC data set name with a Microsoft Access database.

> **NOTE**
>
> Consult your JDBC driver's documentation for information on the subprotocol and subname you should use to establish a database connection.

While the `getDrivers()` and `getConnection()` methods are the most important methods of the `DriverManager` class, the `DriverManager` class provides other methods that support driver and general database management:

- `getDriver()`—Returns a driver that is able to support a connection via a specified URL
- `registerDriver()`—Invoked by drivers to register themselves with `DriverManager`
- `deregisterDriver()`—Invoked by drivers to deregister themselves with `DriverManager`
- `getLoginTimeout()`—Returns the maximum time for drivers to wait while trying to log in to a database
- `setLoginTimeout()`—Sets the maximum time for drivers to wait while trying to log in to a database
- `getLogStream()`—Returns the stream that is to be used for logging and tracking
- `setLogStream()`—Specifies a stream to be used for logging and tracking
- `println()`—Prints data to the log stream

The `Driver` Interface

The `Driver` interface is implemented by JDBC drivers. While you most likely won't have to worry about writing your own JDBC driver, there are a few useful methods in the `Driver` interface that you should be aware of:

- `connect()`—An abstract method that is overridden by a driver to establish a database connection. This method is invoked for the driver by `DriverManager`.

- `acceptsURL()`—Returns a `boolean` value indicating whether a driver is capable of opening a database connection via a specified URL.
- `getPropertyInfo()`—Returns a `DriverPropertyInfo` array that provides information about how to use a driver to connect to a database.
- `getMajorVersion()`—Returns the driver's major version number.
- `getMinorVersion()`—Returns the driver's minor version number.
- `jdbcCompliant()`—Returns a `boolean` value indicating whether a driver is fully JDBC compliant. It must pass the JDBC compliance tests to return `true`.

The `DriverPropertyInfo` Class

An array of objects of the `DriverPropertyInfo` class is returned by the `getPropertyInfo()` method of the `Driver` class to provide information about a `Driver` that can be used to establish a database connection. The `DriverPropertyInfo` class provides the following five field variables to describe a property of a driver:

- `name`—The property's name
- `description`—A description of the property
- `value`—The current value of the property
- `choices`—A list of possible values
- `required`—A variable that indicates whether the property is required

The `DriverApp` Program

The `DriverApp` program, shown in Listing 19.1, illustrates the use of the `DriverManager` and `DriverPropertyInfo` classes and the `Driver` interface.

When I run the program, it provides the following output:

```
C:\jdk1.1.1\jdg\ch19>java DriverApp
Available drivers:
  Driver: ids.sql.IDSDriver
  Major version: 1
  Minor version: 4
  JDBC compliant: true
  Properties:
    Name: dsn
      Description: Data Source Name or Database Name
      Value: null
      Required: true
    Name: user
      Description: User ID
      Value: null
      Required: false
```

```
    Name: password
      Description: Password
      Value: null
      Required: false
   Driver: sun.jdbc.odbc.JdbcOdbcDriver
   Major version: 1
   Minor version: 1001
   JDBC compliant: true
```

If you use a different driver than the IDS driver, you'll have to replace the class name `ids.sql.IDSDriver` in the statement

```
Class.forName("ids.sql.IDSDriver");
```

If you deleted the preceding statement, the program only displays information about the Sun JDBC-ODBC driver.

> **NOTE**
>
> The IDS Server runs on both Windows 95 and Windows NT.

`DriverApp` provides useful information about your driver that you can use to set up a database connection. It loads the `ids.sql.IDSDriver` and the `sun.jdbc.odbc.JdbcOdbcDriver` classes by invoking the `forName()` method of the `Class` class. It then invokes the `getDrivers()` method of `DriverManager` to return an `Enumeration` of the loaded drivers. A `while` loop is used to iterate through the `Enumeration` object and display information about each driver.

The name of the driver is retrieved by invoking the `getClass()` method to retrieve the driver's class and the `getName()` method to retrieve the name of the class. The `getMajorVersion()`, `getMinorVersion()`, and `jdbcCompliant()` methods return additional information about each driver.

An array of `DriverPropertyInfo` objects is returned by the `getPropertyInfo()` method of the `Driver` class. The `name`, `description`, `value`, `choices`, and `required` fields of each object are displayed.

The sample program output shows that the `ids.sql.IDSDriver` driver is version 1.4, is JDBC compliant, and takes the required `dsn` and optional `user` and `password` properties. However, the `sun.jdbc.odbc.JdbcOdbcDriver` driver revealed little information about itself.

Listing 19.1. The `DriverApp` program.

```
import java.sql.*;
import java.util.*;

class DriverApp {
 public static void main(String args[]) {
  try{
```

```
    Class.forName("ids.sql.IDSDriver");
    Class.forName("sun.jdbc.odbc.JdbcOdbcDriver");
    Enumeration drivers = DriverManager.getDrivers();
    System.out.println("Available drivers:");
    while(drivers.hasMoreElements()){
     Driver driver=(Driver)drivers.nextElement();
     System.out.println("  Driver: "+driver.getClass().getName());
     System.out.println("   Major version: "+driver.getMajorVersion());
     System.out.println("   Minor version: "+driver.getMinorVersion());
     System.out.println("   JDBC compliant: "+driver.jdbcCompliant());
     DriverPropertyInfo props[] = driver.getPropertyInfo("",null);
     if(props!=null){
      System.out.println("   Properties: ");
      for(int i=0;i<props.length;++i){
       System.out.println("    Name: "+props[i].name);
       System.out.println("     Description: "+props[i].description);
       System.out.println("     Value: "+props[i].value);
       if(props[i].choices!=null){
        System.out.println("     Choices: ");
        for(int j=0;j<props[i].choices.length;++j)
         System.out.println("       "+props[i].choices[j]);
       }
       System.out.println("     Required: "+props[i].required);
      }
     }
    }
  }catch(Exception ex){
   System.out.println(ex);
   System.exit(0);
  }
 }
}
```

Connecting to the Database

The `getConnection()` method of `DriverManager` is used to establish a connection to a database. In this section, you'll see how a database connection is established. But first let's cover two important interfaces related to database connections—`Connection` and `DatabaseMetaData`. You'll then use the `ConnectApp` program to connect to a database and return information about the database to which you are connected.

The `Connection` Interface

When a database connection is established using the `getConnection()` method of `DriverManager`, the `getConnection()` method returns an object that implements the `Connection` interface. This interface defines methods for interacting with the database via the established connection. It also defines several constants that describe the manner in which the database supports the committing of database transactions. Approaches to committing transactions are covered in Chapter 48. You don't need to understand these concepts to complete this chapter.

The methods of the Connection interface are used to manage a database connection, obtain information about a connection, roll back or commit database transactions, or prepare SQL statements for execution.

A number of methods are defined by the Connection interface. Consult the API documentation of the Connection interface for a complete description of these methods. Particular methods of interest include the following:

- close()—Closes a database connection.
- getMetaData()—Returns an object of the DatabaseMetaData interface that can be used to obtain detailed information about the structure and capabilities of a database.
- createStatement()—Creates an SQL Statement object.
- prepareStatement()—Creates an SQL PreparedStatement object using an SQL string. PreparedStatement objects are precompiled SQL statements that are more efficiently executed.
- prepareCall()—Creates an SQL CallableStatement object using an SQL string. CallableStatement objects are SQL-stored procedure call statements.

> **NOTE**
>
> SQL is the Structured Query Language. It is a language for adding information to a database or retrieving information that is contained in a database. Chapter 48 covers SQL in more detail.

The DatabaseMetaData Interface

The DatabaseMetaData interface provides a vast amount of information about the database to which a connection is established. It defines several constants for describing database attributes and over 100 methods. You can use these methods to retrieve almost any type of information about a database's structure and capabilities. It is well worth the time to scan through the API documentation of DatabaseMetaData to see what kind of information is available through these methods.

> **NOTE**
>
> Databases differ in the extent to which they support the methods of DatabaseMetaData. For example, Microsoft Access 97 supports the simple methods used in the ConnectApp program of the following section, but tends to choke on more advanced metadata queries.

The ConnectApp Program

The ConnectApp program, shown in Listing 19.2, establishes a connection to a database and returns information about that database. It illustrates the use of the Connection and DatabaseMetaData classes. The ConnectApp program connects to a sample database provided with the IDS JDBC driver. (We won't get into developing databases until Part VII.) If you've downloaded and installed an evaluation copy of the IDS Server and JDBC driver, you'll be able to run ConnectApp as shown. Otherwise, if you feel comfortable doing so, you can tailor ConnectApp to your driver and database. Otherwise, just try to read through the program's output and correlate it with its description. In Part VII, I'll lay down the conceptual foundation you'll need to work with your driver and database.

> **WARNING**
>
> If you use a different driver than the IDS driver, you'll have to adjust the parameters you use to establish a database connection. Check your driver's documentation for instructions on how to set up a database connection.

When ConnectApp is run it generates the following output:

```
C:\jdk1.1.1\jdg\ch19>java ConnectApp
Database: ACCESS version 3.5 Jet
User name: admin
```

The name of my database is reported as ACCESS with version number 3.5 Jet. It also identifies me as accessing the database as user admin.

While the output produced by ConnectApp may be underwhelming, don't be concerned—you'll be able to produce mountains of information once you learn to use ResultSet objects. The important point is that we established a successful database connection and were able to access metadata about the database.

ConnectApp begins by loading the IDS driver using the forName() method of the Class class. It then creates a database URL for that driver and the IDSExamples data set that comes with the IDS Server and driver.

> **NOTE**
>
> The IDS Server is a database access server and a Web server. It is used to support the connection of the IDS JDBC driver with a variety of database servers. See Chapter 48 for more information about database access servers.
>
> If you are using the IDS Server and JDBC driver, don't forget to install the IDSExamples data set, as specified in the installation instructions contained in the IDS User Guide.

The URL of the database consists of the JDBC protocol identifier (jdbc:), followed by the IDS subprotocol identifier (ids:), followed by the subname. The subname consists of the host name and port of my database server (atwork.jaworski.com:80), the connection parameter identifier (conn), the database type (dbtype=odbc), and the data set name (dsn='IDSExamples'). Other characters of the URL are used as separators.

> **NOTE**
>
> Substitute your host name for atwork.jaworski.com in the database URL.

The getConnection() method of DriverManager establishes the connection and returns an object of the Connection interface. The getMetaData() method is invoked for this Connection object to obtain information about the database to which the connection is established.

The getDatabaseProductName(), getDatabaseProductVersion(), and getUserName() methods of the DatabaseMetaData interface are used to retrieve information about the database product and the user name associated with the connection.

Listing 19.2. The ConnectApp program.

```
import java.sql.*;
import java.util.*;

class ConnectApp {
 public static void main(String args[]) {
  try{
   Class.forName("ids.sql.IDSDriver");
   String url="jdbc:ids://atwork.jaworski.com:80/";
   url+="conn?dbtype=odbc&dsn='IDSExamples'";
   Connection connection=DriverManager.getConnection(url);
   DatabaseMetaData meta=connection.getMetaData();
   System.out.print("Database: "+meta.getDatabaseProductName());
   System.out.println(" version "+meta.getDatabaseProductVersion());
   System.out.println("User name: "+meta.getUserName());
   connection.close();
  }catch(Exception ex){
   System.out.println(ex);
   System.exit(0);
  }
 }
}
```

Working with Result Sets

When a database query is executed, the results of the query are returned as a table of data organized according to rows and columns. The ResultSet interface is used to provide access to this tabular data. Query results are returned as ResultSet objects that provide access to the tabular data, one row at a time.

A ResultSet object maintains a pointer to a row within the tabular results. This pointer is referred to as a *cursor*. When a ResultSet object is returned from a query, the cursor initially points immediately before the first row of the table. The next() method of the ResultSet class is used to move the cursor to the next row of the table. The next() method returns a boolean value that is true if the next row is returned and false if the end of the table is reached. The next() method is used to successively step through the rows of the tabular results.

The ResultSet interface provides a number of get methods that allow the column entries for a row to be returned as a variety of primitive and reference types ranging from simple integers to streams and arbitrary objects. The getMetaData() method returns a ResultSetMetaData object that contains information about a row.

The ResultSetMetaData Interface

The ResultSetMetaData interface provides constants and methods that are used to obtain information about ResultSet objects. The getColumnCount() method returns the number of columns in the tabular data accessed by a ResultSet. The getColumnName() method returns the names of each column in the database from which the data was retrieved. The getColumnType() method returns a column's SQL type. The Type class defines constants that are used to identify SQL types. Other methods of ResultMetaData are used to access additional column properties, such as the column's display width, number formats, and read-write status.

> **NOTE**
>
> The columns in a ResultSet are accessed beginning with index 1 instead of index 0.

The ResultApp Program

The ResultApp program, shown in Listing 19.3, illustrates the use of the ResultSet and ResultMetaData interfaces. It retrieves information from the IDSExamples database that comes with the IDS JDBC driver. This database defines three tables (courses, departments, and employees) that correspond to those of a typical university. The tables are filled with sample data. The ResultApp program executes an SQL statement that queries the database for the entire contents of the courses table. The program's results follow:

```
C:\jdk1.1.1\jdg\ch19>java ResultApp
Course_ID ¦ Department_ID ¦ CourseNumber ¦ CourseLevel ¦ CourseName
35 ¦ BIOL ¦ 100 ¦ Basic        ¦ Physiology
37 ¦ BIOL ¦ 300 ¦ Intermediate ¦ Plant Biology
38 ¦ BIOL ¦ 600 ¦ Advanced     ¦ Microbiology
```

```
39 | BIOL | 310 | Intermediate | Neurobiology
40 | BIOL | 620 | Advanced     | Neurobiology
41 | CHEM | 100 | Basic        | General Chemistry
42 | CHEM | 300 | Intermediate | Analytical Chemistry
44 | ECON | 100 | Basic        | Financial Accounting
45 | ECON | 110 | Basic        | Business Law
51 | MATH | 100 | Basic        | Calculus I
52 | MATH | 300 | Intermediate | Calculus II
59 | MATH | 600 | Advanced     | Linear Algebra
60 | ECON | 220 | Intermediate | Microeconomics
61 | CHEM | 600 | Advanced     | Organic Chemistry
```

The first line displays the column names of the table. Subsequent lines display the data contained in the table.

NOTE

You'll learn how to execute SQL statements in the next section.

The `ResultApp` program begins by establishing a connection to the `IDSExamples` database in the same manner as the `ConnectApp` program. It invokes the `createStatement()` method of the `Connection` class to create a `Statement` object to be used to query the database. The `SELECT * FROM customer` SQL query statement is then executed using the `executeQuery()` method of the `Statement` class. This statement queries the database, and its results are returned as a `ResultSet` object. The `ResultSet` object is displayed using the `displayResults()` method.

The `displayResults()` method invokes the `getMetaData()` method of a `ResultSet` object to access a `ResultSetMetaData` object that describes the `ResultSet` object. The `getColumnCount()` method of the `ResultSetMetaData` object identifies the number of columns in the `ResultSet` object. The names of these columns are retrieved using the `getColumnName()` method of `ResultSetMetaData`.

A `while` loop steps through each row of the `ResultSet` object using the `next()` method. The `getString()` method of the `ResultSet` class is used to retrieve each row's column entry and display it to the console. Note that the columns are accessed beginning with index 1.

Listing 19.3. The `ResultApp` program.

```java
import java.sql.*;
import java.util.*;

class ResultApp {
 public static void main(String args[]) {
  try{
   Class.forName("ids.sql.IDSDriver");
   String url="jdbc:ids://atwork.jaworski.com:80/";
   url+="conn?dbtype=odbc&dsn='IDSExamples'";
   Connection connection=DriverManager.getConnection(url);
   Statement statement = connection.createStatement();
```

```
  String sql="SELECT * FROM courses";
  ResultSet result = statement.executeQuery(sql);
  displayResults(result);
  connection.close();
 }catch(Exception ex){
  System.out.println(ex);
  System.exit(0);
 }
}
static void displayResults(ResultSet r) throws SQLException {
 ResultSetMetaData rmeta = r.getMetaData();
 int numColumns=rmeta.getColumnCount();
 for(int i=1;i<=numColumns;++i) {
  if(i<numColumns)
   System.out.print(rmeta.getColumnName(i)+" ¦ ");
  else
   System.out.println(rmeta.getColumnName(i));
 }
 while(r.next()){
  for(int i=1;i<=numColumns;++i) {
   if(i<numColumns)
    System.out.print(r.getString(i)+" ¦ ");
   else
    System.out.println(r.getString(i).trim());
  }
 }
}
}
```

Executing SQL Statements

The Structured Query Language (SQL) is the language used to interact with database servers. SQL statements can be used to add information to a database, update or delete existing database information, or retrieve information from a database. The purpose of the `java.sql` package is to let you execute SQL statements from Java. If you are not familiar with SQL, please bear with me. Chapter 48 provides an introduction to SQL. This section discusses the JDBC API interfaces that are used to execute SQL statements.

The `Statement` Interface

In the `ResultApp` program, you created an object of the `Statement` interface by invoking the `createStatement()` method of the `Connection` interface. You then invoked the `executeQuery()` method of the `Statement` interface, passing it the `SELECT * FROM courses` SQL statement as an argument. This resulted in the query being processed by the database and a `ResultSet` object being returned. This example illustrates the simplicity with which SQL statements are executed via the JDBC.

The Statement interface defines methods that are used to interact with databases via the execution of SQL statements. These methods also support the processing of query results returned via ResultSet objects and provide control over the mechanics of query processing. The execute(), executeQuery(), and executeUpdate() methods are the primary methods of interest in the Statement interface.

The executeQuery() method executes an SQL statement (such as the SELECT statement) that queries a database and returns a ResultSet object. The executeUpdate() method executes an SQL statement (such as the INSERT, UPDATE, or DELETE statement) that updates the database and returns the integer value of the row count associated with the SQL statement or 0 if the statement did not return a result.

The execute() method executes an SQL statement that is written as a String object. It returns a boolean value indicating whether a ResultSet object was produced as the result of the statement's execution. The getResultSet() and getMoreResults() methods are used to retrieve the ResultSet object. If the statement's execution returns an update count, execute() returns false. The update count can be retrieved using the getUpdateCount() method.

The PreparedStatement Interface

The PreparedStatement interface extends the Statement interface to define methods that are used to work with precompiled SQL statements. The use of precompiled SQL statements provides a more efficient way of executing frequently used SQL statements.

PreparedStatement objects may be used with parameterized SQL statements. These parameterized SQL statements replace constant SQL expressions with question marks (?). For example, the following parameterized statement retrieves an unspecified column from the classes table:

```
SELECT ? FROM courses
```

The preceding statement needs to be instantiated with the name of the column to be retrieved. The parameterized fields are said to be instantiated by IN parameter values.

> **NOTE**
>
> The implementation of SQL varies from database to database. However, the SQL presented in this book is commonly supported by all databases.

The PreparedStatement interface provides several set methods for setting the values of IN parameters. These methods are organized into the type of value to which a parameter is to be set.

PreparedStatement provides its own version of the execute(), executeQuery(), and executeUpdate() methods of the Statement interface. These methods do not specify the SQL statement to be used in the query. Instead, the SQL statement is specified as an argument to the `prepareStatement()` method of the `Connection` interface that is used to create the `PreparedStatement` object.

The `CallableStatement` Interface

The `CallableStatement` interface extends the `PreparedStatement` interface to implement stored SQL procedures. `CallableStatement` objects are created via the `prepareCall()` method of the `Connection` class. A stored SQL procedure is passed as an argument to the `prepareCall()` method. It may be parameterized using question marks in the same manner as discussed for the `PreparedStatement` interface. However, the `CallableStatement` interface allows some parameters to be OUT parameters. OUT parameters are used to return values from the SQL procedure call. The `registerOutParameter()` method of the `CallableStatement` interface is used to identify the type of OUT parameter. In addition, several get methods are provided to retrieve the value returned by an OUT parameter.

The `StatementApp` Program

The `StatementApp` program, shown in Listing 19.4, allows you to execute an SQL statement that is passed as a command-line parameter. The program uses the IDS driver to link to the `IDSExamples` data set used in the previous examples of this chapter. You can use this program to brush up on your SQL. Execute the program with the `"SELECT * FROM courses"` SQL statement to obtain a listing of the contents of the courses table:

```
C:\jdk1.1.1\jdg\ch19>java StatementApp "SELECT * FROM courses"
SELECT * FROM courses
Course_ID ¦ Department_ID ¦ CourseNumber ¦ CourseLevel ¦ CourseName
35 ¦ BIOL ¦ 100 ¦ Basic        ¦ Physiology
37 ¦ BIOL ¦ 300 ¦ Intermediate ¦ Plant Biology
38 ¦ BIOL ¦ 600 ¦ Advanced     ¦ Microbiology
39 ¦ BIOL ¦ 310 ¦ Intermediate ¦ Neurobiology
40 ¦ BIOL ¦ 620 ¦ Advanced     ¦ Neurobiology
41 ¦ CHEM ¦ 100 ¦ Basic        ¦ General Chemistry
42 ¦ CHEM ¦ 300 ¦ Intermediate ¦ Analytical Chemistry
44 ¦ ECON ¦ 100 ¦ Basic        ¦ Financial Accounting
45 ¦ ECON ¦ 110 ¦ Basic        ¦ Business Law
51 ¦ MATH ¦ 100 ¦ Basic        ¦ Calculus I
52 ¦ MATH ¦ 300 ¦ Intermediate ¦ Calculus II
59 ¦ MATH ¦ 600 ¦ Advanced     ¦ Linear Algebra
60 ¦ ECON ¦ 220 ¦ Intermediate ¦ Microeconomics
61 ¦ CHEM ¦ 600 ¦ Advanced     ¦ Organic Chemistry
```

The economics classes don't belong with all of the math and science courses. Let's delete them using the `"DELETE FROM courses WHERE Department_ID = 'ECON'"` SQL statement:

```
C:\jdk1.1.1\jdg\ch19>java StatementApp "DELETE FROM courses WHERE Department_ID
↪= 'ECON'"
DELETE FROM courses WHERE Department_ID = 'ECON'
```

Use the "SELECT * FROM courses" statement to verify that the economics classes have been deleted:

```
C:\jdk1.1.1\jdg\ch19>java StatementApp "SELECT * FROM courses"
SELECT * FROM courses
Course_ID ¦ Department_ID ¦ CourseNumber ¦ CourseLevel ¦ CourseName
35 ¦ BIOL ¦ 100 ¦ Basic        ¦ Physiology
37 ¦ BIOL ¦ 300 ¦ Intermediate ¦ Plant Biology
38 ¦ BIOL ¦ 600 ¦ Advanced     ¦ Microbiology
39 ¦ BIOL ¦ 310 ¦ Intermediate ¦ Neurobiology
40 ¦ BIOL ¦ 620 ¦ Advanced     ¦ Neurobiology
41 ¦ CHEM ¦ 100 ¦ Basic        ¦ General Chemistry
42 ¦ CHEM ¦ 300 ¦ Intermediate ¦ Analytical Chemistry
51 ¦ MATH ¦ 100 ¦ Basic        ¦ Calculus I
52 ¦ MATH ¦ 300 ¦ Intermediate ¦ Calculus II
59 ¦ MATH ¦ 600 ¦ Advanced     ¦ Linear Algebra
61 ¦ CHEM ¦ 600 ¦ Advanced     ¦ Organic Chemistry
```

What courses are missing from the list? These poor students are being deprived of a Java education. Enter the following INSERT SQL statements to round out their education:

```
C:\jdk1.1.1\jdg\ch19>java StatementApp "INSERT INTO courses VALUES ('34', 'JAVA'
➥, '999', 'Basic', 'Intro to Java')"
INSERT INTO courses VALUES ('34', 'JAVA', '999', 'Basic', 'Intro to Java')

C:\jdk1.1.1\jdg\ch19>java StatementApp "INSERT INTO courses VALUES ('43', 'JAVA'
➥, '999', 'Intermediate', 'AWT Programming')"
INSERT INTO courses VALUES ('43', 'JAVA', '999', 'Intermediate', 'AWT Programmin
➥g')

C:\jdk1.1.1\jdg\ch19>java StatementApp "INSERT INTO courses VALUES ('62', 'JAVA'
➥, '999', 'Advanced', 'Database Programming')"
INSERT INTO courses VALUES ('62', 'JAVA', '999', 'Advanced', 'Database Programmi
➥ng')
```

Use the "SELECT * FROM courses" statement to redisplay the courses table:

```
C:\jdk1.1.1\jdg\ch19>java StatementApp "SELECT * FROM courses"
SELECT * FROM courses
Course_ID ¦ Department_ID ¦ CourseNumber ¦ CourseLevel ¦ CourseName
35 ¦ BIOL ¦ 100 ¦ Basic        ¦ Physiology
37 ¦ BIOL ¦ 300 ¦ Intermediate ¦ Plant Biology
38 ¦ BIOL ¦ 600 ¦ Advanced     ¦ Microbiology
39 ¦ BIOL ¦ 310 ¦ Intermediate ¦ Neurobiology
40 ¦ BIOL ¦ 620 ¦ Advanced     ¦ Neurobiology
41 ¦ CHEM ¦ 100 ¦ Basic        ¦ General Chemistry
42 ¦ CHEM ¦ 300 ¦ Intermediate ¦ Analytical Chemistry
51 ¦ MATH ¦ 100 ¦ Basic        ¦ Calculus I
52 ¦ MATH ¦ 300 ¦ Intermediate ¦ Calculus II
59 ¦ MATH ¦ 600 ¦ Advanced     ¦ Linear Algebra
61 ¦ CHEM ¦ 600 ¦ Advanced     ¦ Organic Chemistry
34 ¦ JAVA ¦ 999 ¦ Basic        ¦ Intro to Java
43 ¦ JAVA ¦ 999 ¦ Intermediate ¦ AWT Programming
62 ¦ JAVA ¦ 999 ¦ Advanced     ¦ Database Programming
```

All the Java courses were appended to the end of the table. Let's sort the result set by the Course_ID column:

```
C:\jdk1.1.1\jdg\ch19>java StatementApp "SELECT * FROM courses ORDER BY Course_ID
↩"
SELECT * FROM courses ORDER BY Course_ID
Course_ID ¦ Department_ID ¦ CourseNumber ¦ CourseLevel ¦ CourseName
34 ¦ JAVA ¦ 999 ¦ Basic          ¦ Intro to Java
35 ¦ BIOL ¦ 100 ¦ Basic          ¦ Physiology
37 ¦ BIOL ¦ 300 ¦ Intermediate   ¦ Plant Biology
38 ¦ BIOL ¦ 600 ¦ Advanced       ¦ Microbiology
39 ¦ BIOL ¦ 310 ¦ Intermediate   ¦ Neurobiology
40 ¦ BIOL ¦ 620 ¦ Advanced       ¦ Neurobiology
41 ¦ CHEM ¦ 100 ¦ Basic          ¦ General Chemistry
42 ¦ CHEM ¦ 300 ¦ Intermediate   ¦ Analytical Chemistry
43 ¦ JAVA ¦ 999 ¦ Intermediate   ¦ AWT Programming
51 ¦ MATH ¦ 100 ¦ Basic          ¦ Calculus I
52 ¦ MATH ¦ 300 ¦ Intermediate   ¦ Calculus II
59 ¦ MATH ¦ 600 ¦ Advanced       ¦ Linear Algebra
61 ¦ CHEM ¦ 600 ¦ Advanced       ¦ Organic Chemistry
62 ¦ JAVA ¦ 999 ¦ Advanced       ¦ Database Programming
```

The Database Programming course could apply to any programming language. Let's use the
UPDATE statement to change it to Advanced JDBC:

```
C:\jdk1.1.1\jdg\ch19>java StatementApp "UPDATE courses SET CourseName = 'Advance
↩d JDBC' WHERE Department_ID = 'JAVA' AND CourseLevel = 'Advanced'"
UPDATE courses SET CourseName = 'Advanced JDBC' WHERE Department_ID = 'JAVA' AND
↩ CourseLevel = 'Advanced'
```

Once again, we'll use display the courses table, sorted by the `Course_ID` column:

```
C:\jdk1.1.1\jdg\ch19>java StatementApp "SELECT * FROM courses ORDER BY Course_ID
↩"
SELECT * FROM courses ORDER BY Course_ID
Course_ID ¦ Department_ID ¦ CourseNumber ¦ CourseLevel ¦ CourseName
34 ¦ JAVA ¦ 999 ¦ Basic          ¦ Intro to Java
35 ¦ BIOL ¦ 100 ¦ Basic          ¦ Physiology
37 ¦ BIOL ¦ 300 ¦ Intermediate   ¦ Plant Biology
38 ¦ BIOL ¦ 600 ¦ Advanced       ¦ Microbiology
39 ¦ BIOL ¦ 310 ¦ Intermediate   ¦ Neurobiology
40 ¦ BIOL ¦ 620 ¦ Advanced       ¦ Neurobiology
41 ¦ CHEM ¦ 100 ¦ Basic          ¦ General Chemistry
42 ¦ CHEM ¦ 300 ¦ Intermediate   ¦ Analytical Chemistry
43 ¦ JAVA ¦ 999 ¦ Intermediate   ¦ AWT Programming
51 ¦ MATH ¦ 100 ¦ Basic          ¦ Calculus I
52 ¦ MATH ¦ 300 ¦ Intermediate   ¦ Calculus II
59 ¦ MATH ¦ 600 ¦ Advanced       ¦ Linear Algebra
61 ¦ CHEM ¦ 600 ¦ Advanced       ¦ Organic Chemistry
62 ¦ JAVA ¦ 999 ¦ Advanced       ¦ Advanced JDBC
```

The `StatementApp` program provides a lot of capability in a few lines of code. That's because it
allows you to directly enter SQL statements to the database. It begins in the same way as
`ResultApp` by loading the `ids.sql.IDSDriver`, connecting to the `IDSExamples` data set, and creating a `Statement` object. It then passes the program's command-line argument to the `execute()`
method of the `Statement` interface. If the `execute()` method returns a `true` value, it invokes the
`getResultSet()` method of the `Statement` interface to retrieve the `ResultSet` object of a query
operation. It then invokes the `displayResults()` method to display the `ResultSet`.

Listing 19.4. The StatementApp program.

```
import java.sql.*;
import java.util.*;

class StatementApp {
 public static void main(String args[]) {
  if(args.length!=1){
   System.out.println("Usage: java StatementApp sql");
   System.exit(0);
  }
  try{
   Class.forName("ids.sql.IDSDriver");
   String url="jdbc:ids://atwork.jaworski.com:80/";
   url+="conn?dbtype=odbc&dsn='IDSExamples'";
   Connection connection=DriverManager.getConnection(url);
   Statement statement = connection.createStatement();
   String sql=args[0];
   System.out.println(sql);
   boolean hasResults = statement.execute(sql);
   if(hasResults){
    ResultSet result = statement.getResultSet();
    if(result!=null) displayResults(result);
   }
   connection.close();
  }catch(Exception ex){
   System.out.println(ex);
   System.exit(0);
  }
 }
 static void displayResults(ResultSet r) throws SQLException {
  ResultSetMetaData rmeta = r.getMetaData();
  int numColumns=rmeta.getColumnCount();
  for(int i=1;i<=numColumns;++i) {
   if(i<numColumns)
    System.out.print(rmeta.getColumnName(i)+" ¦ ");
   else
    System.out.println(rmeta.getColumnName(i));
  }
  while(r.next()){
   for(int i=1;i<=numColumns;++i) {
    if(i<numColumns)
     System.out.print(r.getString(i)+" ¦ ");
    else
     System.out.println(r.getString(i).trim());
   }
  }
 }
}
```

The `Date`, `Time`, and `Timestamp` Classes

The `java.sql` package provides the `Date`, `Time`, and `Timestamp` classes as extensions to `java.util.Date`. They may be used as objects within database transactions. The `Date` class represents ANSI SQL DATE values in the YYYY-MM-DD format. The `Time` class represents ANSI SQL TIME values in the HH:MM:SS format. The `Timestamp` class represents ANSI SQL TIMESTAMP (DATE and TIME) values.

Summary

In this chapter, you were introduced to the JDBC. You covered the classes of the `java.sql` package and learned to work with JDBC drivers, connect to databases, execute SQL statements, and work with result sets. This chapter provides a quick introduction to the `java.sql` package. Part VII of this book provides a comprehensive introduction to Java database programming. The next chapter, "Security and the `java.security` Packages," introduces you to the new JDK 1.1 Security API.

20

Security and the
java.security Packages

From Java's inception, security has been an important factor in all aspects of Java's design and implementation. The Java language is designed to be safe, reliable, and secure. The Java virtual machine and runtime system control the accesses that Java applets may make of local system and network resources. By default, the Java runtime system implements a stringent security policy. More restrictive or more flexible policies can be implemented via the SecurityManager class of java.lang. See Chapter 60, "Java Security," for more information on the SecurityManager class.

The JDK 1.1 has expanded the security capabilities of JDK 1.02 to support application-level security. This new security support is provided by the Security API of the java.security packages and includes support for message digests, digital signatures, key management, and access control lists. These application-level security controls can be used to protect information from unauthorized modification and disclosure as it traverses the Internet. They can also authenticate the contents of messages and files as well as the identity of applications and individuals.

In this chapter, you'll be introduced to the java.security, java.security.acl, and java.security.interfaces packages. You'll learn how to use these packages to create message digests and digital signatures. You'll also learn about the Security API's key management support, and then you'll be introduced to the access control interfaces of java.security.acl. When you finish this chapter, you should be able to use the Security API to add application-level security mechanisms to your Java programs.

The java.security Packages

The Java Security API consists of the packages java.security, java.security.acl, and java.security.interfaces. The java.security package is the core Security API package. It provides the classes and interfaces that support encryption and the computation of message digests and digital signatures. This package also provides key generation and management support. The java.security.acl package consists of interfaces that can be used to implement access control policies. The java.security.interfaces package defines interfaces that are used to access the National Institute of Standards and Technology (NIST) Digital Signature Algorithm.

> **TIP**
>
> The Java Cryptography Architecture document located at http://java.sun.com/ products/JDK/1.1/docs/guide/security/CryptoSpec.html provides additional information about the use of the java.security packages and references to information about specific cryptographic algorithms. The Java Crpytography Extension (JCE) is not part of the Security API; it must be separately downloaded.

Security API Approach

The Java Security API provides a flexible framework for implementing cryptographic functions and other security controls. It contains the "hooks" for message digest and digital signature computation, key generation and management, and access control enforcement. It includes standard algorithms (such as MD5 and DSA) that support these security functions, but leaves out encryption algorithms (due to the restrictions of U.S. export controls). Instead of promoting a small set of cryptographic algorithms, Java Security API implements an approach where different algorithm cryptographic packages may be *provided* by vendors and plugged in and installed within the common Security API framework.

> **NOTE**
>
> JCE is an add-on to the Security API that implements encryption algorithms that are subject to U.S. export controls.

Package Providers

The Provider class of java.security lays the foundation for using pluggable packages of cryptographic algorithms that support common functions such as message digest computation, digital signing, and key generation. The Provider class is a subclass of the Properties class of java.util. It encapsulates the notion of a cryptographic provider in terms of a provider name, version number, and information about the services provided by the provider.

The Provider class has a single constructor that identifies the name of the provider (String), version number (double), and information about the provided services (String). Four access methods are provided:

- getName()—Returns the provider's name
- getVersion()—Returns the version number of the provided package
- getInfo()—Returns a description of the provided services
- toString()—Returns the provider's name and package version number

The rationale for the Provider class is that it can be used to separate specific implementations of a cryptographic function (such as Company A's implementation of MD5, Company B's implementation of SHA-1, and Company C's implementation of MD5) from their provider-specific implementation. For example, several DSA packages may be available—some faster than others, some approved by the U.S. Department of Defense, and others supported by the Citizens Against Big Brother.

> **NOTE**
>
> The default package provided with the JDK 1.1 is named SUN. It includes the MD5 and SHA-1 message digest algorithms, the DSA signature algorithm, and a DSA key-pair generator.

The Security Class

The Security class provides a set of static methods that are used to manage providers. Providers are ranked in order of preference with the most preferred provider receiving a rank of 1 and less preferred providers receiving a larger number. The methods of the Security class can be used to install providers, adjust their preference ranking, and retrieve information about the providers that are installed. These methods are as follows:

- getProviders()—Returns an array of all installed Provider objects
- getProvider()—Returns a named Provider object
- getProperty()—Returns the value of a specific property
- getAlgorithmProperty()—Returns the value of a particular property for a specific algorithm
- setProperty()—Sets a named security property to a String value
- addProvider()—Adds a provider to the next available preference rank
- insertProviderAt()—Inserts a named provider at the specified preference rank
- removeProvider()—Removes a named provider

> **NOTE**
>
> The Security class only allows providers to be installed for the duration of the Java session. Providers can be permanently installed by editing the java.security file located in the \jdk1.1.1\lib\security\ directory. Consult the Java Cryptography Architecture document for more information on installing providers.

The ProviderApp Program

The ProviderApp program, shown in Listing 20.1, may be used to display information about the Provider objects that are installed on your system. If you have not installed any additional providers, it will display the following output:

```
C:\jdk1.1.1\jdg\ch20>java ProviderApp

SUN Security Provider v1.0, DSA signing and key generation,
 SHA-1 and MD5 message digests.
```

Listing 20.1. The `ProviderApp` program.

```
import java.security.*;

public class ProviderApp {
 public static void main(String args[]) {
  Provider providers[] = Security.getProviders();
  for(int i=0;i<providers.length;++i){
   System.out.println("\n"+providers[i].getInfo());
  }
 }
}
```

Cryptographic Engines

The Security API supports the notion of cryptographic *engines*. These engines are generic algorithm types, such as message digest, digital signature, and key generation, that support common cryptographic functions. The engines of the Security API are implemented by the `MessageDigest`, `Signature`, and `KeyPairGenerator` classes. The methods of these classes are mostly static. They apply to the class as a whole, rather than specific instances of the class. Instances of a class are created using each class's `getInstance()` method and not using the class's constructor. The reason for this is that the engine classes have two interfaces—one to the application developer and the other to the package provider. As a user, you use the `getInstance()` method to create a particular instance of an engine, specifying which provider-specific algorithm is to be used. The provider subclasses the engine's class (`MessageDigest`, `Signature`, or `KeyPairGenerator`) to supply an algorithm-specific implementation.

The `MessageDigest` Class

The `MessageDigest` class, as you would expect, supports the computation of a message digest. A message digest is very similar to a checksum, except that it provides much stronger security. The following are the principal advantages of a message digest (versus a checksum):

- It is computationally infeasible to determine another input byte sequence that will result in the same digest value.
- It is computationally infeasible to determine what input was used to generate the digest value.

A message digest can be thought of as a function that is computationally difficult to invert. The digest acts as a fingerprint for an input byte sequence and, as such, can be used to identify and represent that byte sequence.

The `MessageDigest` class provides a single constructor that identifies the name of the algorithm to be used to calculate the digest value. It provides 16 methods that are organized into two categories: service provider methods and application methods. The service provider methods are overridden by a specific service provider implementation of a message digest algorithm. These methods are as follows:

- `engineDigest()`—Completes the calculation of a message digest and returns the digest value as a byte array
- `engineReset()`—Resets the digest calculation so that another digest can be computed
- `engineUpdate()`—Updates the digest calculation based on additional input byte(s)

You won't be using any of the preceding methods unless you are a provider and you are creating your own message digest algorithm.

In order to *use* a provider's message digest algorithm, you must first invoke the static `getInstance()` method with the name of the algorithm and (optionally) the name of the provider. Both arguments are passed as `String` objects to `getInstance()`. An object of the `MessageDigest` class is returned. The default provider name is SUN. The available message digest algorithms are MD5 and SHA-1.

Once you've created an instance of `MessageDigest` (that is, a `MessageDigest` object), you can invoke the application methods of `MessageDigest` to compute a message digest value for a particular input byte sequence. The following are the most commonly used methods:

- `digest()`—Completes the computation of the digest value and returns it as a byte array
- `reset()`—Resets the digest computation so that a new value can be calculated
- `update()`—Updates the digest value based on additional input data
- `getAlgorithm()`—Returns a `String` value that identifies the message digest algorithm being used
- `isEqual()`—Compares two digest values (byte arrays) for equality
- `toString()`—Creates a `String` representation of a digest value
- `clone()`—Creates a clone copy of the `MessageDigest` object if the provided implementation is cloneable

DigestInputStream and DigestOutputStream

The `DigestInputStream` and `DigestOutputStream` classes are used to automatically calculate a message digest from data that is read from or written to a stream.

The `DigestInputStream` class extends the `FilterInputStream` class of `java.io`. It provides a single constructor that takes an `InputStream` object and a `MessageDigest` object as arguments. It defines a single field variable, `digest`, that contains the message digest associated with the input stream. Its access methods override the `read()` and `toString()` methods of `FilterInputStream` and `Object`. The `getMessageDigest()` method returns the `MessageDigest` object that is calculated. The `on()` method is used to turn on and off the digest calculation for various segments of the input stream. The setMessageDigest() method assigns a value to the digest being calculated.

The DigestOutputStream class extends FilterOutputStream of java.io to support message digest calculation on output that is written to the stream. The DataOutputStream constructor takes objects of the OutputStream and MessageDigest classes as arguments. It overrides the write() method of FilterOutputStream and the toString() method of Object. The getMessageDigest(), setMessageDigest(), and on() methods are used in the same manner as discussed for DigestInputStream.

The DigestApp Program

The DigestApp program, shown in Listing 20.2, illustrates the use of the MessageDigest and DigestInputStream classes in calculating the message digest of a file. When you run the program, you must supply the name of the file whose message digest is to be calculated. An example of the program's output follows:

```
C:\jdk1.1.1\jdg\ch20>java DigestApp DigestApp.java

File: DigestApp.java

Algorithm: MD5

Message Digest: sun.security.provider.MD5 Message Digest
 <cbe2674cdee0aeb67f5d5afbad63eddf>
```

Listing 20.2. The DigestApp program.

```
import java.security.*;
import java.io.*;

public class DigestApp {
 public static void main(String args[]) {
  MessageDigest md;
  try{
   md = MessageDigest.getInstance("MD5");
   if(args.length==0) {
    System.out.println("Usage: java DigestApp fileName");
    System.exit(0);
   }else{
    FileInputStream f = new FileInputStream(args[0]);
    DigestInputStream d = new DigestInputStream(f,md);
    int ch;
    while((ch=d.read()) != -1) ;
    md.digest();
    System.out.println("\nFile: "+args[0]);
    System.out.println("\nAlgorithm: "+md.getAlgorithm());
    System.out.println("\nMessage Digest: "+md);
   }
  }catch(Exception ex){
   System.out.println(ex);
  }
 }
}
```

The `main()` method invokes the `getInstance()` method, which passes the MD5 string as an argument. This creates an instance of an MD5 message digest algorithm. A new `FileInputStream` object is created to open the file for reading. It is passed to the `DigestInputStream()` constructor along with the MD5 `MessageDigest` object. Each byte of the file is then read. This causes the `MessageDigest` object to be updated with the file's contents. The `digest()` method is invoked to complete the message digest calculation. The results of the calculation are then displayed to the user. The `getAlgorithm()` method is invoked to retrieve the name of the message digest algorithm.

The `Signature` Class

The `Signature` class is an engine for calculating digital signatures based on provider-furnished digital signature algorithms. A digital signature is an algorithm that produces a string of bytes called a signature that positively identifies the signing party. The signature uses the private key of a public key/private key pair to produce the signature. Because the private key is only known to the signing party, the signature cannot be forged. The signature can be universally verified because the signer's public key is (theoretically) universally accessible. In addition, it is computationally infeasible to deduce the private key from the public key and signature value.

The `Signature` class supports both the creation of a digital signature and the verification of a digital signature. A `Signature` object is in one of three states: `UNINITIALIZED`, `SIGN`, and `VERIFY`. The current state of a `Signature` object is given by the `state` variable.

The `Signature` class provides a single constructor that takes a `String` argument identifying the name of the signature algorithm to be used. Like the `MessageDigest` class, the `Signature` class consists of service provider methods and application methods. The service provider methods are overridden by provider-furnished algorithms. These methods include the following:

- `engineGetParameter()`—Returns the value of a specified signature algorithm parameter.
- `enginerInitSign()`—Initializes a `Signature` object for signing. The `PrivateKey` of the signer is supplied as an argument.
- `engineInitVerify()`—Initializes a `Signature` object for signature verification. The `PrivateKey` of the signer is supplied as an argument.
- `engineSetParameter()`—Sets a named signature algorithm parameter to a specific object.
- `enginerSign()`—Returns the current signature being calculated.
- `engineUpdate()`—Updates a signature based on new input data.
- `engineVerify()`—Verifies that a signature value argument (`byte` array) is valid.

The `getInstance()` method is used to create a `Signature` object for a particular signature algorithm and/or service provider. The name of the algorithm must be supplied to `getInstance()`.

The name of the service provider is optional. The default service provider supplied with the JDK 1.1 is SUN and the default signature algorithm is DSA.

The application methods of the `Signature` class include the following:

- `getAlgorithm()`—Returns the name of the signature algorithm being used.
- `getParameter()`—Returns the value of a named algorithm parameter.
- `initSign()`—Initializes a `Signature` object to perform signature generation. A `PrivateKey` argument must be supplied.
- `initVerify()`—Initializes a `Signature` object to perform signature verification. A `PrivateKey` argument must be supplied.
- `setParameter()`—Sets a named algorithm parameter to a specified object.
- `sign()`—Returns the signature value being calculated as a `byte` array.
- `toString()`—Returns the signature value being calculated as a `String` value.
- `update()`—Updates the signature calculation/verification using a byte or an array of bytes.
- `verify()`—Verifies that a `byte` array is the correct signature for an input byte sequence.
- `clone()`—Returns a copy of the `Signature` instance if the provider implementation is cloneable.

An example of using the `Signature` class is provided in the section "The `SignApp` Program," later in this chapter.

Key Generation Classes and Interfaces

The calculation of a digital signature requires the private key of a public/private key pair. The `KeyPair` class encapsulates a public/private key pair. It has a single constructor that takes two arguments: an object that implements the `PublicKey` interface and an object that implements the `PrivateKey` interface. It provides the `getPrivate()` and `getPublic()` methods to return the `PrivateKey` and `PublicKey` objects that it holds.

The `Key` interface is the parent of the `PublicKey` and `PrivateKey` interfaces. It encapsulates a key in terms of the algorithm with which the key is used (for example, DSA or RSA), an encoded form of the key, and the format used to encode the key. Keys are encoded so that they cannot be read outside the Java runtime system. Various formats, such as X.509 and PKCS#8, may be used to encode a key. The `getAlgorithm()`, `getEncoded()`, and `getFormat()` methods return the algorithm, encoded key, and encoding format values of a `Key` interface object.

The `PublicKey` and `PrivateKey` interfaces extend the `Key` interface but do not add any methods or constants to the `Key` interface. They are used to differentiate publicly accessible keys from those that are not.

The `KeyPairGenerator` class, like `MessageDigest` and `Signature`, is another engine that provides a mechanism by which provider-furnished algorithms may be accessed. `KeyPairGenerator` provides the capability to generate public/private key pairs. Unlike `MessageDigest` and `Signature`, key generation is difficult to implement in an algorithm-independent manner. Because of this, `KeyPairGenerator` supports both algorithm-independent and algorithm-specific key generation—the difference being in the way that the algorithms are initialized.

To be effective, key generation requires good random number generation. Otherwise, generated keys would be statistically predictable and subject to compromise. Key generators are also characterized by their *strength,* which measures the difficulty of an outside party reproducing the generated keys. The algorithm-independent key generation takes a strength value and random number source as arguments. The algorithm-independent key generation allows algorithm-specific parameters to be identified. Algorithm-specific initialization of the DSA key generation algorithm is supported through the interfaces of the `java.security.interfaces` package.

The `KeyPairGenerator()` constructor takes a `String` value identifying the name of the algorithm to be used in key generation as an argument. No service provider methods are declared. Specific instances of a `KeyPairGenerator` object either override the access methods of `KeyPairGenerator()` or implement algorithm-specific interfaces, such as those of `java.security.interfaces`.

A `KeyPairGenerator` object is created using the `getInstance()` method. The name of the key generation algorithm must be supplied as an argument to `getInstance()`. The name of the service provider is optional.

Once a `KeyPairGenerator` object is created, it must be initialized. This can be accomplished in either an algorithm-independent or algorithm-specific manner. The `initialize()` method may be used to initialize an algorithm in an algorithm-independent manner. It takes a strength value (integer) and an optional `SecureRandom` object as arguments. Algorithm-specific initialization is accomplished by casting a `KeyPairGenerator` object to an interface that provides an algorithm-specific `initialize()` method. The section "The `java.security.interfaces` Package," later in this chapter, discusses how this is accomplished.

Once a `KeyPairGenerator` object is initialized, the `generateKeyPair()` method can be used to create a `KeyPair` object. The `getAlgorithm()` method returns the name of the algorithm used in key generation.

The `SecureRandom` Class

The `KeyPairGenerator` class uses an object of the `SecureRandom` class to identify a source of random numbers to be used in key generation. The `SecureRandom` class extends the `Random` class of `java.util` to support cryptographically strong random-number generation. It is based on the NIST SHA-1 hash algorithm.

A `SecureRandom` object can be constructed using a default-seed random number generator or by specifying a `byte` array to be used as the seed of the random number generator. The two forms of the `SecureRandom` constructor support these options. In addition, the `setSeed()` methods may be used to reseed the random number generator using either a `byte` array or a `long` value as the seed.

The `nextBytes()` method is used to generate a random array of bytes. The `next()` method generates a random integer with a specified number of random bits. The `getSeed()` method returns a specified number of bytes of the seed.

The `KeyGenApp` Program

The `KeyGenApp` program, shown in Listing 20.3, illustrates how simple the process of key generation can be. It generates a `KeyPair` object using the DSA key generation algorithm. Sample output of `KeyGenApp` follows:

```
C:\jdk1.1.1\jdg\ch20>java KeyGenApp
Public key: Sun DSA Public Key
parameters:
p: fd7f53811d75122952df4a9c2eece4e7f611b7523cef4400c31e3f80b6512669455d402251fb5
93d8d58fabfc5f5ba30f6cb9b556cd7813b801d346ff26660b76b9950a5a49f9fe8047b1022c24fb
ba9d7feb7c61bf83b57e7c6a8a6150f04fb83f6d3c51ec3023554135a169132f675f3ae2b61d72ae
ff22203199dd14801c7
q: 9760508f15230bccb292b982a2eb840bf0581cf5
g: f7e1a085d69b3ddecbbcab5c36b857b97994afbbfa3aea82f9574c0b3d0782675159578ebad45
94fe67107108180b449167123e84c281613b7cf09328cc8a6e13c167a8b547c8d28e0a3ae1e2bb3a
675916ea37f0bfa213562f1fb627a01243bcca4f1bea8519089a883dfe15ae59f06928b665e807b5
52564014c3bfecf492a

y: 9847b43bfc99738d50912e58e20b303d1670e27e3af28a7a7b02c86ed32c574b854dfc72fdae8
acc47d82eddc402f9fcf6d56433f8d913d61aa99249db16ebcec9b4de5e62faa13c9db6ceea1d209
a7f7407488436b20dedfd31d9e0a33a0ac4e3bdfcb0514a96607b565c40aaa64c3f748edad9eb652
7dbd5682e24eaa35236

Private key: Sun DSA Private Key
parameters:
p: fd7f53811d75122952df4a9c2eece4e7f611b7523cef4400c31e3f80b6512669455d402251fb5
93d8d58fabfc5f5ba30f6cb9b556cd7813b801d346ff26660b76b9950a5a49f9fe8047b1022c24fb
ba9d7feb7c61bf83b57e7c6a8a6150f04fb83f6d3c51ec3023554135a169132f675f3ae2b61d72ae
ff22203199dd14801c7
q: 9760508f15230bccb292b982a2eb840bf0581cf5
g: f7e1a085d69b3ddecbbcab5c36b857b97994afbbfa3aea82f9574c0b3d0782675159578ebad45
94fe67107108180b449167123e84c281613b7cf09328cc8a6e13c167a8b547c8d28e0a3ae1e2bb3a
675916ea37f0bfa213562f1fb627a01243bcca4f1bea8519089a883dfe15ae59f06928b665e807b5
52564014c3bfecf492a

x: 3e562926b77135fae5a7d173dcc9b3feed2ea51c
```

NOTE

Depending on your processor speed, key generation may take from a few seconds to a few minutes.

If you are familiar with DSA key generation, you will recognize the p, q, and g parameters used for key generation. The actual value of the public key is given by y. The value of the private key is given by x.

Listing 20.3. The `KeyGenApp` program.

```
import java.security.*;

public class KeyGenApp {
 public static void main(String args[]) {
  KeyPairGenerator keygen;
  try{
   keygen = KeyPairGenerator.getInstance("DSA");
   keygen.initialize(1024);
   KeyPair keys=keygen.generateKeyPair();
   System.out.println("Public key: "+keys.getPublic());
   System.out.println("Private key: "+keys.getPrivate()+"\n");
  }catch(Exception ex){
   System.out.println(ex);
  }
 }
}
```

The getInstance() method of KeyPairGenerator is invoked to create an instance of the DSA-key generation algorithm from the default SUN-provided package. The KeyPairGenerator object is initialized to a strength value of 1024. The default RandomSource is used. The strength value measures the number of bits in the modulous p.

The generateKeyPair() method is invoked to generate a KeyPair object. The getPublic() and getPrivate() methods of KeyPair return the PublicKey and PrivateKey objects of the key pair.

The SignApp Program

Now that you know how to generate keys, you can create digital signatures. The SignApp program, shown in Listing 20.4, illustrates the process of signature creation. An example of its output follows:

```
C:\jdk1.1.1\jdg\ch20>java SignApp DigestApp.java

Message Digest: sun.security.provider.MD5 Message Digest <cbe2674cdee0aeb67f5d5a
fbad63eddf>


Signature: DSA Signature
        p: fd7f53811d75122952df4a9c2eece4e7f611b7523cef4400c31e3f80b6512669455d4
02251fb593d8d58fabfc5f5ba30f6cb9b556cd7813b801d346ff26660b76b9950a5a49f9fe8047b1
022c24fbba9d7feb7c61bf83b57e7c6a8a6150f04fb83f6d3c51ec3023554135a169132f675f3ae2
b61d72aeff22203199dd14801c7
        q: 9760508f15230bccb292b982a2eb840bf0581cf5
        g: f7e1a085d69b3ddecbbcab5c36b857b97994afbbfa3aea82f9574c0b3d07826751595
78ebad4594fe67107108180b449167123e84c281613b7cf09328cc8a6e13c167a8b547c8d28e0a3a
e1e2bb3a675916ea37f0bfa213562f1fb627a01243bcca4f1bea8519089a883dfe15ae59f06928b6
65e807b552564014c3bfecf492a

Signature verified: true
```

Listing 20.4. The SignApp program.

```java
import java.security.*;
import java.io.*;

public class SignApp {
 public static void main(String args[]) {
  MessageDigest md;
  try{
   md = MessageDigest.getInstance("MD5");
   if(args.length==0) {
    System.out.println("Usage: java SignApp fileName");
    System.exit(0);
   }else{
    FileInputStream f = new FileInputStream(args[0]);
    DigestInputStream d = new DigestInputStream(f,md);
    int ch;
    while((ch=d.read()) != -1) ;
    byte digest[]=md.digest();
    System.out.println("\nMessage Digest: "+md);
    KeyPairGenerator keygen = KeyPairGenerator.getInstance("DSA");
    keygen.initialize(1024);
    KeyPair keys=keygen.generateKeyPair();
    Signature sign=Signature.getInstance("DSA");
    sign.initSign(keys.getPrivate());
    sign.update(digest);
    byte signature[]=sign.sign();
```

continues

Listing 20.4. continued

```
    System.out.println("\nSignature: "+sign);
    sign.initVerify(keys.getPublic());
    sign.update(digest);
    boolean verified=sign.verify(signature);
    System.out.println("\nSignature verified: "+verified);
   }
  }catch(Exception ex){
   System.out.println(ex);
  }
 }
}
```

The `SignApp` program uses the message digest calculation code of the `DigestApp` program (see Listing 20.2) and the key generation code of `KeyGenApp` (see Listing 20.3) to produce a message digest and a public and private key pair. A `Signature` object is created by invoking the `getInstance()` method of `Signature`, passing it the DSA argument. The `initSign()` method is invoked to initialize the signature algorithm with the private key. The `update()` method is invoked with the value of the message digest. This causes the signature to be calculated based on the contents of the specified file (indirectly through digest) and the private key value. The invocation of the `sign()` method completes the signature calculation, and the signature is displayed.

To verify the signature, the `Signature` object is first reinitialized. This is accomplished by invoking the `initVerify()` method and passing it the public key value as an argument. The `update()` method is invoked with the value of the message digest and the `verify()` method is invoked with the value of the `signature` to be checked. The `verify()` method returns a `boolean` value indicating whether the signature was verified.

The `java.security.interfaces` Package

The `java.security.interfaces` package defines five interfaces that are used to generate keys for use in the NIST Digital Signature Algorithm. The `DSAKeyPairGenerator` interface generates keys specifically for the DSA. It is used in conjunction with the `KeyPairGenerator` interface by first creating a `KeyPairGenerator` object and then casting it to an object of the `DSAKeyPairGenerator` interface. The `initialize()` method of `DSAKeyPairGenerator` is then used to initialize the `KeyPairGenerator` using DSA-specific initialization parameters. Two forms of the `initialize()` method are provided—one that accepts a `DSAParams` object and a `SecureRandom` object as arguments and another that accepts an `integer` value, `boolean` value, and a `SecureRandom` object as parameters. The first form allows the p, q, and g values of the DSA to be specified via the `DSAParams` interface. The second form initializes the key generator to the integer-specified modulous length and the specified random source. The `boolean` value indicates whether new p, q, and g parameters should be specified or whether default values should be used.

The `DSAParams` interface provides three methods—`getG()`, `getP()`, and `getQ()`—which return the g, p, and q values associated with DSA key pair generation. The `DSAKey` interface provides the `getParams()` method to return the `DSAParams` interface associated with a DSA public or private key. The `DSAPublicKey` method provides the `getY()` method to return the value of the DSA public key. This value is returned as a `BigInteger` object of `java.math`. The `DSAPrivateKey` method provides the `getX()` method that returns the DSA private key. This value is also returned as a `BigInteger` object.

Managing Keys and Identities

In any system where signatures are used, it is important to be able to verify the signatures with respect to the individuals, organizations, or other entities that are purported to have created the signature. This is accomplished by using the public keys of the signing entities to check their signatures. But how do we keep track of what public keys are associated with individuals, organizations, and other entities? The `Identity` class is the answer.

The `Identity` Class

The `Identity` class encapsulates the name of a real-world entity (such as an individual, organization, or software process) together with its public key and a set of certificates that attest to the fact that the named entity does, in fact, use the specified public key.

The name and public key of an `Identity` must be unique for a particular *scope*. No two `Identity` objects may have the same name or same public key within a scope. A scope is just a set of related `Identity` objects. Examples are the students in a particular class, the employees in a particular company, or the companies using a particular signature service. Scopes are defined using the `IdentityScope` class (covered in a later subsection).

The `Identity` class provides three constructors: a parameterless constructor that creates an unnamed `Identity` object, a constructor that creates a named `Identity` object with an `IdentityScope`, and a constructor that creates a named `Identity` with an `IdentityScope`.

The access methods of the `Identity` class support the management of the certificates of the `Identity` object, comparison of `Identity` objects, and access to specific properties of `Identity` objects, such as their name, scope, and public key values. The `getName()` method returns the name of an `Identity` object. The `getScope()` method returns its `IdentityScope`. The `setInfo()` and `getInfo()` methods allow general information about an `Identity` object to be set and retrieved. The `setPublicKey()` and `getPublicKey()` methods provide access to the `Identity` object's public key.

The `certificates()` method returns a list of the `Identity` object's certificates. The `addCertificate()` method adds an object that implements the `Certificate` interface to the `Identity` object's list of certificates. The `removeCertificate()` method removes a `Certificate` object from this list.

The `equals()` method compares an `Identity` object with an arbitrary object. The `identityEquals()` method compares two `Identity` objects. The `hashCode()` method calculates a hash code value for the `Identity` object.

The `toString()` method overrides that of the `Object` class. A second `toString()` method is provided that takes a `boolean` value as an argument. If the `boolean` value is `true`, additional information is provided in the `Identity` object's `String` description.

The `Principal` Interface

The `Identity` class implements the `Principal` interface. This interface defines methods that are to be implemented by any representation of a real-world object that can have an identity, such as a person, an organization, or an executing program. These methods are as follows:

- `getName()`—Returns the name of the `Principal` object
- `equals()`—Returns a `boolean` value indicating whether the `Principal` object is equal to another object
- `hashCode()`—Returns an integer hash code for the `Principal` object
- `toString()`—Returns a `String` representation of the `Principal` object

The `IdentityScope` Class

The `IdentityScope` class extends the `Identity` class to implement a name scope for an identity. For example, the `Identity` object named "John Doe" could have the `IdentityScope` object named "Java Programming Team," which could have the `IdentityScope` object named "Great Software Company." The `IdentityScope` class allows `Identity` objects to be defined relative to a particular name space (that is, the scope). All `Identity` objects within a scope must have a unique name and public key value. However, `Identity` objects from different scopes may have the same name or public key values. For example, you couldn't have two John Does within the same Java Programming Team, but you could have two John Does at the Great Software Company.

The `IdentityScope` class has three constructors—a parameterless constructor that is used to create an unnamed `IdentityScope`, a constructor that takes the name of the `IdentityScope` object as a `String` argument, and a constructor that takes the name `String` and an `IdentityScope` object as arguments. The `IdentityScope` argument identifies the scope in which the newly created `IdentityScope` object is contained.

The `IdentityScope` class provides methods for adding, deleting, and accessing the `Identity` and `IdentityScope` objects that are within its scope. The `identities()` method returns an `Enumeration` object that contains all `Identity` objects in the identity scope. The `size()` method returns the number of these identities. The `getIdentity()` method returns a specific `Identity` object that is contained in the `IdentityScope` object. The `Identity` object may be specified by its name `String`, its `PublicKey` object, or an object that implements the `Principal` interface. The `addIdentity()` and `removeIdentity()` methods allow `Identity` objects to be added or removed from an `IdentityScope` object. The `toString()` method returns a `String` object that describes an `IdentityScope` object.

The `setSystemScope()` and `getSystemScope()` methods set and retrieve the value of the system's `IdentityScope` object. This object is, by default, an `IdentityDatabase` object defined in the `sun.security.provider` package. This object provides a persistent mechanism for managing identities and their associated keys and certificates. The system's `IdentityScope` object can be changed by `setSystemScope()`. The system's `IdentityScope` object that is currently in use is retrieved by `getSystemScope()`.

The `Certificate` Interface

The `Certificate` interface defines methods that are to be used to manage an identity certificate. `Identity` certificates are objects that guarantee a `Principal` object has a particular public key. A recognized authority digitally signs the identity certificates. Certificates may have different formats, such as X.509 or PGP. The `Certificate` interface provides a common set of methods that can be used with any particular certificate formats.

- `decode()`—Reads and decodes a certificate from an `InputStream` object
- `encode()`—Encodes and writes a certificate to an `OutputStream` object
- `getFormat()`—Returns a `String` that identifies the certificate format, such as X.509 or PGP
- `getGuarantor()`—Returns the `Principal` object that is the guarantor of the certificate—that is, the party that signed the certificate
- `getPrincipal()`—Returns the `Principal` object to which the certificate applies
- `getPublicKey()`—Returns the `PublicKey` object of the `Principal` object to which the certificate applies
- `toString()`—Returns a `String` object description of the certificate

The `Signer` Class

The `Signer` class is a subclass of the `Identity` class that is used for those identities that are capable of creating digital signatures. As such, it provides methods for dealing with private keys. (Private keys are used to create digital certificates. Public keys are used to verify them.)

The `Signer` class, like the `Identity` and `IdentityScope` classes, provides three constructors: a constructor that creates an unnamed `Signer` object, a constructor that creates a named `Signer` object, and a constructor that creates a named `Signer` object within a specified `IdentityScope`.

The `setKeyPair()` method is used to specify the `KeyPair` object of the `Signer` object. The `getPrivateKey()` method returns the `PrivateKey` of the `Signer`. The `toString()` returns a `String` representation of the `Signer`.

Implementing Access Controls

In addition to cryptographic security controls, the `java.security.acl` package provides the capability to implement traditional access control lists. Access control lists are lists of access control entries. Each access control entry identifies the accesses that a `Principal` may or may not make of a resource. These accesses are described in terms of permissions. The `java.security.acl` package defines the `Acl`, `AclEntry`, `Group`, `Owner`, and `Permission` interfaces.

The `Acl` Interface

The `Acl` interface defines methods for adding and removing `AclEntry` objects and for checking access permissions. The `entries()` method returns an `Enumeration` object containing the `AclEntry` objects in the list. The `addEntry()` and `removeEntry()` methods allow `AclEntry` objects to be added or removed from an `Acl` interface. A `Principal` may only have one positive and one negative `AclEntry` object in an `Acl` object.

> **NOTE**
>
> Modifications to an `Acl` object may only be made by its `Owner`. Refer to the subsequent "The `Owner` Interface" section.

The `setName()` and `getName()` methods are used to set and retrieve the name of an `Acl` object. The `checkPermission()` method checks whether a `Principal` has a particular `Permission`. The `getPermissions()` method returns an `Enumeration` object containing all the permissions of a particular `Principal`. The `toString()` method returns a `String` representation of an `Acl`.

> **NOTE**
>
> The `sun.security.acl` package provides a default implementation of the `java.security.acl` interfaces.

The `AclEntry` Interface

The `AclEntry` object identifies the `Permission` objects that are associated with a `Principal`. If the `AclEntry` object is positive (the default case), the accesses specified by the `Permission` objects are allowed. Otherwise, the accesses are denied. The `setPrincipal()` and `getPrincipal()` methods are used to set and retrieve the `Principal` object to which an `AclEntry` applies. The `permissions()` method returns an `Enumeration` object containing the `Permission` objects of an `AclEntry`. The `addPermission()` and `removePermission()` methods are used to update the `Permission` objects contained in an `AclEntry` object. The `checkPermission()` method returns a `boolean` value indicating whether a `Permission` object is contained in an `AclEntry`.

The `setNegativePermissions()` method is used to specify that the permissions of an `AclEntry` object are negative. The `isNegative()` method is used to determine whether the permissions of an `AclEntry` object are negative.

The `clone()` method creates a cloned copy of an `AclEntry` object. The `toString()` method returns a `String` representation of an `AclEntry` object.

The `Permission` Interface

The `Permission` interface encapsulates the concept of a `Principal` having access to a resource. It does not provide the capability to name a resource or the accesses that may take place. It defines two methods, `equal()` and `toString()`, which are used to compare `Permission` objects and display them as String values.

The `Owner` Interface

The `Owner` interface defines methods that are used to specify the owners of an `Acl` object. Only an `Owner` object is allowed to change an `Acl` object. The `addOwner()` method adds a new `Principal` object to a list of `Acl` owners. The `deleteOwner()` method deletes a `Principal` object from ownership of an `Acl`. The `isOwner()` method returns a `boolean` object indicating whether a `Principal` is the owner of an `Acl` object.

The `Group` Interface

The `Group` interface extends the `Principal` interface to organize `Principal` objects into related groups. The `members()` method returns an `Enumeration` object containing the members of a group. The `addMember()` and `removeMember()` methods add and remove `Principal` objects from a `Group`. The `isMember()` method returns a `boolean` value indicating whether a `Principal` object is a member of a `Group`.

Summary

In this chapter, you were introduced to the `java.security`, `java.security.acl`, and `java.security.interfaces` packages. You learned how to use these packages to create message digests and digital signatures. You also learned how to use the Security API's key management support. You then covered the access control interfaces of `java.security.acl`. Chapter 42, "Using `.jar` Files and Signed Applets," and Chapter 60, "Java Security," provide additional information on Java security mechanisms. The following chapter, "Internationalization and the `java.text` Package," illustrates the new JDK 1.1 internationalization capabilities.

21

Internationalization and the java.text Package

Being the de facto programming language of the Web, Java is an international programming language. It is being used in every country connected to the Web, and it is increasingly being called upon to develop applications and applets for use in the native languages of these countries. Fortunately, the developers of Java anticipated its international appeal and designed the language accordingly. The decision to provide comprehensive support of the Unicode character set was a major step toward Java's internationalization. In addition to Unicode support, JDK 1.1 provides classes and interfaces that simplify the process of incorporating locale-specific resources (such as text strings, dates, and currencies) within Java programs. These classes and interfaces allow locale-specific resources to be separately maintained and easily converted.

This chapter covers Java's internationalization support. You'll be introduced to the Unicode character set and you'll learn how to use the `Locale` and `ResourceBundle` classes to maintain locale-specific information. You'll also learn how the `java.text` package facilitates conversion of numbers, dates, and other units. When you finish this chapter, you'll be able to develop Java programs that adjust their output to the language and customs of the locale in which they execute.

What Is Internationalization?

In an age when individuals around the world are globally connected via the Internet, it is often required that programs be tailorable to the language and customs of the locales in which they execute. Programs that provide these capabilities are referred to as *global* programs.

Global programs can be difficult to develop, but they don't have to be. If you write a program that mixes language-dependent text strings throughout its code and displays all its output using the customs of a single country, you will have a terrible time converting it to the language and customs of another locale. If and when you do complete the conversion, you will have to maintain multiple versions of the same program—one for each locale. When you take this kind of approach, developing global programs is complex, difficult, and time-consuming.

On the other hand, if you carefully isolate locale-specific resources, such as text strings, currencies, and dates, and maintain these resources separate from locale-independent code, global programs can be developed with a minimum of additional effort. Tailoring of such programs, for use in specific locales, can often be reduced to providing foreign language equivalents of native language text strings and specifying the use of alternative format sets.

Internationalization is the process of designing and developing global programs in such a way that locale-specific information is separately and efficiently maintained. Internationalization allows global programs to be more easily localized.

The JDK 1.1 supports internationalization by using a multilanguage character set (Unicode 2.0), the `Locale`, `ResourceBundle` and other classes of `java.util`, the format conversion classes of `java.text`, and the Unicode character-stream support of `java.io`. Although this chapter focuses on java.text, it also discusses how the internationalization-related classes and interfaces of other packages are used to develop global Java applications and applets.

Using Unicode

Unlike most other programming languages, Java provides comprehensive support for the Unicode 2.0 character set. Unicode is a 16-bit character set. This means that it is capable of representing 65,536 characters. This is a large character set and can be used to represent the characters used by many of the world's popular languages. The 128 characters of the popular ASCII character set are the first 128 characters of Unicode.

> **NOTE**
>
> ASCII stands for American Standard Code for Information Interchange.
>
> More information about the Unicode character set can be found at http://www.unicode.org.

Unicode characters are written in Java using *Unicode escape character sequences.* These sequences are of the form \u*xxxx* where the four *x*s are replaced with hexadecimal digits. Each of the four hexadecimal digits represents four bits of a 16-bit Unicode character.

To display Unicode characters other than ASCII, you need a Unicode font. In the absence of such a font, Java displays Unicode characters using the \u*xxxx* notation.

Managing Locales and Resources

You learned about the Locale class in Chapter 14, "Useful Tools in the java.util and java.math Packages." This class provides internationalization support by describing geographic, political, or cultural regions. Locale objects are created by supplying the language and country arguments to the Locale() constructor or by using any of the predefined Locale constants. The access methods of Locale support the setting and retrieving of language, country, and variant-related values. The LocaleApp program, shown in Listing 21.1, illustrates the use of the Locale class in describing a locale in terms of a country and a language. Its output is as follows:

```
C:\jdk1.1.1\jdg\Ch21>java LocaleApp
CURRENT LOCALE:
Country: United States
Language: English

OTHER LOCALES:
Country: ROC
Language: Chinese
```

428 Part III ■ *Using the Java API*

```
Country: Korea
Language: Korean

Country: Italy
Language: Italian

Country: Canada
Language: English

Country: Canada
Language: French
```

Listing 21.1. The LocaleApp program.

```java
import java.util.*;

class LocaleApp {
 public static void main(String args[]) {
  Locale currentLocale = Locale.getDefault();
  Locale locales[]={Locale.TAIWAN,Locale.KOREA,
   Locale.ITALY,Locale.CANADA,Locale.CANADA_FRENCH};
  System.out.println("CURRENT LOCALE:");
  describeLocale(currentLocale);
  System.out.println("OTHER LOCALES:");
  for(int i=0;i<locales.length;++i)
   describeLocale(locales[i]);
 }
 static void describeLocale(Locale l){
  System.out.println("Country: "+l.getDisplayCountry());
  System.out.println("Language: "+l.getDisplayLanguage());
  System.out.println();
 }
}
```

The LocaleApp program invokes the getDefault() method of the Locale class to retrieve the current locale that is in effect. It then creates an array of sample Locale objects using the Locale constants to Taiwan, Korea, Italy, Canada, and French Canada. The describeLocale() method is then used to display the country and language associated with each Locale object.

The ResourceBundle Classes

The ResourceBundle class of java.util also supports internationalization. It is used to store locale-specific resources and tailor a program's appearance to the particular locale in which it is being run. The ResourceBundle class is extended by the ListResourceBundle and PropertyResourceBundle classes. The ListResourceBundle class organizes resources in terms of an array of object pairs, where the first object is a String key and the second object is the key's value. The PropertyResourceBundle class organizes locale-specific resources using a property file.

The ResourceBundleApp program of Listing 21.2 shows how resource bundles can be used to tailor a program's output. It is invoked with a two-character ISO-3166 country code and displays the names of five animals in English or Spanish, depending on the country code that was used.

The following examples of program output show how the program tailors the information it displays using the methods of the Locale, ResourceBundle, and ListResourceBundle classes:

```
C:\jdk1.1.1\jdg\Ch21>java ResourceBundleApp CA
cow
horse
cat
elephant
dog

C:\jdk1.1.1\jdg\Ch21>java ResourceBundleApp US
cow
horse
cat
elephant
dog

C:\jdk1.1.1\jdg\Ch21>java ResourceBundleApp GB
cow
horse
cat
elephant
dog

C:\jdk1.1.1\jdg\Ch21>java ResourceBundleApp ES
vaca
caballo
gato
elefante
perro

C:\jdk1.1.1\jdg\Ch21>java ResourceBundleApp MX
vaca
caballo
gato
elefante
perro
```

NOTE

The TextBundle and TextBundle_es classes, introduced later in this section, must be compiled before running ResourceBundleApp.

Listing 21.2. The ResourceBundleApp program.

```
import java.util.*;

class ResourceBundleApp {
 public static void main(String args[]) {
  if(args.length!=1){
   System.out.println("Usage: java ResourceBundleApp country_code");
   System.exit(0);
  }
  Locale mexico = new Locale("es","MX");
  Locale spain = new Locale("es","ES");
  Locale locales[] = {mexico,spain,Locale.US,Locale.CANADA,Locale.UK};
  Locale newLocale=null;
  for(int i=0;i<locales.length;++i){
   if(args[0].equals(locales[i].getCountry())){
    newLocale=locales[i];
    break;
   }
  }
  if(newLocale==null){
   System.out.println("Country not found.");
   System.exit(0);
  }
  ResourceBundle resources=ResourceBundle.getBundle("TextBundle",newLocale);
  Enumeration enum=resources.getKeys();
  while(enum.hasMoreElements()){
   String key=(String) enum.nextElement();
   System.out.println(resources.getString(key));
  }
 }
}
```

The ResourceBundleApp program creates Locale objects for Mexico and Spain and creates a list of supported locales including Mexico, Spain, the United States, Canada, and Great Britain. It checks the two-character country code that is passed to the program as a command-line argument with the list of supported locales. The newLocale variable is assigned the Locale object whose country code matches the one passed via the command line. The getCountry() method of the Locale class returns the two-character country code of a Locale object.

The getBundle() method of the ResourceBundle class is invoked to retrieve the ResourceBundle object associated with the Locale object stored in newLocale. Two resource bundle classes are available: the default (English) resource bundle, shown in Listing 21.3, and the Spanish language resource bundle, shown in Listing 21.4. The getBundle() method looks for classes of the following form until it finds one that matches; *ll* is the two-character (lowercase) language code of the locale, and *CC* is the two-character (uppercase) country code of the locale.

- ■ TextBundle_*ll*_*CC*
- ■ TextBundle_*ll*
- ■ TextBundle

For example, if you pass the GB country code (Great Britain) to ResourceBundleApp, getBundle() will look for resource bundle classes TextBundle_en_GB and TextBundle_en before settling on TextBundle.

> **NOTE**
>
> The language code for English is en. The language code for Spanish is es. The country codes for Mexico, Spain, United States, Canada, and United Kingdom are MX, ES, US, CA, and GB.

The getKeys() method of the ResourceBundle class returns an enumeration of the keys used to access locale-specific resources. The getString() method of ResourceBundle returns a String representation of the resource object associated with the key.

Listing 21.3. The TextBundle class.

```
import java.util.*;

public class TextBundle extends ListResourceBundle {
 public Object[][] getContents() {
  return contents;
 }
 static final Object[][] contents = {
  {"dog","dog"},
  {"cat","cat"},
  {"horse","horse"},
  {"cow","cow"},
  {"elephant","elephant"}
 };
}
```

The TextBundle class is a subclass of ListResourceBundle, which is a subclass of ResourceBundle. The getContents() method of ListResourceBundle is overridden to return an array of keys and their associated language-specific resources. The getContents() method is used to generate the information returned by the getKeys() and getString() methods used in ResourceBundleApp.

contents is an array of two-element arrays: the first element is the key and the second element is its value.

The `TextBundle_es` class is a Spanish language version of the `TextBundle` class. It provides a Spanish translation of the words dog, cat, horse, cow, and elephant.

Listing 21.4. The `TextBundle_es` class.

```
import java.util.*;

public class TextBundle_es extends ListResourceBundle {
 public Object[][] getContents() {
  return contents;
 }
 static final Object[][] contents = {
  {"dog","perro"},
  {"cat","gato"},
  {"horse","caballo"},
  {"cow","vaca"},
  {"elephant","elefante"}
 };
}
```

Performing Locale-Specific Format Conversions

The classes of `java.text` are used to provide locale-specific format conversions for use with numbers, dates, and other objects. `Format` is an abstract class that is extended by other classes to support parsing and format conversion. It declares the `format()` method to convert objects to strings and the `parseObject()` method to convert strings to objects. These methods are overridden by its subclasses.

The `DateFormat` Class

`DateFormat` is an abstract class used to format and parse date and time values using locale-specific customs. It supports four formatting styles defined by the `FULL`, `LONG`, `MEDIUM`, and `SHORT` constants. These styles determine the length of the formatted output. `DateFormat` defines other constants for identifying specific date and time fields. The `getInstance()`, `getDateInstance()`, `getTimeInstance()`, and `getDateTimeInstance()` methods return instances of `DateFormat` that are specific to a locale. Other methods are provided for working with objects of the `Calendar`, `TimeZone`, and other date-related classes covered in Chapter 14.

The `SimpleDateFormat` Class

The `SimpleDateFormat` class extends the `DateFormat` class to provide a default implementation of date formatting and parsing capabilities. It allows date and time formatting patterns to be used to customize formatting and parsing. The `SimpleDateFormat` class makes use of special date and time pattern symbols that are discussed in the class's API description.

The `DateFormatApp` program, shown in Listing 21.5, illustrates the use of the date-formatting capabilities of the `SimpleDateFormat` class. When you run the program, it produces the following type-formatted output. The date and time displayed are the current date and time of the locale in which the program is run:

```
C:\jdk1.1.1\jdg\Ch21>java DateFormatApp
The year is 1997 AD.
The month is April.
It is 12 o'clock AM, Pacific Daylight Time.
```

Although the output may not be that impressive, the formatting capabilities provided by `SimpleDateFormat` are efficient and easy to use. The pattern string places single quotes around text that is not a date/time formatting pattern. The formatting patterns used in the pattern string are as follows:

- yyyy—Year
- GG—Era
- MMMMMMMMM—Month
- hh—Hour
- a—AM/PM designator
- zzzz—Time zone

The pattern is supplied as an argument to the `SimpleDateFormat` constructor to create a format pattern–specific object. The current date is passed to the `format()` method of this object to create a `String` object that is formatted using the current date and the format pattern.

Listing 21.5. The `DateFormatApp` program.

```
import java.text.*;
import java.util.*;

class DateFormatApp {
 public static void main(String args[]) {
  String pattern="'The year is 'yyyy GG'.\n'";
  pattern+="'The month is 'MMMMMMMMM'.\n'";
  pattern+="'It is 'hh 'o''''clock' a, zzzz'.'";
  SimpleDateFormat format = new SimpleDateFormat(pattern);
  String formattedDate = format.format(new Date());
  System.out.println(formattedDate);
 }
}
```

The `DateFormatSymbols` Class

The `DateFormatSymbols` class is used to provide access to locale-specific date symbols, such as the names of days, months, and other date and time units. `DateFormatSymbols` objects are created using the `getDateFormatSymbols` method of the `SimpleDateFormat` class or via the `DateFormatSymbols()` constructor. Several get methods allow locale-specific formatting strings to be retrieved.

The `NumberFormat` Class

The `NumberFormat` class is an abstract class that supports the locale-specific formatting and parsing of numbers. The `INTEGER_FIELD` and `FRACTION_FIELD` constants are used to identify fields within decimal numbers. The `format()` and `parse()` methods support number formatting and parsing. Other methods are provided to access the number of digits to the left and right of the decimal point, to work with locales, and to access other number-formatting attributes.

The `NumberFormatApp` program, shown in Listing 21.6, illustrates the use of the `NumberFormat` class in supporting locale-specific currency formatting. It prints out a value of 1,000,000 currency units using the locale-specific currency value, as shown in the following:

```
C:\jdk1.1.1\jdg\Ch21>java NumberFormatApp
$1,000,000.00
```

Listing 21.6. The `NumberFormatApp` program.

```
import java.text.*;
import java.util.*;

class NumberFormatApp {
 public static void main(String args[]) {
  NumberFormat format = NumberFormat.getCurrencyInstance(
   Locale.getDefault());
  String formattedCurrency = format.format(1000000);
  System.out.println(formattedCurrency);
 }
}
```

The `DecimalFormat` Class

The `DecimalFormat` class extends the `NumberFormat` class to support the formatting of decimal numbers using locale-specific customs. The class supports the specification and use of custom formatting patterns. The `format()` and `parse()` methods are used to perform formatting and parsing. A number of `get` and `set` methods are provided to access specific formatting parameters. The `DecimalFormat` class makes use of special number formatting pattern symbols that are discussed in the class's API description.

The `DecimalFormatSymbols` Class

The `DecimalFormatSymbols` class provides access to the locale-specific symbols used in formatting numbers. These symbols include decimal separators, grouping separators, and others used by objects of the `DecimalFormat` class. Instances of `DecimalFormatSymbols` are created using the `getDecimalFormatSymbols()` method of the `DecimalFormat` class and the `DecimalFormatSymbols()` constructors. Several methods are provided to set and retrieve formatting information, such as the decimal separator character, grouping separators, the minus sign, the infinity symbol, the not-a-number symbol, and the percentage sign.

The `ChoiceFormat` Class

The `ChoiceFormat` class extends the `NumberFormat` class to identify strings that serve as labels for numbers within specific intervals. The `ChoiceFormat` constructor takes an array of `double` values used to specify numeric intervals and an array of `String` objects that identify the labels associated with those intervals. The `double` values are referred to as *limits*. The methods of the `ChoiceFormat` class support the formatting and parsing of strings based on the limits and their labels.

The `ChoiceFormatApp` program of Listing 21.7 illustrates the use of the `ChoiceFormat` class. It uses a random number generator to predict the likelihood of rain. Its output varies every time you run it. Sample output follows:

```
C:\jdk1.1.1\jdg\Ch21>java ChoiceFormatApp
The likelihood of rain today is very low (0.05002163005399529).

C:\jdk1.1.1\jdg\Ch21>java ChoiceFormatApp
The likelihood of rain today is high (0.954441890602895).

C:\jdk1.1.1\jdg\Ch21>java ChoiceFormatApp
The likelihood of rain today is moderate (0.3000466839384621).
```

The `ChoiceFormatApp` program defines five limits: 0.0, 0.1, 0.3, 0.7, and 1.0. It defines four labels that correspond to intervals defined by these limits:

- `very low`—From 0.0 up to, but not including, 0.1
- `low`—From 0.1 up to, but not including, 0.3
- `moderate`—From 0.3 up to, but not including, 0.7
- `high`—From 0.7 up to, but not including, 1.0

An object of the `ChoiceFormat` class is created using the `limits` and `labels` arrays. A random number between 0 and 1 is fed into the `format()` method of the `ChoiceFormat` object to select the label associated with the interval in which the random number generator falls.

Listing 21.7. The ChoiceFormatApp program.

```
import java.text.*;
import java.util.*;

class ChoiceFormatApp {
 public static void main(String args[]) {
  double limits[] = {0.0,0.1,0.3,0.7,1.0};
  String labels[] = {"very low","low","moderate","high"};
  ChoiceFormat format = new ChoiceFormat(limits,labels);
  String prediction = "The likelihood of rain today is ";
  double r = Math.random();
  prediction += format.format(r)+" ("+r+").";
  System.out.println(prediction);
 }
}
```

The MessageFormat Class

The MessageFormat class extends the Format class to format objects as messages that are inserted into a String object. The MessageFormat constructor takes a String argument that specifies a message-formatting pattern. This pattern contains formatting elements where time, date, number, and choice objects may be inserted. Consult the API documentation of the MessageFormat class for a description of the syntax used to create formatting patterns. The format() method is used to insert objects into a message-formatting pattern. The parse() method is used to parse the objects contained in a string according to a message-formatting pattern.

The MessageFormatApp program, shown in Listing 21.8, provides a simple introduction of the use of the MessageFormat class. It generates output of the form:

```
C:\jdk1.1.1\jdg\Ch21>java MessageFormatApp
The time is 1:21:57 AM and your lucky number is 761.
```

MessageFormatApp creates a format pattern with time and number fields and uses this pattern to construct a MessageFormat object. It creates an array of two objects: the current time (as a Date object) and a random Integer object. It then invokes the format() method of the MessageFormat object to produce the formatted output that is displayed to the console window.

Listing 21.8. The MessageFormatApp class.

```
import java.text.*;
import java.util.*;

class MessageFormatApp {
 public static void main(String args[]) {
  String pattern = "The time is {0,time} and ";
  pattern += "your lucky number is {1,number}.";
  MessageFormat format = new MessageFormat(pattern);
  Object objects[] = {new Date(),
```

```
    new Integer((int)(Math.random()*1000))};
  String formattedOutput=format.format(objects);
  System.out.println(formattedOutput);
  }
}
```

The `FieldPosition` and `ParsePosition` Classes

The `FieldPosition` class is used to identify fields in formatted output. It keeps track of the field's position within the formatted output. The `FieldPosition()` constructor takes an integer value that is used to identify the field. Its methods are used to retrieve the indices of the beginning and end of the field and the field's identifier.

The `ParsePosition` class is similar to the `FieldPosition` class. While `FieldPosition` is used for formatting, `ParsePosition` is used for parsing. Its constructor takes an integer that identifies its index within the string being parsed. The `getIndex()` and `setIndex()` methods are used to change this index.

Collation

Different languages have different alphabets and unique ways of sorting text strings written in those languages. *Collation*, as it applies to `java.text`, is the process of sorting or arranging text strings according to locale-specific customs. The `java.text` package supports collation through the `Collator`, `RuleBasedCollator`, `CollationKey`, and `CollationElementIterator` classes.

The `Collator` class is an abstract class that is used to compare `String` objects using locale-specific customs. It is subclassed to provide implement-specific collation algorithms. The `getInstance()` method is used to retrieve a locale-specific `Collation` instance. Some languages recognize different *strengths* in determining whether letters are identical or different; this is common to languages that support accented characters. The `setStrength()` of `Collator` may be used to set different collation strength levels. The `compare()` method compares two strings and returns an `int` value indicating the results of the comparison. The other methods of `Collator` support the decomposition of composite (for example, accented) characters and the creation of `CollationKey` objects.

The `CollationKey` class provides a compact representation of a `String` object according to the collation rules of a `Collator` object. `CollationKey` objects are optimized to support fast `String` comparisons and are preferred to the `compare()` method of the `Collator` class for extensive comparisons, such as those found in sorting algorithms. `CollationKey` objects are generated using the `getCollationKey()` method of the `Collator` class. The `compareTo()` and `equals()` methods of `CollationKey` are used to perform comparisons. The `toByteArray()` method can be used to convert a `CollationKey` object to a `byte` array. The `getSourceString()` method returns the `String` object from which a `CollationKey` object was generated.

The RuleBasedCollator class extends Collator to provide a concrete collator implementation. It allows you to define your own collation rules. However, in most cases, you'll want to use the predefined rules that are specific to your locale. The getRules() method may be used to retrieve the collation rules that are in effect for a RuleBasedCollator object. The getCollationKey() method overrides that of the Collator class. The getCollationElementIterator() method returns a CollationElementIterator object for the collator. Iterator classes are covered in the next section.

The CollateApp program, shown in Listing 21.9, shows how the RulesBasedCollator and CollationKey classes can be used to sort a file. The CollateApp program takes a filename as a command-line argument and produces a sorted version of the file's contents as its output. The following output shows how the file CollateApp.java is sorted. Note how the default collation rules treat blanks that appear at the beginning of a string:

```
C:\jdk1.1.1\jdg\Ch21>java CollateApp CollateApp.java

}
 }
 }
  }
  }
  }
   }
    }
   }catch(Exception ex){
   boolean changes=true;
    BufferedReader in = new BufferedReader(new FileReader(args[0]));
    changes=false;
      changes=true;
class CollateApp {
   CollationKey keys[]=new CollationKey[keyVector.size()];
      CollationKey temp=keys[i];
   Collator.getInstance(defaultLocale);
   for(int i=0;i<keys.length;++i)
   for(int i=0;i<keys.length;++i)
    for(int i=0;i<keys.length-1;++i){
   if(args.length!=1){
      if(compare>0){
import java.io.*;
import java.text.*;
import java.util.*;
    in.close();
    int compare=keys[i].compareTo(keys[i+1]);
   keys[i]=(CollationKey) keyVector.elementAt(i);
      keys[i]=keys[i+1];
      keys[i+1]=temp;
   keys=sort(keys);
     keyVector.addElement(collator.getCollationKey(line));
   Locale defaultLocale = Locale.getDefault();
  public static void main(String args[]) {
   return keys;
   RuleBasedCollator collator = (RuleBasedCollator)
  static CollationKey[] sort(CollationKey keys[]){
   String line;
   System.exit(0);
```

```
   System.exit(0);
   System.out.println("Usage: java CollateApp file");
   System.out.println(ex);
   System.out.println(keys[i].getSourceString());
  try {
 Vector keyVector = new Vector();
   while((line=in.readLine())!=null)
  while(changes){
```

Listing 21.9. The CollateApp program.

```
import java.text.*;
import java.util.*;
import java.io.*;

class CollateApp {
 public static void main(String args[]) {
  if(args.length!=1){
   System.out.println("Usage: java CollateApp file");
   System.exit(0);
  }
  Locale defaultLocale = Locale.getDefault();
  RuleBasedCollator collator = (RuleBasedCollator)
   Collator.getInstance(defaultLocale);
  Vector keyVector = new Vector();
  try {
   BufferedReader in = new BufferedReader(new FileReader(args[0]));
   String line;
   while((line=in.readLine())!=null)
    keyVector.addElement(collator.getCollationKey(line));
   in.close();
  }catch(Exception ex){
   System.out.println(ex);
   System.exit(0);
  }
  CollationKey keys[]=new CollationKey[keyVector.size()];
  for(int i=0;i<keys.length;++i)
   keys[i]=(CollationKey) keyVector.elementAt(i);
  keys=sort(keys);
  for(int i=0;i<keys.length;++i)
   System.out.println(keys[i].getSourceString());
 }
 static CollationKey[] sort(CollationKey keys[]){
  boolean changes=true;
  while(changes){
   changes=false;
   for(int i=0;i<keys.length-1;++i){
    int compare=keys[i].compareTo(keys[i+1]);
    if(compare>0){
     changes=true;
     CollationKey temp=keys[i];
     keys[i]=keys[i+1];
     keys[i+1]=temp;
    }
   }
  }
  return keys;
 }
}
```

The `CollateApp` program creates a `RulesBasedCollator` object using the `getInstance()` method of the `Collator` class. It selects the collator corresponding to the default locale. It reads in each line of the file, creates a `CollationKey` object corresponding to the input line, and stores the line in a `Vector` object. It then converts the vector to an array to simplify the sorting process. The `sort()` method is invoked to sort the `CollationKey` array. The `String` objects corresponding to the sorted `CollationKey` objects are retrieved via the `getSourceString()` method. These `String` objects are then printed.

The `sort()` method sorts the `CollationKey` array using `CollationKey`'s `compareTo()` method. This method returns a positive integer if the `CollationKey` object being compared is greater than the one it is being compared to. It returns `0` if they are equal and a negative integer if the `CollationKey` object being compared is less than the one it is being compared to.

The Iterator Classes and Interfaces of `java.text`

The `CharacterIterator` interface defines methods that are implemented by classes that provide the ability to step through (iterate) a sequence of characters. These methods allow you to set your position within the text, move to other positions, and return the character at a specific position. The `StringCharacterIterator` class implements `CharacterIterator` to support string iteration and parsing.

The `BreakIterator` class is used to find text boundaries. It provides useful static methods for locale-specific parsing of character sequences by word, line, or sentence.

The `CollationElementIterator` class supports string iteration and returns information used to collate strings using locale-specific customs.

Summary

In this chapter you were introduced to Java's internationalization support. You covered the Unicode character set and learned how to use the `Locale` and `ResourceBundle` classes to maintain locale-specific information. You also learned how the classes of the `java.text` package facilitate the conversion of numbers, dates, and other units. In the next chapter you'll be introduced to JavaBeans and learn about the benefits of this component-based approach to Java software development.

22

Building Reusable Components with java.beans

In this book you develop almost all of your applications and applets from scratch because you're trying to learn Java. Once you become comfortable in Java programming and go out to develop real-world Java applications and applets, you won't be so eager to start from scratch. You'll want to use available off-the-shelf Java components whenever possible.

There are a number of forms that Java components may distribute. For example, you can go down to your local software superstore and purchase a set of Java API packages. Then you can use these new APIs to create objects that are instances of the classes and interfaces of the new APIs. You're familiar with this process because you've been learning to do this with the API of JDK 1.1.

If you purchase a visual Java development tool, such as Symantec's Visual Café, you'll be able to drag and drop GUI components onto the interface design of your applications and applets. Some of these GUI components may be new components that are not included with the JDK 1.1. These components are not made available as API classes and interfaces and are similar to Java beans.

In this chapter, you'll be introduced to Java beans and learn how the JavaBeans software component assembly model can be used to quickly and easily develop applications and applets. You'll cover the classes and interfaces of the java.beans package and learn how they are used to support the software component assembly model. Chapter 44, "Using JavaBeans," provides additional information on the development and use of Java beans.

The Software Component Assembly Model

Java beans are Java software components that are designed for maximum reuse. They are often visible GUI components, but can also be invisible algorithmic components. They support the software component assembly model pioneered by Microsoft's Visual Basic and Borland's Delphi. This model focuses on the use of components and containers.

Components are specialized, self-contained software entities that may be replicated, customized, and inserted into applications and applets. Component interfaces are well-defined and may be *discovered* during a component's execution. This feature, referred to as *introspection*, allows visual programming tools to drag and drop a component onto an application or applet design and dynamically determine what component *interface methods* and *properties* are available. Interface methods are public methods of a class that are available for use by other components. Properties are attributes of a bean that are implemented by the bean class's field variables and accessed via *accessor* methods.

Properties determine the appearance or behavior of a bean. A component's properties may be modified during the visual design of an application. The modified properties can be stored in such a manner that they remain with the component from design to execution. The capability to store changes to a component's properties is known as *persistence*. Persistence allows components to be customized for later use. For example, during design, you may create two button beans—one with a blue background color and a yellow foreground color and another with a red background color and a white foreground color. The color modifications are stored along with instances of each bean object. When the beans are displayed during a program's execution, they are displayed using the modified colors.

As mentioned earlier, a software component assembly model deals with components and containers. *Containers* are simply components that contain other components. A container is used as a framework for visually organizing components. Visual development tools allow components to be dragged and dropped into a container, resized, and positioned. The visual design nature of these tools greatly simplifies the development of a user interface. However, component-based visual development tools go beyond simple screen layout. They also allow component event handling to be described in a visual manner.

You should be familiar with events from Chapter 15, "Window Programming with the `java.awt` Packages." You will master event handling in Part IV, "Window Programming." For now, you just need to know that events are generated in response to certain actions, such as the user clicking or moving the mouse or pressing a keyboard key. The event is then handled by an event handler. Beans may handle events that occur local to them. For example, a button-based bean is required to handle the clicking of a button. Beans may also call upon other beans to complete the handling of an event. For example, a button bean may handle the button-clicked event by causing a text string to be displayed in a status-display bean. Visual development tools support the connection of *event sources* (for example, the button bean) with *event listeners* (for example, the status-display bean) using graphical design tools.

If the terminology of the software component development model seems abstract and confusing to you, don't worry—some visual explanations of these concepts will follow shortly. In order to *see* what these terms mean, however, you'll have to download and install the Beans Development Kit (BDK) as described in the next section. We'll use the BDK to cover component-based software development using JavaBeans. After you get the picture of what beans are all about, then we'll cover the classes and interfaces of the `java.beans` API.

The Beans Development Kit

The Beans Development Kit (BDK) provides several examples of Java beans, a tutorial, and supporting documentation. But most important, it provides a tool, referred to as the BeanBox, that can be used to display, customize, and test the beans that you'll develop. The BeanBox also serves as a primitive visual development tool. We'll use the BeanBox to illustrate the important aspects of visual component-based software development as it applies to JavaBeans.

The BDK can be downloaded by following the appropriate links from `http://splash.javasoft.com/beans/`. Online installation instructions are also provided. Download and install the BDK before continuing on to the next section. Once you've installed the BDK, re-start your system to make sure that all installation changes take effect.

> **NOTE**
>
> Through the rest of the chapter, I will assume that you've installed the BDK in its default location, the `c:\bdk` directory. If you install the BDK in a different directory, you'll have to map between `c:\bdk` and your installation directory.

The BeanBox

The BeanBox of the BDK is an example of a simple visual development tool for JavaBeans. It is located in the `c:\bdk\beanbox` directory. Change to this directory and start the BeanBox as follows:

```
C:\BDK\beanbox>run
```

The BeanBox application loads and displays three windows labeled ToolBox, BeanBox, and PropertySheet, as shown in Figures 22.1, 22.2, and 22.3.

The ToolBox window contains a list of available Java beans. These beans are components that can be used to build more complex beans, Java applications, or applets.

FIGURE 22.1.

The ToolBox window.

FIGURE 22.2.
The BeanBox window.

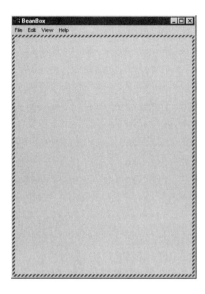

FIGURE 22.3.
The PropertySheet window.

Visual software development tools, such as the BeanBox, allow beans to be visually organized by placing them at the location where you want them to be displayed. Click on the Juggler bean in the ToolBox window and then click in the BeanBox—the Juggler bean is placed in the BeanBox, as shown in Figure 22.4. The Juggler bean juggles when it is placed in the BeanBox.

Note that the PropertySheet is updated to display the properties of the Juggler bean. (See Figure 22.5.) You can customize the Juggler bean by changing its properties. Change the `animationRate` property to 500, as shown in Figure 22.6. Note how the Juggler slows the rate at which it juggles the beans.

FIGURE 22.4.

Adding a bean to the BeanBox.

FIGURE 22.5.

The Juggler's PropertySheet.

FIGURE 22.6.

Changing the Juggler's animationRate *property.*

Let's add a couple of buttons to the BeanBox. Select an ourButton bean in the ToolBox and then place it in the BeanBox, as shown in Figure 22.7. A button labeled press is displayed. Use the button's property sheet to change its label to Start, as shown in Figure 22.8. Now create a second button labeled Stop, as shown in Figure 22.9.

FIGURE 22.7.
Adding a button to the BeanBox.

FIGURE 22.8.
Editing the button's label.

By now you can see where this application is going. You're going to use the Start and Stop buttons to control the animation. To do this, connect the Start button's `actionPerformed()` event handler to the `startJuggling()` method of the Juggler bean and the Stop button's `actionPerformed()` event handler to the `stopJuggling()` method of the Juggler bean. If you forgot what events are, refer to the description of events in Chapter 15. If you still don't get it, don't worry—you'll write plenty of event-driven programs in Part IV.

Click the Start button and then select Edit | Events | action | actionPerformed from the BeanBox menu bar, as shown in Figure 22.10. A red line is now shown emanating from the Start button. This line represents a logical connection from the Start button's `actionPerformed()` event handler. Click on the Juggler bean to close the connection. When you do, the

EventTargetDialog, shown in Figure 22.11, is displayed. This dialog lists the interface methods of the Juggler bean. Select startJuggling. By doing so, you connect the clicking of the Start button to the `startJuggling()` method via the `actionPerformed()` event handler of the Start button bean. The EventTargetDialog notifies you that it is compiling an adapter class. The BeanBox creates a special class, referred to as an *adapter* class, to connect the clicking of the button with the `startJuggling()` method of the Juggler. It must compile this class and add it in to the running BeanBox to support this connection.

FIGURE 22.9.

Adding a second button to the BeanBox.

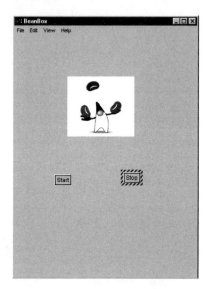

FIGURE 22.10.

Selecting the `actionPerformed()` *event handler.*

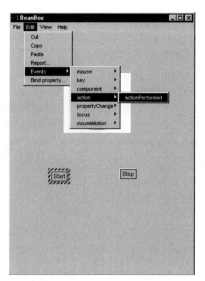

FIGURE 22.11.
Connecting to the
`startJuggling()`
method.

Now that you know how to associate events with interface methods, let's connect the Stop button to the `stopJuggling()` method of the Juggler bean. Click on the Stop button and select Edit | Events | action | actionPerformed from the BeanBox menubar. Connect the red connector to the Juggler bean and select the `stopJuggling()` method.

Now you can have some fun with the Juggler. Click the Stop button to stop the juggling and click the Start button to get it going again.

How Do Beans Work?

The point of the BeanBox tutorial is to give you a general idea of how beans are used in software development. This section covers some of the underlying mechanisms that enable beans to be used in this manner.

Graphic Representation and Visual Layout

One of the first things that you probably noticed when you started up the BeanBox was the ToolBox full of Java beans. Several of these beans had icons. Java beans have the capability to support a variety of icons for display by visual development tools.

Beans themselves can also be graphically displayed by visual development tools. When you placed the Juggler and ourButton beans in the BeanBox, they were displayed exactly how they appear in a final application. You can move them to their intended position and resize them to the desired dimensions.

Some beans are invisible in the sense that they do not have a graphical display. An example of an invisible bean could be a specialized algorithm, such as an image filter. Visual development tools usually create special graphical objects that allow the invisible beans to be manipulated in the same manner as visible beans during software development. Of course, the special graphical objects of the invisible beans are not displayed by the final application or applet.

Customizable and Persistent Properties

Properties are attributes of a bean that can be modified to change the appearance or behavior of a bean. Properties are accessed through special methods, referred to as *accessor* methods. (You'll learn about accessor methods shortly.) Visual development tools allow properties to be changed through the use of *property sheets*. A property sheet is a list of properties that can be specified for a bean. Visual building tools, like the BeanBox, display a property sheet in response to a bean's selection. You used property sheets to change the `animationRate` property of the Juggler bean and the `label` property of the ourButton bean.

In addition to the simple property-editing capabilities exhibited by the BeanBox example, individual beans can define custom property editors that allow properties to be edited using specialized dialog boxes. These custom property editors are implemented as special classes that are associated with the bean's class. The custom property editors are available to visual development tools, but because they are not part of the bean's class, they do not need to be compiled into applications or applets. This lets you provide extra *design* capabilities for a bean without having to develop bloated applications.

Suppose that you are using a bean that provides extensive customization support. You change the bean's background color to red and its foreground color to white, change a label associated with the bean, and alter a few other properties. You may wonder what happens to the property changes. How are the changes packaged along with the bean's class?

Beans store any property changes so that new property values come into effect and are displayed when the modified bean is used in an application. The capability to permanently store property changes is known as persistence. Java beans implement persistence by serializing bean objects that are instances of a bean class. *Serialization* is the process of writing the current state of an object to a stream. Because beans are serialized, they must implement the `java.io.Serializable` or `java.io.Externalizable` interfaces. Beans that implement `java.io.Serializable` are automatically saved. Beans that implement `java.io.Externalizable` are responsible for saving themselves. Chapter 53, "Using Object Serialization," covers object serialization in more detail.

When a bean object is saved through serialization, all the values of the object's variables are saved. In this way, any property changes are carried along with the object. The only exceptions to this are variables that are identified as `transient`. The values of `transient` variables are not serialized.

Bean Properties

Beans support a few different types of properties. In the BeanBox tutorial you saw examples of *simple* properties. The `animationRate` property of the Juggler bean used a simple numeric value and the `label` property of the ourButton bean used a text value.

An *indexed property* is a property that can take on an array of values. Indexed properties are used to keep track of a group of related values of the same type. For example, an indexed property could be used to maintain the values of a scrollable list.

A *bound* property is a property that alerts other objects when its value changes. For example, you could use a bound property to implement a temperature control dial. Whenever the user changes the control, notification of the change is propagated to objects that regulate temperature.

A *constrained* property is similar to a bound property in that it notifies other objects of an *impending* change. Constrained properties give the notified objects the power to veto a property change. You could use a constrained property to implement a bean that fires a missile under two-person control. When one person initiates a missile launch, a notification is sent to a second user, who could either confirm or deny the launch. (Hopefully, extra security protections other than the bean would be provided!)

Accessor Methods

All properties are accessed through accessor methods. There are two types of accessor methods: *getter* methods and *setter* methods. Getter methods retrieve the values of properties, and setter methods set property values. The names of getter methods begin with `get` and are followed by the name of the property to which they apply. The names of setter methods begin with `set` and are followed by the property name.

Methods Used with Simple Properties

If a bean has a property named `fooz` of type `foozType` that can be read and written, it should have the following accessor methods:

```
public foozType getFooz()
public void setFooz(foozType foozValue)
```

A property is read-only or write-only if one of the preceding accessor methods are missing.

> **NOTE**
>
> If a property is `boolean`, then getter methods are written using `is` instead of `get`. For example, `isFooz()` would be used instead of `getFooz()` if `fooz` is a `boolean` property.

Methods Used with Indexed Properties

A bean that has an indexed property will have methods that support the reading and writing of individual array elements as well as the entire array. For example, if a bean has an indexed widget property where each element of the array is of type widgetType, it will have the following accessor methods:

```
public widgetType getWidget(int index)
public widgetType[] getWidget()
public void setWidget(int index, widgetType widgetValue)
public void setWidget(widgetType[] widgetValues)
```

Methods Used with Bound Properties

Beans with bound properties have getter and setter methods as previously identified, depending upon whether the property values are simple or indexed. Bound properties require certain objects to be notified when they change. The change notification is accomplished through the generation of a PropertyChangeEvent. Objects that wish to be notified of a property change of a bound property must register as listeners. Accordingly, the bean implementing the bound property supplies methods of the form:

```
public void addPropertyChangeListener(PropertyChangeListener l)
public void removePropertyChangeListener(PropertyChangeListener l)
```

> **NOTE**
>
> The PropertyChangeEvent class and PropertyChangeListener interface are defined in java.beans.

The preceding listener registration methods do not identify specific bound properties. To register listeners for the PropertyChangeEvent of a specific property, the following methods must be provided:

```
public void add*PropertyName*Listener(PropertyChangeListener l)
public void remove*PropertyName*Listener(PropertyChangeListener l)
```

In the preceding methods, PropertyName is replaced by the name of the bound property.

Objects that implement the PropertyChangeListener interface must implement the propertyChange() method. This method is invoked by the bean for all of its registered listeners to inform the listeners of a property change.

Methods Used with Constrained Properties

The previously discussed methods used with simple and indexed properties apply to constrained properties. In addition, the following event registration methods are provided:

```
public void addVetoableChangeListener(VetoableChangeListener l)
public void removeVetoableChangeListener(VetoableChangeListener l)
public void add*PropertyName*Listener(VetoableChangeListener l)
public void remove*PropertyName*Listener(VetoableChangeListener l)
```

Objects that implement the `VetoableChangeListener` interface must implement the `vetoableChange()` method. This method is invoked by the bean for all of its registered listeners to inform the listeners of a property change. Any object that does not approve of a property change can throw a `PropertyVetoException` within its `vetoableChange()` method to inform the bean, whose constrained property was changed, that the change was not approved.

Introspection

In order for beans to be used by visual development tools, the beans must be able to dynamically inform the tools of their interface methods and properties and also what kind of events they may generate or respond to. This capability is referred to as *introspection*. The `Introspector` class of `java.beans` provides a set of static methods for tools to obtain information about the properties, methods, and events of a bean.

The `Introspector` supports introspection in two ways:

- Reflection and Design Patterns—The `java.lang.reflect` package provides the capability to identify the fields and methods of a class. The `Introspector` uses this capability to review the names of the methods of a bean's class. It identifies a bean's properties by looking at the method names for the getter and setter naming patterns identified in previous sections of this chapter. It identifies a bean's event generation and processing capabilities by looking for methods that follow the naming conventions for event generation and event listening. The `Introspector` automatically applies reflection and design (naming) patterns to a bean class to obtain information for design tools in the absence of explicitly provided information.

- Explicit Specification—Information about a bean may be optionally provided by the use of a special bean information class that implements the `BeanInfo` interface. The `BeanInfo` interface provides methods for explicitly conveying information about a bean's methods, properties, and events. The `Introspector` recognizes `BeanInfo` classes by their name. The name of a `BeanInfo` class is the name of the bean class followed by `BeanInfo`. For example, suppose a bean is implemented via the `MyGizmo` class. The related `BeanInfo` class would be named `MyGizmoBeanInfo`.

Connecting Events to Interface Methods

Beans, being primarily GUI components, generate and respond to events. Visual development tools provide the capability to link events generated by one bean with event-handling methods implemented by other beans. For example, a button component may generate an event as the result of the user clicking on that button. A visual development tool would enable you to connect the handling of this event to the interface methods of other beans. The bean generating the event is referred to as the *event source*. The bean listening for (and handling) the event is referred to as the *event listener*. Events and event handling are introduced in Chapter 15. They are covered extensively in Part IV.

Inside `java.beans`

Now that you have a feel for what beans are and how they are used and have been introduced to some of the mechanisms they employ, let's take a look at the classes and interfaces of `java.beans`. These classes and interfaces are organized into the categories of design support, introspection support, and change event-handling support.

Design Support

The classes in this category help visual development tools to use beans in a design environment.

The `Beans` class provides seven static methods that are used by application builders:

- `instantiate()`—Creates an instance of a bean from a serialized object
- `isInstanceOf()`—Determines if a bean is of a specified class or interface
- `getInstanceof()`—Returns an object that represents a particular view of a bean
- `isDesignTime()`—Determines whether beans are running in an application builder environment
- `setDesignTime()`—Identifies the fact that beans are running in an application builder environment
- `isGuiAvailable()`—Determines whether a GUI is available for beans
- `setGuiAvailable()`—Identifies the fact that a GUI is available for beans

The `Visibility` interface is implemented by classes that support the capability to answer questions about the availability of a GUI for a bean. It provides the `avoidingGui()`, `dontUseGui()`, `needsGui()`, and `okToUseGui()` methods.

The methods of the `PropertyEditor` interface are implemented by classes that support custom property editing. These methods support a range of property editors from simple to complex. The `setValue()` method is used to identify the object that is to be edited. The `getValue()` method returns the edited value. The `isPaintable()` and `paintValue()` methods support the painting of property values on a `Graphics` object. The `getJavaInitializationString()` method returns a string of Java code that is used to initialize a property value. The `setAsText()` and `getAsText()` methods are used to set and retrieve a property value as a `String` object. The `getTags()` method returns an array of `String` objects that are acceptable values for a property. The `supportsCustomEditor()` method returns a `boolean` value indicating whether a custom editor is provided by a `PropertyEditor`. The `getCustomEditor()` method returns an object that is of a subclass of `Component` and is used as a custom editor for a bean's property. The `addPropertyChangeListener()` and `removePropertyChangeListener()` methods are used to register event handlers for the `PropertyChangeEvent` associated with a property.

The `PropertyEditorManager` class provides static methods that help application builders find property editors for specific properties. The `registerEditor()` method is used to register an editor class for a particular property class. The `getEditorSearchPath()` and `setEditorSearchPath()`methods support package name lists for finding property editors. The `findEditor()` method finds a property editor for a specified class. Unregistered property editors are identified by the name of the property followed by `Editor`.

The `PropertyEditorSupport` class is a utility class that implements the `PropertyEditor` interface. It is subclassed to simplify the development of property editors.

The methods of the `Customizer` interface are implemented by classes that provide a graphical interface for customizing a bean. These classes are required to be a subclass of `java.awt.Component` so that they can be displayed in a panel. The `addPropertyChangeListener()` method is used to enable an object that implements the `PropertyChangeListener` interface as an event handler for the `PropertyChangeEvent` of the object being customized. The `removePropertyChangeListener()` method is used to remove a `PropertyChangeListener`. The `setObject()` method is used to identify the object that is to be customized.

Introspection Support

The classes and interfaces in this category provide information to application builders about the interface methods, properties, and events of a bean.

The `Introspector` Class

The `Introspector` class provides static methods that are used by application builders to obtain information about a bean's class. The `Introspector` gathers this information using explicitly provided information (by the bean designer) whenever possible and uses reflection and design patterns when explicit information is not available. The `getBeanInfo()` method returns information about a class as a `BeanInfo` object. The `getBeanInfoSearchPath()` method returns a `String` array to be used as a search path for finding `BeanInfo` classes. The `setBeanInfoSearchPath()` method updates the list of package names used to find `BeanInfo` classes. The `decapitalize()` method is used to convert a `String` object to a standard variable name in terms of capitalization.

The `BeanInfo` Interface

The methods of the `BeanInfo` interface are implemented by classes that want to provide additional information about a bean. The `getBeanDescriptor()` method returns a `BeanDescriptor` object that provides information about a bean. The `getIcon()` method returns an `Image` object that is used as an icon to represent a bean. It uses the icon constants defined in `BeanInfo` to determine what type of icon should be returned. The getEventSetDescriptors() method returns an array of EventSetDescriptor objects that describe the events generated (fired) by a bean. The getDefaultEventIndex() method returns the index of the most commonly used event of a bean. The getPropertyDescriptors() method returns an array of PropertyDescriptor objects that support the editing of a bean's properties. The getDefaultPropertyIndex() method returns the most commonly updated property of a bean. The getMethodDescriptors() method returns an array of MethodDescriptor objects that describe a bean's externally accessible methods. The getAdditionalBeanInfo() method returns an array of objects that implement the BeanInfo interface.

The SimpleBeanInfo Class

The SimpleBeanInfo class provides a default implementation of the BeanInfo interface. It is subclassed to implement BeanInfo classes.

The FeatureDescriptor Class and its Subclasses

The FeatureDescriptor class is the top-level class of a seven class hierarchy that is used by BeanInfo objects to report information to application builders. It provides 13 methods that are used by its subclasses for information gathering and reporting.

The BeanDescriptor class provides global information about a bean, such as the bean's class and its Customizer class, if any. The EventSetDescriptor class provides information on the events generated by a bean. The PropertyDescriptor class provides information on a property's accessor methods and property editor. It is extended by the IndexedPropertyDescriptor class, which provides access to the type of the array implemented as an indexed property and information about the property's accessor methods.

The MethodDescriptor and ParameterDescriptor classes provide information about a bean's methods and parameters.

Change Event-Handling Support

The PropertyChangeEvent is generated by beans that implement bound and constrained properties as the result of a change in the values of these properties. The PropertyChangeListener interface is implemented by those classes that listen for the PropertyChangeEvent. It consists of a single method, propertyChange(), that is used to handle the event.

The VetoableChangeListener interface is implemented by classes that handle the PropertyChangeEvent and throw a VetoableChangeEvent in response to certain property changes. The vetoableChange() method is used to handle the PropertyChangeEvent.

The `PropertyChangeSupport` class is a utility class that can be subclassed by beans that implement bound properties. This class provides a default implementation of the `addPropertyChangeListener()`, `removePropertyChangeListener()`, and `firePropertyChange()` methods.

`VetoableChangeSupport` is similar to `PropertyChangeSupport` in that it is a utility class that can be subclassed by beans that implement constrained properties. It provides a default implementation of the `addVetoableChangeListener()`, `removeVetoableChangeListener()`, and `fireVetoableChange()` methods.

Summary

In this chapter, you were introduced to Java beans and you learned how the JavaBeans software component assembly model is used to quickly and easily develop applications and applets. You covered the classes and interfaces of the `java.beans` package and learned how they support the software component assembly model. This is the last chapter of Part III, "Using the Java API"; you now have covered the JDK 1.1 API. In the remaining parts of this book, you'll learn how to use the JDK 1.1 API to create Java applications and applets. Chapter 23 begins Part IV and shows you how to develop window-based Java programs using the `java.awt` packages.

IV

Window Programming

23

Opening Windows

This chapter is the first of 11 chapters that cover window programming. It introduces you to Java windows by way of several examples that illustrate different aspects of the classes and methods used to implement simple window applications. Its purpose is to quickly get you up to speed developing window-based programs. Subsequent chapters will fill in the details of the classes and methods that are introduced here. You should approach this chapter by trying to get a good general understanding of what is going on in the sample programs without dwelling on the details. You will learn the details when you study them in later chapters.

Hello Windows!

The first program you wrote in Chapter 4, "First Programs: Hello World! to BlackJack," is the `HelloWorldApp` program. It displays the traditional `Hello World!` text to the console window. The main purpose of the program was to show you how to develop a simple Java program that actually produced some noticeable effect. The same rationale applies to the `HelloWindowsApp` program that you'll develop shortly. The program shows you how to open an application window and write the text `Hello Windows!` to the window. The code for the `HelloWindowsApp` program is shown in Listing 23.1.

Listing 23.1. The source code of the `HelloWindowsApp` program.

```
import java.awt.*;
import java.awt.event.*;

public class HelloWindowsApp extends Frame {
 public static void main(String args[]){
  HelloWindowsApp app = new HelloWindowsApp();
 }
 public HelloWindowsApp() {
  super("Hello Windows!");
  setSize(200,200);
  addWindowListener(new HelloWindowsApp.WindowEventHandler());
  show();
 }
 public void paint(Graphics g) {
  g.drawString("Hello Windows!",50,90);
 }
 class WindowEventHandler extends WindowAdapter {
  public void windowClosing(WindowEvent e){
   System.exit(0);
  }
 }
}
```

When you compile and run the program it opens a small window in the upper-left corner of your desktop and displays the text `Hello Windows!` in the middle of the window. This program is no giant feat for mankind, but it's a large step for us. It marks our transition from console to window-based programs. Up to this point in the book, console programs served admirably in helping cover the different aspects of the Java language and many of the classes of the API.

However, window-based programs and applets (which you learn about in Part VI, "Web Programming") are the primary areas of interest for most Java programmers. Figure 23.1 shows the window displayed by the HelloWindowsApp program.

FIGURE 23.1.

The HelloWindowsApp *program display.*

Let's take a look at HelloWindowsApp to find out what makes it work. You probably noticed right off the bat that we are now importing classes from the java.awt and java.awt.event packages. The Frame, Graphics, and WindowAdapter classes are the primary classes that are imported. The Frame and Graphics classes are fundamental to developing window programs. The Frame class is used to create Frame objects that implement application main windows. The Graphics class is used to update the screen display. The WindowAdapter class is used to process user-generated window events, such as closing the window.

The HelloWindowsApp class extends the Frame class. This is a typical approach to developing window programs. By subclassing Frame, your application class implements a main application window. You still use the same old main() method for implementing the entry point to your program. In HelloWindowsApp, the main() method simply creates a default object of class HelloWindowsApp.

The HelloWindowsApp constructor uses the super() constructor call statement to invoke the Frame constructor with the string "Hello Windows!". The Frame constructor creates a new application window frame with the specified text as its title. The setSize() method sets the size of the window to a 200×200-pixel dimension. The setSize() method is inherited from the Component class by way of the Container, Window, and Frame classes. The addWindowListener() method is invoked to associate window-related events with a newly created object of class WindowEventHandler. Finally, the show() method causes the window to be displayed. It is inherited from the Window class.

You might be wondering how the `"Hello Windows!"` text is actually displayed because there is no call from `main()` or `HelloWindowsApp()` to the `paint()` method. When a window or any other object that is in a subclass of `Component` is initially displayed or redisplayed as the result of the window being uncovered or brought to the foreground, the `paint()` method is invoked. It then paints the window according to the current application state.

The `paint()` method used by `HelloWindowsApp` overrides the `paint()` method inherited from the `Component` class. It takes a `Graphics` object as a parameter. The `Graphics` class provides numerous easy-to-use methods for drawing on `Graphics` objects. The `paint()` method uses the `drawString()` method to display the text `"Hello Windows!"` at the screen coordinate 50,90 within the application window.

Window coordinates are organized with the upper-left corner of the window being 0,0. The coordinates of the upper-right corner of the window are *width*,0, where *width* is the horizontal width of the window in pixels. The coordinates of the lower-left corner of the window are 0,*height*, where *height* is the vertical height of the window in pixels. Finally, the coordinates of the lower-right corner of the window are *width,height*. Figure 23.2 illustrates the window coordinate system.

FIGURE 23.2.

Window coordinates.

(0,0)	(1,0)	(2,0)	(3,0)	(4,0)	(5,0)
(0,1)	(1,1)	(2,1)	(3,1)	(4,1)	(5,1)
(0,2)	(1,2)	(2,2)	(3,2)	(4,2)	(5,2)

You probably have been wondering what the `WindowEventHandler` class is doing inside the `HelloWindowsApp` class. The `WindowEventHandler` class is an example of an inner class. *Inner classes* are classes (introduced in Java 1.1) that are declared within another class, a block of statements, or even anonymously (unnamed) in an expression. Inner classes are limited to the scope in which they are declared. This makes inner classes useful for creating specialized classes that are used in limited situations.

Inner classes are especially appropriate for event handling. *Events* represent actions that occur during the course of program execution. Most events are generated as the result of user actions such as mouse clicks and keyboard actions. Events are *handled* by responding to their occurrence and providing feedback to the user. Java 1.1 provides the capability to deliver events to specific objects, a capability that was lacking in Java 1.0. This new approach to event handling is both less complex and more efficient. It makes use of special classes, called *adapter classes*, whose objects *listen* for the occurrence of events on behalf of objects of other classes. Given their specialized purpose, adapter classes are often most conveniently implemented as inner classes of the classes that implement GUI functions.

The WindowEventHandler class is an example of an adapter class. It subclasses the WindowAdapter class of java.awt.event. The WindowAdapter class provides methods that can be overridden to handle window events. Window-related events are defined by the WindowEvent class of java.awt.event. Additional event classes defined in java.awt.event are used to handle other GUI events. The event handled by the windowClosing() method is the event associated with the closing of the program's main application window. This event occurs when the user closes the main application window by clicking the Close Window icon, as shown in Figure 23.3.

FIGURE 23.3.

Terminating the
HelloWindowsApp
program.

The window closing event is handled by invoking the exit() method of the System class to terminate the program. You might be wondering what would happen if the windowClosing() method did not handle the window closing event. Try deleting the line with the System.exit(0) method invocation, recompiling, and rerunning HelloWindowsApp to see what happens when you try to terminate the application. Your program will no longer terminate when you attempt to close it.

Going Round in Ovals: A Graphics Program

The HelloWindowsApp program provided a simple introduction to window programming. It illustrated many of the basics of writing a window program, but it didn't actually *do* all that much. The OvalApp program is also an introductory window program. It introduces more window programming classes and methods such as panels, buttons, layouts, additional event handling, and, of course, oval drawing. The source code of OvalApp is shown in Listing 23.2.

Listing 23.2. The source code of the OvalApp program.

```
import java.awt.*;
import java.awt.event.*;
import java.util.Random;

public class OvalApp extends Frame {
 int screenWidth = 400;
 int screenHeight = 400;
 Oval oval;
```

continues

Listing 23.2. continued

```
public static void main(String args[]){
 OvalApp app = new OvalApp();
}
public OvalApp() {
 super("Let's Draw Ovals!");
 Panel buttons = new Panel();
 Button nextButton=new Button("Next");
 Button quitButton=new Button("Quit");
 OvalApp.ButtonHandler bh=new OvalApp.ButtonHandler();
 nextButton.addActionListener(bh);
 quitButton.addActionListener(bh);
 buttons.add(nextButton);
 buttons.add(quitButton);
 add("South",buttons);
 oval = new Oval(screenWidth,screenHeight);
 setSize(screenWidth,screenHeight);
 addWindowListener(new OvalApp.WindowEventHandler());
 show();
}
public void paint(Graphics g) {
 oval.paint(g);
}
class ButtonHandler implements ActionListener {
 public void actionPerformed(ActionEvent ev){
  String s=ev.getActionCommand();
  if(s=="Next"){
   oval.update();
   repaint();
  }else if(s=="Quit") System.exit(0);
 }
}
class WindowEventHandler extends WindowAdapter {
 public void windowClosing(WindowEvent e){
  System.exit(0);
 }
}
}

class Oval {
 int x, y, width, height, maxWidth, maxHeight;
 Color color;
 static Random r = new Random();
 public Oval(int w,int h) {
  super();
  maxWidth = w;
  maxHeight = h;
  update();
 }
 public void update() {
  x = Math.abs(r.nextInt() % (maxWidth-100));
  y = Math.abs(r.nextInt() % (maxHeight-100));
  width = (maxWidth - x)/3;
  height = (maxHeight - y)/3;
  int rgb[] = new int[3];
  for(int i=0;i<3;++i) rgb[i]=Math.abs(r.nextInt()%256);
  color = new Color(rgb[0],rgb[1],rgb[2]);
 }
```

```
public void paint(Graphics g) {
  g.setColor(color);
  g.fillOval(x,y,width,height);
 }
}
```

When you run the `OvalApp` program it displays a window with the title Let's Draw Ovals!. A colored oval is displayed somewhere in the application window, as shown in Figure 23.4.

FIGURE 23.4.

The `OvalApp` *startup display.*

The window has two buttons, labeled Next and Quit. When you click on the Next button, as shown in Figure 23.5, a different oval is displayed.

FIGURE 23.5.

The Next button.

You can continue clicking on the Next button to cause different colored ovals to be displayed in different parts of the window, as shown in Figure 23.6.

FIGURE 23.6.
A new oval is displayed.

When you have thoroughly amused yourself by drawing ovals, you can click on the Quit button, as shown in Figure 23.7, and terminate the program's execution.

FIGURE 23.7.
The Quit button.

The OvalApp program is cute and entertaining, but doesn't perform any useful processing. It does, however, provide a good example of some new window programming constructs.

The program begins by doing an import of the relevant classes of the java.awt and java.awt.event packages. The program uses a large number of these classes. Rather than listing each one individually, it uses the more general package import statement. The only other class that is included is the Random class of the java.util package. This class provides the capability to generate random numbers used in the oval drawing.

The OvalApp class extends Frame in the same manner as the HelloWindowsApp. Three variables are defined for the OvalApp class. The screenWidth and screenHeight variables define the dimensions of the main window. The oval variable is used to refer to the current Oval object being displayed. The main() method simply creates a new object of class OvalApp.

The OvalApp constructor sets the window title using the superclass constructor call statement, super(). It then creates a Panel object called buttons. Panels are window objects that are used as containers for other objects. They help to organize the way GUI controls are placed in windows. The buttons panel is used to organize the Next and Quit buttons that are created and assigned to the nextButton and quitButton variables. The Button constructor takes a string argument that is the label for the buttons. A new object of the ButtonHandler inner class is created to handle button-related events. It is assigned to the bh variable and then is identified as the "listener" for the events of the Next and Quit buttons. The add() method is used with buttons to add two new objects of class Button to the panel. The add() method is then invoked for the OvalApp object being constructed to add the panel to the OvalApp application window. The OvalApp add() method is inherited from the Container class. The "South" string identifies where the panel should be added in the application window.

The organization of objects within a window container is governed by the *layout* of the container. (Layouts are described in detail in Chapter 24, "Organizing Window Programs.") The default layout for Frame objects and their subclasses is BorderLayout. This type of layout organizes objects within a container by their north, south, east, and west borders. Objects can also be placed in the center of a container. The add("South",buttons); method invocation adds the buttons panel to the southern (bottom) border of the OvalApp window.

The buttons panel is also associated with a layout. Panels use a FlowLayout object, by default. The FlowLayout class organizes objects in a container in a left to right fashion, fitting as many objects as possible in a row before moving on to fill the next row.

The oval variable is assigned a new object of class Oval that is parameterized by the screenWidth and screenHeight dimensions. These arguments are passed to the Oval constructor to make sure that an Oval object is created that is appropriate for the screen size of the OvalApp window. The Oval class is discussed after the OvalApp class's description is completed.

After adding the buttons panel to the window and creating an Oval object, the setSize() method is invoked to adjust the window size to the specified width and height dimensions. The addWindowListener() method is invoked to cause a newly created WindowEventHandler object to be the window's event handler. Finally, the show() method causes the window to be displayed.

The paint() method for the OvalApp class simply passes the task of drawing the window to the Oval class. Notice that it passes the Graphics object that it receives on to the Oval paint() method. Without the Graphics object, Oval's paint() method would have nothing to draw on.

The ButtonHandler inner class is defined to handle button-related events. It does this by implementing the ActionListener interface. ActionListener provides the actionPerformed() method for handling action events. Action events are the type of event associated with button clicks and other user actions. ButtonHandler implements actionPerformed() to handle the clicking of the Next and Quit buttons. It determines which button was clicked by invoking the getActionCommand() method for the ActionEvent object that is passed in the actionPerformed()

method invocation. The getActionCommand() returns a String value that identifies the name of the button that is clicked. If the Next button is clicked, the update() method is invoked for the Oval object assigned to the oval variable. This causes the Oval object to be changed in color, size, and position. The repaint() method causes the paint() method to be reinvoked to redraw an object—in this case, the OvalApp window. You should never invoke paint() directly—it is under the control of the native windows implementation. Always access it by invoking repaint().

The Quit button is handled by invoking the exit() method of the System class to cause the program's execution to be terminated. The WindowEventHandler inner class handles the window closing event in the same manner as in the HelloWindowsApp program. It also invokes the exit() method of the System class to terminate the program's execution.

The Oval class is used to randomly generate ovals of a different color, size, and position and display them in the OvalApp window. It defines a number of variables that specify these parameters. The maxWidth and maxHeight variables store the dimensions of the application window. The width and height parameters store the actual width and height of an Oval object. The x and y parameters identify its position within the application window. The color parameter identifies the color in which the oval is to be drawn. The static r variable is an object of class Random that is used to generate random numbers that determine the oval's characteristics.

The Oval constructor explicitly calls the default constructor call statement, sets the maxWidth and maxHeight variables, and invokes its update() method to randomly generate the values of the rest of the variables defined by the Oval class.

The update() method sets the upper-left corner of the oval to a random value between (0,0) and (maxWidth=100,maxHeight=100). This keeps the oval from scrunching up against the window's borders. The width and height of the rectangle are set to one-third of the distance between the upper-left corner of the rectangle and the lower-right corner of the application window.

The red, blue, and green color intensities of the rectangle are randomly generated as values between 0 and 255. In order for the full range of color values to be displayed, your screen must support 24-bit color in its current screen resolution; otherwise, the randomly generated color will be approximated by the next closest color supported by your video card. I rarely set my screen to 24-bit color and usually use 8-bit color to cut down on my video display memory requirements.

The paint() method of the Oval class uses the Graphics object passed to it by the OvalApp paint() method to display the oval. It sets the current color of the Graphics object based on the randomly generated color stored in the color variable. It then invokes the fillOval() method of the Graphics class to draw an oval that is filled with the current color. The fillOval() method takes the upper-left corner of the Oval and its width and height dimensions as parameters.

A Text Editor

Now let's extend your exploration of window applications by developing a primitive text editor. The `TextEditApp` program illustrates more window programming constructs. It introduces menus, dialog boxes, fonts, text processing, and window-based file I/O. It also builds on the event-handling skills that you've developed so far. The source code of the `TextEditApp` program is shown in Listing 23.3.

Listing 23.3. The source code of the `TextEditApp` program.

```java
import java.awt.*;
import java.awt.event.*;
import java.io.*;

public class TextEditApp extends Frame {
 TextArea text;
 MenuBar menuBar;
 FileDialog openFile;
 FileDialog saveFile;
 public static void main(String args[]){
  TextEditApp app = new TextEditApp();
 }
 public TextEditApp() {
  super("Text Editor");
  setup();
  pack();
  addWindowListener(new TextEditApp.WindowEventHandler());
  show();
 }
 void setup() {
  setFont(new Font("System",Font.PLAIN,12));
  setBackground(Color.white);
  text = new TextArea(25,80);
  add("Center",text);
  setupMenuBar();
  openFile = new FileDialog(this,"Open File",FileDialog.LOAD);
  saveFile = new FileDialog(this,"Save File As",FileDialog.SAVE);
 }
 void setupMenuBar(){
  menuBar = new MenuBar();
  Menu fileMenu = new Menu("File");
  MenuItem fileNew = new MenuItem("New");
  MenuItem fileOpen = new MenuItem("Open");
  MenuItem fileSaveAs = new MenuItem("Save As");
  MenuItem fileExit = new MenuItem("Exit");
  TextEditApp.MenuItemHandler mih = new TextEditApp.MenuItemHandler();
  fileNew.addActionListener(mih);
  fileOpen.addActionListener(mih);
  fileSaveAs.addActionListener(mih);
  fileExit.addActionListener(mih);
  fileMenu.add(fileNew);
  fileMenu.add(fileOpen);
  fileMenu.addSeparator();
  fileMenu.add(fileSaveAs);
```

continues

Listing 23.3. continued

```
 fileMenu.addSeparator();
 fileMenu.add(fileExit);
 menuBar.add(fileMenu);
 setMenuBar(menuBar);
}
public void readFile(String file) {
 BufferedReader inStream;
 try{
  inStream = new BufferedReader(new FileReader(file));
 }catch (IOException ex){
  notifyDialog("Error opening file");
  return;
 }
 try{
  String newText="";
  String line;
  while((line=inStream.readLine())!=null)
   newText=newText+line+"\n";
  text.setText(newText);
  inStream.close();
 }catch (IOException ex){
  notifyDialog("Error reading file");
 }
}
public void writeFile(String file) {
 BufferedWriter outStream;
 try{
  outStream = new BufferedWriter(new FileWriter(file));
 }catch (IOException ex){
  notifyDialog("Error opening file");
  return;
 }
 try{
  outStream.write(text.getText());
  outStream.close();
 }catch (IOException ex){
  notifyDialog("Error writing file");
 }
}
public void notifyDialog(String msg) {
 Notification notification = new Notification(this,msg);
 notification.show();
}
class MenuItemHandler implements ActionListener {
 public void actionPerformed(ActionEvent ev){
  String s=ev.getActionCommand();
  if(s=="New"){
   text.setText("");
  }else if(s=="Open"){
   openFile.show();
   String inFile = openFile.getFile();
   readFile(inFile);
```

```
   }else if(s=="Save As"){
    saveFile.show();
    String outFile = saveFile.getFile();
    writeFile(outFile);
   }else{
    System.exit(0);
   }
  }
 }
 class WindowEventHandler extends WindowAdapter {
  public void windowClosing(WindowEvent e){
   System.exit(0);
  }
 }
}
class Notification extends Dialog {
 String msg;
 public Notification(Frame f,String s) {
  super(f,"Notification",true);
  msg = s;
  addWindowListener(new Notification.WindowEventHandler());
 }
 public void show() {
  add("North",new Label(msg,Label.CENTER));
  Panel p = new Panel();
  Button okButton=new Button("OK");
  okButton.addActionListener(new Notification.ButtonHandler());
  p.add(okButton);
  add("South",p);
  setBackground(Color.gray);
  setSize(160,100);
  super.show();
 }
 class ButtonHandler implements ActionListener {
  public void actionPerformed(ActionEvent ev){
   dispose();
  }
 }
 class WindowEventHandler extends WindowAdapter {
  public void windowClosing(WindowEvent e){
   dispose();
  }
 }
}
```

The `TextEditApp` program provides quite a bit more functionality than the other window programs that you've written so far. After you've compiled it, run the program. It will begin by launching a blank text-editing window with the Text Editor title, as shown in Figure 23.8.

FIGURE 23.8.
The TextEditApp
opening window.

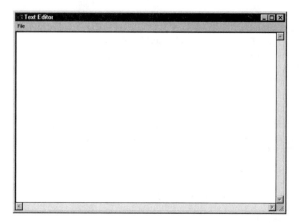

Click in the editor window and begin experimenting with editing text. Type in whatever text comes to your mind. Experiment with tabs to see how they work. Try typing past the right margin to see how the horizontal scrollbars work. Select text with your cursor and use the keyboard copy, cut, and paste commands. Double-click on a word to select it, and then type another word over it. Try typing a few lines to cause the vertical scrollbars to come into play. Your screen should look somewhat similar to Figure 23.9.

FIGURE 23.9.
Editing text.

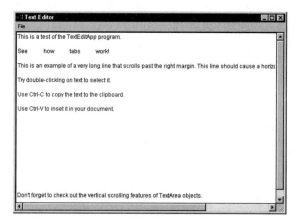

When you have finished editing the text, check out the File pull-down menu, shown in Figure 23.10. You'll notice that the File menu supports four commands and contains two separator lines that help organize these commands.

FIGURE 23.10.

The File pull-down menu.

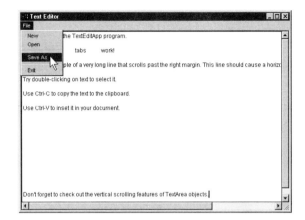

Save your text in the file test.txt. A File Save As dialog box appears to help you save your file. The Windows 95 implementation of Java displays a dialog box as shown in Figure 23.11. If you are using Java on another operating system, the dialog box will look different.

FIGURE 23.11.

Saving text to a file.

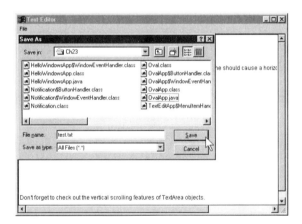

After you have saved your file, select New from the File menu. A new text-editing buffer is displayed. Having cleared the buffer, select Open from the File menu and open the test.txt file that you just saved. (See Figure 23.12.) This file will be read in and loaded into the text-editing buffer.

If this seems like a lot of functionality for two pages of code, you're right. Java does most of the work for you. You just need to invoke the correct methods for the java.awt API classes.

FIGURE 23.12.

Opening a file.

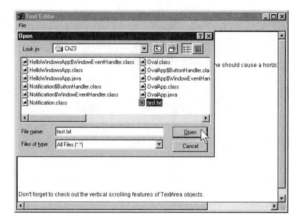

Let's explore the TextEditApp program to see how it works. You'll first notice that it imports the classes of the java.awt, java.awt.event, and java.io packages. The java.awt package provides the required window classes, the java.awt.event package provides event-handling classes and interfaces, and the java.io package provides needed file I/O classes.

TextEditApp follows the lead of the other window programs developed earlier in this chapter and subclasses the Frame class. It declares four field variables: text, menuBar, openFile, and saveFile. The text variable is of class TextArea. It holds the object that implements the functionality of the text-editing buffer. The menuBar variable sets up the File menu. The openFile and saveFile variables support the file dialog boxes shown in Figures 23.11 and 23.12.

The main() method simply creates an object of TextEditApp. The TextEditApp constructor sets the window title using the constructor of the Frame class and then invokes its setup() method to set up all the objects in the TextEditApp window. The pack() method is called to adjust the window to the appropriate size for the editing area. It resizes the window so that its components are at their default size. The addWindowListener() method is invoked to set up a WindowEventHandler object for event handling, and the show() method is invoked to display the window.

The setup() method sets the font to be used in the TextArea object, changes the window's background color, and then sets up the TextArea object, the menu bar, and the file dialog boxes. The setFont() method sets the current font to a newly constructed font. It is inherited from the Component class. The Font class constructor used to create the new font uses the font name (System), text type (PLAIN), and point size (12) of the font as parameters. The Font class defines a number of font parameters that can be used in constructing new font variations.

The setBackground() method sets the background color to white. It is inherited from the Component class. The Color class provides a number of predefined color constants. Check the API description of this class for a description of these constants. The text variable is assigned an object of class TextArea that is at least 25 rows by 80 columns. This object implements most of the text-editing capabilities of `TextEditApp`. It is then added to the center of the `TextEditApp` window. The `setupMenuBar()` method is called to set up the File menu.

The `openFile` and `saveFile FileDialog` variables are assigned newly created `FileDialog` objects. The `FileDialog` constructor takes three arguments. The first is the window that "owns" the dialog box. This is the window to which the file dialog box is attached. The window is attached to the `TextEditApp` object created by the `main()` method, so the `this` argument is supplied to identify the current `TextEditApp` object. The second parameter is the text string to be displayed at the top of the dialog box. Refer to Figures 23.11 and 23.12 to see how the text string is displayed. The third parameter is either the `FileDialog.LOAD` or the `FileDialog.SAVE` constant indicating whether a file is to be loaded from disk or saved to disk.

The `setupMenuBar()` method shows how menu bars are created and added to a window. The `menuBar` variable is assigned an object of class `MenuBar`. Four `MenuItem` objects are created and assigned to the `fileNew`, `fileOpen`, `fileSaveAs`, and `fileExit` variables. A `MenuItemHandler` object is created and then added as an `ActionListener` for the four `MenuItem` objects.

A `Menu` object is created with the `File` label and assigned to the `fileMenu` variable. Menu items and separators are then added to the menu. A `Menu` object represents a single pull-down menu. A `MenuItem` object is a pull-down menu selection. A `MenuBar` is a collection of `Menu` objects that is attached to a window.

The `MenuItem` objects are assigned a label when they are created. They are added to the `fileMenu` in a top-down fashion. The `addSeparator()` method is used to add a separator line to a menu. Refer to Figure 23.10 to see how the resulting `fileMenu` is displayed. The `fileMenu` is added to the `menuBar` object using the `add()` method of the `MenuBar` class. The resulting menu bar is added to the `TextEditApp` window using the `setMenuBar()` method inherited from the `Frame` class.

At this point you might have noticed that the `TextEditApp` class has no `paint()` method. The `TextArea` object takes care of drawing itself and does not require an external `paint()` method. `TextArea` is a remarkably self-contained and easy-to-use class. Without `TextArea`, implementing `TextEditApp` would be considerably more difficult.

The `MenuItemHandler` and `WindowEventHandler` classes are inner classes of `TextEditApp` that support event handling. The `WindowEventHandler` class is the same as in the `HelloWindowsApp` and `OvalApp` programs. The `MenuItemHandler` class implements the `ActionListener` interface and provides the `actionPerformed()` method. The `actionPerformed()` method uses the `getActionCommand()` method to retrieve the label of the menu item that was selected and then handles the event according to the label.

The New menu item is handled by invoking the `setText()` method of the `TextArea` class to delete all text in the `text` variable. The Open menu item is handled by invoking the `show()` method for the `openFile FileDialog`, causing the dialog box to be displayed. The `getFile()` method is invoked to get the name of the file selected for opening by the user. The returned string is then passed to the `readFile()` method of `TextEditApp`. The handling of the Save As menu item is similar to that of the Open menu item. The saveFile FileDialog is displayed. A filename is returned and then passed to the writeFile() method of the TextEditApp class. The Exit menu item is handled in the same way as the window closing event. A full-featured editor would prompt the user to save changes before exiting.

The readFile() method reads the file whose name was retrieved via the openFile FileDialog. It first opens the file by creating a new FileReader object using the filename and then filtering this stream as a BufferedReader object. The resulting input stream is then assigned to the inStream variable. The try statement has a catch clause that checks for the occurrence of an IOException. If an exception occurs, the notifyDialog() method is used to warn the user. It displays a dialog box as shown in Figure 23.13. You can cause this dialog box to be generated by trying to open a nonexistent file. Try it!

FIGURE 23.13.

The Notification dialog box.

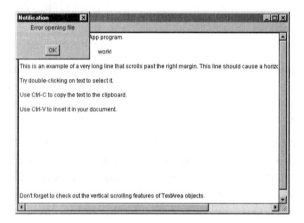

After the file has been opened, its text is read in a line at a time and appended to the newText variable. This results in the input being placed in one long string. The setText() method of the TextArea class is used to move the text into the TextArea object assigned to the text variable. Any I/O errors occurring while the file is being read result in the display of a Notification dialog box with the Error reading file message.

The writeFile() method operates in a similar but reverse manner than the readFile() method. It uses the filename retrieved via the saveFile FileDialog to create a FileWriter object. It then filters this stream as a BufferedWriter and assigns it to the outStream variable. If any errors occur in the creation of these streams, a dialog box is displayed with the message Error opening file.

After saving the file, the write() method of the BufferedWriter class is invoked to write the data stored in the TextArea object assigned to the text variable to the output stream. The close() method is then invoked to close the output stream. Any write errors result in the display of an error-notification dialog box.

The `notifyDialog()` method supports the generation and display of dialog boxes by creating new instances of the `Notification` class and passing them the error message. It then invokes their `show()` method to display them.

The `Notification` class implements the dialog boxes that are displayed when an error occurs by extending the `Dialog` class. The `Dialog` class, like the `Frame` class, extends the `Window` class. It provides a different set of methods to display dialog boxes as opposed to main application windows. It has one variable, `msg`, that stores the message to be displayed in the dialog box. Its constructor takes two arguments: the application window object to which it is attached and the message to be displayed. It invokes the `Dialog` class constructor using the superclass constructor call statement and passes it the `Frame` object, the string `"Notification"` to be used as the title of the dialog box, and the `true boolean` value, which determines whether the dialog box will be modal. A *modal* dialog box is one that must be closed before the user can return to the main application window. The constructor then saves the error message argument in the `msg` variable. Objects of the `Notification` class handle their own window events via the `WindowEventHandler` inner class. An object of the `WindowEventHandler` class is added as an event handler via the `addWindowListener()` method.

The `show()` method of the `Notification` class causes the dialog box to be displayed. It first creates an object of class `Label` with the contents of the `msg` variable being the text assigned to the `Label` object. The `Label.CENTER` constant is used to center the text in the `Label` object. The new label is then added to the north end of the dialog box. `Dialog` objects, like `Frame` objects, use a `BorderLayout` object by default. A `Panel` object is then created, and the OK button is created and added to the panel. An object of the `ButtonHandler` inner class is used to handle the button's action event (that is, the clicking of the button).

The panel is added to the south end of the dialog box. The single button is placed in the panel to cause the button into be displayed in its default dimensions. Instead of the button being stretched to fit the dialog box, the panel in which the button resides is stretched. To see this, try directly inserting the button to the dialog box without using a panel. For example, change `p.add(okButton)` to `add(okButton)` in the `show()` method of the `Notification` class.

The background color of the dialog box is set to gray using the `setBackground()` method inherited from the `Component` class and the `Color` class constants. The window is sized to 160×100 pixels and then displayed using the `show()` method of the `Dialog` class. The `super` keyword is used to indicate that the `show()` method of the superclass (`Dialog`) should be used instead of the `show()` method of the current class (`Notification`).

The `Notification` class uses the `ButtonHandler` and `WindowEventHandler` classes to handle events. `ButtonHandler` handles the clicking of the OK button of a dialog box by invoking the `dispose()` method inherited from the `Window` class. The `dispose()` method causes the dialog window to be closed and its resources to be returned to the system. The `WindowEventHandler` class handles the window closing event in the same manner.

Summary

This chapter introduces you to window programming by way of several sample programs that illustrate the classes and methods used to implement simple window applications. You should now be comfortable with analyzing window-based programs. Subsequent chapters fill in the details of the classes and methods introduced here. They will help you to become proficient in developing your own window programs. Chapter 24, "Organizing Window Programs," lays the framework for developing window programs by expanding on the basics introduced here.

24

Organizing Window Programs

This chapter covers the basics of writing window programs. It shows you how window programs are structured and organized and identifies the basic approach to designing most window programs. It covers the details of the Frame class and explains how windows are opened and closed. The five basic window layouts are introduced and illustrated through a sample program. The finer points of window event handling are then described. Finally, a window program is created that introduces the most common window GUI controls. When you finish this chapter, you will have had a broad introduction to window programming and will be familiar with most of the common window GUI controls.

Designing Window Programs

The design of most window programs usually involves two basic steps: laying out the program's graphical user interface and providing the functionality that implements the interface.

The first step addresses one of the most important features of window programs—its look and feel. Window programs are preferred to console programs when their look and feel are interesting, innovative, and help the user to accomplish a particular purpose.

A program's look is determined by how it presents itself to users. It consists of all those characteristics that determine its appearance, such as window size, layout, background and foreground colors, menus, and GUI controls. A program's feel is determined by the availability of easy-to-use GUI controls and the contribution of these controls to the program's ultimate intended use. It is the result of the designer's ability to select and implement those GUI controls that enhance a program's capability to satisfy user expectations.

The window's GUI design begins by creating an application window, using the Frame class, and determining the basic characteristics of the window, such as its size, title, background and foreground colors, and general layout. Next a menu bar is added to the window and the program's menus and menu items are added to the menu bar. The GUI controls that are to be used in the window are determined, designed, and attached to the window's panels and frame.

At this point, you know what your program will look like and you can concentrate on what it will do. The first step in bringing your program's user interface to life is to add the event-handling software required to respond to events generated as the result of user interaction. The event-handling software will not immediately implement all user actions, but it should respond to them and provide hooks for eventual implementation of all user interface actions. The event-handling software is then fleshed out to provide all the functionality required of the application program. The program's design and implementation reaches an Alpha stage when all required user-interface functions have been implemented.

The next stage of program development is to refine and test the program to make it more responsive to its intended purpose. A series of Beta versions of the program are developed that implement user feedback and fix any identified errors or deficiencies. Finally, the program is refined to handle unusual user inputs and to process errors and exceptions.

Figure 24.1 provides an overview of the process of designing and implementing window programs. This chapter covers the basics of creating and organizing window programs and shows how to connect event-handling code to general window components. A window sampler program is provided that illustrates basic use of common window GUI controls. Subsequent chapters explore the use of these GUI controls in more detail.

FIGURE 24.1.

The process for window design and implementation.

Lay out the program's graphical user interface.

    Create a frame and specify its characteristics.

    Determine the frame's layout.

    Add a menu bar.

    Add panels and GUI components.

Add the functionality that implements the interface.

    Add event-handling software.

    Provide hooks for handling all user interface actions.

    Flesh out event-handling software.

    Refine and test software functions.

    Handle errors and exceptions.

    Response to user feedback.

Opening and Closing Windows

The opening and closing of windows marks the beginning and end of any window program. The `Frame` class enables these fundamental window operations to be accomplished. A `Frame` object implements an application main window, inheriting many methods from the `Window`, `Container`, and `Component` classes.

To open an application window, a `Frame` object is created and its `show()` method is invoked. The `show()` method is inherited from the `Window` class. To close an application window, the window closing event must be handled. The window is disposed of using the `dispose()` method of the `Window` class or more commonly by invoking the `System.exit()` method after performing any necessary program-termination processing.

The `Frame` class and its ancestors provide a number of methods that control the way in which a window is displayed. The `setBackground()` and `setForeground()` methods inherited from the `Component` class are used to specify a window's background and foreground colors. The `setFont()`

method, also inherited from `Component`, is used to specify the default font to be used with a window. The `Frame` class itself provides a number of methods that control a window's appearance. The `setTitle()` method allows a window's title to be changed. The `setMenuBar()` method enables a menu bar to be attached to a window, and the `setResizable()` method toggles whether a window can or cannot be resized. The `setIconImage()` method allows the window's minimized icon to be changed. This method is not supported by all Java implementations and therefore should be avoided if cross-platform compatibility is a concern.

The `FrameApp` program, shown in Listing 24.1, illustrates the window concepts covered so far and shows the effect of using the basic window controls identified in the previous paragraph.

Listing 24.1. The source code of the `FrameApp` program.

```
import java.awt.*;
import java.awt.event.*;

public class FrameApp extends Frame {
 String defaultTitle;
 MenuBar defaultMenuBar;
 MenuBar alternativeMenuBar;
 int cursors[] = {CROSSHAIR_CURSOR,DEFAULT_CURSOR,E_RESIZE_CURSOR,HAND_CURSOR,
  MOVE_CURSOR,NE_RESIZE_CURSOR,NW_RESIZE_CURSOR,N_RESIZE_CURSOR,
  SE_RESIZE_CURSOR,SW_RESIZE_CURSOR,S_RESIZE_CURSOR,TEXT_CURSOR,
  WAIT_CURSOR,W_RESIZE_CURSOR};
 Color colors[] = {Color.black,Color.blue,Color.cyan,Color.darkGray,Color.gray,
  Color.green,Color.lightGray,Color.magenta,Color.orange,Color.pink,Color.red,
  Color.white,Color.yellow};
 String fontNames[] = {"Helvetica","TimesRoman","Courier","Dialog",
  "DialogInput","ZapfDingbats"};
 int cursorIndex = 1;
 int backgroundColorIndex = 0;
 int foregroundColorIndex = 0;
 int fontIndex = 0;
 public static void main(String args[]){
  FrameApp app = new FrameApp();
 }
 public FrameApp() {
  super("Exploring Frames");
  defaultTitle = getTitle();
  setup();
  setSize(400,400);
  addWindowListener(new FrameApp.WindowEventHandler());
  show();
 }
 void setup() {
  setupPanels();
  setupMenuBars();
  setFont(new Font(fontNames[fontIndex],Font.PLAIN,14));
 }
 void setupPanels() {
  Panel mainPanel = new Panel();
  mainPanel.setLayout(new GridLayout(4,1));
  Label label1 =
   new Label("Change these windows characteristics:",Label.CENTER);
```

```
 mainPanel.add(label1);
 Panel panel1 = new Panel();
 Button titleButton = new Button("Title");
 Button menuButton = new Button("Menu Bar");
 Button resizeButton = new Button("Resizable");
 FrameApp.ButtonHandler bh=new FrameApp.ButtonHandler();
 titleButton.addActionListener(bh);
 menuButton.addActionListener(bh);
 resizeButton.addActionListener(bh);
 panel1.add(titleButton);
 panel1.add(menuButton);
 panel1.add(resizeButton);
 mainPanel.add(panel1);
 Label label2 = new Label("Check out these windows options:",Label.CENTER);
 mainPanel.add(label2);
 Panel panel2 = new Panel();
 Button cursorButton = new  Button("Cursor");
 Button bgButton = new  Button("Background");
 Button fgButton = new  Button("Foreground");
 Button fontButton = new  Button("Font");
 cursorButton.addActionListener(bh);
 bgButton.addActionListener(bh);
 fgButton.addActionListener(bh);
 fontButton.addActionListener(bh);
 panel2.add(cursorButton);
 panel2.add(bgButton);
 panel2.add(fgButton);
 panel2.add(fontButton);
 mainPanel.add(panel2);
 add("South",mainPanel);
}
void setupMenuBars() {
 defaultMenuBar = new MenuBar();
 Menu fileMenu = new Menu("File");
 MenuItem fileExit = new MenuItem("Exit");
 FrameApp.MenuItemHandler mh = new FrameApp.MenuItemHandler();
 fileExit.addActionListener(mh);
 fileMenu.add(fileExit);
 defaultMenuBar.add(fileMenu);
 setMenuBar(defaultMenuBar);
 alternativeMenuBar = new MenuBar();
 Menu otherMenu = new Menu("Program");
 MenuItem fileQuit = new MenuItem("Quit");
 fileQuit.addActionListener(mh);
 otherMenu.add(fileQuit);
 alternativeMenuBar.add(otherMenu);
}
public void paint(Graphics g) {
 g.drawString("Sample Text",160,100);
}
class WindowEventHandler extends WindowAdapter {
 public void windowClosing(WindowEvent e){
  System.exit(0);
 }
}
class ButtonHandler implements ActionListener {
 public void actionPerformed(ActionEvent ev){
```

continues

Listing 24.1. continued

```
    String s=ev.getActionCommand();
    if(s=="Title"){
     if(defaultTitle.equals(getTitle()))
      setTitle("Here's an alternative title.");
     else setTitle(defaultTitle);
    }else if(s=="Menu Bar"){
     if(defaultMenuBar.equals(getMenuBar()))
      setMenuBar(alternativeMenuBar);
     else setMenuBar(defaultMenuBar);
    }else if(s=="Resizable"){
     setResizable(!isResizable());
    }else if(s=="Cursor"){
     ++cursorIndex;
     cursorIndex %= cursors.length;
     setCursor(new Cursor(cursorIndex));
    }else if(s=="Background"){
     ++backgroundColorIndex;
     backgroundColorIndex %= colors.length;
     setBackground(colors[backgroundColorIndex]);
     repaint();
    }else if(s=="Foreground"){
     ++foregroundColorIndex;
     foregroundColorIndex %= colors.length;
     setForeground(colors[foregroundColorIndex]);
     repaint();
    }else if(s=="Font"){
     ++fontIndex;
     fontIndex %= fontNames.length;
     setFont(new Font(fontNames[fontIndex],Font.PLAIN,14));
     repaint();
    }
   }
  }
  class MenuItemHandler implements ActionListener {
   public void actionPerformed(ActionEvent ev){
    String s=ev.getActionCommand();
    if(s=="Exit") System.exit(0);
    else if(s=="Quit") System.exit(0);
   }
  }
 }
```

After you have compiled FrameApp, run it and check out the buttons and menus it provides. When you first launch FrameApp it displays the text Sample Text followed by two rows of buttons, as shown in Figure 24.2. The first row of buttons provides the capability to change the window's title, menu bar, and resizable properties. These buttons are *toggles*—the second time you click a button the window's characteristic being changed is reverted to its initial default value. The second row of buttons allows you to step through a sequence of values for the window's cursor, background and foreground colors, and text font. If you are using Windows 95, you will find that it does not support all cursors defined by Java. You will find out which cursors are not supported when you analyze this program's code.

FIGURE 24.2.

The FrameApp *initial display.*

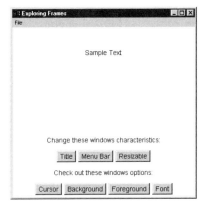

Let's investigate each of the program's features. Click on the Title button and you will notice that the window's title text is changed from Exploring Frames to Here's an alternative title, as shown in Figure 24.3. Click on the button a second time and the title changes back to Exploring Frames.

FIGURE 24.3.

Here's an alternative title.

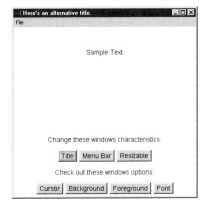

Click on the File menu, but don't select the Exit option. The File menu is replaced by the Program menu, shown in Figure 24.4, when you click on the Menu Bar button. Adding, deleting, and modifying menus are common operations for many window programs.

You will notice that your program window is initially resizable. This means that you can use the cursor at the window's edge to make the window larger or smaller. The cursor changes from a pointer to a resizable icon to let you know that the window can be resized. If you click on the Resizable button, the window is no longer capable of being resized. You can check this by placing your cursor at the window's boundary.

FIGURE 24.4.

The Program menu.

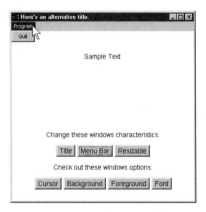

Click on the Cursor button to change the cursor associated with your program's window to the I-beam cursor. Step through the list of available cursors until you reach the crosshair cursor. Then click the Cursor button one more time to return to the default cursor.

Click the Background button and the program's background color is changed to blue, as shown in Figure 24.5. You can continue to click the Background button to look at other background colors. Notice that the color does not change in the panel used by the program's buttons. Now try clicking on the Foreground button a few times to change the window's foreground color.

FIGURE 24.5.

Changing the window background.

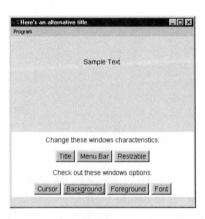

The Font button allows you to change the font used with the sample text display, as shown in Figure 24.6.

FIGURE 24.6.

Using a Courier font.

You have covered the program's features. Now let's look at its code to see how it works.

The FrameApp class defines a number of variables. The defaultTitle variable is used to store the default window title so that it can be restored after it has been changed. The defaultMenuBar and alternativeMenuBar variables are used to store the File and Program menu bars. The cursors[] array stores the cursor constants that are defined for the Frame class. These constants are stored in an array to make it easier to cycle through them. The cursorIndex variable maintains an index to the current cursor being displayed.

The colors[] array stores a subset of the colors defined by the Color class. These colors are used when the background and foreground colors are changed. The backgroundColorIndex and foregroundColorIndex variables are used to keep track of the current background and foreground colors. Note that in Java 1.1, the java.awt.SystemColor class may be used to access the desktop and GUI component colors that are currently in use by the desktop. This class allows you to develop your window-based programs in a way that is consistent with other programs that you run from your desktop.

The fontNames[] array stores the names of the fonts known to Java. The fontIndex variable is used to point to the current window font.

FrameApp has a simple standard main() method that creates a new FrameApp object. The FrameApp constructor invokes the superclass constructor call statement to set the window's title and then uses the getTitle() method inherited from Frame to store the title in the defaultTitle variable. It then invokes the setup() method to set up panels, buttons, menu bars, and the default window font. The setSize() method adjusts the window to the desired size and the addWindowListener() method sets up the window's event handler. The show() method then causes the window to be opened and displayed.

The setup() method invokes the setupPanels() and setupMenuBars() methods to set up the program's panels, buttons, and menu bars. It invokes the setFont() method inherited from the Component class to set the default font to be used with the window. The setFont() method takes three arguments: the name of the font, the font style, and the size of the font in points. The font names are stored in the fontNames[] array. The font style constants are defined in the Font class.

The setupPanels() method constructs a Panel object named mainPanel that is to hold the subpanels corresponding to the rows of buttons. The layout of the mainPanel is set to a GridLayout object of four rows and one column. Layouts are used to specify how objects are to be placed in a container. They are covered in the "Using Layouts" section later in this chapter.

A new Label object is created with the text Change these windows characteristics: and added to the mainPanel. The Label.CENTER constant specifies how the label should be aligned within its available space. A Panel object named panel1 is created to hold the Title, Menu Bar, and Resizable buttons that are subsequently created and added to the panel. A ButtonHandler object, bh, is created and identified as the event handler for each of the buttons. The panel1 object is then added to the mainPanel.

A second Label object named label2 is created to hold the text Check out these windows options:. The label is then added to the mainPanel. A second Panel object named panel2 is created. The Cursor, Background, Foreground, and Font buttons are then added to panel2. The ButtonHandler object stored in bh is added as the event handler for these buttons. The panel2 object is then added to the mainPanel. The mainPanel is then added to the southern (bottom) region of the FrameApp object being constructed. The "Using Layouts" section in this chapter describes why the FrameApp object was organized with a mainPanel and two subpanels.

The setupMenuBars() method creates a new MenuBar object and assigns it to the defaultMenuBar variable. It declares the fileMenu variable and assigns it a new Menu object with the File label. It creates a MenuItem object with the Exit label and adds it to the fileMenu. A MenuItemHandler object is created and assigned to the mh variable. This object is set as the event handler for the Exit menu item via the addActionListener() method.

The Menu object stored in fileMenu is added to the MenuBar object stored in defaultMenuBar. This MenuBar object is then set as the menu bar of the FrameApp object being constructed via the setMenuBar() method of the Frame class. Menus are covered in Chapter 25, "Menus, Buttons, and Dialog Boxes." For now, just remember that a Frame has a MenuBar that consists of one or more Menus that each have one or more MenuItems.

The alternativeMenuBar is constructed in the same manner as the defaultMenuBar except that it contains an otherMenu with the File and Exit labels replaced by Program and Quit labels. This menu bar uses the same event handler as the other menu bar.

The alternativeMenuBar is not set to the FrameApp using the setMenuBar() method. A Frame object can have only one menu bar at a time.

The paint() method is used to initially draw the window display and then to update it as the result of window operations. It simply displays the text Sample Text at pixel location (160,100) within the window Graphics object.

The WindowEventHandler inner class handles the window closing event in the same way as in the sample programs of Chapter 23, "Opening Windows."

The ButtonHandler inner class handles the event that occurs when the user clicks on a button. It implements the ActionListener interface, the interface used to handle all action events. This interface consists of one method—the actionPerformed() method, which is invoked to process action events. The getActionCommand() method is invoked to retrieve the label of the button that was clicked to generate the event. This value is assigned to the s variable and is checked via an extended if-then-else statement to see if it contains the strings Title, Menu Bar, Resizable, Cursor, Background, Foreground, or Font. These strings correspond to the buttons displayed in the program's window.

When the Title button is clicked, the getTitle() method is used to determine whether the current window title equals the title stored in defaultTitle. If they are equal, the window's title is set to Here's an alternative title. If the current title differs from the value stored in defaultTitle, the window's title is set using defaultTitle.

When the Menu Bar button is clicked, the getMenuBar() method is used to check whether the window's current menu bar is the same as the value of defaultMenuBar. If they are the same, the window's menu bar is set to the value of alternativeMenuBar. If they are different, the window's menu bar is set to the value of defaultMenuBar.

When the Resizable button is clicked, the isResizable() method is used to determine whether the window is currently resizable and then sets it to the opposite value.

When the Cursor button is clicked, actionPerformed() cycles the cursorIndex to the next cursor value within the cursors[] array and sets the cursor to this value using the setCursor() method. Note that in Java 1.1, the setCursor() method is a method of the Component class. This allows each GUI component to set its cursor in a unique fashion.

When the Background button is clicked, actionPerformed() cycles the backgroundIndex variable to the next color value within the color[] array and sets the background to this value using the setBackground() method. It then invokes the repaint() method of the Component class to cause the screen to be repainted. The Foreground button is handled in a similar manner.

When the Font button is clicked, actionPerformed() cycles the fontIndex to the next font name and creates a new 14-point plain font of that type. It then invokes the setFont() method of the Component class to change the current font. The repaint() method is used to cause the screen to be repainted.

Using Layouts

The FrameApp program uses a number of panels and layouts to organize the way that labels and buttons are presented in the application window. The organization of any object that is a subclass of the Container class is governed by a layout. The layout determines how objects of class Component are positioned when they are added via the add() method to the Container object. There are five types of layouts that are provided by Java: BorderLayout, CardLayout, FlowLayout, GridLayout, and GridBagLayout. Other, custom layouts can also be defined.

In addition to using layouts, components can be absolutely positioned within a container. However, absolute positioning should be avoided at all costs; it does not allow window managers to lay out windows according to the capabilities of their native windowing implementation.

The BorderLayout class is the default layout used by Frame objects. An object of the Component class is added to either the North, South, East, West, or Center of the component, as shown in Figure 24.7.

FIGURE 24.7.

A BorderLayout *example.*

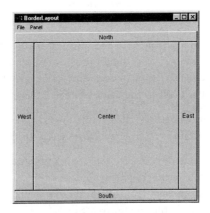

In the FrameApp program, the mainPanel was added to the South region of the window. The remainder of the program window was used by the program's default Graphics object that was placed in the North region of the window. No Component objects were added to the East, West, or Center regions.

The FlowLayout class is the default layout used for Panel objects. If a container uses FlowLayout, the container is filled left to right from top to bottom. Examples of this layout are the two rows of buttons that were added to panel1 and panel2. The FlowLayout class causes each component to be centered in its container, by default.

The GridLayout class organizes a container as a grid of *n* rows and *m* columns. Each grid cell is of the same size, as shown in Figure 24.8.

FIGURE 24.8.
A `GridLayout`
example.

The `GridLayout` class is used with the `mainPanel` in the `FrameApp` program. A grid of four rows and one column is used to stack `panel1` and `panel2` with the two labels to produce the display shown in Figure 24.2.

The `CardLayout` class organizes a container like a deck of cards. The first component in the container is initially displayed. Other components are then displayed using the `next()`, `previous()`, `first()`, `last()`, and `show()` methods of the `CardLayout` class. The `CardLayout` class is illustrated in Listing 24.2.

The `GridBagLayout` class is the most complex and flexible of the layout classes. It is similar to the `GridLayout` class in that it organizes its components in a grid, but it is more flexible because it allows the rows and columns to have different sizes. In addition, components are allowed to span multiple rows and columns. The positioning of each component is controlled by the use of objects of class `GridBagConstraints`. The `GridBagConstraints` objects identify the preferred size of each component and specify constraints on how they should be laid out. You should refer to the API documentation for the `GridBagLayout` and `GridBagConstraints` classes to read the detailed description of the variables and methods of these classes. The `GridBagLayout` class is demonstrated in the `LayoutApp` program in Listing 24.2.

The `LayoutApp` program illustrates the use of each of the five predefined Java layouts. These layouts position buttons within panels to show how the various layouts are organized and displayed. A pull-down menu is used to switch to each of the layout classes.

Listing 24.2. The source code of the `LayoutApp` program.

```
import java.awt.*;
import java.awt.event.*;

public class LayoutApp extends Frame {
 MenuBar menuBar;
 Panel panels[];
```

continues

Listing 24.2. continued

```
Panel currentPanel;
static int border=0;
static int card=1;
static int flow=2;
static int grid=3;
static int gridBag=4;
Menu fileMenu;
Menu panelMenu;
Menu cardMenu;
public static void main(String args[]){
 LayoutApp app = new LayoutApp();
}
public LayoutApp() {
 super("BorderLayout");
 setup();
 setSize(400,400);
 addWindowListener(new LayoutApp.WindowEventHandler());
 show();
}
void setup() {
 setupMenuBar();
 setupPanels();
}
void setupMenuBar() {
 menuBar = new MenuBar();
 fileMenu = new Menu("File");
 MenuItem fileExit = new MenuItem("Exit");
 LayoutApp.MenuItemHandler mh = new LayoutApp.MenuItemHandler();
 fileExit.addActionListener(mh);
 fileMenu.add(fileExit);
 menuBar.add(fileMenu);
 panelMenu = new Menu("Panel");
 MenuItem borderLayoutMenuItem = new MenuItem("BorderLayout");
 MenuItem cardLayoutMenuItem = new MenuItem("CardLayout");
 MenuItem flowLayoutMenuItem = new MenuItem("FlowLayout");
 MenuItem gridLayoutMenuItem = new MenuItem("GridLayout");
 MenuItem gridBagLayoutMenuItem = new MenuItem("GridBagLayout");
 borderLayoutMenuItem.addActionListener(mh);
 cardLayoutMenuItem.addActionListener(mh);
 flowLayoutMenuItem.addActionListener(mh);
 gridLayoutMenuItem.addActionListener(mh);
 gridBagLayoutMenuItem.addActionListener(mh);
 panelMenu.add(borderLayoutMenuItem);
 panelMenu.add(cardLayoutMenuItem);
 panelMenu.add(flowLayoutMenuItem);
 panelMenu.add(gridLayoutMenuItem);
 panelMenu.add(gridBagLayoutMenuItem);
 menuBar.add(panelMenu);
 cardMenu = new Menu("Card");
 MenuItem firstMenuItem = new MenuItem("First");
 MenuItem lastMenuItem = new MenuItem("Last");
 MenuItem nextMenuItem = new MenuItem("Next");
 MenuItem previousMenuItem = new MenuItem("Previous"); .
 firstMenuItem.addActionListener(mh);
 lastMenuItem.addActionListener(mh);
 nextMenuItem.addActionListener(mh);
```

```
  previousMenuItem.addActionListener(mh);
  cardMenu.add(firstMenuItem);
  cardMenu.add(lastMenuItem);
  cardMenu.add(nextMenuItem);
  cardMenu.add(previousMenuItem);
  setMenuBar(menuBar);
}
void setupPanels() {
  panels = new Panel[5];
  for(int i=0;i<5;++i) panels[i]=new Panel();
  panels[border].setLayout(new BorderLayout());
  panels[card].setLayout(new CardLayout());
  panels[flow].setLayout(new FlowLayout());
  panels[grid].setLayout(new GridLayout(2,3));
  GridBagLayout gridBagLayout = new GridBagLayout();
  panels[gridBag].setLayout(gridBagLayout);
  panels[border].add("North",new Button("North"));
  panels[border].add("South",new Button("South"));
  panels[border].add("East",new Button("East"));
  panels[border].add("West",new Button("West"));
  panels[border].add("Center",new Button("Center"));
  String cardButtons[] = {"First","Second","Third","Fourth","Last"};
  String flowButtons[] = {"One","Two","Three","Four","Five"};
  String gridButtons[] = {"(0,0)","(1,0)","(2,0)","(0,1)","(1,1)","(2,1)"};
  for(int i=0;i<cardButtons.length;++i)
   panels[card].add("next card",new Button(cardButtons[i]));
  for(int i=0;i<flowButtons.length;++i)
   panels[flow].add(new Button(flowButtons[i]));
  for(int i=0;i<gridButtons.length;++i)
   panels[grid].add(new Button(gridButtons[i]));
  Button gridBagButtons[] = new Button[9];
  for(int i=0;i<9;++i) gridBagButtons[i] = new Button("Button"+i);
  int gridx[] = {0,1,2,0,2,0,1,1,0};
  int gridy[] = {0,0,0,1,1,2,2,3,4};
  int gridwidth[] = {1,1,1,2,1,1,1,2,3};
  int gridheight[] = {1,1,1,1,2,2,1,1,1};
  GridBagConstraints gridBagConstraints[] = new GridBagConstraints[9];
  for(int i=0;i<9;++i) {
   gridBagConstraints[i] = new GridBagConstraints();
   gridBagConstraints[i].fill=GridBagConstraints.BOTH;
   gridBagConstraints[i].gridx=gridx[i];
   gridBagConstraints[i].gridy=gridy[i];
   gridBagConstraints[i].gridwidth=gridwidth[i];
   gridBagConstraints[i].gridheight=gridheight[i];
   gridBagLayout.setConstraints(gridBagButtons[i],gridBagConstraints[i]);
   panels[gridBag].add(gridBagButtons[i]);
  }
  add("Center",panels[border]);
  currentPanel=panels[border];
}
void switchPanels(Panel newPanel,String newTitle,boolean setCardMenu) {
  remove(currentPanel);
  currentPanel=newPanel;
  add("Center",currentPanel);
  setTitle(newTitle);
  menuBar.add(cardMenu);
```

continues

Listing 24.2. continued

```
 if(setCardMenu){
  menuBar = new MenuBar();
  menuBar.add(fileMenu);
  menuBar.add(panelMenu);
  menuBar.add(cardMenu);
  setMenuBar(menuBar);
 }else menuBar.remove(cardMenu);
 setSize(400,400);
 show();
}
class MenuItemHandler implements ActionListener {
 public void actionPerformed(ActionEvent ev){
  String s=ev.getActionCommand();
  if(s=="Exit"){
   System.exit(0);
  }else if(s=="BorderLayout"){
   switchPanels(panels[border],"BorderLayout",false);
  }else if(s=="CardLayout"){
   switchPanels(panels[card],"CardLayout",true);
  }else if(s=="FlowLayout"){
   switchPanels(panels[flow],"FlowLayout",false);
  }else if(s=="GridLayout"){
   switchPanels(panels[grid],"GridLayout",false);
  }else if(s=="GridBagLayout"){
   switchPanels(panels[gridBag],"GridBagLayout",false);
  }else if(s=="First"){
   CardLayout currentLayout=(CardLayout)currentPanel.getLayout();
   currentLayout.first(currentPanel);
  }else if(s=="Last"){
   CardLayout currentLayout=(CardLayout)currentPanel.getLayout();
   currentLayout.last(currentPanel);
  }else if(s=="Next"){
   CardLayout currentLayout=(CardLayout)currentPanel.getLayout();
   currentLayout.next(currentPanel);
  }else if(s=="Previous"){
   CardLayout currentLayout=(CardLayout)currentPanel.getLayout();
   currentLayout.previous(currentPanel);
  }
 }
}
class WindowEventHandler extends WindowAdapter {
 public void windowClosing(WindowEvent e){
  System.exit(0);
 }
 }
}
```

When you compile and run LayoutApp, the opening window should look like the one shown in Figure 24.9.

FIGURE 24.9.

The opening window of the LayoutApp *program.*

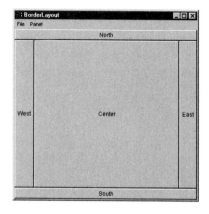

The opening window illustrates the use of the BorderLayout class by displaying a panel that uses the BorderLayout. Notice that the window's title is BorderLayout. The title is updated when a new layout class is displayed. To switch layouts, use the Panel pull-down menu as shown in Figure 24.10.

FIGURE 24.10.

The Panel menu.

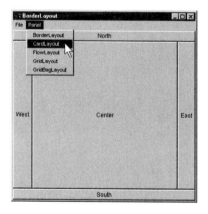

Select the CardLayout menu item from the Panel menu. The window displays a panel that uses a CardLayout object, and the window's title is updated to identify the new layout. An additional Card pull-down menu is added to the menu bar so that the different button components in the CardLayout object can be displayed. (See Figure 24.11.) There are five buttons, labeled First, Second, Third, Fourth, and Last. Use the Next menu item of the Card menu to step through these buttons. After you have reached the button labeled Last, use the Previous menu item to step back through the list of buttons. Next, try using the First and Last menu items to go to the first and last buttons in the panel governed by the CardLayout object.

FIGURE 24.11.
A CardLayout
example.

Select the FlowLayout menu item from the Panel menu. The window displays five buttons, labeled One through Five, across the top of the window as shown in Figure 24.12. The Card pull-down menu is removed and the window's title is changed to FlowLayout.

FIGURE 24.12.
A FlowLayout
example.

Select the GridLayout menu item from the Panel menu. The window displays six buttons in a rectangular grid that is two rows by three columns, with each button labeled with its x,y-coordinate, as shown in Figure 24.13. The window's title is changed to GridLayout.

Select the GridBagLayout menu item from the Panel menu. The window displays nine buttons arranged in a free-form manner in a rectangular grid, five rows by three columns, as shown in Figure 24.14. The window's title is changed to GridBagLayout.

FIGURE 24.13.
A GridLayout
example.

FIGURE 24.14.
A GridBagLayout
example.

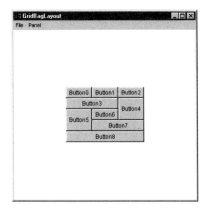

Now that you have an idea of what the LayoutApp program does, let's see how it works.

The LayoutApp class declares several variables and constants. The menuBar variable provides the program's menu bar. It is updated by different class methods when it is initially set up and displayed and when the Card menu is added and removed. The cardMenu variable is also declared. The panels[] array consists of five panels that illustrate the five predefined Java layouts. It is indexed by the border, card, flow, grid, and gridBag constants. The currentPanel variable is used to keep track of the current panel being displayed. The fileMenu, panelMenu, and cardMenu variables are used to hold the Menu objects that are displayed on the program's menu bar.

The main() function should seem to be pretty standard to you by now. It is typical of the main() function found in most window programs—it simply creates a new object of the application class.

The LayoutApp class invokes the superclass constructor with the BorderLayout title. BorderLayout is the layout of the first panel to be displayed and is the default layout for Frame objects. The setup() method is invoked to set up the menu bar and panels used in the program. The rest of the LayoutApp constructor is fairly standard. The setSize(), addWindowListener(), and show() methods are used to resize the application window, set its event handler, and display it to the user.

The setup() method invokes setupMenuBar() to set up the program's menu bar and setupPanels() to set up the panels used by the program.

The setupMenuBar()method creates a new menu bar and assigns it to the menuBar variable. A File menu is created with an Exit menu item. A MenuItemHandler object is created to handle menu item events and assigned to the mh variable. This object is used as the menu item event handler of all menu items created in the program. After the Exit menu item is added to the File menu, the File menu is added to the object referenced by menuBar. A Panel menu is created and added to the menuBar in a similar fashion. The Panel menu is given buttons that identify each of the five layouts. A third Card menu is also created, but is not added to the menuBar. It is given the First, Last, Next, and Previous menu items. Finally, the object referenced by menuBar is set as the menu bar by invoking the setMenuBar() method of the Frame class.

The setupPanels() method is the most complicated method in this program. It is where all of the five different panels are created and laid out. First, the panels[] array is allocated and then five new Panel objects are assigned to the array's elements. Then each of the panels is laid out.

The panels[border] array element has its layout set to a BorderLayout object using the setLayout() method of the Container class. The panels[card] array element has its layout set to a CardLayout object. The panels[flow] array element has its layout set to a FlowLayout object. The panels[grid] array element has its layout set to a GridLayout object, two rows by three columns. The layout of the panels[gridBag] array element is separately created and assigned to the gridBagLayout variable. It is used later on when the panel is laid out with objects of class GridBagConstraints.

After each of the panels has had its layout set, buttons are added to illustrate how the individual layouts are displayed. The panels[border] panel is given five buttons, labeled North, South, East, West, and Center. These buttons are added to the positions identified by their labels. The buttons for the panels[card], panels[flow], and panels[grid] panels are added by first creating an array of labels for each panel and then using a for statement to step through the arrays, creating buttons and adding them to their respective panels. This approach greatly simplifies the process of creating buttons and adding them to panels.

The buttons for the panels[gridBag] panel are created a little differently by iterating from 0 through 8 and appending the number on to the end of the "Button" string. The gridx[], gridy[], gridwidth[], and gridheight[] arrays are used to produce the objects of class GridBagConstraints that are used to lay out the buttons in the panels[gridBag] panel. The gridx[] array identifies the x-coordinate of each button within the 5-by-3 grid. The gridy[] array identifies the y-coordinate. The `gridwidth[]` array identifies button widths in terms of number of grid cells. The `gridheight[]` array identifies the height of each button in grid cells.

An array of `GridBagConstraint` objects is created and assigned to the `gridBagConstraints` variable. Each of the array's elements is then created and initialized using the `gridx[]`, `gridy[]`, `gridwidth[]`, and `gridheight[]` arrays. The fill variable of each array element is set to the `GridBagConstraints.BOTH` constant, indicating that the buttons may grow both vertically and horizontally to fill the space assigned to them as the result of the way they are laid out. The `setConstraints()` method is used to associate each button with its `gridBagConstraints[]` element within the `GridBagLayout` object referenced by `gridBagLayout`. The last line in the `for` statement adds each button to the `panels[gridBag]` panel.

Finally, the `panels[border]` panel is assigned as the initial panel to be displayed when the program starts up. The `currentPanel` variable is also initialized to `panels[border]`.

The `switchPanels()` method is used to provide a common method of switching from one panel to another. It begins by using the `remove()` method of the `Container` class to remove the current panel from the `LayoutApp` main window. The current panel is set based on the `Panel` object passed to the method via the `newPanel` parameter. The new current panel is then added to the center of the main window and the window's title is set based on the `newTitle` string parameter. The `cardMenu` is added or removed from the menu bar based on the `boolean setCardMenu` parameter. Finally, the new panel is displayed by invoking the `show()` method of the `Window` class.

The `actionPerformed()` method of the `MenuItemHandler` inner class handles events for all menu items. It handles the Exit menu item by invoking the `exit()` method of the `System` class to terminate the program's execution. It handles the `BorderLayout` menu item by invoking `switchPanels()` to switch to a border layout panel. It handles the CardLayout, FlowLayout, GridLayout, and GridBagLayout menu items in a similar manner. The First, Last, Next, and Previous menu items are only available when the panel is organized according to a card layout. These menu items are implemented by invoking the `first()`, `last()`, `next()`, and `previous()` methods of the `CardLayout` class to switch between the "cards" of the panel.

The `WindowEventHandler` inner class is the standard window event handler that we've been using in all window programming examples.

Connecting Code to Events

Although the various graphical user interface subclasses of the `Component` class are what is seen by the user when he interacts with a window program, the event-handling software is what actually connects these components to the code that implements the program's behavior.

Events are generated as the result of the user's interaction with the program's GUI components. These events are defined in the `java.awt.event` package and cover a large variety of user actions related to the mouse and keyboard.

The Java 1.1 event model is a significant improvement over that of Java 1.0. The Java 1.0 model required GUI components to be subclassed in order to handle events. While it is still possible to do so in Java 1.1, it is no longer necessary. Events can be handled by adapter classes that are separate from the component from which the event is generated.

The Java 1.1 event model is referred to as a *delegation* model. This means that event handling is delegated to specific event-handling adapter classes. In this model, a source object generates events that are listened for by a listener object. The source object is usually a window GUI component, such as a button or menu item. The listener object is an adapter class that implements an event listener interface. The source object provides methods that allow listener objects to register themselves to listen for its events. The addWindowListener() and addActionListener() methods are examples of these event handler registration methods.

The Window Sampler Program

The SamplerApp program serves a dual purpose. It shows how each of the most common GUI components are displayed and accessed and also demonstrates local event-handling approaches for each of these components. The program displays Label, TextField, TextArea, Button, Canvas, Checkbox, Choice, List, and Scrollbar objects and shows how to handle events associated with these objects.

The program makes use of the Java 1.1 event-handling methods, but for the most part, handles events locally with each GUI component subclass. In this respect, it is similar to a Java 1.0 program. The reason for this is to show how GUI components can be subclassed to build new custom components. Java 1.1 provides what is referred to as a lightweight user interface framework. This means that GUI components may be subclassed to create components that do not depend on the native window implementation. This makes them less resource intensive and more portable. The SamplerApp program's source code is shown in Listing 24.3.

Listing 24.3. The source code of the SamplerApp program.

```
import java.awt.*;
import java.awt.event.*;

public class SamplerApp extends Frame {
 TextArea textArea;
 public static void main(String args[]){
  SamplerApp app = new SamplerApp();
 }
 public SamplerApp() {
  super("Windows Sampler");
  setup();
  setSize(480,480);
  addWindowListener(new SamplerApp.WindowEventHandler());
  show();
 }
 void setup() {
```

```
 setupMenuBars();
 setupPanels();
}
void setupMenuBars() {
 MenuBar menuBar = new MenuBar();
 Menu fileMenu = new Menu("File");
 MenuItem fileExit = new MenuItem("Exit");
 SamplerApp.MenuItemHandler mh = new SamplerApp.MenuItemHandler();
 fileExit.addActionListener(mh);
 fileMenu.add(fileExit);
 menuBar.add(fileMenu);
 setMenuBar(menuBar);
}
void setupPanels() {
 Panel mainPanel = new Panel();
 mainPanel.setLayout(new GridLayout(3,3));
 Panel panels[][] = new Panel[3][3];
 for(int i=0;i<3;++i){
  for(int j=0;j<3;++j){
   panels[j][i] = new Panel();
   panels[j][i].setLayout(new FlowLayout(FlowLayout.LEFT));
  }
 }
 panels[0][0].add(new Label("Text Field:"));
 panels[0][0].add(new MyTextField("A text field.",15));
 panels[1][0].add(new Label("Text Area:"));
 textArea = new TextArea("A text area.",5,15);
 panels[1][0].add(textArea);
 panels[2][0].add(new Label("Button:"));
 panels[2][0].add(new MyButton("Blank Text Area",textArea));
 panels[0][1].add(new Label("Canvas:"));
 panels[0][1].add(new MyCanvas());
 String checkboxStrings[] = {"Checkboxes:","Java","Developer's","Guide"};
 panels[1][1].add(new MyCheckboxGroup(checkboxStrings));
 panels[2][1].add(new Label("Choices:"));
 String choiceStrings[] = {"Yes","No","Maybe"};
 panels[2][1].add(new MyChoice(choiceStrings,textArea));
 panels[0][2].add(new Label("List:"));
 String listStrings[] = {"Sleepy","Sneezy","Grumpy","Dopey","Doc",
  "Happy","Bashful"};
 panels[0][2].add(new MyList(listStrings,textArea));
 panels[1][2].setLayout(new BorderLayout());
 panels[1][2].add("Center",new Label("Horizontal Scrollbar:"));
 panels[1][2].add("South",new MyScrollbar(Scrollbar.HORIZONTAL,50,10,0,
  100,textArea));
 panels[2][2].setLayout(new BorderLayout());
 panels[2][2].add("North",new Label("Vertical Scrollbar:"));
 panels[2][2].add("East",new MyScrollbar(Scrollbar.VERTICAL,50,10,0,
  1000,textArea));
 for(int i=0;i<3;++i)
  for(int j=0;j<3;++j)
   mainPanel.add(panels[j][i]);
 add("Center",mainPanel);
}
class WindowEventHandler extends WindowAdapter {
 public void windowClosing(WindowEvent e){
  System.exit(0);
```

continues

Listing 24.3. continued

```
  }
 }
 class MenuItemHandler implements ActionListener {
  public void actionPerformed(ActionEvent ev){
   String s=ev.getActionCommand();
   if(s=="Exit") System.exit(0);
  }
 }
}
class MyTextField extends TextField {
 public MyTextField(String text,int columns) {
  super(text,columns);
  addActionListener(new MyTextField.HandleTextField());
 }
 class HandleTextField implements ActionListener {
  public void actionPerformed(ActionEvent ev){
   String text = getText();
   setText(text.toUpperCase());
  }
 }
}
class MyButton extends Button {
 TextArea textArea;
 public MyButton(String text,TextArea newTextArea) {
  super(text);
  textArea = newTextArea;
  addActionListener(new MyButton.HandleButton());
 }
 class HandleButton implements ActionListener {
  public void actionPerformed(ActionEvent ev){
   textArea.setText("");
  }
 }
}
class MyCanvas extends Canvas {
 int x = -1;
 int y = -1;
 int boxSize = 10;
 public MyCanvas() {
  super();
  setSize(100,100);
  setVisible(true);
  addMouseListener(new MyCanvas.MouseHandler());
  repaint();
 }
 public void paint(Graphics g) {
  setBackground(Color.gray);
  setForeground(Color.red);
  if(x>=0 && y>=0) g.fillRect(x,y,boxSize,boxSize);
 }
 class MouseHandler extends MouseAdapter {
  public void mouseClicked(MouseEvent ev){
   x = ev.getX();
   y = ev.getY();
   repaint();
  }
```

```
  }
}
class MyCheckboxGroup extends Panel {
 String labelString;
 String checkboxLabels[];
 Checkbox checkboxes[];
 int numBoxes;
 TextField results;
 public MyCheckboxGroup(String strings[]) {
  super();
  labelString = strings[0];
  numBoxes = strings.length-1;
  checkboxLabels = new String[numBoxes];
  for(int i=0;i<numBoxes;++i)
   checkboxLabels[i] = strings[i+1];
  results = new TextField("",15);
  setupPanel();
  setVisible(true);
 }
 void setupPanel() {
  setLayout(new GridLayout(numBoxes+2,1));
  add(new Label(labelString));
  checkboxes = new Checkbox[numBoxes];
  MyCheckboxGroup.HandleCheck hrc =
   new MyCheckboxGroup.HandleCheck();
  for(int i=0;i<numBoxes;++i){
   checkboxes[i] = new Checkbox(checkboxLabels[i]);
   checkboxes[i].addItemListener(hrc);
   add(checkboxes[i]);
  }
  add(results);
 }
 class HandleCheck implements ItemListener {
  public void itemStateChanged(ItemEvent e){
   String newResults = "";
   for(int i=0;i<numBoxes;++i)
    if(checkboxes[i].getState())
     newResults = newResults + " " +checkboxes[i].getLabel();
   results.setText(newResults);
  }
 }
}
class MyChoice extends Choice {
 TextArea text;
 public MyChoice(String strings[],TextArea textArea) {
  super();
  try {
   for(int i=0;i<strings.length;++i)
    addItem(strings[i]);
   text = textArea;
  }catch(NullPointerException ex){
   System.exit(0);
  }
  addItemListener(new MyChoice.HandleChoice());
 }
 class HandleChoice implements ItemListener {
```

continues

Listing 24.3. continued

```java
  public void itemStateChanged(ItemEvent e){
   Choice ch = (Choice) e.getItemSelectable();
   text.setText(ch.getSelectedItem());
  }
 }
}
class MyList extends List {
 TextArea text;
 public MyList(String strings[],TextArea textArea) {
  super(3,false);
  for(int i=0;i<strings.length;++i)
   addItem(strings[i]);
  text = textArea;
  addItemListener(new MyList.HandleListSelect());
  addActionListener(new MyList.HandleListDoubleClick());
 }
 class HandleListSelect implements ItemListener {
  public void itemStateChanged(ItemEvent e){
   int change = e.getStateChange();
   List l = (List) e.getItemSelectable();
   if(change==ItemEvent.SELECTED){
    text.setText("Selected:\n"+l.getSelectedItem());
   }else if(change==ItemEvent.DESELECTED){
    text.setText("Selected:");
   }
  }
 }
 class HandleListDoubleClick implements ActionListener {
  public void actionPerformed(ActionEvent e){
   text.setText("Double-clicked:\n "+e.getActionCommand());
  }
 }
}
class MyScrollbar extends Scrollbar {
 TextArea text;
 public MyScrollbar(int orientation,int value,int visible,int min,int max,
  TextArea textArea) {
  super(orientation,value,visible,min,max);
  text=textArea;
  addAdjustmentListener(new MyScrollbar.HandleScrolling());
 }
 class HandleScrolling implements AdjustmentListener {
  public void adjustmentValueChanged(AdjustmentEvent e){
   text.setText("Position: "+e.getValue());
  }
 }
}
```

After compiling and running the program, the main application window should be displayed as shown in Figure 24.15. The program presents a number of GUI components at various locations within the window. Labels are used to identify these components.

FIGURE 24.15.

The `SamplerApp`
program display.

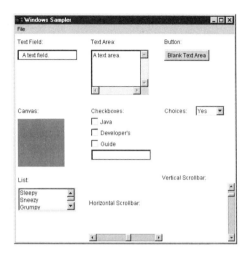

The `TextField` object presented in the upper-left corner of the window allows a user to type some text. When the user presses the Enter key from within the text field, the text is automatically converted to uppercase.

The `TextArea` object allows the user to type in and edit text in a multiline text field. This object is used in the `SamplerApp` program to display the results of operations on other objects such as the Blank Text Area button, the choices list, the scrollable list, and the horizontal and vertical scrollbars.

The Blank Text Area button causes all text displayed in the `TextArea` object to be erased. The `Canvas` object displays a red square at the point where the user clicks within the canvas. When the `Checkbox` objects are selected, they display the text of their labels in the underlying text field. The value selected from the `Choice` and `List` objects is displayed in the `TextArea` object. The horizontal and vertical scrollbars also display their scrollbar position in the `TextArea` object.

Play around with each of the GUI components to familiarize yourself with their operation before moving on to analyze the `SamplerApp` source code.

The `SamplerApp` class defines only one variable—the `textArea` variable that is used to hold the `TextArea` object written to by several GUI components. The `main()` method and `SamplerApp` constructor are defined in the standard manner. The `setup()`, `setupMenuBars()`, and `setupPanels()` methods provide the primary setup processing for this class, with the bulk of the processing being performed in `setupPanels()`.

The `setupMenuBars()` method creates a File menu with an Exit menu item. The `MenuItemHandler` class handles the clicking of the Exit menu item. All other event handling is performed locally by the window components.

The setupPanels() method creates a Panel with a 3-by-3 GridLayout and assigns it to mainPanel. It then declares and initializes a 3-by-3 panels array to hold the nine subpanels of the mainPanel. The layout of elements of the panels array is set to a left-justified FlowLayout. Subsequent code adds GUI components to each of the panels elements.

A TextField: label and an object of MyTextField are added to panels[0][0]. The MyTextField object is assigned a default value of "A text field." and is set to 15 columns. A TextArea: label and a 5-row by 15-column TextArea object with the default text of "A text area." are added to panels[1][0]. A Button: label and a MyButton object are added to panels[2][0]. The MyButton object is given the Blank Text Area label and is passed the name of a TextArea to be updated.

A Canvas: label and a MyCanvas object are added to panels[0][1]. An array of strings is created and passed to the MyCheckBoxGroup() constructor. The resulting MyCheckBoxGroup object is added to panels[1][1]. A Choices: label is added to panels[2][1]. A MyChoice object is created using the choiceStrings[] array and the textArea variable. The object is also added to panels[2][1].

A List: label is added to panels[0][2]. A MyList object is created using the names of the Seven Dwarfs and the textArea variable and is added to panels[1][2]. The layouts for panels[1][2] and panels[2][2] are changed to a BorderLayout object. A Horizontal Scrollbar: label is added to the center of panels[1][2], and a MyScrollBar object is created and added to the southern region of panels[1][2]. A Vertical Scrollbar: label is added to the northern region of panels[2][2], and a MyScrollBar object is created and added to the eastern region of panels[2][2].

After the components of all the panels have been created and added to their respective panels, each of the elements of the panels array is added to the mainPanel object. The mainPanel is then added to the center of the SamplerApp window.

The WindowEventHandler and MenuItemHandler inner classes handle the window closing event and the Exit menu item event by terminating the program's execution.

After the SamplerApp class is declared, seven new classes are declared that subclass the standard GUI components and provide custom display and event handling.

MyTextField

The TextField class provides the capability for the user to enter and edit a single line of text. The MyTextField() constructor passes the text and columns parameters to the TextField constructor via the superclass constructor call statement. The text parameter identifies a string of text that is to be initially displayed within the text field. The columns parameter specifies the displayed width of the text field in character columns. The HandleTextField inner class handles the event generated when the user presses the Enter key while editing within the text field. The actionPerformed() method handles the event occurring when the user presses the Enter key while editing the text field. It uses the getText() method inherited from the TextComponent class to retrieve the current text displayed within the text field, converts it to uppercase, and then sets the converted text in the text field using the setText() method inherited from TextComponent. The TextComponent class is the parent of both TextField and TextArea.

MyButton

The MyButton class extends the Button class. Its constructor takes two parameters: the string label to be displayed on the button and a reference to the TextArea object that is to be cleared when the button is clicked. The actionPerformed() method of the HandleButton inner class handles the button click and uses the setText() method of TextComponent to set the text of the TextArea object to an empty string.

MyCanvas

The Canvas class provides the capability to add individual drawing components to a container. It is covered extensively in Chapter 28, "The Canvas." The MyCanvas class extends Canvas and provides a minimal drawing capability. It declares the x and y variables to record the last position in which the mouse is clicked within the canvas. Their default values are set to -1 to indicate that the mouse has not yet been clicked on the canvas. The boxSize variable specifies the size of the box to be displayed at the position of the last mouse click.

The MyCanvas constructor sets the canvas size to an area of 100×100 pixels. The setVisible() method is used to cause the canvas to be initially displayed. The addMouseListener() method is invoked to set up the MouseHandler() class to handle mouse events that occur with respect to the canvas. The repaint() method is invoked to cause the canvas to be painted with a gray background and red foreground.

The paint() method checks to make sure that a click has occurred and fills a rectangle with the upper-left corner at the point of the last click and with boxSize dimensions.

The mouseClicked() method of the MouseHandler inner class handles the event generated when the user clicks a mouse button. Java assumes a one-button mouse to provide the widest compatibility. The mouseClicked() method stores the position of the user's click and then invokes the repaint() method to repaint the canvas. Note that MouseHandler subclasses the MouseAdapter class. MouseAdapter provides other methods that may be overridden to support mouse event handling.

MyCheckBoxGroup

The MyCheckBoxGroup class extends the Panel class. It implements a custom panel consisting of a label, an array of Checkbox objects, and a TextField object. The results of clicking on any of the checkboxes are displayed in the results TextField. The MyCheckBoxGroup constructor takes an array of strings as its parameter. It sets the label string to the first string in the array and sets the labels of the checkboxes to the rest of the strings. The numBoxes variable specifies the number of Checkbox objects to be created. The results TextField is created as an empty 15-character TextField object.

The setupPanel() method sets the layout of the panel to a GridLayout that is one column wide and with enough rows to accommodate the label, checkboxes, and text field. An object of the HandleCheck inner class is created and assigned to the hrc variable. A for loop is used to create new checkboxes, assign the HandleCheck object as an event handler, and add the checkboxes to the panel. The results TextField is then added to the end of the panel.

The itemStateChanged() method of the HandleCheck inner class is used to handle the checking of the checkboxes. It uses the getState() and getLabel() methods of the Checkbox class to query the checked status of each checkbox and to retrieve the labels associated with the checkboxes that are checked. It then displays these labels in the results TextField using the setText() method. Note that HandleCheck implements the ItemListener interface.

MyChoice

The Choice class is used to implement Motif option menus, which are free-standing pull-down menus that can be used to select a single value from a list. The MyChoice class extends the Choice class and provides the capability to display selected choices in a TextArea object.

The MyChoice constructor takes an array of strings to be used as the choices and a TextArea object as its parameters. The addItem() method of the Choice class is used to add the choice strings to the list of choices. The constructor checks for a NullPointerException when the strings are added to the Choice list because the addItem() method throws this exception. The addItemListener() method is used to set up an object of the HandleChoice inner class as an event handler.

The itemStateChanged() method of the HandleChoice inner class handles the event generated when a user makes a selection from the list. The getItemSelectable() method of the ItemEvent class returns the label of the selected choice. It is displayed in the TextArea object using the setText() method.

MyList

The List class implements scrollable lists from which a user can select one or more list items. The MyList class extends the List class and provides support for displaying the selected list items in a TextArea field.

The MyList constructor takes an array of strings and the TextArea object as its parameters. The strings are used as the items of the list. The super(3,false) superclass constructor call statement invokes the List class constructor and specifies a three-row list with multiple list selections being disabled. Lists are covered in more detail in Chapter 26, "Checkboxes, Choices, and Lists." The addItem() method of the List class is used to add the strings as items of the list. The addItemListener() method is used to set up an object of the HandleListSelect inner class as the event handler for single-click selections of list items. The addActionListener() method is used to set up an object of HandleListDoubleClick as an event handler for double-clicked list selections.

The itemStateChanged() method of the HandleListSelect inner class handles the event that occurs when a list item is selected through a single click. It uses the getStateChange() method of the ItemEvent object passed through the e parameter to get the type of list item change that occurred. It uses the getItemSelectable() method to retrieve the list from which the selection was made. If the change variable indicates that a list item was selected, it displays the label of the selected item in the text area. If the change variable indicates that a list item was deselected, it simply displays the text Selected: in the text area. Note that the Windows 95 implementation of Java does not correctly handle the deselection of a list item event.

The actionPerformed() method of the HandleListDoubleClick inner class handles the event associated with the double-clicking of a list item by indicating which item was double-clicked in the text area. The getActionCommand() method of the ActionEvent class is used to get the label of the selected list item.

MyScrollbar

The Scrollbar class encapsulates vertical and horizontal scrollbars. The MyScrollbar class extends Scrollbar and provides the capability to display the results of scrollbar operations using a TextArea object. (See Chapter 29, "Scrollbars," for more information on using scrollbars.)

The MyScrollbar constructor takes a number of parameters that determine the characteristics of a scrollbar. These parameters are forwarded to the superclass constructor. A TextArea object is also passed as a parameter. The orientation parameter is set to the HORIZONTAL and VERTICAL constants of the Scrollbar class. These constants specify whether the scrollbar should be displayed horizontally or vertically. The min and max parameters specify a range of integer values that are associated with the scrollbar. The value parameter sets the initial position of the scrollbar between the min and max values. The visible parameter identifies the size of the visible portion of the scrollable area. This determines how the current scrollbar position is updated as the result of a page-up or page-down scrollbar operation. The addAdjustmentListener() method is used to set up an object of the HandleScrolling inner class as a scrollbar event handler.

The adjustmentValueChanged() method of the HandleScrolling class handles scrollbar events by using the getValue() method of the AdjustmentEvent class to obtain the current scrollbar position and displaying this value in the text area. Note that the HandleScrolling class implements the AdjustmentListener interface.

Summary

This chapter covers the basics of writing window programs. It shows how window programs are structured and organized and identifies the basic approach used to design most window programs. It covers the details of the `Frame` class and the five basic window layouts. The process of window event handling is described and illustrated through the `SamplerApp` program. `SamplerApp` also introduces the most common window GUI controls. Subsequent chapters investigate these components in more detail.

25

Menus, Buttons, and Dialog Boxes

This chapter covers the details of using the Menu, Button, and Dialog classes. It describes the available menu and button options, and shows you how to quickly and easily construct menus and buttons for your window programs. The use of dialog boxes is explained, and a generic MessageDialog component is constructed and explained as part of an example. When you finish this chapter, you will be able to use menus, buttons, and dialog boxes effectively in your Java window programs.

Adding Menus to Windows

Java provides a rich set of menu-related classes to create and interact with pull-down menus. The MenuComponent class is the superclass of all menu-related classes. It extends the Object class. The getFont()and setFont() methods are the most useful methods provided by MenuComponent. Its two direct superclasses, MenuBar and MenuItem, provide most of the methods for creating and using menus. The CheckboxMenuItem class extends the MenuItem class and supports menu items that can be checked on or off. The Menu class extends the MenuItem class and implements a collection of MenuItem objects that can be assigned to a MenuBar object. The PopupMenu class extends the Menu class to provide a menu that can be popped up inside a component to enable user menu selections. Finally, the MenuShortcut class can be used to create a keyboard shortcut to a menu item.

You are probably somewhat familiar with menus from Chapters 23, "Opening Windows," and 24, "Organizing Window Programs." A program's application window is implemented by a Frame object. It can have one and only one MenuBar object, which is set using the setMenuBar() method. A *menu bar* is a collection of menus. Each menu is represented as a separate pull-down menu on the menu bar. Common examples are the File, Edit, and Help pull-down menus found in many window applications. The MenuBar class allows a special menu to be designated as a Help menu, but this feature is not implemented in Windows 95 or NT. It is implemented by Solaris and other flavors of UNIX.

A Menu object contains one or more MenuItem objects, which can be a normal user-selectable MenuItem object, a CheckboxMenuItem object, or another Menu object. Java supports *tear-off menus*, which are menus that can be removed from a menu bar. A tear-off menu is constructed in the same manner as a regular menu—you only need to set the boolean tear-off value in the Menu() constructor. Tear-off menus, however, are not implemented within Windows 95 or NT. They are implemented in Solaris and other UNIX derivatives.

The MenuItem class is the superclass of the Menu class. This allows a menu to be a menu item and is used in constructing cascading, multilevel menus. MenuItem is also the superclass of the CheckboxMenuItem class and provides the capability to implement menu items that can be checked or unchecked. If a MenuItem object is constructed directly with the MenuItem constructor, it becomes a normal menu item that is selected from a pull-down menu.

The MyMenu **Class**

The creation and organization of menu bars, menus, and menu items into a program's menu is a straightforward, but tedious, process. You have to create a menu bar, create and add menus to the menu bar, add menu items to the menus, and then add the menu bar to the program's application window. This usually involves the use of a large number of constructors and access methods. To illustrate the use of the menu-related classes and to simplify the menu-creation process, you'll create two classes, MyMenu and MyMenuBar, that can be used to quickly construct menus for Java programs. These classes implement multiple levels of menus, checkbox menu items, and menu-disabling options. The special Help and tear-off menus are not implemented, however, because they are transparent to Windows 95 and NT.

The MyMenu class is used to construct menus using an array of objects consisting of String objects that represent menu labels, or arrays of objects that represent submenus. Menu labels can be either checkbox menu items or normal menu items and can be either initially enabled or disabled (grayed out). Checkbox menu items can be initially checked or unchecked. The first character of the label's text string is used to indicate what type of label it is. The character conventions are as follows:

+   A checkbox menu item that is initially checked and enabled.

\#   A checkbox menu item that is initially checked and disabled.

-      A checkbox menu item that is initially unchecked and enabled. If the label consists of just -, it indicates a separator.

=   A checkbox menu item that is initially unchecked and disabled.

~   A normal menu item that is initially disabled.

Any other character indicates a normal, enabled menu item. If the first character is !, it is ignored. This allows any menu item to begin with any character.

These conventions apply to menu options. Only the ~ and ! options are used with the menu's main label. Using these options greatly simplifies the process of a menu creation. The source code for the MyMenu class is shown in Listing 25.1.

Listing 25.1. The source code of the MyMenu class.

```
package jdg.ch25;

import java.awt.*;
import java.awt.event.*;

public class MyMenu extends Menu {
 public MyMenu(Object labels[],ActionListener al,ItemListener il) {
  super((String)labels[0]);
  String menuName = (String) labels[0];
  char firstMenuChar = menuName.charAt(0);
```

continues

Listing 25.1. continued

```
if(firstMenuChar == '~' || firstMenuChar =='!'){
 setLabel(menuName.substring(1));
 if(firstMenuChar == '~') setEnabled(false);
}
for(int i=1;i<labels.length;++i) {
 if(labels[i] instanceof String){
  if("-".equals(labels[i])) addSeparator();
  else{
   String label = (String)labels[i];
   char firstChar = label.charAt(0);
   switch(firstChar){
   case '+':
    CheckboxMenuItem checkboxItem = new CheckboxMenuItem(label.substring(1));
    checkboxItem.setState(true);
    add(checkboxItem);
    checkboxItem.addItemListener(il);
    break;
   case '#':
    checkboxItem = new CheckboxMenuItem(label.substring(1));
    checkboxItem.setState(true);
    checkboxItem.setEnabled(false);
    add(checkboxItem);
    checkboxItem.addItemListener(il);
    break;
   case '-':
    checkboxItem = new CheckboxMenuItem(label.substring(1));
    checkboxItem.setState(false);
    add(checkboxItem);
    checkboxItem.addItemListener(il);
    break;
   case '=':
    checkboxItem = new CheckboxMenuItem(label.substring(1));
    checkboxItem.setState(false);
    checkboxItem.setEnabled(false);
    add(checkboxItem);
    checkboxItem.addItemListener(il);
    break;
   case '~':
    MenuItem menuItem = new MenuItem(label.substring(1));
    menuItem.setEnabled(false);
    add(menuItem);
    menuItem.addActionListener(al);
    break;
   case '!':
    menuItem = new MenuItem(label.substring(1));
    add(menuItem);
    menuItem.addActionListener(al);
    break;
   default:
    menuItem = new MenuItem(label);
    add(menuItem);
    menuItem.addActionListener(al);
   }
  }
 }else{
  add(new MyMenu((Object[])labels[i],al,il));
 }
```

```
   }
  }
  public MenuItem getItem(String menuItem) {
   int numItems = getItemCount();
   for(int i=0;i<numItems;++i)
    if(menuItem.equals(getItem(i).getLabel())) return getItem(i);
   return null;
  }
 }
```

The MyMenu class specifies that it is in the jdg.ch25 package. Make sure that you place it in the jdg/ch25 directory and compile it. You'll be using it quite a bit in subsequent chapters.

MyMenu contains no field variables. It consists of a single constructor and the getItem()access method. The getItem() method retrieves a menu item contained in the menu and based on the menu item's label. It uses the getItemCount() and getItem() methods of the Menu class to retrieve the menu items contained in a menu and the getLabel() method of the MenuItem class to match a menu item with the search string.

The MyMenu constructor constructs a menu from an array of menu labels and nested menu arrays (representing submenus). It also takes ActionListener and ItemListener objects as arguments. These objects are set up as the event handlers for the regular and checkbox menu items of the menu. For example, to construct a typical File menu, labeled File, with the New and Open menu items followed by a separator and an Exit menu item, you would use the following MyMenu constructor:

```
String fileMenuLabels[] = {"File","New","Open","-","Exit"};
// EventHandler must implement the ActionListener and ItemListener interfaces.
EventHandler eh = new EventHandler();
MyMenu fileMenu = new MyMenu(fileLabelMenus,eh,eh);
```

The first object in the array must be a String object that is the main label associated with the menu. The following objects are either String objects identifying the labels of the menu items contained in the menu, separators, or second-level arrays representing submenus. For example, the following creates a multilevel menu:

```
String goMenuLabels[] = {"Go","Beginning","End","Previous","Next"};
String editMenuLabels[] = {"Edit","Copy","Cut","-","Paste","-",goMenuLabels};
// EventHandler must implement the ActionListener and ItemListener interfaces.
EventHandler eh = new EventHandler();
MyMenu editLabel = new MyMenu(editMenuLabels,eh,eh);
```

Using the MyMenu class is much easier than constructing each of the individual menu items and adding them to a menu.

Let's step through the MyMenu constructor to see how it works. It uses the super() class constructor call statement to construct a Menu object using the first label in the labels array. This label may contain the ~ or ! character as the first character. MyMenu() checks for these characters and readjusts the menu's label accordingly. If the first character of the menu's label is ~, MyMenu() will disable the entire menu using the setEnabled() method of the MenuItem class.

After setting up the menu's main label, MyMenu() iterates through the list of objects contained in labels. If the object is an instance of the String class and is therefore a label, MyMenu() checks the first letter of the label and processes it accordingly. If the object is not an instance of the String class, MyMenu() calls itself again, passing the object to itself as another array of objects. It then adds the resulting MyMenu object to itself using the add() method of the Menu class. This allows submenus to be processed in a recursive fashion.

MyMenu() processes the menu item labels by using a switch statement to check the first character of the label to see if it matches the +, #, -, =, ~, or ! characters. If it does not match any of these characters, the label is added as a normal menu item. If the label equals -, a separator is added.

If the first character is +, an enabled and checked CheckboxMenuItem object is added to the menu. The setState() method of the CheckboxMenuItem class is used to set the state of the menu item to checked. If the first character is #, a checked, but disabled, CheckboxMenuItem object is added. The setEnabled() method of the MenuItem class is used to disable the menu item. The cases in which the first character of the label is - or = are processed in a similar manner, except that the CheckboxMenuItem object is initially unchecked.

When the first character of the label is ~, a normal MenuItem object is added to the menu. The menu item is disabled.

The ! character is an escape character that is used to create a normal menu item beginning with any of the special characters previously mentioned. When the first character of a label is !, the actual label generated begins with the subsequent character.

The MyMenuBar Class

The MyMenuBar class uses the MyMenu class presented in the previous section to quickly create an entire menu bar. Whereas the MyMenu class uses an array of labels and submenus to create a menu, the MyMenuBar class uses an array of these arrays to create the entire menu bar. For example, the following statements will construct a menu bar with File, Edit, and Help menus, each consisting of individual menu items:

```
String menuBarLabels[] = {
  {"File","New","Open","-","~Save As","-","Exit"};
  {"Edit","Copy","Cut","-","~Paste"};
  {"Help","Index"};
};
// EventHandler must implement the ActionListener and ItemListener interfaces.
EventHandler eh = new EventHandler();
MyMenuBar menuBar = new MyMenuBar(menuBarLabels,eh,eh);
```

Note that the Save As and Paste menu items are initially disabled.

The source code of the MyMenuBar class is shown in Listing 25.2.

Listing 25.2. The source code of the MyMenuBar class.

```
package jdg.ch25;

import java.awt.*;
import java.awt.event.*;

public class MyMenuBar extends MenuBar {
 public MyMenuBar(Object labels[][],ActionListener al,
   ItemListener il) {
  super();
  for(int i=0;i<labels.length;++i)
   add(new MyMenu(labels[i],al,il));
 }
 public MyMenu getMenu(String menuName) {
  int numMenus = getMenuCount();
  for(int i=0;i<numMenus;++i)
   if(menuName.equals(getMenu(i).getLabel())) return((MyMenu)getMenu(i));
  return null;
 }
}
```

The MyMenuBar constructor simply iterates through the outer array and passes the first-level elements (which are themselves Object arrays) to the MyMenu constructor to construct MyMenu objects. These objects are then added to the MyMenuBar object being constructed using the add() method inherited from the MenuBar class.

The getMenu() method retrieves a MyMenu object from a MyMenuBar object based on the label associated with the MyMenu object. It uses the getMenuCount() and getMenu() methods of the MenuBar class to retrieve each MyMenu object contained in the menu bar. The getLabel() method of the MenuItem class is used to check the labels of the MyMenu objects against the search string.

The MenuApp Program

The MenuApp program illustrates the use of the MyMenuBar and MyMenu classes. Its source code is shown in Listing 25.3.

Listing 25.3. The source code of the MenuApp program.

```
import java.awt.*;
import java.awt.event.*;
import jdg.ch25.MyMenu;
import jdg.ch25.MyMenuBar;

public class MenuApp extends Frame {
 MyMenuBar menuBar;
 MenuApp.EventHandler eh = new MenuApp.EventHandler();
 public static void main(String args[]){
  MenuApp app = new MenuApp();
```

continues

Listing 25.3. continued

```
  }
public MenuApp() {
 super("Menu Madness");
 setup();
 setSize(400,400);
 addWindowListener(eh);
 show();
}
void setup() {
 setBackground(Color.white);
 setupMenuBar();
}
void setupMenuBar(){
 String gotoMenu[] = {"Go To","Beginning","End","-","Line Number"};
 Object menuItems[][] = {
  {"File","New","Open","-","~Save","~Save As","-","Exit"},
  {"Edit","Copy","Cut","-","~Paste"},
  {"Search","Find","~Find Next","~Find Previous","-", gotoMenu},
  {"View","-Hex","+Line Number","+Column Number"},
  {"Help","About Menu Madness"},
 };
 menuBar = new MyMenuBar(menuItems,eh,eh);
 setMenuBar(menuBar);
}
class EventHandler extends WindowAdapter implements ActionListener,
  ItemListener {
 public void actionPerformed(ActionEvent e){
  String selection=e.getActionCommand();
  if("Exit".equals(selection)){
   System.exit(0);
  }else if("New".equals(selection) ¦¦ "Open".equals(selection)){
   menuBar.getMenu("File").getItem("Save").setEnabled(true);
   menuBar.getMenu("File").getItem("Save As").setEnabled(true);
  }else if("Copy".equals(selection) ¦¦ "Cut".equals(selection)){
   menuBar.getMenu("Edit").getItem("Paste").setEnabled(true);
  }else if("Find".equals(selection)){
   menuBar.getMenu("Search").getItem("Find Next").setEnabled(true);
   menuBar.getMenu("Search").getItem("Find Previous").setEnabled(true);
  }else if("About Menu Madness".equals(selection)){
   menuBar.getMenu("Help").setEnabled(false);
  }
 }
 public void itemStateChanged(ItemEvent e){
 }
 public void windowClosing(WindowEvent e){
  System.exit(0);
 }
}
}
```

MenuApp shows how the `MyMenuBar` and `MyMenu` classes are used to easily create a menu bar and to support the processing of menu-related events. When the program is executed, it displays a blank opening screen and a menu bar with five pull-down menus, as shown in Figure 25.1.

FIGURE 25.1.

The MenuApp *opening window.*

Click on the File menu and select the New menu item, as shown in Figure 25.2. This will cause the Save and Save As menu items to become enabled. You can verify this by clicking on the File menu once again.

FIGURE 25.2.

The File menu.

Click on the Edit menu and select the Copy menu item, as shown in Figure 25.3. This results in the Paste menu item becoming enabled.

FIGURE 25.3.
The Edit menu.

Click on the Search menu and then on the Go To menu item, as shown in Figure 25.4. The Go To menu item is a second-level menu that is attached to the Search menu.

FIGURE 25.4.
The Search menu.

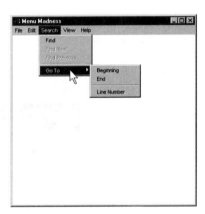

Click on the View menu and select the Hex checkbox menu item, as shown in Figure 25.5. Notice that the Hex checkbox becomes checked, as shown in Figure 25.6.

Click on the Help menu and select About Menu Madness, as shown in Figure 25.7. This Help menu isn't much help at all because it is programmed to disable itself, as shown in Figure 25.8.

FIGURE 25.5.
The View menu.

FIGURE 25.6.
The View menu after checking Hex.

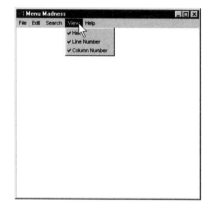

FIGURE 25.7.
The Help menu.

FIGURE 25.8.

The Help menu disabled.

You've completed the tour of the MenuApp program. Select Exit from the File menu to terminate the program's operation.

Inside MenuApp

The MenuApp class consists of two variables: menuBar and eh. The menuBar variable is an object of class MyMenuBar that is used to hold the application's menu bar. The eh variable is assigned an object of the EventHandler class. This object is used to handle both window and menu-related events. It is used to show how multiple event handlers can be combined into a single event handler.

The MenuApp constructor creates a 400×400 frame window with the title Menu Madness and invokes the setup() method to set up the background color and the menu bar. The setup() method invokes setupMenuBar() to actually perform the menu bar setup.

The setupMenuBar() method creates a gotoMenu array as the labels of a submenu that will be attached to the Search menu. The menuItems array is used to define the labels associated with the menu bar and its first-level menus. The gotoMenu array is included as an object in this array. Notice the use of the first-character conventions for disabling menu items and specifying menu items that are checkboxes. The menu bar is created, assigned to the menuBar variable, and set as the menu bar for the MenuApp frame.

Creating the menu bar was a snap using the MyMenuBar class. However, creating the menu bar is only half of the work. You also need to write event-handling code that acts on the menu items selected by the user. The EventHandler inner class illustrates the use of a single event handler to handle multiple types of events. EventHandler extends the WindowAdapter class. This allows it to handle window events, such as the window closing event. It handles this event in the standard way, by overriding the windowClosing() method.

`EventHandler` also implements the `ActionListener` and `ItemListener` interfaces and therefore the `actionPerformed()` and `itemStateChanged()` methods. The `actionPerformed()` method is used to handle the events associated with the selection of normal menu items, and the `itemStateChanged()` method is used to handle events associated with checkbox menu items.

The Exit menu item is handled by terminating the program's execution. The New and Open menu items cause the Save and Save As menu items to be enabled. The `getMenu()` method of `MyMenuBar` and the `getItem()` method of `MyMenu` are used to retrieve the Save and Save As `MenuItem` objects. The `setEnabled()` method of the `MenuItem` class is used to enable these menu items. Note that the Save and Save As menu items, as well as some other menu items, are not handled. Selecting these menu items does not result in any action being performed.

The Copy and Cut menu items are processed in a similar manner as the New and Open menu items. Selecting Copy or Cut menu items results in the Paste menu item being enabled.

The Find menu item causes the Find Next and Find Previous menu items to be enabled.

The handling of the About Menu Madness menu item shows how an entire menu can be disabled.

Popup Menus

In addition to the traditional menus that are pulled down from a menu bar, Java 1.1 provides support of popup menus. Popup menus are menus that appear when you perform a mouse action that triggers these menus. In Windows 95 platforms, this is the right-button click. Try right-clicking on your Windows 95 desktop. This should cause a popup menu to be displayed.

Popup menus are supported via the `PopupMenu` class, which is a subclass of the `Menu` class. This class provides two constructors—a default parameterless constructor and a constructor that takes a `String` parameter. The `String` parameter is used as the popup menu's title. In Windows 95, the title is not displayed.

The `show()` method of the `PopupMenu` class causes a popup menu to be displayed. Its arguments are the `Component` object in which the menu is to be popped up and the x- and y-coordinates where the menu is to be placed (relative to the component).

Additional support of popup menus is provided in the `MouseEvent` and `ComponentEvent` classes of the `java.awt.event` package. The `isPopupTrigger()` method of `MouseEvent` is used to determine whether a mouse event is the native window event associated with popup menus. The `getComponent()` method of `ComponentEvent` returns the component in which a mouse event takes place. The use of popup menus is illustrated in the `PopupApp` program of Listing 25.4.

Listing 25.4. The source code of the PopupApp program.

```
import java.awt.*;
import java.awt.event.*;
import jdg.ch25.MyMenu;
import jdg.ch25.MyMenuBar;

public class PopupApp extends Frame {
 MyMenuBar menuBar;
 PopupMenu popup;
 PopupApp.EventHandler eh = new PopupApp.EventHandler();
 public static void main(String args[]){
  PopupApp app = new PopupApp();
 }
 public PopupApp() {
  super("PopupApp");
  setup();
  setSize(400,400);
  addWindowListener(eh);
  show();
 }
 void setup() {
  Object menuItems[][] = {{"File","Exit"}};
  menuBar = new MyMenuBar(menuItems,eh,eh);
  setMenuBar(menuBar);
  Panel panel = new Panel();
  popup = new PopupMenu("Popup");
  popup.add(new MenuItem("Item 1"));
  popup.add(new MenuItem("Item 2"));
  popup.add(new MenuItem("Item 3"));
  panel.add(popup);
  panel.addMouseListener(new MouseHandler());
  add(panel,"Center");
 }
 class MouseHandler extends MouseAdapter {
  public void mouseReleased(MouseEvent e) {
   if(e.isPopupTrigger()){
    popup.show(e.getComponent(), e.getX(), e.getY());
   }
  }
 }
 class EventHandler extends WindowAdapter implements ActionListener,
   ItemListener {
  public void actionPerformed(ActionEvent e){
   String selection=e.getActionCommand();
   if("Exit".equals(selection)){
    System.exit(0);
   }
  }
  public void itemStateChanged(ItemEvent e){
  }
  public void windowClosing(WindowEvent e){
   System.exit(0);
  }
 }
}
```

When you run the PopupApp program, right-click anywhere in the program's window area and a popup menu similar to the one shown in Figure 25.9 is displayed.

FIGURE 25.9.
Creating a popup menu.

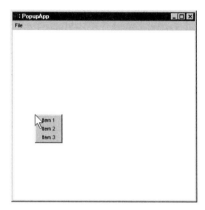

The PopupApp class declares the menuBar variable for referencing the program's menu bar, the popup variable for holding the popup menu, and the eh variable for performing most of the event handling. The main() method and constructor are similar to those that we've used with previous window programs.

The setup() method creates a menu bar using the MyMenuBar class that you studied earlier in this chapter. A panel is created to provide a GUI component to which the popup menu is added. A popup menu is created with the name Popup. Three menu items are also created and added to the popup menu. The PopupMenu object is then added to the Panel object. A MouseHandler object is created to handle mouse events associated with the Panel object. Finally, the Panel object is added to the center of the application window.

The MouseHandler inner class extends the MouseAdapter class in order to handle mouse-related events. It overrides the mouseReleased() method so that it can process the mouse event associated with popup menus on Windows 95. MouseHandler invokes the isPopupTrigger() method of the MouseEvent class to determine whether the mouse event is the correct event for displaying a popup menu. If it is the correct event, MouseHandler invokes the show() method to display the popup menu. The getComponent(), getX(), and getY() methods are used to retrieve the information needed from the MouseEvent in order to correctly display the menu.

The EventHandler class handles events associated with program termination.

Working with Buttons

Buttons are one of the easiest GUI components to use in a Java window program. You create them using the Button constructor and add them to your program using the add() method of their container. After that, all you need to do is handle their events.

The ButtonBar Class

To do something a little bit creative with labels, you can design a ButtonBar class. This class creates a dialog box with a specified label and adds a list of buttons to the dialog box, in the form of a button bar. It also allows the buttons in the button bar to be arranged in a vertical or horizontal fashion. The source code for the ButtonBar class is shown in Listing 25.5.

Listing 25.5. The source code of the ButtonBar class.

```
package jdg.ch25;

import java.awt.*;
import java.awt.event.*;

public class ButtonBar extends Dialog {
 public static int HORIZONTAL = 0;
 public static int VERTICAL = 1;
 public ButtonBar(Frame parent,String title,String labels[],
  int orientation,WindowListener wh,ActionListener bh) {
  super(parent,title,false);
  int length = labels.length;
  if(orientation == HORIZONTAL) setLayout(new GridLayout(1,length));
  else setLayout(new GridLayout(length,1));
  for(int i=0;i<length;++i){
   Button b=new Button(labels[i]);
   b.addActionListener(bh);
   add(b);
  }
  pack();
  addWindowListener(wh);
 }
}
```

The HORIZONTAL and VERTICAL constants are used to specify the orientation of the button bar. The constructor uses the parent, title, labels, orientation, wh, and bh parameters. The parent and title parameters are passed to the Dialog class constructor via the super() constructor call statement. The false value indicates that the button bar is not modal. The orientation parameter is used to determine the type of GridLayout associated with the button bar. After the orientation is specified, the Button objects, whose labels are specified by the labels array, are added to the button bar. The ActionListener object passed via bh is set up as the buttons' event handler. The button bar dialog box is then packed and the WindowListener object passed via wh is set up as the dialog box's event handler.

The ButtonApp Program

The ButtonApp program illustrates the operation of the ButtonBar class. Its source code is shown in Listing 25.6.

Listing 25.6. The source code of the `ButtonApp` program.

```java
import java.awt.*;
import java.awt.event.*;
import jdg.ch25.MyMenu;
import jdg.ch25.MyMenuBar;
import jdg.ch25.ButtonBar;

public class ButtonApp extends Frame {
 MyMenuBar menuBar;
 ButtonBar buttonBar;
 public static void main(String args[]){
  ButtonApp app = new ButtonApp();
 }
 public ButtonApp() {
  super("ButtonApp");
  setup();
  setSize(400,400);
  show();
  addWindowListener(new WindowEventHandler());
 }
 void setup() {
  setupMenuBar();
  String buttons[] = {"this","is","a","test"};
  ButtonBarHandler bbh = new ButtonBarHandler();
  buttonBar = new ButtonBar(this,"Button Bar",buttons,
   ButtonBar.HORIZONTAL,bbh,bbh);
 }
 void setupMenuBar(){
  Object menuItems[][] = {
   {"File","Exit"},
   {"View","-Button Bar"},
  };
  MenuItemHandler meh = new MenuItemHandler();
  menuBar = new MyMenuBar(menuItems,meh,meh);
  setMenuBar(menuBar);
 }
 class ButtonBarHandler extends WindowAdapter implements ActionListener {
  public void actionPerformed(ActionEvent e){
  }
  public void windowClosing(WindowEvent e){
  }
 }
 class MenuItemHandler implements ActionListener, ItemListener {
  public void actionPerformed(ActionEvent ev){
   String s=ev.getActionCommand();
   if(s=="Exit"){
    System.exit(0);
   }
  }
  public void itemStateChanged(ItemEvent e){
   buttonBar.setVisible(!buttonBar.isShowing());
  }
 }
 class WindowEventHandler extends WindowAdapter {
  public void windowClosing(WindowEvent e){
   System.exit(0);
  }
 }
}
```

When you execute `ButtonApp`, it displays the opening window, shown in Figure 25.10.

FIGURE 25.10.

The `ButtonApp`
opening window.

Select Button Bar from the View menu, as shown in Figure 25.11.

FIGURE 25.11.

Selecting Button Bar
from the View menu.

The button bar shown in Figure 25.12 is displayed on top of the main `ButtonApp` window. If you select the View menu once more, you will notice that the Button Bar menu item is implemented as a pull-down menu. It is checked or unchecked depending on whether the button bar is displayed.

The `ButtonApp` program consists mostly of setup and event-handling software. It declares two variables, `menuBar` and `buttonBar`, that are used to reference the program's menu bar and the button bar. The constructor follows the typical approach to constructing a frame window and creates a 400×400 window with the `ButtonApp` title.

FIGURE 25.12.
The button bar.

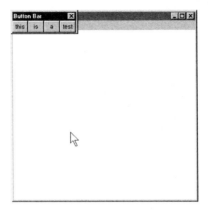

The setup() method invokes setupMenuBar() to create a menu bar using the MyMenuBar class and constructs a horizontal button bar using the ButtonBar class constructor introduced in the previous section. The rest of the program consists of event handling.

The ButtonBarEventHandler class is used to handle events associated with the button bar. It implements the WindowAdapter interface so that it can handle window-related events associated with the button bar. Note that it does nothing in response to the window closing event. This forces the user to use the View menu to hide or show the button bar. ButtonBarEventHandler also implements the ActionListener interface. This allows it to handle the events associated with the clicking of the individual buttons of the button bar via the actionPerformed() method.

Using Dialog Boxes

The ButtonBar class illustrates some of the typical methods used with dialog boxes. Most of these methods are not specific to the Dialog class, which provides few methods of its own. Rather, they are inherited from the Window and Component superclasses of the Dialog class.

The Dialog class is used to construct a window that is displayed separately from the application menu. The window associated with a Dialog object is not allowed to contain a menu bar. It may be specified as being *modal*, meaning that it is displayed on top of the main application window until it is hidden or disposed of using the show() and dispose() methods. Most dialog boxes are not as elaborate as that made with the ButtonBar class. They are mainly used to display information to the user and get the user's response via a button click.

The MessageDialog Class

The MessageDialog class provides a custom component that implements the most common types of dialog boxes. Its source code is shown in Listing 25.7.

Listing 25.7. The source code of the MessageDialog class.

```
package jdg.ch25;

import java.awt.*;
import java.awt.event.*;

public class MessageDialog extends Dialog {
 public MessageDialog(Frame parent,String title,boolean modal,String text[],
  String buttons[], WindowListener wh, ActionListener bh) {
  super(parent,title,modal);
  int textLines = text.length;
  int numButtons = buttons.length;
  Panel textPanel = new Panel();
  Panel buttonPanel = new Panel();
  textPanel.setLayout(new GridLayout(textLines,1));
  for(int i=0;i<textLines;++i) textPanel.add(new Label(text[i]));
  for(int i=0;i<numButtons;++i){
   Button b = new Button(buttons[i]);
   b.addActionListener(bh);
   buttonPanel.add(b);
  }
  add("North",textPanel);
  add("South",buttonPanel);
  setBackground(Color.lightGray);
  setForeground(Color.black);
  pack();
  addWindowListener(wh);
 }
}
```

The MessageDialog constructor uses the parent, title, modal, text, buttons, wh, and bh parameters. The parent, title, and modal parameters are passed to the Dialog constructor of their parent class. Two Panel objects are created and assigned to textPanel and buttonPanel. The textPanel layout is specified as a GridLayout object and the buttonPanel layout is the default FlowLayout object. The text lines are arranged in a vertical grid in the textPanel. The buttons are laid out in a centered horizontal fashion within the buttonPanel. The layout for the MessageDialog object is BorderLayout, by default. The ActionListener object passed via bh is set up as the event handler for each button. The textPanel is added to the top of the dialog box, and the buttonPanel is added to the bottom. The foreground and background colors are set to light gray and black. The dialog box is packed and the WindowListener object passed via wh is set up as the event handler for the dialog box.

The MessageApp Program

The MessageApp program shows how the MessageDialog class can be used to implement traditional dialog box functions found in typical window programs. Its source code is shown in Listing 25.8.

Listing 25.8. The source code of the MessageApp program.

```
import java.awt.*;
import java.awt.event.*;
import jdg.ch25.MyMenu;
import jdg.ch25.MyMenuBar;
import jdg.ch25.MessageDialog;

public class MessageApp extends Frame {
 MyMenuBar menuBar;
 MessageDialog dialog;
 DialogHandler dh = new DialogHandler();
 public static void main(String args[]){
  MessageApp app = new MessageApp();
 }
 public MessageApp() {
  super("MessageApp");
  setup();
  setSize(400,400);
  addWindowListener(new WindowEventHandler());
  show();
 }
 void setup() {
  Object menuItems[][] = {
   {"File","Exit"},
   {"View","Information","Confirmation","Selection"},
  };
  MenuItemHandler mih = new MenuItemHandler();
  menuBar = new MyMenuBar(menuItems,mih,mih);
  setMenuBar(menuBar);
 }
 class MenuItemHandler implements ActionListener, ItemListener {
  public void actionPerformed(ActionEvent ev){
   String s=ev.getActionCommand();
   if(s=="Exit"){
    System.exit(0);
   }else if(s=="Information"){
    String text[] = {"Don't look now, but your shoelace is untied."};
    String buttons[] = {"OK"};
    dialog = new MessageDialog(MessageApp.this,"Information",true,
    text,buttons,dh,dh);
    dialog.show();
   }else if(s=="Confirmation"){
    String text[] = {"Do you really want to do this?"};
    String buttons[] = {"Yes","No","Cancel"};
    dialog = new MessageDialog(MessageApp.this,"Confirmation",true,
    text,buttons,dh,dh);
    dialog.show();
   }else if(s=="Selection"){
    String text[] = {"What direction do you want to go?",
     "North: cold", "South: warm", "East: humid", "West: arid"};
    String buttons[] = {"North","South","East","West"};
    dialog = new MessageDialog(MessageApp.this,"Selection",true,
    text,buttons,dh,dh);
    dialog.show();
```

continues

Listing 25.8. continued

```
  }
 }
 public void itemStateChanged(ItemEvent e){
 }
}
class WindowEventHandler extends WindowAdapter {
 public void windowClosing(WindowEvent e){
  System.exit(0);
 }
}
class DialogHandler extends WindowAdapter implements ActionListener {
 public void windowClosing(WindowEvent e){
  dialog.dispose();
 }
 public void actionPerformed(ActionEvent e){
  dialog.dispose();
 }
 }
}
```

The MessageApp opening window is shown in Figure 25.13. It supports the File and View pull-down menus.

FIGURE 25.13.

The MessageApp
opening window.

Select the Information menu item from the View pull-down menu, as shown in Figure 25.14.

A helpful Information dialog box is displayed, as shown in Figure 25.15. This type of dialog box is typically used to provide information to the user. When the dialog box is displayed, the user acknowledges the information by clicking the OK button.

FIGURE 25.14.

Selecting Information from the View menu.

FIGURE 25.15.

The Information dialog box.

Selecting Confirmation from the View menu results in a Confirmation dialog box being displayed to the user, as shown in Figure 25.16. This type of dialog box requests confirmation from the user before attempting to perform an operation that may require the user's approval. If the user clicks the Yes button, the action is performed. If the user clicks No, the operation is not performed. If the user clicks Cancel, an entire series of actions leading up to the confirmation dialog box is aborted.

Choosing the Selection menu item from the View menu results in a multiple-choice Selection dialog box displayed to the user. The user is allowed to pick one from several alternative paths of program execution. (See Figure 25.17.)

FIGURE 25.16.

The Confirmation dialog box.

FIGURE 25.17.

The Selection dialog box.

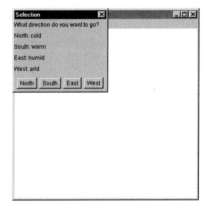

The MessageApp constructor creates a 400×400 window, titled MessageApp. It uses the MyMenuBar class to construct the program's menu bar. No special processing of note is performed in the application window's construction. The dialog boxes, previously shown, are created by the program's event-handling software.

The MenuItemHandler class handles the events associated with the program's menu bar. The Exit menu item is handled by terminating the program. If the Information menu item is selected, a new MessageDialog object is created with the information shown in Figure 25.15 and the dialog box is displayed to the user using the show() method. The dialog box is modal. The Confirmation and Selection menu items are handled in a similar manner. They create the dialog boxes shown in Figures 25.16 and 25.17 using the MessageDialog() constructor.

The event handling for each dialog box is performed by the DialogHandler class. This class simply disposes of the dialog box when a window or action event occurs.

The `FileDialog` Class

The `FileDialog` class is a custom subclass of the `Dialog` class. The `FileDialog` class uses the operating system's native dialog boxes to query the user for the name of a file to be loaded or saved. The `getDirectory()` and `getFile()` methods return the file's directory and filename. The `setDirectory()` and `setFile()` methods are used to set the state of the dialog box to a particular directory and file when it is initially opened. The `getMode()` method returns the LOAD or SAVE mode of the dialog box. The `setFileNameFilter()` and `getFileNameFilter()` methods are used to associate an object of the `FileNameFilter` interface with the dialog box. The `TextEdit` example in Chapter 23 illustrates the use of the `FileDialog` class in performing file load and save operations.

Summary

This chapter shows you how to use the `Menu`, `Button`, and `Dialog` classes. It describes the available menu and button options and shows you how to quickly and easily construct menus and buttons for your window programs using the `MyMenu`, `MyMenuBar`, and `ButtonBar` classes. The use of dialog boxes is also covered. You created the `MessageDialog` class, which you can also reuse in other programs. Chapter 26, "Checkboxes, Choices, and Lists," shows you how to work with those elements.

26

Checkboxes, Choices, and Lists

This chapter covers the details of using the Checkbox, Choice, and List classes. It shows you how to create and use objects of these classes and how to create custom components that simplify the use of these GUI controls. When you finish this chapter, you will be able to effectively use checkboxes, radio buttons, choices, and lists in your Java window programs.

Using Checkboxes

Checkboxes are a common type of GUI control. They are typically used in form-like windows to simplify yes/no or true/false selections. The user checks a checkbox to indicate yes or true, and leaves it unchecked to indicate no or false.

The name of the Checkbox class is somewhat misleading in that Checkbox objects are used to implement traditional checkboxes as well as radio buttons.

Radio buttons are similar to traditional checkboxes in that they are in either an on or off state. They are different from traditional checkboxes in that only one radio button in a group may be on at a given time. They are aptly named after a car radio's buttons, which can only be used to select a single radio channel at a given time.

When Checkbox objects are used as radio buttons, they are associated with a CheckboxGroup object that enforces mutual exclusion among the Checkbox objects in its group.

The CheckboxPanel Class

Checkboxes, like menus, are easy to use but tedious to construct and organize. The CheckboxPanel class provides a more convenient approach to creating and organizing checkboxes. (See Listing 26.1.) Typically, checkboxes are created in groups and organized in a panel that is given a title. The CheckboxPanel class provides a constructor for quickly creating objects of this type. It also provides access methods for getting and setting the value of an individual checkbox within the panel, based on the checkbox's label.

Listing 26.1. The CheckboxPanel class source code.

```
package jdg.ch26;

import java.awt.*;
import java.awt.event.*;

public class CheckboxPanel extends Panel {
 public static int HORIZONTAL = 0;
 public static int VERTICAL = 1;
 public CheckboxPanel(String title,String labels[],int orientation,
   ItemListener ih) {
  super();
  int length = labels.length;
  if(orientation == HORIZONTAL) setLayout(new GridLayout(1,length+1));
  else setLayout(new GridLayout(length+1,1));
```

```
   add(new Label(title));
   for(int i=0;i<length;++i){
    Checkbox ch = new Checkbox(labels[i]);
    ch.addItemListener(ih);
    add(ch);
   }
  }
 public CheckboxPanel(String title,String labels[],boolean state[],
  int orientation,ItemListener ih) {
  super();
  int length = labels.length;
  if(orientation == HORIZONTAL) setLayout(new GridLayout(1,length+1));
  else setLayout(new GridLayout(length+1,1));
  add(new Label(title));
  for(int i=0;i<length;++i){
   Checkbox ch = new Checkbox(labels[i]);
   ch.setState(state[i]);
   ch.addItemListener(ih);
   add(ch);
  }
 }
 public boolean getState(String label) {
  Checkbox boxes[] = (Checkbox[])getComponents();
  for(int i=0;i<boxes.length;++i)
   if(label.equals(boxes[i].getLabel())) return boxes[i].getState();
  return false;
 }
 public void setState(String label,boolean state) {
  Checkbox boxes[] = (Checkbox[])getComponents();
  for(int i=0;i<boxes.length;++i)
   if(label.equals(boxes[i].getLabel())) boxes[i].setState(state);
 }
}
```

Two CheckboxPanel constructors are provided. The first constructor uses a title string for the panel, an array of labels[] to be associated with checkboxes, an orientation parameter that specifies whether the panel is to be organized in a vertical or horizontal fashion, and an ItemListener object that is to be used to handle checkbox events.

A GridLayout object is used to organize the Label and Checkbox objects placed within the panel. The title Label is added at the top of vertical panels and on the left side of horizontal panels. Then the checkboxes are created, one at a time, and fill in the rest of the panel.

The second constructor is similar to the first constructor, except that it uses an additional state[] array to set the initial state of the checkboxes that are added to the panel. The state of each checkbox is set using the setState() method of the Checkbox class.

The getState() method takes the label of a checkbox as its parameter and searches the checkboxes contained in the panel for one whose label matches the specified label. It then returns the state of this checkbox. If no matching checkbox is found, it returns false.

The setState() method is similar to the getState() method. It is used to update a checkbox with a given label.

Working with Radio Buttons

Radio buttons are created using the Checkbox class and are transformed from checkboxes into radio buttons when they are associated with a CheckboxGroup object. A CheckboxGroup can be assigned with the Checkbox constructor or using the setCheckboxGroup() method. Only one object in the checkbox group is allowed to be set at any given time.

The CheckboxGroupPanel Class

The CheckboxGroupPanel class extends the CheckboxPanel class to work with radio buttons. Its source code is shown in Listing 26.2.

Listing 26.2. The source code for the CheckboxGroupPanel class.

```
package jdg.ch26;

import java.awt.*;
import java.awt.event.*;

public class CheckboxGroupPanel extends CheckboxPanel {
 public CheckboxGroupPanel(String title,String labels[],int orientation,
   ItemListener ih) {
  super(title,labels,orientation,ih);
  putInGroup();
 }
 public CheckboxGroupPanel(String title,String labels[],boolean state[],
   int orientation, ItemListener ih) {
  super(title,labels,state,orientation,ih);
  putInGroup();
 }
 void putInGroup() {
  Component components[] = getComponents();
  int length = components.length;
  CheckboxGroup group = new CheckboxGroup();
  for(int i=1;i<length;++i){
   Checkbox checkBox = (Checkbox) components[i];
   checkBox.setCheckboxGroup(group);
  }
 }
}
```

The Checkbox panel constructors are overridden to place the checkboxes in the panel of a single group. If the second constructor is used, only one checkbox should be specified as being in the "on" state.

The putInGroup() method uses the getComponents() method inherited from the Container class to create an array of the components contained in the panel. It creates a CheckboxGroup object and then indexes through the array, putting all checkboxes into this group using the setCheckboxGroup() method. The first component is skipped because it is the title of the panel.

The CheckboxApp Program

The CheckboxApp program illustrates the use of the CheckboxPanel and CheckboxGroupPanel classes.
Its source code is shown in Listing 26.3.

Listing 26.3. The source code for the CheckboxApp program.

```
import java.awt.*;
import java.awt.event.*;
import jdg.ch25.MyMenu;
import jdg.ch25.MyMenuBar;
import jdg.ch26.CheckboxPanel;
import jdg.ch26.CheckboxGroupPanel;

public class CheckboxApp extends Frame {
 MyMenuBar menuBar;
 CheckboxPanel checkboxPanel;
 CheckboxGroupPanel checkboxGroupPanel;
 TextArea textArea = new TextArea(5,20);
 public static void main(String args[]){
  CheckboxApp app = new CheckboxApp();
 }
 public CheckboxApp() {
  super("CheckboxApp");
  setup();
  pack();
  show();
  addWindowListener(new WindowEventHandler());
 }
 void setup() {
  setupMenuBar();
  setupCheckboxes();
 }
 void setupMenuBar(){
  Object menuItems[][] = {
   {"File","Exit"},
  };
  MenuItemHandler mih = new MenuItemHandler();
  menuBar = new MyMenuBar(menuItems,mih,mih);
  setMenuBar(menuBar);
 }
 void setupCheckboxes(){
  CheckboxHandler ch = new CheckboxHandler();
  String sports[] = {"Baseball","Basketball","Football","Hockey","Soccer"};
  checkboxPanel = new CheckboxPanel("What team sports do you like?  ",
   sports,CheckboxPanel.VERTICAL,ch);
  add(checkboxPanel,"West");
  String ages[] = {"under 20","20 - 39","40 - 59","60 - 79","80 and over"};
  checkboxGroupPanel = new CheckboxGroupPanel("What is your age?  ",
   ages,CheckboxPanel.VERTICAL,ch);
  add(checkboxGroupPanel,"East");
  add(textArea,"South");
 }
 class CheckboxHandler implements ItemListener {
  public void itemStateChanged(ItemEvent e){
```

continues

Listing 26.3. continued

```
  String status;
  Checkbox checkbox = (Checkbox) e.getItemSelectable();
  if(checkbox.getState()) status = "You checked: ";
  else status = "You unchecked: ";
  status+=checkbox.getLabel();
  textArea.setText(status);
 }
}
class MenuItemHandler implements ActionListener, ItemListener {
 public void actionPerformed(ActionEvent ev){
  String s=ev.getActionCommand();
  if(s=="Exit"){
   System.exit(0);
  }
 }
 public void itemStateChanged(ItemEvent e){
 }
}
class WindowEventHandler extends WindowAdapter {
 public void windowClosing(WindowEvent e){
  System.exit(0);
 }
}
}
```

When you execute the program, it displays the window shown in Figure 26.1. The left side of the window displays a `CheckboxPanel` object and the right side displays a `CheckboxPanelGroup` object. Notice that traditional checkboxes are displayed on the left and radio buttons are displayed on the right. The bottom of the panel contains a `TextArea` object that is used to display the results of user-generated checkbox events.

FIGURE 26.1.

The `CheckboxApp`
opening window.

Click in the Basketball checkbox, as shown in Figure 26.2. The checkbox is checked and the text area is updated as the result of handling this event. Click on the Basketball checkbox again and the text area is updated, as shown in Figure 26.3.

Go ahead and check your favorite sports and then turn your attention to the radio buttons. Select your age group, as shown in Figure 26.4. The program notifies you of your selection. Go ahead and select another age group, as shown in Figure 26.5. Notice that you can't select more than one age group at a given time. That's the idea behind radio buttons.

FIGURE 26.2.
Checking Basketball.

FIGURE 26.3.
Unchecking Basketball.

FIGURE 26.4.
Select your age group.

FIGURE 26.5.
Now select a different age group.

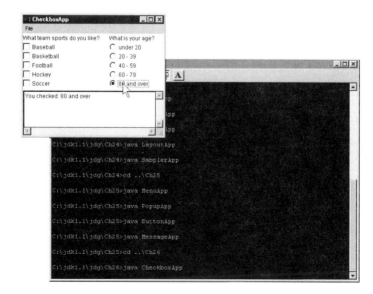

The CheckboxApp program makes use of several custom components that you've built so far, including the MyMenu, MyMenuBar, CheckboxPanel, and CheckboxGroupPanel classes. Try rewriting this program without using these classes and you'll find out how time-consuming and tedious it can be to write programs without custom classes. You should now be getting used to using this class-building approach to simplify your Java programming.

The setupCheckboxes() method sets up the checkbox and radio button panels displayed in the previous figures. The default BorderLayout object is used to organize the main application window. The checkboxPanel variable is assigned the CheckboxPanel object that is created using the sports array, and the checkboxGroupPanel variable is assigned the CheckboxGroupPanel object that is created using the ages array. Both panels are added to the Frame object being constructed. Then the TextArea object is added. That's all the code required to create the GUI controls shown in Figure 26.1.

The CheckboxHandler class handles the events associated with checking and unchecking checkboxes. Its itemStateChanged() method invokes the getItemSelectable() method of the ItemEvent class to access the checkbox for which the event is associated. It uses the getState() method of the Checkbox class to determine whether the checkbox was checked or unchecked. It then uses the getLabel() method of the Checkbox class to retrieve the label associated with the checkbox.

Making Choices

The Choice class allows Motif-style choice lists to be used in Java window programs. These GUI controls are also supported in Windows 95 and NT programs. A *choice list* is a pull-down menu that allows a user to select a single item from a list. When a choice selection is made, an ItemEvent is generated and the program is then able to respond to that selection. Choices are like menus that are placed in the middle of a window.

The MyChoice Class

MyChoice is a short and sweet class that simplifies the construction of a Choice object. Its source code is shown in Listing 26.4.

Listing 26.4. The source code for the MyChoice class.

```
package jdg.ch26;

import java.awt.*;

public class MyChoice extends Choice {
 public MyChoice(String labels[]) {
  super();
  int length = labels.length;
  for(int i=0;i<length;++i) {
```

```
  try {
   addItem(labels[i]);
  }catch (NullPointerException ex) {
   addItem("");
  }
 }
 }
}
```

Rather than constructing a `Choice` object and adding all of the items in the choice list, the `MyChoice` constructor takes an array of labels and adds them to the `Choice` object as it is constructed. The `addItem()` method of the `Choice` class throws the `NullPointerException` and is handled by adding a blank item to the choice list when a `null` pointer is encountered.

Selecting from Lists

The `List` class is a tad more sophisticated than the `Choice` class. It is similar in that it allows a user to select from a list of items that are displayed in a window component. It is different because it provides the capability to support multiple item selections within the list, to specify the size of the list window, and to dynamically update the list during program execution.

The `List` class provides two constructors. The default constructor takes no parameters. The second constructor specifies the number of visible rows to be displayed and whether multiple selections are allowed.

The access methods supported by the `List` class are also more extensive than the `Choice` class. In particular, the `delItem()` and `replaceItem()`methods allow `List` objects to be dynamically updated.

The `MyList` Class

The `MyList` class is similar to the `MyChoice` class in that it enables a list to be constructed using an array of list items. (See Listing 26.5.) The `MyList` constructor also allows the number of rows displayed in the list and the multiple-selection parameter to be specified.

Listing 26.5. The source code for the `MyList` class.

```
package jdg.ch26;

import java.awt.*;

public class MyList extends List {
 public MyList(int rows,boolean multiple,String labels[]) {
  super(rows,multiple);
  int length = labels.length;
  for(int i=0;i<length;++i) {
```

continues

Listing 26.5. continued

```
  try {
    addItem(labels[i]);
  }catch (NullPointerException ex) {
    addItem("");
  }
 }
}
}
```

The ChoiceListApp Program

The ChoiceListApp program illustrates the use of the MyChoice and MyList classes. (See Listing 26.6.) It provides the capability to decide what you want to eat for your next meal and can be very handy when a moment of indecision arrives. The following source code lists only a basic set of menu items, but additional menu items can be added easily.

Listing 26.6. The source code for the ChoiceListApp program.

```
import java.awt.*;
import java.awt.event.*;
import jdg.ch25.MyMenu;
import jdg.ch25.MyMenuBar;
import jdg.ch26.MyChoice;
import jdg.ch26.MyList;

public class ChoiceListApp extends Frame {
 MyMenuBar menuBar;
 MyChoice mealChoice;
 MyList currentList;
 MyList mealList[];
 String meals[] = {"Breakfast","Lunch","Dinner"};
 String mealChoices[][] = {
  {"pancakes","eggs","bacon","ham","sausage","cereal",
   "toast","coffee","juice"},
  {"pizza","hamburger","hot dog","burrito","salad","fries",
   "chips","soda","milk"},
  {"spaghetti","carne asada","barbequed chicken","soup","salad",
   "bread","wine","beer","soda","milk"}
 };
 TextField text;
 public static void main(String args[]){
  ChoiceListApp app = new ChoiceListApp();
 }
 public ChoiceListApp() {
  super("ChoiceListApp");
  setup();
  setSize(275,175);
  addWindowListener(new WindowEventHandler());
  show();
 }
```

```
void setup() {
 setupMenuBar();
 setupChoice();
 setupLists();
 text = new TextField(40);
 add("North",new Label("Place your order:"));
 add("South",text);
 add("West",mealChoice);
 currentList = mealList[0];
 add("East",currentList);
}
void setupMenuBar(){
 Object menuItems[][] = {
  {"File","Exit"},
 };
 MenuItemHandler mih = new MenuItemHandler();
 menuBar = new MyMenuBar(menuItems,mih,mih);
 setMenuBar(menuBar);
}
void setupChoice(){
 mealChoice = new MyChoice(meals);
 mealChoice.addItemListener(new ChoiceHandler());
}
void setupLists(){
 mealList = new MyList[meals.length];
 ListHandler lh = new ListHandler();
 for(int i=0;i<meals.length;++i){
  mealList[i] = new MyList(5,true,mealChoices[i]);
  mealList[i].addItemListener(lh);
 }
}
class ChoiceHandler implements ItemListener {
 public void itemStateChanged(ItemEvent e){
  for(int i=0;i<meals.length;++i)
   if(meals[i].equals(mealChoice.getSelectedItem())){
    ChoiceListApp.this.remove(currentList);
    currentList = mealList[i];
    ChoiceListApp.this.add("East",currentList);
    text.setText(meals[i]);
   }
  ChoiceListApp.this.show();
 }
}
class ListHandler implements ItemListener {
 public void itemStateChanged(ItemEvent e){
  String order = mealChoice.getSelectedItem()+": ";
  String items[] = currentList.getSelectedItems();
  for(int i=0;i<items.length;++i) order += items[i]+" ";
  text.setText(order);
 }
}
class MenuItemHandler implements ActionListener, ItemListener {
 public void actionPerformed(ActionEvent ev){
  String s=ev.getActionCommand();
  if(s=="Exit"){
   System.exit(0);
  }
 }
```

continues

Listing 26.6. continued

```
public void itemStateChanged(ItemEvent e){
  }
}
class WindowEventHandler extends WindowAdapter {
 public void windowClosing(WindowEvent e){
  System.exit(0);
  }
 }
}
```

Make sure that you have food on hand when you run the ChoiceListApp program. Its opening window is shown in Figure 26.6.

FIGURE 26.6.

The ChoiceListApp *opening window.*

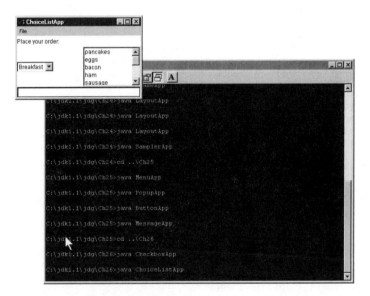

The choice list shown on the left side of the window is used to select a meal. This selection determines what menu items are displayed in the list shown on the right side of the window. More than one item can be selected from the entrée list. The text field on the bottom of the screen identifies the selections that you have made. Go ahead and select Lunch from the choice list, as shown in Figure 26.7. Notice that the entrée list is updated with some typical lunch items. The text field tells you that you are now ordering lunch.

FIGURE 26.7.

Selecting lunch.

Go ahead and select some menu items form the entrée list. They are displayed in the text field as shown in Figure 26.8.

FIGURE 26.8.
Ordering lunch.

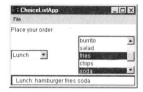

Now select Dinner from the choice list and select some dinner entrées, as shown in Figure 26.9. The text field is updated to list your new selections.

FIGURE 26.9.
Selecting another meal.

The `ChoiceListApp` program declares several field variables. The `menuBar` variable is the now-standard variable used to identify the program's menu bar. The `mealChoice` variable is used to refer to the `MyChoice` object that displays the meals identified in the `meals` array. Two `MyList` variables are declared. The `mealList` array holds the three `MyList` objects used for breakfast, lunch, and dinner. These items are stored in the `mealChoices` array. The `currentList` variable points to the current menu entrée list being displayed. The `text` variable refers to the `TextField` object displayed on the bottom of the window.

The `main()` method and `ChoiceListApp()` constructor follow the pattern that's been developed so far. The window is resized to make its display more visually appealing. A `GridBagLayout` layout would have been more appropriate for this type of application, but the overhead of implementing it would obscure the important points associated with the `MyChoice` and `MyList` classes.

The `setup()` method sets up the menu bar and then invokes the `setupChoice()` and `setupLists()` methods to set up the `MyChoice` and `MyList` objects. The text field is initialized to be 40 characters wide, and then the user interface objects are placed in the appropriate places in the `ChoiceListApp` window.

The `setupChoice()` method constructs the `mealChoice` object and sets up its event handler. The `setupLists()` method sets up the `mealList` object by indexing through the `mealChoices[]` array and setting up the individual `MyList` objects.

The `ChoiceHandler` inner class handles the events associated with the `MyChoice` object assigned to `mealChoice`. It does so by updating the `MyList` object displayed in the right side of the window. It uses the `remove()` method of the `Container` class to remove the currently displayed `MyList` object and then adds the `MyList` object corresponding to the selected meal choice. The `show()` method is invoked to update the window's display.

The `ListHandler` inner class handles the events associated with the meal lists that are implemented as `MyList` objects. It invokes the `getSelectedItem()` method of the `Choice` class to determine which meal was selected and the `getSelectedItems()` method of the `List` class to obtain an array containing the selected list items associated with the meal. It combines the meal choice and associated entrées into a string that is displayed in the `TextArea` object.

Summary

This chapter shows you how to use the `Checkbox`, `Choice`, and `List` classes. It describes their available constructors and access methods and shows you how to use them as the basis for creating custom GUI components. Chapter 27, "Text and Fonts," will show you how to work with these features.

27

Text and Fonts

This chapter covers the details of Java's text- and font-related classes. It shows how to use the TextComponent subclasses and how to display text with the canvas. It explains Java's use of fonts and shows how the Font and FontMetrics classes are used to provide custom control of text display. When you finish this chapter, you will be able to effectively use text and fonts in your Java window programs.

The Text Classes

You should now be fairly familiar with the text-related classes supported by Java because you've used TextArea and TextField objects in some of the examples presented so far. Let's review these classes and then you can learn how to use font-related classes to alter the way text is displayed to the user.

The TextComponent class is the superclass of the TextField and TextArea classes. It extends the Component class to support text-related processing. TextComponent provides several methods that are used to process text that is selected by the user. The setEditable() method determines whether a TextComponent object is read-only or can be edited. The getText() and setText()methods are its most popular methods and are used with all text-related classes.

The TextField class implements a simple, one-line text field. The visible length of the field (in characters) can be specified. Character echoing can be disabled to implement password-like text fields.

The TextArea class implements a multiple-line text field and supports a number of methods for updating the field by inserting, appending, and replacing text. The number of rows and columns associated with a text field can be specified.

Font Basics

The Font class provides a platform-independent method of specifying and using fonts. The Font class constructor constructs Font objects using the font's name, style (PLAIN, BOLD, ITALIC, or BOLD + ITALIC), and point size. Java's fonts are named in a platform-independent manner and then mapped to local fonts that are supported by the operating system on which it executes. The getName()method returns the logical Java font name of a particular font, and the getFamily() method returns the operating system–specific name of the font. You'll learn the name of the standard Java fonts in the first programming example of this chapter.

The FontMetrics class is used to return the specific parameters for a particular Font object. An object of this class is created using the getFontMetrics() methods supported by the Component class and other classes, such as the Graphics and Toolkit classes. The FontMetrics methods provide access to the details of the implementation of a Font object.

The `bytesWidth()`, `charWidth()`, `charsWidth()`, `getWidths()`, and `stringWidth()` methods are used to determine the width of a text object in pixels. These methods are essential for determining the horizontal position of text on the screen.

When text characters are displayed, they are displayed relative to a baseline. The *baseline* is the line drawn through the bottom of nondescending characters. For example, if you drew a line at the bottom of most text displayed on this line, you would get the text's baseline. Some characters, such as g and y, descend below the baseline. The number of pixels that the characters of a font descend below the baseline is known as the font's *descent*. The number of pixels that the characters of a font extend above the baseline is known as the font's *ascent*. In addition to a font's ascent and descent, a third parameter, referred to as the font's *leading*, is used to describe the amount of vertical spacing, in pixels, used between the descent of a line of text and the ascent of the line of text below it. The overall height of a font is the sum of its leading, ascent, and descent and is equal to the distance between baselines (in pixels) of vertically adjacent lines of text. The `getLeading()`, `getAscent()`, `getDescent()`, and `getHeight()` methods of the `FontMetrics` class are used to access these important font-related parameters. Figure 27.1 provides a graphical description of these parameters.

FIGURE 27.1.
Font parameters.

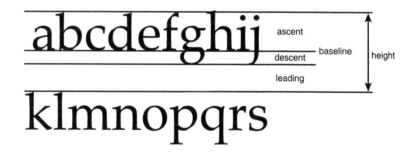

The `getMaxAdvance()`, `getMaxAscent()`, and `getMaxDescent()` methods are provided for backward compatibility with earlier Java versions.

Using the `Toolkit` Class

The `Toolkit` class provides a link between the platform-independent Java implementation and its platform-specific characteristics. Among the many interesting methods implemented by this class are the `getFontList()`, `getFontMetrics()`, `getScreenSize()`, and `getScreenResolution()` methods. The `getFontList()` method returns a list of fonts that are accessible from Java. The `getFontMetrics()` method identifies the font metrics for a particular font. The `getScreenSize()` method identifies the screen dimension in terms of horizontal and vertical dots. The `getScreenResolution()` method identifies the screen resolution in dots per inch.

The `getFontList()` is the method of interest for this chapter. In the next section, you'll use it to get a list of the fonts available to Java.

The FontApp Program

The FontApp program illustrates the use of the Font, FontMetrics, and Toolkit classes and shows you how to draw text on a Graphics object. Its source code is shown in Listing 27.1.

Listing 27.1. The source code of the FontApp program.

```
import java.awt.*;
import java.awt.event.*;
import jdg.ch25.*;

public class FontApp extends Frame {
 MyMenuBar menuBar;
 Toolkit toolkit;
 Font defaultFont;
 String fontNames[];
 int screenWidth = 400;
 int screenHeight = 500;
 public static void main(String args[]){
  FontApp app = new FontApp();
 }
 public FontApp() {
  super("FontApp");
  setup();
  setSize(screenWidth,screenHeight);
  addWindowListener(new WindowEventHandler());
  show();
 }
 void setup() {
  setupMenuBar();
  setMenuBar(menuBar);
  setupFonts();
 }
 void setupMenuBar() {
  String menuItems[][] = {{"File","Exit"}};
  MenuItemHandler mih = new MenuItemHandler();
  menuBar = new MyMenuBar(menuItems,mih,mih);
 }
 void setupFonts() {
  toolkit = getToolkit();
  defaultFont = getFont();
  fontNames = toolkit.getFontList();
 }
 public void paint(Graphics g) {
  int styles[] = {Font.PLAIN,Font.BOLD,Font.ITALIC};
  String styleNames[] = {"Plain","Bold","Italic"};
  int size = 12;
  int y=50;
  for(int i=0;i<fontNames.length;++i) {
   for(int j=0;j<styles.length;++j) {
    Font newFont = new Font(fontNames[i],styles[j],size);
    FontMetrics fm = g.getFontMetrics(newFont);
    g.setFont(newFont);
    String text = fontNames[i]+"-"+styleNames[j];
    int x = (screenWidth - fm.stringWidth(text))/2;
    g.drawString(text,x,y+fm.getLeading()+fm.getAscent());
```

```
  y += fm.getHeight();
  }
 }
}
class MenuItemHandler implements ActionListener, ItemListener {
 public void actionPerformed(ActionEvent ev){
  String s=ev.getActionCommand();
  if(s=="Exit"){
   System.exit(0);
  }
 }
 public void itemStateChanged(ItemEvent e){
 }
}
class WindowEventHandler extends WindowAdapter {
 public void windowClosing(WindowEvent e){
  System.exit(0);
 }
 }
}
```

The FontApp program does not provide much functionality. Just run it and it will display a list of the fonts that are currently available to Java, with each name written in its font. Figure 27.2 shows its display. The program's importance is not in what it does, but in how it does it. By closely examining this program, you'll be able to quickly come up to speed on working with Java fonts.

FIGURE 27.2.

The FontApp *opening window.*

The FontApp class declares a number of field variables. The toolkit variable is used to refer to the Toolkit object associated with the program window. The defaultFont variable identifies the default font used by the program. The `fontNames[]` array is used to store the names of the fonts that are accessible to Java.

The `setupFonts()` method obtains the `Toolkit` object associated with the program's window, using the `getToolkit()` method, and assigns this object to the `toolkit` variable. The current font used by the program is accessed by `getFont()` and assigned to the `defaultFont` variable. The `Toolkit` object is then used to obtain the current list of font names via the `getFontList()` method of the `Toolkit` class. That's all for the program's setup. The program's event handling is the standard Exit menu item and window closing event processing.

The `paint()` method is where the primary processing of interest takes place. The `styles[]` and `styleNames[]` arrays are used to identify the various text styles and their associated string descriptions. The `y` variable identifies the vertical screen position where text is displayed. The `size` variable identifies the point size used to display a font.

The `paint()` method uses two `for` statements. The outer statement iterates through the list of font names, and the inner statement iterates through the font styles. At each pass through the inner loop, a new font is created with the specified name, style, and size. The `getFontMetrics()` method of the `Graphics` class is used to obtain the `FontMetrics` object associated with the newly created font, and this object is assigned to the `fm` variable. The `setFont()` method of the `Graphics` class is used to set the current font to the new font.

The next line of text to be displayed is created by concatenating the font name and its style name. The horizontal position at which the text is to be displayed in order for it to be centered is calculated based upon the width of the text (in pixels) returned by the `stringWidth()` method of the `FontMetrics` class and the initial width of the program window. The vertical position where the text is to be displayed is its baseline and is determined by adding the leading and ascent values of the font with the `y` variable. These values are obtained using the `getLeading()` and `getAscent()` methods of the current `FontMetric` object. The `y` variable identifies the point of maximum descent of the previously displayed line of text. It is then updated for the current line of text by adding the height of the current font returned by the `getHeight()` method of the `FontMetric` class.

WYSIWYG Editors

The `Font` and `FontMetrics` classes are not confined to text that is drawn on `Graphics` objects. These classes can also be used with the `TextField` and `TextArea` classes. These classes automatically calculate the correct text-display locations using the native text objects supported by the local operating-system platform. In addition to changing text fonts, the `TextField` and `TextArea` classes also support the display of text using different foreground and background colors. The following program shows how fonts and colors can be quickly incorporated into a Java program to implement features associated with What-You-See-Is-What-You-Get (WYSIWYG) editors.

The EditApp Program

The EditApp program shows how the Font and Color classes can be incorporated into the TextEdit program introduced in Chapter 23, "Opening Windows." Its source code is shown in Listing 27.2.

The EditApp program uses the FontDialog and ColorDialog classes that are introduced in subsequent sections. In order to compile and run EditApp.java, you will need to type in the FontDialog.java and ColorDialog.java files. Java will automatically compile the FontDialog.java and ColorDialog.java files when EditApp.java is compiled.

Listing 27.2. The source code of the EditApp program.

```
import java.awt.*;
import java.awt.event.*;
import java.io.*;
import jdg.ch25.*;
import jdg.ch27.FontDialog;
import jdg.ch27.ColorDialog;

public class EditApp extends Frame {
 String programName;
 Object menuItems[][] = {
  {"File","New","Open","-","Save As","-","Exit"},
  {"Format","Font","Color"}
 };
 MenuItemHandler mih = new MenuItemHandler();
 MyMenuBar menuBar = new MyMenuBar(menuItems,mih,mih);
 TextArea text;
 FileDialog openFile = new FileDialog(this,"Open File",FileDialog.LOAD);
 FileDialog saveFile = new FileDialog(this,"Save File As",FileDialog.SAVE);
 MessageDialog notification;
 DialogHandler dh = new DialogHandler();
 FontDialog fd;
 ColorDialog cd;
 Font currentFont = new Font("Courier",Font.PLAIN,12);
 Color currentColor = Color.black;
 public static void main(String args[]){
  EditApp app = new EditApp();
 }
 public EditApp() {
  super("WYSIWYG Text Editor");
  programName = getTitle();
  setup();
  pack();
  addWindowListener(new WindowEventHandler());
  show();
 }
 void setup() {
  setBackground(Color.white);
  text = new TextArea(25,80);
  text.setFont(currentFont);
  text.addFocusListener(new FocusHandler());
  add("Center",text);
```

continues

Listing 27.2. continued

```java
  setMenuBar(menuBar);
  setCursor(new Cursor(TEXT_CURSOR));
 }
 public void readFile(String file) {
  BufferedReader inStream;
  try{
   inStream = new BufferedReader(new FileReader(file));
  }catch (IOException ex){
   notifyUser("Error opening file");
   return;
  }
  try{
   String newText="";
   String line;
   while((line=inStream.readLine())!=null)
    newText=newText+line+"\n";
   text.setText(newText);
   inStream.close();
  }catch (IOException ex){
   notifyUser("Error reading file");
  }
 }
 public void writeFile(String file) {
  BufferedWriter outStream;
  try{
   outStream = new BufferedWriter(new FileWriter(file));
  }catch (IOException ex){
   notifyUser("Error opening file");
   return;
  }
  try{
   outStream.write(text.getText());
   outStream.close();
  }catch (IOException ex){
   notifyUser("Error writing file");
  }
 }
 public void notifyUser(String s) {
  String text[] = {s};
  String buttons[] = {"OK"};
  notification = new MessageDialog(this,"Error",true,
   text,buttons,dh,dh);
 }
 class FocusHandler extends FocusAdapter {
  public void focusGained(FocusEvent e){
   setCursor(new Cursor(TEXT_CURSOR));
  }
  public void focusLost(FocusEvent e){
   setCursor(new Cursor(DEFAULT_CURSOR));
  }
 }
 class MenuItemHandler implements ActionListener, ItemListener {
  public void actionPerformed(ActionEvent ev){
   String s=ev.getActionCommand();
   if(s=="Exit"){
    System.exit(0);
   }else if(s=="New"){
```

```
   text.setText("");
  }else if(s=="Open"){
   openFile.show();
   String inFile = openFile.getFile();
   readFile(inFile);
  }else if(s=="Save As"){
   saveFile.show();
   String outFile = saveFile.getFile();
   writeFile(outFile);
  }else if(s=="Font"){
   fd = new FontDialog(EditApp.this,currentFont,
    new FontSelectHandler());
   fd.show();
  }else if(s=="Color"){
   cd = new ColorDialog(EditApp.this,currentColor,
    new ColorSelectHandler());
   cd.show();
  }
 }
 public void itemStateChanged(ItemEvent e){
 }
}
class FontSelectHandler implements ActionListener {
 public void actionPerformed(ActionEvent e){
  currentFont = fd.getFont();
  fd.dispose();
  text.setFont(currentFont);
 }
}
class ColorSelectHandler implements ActionListener {
 public void actionPerformed(ActionEvent e){
  currentColor = cd.getColor();
  cd.dispose();
  text.setForeground(currentColor);
  text.setText(text.getText());
  text.setVisible(true);
 }
}
class WindowEventHandler extends WindowAdapter {
 public void windowClosing(WindowEvent e){
  System.exit(0);
 }
}
class DialogHandler extends WindowAdapter implements ActionListener {
 public void windowClosing(WindowEvent e){
  notification.dispose();
 }
 public void actionPerformed(ActionEvent e){
  notification.dispose();
 }
}
}
```

The EditApp program displays the opening window shown in Figure 27.3.

FIGURE 27.3.

The EditApp *opening window.*

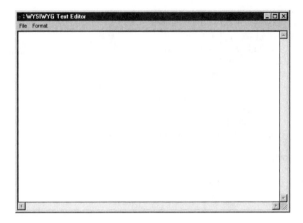

Select Open from the File menu, as shown in Figure 27.4, and use the Open File dialog box, shown in Figure 27.5, to open the EditApp.java source code file.

FIGURE 27.4.

The File menu.

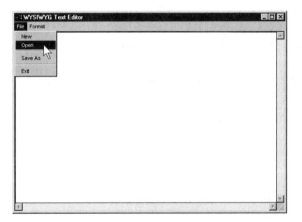

FIGURE 27.5.

The Open File dialog box.

The text of the EditApp.java source file is read into the program and displayed in the window using a 12-point Courier font, as shown in Figure 27.6.

FIGURE 27.6.
Editing
`EditApp.java.`

Select the Font menu item from the Format menu to change the current font used to display the text, as shown in Figure 27.7.

FIGURE 27.7.
The Format menu.

The Select a font: dialog box is displayed, as shown in Figure 27.8. Use this dialog box to select a 14-point Bold Italic Helvetica font, as shown in Figure 27.9.

The text's display is updated, as shown in Figure 27.10.

FIGURE 27.8.
The Select a font:
dialog box.

FIGURE 27.9.

Selecting a new font.

FIGURE 27.10.

Updated text.

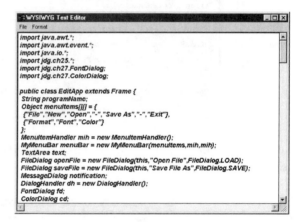

Select the Color menu item from the Format menu. The Select a color: dialog box is displayed, as shown in Figure 27.11. Use this dialog box to change the color associated with the text's display. Try using primary colors such as blue or green. Other colors might not display correctly, depending on the number of colors supported by your video card and the current color map associated with the display.

FIGURE 27.11.

The Select a color: dialog box.

The EditApp program makes use of the FontDialog and ColorDialog classes covered in the following sections. The basic functionality of the EditApp program remains the same as the TextEdit program. It has been streamlined to use the MyMenuBar and MyMenu classes and adds the fd and cd variables to refer to the FontDialog and ColorDialog objects created by the program.

The setup() method specifies that a TEXT_CURSOR should be used, by default, and extra event-handling code has been added to switch between the TEXT_CURSOR and the DEFAULT_CURSOR, depending on whether the cursor is in the locus of the text area or the menu bar.

The Notification class has been replaced by the MessageDialog class.

The main changes to the EditApp program are to its event handling. The FocusHandler class is used to handle the event associated with the TextArea object gaining and losing focus. The addFocusListener() method of the Component class is used in the setup() method to register an object of FocusHandler as the event handler for the TextArea object. FocusHandler overrides the focusGained() and focusLost() methods to switch the cursor between a TEXT_CURSOR and the DEFAULT_CURSOR.

The MenuItemHandler class handles menu item selections. The File menu items are handled in the same way as in Chapter 23. The Format menu contains the Font and Color menu items. The Font menu item results in a new FontDialog object being created to solicit the user to change the current font. You'll learn about this class in the next section. The Color menu item results in a ColorDialog object being created to provide the user with an opportunity to change the color of the current text. The ColorDialog class is covered later in the chapter.

The FontSelectHandler class handles the event that occurs when the user closes a font dialog box. This event is an event that you'll create in the FontDialog class. The actionPerformed() method invokes the getFont() method of the FontDialog class to retrieve the font selected by the user. It then disposes of the dialog box and sets the current font of the TextArea object to the retrieved font.

The ColorSelectHandler class handles the event that occurs when the user closes a color dialog box. You'll create this event in the ColorDialog class. The actionPerformed() method invokes the getColor() method of the ColorDialog class to retrieve the color selected by the user. It then disposes of the dialog box and sets the current color of the TextArea object to the retrieved font. The setText() and getText() methods are used to reset the text using the new color. The setVisible() method causes the TextArea object to be redisplayed.

The DialogHandler class is used to dispose of the dialog box displayed by objects of the MessageDialog class.

The FontDialog Class

The FontDialog class provides a handy encapsulation of the dialog boxes commonly used to select a font from the list of available fonts provided by the system. The source code of the FontDialog class is shown in Listing 27.3.

Listing 27.3. The source code of the FontDialog class.

```
package jdg.ch27;

import java.awt.*;
import java.awt.event.*;
import jdg.ch26.MyList;

public class FontDialog extends Dialog {
 String fontName;
```

continues

Listing 27.3. continued

```
int fontStyle;
int fontSize;
String fontNames[];
String styleNames[] = {"Plain","Bold","Italic","Bold Italic"};
String sizeNames[] = {"10","12","14","18","24","36","72"};
int styles[] = {Font.PLAIN,Font.BOLD,Font.ITALIC,Font.BOLD+Font.ITALIC};
int sizes[] = {10,12,14,18,24,36,72};
MyList fontList;
MyList styleList = new MyList(5,false,styleNames);
MyList sizeList = new MyList(5,false,sizeNames);
Toolkit toolkit;
Font newFont;
boolean fontChanged;
ActionListener ah;
public FontDialog(Frame parent,Font currentFont,ActionListener ah) {
 super(parent,"Select a font:",true);
 toolkit = parent.getToolkit();
 newFont = currentFont;
 setupFonts();
 setupPanels();
 setBackground(Color.lightGray);
 setForeground(Color.black);
 this.ah=ah;
 pack();
 addWindowListener(new WindowEventHandler());
}
void setupFonts() {
 fontName=newFont.getName();
 fontStyle=newFont.getStyle();
 fontSize=newFont.getSize();
 fontNames = toolkit.getFontList();
 fontList = new MyList(5,false,fontNames);
}
void setupPanels() {
 Panel mainPanel = new Panel();
 mainPanel.setLayout(new GridLayout(1,3));
 Panel fontPanel = new Panel();
 fontPanel.setLayout(new BorderLayout());
 Label fontLabel = new Label("Font:");
 fontPanel.add("North",fontLabel);
 fontPanel.add("Center",fontList);
 Panel stylePanel = new Panel();
 stylePanel.setLayout(new BorderLayout());
 Label styleLabel = new Label("Style:");
 stylePanel.add("North",styleLabel);
 stylePanel.add("Center",styleList);
 Panel sizePanel = new Panel();
 sizePanel.setLayout(new BorderLayout());
 Label sizeLabel = new Label("Size:");
 sizePanel.add("North",sizeLabel);
 sizePanel.add("Center",sizeList);
 mainPanel.add(fontPanel);
 mainPanel.add(stylePanel);
 mainPanel.add(sizePanel);
 Font plainFont = new Font("Helvetica",Font.PLAIN,12);
 Font boldFont = new Font("Helvetica",Font.BOLD,12);
 mainPanel.setFont(plainFont);
```

```
      fontLabel.setFont(boldFont);
      styleLabel.setFont(boldFont);
      sizeLabel.setFont(boldFont);
      Panel buttonPanel = new Panel();
      buttonPanel.setLayout(new FlowLayout());
      Button selectButton = new Button("Select");
      Button cancelButton = new Button("Cancel");
      ButtonHandler bh = new ButtonHandler();
      selectButton.addActionListener(bh);
      cancelButton.addActionListener(bh);
      buttonPanel.add(selectButton);
      buttonPanel.add(cancelButton);
      buttonPanel.setFont(boldFont);
      add("Center",mainPanel);
      add("South",buttonPanel);
   }
   public boolean isChanged() {
    return fontChanged;
   }
   public Font getFont() {
    return newFont;
   }
   void updateNewFont() {
    if(fontList.getSelectedIndex() != -1) fontName = fontList.getSelectedItem();
    if(styleList.getSelectedIndex() != -1)
     fontStyle = styles[styleList.getSelectedIndex()];
    if(sizeList.getSelectedIndex() != -1)
     fontSize = sizes[sizeList.getSelectedIndex()];
    newFont = new Font(fontName,fontStyle,fontSize);
    fontChanged = true;
   }
   class ButtonHandler implements ActionListener {
    public void actionPerformed(ActionEvent e){
     String s = e.getActionCommand();
     if("Select".equals(s)) {
      updateNewFont();
      ah.actionPerformed(new ActionEvent(FontDialog.this,
       ActionEvent.ACTION_PERFORMED,"Select"));
      FontDialog.this.setVisible(false);
     }else if("Cancel".equals(s)) {
      FontDialog.this.dispose();
     }
    }
   }
   class WindowEventHandler extends WindowAdapter {
    public void windowClosing(WindowEvent e){
     FontDialog.this.dispose();
    }
   }
}
```

The FontDialog class creates the font dialog box, shown in Figure 27.8. This type of dialog box is used in most text-processing applications. You can reuse the FontDialog class, as it is currently defined, in your Java programs. You can also subclass FontDialog and add your own custom enhancements.

The `FontDialog` class declares a number of variables that are used in the generation and processing of the Font dialog box. The `fontName`, `fontStyle`, and `fontSize` variables are used to keep track of the parameters of the currently selected font. The `fontNames` array identifies the names of the fonts that are currently supported by the system. The `styles`, `styleNames`, `sizes`, and `sizeNames` arrays are used to maintain `int` and `String` lists of the font styles and sizes that are displayed in the dialog box. The `fontList`, `styleList`, and `sizeList` variables refer to the `MyList` objects displayed in the dialog box. The `toolkit` variable refers to the `Toolkit` object of the window containing the font dialog box. The `fontChanged` variable keeps track of whether the user has selected a new font, and the `newFont` variable maintains the `Font` object that is selected by the user.

The `FontDialog` constructor uses the superclass constructor call statement to create a modal dialog box with the title Select a font:. The toolkit associated with the window containing the dialog box is obtained using the `getToolkit()` method of the `Window` class. The `newFont` variable, representing the user's font selection, is set to the default value of the currently selected font. This font is passed to the `FontDialog` constructor using the `currentFont` parameter. The `FontDialog` constructor invokes the `setupFonts()` and `setupPanels()` methods to perform the bulk of the dialog box setup. It then sets the background and foreground colors and stores the `ActionListener` object passed via the `ah` variable. This `ActionListener` object is used to handle an event generated by the `FontDialog` class. The constructor then packs the dialog box window and assigns an event handler to it.

The `setupFonts()` method assigns default values to the `fontName`, `fontStyle`, and `fontSize` variables based on the values of the current font stored in the `newFont` variable. The `getFontList()` method of the `Toolkit` class is used to set the `fontNames[]` array to the list of fonts currently supported by the system. These names are converted to a list using the `MyList()` constructor.

The `setupPanels()` method performs all of the grunt work, adding the lists to the dialog box and rearranging them in an appealing fashion. The `mainPanel` variable is used to refer to the overall panel into which the `fontPanel`, `stylePanel`, and `sizePanel` objects are inserted. The `mainPanel` is laid out as a three-column set of subpanels. These subpanels are identified by the `fontPanel`, `stylePanel`, and `sizePanel` variables. Each of these subpanels is laid out using a `BorderLayout` object. The label identifying the contents of the panel is added to the top of the panel. The center of each panel contains the three `MyList` objects identified by the `fontList`, `styleList`, and `sizeList` variables.

The Helvetica font is used for the contents of the font dialog box. The labels at the top of each column are set in a boldface style. A second panel, referred to by the `buttonPanel` variable, is created with two buttons: Select and Cancel. These buttons provide the user with controls needed to accept or abort a font selection. An object of the `ButtonHandler` class is used as the buttons' event handler. The `mainPanel` is added to the center of the font dialog box and the `buttonPanel` is added to the bottom.

Two access methods are provided with the FontDialog class. The isChanged()method is used to query a FontDialog object to determine whether the user made a font selection. The getFont()method returns the font selected by the user.

The ButtonHandler class handles the clicking of the Select and Cancel buttons. The Cancel button results in the destruction of the FontDialog object. The object is destroyed using the dispose() method of the Window class. The Select button invokes the updateNewFont() method to create a font based on the user's current list selections and assign that font to the newFont variable. The actionPerformed() method of the ActionListener object passed to the FontDialog constructor is invoked. This enables additional event handling to be performed outside the FontDialog class. The font dialog box is then hidden but not destroyed. Note that an ActionEvent object is passed as an argument to the actionPerformed() method. The setVisible() method of the Component class is used to hide the dialog box.

The updateNewFont() method checks the MyList objects referred to by the fontList, styleList, and sizeList variables to update the fontName, fontStyle, and fontSize variables based on the user's selection. These variables are then used to construct a new Font object, which is assigned to the newFont variable. The fontChanged flag is then set to indicate that a user font selection has occurred.

The ColorDialog Class

The ColorDialog class is very similar to, but simpler than, the FontDialog class. It allows the user to select a color from the list of colors defined in the Color class. It provides a dialog box that is similar to that of FontDialog, but is much simpler because only one list—the list of available colors—is supported. The source code of the ColorDialog class is shown in Listing 27.4.

Listing 27.4. The source code of the ColorDialog class.

```
package jdg.ch27;

import java.awt.*;
import java.awt.event.*;
import jdg.ch26.MyList;

public class ColorDialog extends Dialog {
 Color colors[] = {Color.black,Color.blue,Color.cyan,Color.darkGray,Color.gray,
  Color.green,Color.lightGray,Color.magenta,Color.orange,Color.pink,Color.red,
  Color.white,Color.yellow};
 String colorNames[] = {"black","blue","cyan","darkGray","gray","green",
  "lightGray","magenta","orange","pink","red",
  "white","yellow"};
 MyList colorList = new MyList(5,false,colorNames);
 Color newColor;
 boolean colorChanged;
 ActionListener ah;
 public ColorDialog(Frame parent,Color currentColor,ActionListener ah) {
  super(parent,"Select a color:",true);
```

continues

Listing 27.4. continued

```java
  setupPanels();
  setBackground(Color.lightGray);
  setForeground(Color.black);
  this.ah=ah;
  pack();
  addWindowListener(new WindowEventHandler());
 }
 void setupPanels() {
  Panel colorPanel = new Panel();
  colorPanel.setLayout(new BorderLayout());
  Label colorLabel = new Label("Color:");
  colorPanel.add("North",colorLabel);
  colorPanel.add("Center",colorList);
  Font plainFont = new Font("Helvetica",Font.PLAIN,12);
  Font boldFont = new Font("Helvetica",Font.BOLD,12);
  colorLabel.setFont(boldFont);
  colorList.setFont(plainFont);
  Panel buttonPanel = new Panel();
  buttonPanel.setLayout(new FlowLayout());
  Button selectButton = new Button("Select");
  Button cancelButton = new Button("Cancel");
  ButtonHandler bh = new ButtonHandler();
  selectButton.addActionListener(bh);
  cancelButton.addActionListener(bh);
  buttonPanel.add(selectButton);
  buttonPanel.add(cancelButton);
  buttonPanel.setFont(boldFont);
  add("Center",colorPanel);
  add("South",buttonPanel);
 }
 public boolean isChanged() {
  return colorChanged;
 }
 public Color getColor() {
  return newColor;
 }
 class ButtonHandler implements ActionListener {
  public void actionPerformed(ActionEvent e){
   String s = e.getActionCommand();
   if("Select".equals(s)) {
    if(colorList.getSelectedIndex() != -1)
     newColor = colors[colorList.getSelectedIndex()];
    colorChanged = true;
    ah.actionPerformed(new ActionEvent(ColorDialog.this,
     ActionEvent.ACTION_PERFORMED,"Select"));
    ColorDialog.this.setVisible(false);
   }else if("Cancel".equals(s)) {
    ColorDialog.this.dispose();
   }
  }
 }
 class WindowEventHandler extends WindowAdapter {
  public void windowClosing(WindowEvent e){
   ColorDialog.this.dispose();
  }
 }
}
```

The ColorDialog class declares the colors array as an array of color constants and the colorNames array as the names associated with these color constants. The colorList variable refers to the MyList object that presents the colorNames array to the user. The newColor variable identifies the color selected by the user, and the colorChanged variable indicates whether a user color selection has been made.

The ColorDialog constructor invokes the Dialog constructor to set the title of the dialog box. It then invokes the setupPanels() method to perform most of the setup of the dialog box's internal components. The foreground and background colors are set and then the dialog box is packed and resized.

The setupPanels() method creates and adds two panels to the dialog box. These panels are identified by the colorPanel and buttonPanel variables. The panel identified by the colorPanel variable contains the Color: label and the MyList object referred to by the colorList variable. The button panel is implemented in the same manner as in the FontDialog class.

The isChanged()and getColor()methods are used to determine whether the user has selected a color and, if so, to return the color selected.

The ButtonHandler class handles the clicking of the Select and Cancel buttons. The Select button is handled by invoking the getSelectedIndex() method of the List class to see if a color was selected and setting the newColor variable to the selected color. The colorChanged flag is updated to indicate that a color has been selected. The actionPerformed() method of the ActionListener object passed to the ColorDialog constructor is invoked in the same manner as in the FontDialog class. The setVisible() method causes the dialog box to be hidden.

The Cancel button is handled by simply disposing of the dialog box.

Summary

This chapter covers the details of using the text- and font-related classes. It shows you how to use the text-based classes provided by Java and how to display text with the canvas. It also explains how the Font and FontMetrics classes are used to provide custom control of text display. Chapter 28, "The Canvas," covers the Canvas and Graphics classes.

28

The Canvas

This chapter covers the details of using the `Canvas` and `Graphics` classes. It also shows you how to use the image processing–related classes of the `java.awt.image` package. Java's support of bitmapped images is explained and the drawing methods of the `Graphics` class are illustrated as part of an example. When you finish this chapter, you'll be able to effectively use graphics in your Java window programs.

The `Canvas` and `Graphics` Classes

The `Canvas` class provides a general GUI component for drawing images and text on the screen. It does not support any drawing methods of its own, but provides access to a `Graphics` object through its `paint()` method. The `paint()` method is invoked upon creation and update of a canvas so that the `Graphics` object associated with a `Canvas` object can be updated. The `paint()` method should not be directly invoked, but it can be indirectly accessed using the `repaint()` method. The `Canvas` class is used to provide custom drawing and event handling. You can also use the `Graphics` object associated with your application's `Frame` subclass by overriding its `paint()`method. This is typically done in small applications.

The `Graphics` class is where all of the low-level drawing methods are implemented. These methods can be used directly to draw objects and text or can be combined to display more elaborate screen objects. The `Graphics` drawing methods allow a number of geometrical shapes to be drawn and filled, including lines, arcs, ovals, rectangles, rounded rectangles, and polygons. A special `draw3DRect()`method is provided for drawing rectangles that are shaded to give them a three-dimensional appearance. The `Graphics` class also provides the capability to draw bitmapped images and text on the canvas. Chapter 27, "Text and Fonts," covers the drawing of text and introduces the `Font` and `FontMetrics` classes. These classes control the specific manner in which text is displayed.

Displaying Bitmapped Images

The `drawImage()` method of the `Graphics` class is used to display bitmapped images on the `Graphics` object associated with a canvas. It takes an object of the `Image` class, an object that implements the `ImageObserver` interface, the x,y-coordinates where the image is to be displayed, and other parameters as its arguments.

The `Image` class is an abstract class that provides format-independent access to graphical images. `Image` objects are created by invoking methods of other classes that create images. Examples of these image-creating methods are the `createImage()` methods of the `Component` and `Applet` classes and the `getImage()` methods of the `Toolkit` and `Applet` classes. The `getImage()` methods are the most handy methods for retrieving an image that is stored in a disk file. Java currently supports GIF- and JPEG-formatted images through these methods.

The ImageObserver interface is defined in the java.awt.image package. This interface provides a set of constants and methods that support the creation and loading of images. The Component class implements the ImageObserver interface, and in most cases, the ImageObserver object used as the parameter to the drawImage() method can be supplied using the this identifier to reference the current Canvas or Frame object being painted.

The DisplayImageApp Program

The DisplayImageApp program shows how bitmapped images can be drawn on the screen using the drawImage() method of the Graphics class. Its source code is shown in Listing 28.1.

Listing 28.1. The source code for the DisplayImageApp program.

```
import java.awt.*;
import java.awt.event.*;
import jdg.ch25.*;

public class DisplayImageApp extends Frame {
 MyMenuBar menuBar;
 Toolkit toolkit;
 int screenWidth = 400;
 int screenHeight = 400;
 Image image;
 public static void main(String args[]){
  DisplayImageApp app = new DisplayImageApp();
 }
 public DisplayImageApp() {
  super("DisplayImageApp");
  setup();
  setSize(screenWidth,screenHeight);
  addWindowListener(new WindowEventHandler());
  show();
 }
 void setup() {
  setBackground(Color.white);
  setupMenuBar();
  setMenuBar(menuBar);
  setupImage();
 }
 void setupMenuBar() {
  String menuItems[][] = {{"File","Exit"}};
  MenuItemHandler mih = new MenuItemHandler();
  menuBar = new MyMenuBar(menuItems,mih,mih);
 }
 void setupImage() {
  toolkit = getToolkit();
  image = toolkit.getImage("test.gif");
 }
 public void paint(Graphics g) {
  g.drawImage(image,0,0,this);
 }
 class MenuItemHandler implements ActionListener, ItemListener {
  public void actionPerformed(ActionEvent ev){
```

continues

Listing 28.1. continued

```
  String s=ev.getActionCommand();
  if(s=="Exit"){
   System.exit(0);
  }
 }
 public void itemStateChanged(ItemEvent e){
 }
}
class WindowEventHandler extends WindowAdapter {
 public void windowClosing(WindowEvent e){
  System.exit(0);
 }
 }
}
```

Before running the DisplayImageApp program, copy the test.gif and aviris.gif images from the \jdg\ch28 directory of the CD-ROM to your jdg\ch28 directory. The DisplayImageApp program uses the test.gif file. The ImageApp program, which you'll develop later in this chapter, displays the aviris.gif image.

DisplayImageMap shows how a bitmapped image can be displayed using the Graphics class. When you run the program, it will display the bitmapped image shown in Figure 28.1.

FIGURE 28.1.

The
DisplayImageApp
opening window.

The functionality of the DisplayImageApp program isn't all that astounding. Its purpose is to illustrate the use of the methods involved in loading and displaying image files. You can easily upgrade the program to display arbitrary GIF or JPEG files by adding and implementing an Open option on the File menu.

DisplayImageApp declares several field variables. The menuBar variable is used to identify the program's menu bar. The toolkit variable is used to reference the toolkit associated with the application window. The screenWidth and screenHeight variables control the size at which the window is displayed. The image variable is used to refer to the loaded image.

The `DisplayImageApp` window is created, set up, and displayed using the methods covered in previous chapters. The `setupImage()` method uses the `getToolkit()` method of the `Window` class to get the `Toolkit` object associated with the application window. The `getImage()` method of the `Toolkit` class is used to load the image in the `test.gif` file and assign it to the `image` variable.

The `paint()` method draws the image referenced by the `image` variable on the default `Graphics` object of the application window. It accomplishes this using the `drawImage()` method of the `Graphics` class. The arguments to `drawImage()` are the image to be displayed, the x- and y-coordinates where the image is to be drawn, and the object implementing the `ImageObserver` interface associated with the image. The `this` identifier is used to indicate that the application window is the `ImageObserver`.

Drawing and Painting

Some programs, such as the Microsoft Windows Paint program, are used to construct images by *painting* on the screen. These paint programs create an image array of color pixels and update the array based on user paint commands. These commands may consist of pixel-level drawing operations or more general operations that draw geometrical objects such as circles, rectangles, and lines. Painting programs are characterized by the fact that the pixel array is the focus for the drawing that takes place.

Drawing programs, such as CorelDRAW!, support drawing operations using a more object-oriented approach. When you draw a circle or line with a drawing program, you do not merely update the pixels of the canvas—you add an object to the list of objects that are displayed on the canvas. Because drawing programs operate at a higher object level, you can select, move, resize, group, and perform other operations on the objects that you've drawn.

The `Graphics` class is oriented toward providing the methods that are needed to support higher-level drawing programs rather than lower-level painting programs, although it does support important painting operations, such as displaying bitmapped images, as you saw in the `DisplayImageApp` program.

When using the `Graphics` class to support graphical operations, you will generally maintain a list of the objects that you've drawn and use that list of objects to repaint the screen, as required.

The DrawApp Program

The `DrawApp` program shows how the higher-level drawing operations of the `Graphics` class are used to display and maintain a list of the objects that are drawn on a canvas. The source code of the `DrawApp` program is shown in Listing 28.2.

Listing 28.2. The source code for the DrawApp program.

```java
import java.awt.*;
import java.awt.event.*;
import java.lang.Math;
import java.util.Vector;
import jdg.ch25.*;

public class DrawApp extends Frame {
 Object menuItems[][] = {
  {"File","New","-","Exit"},
  {"Draw","+Line","-Oval","-Rectangle"}
 };
 MenuItemHandler mih = new MenuItemHandler();
 MyMenuBar menuBar = new MyMenuBar(menuItems,mih,mih);
 MyCanvas canvas = new MyCanvas(TwoPointObject.LINE);
 int screenWidth = 400;
 int screenHeight = 400;
 public static void main(String args[]){
  DrawApp app = new DrawApp();
 }
 public DrawApp() {
  super("DrawApp");
  setup();
  setSize(screenWidth,screenHeight);
  addWindowListener(new WindowEventHandler());
  show();
 }
 void setup() {
  setBackground(Color.white);
  setMenuBar(menuBar);
  setCursor(new Cursor(CROSSHAIR_CURSOR));
  canvas.addFocusListener(new FocusHandler());
  add("Center",canvas);
 }
 class FocusHandler extends FocusAdapter {
  public void focusGained(FocusEvent e){
   setCursor(new Cursor(CROSSHAIR_CURSOR));
  }
  public void focusLost(FocusEvent e){
   setCursor(new Cursor(DEFAULT_CURSOR));
  }
 }
 class MenuItemHandler implements ActionListener, ItemListener {
  public void actionPerformed(ActionEvent ev){
   String s=ev.getActionCommand();
   if(s=="Exit"){
    System.exit(0);
   }else if(s=="New"){
    canvas.clear();
   }
  }
  public void itemStateChanged(ItemEvent e){
   CheckboxMenuItem ch = (CheckboxMenuItem) e.getItemSelectable();
   String s = ch.getLabel();
   MyMenu menu = menuBar.getMenu("Draw");
   CheckboxMenuItem lineItem = (CheckboxMenuItem) menu.getItem("Line");
   CheckboxMenuItem ovalItem = (CheckboxMenuItem) menu.getItem("Oval");
```

```
   CheckboxMenuItem rectangleItem =
    (CheckboxMenuItem) menu.getItem("Rectangle");
   if(s.equals("Line")){
    canvas.setTool(TwoPointObject.LINE);
    lineItem.setState(true);
    ovalItem.setState(false);
    rectangleItem.setState(false);
   }else if(s.equals("Oval")){
    canvas.setTool(TwoPointObject.OVAL);
    lineItem.setState(false);
    ovalItem.setState(true);
    rectangleItem.setState(false);
   }else if(s.equals("Rectangle")){
    canvas.setTool(TwoPointObject.RECTANGLE);
    lineItem.setState(false);
    ovalItem.setState(false);
    rectangleItem.setState(true);
   }
  }
 }
 class WindowEventHandler extends WindowAdapter {
  public void windowClosing(WindowEvent e){
   System.exit(0);
  }
 }
}
class MyCanvas extends Canvas {
 int tool = TwoPointObject.LINE;
 Vector objects = new Vector();
 TwoPointObject current;
 boolean newObject = false;
 public MyCanvas(int toolType) {
  super();
  tool = toolType;
  addMouseListener(new MouseHandler());
  addMouseMotionListener(new MouseMotionHandler());
 }
 public void setTool(int toolType) {
  tool = toolType;
 }
 public void clear() {
  objects.removeAllElements();
  repaint();
 }
 public void paint(Graphics g) {
  int numObjects = objects.size();
  for(int i=0;i<numObjects;++i) {
   TwoPointObject obj = (TwoPointObject) objects.elementAt(i);
   obj.draw(g);
  }
  if(newObject) current.draw(g);
 }
 class MouseHandler extends MouseAdapter {
  public void mousePressed(MouseEvent e){
   current = new TwoPointObject(tool,e.getX(),e.getY());
   newObject = true;
  }
```

continues

Listing 28.2. continued

```java
  public void mouseReleased(MouseEvent e){
    if(newObject) {
      objects.addElement(current);
      newObject = false;
    }
  }
}
class MouseMotionHandler extends MouseMotionAdapter {
  public void mouseDragged(MouseEvent e){
    int x = e.getX();
    int y = e.getY();
    if(newObject) {
      int oldX = current.endX;
      int oldY = current.endY;
      if(tool != TwoPointObject.LINE) {
        if(x > current.startX) current.endX = x;
        if(y > current.startY) current.endY = y;
        int width = Math.max(oldX,current.endX) - current.startX + 1;
        int height = Math.max(oldY,current.endY) - current.startY + 1;
        repaint(current.startX,current.startY,width,height);
      }else{
        current.endX = x;
        current.endY = y;
        int startX = Math.min(Math.min(current.startX,current.endX),oldX);
        int startY = Math.min(Math.min(current.startY,current.endY),oldY);
        int endX = Math.max(Math.max(current.startX,current.endX),oldX);
        int endY = Math.max(Math.max(current.startY,current.endY),oldY);
        repaint(startX,startY,endX-startX+1,endY-startY+1);
      }
    }
  }
}
}
class TwoPointObject {
  public static int LINE = 0;
  public static int OVAL = 1;
  public static int RECTANGLE = 2;
  public int type, startX, startY, endX, endY;
  public TwoPointObject(int objectType,int x1,int y1,int x2,int y2) {
    type = objectType;
    startX = x1;
    startY = y1;
    endX = x2;
    endY = y2;
  }
  public TwoPointObject(int objectType,int x,int y) {
    this(objectType,x,y,x,y);
  }
  public TwoPointObject() {
    this(LINE,0,0,0,0);
  }
  public void draw(Graphics g) {
    if(type == LINE) g.drawLine(startX,startY,endX,endY);
    else{
      int w = Math.abs(endX - startX);
      int l = Math.abs(endY - startY);
```

```
    if(type == OVAL) g.drawOval(startX,startY,w,l);
    else g.drawRect(startX,startY,w,l);
  }
 }
}
```

The DrawApp program is quite a bit more sophisticated than the DisplayImageApp program with respect to the capabilities that it provides. When you run DrawApp you will see the opening window, which is shown in Figure 28.2.

FIGURE 28.2.
The DrawApp *opening window.*

The DrawApp program is initially configured to draw lines in its window. You can draw a line by clicking the left mouse button and dragging the mouse. When you have finished drawing a line, release the left mouse button and the drawn line will be completed. The coordinate where you press the left mouse button is the beginning of the line, and the coordinate where you release the left mouse button is the end of the line. Go ahead and draw several lines, as shown in Figure 28.3.

FIGURE 28.3.
Drawing some lines.

The DrawApp program supports the drawing of lines, ovals, and rectangles. To draw an oval, select the Oval menu item from the Draw pull-down menu, as shown in Figure 28.4.

FIGURE 28.4.

The Draw menu.

You draw an oval in the same way that you draw a line. When you click the left button of your mouse, you mark the upper-left corner of the oval. Drag the mouse to where you want the lower-right corner of the oval and release the left mouse button. Try drawing a few ovals, as shown in Figure 28.5.

FIGURE 28.5.

Drawing some ovals.

Now select the Rectangle menu item from the Draw pull-down menu. You draw rectangles in the same way that you draw ovals. Go ahead and draw a rectangle, as shown in Figure 28.6.

You can experiment with the program before going on to find out how it works. If you want to clear the drawing screen, select New from the File pull-down menu.

The DrawApp program is a little (but not much) longer than the programs you've developed so far. It consists of three major classes. The DrawApp class is the main class used to implement the program. The MyCanvas class is used to implement the main canvas component of the program.

The `TwoPointObject` class is used to implement the line, oval, and rectangle objects that are drawn on the screen. It is called `TwoPointObject` because it supports objects that can be characterized by a starting point (mouse down) and an ending point (mouse up).

FIGURE 28.6.

Drawing a rectangle.

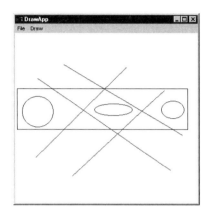

The `DrawApp` program declares several variables. The `menuItems` array is used to construct the menu bar identified by the `menuBar` variable. The `canvas` variable is used to refer to the `MyCanvas` object that implements the program drawing. This object is constructed by passing the `TwoPointObject.LINE` constant as an argument. This tells the constructed object that the line tool should be initially used to support drawing. The height and width of the `DrawApp` window is set to 400×400 pixels.

The `DrawApp` window is constructed using the standard approach that you've been following in previous chapters. The `setup()` method sets the background color to white, invokes `setupMenuBar()` to set up the menu bar, and invokes the `setCursor()` method of the `Component` class to set the initial cursor to the `CROSSHAIR_CURSOR` typically used in drawing programs. The `MyCanvas` object referenced by the `canvas` variable is associated with a focus event handler and then it is added to the center of the main application window.

The focus event handler is used to change the cursor as the mouse enters and exits the drawing area. It is implemented by the `FocusHandler` class, which extends the `FocusAdapter` class. `FocusHandler` overrides the `focusGained()` and `focusLost()` methods of `FocusAdapter` in order to change the cursor based on the occurrence of a `FocusEvent`.

The `actionPerformed()` method of the `MenuItemHandler` class handles the New and Exit menu items. The New menu item is handled by invoking the `clear()` method of the `MyCanvas` class to clear the canvas to a blank state. The Exit menu item is handled in the usual manner.

The `itemStateChanged()` method begins by retrieving the `CheckboxMenuItem` object that was selected using the `getItemSelectable()` method of the `ItemEvent` class. It then uses the `getLabel()` method of the `MenuItem` class to get access to the label associated with the menu item. It continues by assigning the `CheckboxMenuItem` objects in the Draw menu to the `lineItem`, `ovalItem`, and `rectangleItem` variables. These variables are used to determine which menu items are checked.

The `itemStateChanged()` method handles the Line menu item by invoking the `setTool()` method to set the current drawing tool to the line tool. It uses the `LINE` constant defined in the `TwoPointObject` class. The `lineItem`, `ovalItem`, and `rectangleItem` variables are used to update the `CheckboxMenuItem` objects contained in the Draw menu using the `setState()` method of the `CheckboxMenuItem` class. The Oval and Rectangle menu items are handled in a similar manner. The Oval menu item is handled by invoking the `setTool()` method with the `OVAL` constant, and the Rectangle menu item is handled by invoking the `setTool()` method with the `RECTANGLE` constant. The state of the menu items of the Draw menu is updated to reflect the selected drawing tool.

MyCanvas

The `MyCanvas` class subclasses the `Canvas` class to provide custom drawing capabilities. The `tool` variable is used to identify the current drawing tool that is in effect. The `objects` variable is declared as a `Vector`. It is used to store all of the objects drawn by the user. The `current` variable is used to refer to the current `TwoPointObject` object being drawn by the user. The `newObject` flag is used to track whether the user has begun drawing a new object.

The `MyCanvas` constructor invokes the constructor of the `Canvas` class using the superclass constructor call statement and then sets the `tool` variable to the `toolType` argument passed to the constructor.

The `setTool()` method changes the tool used to draw an object.

The `clear()` method invokes the `removeAllElements()` method of the vector class to remove all drawing objects stored in the `Vector` referenced by the `objects` variable.

The `paint()` method is used to paint and repaint the screen. It uses the `size()` method of the `Vector` class to determine how many objects are stored in the `objects` vector and sets the `numObjects` variable to this value. It then iterates through each object stored in `objects` and draws it on the canvas. The `elementAt()` method of the `Vector` class is used to retrieve an object from the `objects` vector. The object is cast into an object of class `TwoPointObject` and assigned to the `obj` variable. The `draw()` method of the `TwoPointObject` class is invoked to draw the object on the current `Graphics` context.

Notice that the `paint()` method does not have to know how to support limited area repainting. Only full canvas painting needs to be implemented by `paint()`. Support of limited area repainting is provided by the local AWT implementation.

The `MouseHandler` and `MouseMotionHandler` inner classes handle the events associated with pressing, releasing, and dragging the mouse. They do this by extending the `MouseAdapter` and `MouseMotionAdapter` classes of `java.awt.event`. The `MouseHandler` class handles the pressing and releasing of the mouse button via the `mousePressed()` and `mouseReleased()` methods. The `MouseMotionHandler` class handles the dragging of the mouse via the `mouseDragged()` method.

The `mousePressed()` method handles the event that is generated when the user clicks the left mouse button in the canvas. The method is called by the Java runtime system with the position of the mouse click. A new `TwoPointObject` object is created, with the `tool` variable and the position of the mouse click as its arguments. The newly created object is assigned to the `current` variable, and the `newObject` flag is set to `true`.

The `mouseReleased()` method is used to handle the event that is generated when the user releases the left mouse button. This action marks the completion of the drawing of an object. The event is handled by adding the object referenced by the `current` variable to the `objects` vector. The `newObject` flag is then set to `false`. The object referenced by the `current` variable is updated with its ending position during the processing of the `mouseDragged()` event-handling method. The `newObject` flag is checked to make sure that the mouse was not clicked outside of the current window and then released.

The `mouseDragged()` method performs somewhat more sophisticated event handling than the `mousePressed()` and `mouseReleased()` methods. It checks the `newObject` flag to make sure that an object is currently being drawn. It then sets the `oldX` and `oldY` variables to the ending position of the object being drawn. These variables will be used to determine what portion of the canvas needs to be repainted. Repainting of the entire canvas is not visually appealing because it causes previously drawn objects to flicker.

If the current drawing tool is not a line, then an oval or a rectangle is the object being drawn by the user. The x- and y-coordinates of the mouse motion are provided via the `MouseEvent` argument to the `mouseDragged()` method. These coordinates are checked to determine whether the mouse was dragged below and to the right of the object being drawn. If this is the case, the ending position of the current object is updated. If the mouse is dragged to the left or above the starting point of the object, the current position of the mouse is ignored. This is to ensure that the starting position of the oval or rectangle is indeed its upper-left corner. The new `width` and `height` of the area to be repainted are calculated as the maximum area covered by the previous ending position and the current object ending position. This is to ensure that the repaint operation will erase any previous boundaries of the object being drawn. The `max()` method of the `java.lang.Math` class is used to determine this maximum area. The `repaint()` method of the `Component` class is then used to repaint the area updated as the result of the mouse drag. This version of the `repaint()` method takes the x,y-coordinates of the upper-left corner of the area to be redrawn and the width and height of this area as its parameters.

Line drawing is not restricted in the same manner as oval and rectangle drawing. If it were, you would not be able to draw lines that go up and to the right or down and to the left. The `else` part of the `if` statement updates the starting position of the area to be repainted as the upper leftmost point of the line being redrawn. It then updates the ending position of the area to be repainted as the lower rightmost point of the line. The canvas is then repainted using the starting coordinates and the updated width and height of the repaint area.

To get a better feel for the process of local screen repainting, try experimenting with the way the repaint() method is used to update the canvas display.

TwoPointObject

The TwoPointObject class is used to keep track of the objects drawn by the user. It records the type of object and its starting and ending coordinates. It also draws the objects on a Graphics object passed as a parameter.

TwoPointObject defines the LINE, OVAL, and RECTANGLE constants, which are also used by the MyCanvas class. The type variable is used to record the type of object being drawn. The startX, startY, endX, and endY variables identify the starting and ending coordinates of the object.

Three TwoPointObject constructors are declared. The first constructor takes the type of object being drawn and its starting and ending coordinates as its parameters. The second constructor leaves out the ending coordinates and sets them to be the same as the starting coordinates. The last constructor takes no parameters and creates a line that is at the coordinate 0,0.

The draw() method checks the type variable to determine what type of object is to be drawn. If the object is a line, it uses the drawLine() method of the Graphics class to draw a line from its starting to ending coordinates. If the object is an oval or a line, the w and l variables are assigned the width and length of the object to be drawn. The drawOval() and drawRect() methods are used to draw an oval or rectangle, respectively.

Combining Graphics and Text

The Graphics class treats text in the same way as it handles other graphics objects. To include text drawing in your graphics applications, use the drawString() method of the Graphics class, as illustrated in Chapter 27. You will need to use the Font and FontMetrics classes to determine the size of the text that is drawn. Otherwise, text and graphics objects can be easily combined in any Graphics-based application.

The Image-Processing Classes of java.awt.image

The java.awt.image package provides a number of classes and interfaces that support image processing. These classes are described in Chapter 15, "Window Programming with the java.awt Packages." For the most part, you will not need to use these classes unless your application program is oriented toward low-level image processing.

The java.awt.image package is based on the concept of an image producer and image consumer. The *image producer* provides the data associated with an image. This data is used or consumed by an *image consumer*. The ImageProducer and ImageConsumer interfaces are used to map this producer–consumer concept to specific image-processing classes.

An image filter is used to alter data that is produced by an image producer before it is consumed by an image consumer. Image filters are similar to the I/O stream filters discussed in Chapter 13, "Stream-Based Input/Output and the java.io Package." An *image filter* reads the data produced by an image producer, modifies it, and then passes it on to the image consumer.

The ImageApp Program

The ImageApp program shows how to perform image processing using a custom-built image filter. Its source code is shown in Listing 28.3.

Listing 28.3. The source code for the ImageApp program.

```
import java.awt.*;
import java.awt.event.*;
import java.awt.image.*;
import jdg.ch25.*;

public class ImageApp extends Frame {
 MyMenuBar menuBar;
 Toolkit toolkit;
 int screenWidth = 500;
 int screenHeight = 480;
 Image filteredImage;
 public static void main(String args[]){
  ImageApp app = new ImageApp();
 }
 public ImageApp() {
  super("ImageApp");
  setup();
  setSize(screenWidth,screenHeight);
  addWindowListener(new WindowEventHandler());
  show();
 }
 void setup() {
  setBackground(Color.white);
  setupMenuBar();
  setMenuBar(menuBar);
  setupImage();
 }
 void setupMenuBar() {
  String menuItems[][] = {{"File","Exit"},{"Filter","-Red","-Green","-Blue"}};
  MenuItemHandler mih = new MenuItemHandler();
  menuBar = new MyMenuBar(menuItems,mih,mih);
 }
 void setupImage() {
  toolkit = getToolkit();
  filteredImage = toolkit.getImage("aviris.gif");
 }
 public void paint(Graphics g) {
  g.drawImage(filteredImage,0,50,this);
 }
 public void filterImage(){
  Image image = toolkit.getImage("aviris.gif");
```

continues

Listing 28.3. continued

```
   ImageFilter filter = new MyImageFilter(getMask());
   filteredImage =
    createImage(new FilteredImageSource(image.getSource(),filter));
   repaint();
  }
 public int getMask() {
  int red = 0xff00ffff;
  int green = 0xffff00ff;
  int blue = 0xffffff00;
  int mask = 0xffffffff;
  MyMenu menu = menuBar.getMenu("Filter");
  CheckboxMenuItem redItem = (CheckboxMenuItem) menu.getItem("Red");
  CheckboxMenuItem greenItem = (CheckboxMenuItem) menu.getItem("Green");
  CheckboxMenuItem blueItem = (CheckboxMenuItem) menu.getItem("Blue");
  if(redItem.getState()) mask &= red;
  if(greenItem.getState()) mask &= green;
  if(blueItem.getState()) mask &= blue;
  return mask;
 }
 class MenuItemHandler implements ActionListener, ItemListener {
  public void actionPerformed(ActionEvent ev){
   String s=ev.getActionCommand();
   if(s=="Exit"){
    System.exit(0);
   }
  }
  public void itemStateChanged(ItemEvent e){
   filterImage();
  }
 }
 class WindowEventHandler extends WindowAdapter {
  public void windowClosing(WindowEvent e){
   System.exit(0);
  }
 }
}
class MyImageFilter extends RGBImageFilter {
 int filter;
 public MyImageFilter(int mask) {
  canFilterIndexColorModel = true;
  filter = mask;
 }
 public int filterRGB(int x,int y,int rgb) {
  return rgb & filter;
 }
}
```

When you first run ImageApp it loads the image contained in the file aviris.gif. (See Figure 28.7.) This is a public-domain image provided by the NASA Jet Propulsion Laboratory. It is produced by the Airborne Visible InfraRed Imaging Spectrometer (AVIRIS). The aviris.gif file is fairly large; you might have to wait a couple seconds for it to complete its loading.

FIGURE 28.7.
The ImageApp *opening window.*

The AVIRIS image is not provided to introduce you to NASA's advanced airborne-imaging algorithms. Instead, you will use this image as an example to understand how basic image filtering works. Unfortunately, the images displayed in this book are in black and white, so you will not be able to see how the image filtering works by looking at the book.

Click on the Filter pull-down menu and select the Blue menu item, as shown in Figure 28.8.

FIGURE 28.8.
The Filter menu.

Selecting the blue filter causes all blue color components to be filtered out of the image. The resulting image is comprised only of green and red color components. (See Figure 28.9.)

FIGURE 28.9.

A filtered image.

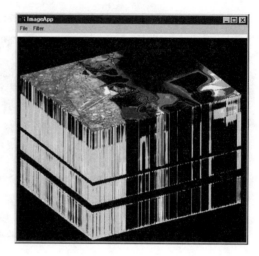

Go ahead and try the red and green filters by selecting Red and Green from the Filter menu. Also, try various filter combinations to get a better feel for how filtering works.

Although the ImageApp program may seem to perform some amazing processing, it is actually quite small. Two classes are defined: the ImageApp class, used to implement the main program window, and the MyImageFilter class, used to implement the actual image filter.

The ImageApp class declares the menuBar, toolkit, screenWidth, screenHeight, and filteredImage variables. The menuBar, screenWidth, and screenHeight variables are used in their usual manner. The toolkit variable is used to refer to the Toolkit object associated with the application window. The filteredImage variable is used to refer to the image that is being manipulated.

The setupImage() method uses the getToolkit() method of the Window class to retrieve the toolkit that is associated with the application window. It then invokes the getImage() method of the Toolkit class to load the image contained in the file into an Image object that is referenced by the filteredImage variable.

The paint() method draws the image identified by the filteredImage variable on the screen using the drawImage() method of the Graphics class.

The filterImage()method oversees the image-filtering process. It loads the aviris.gif image into an object assigned to the image variable. It creates a new object of the MyImageFilter class and assigns it to the filter variable. The MyImageFilter object is provided with a filter mask that is generated by a call to the getMask() method. You'll.learn what a filter mask is shortly.

The filterImage() method uses the createImage() method of the Component class to create a new image and assign it to the filteredImage variable. The repaint() method is invoked to redisplay the new image assigned to the filteredImage variable. The actual image filtering is performed as part of the creation of the arguments supplied to the createImage() method. When createImage() is invoked, a new object of the java.awt.image.FilteredImageSource class is created. This object assigns the source (ImageProducer) of the image being created to the newly created FilteredImageSource object. This object is created using the source (ImageProducer) of the aviris.gif image assigned to the image variable. The getSource() method is invoked to get the ImageProducer of the original image. The FilteredImageSource object is filtered using the MyImageFilter object assigned to the filter variable. To complete this examination of the image-filtering process, you only need to figure out how the MyImageFilter class works and what was returned by the getMask() method.

The getMask() method returns an integer value that is used to mask out certain RGB color combinations. The red variable is assigned the 0xff00ffff hexadecimal constant. The red component of an RGB color is stored in the bits that are set to zero in this constant. So when you logically AND this value with any color, its red bits are stripped out. The hexadecimal constants assigned to the green and blue variables are defined in an analogous fashion to strip out the green and blue bits of a color when they are logically ANDed with the color. Note that the first byte of the hexadecimal constant is always 0xff. This allows it to be ANDed without affecting the result. The mask variable is used to compute the returned result. The constant assigned to the mask variable will have no effect on any color that it is ANDed with.

The getMask() method checks each of the CheckboxMenuItem objects contained in the Filter menu to determine which objects are set. If a menu item is set, the color mask associated with that item is logically ANDed with the mask variable. The resulting mask value is a value that will strip out the colors specified by the set menu items.

The itemStateChanged() method of the MenuItemHandler class handles the selection of the Red, Green, and Blue checkbox menu items by invoking the filterImage() method. This causes the aviris.gif image to be filtered as specified by the mask generated according to the state of the Red, Green, and Blue checkbox menu items.

The MyImageFilter class performs the actual image filtering. It extends the RGBImageFilter class defined in java.awt.image package and overrides the filterRGB() method.

The MyImageFilter constructor takes a mask value as its parameter and assigns it to the filter variable. It also sets the canFilterIndexColorModel variable to true. This allows filtering to take place on the color map associated with the image, rather than on the actual image.

The filterRGB() method performs the image filtering. It takes the x,y-coordinate of each pixel to be filtered and the RGB color of the pixel as its parameters. It then logically ANDs the color value with the mask stored in the filter variable and returns the resulting filtered color.

Summary

This chapter covers the details of using the Canvas and Graphics classes. It also shows you how to use the image processing–related classes of the java.awt.image package. Java's support of bitmapped images is demonstrated with the DisplayImageApp program. The DrawApp program illustrates the drawing methods of the Graphics class, and the ImageApp program shows you how to use the classes of java.awt.image. Chapter 29, "Scrollbars," shows you how to use scrollbars to scroll text and graphics drawn on the canvas.

29

Scrollbars

This chapter is dedicated to explaining the use of the `Scrollbar` and `ScrollPane` classes. It describes the methods provided by these classes and shows how to use vertical and horizontal scrollbars to scroll text and graphics displayed in a window. The event handling supported by scrollbars is also explained. When you finish this chapter, you will be able to use scrollbars effectively in your Java window programs.

How Scrollbars Work

Scrollbars are used to scroll through an object contained in a window that is too large to be completely displayed within the window. Vertical scrollbars are used to scroll up and down from the beginning of the object to its end. Horizontal scrollbars are used to scroll right and left between the right and left sides of the object. Horizontal and vertical scrollbars are implemented in the same fashion. The only differences between them are their placement around the object to be scrolled and the direction in which they move the scrolled object through the window.

Users interact with scrollbars in three ways. By clicking on the arrows at the end of the scrollbars, they move the scrolled object one scrollable unit in the opposite direction of the arrow. This causes the window to appear as though it has moved in the direction of the arrow over the object.

NOTE

A *scrollable unit* is defined by the application program. Vertical and horizontal units differ. Most text-processing applications define a vertical unit as a single line of text and a horizontal unit as a percentage of the horizontal screen size. Graphical applications define vertical and horizontal units as a percentage of the visible screen size.

Scrollbars contain tabs that identify the relative location of the object being viewed with respect to the total size of the object. By clicking between the tab and the end of a scrollbar, the view of the object is updated in a one-page increment in the direction of the arrow. This is the second way that scrollbars can be used. The definition of a *page* is also application specific. Vertical scrollbars usually define a page as the vertical size of the viewing window or some percentage of this size. Horizontal scrollbars tend to operate in the same manner. A horizontal page is defined as a fixed percentage of the horizontal viewing area.

The third way that a user can interact with a scrollbar is to drag the scrollbar's tab to a specific location within the scrollbar. When the user drags the tab of a vertical scrollbar, he moves the object being viewed up or down in the viewing window. When the user drags the tab of a horizontal scrollbar, he moves the object being viewed left or right in the viewing window.

Using Scrollbars

When you use scrollbars in your Java programs, you will most likely be using them to scroll through a `Graphics` object that is associated with a `Canvas` object or the main application window. You create and place scrollbars in your window in the same manner as any other window component. Their position and size within the window are determined by the layout associated with the window.

Scrollbars are created using the `Scrollbar()` constructor. Three forms of this constructor are provided. The default constructor takes no parameters and is not particularly useful unless you want to create a `Scrollbar` object and then specify its orientation and use later in your program. The second constructor allows the orientation of a `Scrollbar` object to be specified. The third `Scrollbar()` constructor uses the five parameters that are needed to create a working scrollbar: `orientation`, `value`, `visible`, `minimum`, and `maximum`.

The `orientation` parameter of a scrollbar is specified by the VERTICAL and HORIZONTAL constants defined by the `Scrollbar` class. The `minimum` and `maximum` parameters specify the minimum and maximum values associated with the scrollbar's position. These values should map to the object being scrolled. For example, if you are scrolling a 1,000-line text object, appropriate minimum and maximum values for a vertical scrollbar would be `0` and `999`. Horizontal values could be determined using the maximum width of the text to be scrolled (in pixels).

The `value` parameter identifies the starting value associated with the scrollbar. The `value` parameter is usually set to the `minimum` value of the scrollbar. However, suppose you wanted to initiate the display of an object with its center displayed on the screen. You would then set the scrollbar's `value` parameter to the average of its minimum and maximum values.

The `visible` parameter is used to specify the size of the viewable area of the object being scrolled. For example, if you are scrolling a 1,000-line text object and the viewable area of the window is 25 lines long, you would set the `visible` variable to 25.

The `Scrollbar` class provides several methods for getting and setting the parameters of a `Scrollbar` object. The `getOrientation()`, `getValue()`, `getVisibleAmount()`, `getMinimum()`, and `getMaximum()` methods retrieve the parameter values discussed so far. The `getValue()` method is used to determine to what position the user has scrolled.

The `setUnitIncrement()` and `setBlockIncrement()` methods are used to specify the size of a scrollable unit and page relative to the minimum and maximum values associated with a scrollbar. For example, when scrolling text, you can set the line increment of a vertical scrollbar to `1`, so that only one line of text is vertically scrolled. You can set the page increment to `10`, to allow 10 lines of text to be scrolled when the user clicks between the tab and arrows of a scrollbar. The `getUnitIncrement()` and `getBlockIncrement()` methods provide access to the current line- and page-increment values.

The setValue() method allows you to set the current position of a scrollbar directly. The setValues() method allows you to specify a scrollbar's value, visible, minimum, and maximum parameters.

Scrollbars implement the Adjustable interface. In order to respond to user scrollbar operations and implement scrolling of the object associated with a scrollbar, you must handle the AdjustmentEvent generated by user manipulation of the scrollbar. This event is handled by implementing the AdjustmentListener interface. The adjustmentValueChanged() method of AdjustmentListener is invoked to handle scrollbar events. It is passed an object of class AdjustmentEvent.

The AdjustmentEvent class provides methods that can be used to retrieve the scrollbar for which the event was generated, the new value of the scrollbar, and the type of scrolling action that took place.

Scrolling Text

In order to handle scrollbar events and implement scrolling, you must repaint the area of the scrollable window based on the mapping between the object being scrolled and the vertical and horizontal scrollbar positions. If you are scrolling text, you are most likely displaying the text on the Graphics object associated with a Canvas object or the main application window. The TextArea object implements its own scrollbars and does not require any additional event handling.

When vertically scrolling text, you should adjust the minimum and maximum values of the vertical scrollbar based on the number of lines of text that are contained in the object being scrolled. In this way, when the user moves the scrollbar's tab to its topmost position, the beginning of the text is displayed, and when the user moves the tab to the bottom of the scrollbar, the end of the text is displayed.

When horizontally scrolling text, you should set the minimum and maximum values of the horizontal scrollbar according to the maximum width of the text being displayed.

The TextScrollApp Program

The TextScrollApp program show how scrollbars can be used to scroll text that is drawn on a Graphics object. This program provides the capability to read in a text file and display it on the screen using the default 12-point plain font. It allows the text file to be scrolled vertically and horizontally through the application window. The source code of the TextScrollApp program is shown in Listing 29.1.

Listing 29.1. The source code of the TextScrollApp program.

```java
import java.awt.*;
import java.awt.event.*;
import java.io.*;
import java.util.Vector;
import jdg.ch25.*;

public class TextScrollApp extends Frame {
 Object menuItems[][] = {{"File","Open","-","Exit"}};
 MenuItemHandler mih = new MenuItemHandler();
 MyMenuBar menuBar = new MyMenuBar(menuItems,mih,mih);
 FileDialog openFile = new FileDialog(this,"Open File",FileDialog.LOAD);
 MessageDialog notification;
 DialogHandler dh = new DialogHandler();
 Font defaultFont = new Font("default",Font.PLAIN,12);
 int screenWidth = 400;
 int screenHeight = 400;
 Vector text = new Vector();
 int topLine;
 Toolkit toolkit;
 FontMetrics fm;
 int baseline;
 int lineSize;
 int maxWidth;
 Canvas canvas = new MyCanvas();
 Scrollbar hbar, vbar;
 public static void main(String args[]){
  TextScrollApp app = new TextScrollApp();
 }
 public TextScrollApp() {
  super("TextScrollApp");
  setup();
  setSize(screenWidth,screenHeight);
  addWindowListener(new WindowEventHandler());
  show();
 }
 void setup() {
  setMenuBar(menuBar);
  setupFontData();
  setupScrollbars();
 }
 void setupFontData() {
  setFont(defaultFont);
  toolkit = getToolkit();
  fm - toolkit.getFontMetrics(defaultFont);
  baseline = fm.getLeading()+fm.getAscent();
  lineSize = fm.getHeight();
 }
 void setupScrollbars() {
  hbar = new Scrollbar(Scrollbar.HORIZONTAL,0,0,0,0);
  vbar = new Scrollbar(Scrollbar.VERTICAL,0,0,0,0);
  hbar.setBackground(Color.lightGray);
  vbar.setBackground(Color.lightGray);
  hbar.addAdjustmentListener(new ScrollHandler());
  vbar.addAdjustmentListener(new ScrollHandler());
  add("Center",canvas);
  add("South",hbar);
```

continues

Listing 29.1. continued

```java
  add("East",vbar);
}
void resetScrollbars() {
 hbar.setValues(0,10,0,maxWidth+5);
 vbar.setValues(0,10,0,text.size()+5);
}
public void readFile(String file) {
 BufferedReader inStream;
 try{
  inStream = new BufferedReader(new FileReader(file));
 }catch (IOException ex){
  notifyUser("Error opening file");
  return;
 }
 try{
  Vector newText = new Vector();
  String line;
  maxWidth = 0;
  while((line=inStream.readLine())!=null) {
   int lineWidth = fm.stringWidth(line);
   if(lineWidth > maxWidth) maxWidth = lineWidth;
   newText.addElement(line);
  }
  text = newText;
  topLine = 0;
  inStream.close();
  resetScrollbars();
  repaint();
 }catch (IOException ex){
  notifyUser("Error reading file");
 }
}
public void notifyUser(String s) {
 String text[] = {s};
 String buttons[] = {"OK"};
 notification = new MessageDialog(this,"Error",true,text,
  buttons,dh,dh);
}
public void paint(Graphics g) {
 canvas.repaint();
}
class ScrollHandler implements AdjustmentListener {
 public void adjustmentValueChanged(AdjustmentEvent e){
  repaint();
 }
}
class MenuItemHandler implements ActionListener, ItemListener {
 public void actionPerformed(ActionEvent ev){
  String s=ev.getActionCommand();
  if(s=="Exit"){
   System.exit(0);
  }else if(s=="Open"){
   openFile.show();
   if(openFile.getFile() != null) {
    String inFile = openFile.getFile();
    readFile(inFile);
```

```
    }
   }
  }
  public void itemStateChanged(ItemEvent e){
  }
 }
 class WindowEventHandler extends WindowAdapter {
  public void windowClosing(WindowEvent e){
   System.exit(0);
  }
 }
 class DialogHandler extends WindowAdapter implements ActionListener {
  public void windowClosing(WindowEvent e){
   notification.dispose();
  }
  public void actionPerformed(ActionEvent e){
   notification.dispose();
  }
 }
 class MyCanvas extends Canvas {
  public void paint(Graphics g) {
   topLine = vbar.getValue();
   int xOffset = hbar.getValue();
   int numLines = text.size();
   screenHeight = getSize().height;
   int y = baseline;
   for(int i = topLine;(i < numLines) && (y < screenHeight + lineSize);++i) {
    g.drawString((String) text.elementAt(i),-xOffset,y);
    y += lineSize;
   }
  }
 }
}
```

When you run the TextScrollApp program, you will see the opening window, shown in Figure 29.1. Notice that vertical and horizontal scrollbars are added to the application window.

FIGURE 29.1.

The TextScrollApp *opening window.*

Click on the File pull-down menu and select the Open menu item. An Open File dialog box is displayed. Open the TextScrollApp.java file. The window is updated, as shown in Figure 29.2.

FIGURE 29.2.

Displaying
TextScrollApp.java.

Use the horizontal scrollbar to scroll the view of the text to the right. (See Figure 29.3.)

FIGURE 29.3.

Scrolling horizontally.

Scroll the text all the way back to the left and then click once on the down arrow of the vertical scrollbar. This causes the window to move the view of the text down one line. (See Figure 29.4.)

Click on the vertical scrollbar between the tab and the down arrow at the bottom of the scrollbar. This causes the view of the text to be scrolled down 10 lines. (See Figure 29.5.)

Now drag the tab of the vertical scrollbar to the middle of the scrollbar. The view of the text is scrolled to the middle of the text file. (See Figure 29.6.)

Experiment with both the vertical and horizontal scrollbars to familiarize yourself with their operation before going on to study the TextScrollApp program.

FIGURE 29.4.

Scrolling vertically one line.

FIGURE 29.5.

Scrolling vertically using one page.

FIGURE 29.6.

Scrolling vertically with the tab.

The TextScrollApp program declares a number of field variables. The menuItems array and menuBar variable are used to construct the program's menu bar. The openFile variable implements the dialog box used to load in the text file to be displayed. The defaultFont variable is used to set the text font to a default 12-point plain style font. The screenWidth and screenHeight variables are used to specify the dimensions of the application window.

The text variable is declared as a Vector object. It is used to store the individual lines of text that are read from the text file. The topLine variable identifies the number of the line that is currently displayed at the top of the window. The toolkit variable is used to refer to the Toolkit associated with the application window. The fm variable is used to refer to the FontMetrics object associated with the default font.

The baseline variable is the vertical offset where the baseline of the first line of text should be displayed. The lineSize variable refers to the total height of the font being displayed. The maxWidth variable is calculated when a file is read. It refers to the maximum length of a text line in pixels. The canvas variable holds an object of the MyCanvas class. The hbar and vbar variables identify the horizontal and vertical scrollbars that are created and attached to the main window.

The setupFontData() method sets the window's font to the default font identified with the defaultFont variable. It then obtains the Toolkit object associated with the window and uses the getFontMetrics() method of the Toolkit to get the FontMetrics object associated with the default font. This object is assigned to the fm variable. The baseline variable is set to the sum of the leading and ascent of the current font as returned by the getLeading() and getAscent() methods of the FontMetrics class. The lineSize variable is set to the total height of the font using the getHeight() method of the FontMetrics class.

The setupScrollbars() method creates and initializes the horizontal and vertical scrollbars. A horizontal scrollbar is created with all of its parameters set to zero and is assigned to the hbar variable. A vertical scrollbar is created in the same manner and is assigned to the vbar variable. The specific parameters associated with these scrollbars are set when the text file that is to be scrolled is initially loaded. ScrollHandler objects are registered as event handlers for both scrollbars.

The background color of both scrollbars is set to light gray, and then the scrollbars are added to the main application window. Using BorderLayout simplifies the positioning of the scrollbars.

The resetScrollbars() method resets the parameters associated with both scrollbars based on the text that is loaded from the file. The horizontal scrollbar assigned to hbar is assigned a minimum value of 0 and a maximum value of maxWidth + 5, where maxWidth is the maximum width of a text line in pixels. The constant 5 is added to maxWidth to allow some scrolling to the right of the end of the widest line. The value parameter of the scrollbar is set to 0 so that the leftmost end of a text line is initially visible. The visible parameter is set to 10 to allow horizontal scrolling of 10 pixels at a time.

The vertical scrollbar assigned to vbar is initialized by setting its maximum parameter to the number of text lines plus the constant 5. The number of text lines is determined by invoking the size() method of the Vector class for the text Vector used to hold the text that was loaded from the selected text file. Specifying the visible parameter as 10 results in 10 lines being scrolled at a time. Note that the parameters of the horizontal scrollbar are specified in pixels, and those of the vertical scrollbar are specified in text lines.

The readFile() method is almost the same as the one used in previous examples. It has been modified to store each line of text that is read within the vector that is assigned to the text variable. The notifyUser() method creates and displays a dialog box if a read error occurs. The paint() method simply invokes the paint() method of the MyCanvas class (via repaint()).

The adjustmentValueChanged() method of the ScrollHandler class implements scrolling by invoking the repaint() method to cause the MyCanvas object to be redrawn.

The paint() method of MyCanvas reads the scrollbar positions in order to determine how to paint the canvas. It displays the text Vector on the screen. It sets the topLine variable to the value of the vertical scrollbar. It obtains this value by invoking the getValue() method of the Scrollbar class for vbar. It sets the xOffset variable to the value of the horizontal scrollbar. The scrollbar values are maintained and updated internally by the Scrollbar objects.

The numLines variable is set to the number of lines of text that are stored in the text Vector. The screenHeight variable is recalculated to adjust the text display for any window-resizing operations that may have occurred.

The y variable is used to specify the vertical position where each line of text should be drawn on the Graphics object referenced by the g variable. A for statement is used to draw the text. The text drawing begins with the line specified by the topLine variable and continues until the last line of the text file is displayed or the vertical display position assigned to the y variable is one line past the end of the screen. The drawString() method of the Graphics class is used to draw the text on the screen. It is invoked with the text lines stored in the Vector object assigned to the text variable. The elementAt() method of the Vector class is used to retrieve the required line of text. Note that the xOffset variable is passed to the drawString() method as a negative value. This causes text drawing to begin before the left edge of the display window and enables horizontal scrolling toward the right to be implemented.

Scrolling Graphics

The scrolling of graphics is handled in the same way as text. The only difference between text scrolling and graphics scrolling is that vertical text scrolling results in an integral number of lines being scrolled at a time and graphics scrolling does not. The minimum and maximum values associated with a vertical text scrollbar are generally set based on the number of lines to be scrolled. The parameters of the horizontal and vertical scrollbars associated with graphics applications are set based on the dimensions of the Graphics object being scrolled and the size of the window in which the object is being viewed.

The `ImageScrollApp` Program

The `ImageScrollApp` program shows how scrollbars can be used to scroll objects that are drawn on a `Graphics` object. This program upgrades the `DrawApp` program developed in the previous chapter with the capability to support horizontal and vertical scrolling. The source code of the `ImageScrollApp` program is shown in Listing 29.2.

Listing 29.2. The source code of the `ImageScrollApp` program.

```java
import java.awt.*;
import java.awt.event.*;
import java.lang.Math;
import java.util.Vector;
import jdg.ch25.*;

public class ImageScrollApp extends Frame {
 Object menuItems[][] = {
  {"File","New","-","Exit"},
  {"Draw","+Line","-Oval","-Rectangle"}
 };
 MenuItemHandler mih = new MenuItemHandler();
 MyMenuBar menuBar = new MyMenuBar(menuItems,mih,mih);
 MyCanvas canvas = new MyCanvas(TwoPointObject.LINE);
 int screenWidth = 400;
 int screenHeight = 400;
 int canvasWidth = 1000;
 int canvasHeight = 1000;
 Scrollbar hbar, vbar;
 public static void main(String args[]){
  ImageScrollApp app = new ImageScrollApp();
 }
 public ImageScrollApp() {
  super("ImageScrollApp");
  setup();
  pack();
  setSize(screenWidth,screenHeight);
  addWindowListener(new WindowEventHandler());
  show();
 }
 void setup() {
  setBackground(Color.white);
  setMenuBar(menuBar);
  setCursor(new Cursor(CROSSHAIR_CURSOR));
  canvas.addFocusListener(new FocusHandler());
  add("Center",canvas);
  setupScrollbars();
 }
 void setupScrollbars() {
  hbar = new Scrollbar(Scrollbar.HORIZONTAL,0,10,0,canvasWidth);
  vbar = new Scrollbar(Scrollbar.VERTICAL,0,10,0,canvasHeight);
  hbar.setBackground(Color.lightGray);
  vbar.setBackground(Color.lightGray);
  hbar.addAdjustmentListener(new ScrollHandler());
  vbar.addAdjustmentListener(new ScrollHandler());
  add("South",hbar);
  add("East",vbar);
```

```java
}
class ScrollHandler implements AdjustmentListener {
 public void adjustmentValueChanged(AdjustmentEvent e){
  canvas.updateOffsets(hbar.getValue(),vbar.getValue());
 }
}
class FocusHandler extends FocusAdapter {
 public void focusGained(FocusEvent e){
  setCursor(new Cursor(CROSSHAIR_CURSOR));
 }
 public void focusLost(FocusEvent e){
  setCursor(new Cursor(DEFAULT_CURSOR));
 }
}
class MenuItemHandler implements ActionListener, ItemListener {
 public void actionPerformed(ActionEvent ev){
  String s=ev.getActionCommand();
  if(s=="Exit"){
   System.exit(0);
  }else if(s=="New"){
   canvas.clear();
  }
 }
 public void itemStateChanged(ItemEvent e){
  CheckboxMenuItem ch = (CheckboxMenuItem) e.getItemSelectable();
  String s = ch.getLabel();
  MyMenu menu = menuBar.getMenu("Draw");
  CheckboxMenuItem lineItem = (CheckboxMenuItem) menu.getItem("Line");
  CheckboxMenuItem ovalItem = (CheckboxMenuItem) menu.getItem("Oval");
  CheckboxMenuItem rectangleItem =
   (CheckboxMenuItem) menu.getItem("Rectangle");
  if(s.equals("Line")){
   canvas.setTool(TwoPointObject.LINE);
   lineItem.setState(true);
   ovalItem.setState(false);
   rectangleItem.setState(false);
  }else if(s.equals("Oval")){
   canvas.setTool(TwoPointObject.OVAL);
   lineItem.setState(false);
   ovalItem.setState(true);
   rectangleItem.setState(false);
  }else if(s.equals("Rectangle")){
   canvas.setTool(TwoPointObject.RECTANGLE);
   lineItem.setState(false);
   ovalItem.setState(false);
   rectangleItem.setState(true);
  }
 }
}
class WindowEventHandler extends WindowAdapter {
 public void windowClosing(WindowEvent e){
  System.exit(0);
 }
}
}
class MyCanvas extends Canvas {
 int tool = TwoPointObject.LINE;
 Vector objects = new Vector();
```

continues

Listing 29.2. continued

```
TwoPointObject current;
boolean newObject = false;
int xOffset = 0;
int yOffset = 0;
public MyCanvas(int toolType) {
 super();
 tool = toolType;
 addMouseListener(new MouseHandler());
 addMouseMotionListener(new MouseMotionHandler());
}
public void setTool(int toolType) {
 tool = toolType;
}
public void clear() {
 objects.removeAllElements();
 repaint();
}
public void updateOffsets(int x,int y) {
 xOffset = x;
 yOffset = y;
 repaint();
}
public void paint(Graphics g) {
 int numObjects = objects.size();
 for(int i=0;i<numObjects;++i) {
  TwoPointObject obj = (TwoPointObject) objects.elementAt(i);
  obj.draw(g,xOffset,yOffset);
 }
 if(newObject) current.draw(g,xOffset,yOffset);
}
class MouseHandler extends MouseAdapter {
 public void mousePressed(MouseEvent e){
  current = new TwoPointObject(tool,e.getX()+xOffset,e.getY()+yOffset);
  newObject = true;
 }
 public void mouseReleased(MouseEvent e){
  if(newObject) {
   objects.addElement(current);
   newObject = false;
  }
 }
}
class MouseMotionHandler extends MouseMotionAdapter {
 public void mouseDragged(MouseEvent e){
  int newX = e.getX()+xOffset;
  int newY = e.getY()+yOffset;
  if(newObject) {
   int oldX = current.endX;
   int oldY = current.endY;
   if(tool != TwoPointObject.LINE) {
    if(newX > current.startX) current.endX = newX;
    if(newY > current.startY) current.endY = newY;
   }else{
    current.endX = newX;
    current.endY = newY;
   }
```

```
    repaint();
    }
   }
  }
}
class TwoPointObject {
 public static int LINE = 0;
 public static int OVAL = 1;
 public static int RECTANGLE = 2;
 public int type, startX, startY, endX, endY;
 public TwoPointObject(int objectType,int x1,int y1,int x2,int y2) {
  type = objectType;
  startX = x1;
  startY = y1;
  endX = x2;
  endY = y2;
 }
 public TwoPointObject(int objectType,int x,int y) {
  this(objectType,x,y,x,y);
 }
 public TwoPointObject() {
  this(LINE,0,0,0,0);
 }
 public void draw(Graphics g,int xOffset,int yOffset) {
  if(type == LINE)
   g.drawLine(startX - xOffset,startY - yOffset,endX - xOffset,endY -yOffset);
  else{
   int w = Math.abs(endX - startX);
   int l = Math.abs(endY - startY);
   if(type == OVAL) g.drawOval(startX - xOffset,startY - yOffset,w,l);
   else g.drawRect(startX - xOffset,startY - yOffset,w,l);
  }
 }
}
```

When you run the ImageScrollApp program, the window shown in Figure 29.7 is displayed. If this program looks similar to the DrawApp program of the previous chapter, it should. The DrawApp program has been upgraded to support vertical and horizontal scrolling.

FIGURE 29.7.

The ImageScrollApp *opening window.*

Use the Draw menu to select drawing tools; then draw some objects in the visible window as I have done in Figure 29.8.

FIGURE 29.8.

Drawing some objects.

Use the vertical and horizontal scrollbars to move throughout the extended canvas and draw more objects as I have done in Figure 29.9.

FIGURE 29.9.

Scrolling and drawing more.

Experiment with the scrollbars and drawing tools to become more familiar with the program's operation.

The `ImageScrollApp` program upgrades the `DrawApp` program to use scrollbars. Because the operation of the `DrawApp` program is extensively described in the previous chapter, I'll assume that it is still fresh in your mind and describe only the coding differences required to implement the scrollbars.

The `ImageScrollApp` class uses the `canvasWidth` and `canvasHeight` variables to represent the horizontal and vertical dimensions of the canvas. The area of the canvas is over six times the area of the default window size. This provides enough canvas to implement a reasonable amount of scrolling. The `hbar` and `vbar` variables are used to identify the horizontal and vertical scrollbars.

The `setupScrollBars()` method creates a horizontal scrollbar with the maximum size parameter set to the `canvasWidth`. It assigns this object to the `hbar` variable. A vertical scrollbar is created with its maximum parameter set to the `canvasHeight` and assigned to the `vbar` variable. The `visible` parameter of both scrollbars is set to the value of `10`. This enables page up and down operations to scroll 10 pixels at a time, a relatively small distance. Both scrollbars use an object of the `ScrollHandler` class to handle scrolling events.

The `adjustmentValueChanged()` method of the `ScrollHandler` class handles scrollbar-related events by invoking the `updateOffsets()` method of the `MyCanvas` class with the current values of the horizontal and vertical scrollbars. The method is invoked for the `MyCanvas` object assigned to the `canvas` variable.

The `MyCanvas` class adds two new variables to its definition. The `xOffset` and `yOffset` variables maintain the current position of the canvas that is displayed in the upper-left corner of its `Graphics` object. These variables are modified via the `updateOffsets()` method, which also invokes the `repaint()` method to cause the canvas to be repainted.

The `paint()` method adds the `xOffset` and `yOffset` variables to the `draw()` method used to draw objects of the `TwoPointObject` class.

The `xOffset` and `yOffset` variables are used in the `mousePressed()` and `mouseDragged()` event-handling methods to translate the x,y-coordinates supplied as arguments in the method invocation to coordinates that are relative to the overall canvas.

The `draw()` method of the `TwoPointObject` class uses the `xOffset` and `yOffset` parameters to translate the x,y-coordinates of the objects being drawn from coordinates that are relative to the overall canvas to coordinates that are relative to the current `Graphics` object being updated.

Using the `ScrollPane` Class

Java 1.1 introduces the `ScrollPane` class in order to simplify the development of scrollable applications. The `ScrollPane` class is like a combination of a panel and vertical and horizontal scrollbars. The great thing about it is that it performs all of the scrollbar event handling and screen redrawing internally. The fact that the `ScrollPane` class handles events is significant. By handling events internally, it allows scrolling-related operations to run significantly faster.

The `ScrollPane` class extends the `Container` class and therefore can contain other components. It is designed to automate scrolling for a single contained component, such as a `Canvas` object. It provides two constructors: a single parameterless constructor and a constructor that takes an `int` argument. The parameterless constructor creates a `ScrollPane` object that displays scrollbars only when they are needed. The other constructor takes one of the three constants:

SCROLLBARS_ALWAYS, SCROLLBARS_AS_NEEDED, and SCROLLBARS_NEVER. These constants determine if and when scrollbars are displayed by the ScrollPane object.

The initial size of the ScrollPane object is 100×100 pixels. The setSize() method can be used to resize it. The ScrollPane class provides methods for accessing and updating its internal scrollbars, although, in most cases, this is both unnecessary and ill-advised. Other methods are provided to get and set the current scrollbar positions.

The ScrollPaneApp Program

The following program illustrates the use of the ScrollPane class. Its code is shown in Listing 29.3. It is a remake of the TextScrollApp program of Listing 29.1.

Listing 29.3. The source code of the ScrollPaneApp program.

```
import java.awt.*;
import java.awt.event.*;
import java.io.*;
import java.util.Vector;
import jdg.ch25.*;

public class ScrollPaneApp extends Frame {
 Object menuItems[][] = {{"File","Open","-","Exit"}};
 MenuItemHandler mih = new MenuItemHandler();
 MyMenuBar menuBar = new MyMenuBar(menuItems,mih,mih);
 FileDialog openFile = new FileDialog(this,"Open File",FileDialog.LOAD);
 MessageDialog notification;
 DialogHandler dh = new DialogHandler();
 Font defaultFont = new Font("default",Font.PLAIN,12);
 Vector text = new Vector();
 int topLine;
 Toolkit toolkit;
 FontMetrics fm;
 int baseline;
 int lineSize;
 int maxWidth;
 Canvas canvas = new MyCanvas();
 ScrollPane scrollPane;
 public static void main(String args[]){
  ScrollPaneApp app = new ScrollPaneApp();
 }
 public ScrollPaneApp() {
  super("ScrollPaneApp");
  setup();
  setSize(400,400);
  addWindowListener(new WindowEventHandler());
  show();
 }
 void setup() {
  setMenuBar(menuBar);
  setupFontData();
  setupScrollPane();
 }
 void setupFontData() {
```

```
 setFont(defaultFont);
 toolkit = getToolkit();
 fm = toolkit.getFontMetrics(defaultFont);
 baseline = fm.getLeading()+fm.getAscent();
 lineSize = fm.getHeight();
}
void setupScrollPane() {
 scrollPane = new ScrollPane(ScrollPane.SCROLLBARS_ALWAYS);
 canvas.setSize(1000,3000);
 scrollPane.add(canvas);
 add("Center",scrollPane);
}
void resetScrollbars() {
 scrollPane.setScrollPosition(0,0);
}
public void readFile(String file) {
 BufferedReader inStream;
 try{
  inStream = new BufferedReader(new FileReader(file));
 }catch (IOException ex){
  notifyUser("Error opening file");
  return;
 }
 try{
  Vector newText = new Vector();
  String line;
  maxWidth = 0;
  while((line=inStream.readLine())!=null) {
   int lineWidth = fm.stringWidth(line);
   if(lineWidth > maxWidth) maxWidth = lineWidth;
   newText.addElement(line);
  }
  text = newText;
  topLine = 0;
  inStream.close();
  resetScrollbars();
  repaint();
 }catch (IOException ex){
  notifyUser("Error reading file");
 }
}
public void notifyUser(String s) {
 String text[] = {s};
 String buttons[] = {"OK"};
 notification = new MessageDialog(this,"Error",true,text,
  buttons,dh,dh);
}
public void paint(Graphics g) {
 canvas.repaint();
}
class MenuItemHandler implements ActionListener, ItemListener {
 public void actionPerformed(ActionEvent ev){
  String s=ev.getActionCommand();
  if(s=="Exit"){
   System.exit(0);
  }else if(s=="Open"){
   openFile.show();
```

continues

Listing 29.3. continued

```
  if(openFile.getFile() != null) {
   String inFile = openFile.getFile();
   readFile(inFile);
  }
 }
}
 public void itemStateChanged(ItemEvent e){
 }
}
class WindowEventHandler extends WindowAdapter {
 public void windowClosing(WindowEvent e){
  System.exit(0);
 }
}
class DialogHandler extends WindowAdapter implements ActionListener {
 public void windowClosing(WindowEvent e){
  notification.dispose();
 }
 public void actionPerformed(ActionEvent e){
  notification.dispose();
 }
}
class MyCanvas extends Canvas {
 public void paint(Graphics g) {
  int numLines = text.size();
  int y = baseline;
  for(int i = 0;i < numLines;++i) {
   g.drawString((String) text.elementAt(i),0,y);
   y += lineSize;
  }
 }
}
}
```

The ScrollPaneApp program operates in the same way as the TextScrollApp program. To verify this, use it to open the ScrollPaneApp.java file and scroll through it, as shown in Figure 29.10.

FIGURE 29.10.

Using the
ScrollPaneApp
program.

Only a few changes were made to TextScrollApp to switch from the use of Scrollbar class to the ScrollPane class:

■ The hbar and vbar variables were removed and replaced by the scrollPane variable.

■ The setupScrollbars() method was replaced by the setupScrollPane() method.

■ The setupScrollPane() method creates a ScrollPane object with scrollbars always displayed and adds a 1,000×3,000 pixel MyCanvas object to it.

■ The resetScrollbars() method is revised to reset the scrollbars of the ScrollPane object using the setScrollPosition() method.

■ The paint() method of the MyCanvas class is simplified to display all lines of a file to the canvas without having to worry about the current scrollbar position.

As you can see, use of the ScrollPane class greatly simplifies screen drawing. That's one of the benefits of using it over simple scrollbars.

Summary

This chapter explains the use of the Scrollbar and ScrollPane classes. It shows you how to use vertical and horizontal scrollbars to scroll text and graphics displayed on the canvas. The event handling supported by scrollbars also was explained. Chapter 32, "Using Animation," shows you how to add multimedia features, such as sound and animation, to your Java programs.

30

Printing

The phenomenal success of the JDK 1.0 was due in a large part to the capabilities provided by the Abstract Window Toolkit (AWT). Although the AWT of JDK 1.0 included a number of powerful platform-independent features for window program development, it also lacked some important capabilities. One of the most glaring capabilities that was missing from the AWT of JDK 1.0 was printing support. JDK 1.1 now provides the printing support that was left out of JDK 1.0.

This chapter shows you how to print from your window programs. It identifies the classes and methods used to print from the AWT. It covers several programming examples that explain how to print text and graphics and to work with print jobs. When you finish this chapter, you'll be able to include printing capabilities in your window programs.

Printing Classes and Methods

JDK 1.1 supports AWT printing through the use of the PrintJob class of java.awt. This is an abstract class used to encapsulate print requests. An object of the PrintJob class is returned by the getPrintJob() method of the Toolkit class. This method initiates a platform-dependent print request using platform-specific dialog boxes. It has three parameters: a Frame object that identifies the application window from which the print request is generated, a String object that provides a title for the print job, and a Properties object that allows job-specific print properties to be specified and retrieved.

> **NOTE**
>
> In the Java vernacular, you *draw* on a Graphics object to display information to the screen or printer.

The PrintJob class provides the following six access methods:

- getGraphics()—Returns a Graphics object that is drawn on to accomplish printing. The Graphics object is sent to the printer when its disposed() method is invoked.
- getPageDimension()—Returns a Dimension object that identifies the width and height in pixels of the page to be printed.
- getPageResolution()—Identifies the page resolution in pixels per inch.
- lastPageFirst()—Returns a boolean value indicating whether the pages of a print job are printed in reverse order.
- end()—Completes the printing of the print job.
- finalize()—Invoked by the garbage collector when the PrintJob is no longer in use.

The getGraphics() method is key to printing—it provides a Graphics object that is used for drawing text and graphics. This Graphics object implements the PrintGraphics interface. This interface can be used to distinguish between a Graphics object that is used for printing and one that is used for screen display. The PrintGraphics interface consists of a single method, getPrintJob(), which returns the PrintJob associated with the Graphics object.

After drawing has been completed for a Graphics object, the object's dispose() method is invoked, which causes it to be printed. The end() method is invoked to end a print job.

The getPageResolution() and getPageDimension() methods are used to determine how a page is to be laid out. The getPageResolution() method returns the number of pixels per inch supported by a printer. The page dimensions returned by getPageDimension() are not the actual pixel dimensions of the page to be printed. Rather, the dimensions are an (often unsuccessful) mapping of screen coordinates to the graphics context used for printing. Because the dimensions returned by this method (as of the JDK 1.1.1) are inaccurate (as you'll see in the example of the next section), it should not be used for page layout.

Working with Print Jobs

The PrintJob class is easy to use. To create a PrintJob object, simply invoke the getPrintJob() method of the Toolkit class. You can then invoke the methods of the PrintJob class to retrieve printer information, obtain a PrintGraphics object, or to complete a print job. The PrintTestApp program, shown in Listing 30.1, shows how to work with PrintJob objects to obtain printer-related information. When you run this program, the opening window, shown in Figure 30.1, is displayed. Select Print from the File menu, and a Print dialog box, similar to the one shown in Figure 30.2, is displayed. Click the OK button and the Print dialog box goes away. The program window is updated to display the following information, as shown in Figure 30.3:

- The name of the print job
- Any Properties object returned by the getPrintJob() request
- The dimensions of the page in pixels
- The printer's resolution in pixels per inch
- Whether the printer prints the last page first

NOTE

Depending on your printer and printer driver, the program may cause a blank page to be ejected.

Listing 30.1. The source code of the `PrintTestApp` program.

```java
import java.awt.*;
import java.awt.event.*;
import java.util.Properties;
import jdg.ch25.*;

public class PrintTestApp extends Frame {
 Object menuItems[][] = {{"File","Print","-","Exit"}};
 MenuItemHandler mih = new MenuItemHandler();
 MyMenuBar menuBar = new MyMenuBar(menuItems,mih,mih);
 TextArea textArea = new TextArea();
 Toolkit toolkit;
 int screenWidth = 300;
 int screenHeight = 300;
 public static void main(String args[]){
  PrintTestApp app = new PrintTestApp();
 }
 public PrintTestApp() {
  super("PrintTestApp");
  setup();
  setSize(screenWidth,screenHeight);
  addWindowListener(new WindowEventHandler());
  show();
 }
 void setup() {
  setMenuBar(menuBar);
  toolkit=getToolkit();
  add("Center",textArea);
 }
 class MenuItemHandler implements ActionListener, ItemListener {
  public void actionPerformed(ActionEvent ev){
   String s=ev.getActionCommand();
   String name="Test print job";
   Properties properties=new Properties();
   if(s=="Exit"){
    System.exit(0);
   }else if(s=="Print"){
    PrintJob pj=toolkit.getPrintJob(PrintTestApp.this,
      name,properties);
    if(pj==null) textArea.setText("A null PrintJob was returned.");
    else{
     String output="Name: "+name+"\nProperties: "+properties.toString();
     Dimension pageDim=pj.getPageDimension();
     int resolution=pj.getPageResolution();
     boolean lastPageFirst=pj.lastPageFirst();
     output+="\nPage dimension (in pixels):";
     output+="\n height: "+String.valueOf(pageDim.height);
     output+="\n width: "+String.valueOf(pageDim.width);
     output+="\nResolution (pixels/inch): "+String.valueOf(resolution);
     output+="\nLast Page First: "+String.valueOf(lastPageFirst);
     textArea.setText(output);
     pj.getGraphics().dispose();
     pj.end();
    }
   }
  }
 }
```

```
  public void itemStateChanged(ItemEvent e){
  }
 }
 class WindowEventHandler extends WindowAdapter {
  public void windowClosing(WindowEvent e){
   System.exit(0);
  }
 }
}
```

FIGURE 30.1.

The opening window of the PrintTestApp *program.*

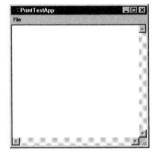

FIGURE 30.2.

A Windows 95 Print dialog box.

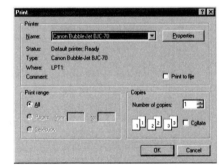

Figure 30.3 shows the parameters that are displayed for my Canon BJC-70 printer. If you have access to more than one printer (for example, a network printer), you can use the Print dialog box to retrieve the parameters for that printer, as shown in Figure 30.4. Figure 30.5 shows the parameters that are displayed for my HP 660C printer.

FIGURE 30.3.

The printer information of a Canon BJC-70 printer.

FIGURE 30.4.
Using the Print dialog box to select another printer.

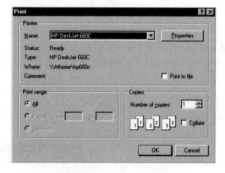

FIGURE 30.5.
The printer information of an HP 660C printer.

The setup() method of the PrintTestApp class creates a Toolkit object and assigns it to the toolkit variable. It also creates a TextArea object to be used to display results to the user. The MenuItemHandler class handles the selection of the Print menu item by invoking the getPrintJob() method of the Toolkit class to return a PrintJob object to be used for printing. This object is assigned to the pj variable. The pj variable is checked to make sure that the print job is not null. In this case, the getPageDimension(), getPageResolution(), and lastPageFirst() methods are invoked to retrieve information about the printer. This information is displayed to the screen along with the Properties object returned by the getPrintJob() method. The getGraphics() method of the PrintJob class is invoked to retrieve a Graphics object for printing. This object is immediately disposed of by invoking its dispose() method. The end() method of the PrintJob class is then invoked to complete the processing of the print job.

The values of the page dimensions reported for the Canon BJC-70 printer were 252 × 252 pixels. The values returned for the HP 660C printer were 792 × 612 pixels. These dimensions are not the physical dimensions of a printed page as you'll see in the next section; however, the printer resolutions of 360 pixels per inch and 300 pixels per inch are accurate.

Page Layout Controls

Java programs are required to perform their own page layout and pagination. The getPageDimension() and getPageResolution() methods provide the mechanism to do this.

Unfortunately, these methods are not compatible. As shown in the previous example, the `getPageResolution()` method returns the actual printer resolution, while the `getPageDimension()` method returns logical page dimensions that are used to provide compatibility with the screen display.

The `PrintDimApp` program, shown in Listing 30.2, illustrates the use of (and inconsistency of) the `getPageDimension()` method in laying out pages for printing. The `PrintDimApp` opening screen is shown in Figure 30.6. When you select Print from the File menu, it prints a rectangle around the border of a page. On some printers, such as my HP 660C, it prints the rectangle using a border that is 10% of the page width and height. On other printers, such as my Canon BJC-70, it prints the rectangle in the upper-left corner of the page. You can use this program to determine how well the page dimensions returned by `getPageDimension()` work with your printer.

FIGURE 30.6.

The opening window of the `PrintDimApp` *program.*

Listing 30.2. The source code of the `PrintDimApp` program.

```
import java.awt.*;
import java.awt.event.*;
import java.util.Properties;
import jdg.ch25.*;

public class PrintDimApp extends Frame {
 Object menuItems[][] = {{"File","Print","-","Exit"}};
 MenuItemHandler mih = new MenuItemHandler();
 MyMenuBar menuBar = new MyMenuBar(menuItems,mih,mih);
 Toolkit toolkit;
 int screenWidth = 200;
 int screenHeight = 200;
 public static void main(String args[]){
  PrintDimApp app = new PrintDimApp();
 }
 public PrintDimApp() {
  super("PrintDimApp");
  setup();
  setSize(screenWidth,screenHeight);
  addWindowListener(new WindowEventHandler());
  show();
 }
 void setup() {
  setMenuBar(menuBar);
  toolkit=getToolkit();
 }
```

continues

Listing 30.2. continued

```
void printDimensions(Graphics g,Dimension size){
 int width=size.width;
 int height=size.height;
 int x1=(int) (width*0.1);
 int x2=(int) (width*0.9);
 int y1=(int) (height*0.1);
 int y2=(int) (height*0.9);
 g.drawRect(x1,y1,x2-x1,y2-y1);
 g.dispose();
}
class MenuItemHandler implements ActionListener, ItemListener {
 public void actionPerformed(ActionEvent ev){
  String s=ev.getActionCommand();
  String name="Test print job";
  Properties properties=new Properties();
  if(s=="Exit"){
   System.exit(0);
  }else if(s=="Print"){
   PrintJob pj=toolkit.getPrintJob(PrintDimApp.this,
    name,properties);
   if(pj!=null){
    printDimensions(pj.getGraphics(),pj.getPageDimension());
    pj.end();
   }
  }
 }
 public void itemStateChanged(ItemEvent e){
 }
}
class WindowEventHandler extends WindowAdapter {
 public void windowClosing(WindowEvent e){
  System.exit(0);
 }
}
}
```

The overall structure of PrintDimApp is similar to PrintTestApp. The major difference between the two programs is the way that the Print menu item is handled.

The PrintDimApp program creates a PrintJob object using the getPrintJob() method of the Toolkit class. It invokes the printDimensions() method, passing it a Graphics object and Dimension object retrieved via the getGraphics() and getPageDimension() methods of PrintJob.

The printDimensions() method uses the Dimension object to draw a rectangle on the Graphics object. This rectangle is drawn with margins that are 10% of the page width and page height. The dispose() method is invoked to initiate printing of the Graphics object.

Printing Text and Graphics

The PrintJob class provides an easy-to-use interface for printing. Text and graphics are drawn to the printer in the same way as they are drawn to the screen—you just display them to a different `Graphics` object. In fact, you can copy everything that is displayed to the screen to the printer by using a common drawing method for both. The `PrintSampleApp` program, shown in Listing 20.3, demonstrates how this can be accomplished.

When you run `PrintSampleApp`, it displays the opening window, shown in Figure 30.7. If you select Print from the File menu, the contents of the window can be sent to your printer. The `PrintSampleApp` program shows how graphics (rectangles, circles, and lines) and text are printed.

FIGURE 30.7.

The opening window of the PrintSampleApp *program.*

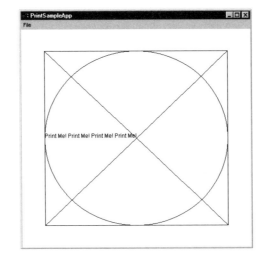

Listing 30.3. The source code for the `PrintSampleApp` program.

```java
import java.awt.*;
import java.awt.event.*;
import java.util.Properties;
import jdg.ch25.*;

public class PrintSampleApp extends Frame {
 Object menuItems[][] = {{"File","Print","-","Exit"}};
 MenuItemHandler mih = new MenuItemHandler();
 MyMenuBar menuBar = new MyMenuBar(menuItems,mih,mih);
 MyCanvas canvas = new MyCanvas();
 Toolkit toolkit;
 int screenWidth = 500;
 int screenHeight = 500;
 public static void main(String args[]){
  PrintSampleApp app = new PrintSampleApp();
 }
 public PrintSampleApp() {
  super("PrintSampleApp");
  setup();
  setSize(screenWidth,screenHeight);
  addWindowListener(new WindowEventHandler());
  show();
```

continues

Listing 30.3. continued

```
 }
 void setup() {
  setMenuBar(menuBar);
  toolkit=getToolkit();
  add("Center",canvas);
 }
 class MenuItemHandler implements ActionListener, ItemListener {
  public void actionPerformed(ActionEvent ev){
   String s=ev.getActionCommand();
   String name="Test print job";
   Properties properties=new Properties();
   if(s=="Exit"){
    System.exit(0);
   }else if(s=="Print"){
    PrintJob pj=toolkit.getPrintJob(PrintSampleApp.this,
     name,properties);
    if(pj!=null){
     canvas.printAll(pj.getGraphics());
     pj.end();
    }
   }
  }
  public void itemStateChanged(ItemEvent e){
  }
 }
 class WindowEventHandler extends WindowAdapter {
  public void windowClosing(WindowEvent e){
   System.exit(0);
  }
 }
}
class MyCanvas extends Canvas {
 public void paint(Graphics g){
  Dimension size=getSize();
  int width=size.width;
  int height=size.height;
  int x1=(int) (width*0.1);
  int x2=(int) (width*0.9);
  int y1=(int) (height*0.1);
  int y2=(int) (height*0.9);
  g.drawRect(x1,y1,x2-x1,y2-y1);
  g.drawOval(x1,y1,x2-x1,y2-y1);
  g.drawLine(x1,y1,x2,y2);
  g.drawLine(x2,y1,x1,y2);
  String text = "Print Me! ";
  text+=text;
  text+=text;
  g.drawString(text,x1,(int)((y1+y2)/2));
  g.dispose();
 }
}
```

The `PrintSampleApp` program creates an object of the `MyCanvas` class and adds it to the center of the application window. The `paint()` method of the `MyCanvas` class draws a rectangle, oval, two lines, and the text `Print Me! Print Me! Print Me!` on a graphics object. When the screen is initially painted and then repainted, the `Graphics` object is displayed to the application window. When the Print menu item is selected from the File menu, the `printAll()` method of the `Component` class is invoked for the `MyCanvas` object displayed in the application window. The `printAll()` method is passed the `Graphics` object of a `PrintJob` as an argument. The `printAll()` method prints a `Component` object (and all subcomponents) to a `Graphics` object. This causes the contents of the screen to be copied to the printer.

Summary

This chapter shows you how to include printing capabilities in your window programs. It covers the classes and methods used to support printing. You created examples that showed you how to print text and graphics and to work with print jobs. Chapter 31, "Using the Clipboard," covers the new Java classes that help you to implement cut, copy, and paste operations using the system clipboard.

31

Using the Clipboard

Copying and pasting data to and from the clipboard is a fundamental capability that is expected by users of all window-based operating systems. However, as of JDK 1.02, this capability was not widely supported in Java window programs. Only objects of the TextField and TextArea classes supported clipboard operations. JDK 1.1 provides the basis for full support of clipboard operations through the Clipboard class and other classes and interfaces of the java.awt.transfer package.

This chapter introduces you to the classes of java.awt.transfer. You'll learn how to copy Java objects to the clipboard and paste them in other windows or programs. When you finish this chapter, you'll be able to implement clipboard support in your Java applications.

Clipboard Basics

As of JDK 1.1, the java.awt.datatransfer class was created to support clipboard operations. It consists of two interfaces (ClipboardOwner and Transferable) and three classes (Clipboard, DataFlavor, and StringSelection). Each of these classes and interfaces are covered in the following sections.

The Clipboard Class

The Clipboard class, as you would expect, is the core class for implementing clipboard operations. It provides access to the system clipboard as well as to Java-internal clipboard objects. The system clipboard can be used to copy and paste data between Java and non-Java programs. The Clipboard object is returned by the getSystemClipboard() method of the Toolkit class. Other Java-internal Clipboard objects can be created using the Clipboard() constructor, which takes a String object (the name of the clipboard) as an argument.

The Clipboard class has two field variables: owner and contents. The owner variable refers to an object that implements the ClipboardOwner interface and identifies the process that owns the clipboard. The contents variable refers to an object that is placed on the clipboard. This object implements the Transferable interface.

The three clipboard access methods—getName(), getContents(), and setContents()—are used to identify a Clipboard object, get the contents of the clipboard, and put new data on the clipboard.

The getContents() method takes a single argument—the object requesting the clipboard's contents. It returns an object that implements the Transferable interface. This object is used to access the clipboard's contents.

The setContents() method takes two arguments: an object that implements the Transferable interface and an object that implements the Clipboard owner interface. The first object contains the data that is to be placed on the clipboard. The second object identifies the object that placed the data on the clipboard.

The `Transferable` Interface

Objects that implement the `Transferable` interface are copied to and from `Clipboard` objects via the `setContents()` and `getContents()` method of the `Clipboard` class. The `Transferable` interface has three methods that allow the clipboard data to be read:

- `getTransferDataFlavors()`—Returns an array of `DataFlavor` objects that describe the type of data that is on the clipboard and the various format options in which the data can be accessed.

- `isDataFlavorSupported()`—Returns a `boolean` value indicating whether a particular `DataFlavor` object is supported. The `DataFlavor` object of interest is passed as an argument to this method.

- `getTransferData()`—Returns an object that identifies the actual data to be retrieved from the clipboard. The object returned depends on the `DataFlavor` object that is passed as an argument. This object must be cast to a class that is appropriate for the `DataFlavor` object.

The key to reading data from the clipboard is to read the data using the most appropriate data flavor (for example, PostScript, HTML, plain text, and so on). At present, choosing the correct flavor is easy because the `java.awt.datatransfer` package only provides useful support for simple text transfers. However, the classes and interfaces of `java.awt.datatransfer` provide a foundation from which more complex data flavors can be created.

The `DataFlavor` Class

The `DataFlavor` class encapsulates data types used to pass data to and from the clipboard. A `DataFlavor` object consists of the following information:

- A human-readable name
- A MIME type
- The Java class of the object to be returned (referred to as its *representation* class)

The naming scheme of the `DataFlavor` class bridges the gap between humans, MIME types, and Java. It provides a sound foundation from which complex clipboard operations can be supported.

The `DataFlavor` class provides two constructors—one that creates a `DataFlavor` object for a particular Java class and one that creates a `DataFlavor` object for a specified MIME type. In the first case, a `Class` object (representing the class of the data to be sent to the keyboard) and a `String` that provides a human-readable name for the data are provided as arguments to the constructor. The MIME type associated with the `DataFlavor` object defaults to `application/x-java-serialized-object`.

In the second case, the MIME type and human-readable name are provided as arguments to the constructor and the Java class name of the object defaults to either `InputStream` or `null`.

Nine access methods of `DataFlavor` are used to get and set the human-readable name, MIME type, and Java class associated with `DataFlavor` objects:

- The `getHumanPresentableName()` and `setHumanPresentableName()` methods provide access to the human-readable name of a `DataFlavor` object.
- The `getMimeType()`, `normalizeMimeType()`, `normalizeMimeTypeParameter()`, and the two versions of the `isMimeTypeEqual()` method provide access to the MIME type of a `DataFlavor` object.
- The `getRepresentationClass()` method returns the Java class that is associated with a `DataFlavor` object.
- The `equals()` method is used to compare `DataFlavor` objects.

The `DataFlavor` class defines two constants, `plainTextFlavor` and `stringFlavor`, that are used to identify specific data flavors. The `plainTextFlavor` constant identifies data that is of the text/plain MIME type and that is associated with an `InputStream` class or with no class (`null`). The `stringFlavor` constant identifies an object of the `java.lang.String` class that has the `application/x-java-serialized-object` MIME type.

The `ReadClipApp` Program

The `ReadClipApp` program of Listing 31.1 shows how the `Clipboard` class, `Transferable` interface, and `DataFlavor` class are used to obtain information about data that is contained on the clipboard. Figure 31.1 shows the program's opening display. Copy some text to the clipboard using a text editor such as Notepad. When you switch to `ReadClipApp` and select Clipboard from the Read menu, `ReadClipApp` displays information about the flavor of the data contained on the clipboard, as shown in Figure 31.2. Try copying nontext objects to the clipboard, such as an image that you create using the Paint program. When you try to read information about these objects, the `ReadClipApp` program displays the information shown in Figure 31.3. The reason why the program does not see the image data is because the `DataFlavor` class for the image data is not available.

FIGURE 31.1.

The opening window of the ReadClipApp *program.*

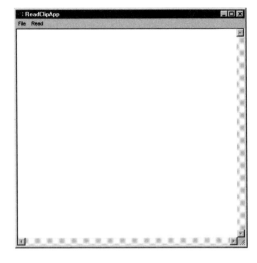

FIGURE 31.2.

Displaying information about the clipboard's contents.

FIGURE 31.3.

How unknown data flavors are handled.

Listing 31.1. The source code of the `ReadClipApp` program.

```java
import java.awt.*;
import java.awt.event.*;
import java.awt.datatransfer.*;
import jdg.ch25.*;

public class ReadClipApp extends Frame {
 Object menuItems[][] = {{"File","Exit"},
  {"Read","Clipboard"}};
 MenuItemHandler mih = new MenuItemHandler();
 MyMenuBar menuBar = new MyMenuBar(menuItems,mih,mih);
 TextArea textArea = new TextArea();
 Toolkit toolkit;
 int screenWidth = 500;
 int screenHeight = 500;
 public static void main(String args[]){
  ReadClipApp app = new ReadClipApp();
 }
 public ReadClipApp() {
  super("ReadClipApp");
  setup();
  setSize(screenWidth,screenHeight);
  addWindowListener(new WindowEventHandler());
  show();
 }
 void setup() {
  setMenuBar(menuBar);
  toolkit=getToolkit();
  add("Center",textArea);
 }
 class MenuItemHandler implements ActionListener, ItemListener {
  public void actionPerformed(ActionEvent ev){
   String s=ev.getActionCommand();
   if(s=="Exit"){
    System.exit(0);
```

```
  }else if(s=="Clipboard"){
   Clipboard clip=toolkit.getSystemClipboard();
   String text="Object Name: ";
   text+=clip.getName();
   text+="\n\nData Flavors:";
   Transferable contents=clip.getContents(ReadClipApp.this);
   if(contents==null) text+="\n\nThe clipboard is empty.";
   else{
    DataFlavor flavors[]=contents.getTransferDataFlavors();
    for(int i=0;i<flavors.length;++i){
     text+="\n\n Name: "+flavors[i].getHumanPresentableName();
     text+="\n MIME Type: "+flavors[i].getMimeType();
     text+="\n Class: ";
     Class cl = flavors[i].getRepresentationClass();
     if(cl==null) text+="null";
     else text+=cl.getName();
    }
   }
   textArea.setText(text);
  }
 }
 public void itemStateChanged(ItemEvent e){
 }
}
class WindowEventHandler extends WindowAdapter {
 public void windowClosing(WindowEvent e){
  System.exit(0);
 }
 }
}
```

The code that implements clipboard operations is contained in the `actionPerfomed()` method of the `MenuItemHandler` class. When the Clipboard menu item is selected, the `getSystemClipboard()` method of the `Toolkit` class is invoked to gain access to the system clipboard. This object is assigned to the `clip` variable. The `getName()` method of the `Clipboard` class is used to get the name of the `Clipboard` object that is returned.

A `Transferable` object representing the contents of the clipboard is returned by invoking the `getContents()` method of the `Clipboard` class. This object is assigned to the `contents` variable.

If a `null` value is returned by `getContents()`, the clipboard is identified as empty. Otherwise, the `getTransferDataFlavors()` method of the `Transferable` interface is invoked to obtain an array of data flavors corresponding to the clipboard data. The `getHumanPresentableName()`, `getMimeType()`, and `getRepresentationClass()` methods are used to obtain information about each of the supported `DataFlavor` objects. This information is then displayed to the user.

Clipboard Ownership

The `ClipboardOwner` interface of `java.awt.datatransfer` is used to provide a callback method, `lostOwnership()`, that notifies the current clipboard owner that it has lost ownership of the clipboard. The ClipboardOwner object can then take whatever action is necessary as the result of lost ownership. In most cases no action is required at all.

The StringSelection Class

The StringSelection class implements both the Transferable and ClipboardOwner interfaces to support the transfer of String objects to and from the clipboard. This is a useful class that simplifies the copying and pasting of text.

The StringSelection class has a single constructor that takes a String object as an argument. This object is the data that is to be transferred via the clipboard. StringSelection implements the getTransferData(), getTransferDataFlavors(), and isDataFlavorSupported() methods of the Transferable interface and the lostOwnership() method of the ClipboardOwner interface. These methods provide all that is needed to copy and paste String objects, as you'll learn in the next section.

Copying and Pasting Text

The ClipTextApp program of Listing 31.2 shows how text can be copied to or pasted from the clipboard. Figure 31.4 shows the ClipTextApp opening window. Copy some text to the clipboard using a text editor and then switch back to the ClipTextApp program. Select Paste from the Edit menu. The text that you copied to the clipboard is pasted to the ClipTextApp window, as shown in Figure 31.5.

You have seen how ClipTextApp supports pasting from the system clipboard. It is also designed to copy the text Hello from Java! to the system clipboard. Select Copy from the Edit menu to copy text from ClipTextApp to the clipboard. Then select Paste to see what text was copied, as shown in Figure 31.6. ClipTextApp copied the text Hello from Java! to the clipboard. You can verify this by pasting the clipboard's contents using another program, such as Notepad, as shown in Figure 31.7.

FIGURE 31.4.
The opening window of the ClipTextApp *program.*

FIGURE 31.5.

Pasting text to the
ClipTextApp
window.

FIGURE 31.6.

The result of copying
and pasting.

FIGURE 31.7.

The text copied by
ClipTextApp *can be*
retrieved by other
programs.

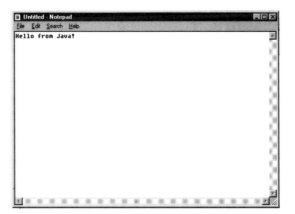

Listing 31.2. The source code of the `ClipTextApp` program.

```java
import java.awt.*;
import java.awt.event.*;
import java.awt.*;
import java.awt.datatransfer.*;
import java.util.*;
import java.io.*;
import jdg.ch25.*;

public class ClipTextApp extends Frame {
 Object menuItems[][] = {{"File","Exit"},
  {"Edit","Copy","Paste"}};
 MenuItemHandler mih = new MenuItemHandler();
 MyMenuBar menuBar = new MyMenuBar(menuItems,mih,mih);
 Font defaultFont = new Font("default",Font.PLAIN,12);
 int screenWidth = 400;
 int screenHeight = 400;
 Toolkit toolkit;
 int baseline;
 int lineSize;
 FontMetrics fm;
 Canvas canvas = new MyCanvas();
 Vector text = new Vector();
 int topLine;
 public static void main(String args[]){
  ClipTextApp app = new ClipTextApp();
 }
 public ClipTextApp() {
  super("ClipTextApp");
  setup();
  setSize(screenWidth,screenHeight);
  addWindowListener(new WindowEventHandler());
  show();
 }
 void setup() {
  setMenuBar(menuBar);
  setupFontData();
  text.addElement("");
  add("Center",canvas);
 }
 void setupFontData() {
  setFont(defaultFont);
  toolkit = getToolkit();
  fm = toolkit.getFontMetrics(defaultFont);
  baseline = fm.getLeading()+fm.getAscent();
  lineSize = fm.getHeight();
 }
 public void paint(Graphics g) {
  canvas.repaint();
 }
 void copyToClipboard() {
  String toClipboard="Hello from Java!";
  StringSelection ss = new StringSelection(toClipboard);
  Clipboard clip=toolkit.getSystemClipboard();
  clip.setContents(ss,ss);
 }
```

```java
void pasteFromClipboard() {
 Clipboard clip=toolkit.getSystemClipboard();
 Transferable contents=clip.getContents(ClipTextApp.this);
 text.removeAllElements();
 if(contents==null) text.addElement("The clipboard is empty.");
 else{
  if(contents.isDataFlavorSupported(DataFlavor.stringFlavor)){
   try{
    String data = (String) contents.getTransferData(
     DataFlavor.stringFlavor);
    if(data==null) text.addElement("null");
    else{
     StringTokenizer st = new StringTokenizer(data,"\n");
     while(st.hasMoreElements()) text.addElement(st.nextToken());
    }
   } catch(IOException ex){
    text.addElement("IOException");
   } catch(UnsupportedFlavorException ex){
    text.addElement("UnsupportedFlavorException");
   }
  }else text.addElement("Wrong flavor.");
 }
 repaint();
}
class MenuItemHandler implements ActionListener, ItemListener {
 public void actionPerformed(ActionEvent ev){
  String s=ev.getActionCommand();
  if(s=="Exit"){
   System.exit(0);
  }else if(s=="Copy") copyToClipboard();
  else if(s=="Paste") pasteFromClipboard();
 }
 public void itemStateChanged(ItemEvent e){
 }
}
class WindowEventHandler extends WindowAdapter {
 public void windowClosing(WindowEvent e){
  System.exit(0);
 }
}
class MyCanvas extends Canvas {
 public void paint(Graphics g) {
  topLine = 0;
  int numLines = text.size();
  screenHeight = getSize().height;
  int y = baseline*2;
  int x = y;
  for(int i = topLine;(i < numLines) && (y < screenHeight + lineSize);++i) {
   g.drawString((String) text.elementAt(i),x,y);
   y += lineSize;
  }
 }
}
}
```

The copying of text to the clipboard is implemented by the `copyToClipboard()` method of `ClipTextApp`. This method creates a `StringSelection` object with the text `Hello from Java!`. It invokes the `getSystemClipboard()` method of the `Toolkit` class to access the system clipboard and the `setContents()` method of the `Clipboard` class to set the `StringSelection` object as the clipboard's contents.

The pasting of text from the clipboard is performed by the `pasteFromClipboard()` method. This method invokes `getSystemClipboard()` to access the system clipboard and `getContents()` to retrieve the clipboard contents as a `Transferable` object. If the `Transferable` object is `null`, a clipboard empty message is displayed to the user. Otherwise, the `isDataFlavorSupported()` method of the `Transferable` interface is used to determine whether an object that is compatible with the `StringSelection` class is contained on the clipboard. If not, a `Wrong flavor.` message is displayed to the user.

If the data on the clipboard can be accessed as a `StringSelection` object, the data is retrieved using the `getTransferData()` method of the `Transferable` interface and assigned to the `data` variable. A `StringTokenizer` object is constructed to parse the data into separate lines and assign them to the `Vector` object referenced by the `text` variable. The contents of `text` are then displayed to the screen via the `paint()` method of the `MyCanvas` class.

Summary

In this chapter you were introduced to the classes of `java.awt.transfer`. You learned how to copy data to and from the clipboard using the Clipboard API. In the next chapter, you'll learn how to use the AWT to perform simple animation.

32

Using Animation

This chapter shows you how to include animation sequences in your window programs. It identifies the basic elements of implementing an animation and then describes approaches to improving the quality of an animation's display by selectively repainting parts of a window and using the MediaTracker class to support the loading of the images used in an animation. When you finish this chapter, you'll be able to include animation in your window programs.

Animation Basics

While including animation sequences in your Java programs may at first appear to be complicated, it is, in fact, rather easy, once you learn the basics. Animations are nothing more than the rapid display of still images such that the pattern of image display causes the appearance of movement for the objects contained in the image. To create an animation, you need to produce the sequence of objects that are to be displayed and then write a Java program that will display that sequence at a particular display rate.

For me, the hardest part of developing an animation is producing the images that are to be displayed. This part requires drawing skills and is completely separate from Java programming. Don't fret if you are unable to easily draw these animation sequences. Chances are that you're better at it than I am. The important point of this chapter is to learn how to display, in the form of an animation, the sequences that you do come up with.

Many animations display their image sequences in a looping fashion. A looping animation gives the appearance that it is much longer than it actually is and it can run indefinitely. Looping animations also requires fewer image frames. If your animation displays 10 to 20 image frames per second and you want it to run for a minute, you will need 600 to 1,200 images. That's a lot of work for a one-minute animation. It is much easier to develop a small but varied looping animation and have it loop several times during the course of a minute.

The major parameter of an animation, besides the type and quality of the images it displays, is the number of image frames that it displays per second. This is typically a fixed number between 5 and 25. The more frames per second that are displayed, the smoother the animation appears to be. The frames-per-second parameter translates into a frame delay parameter that is used to determine how long a program should wait before it displays the next image frame. This is typically measured in milliseconds. For example, frames-per-second rates of 5, 10, and 20 translate into frame delays of 200, 100, and 50 milliseconds.

A common approach to implementing an animation is to create a program thread that runs in an infinite loop and displays the frames of the animation sequence one at a time, waiting milliseconds between each frame's display.

A Simple Animation

In order to get a better understanding of the basics of the animation process, you can develop a simple, character-based animation. The source code of the SimpleAnimationApp program is shown in Listing 32.1.

Listing 32.1. The source code of the SimpleAnimationApp program.

```
import java.awt.*;
import java.awt.event.*;
import jdg.ch25.*;

public class SimpleAnimationApp extends Frame implements Runnable {
 Thread animation;
 int frameDelay = 100;
 String frames[] = {"*","**","***","****","*****","****","***","**","*"};
 int numFrames = frames.length;
 int currentFrame = 0;
 long lastDisplay = 0;
 String menuItems[][] = {{"File","Exit"}};
 MenuItemHandler mih = new MenuItemHandler();
 MyMenuBar menuBar = new MyMenuBar(menuItems,mih,mih);
 int screenWidth = 200;
 int screenHeight = 200;
 public static void main(String args[]) {
  SimpleAnimationApp app = new SimpleAnimationApp();
 }
 public SimpleAnimationApp() {
  super("Simple Animation");
  setup();
  setSize(screenWidth,screenHeight);
  addWindowListener(new WindowEventHandler());
  show();
  animation = new Thread(this);
  animation.start();
 }
 void setup() {
  setMenuBar(menuBar);
  setFont(new Font("default",Font.BOLD,18));
 }
 public void paint(Graphics g) {
  g.drawString(frames[currentFrame],60,60);
 }
 public void run() {
  do {
   long time = System.currentTimeMillis();
   if(time - lastDisplay > frameDelay) {
    repaint();
    try {
     Thread.sleep(frameDelay);
    }catch(InterruptedException ex){
    }
    ++currentFrame;
    currentFrame %= numFrames;
    lastDisplay = time;
```

continues

Listing 32.1. continued

```
  }
 } while (true);
}
class MenuItemHandler implements ActionListener, ItemListener {
 public void actionPerformed(ActionEvent ev){
  String s=ev.getActionCommand();
  if(s=="Exit"){
   System.exit(0);
  }
 }
 public void itemStateChanged(ItemEvent e){
 }
}
class WindowEventHandler extends WindowAdapter {
 public void windowClosing(WindowEvent e){
  System.exit(0);
 }
 }
}
```

Compile and run SimpleAnimationApp. Your program's display should look like the one shown in Figure 32.1.

FIGURE 32.1.

A simple animation.

A string of asterisks is modulated to give the appearance of movement.

While this short animation is by no means in line for any awards, it does illustrate all the basic elements of more complex and entertaining animations.

The SimpleAnimationApp class declares the animation thread, the frameDelay variable, the array of frames[] used to implement the animation's display, the numFrames variable, the currentFrame variable, the time of the lastDisplay of a frame, and the standard menu bar and window size variables.

The setup of the SimpleAnimationApp program is fairly standard, with the exception of the creation of the animation thread at the end of the class constructor and the invocation of the animation thread's start() method.

The paint() method contains a single statement that is used to display a string of asterisks on the console window.

The run() method implements the animation loop. It checks the current system time and the time of the last image display to see if it is time to display a new frame. It uses the currentTimeMillis() method of the System class to read the current time in milliseconds. If it is time to display another frame, the run() method invokes the repaint() method to display the current frame and then tries to sleep for frameDelay milliseconds. It updates the currentFrame using modular arithmetic and changes the time of lastDisplay.

A Graphics Animation

Because the SimpleAnimationApp program provides all the basic elements required of an animation, we can easily modify the animation to support graphics. Figures 32.2 through 32.5 provide four stick figures I drew using the Windows Paint program. These crude figures can be used to create an animation of a stick figure that attempts to fly (or exercise).

FIGURE 32.2.
stickman1.gif.

FIGURE 32.3.
stickman2.gif.

FIGURE 32.4.
stickman3.gif.

FIGURE 32.5.
stickman4.gif.

You may easily substitute your own figures for the ones used in this example.

The source code of the GraphicAnimationApp program is shown in Listing 32.2.

Listing 32.2. The source code of the GraphicAnimationApp program.

```
import java.awt.*;
import java.awt.event.*;
import jdg.ch25.*;

public class GraphicAnimationApp extends Frame implements Runnable {
 Thread animation;
 int frameDelay = 100;
 Image frames[];
 int numFrames;
```

```
int currentFrame = 0;
long lastDisplay = 0;
String menuItems[][] = {{"File","Exit"}};
MenuItemHandler mih = new MenuItemHandler();
MyMenuBar menuBar = new MyMenuBar(menuItems,mih,mih);
int screenWidth = 400;
int screenHeight = 400;
public static void main(String args[]) {
 GraphicAnimationApp app = new GraphicAnimationApp();
}
public GraphicAnimationApp() {
 super("Graphic Animation");
 setup();
 setSize(screenWidth,screenHeight);
 addWindowListener(new WindowEventHandler());
 show();
 animation = new Thread(this);
 animation.start();
}
void setup() {
 setMenuBar(menuBar);
 setFont(new Font("default",Font.BOLD,18));
 Toolkit toolkit = getToolkit();
 frames = new Image[4];
 frames[0] = toolkit.getImage("stickman1.gif");
 frames[1] = toolkit.getImage("stickman2.gif");
 frames[2] = toolkit.getImage("stickman3.gif");
 frames[3] = toolkit.getImage("stickman4.gif");
 numFrames = frames.length;
}
public void paint(Graphics g) {
 g.drawImage(frames[currentFrame],125,80,this);
}
public void run() {
 do {
  long time = System.currentTimeMillis();
  if(time - lastDisplay > frameDelay) {
   repaint();
   try {
    Thread.sleep(frameDelay);
   }catch(InterruptedException ex){
   }
   ++currentFrame;
   currentFrame %= numFrames;
   lastDisplay = time;
  }
 } while (true);
}
class MenuItemHandler implements ActionListener, ItemListener {
 public void actionPerformed(ActionEvent ev){
  String s=ev.getActionCommand();
  if(s=="Exit"){
   System.exit(0);
  }
 }
 public void itemStateChanged(ItemEvent e){
 }
}
```

continues

Listing 32.2. continued

```
class WindowEventHandler extends WindowAdapter {
 public void windowClosing(WindowEvent e){
  System.exit(0);
 }
 }
}
```

When you run `GraphicAnimationApp`, your display should look like the one shown in Figure 32.6.

FIGURE 32.6.

The
GraphicAnimationApp
program display.

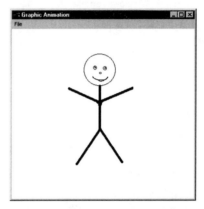

Unless you have a really fast computer and video card, your program display probably has some very noticeable flickering. Don't worry about that problem now. We'll cover ways to improve the quality of an animation's display in the following section. For now, just focus on how we modified the `SimpleAnimationApp` program to support graphic-based animation.

The `GraphicAnimationApp` program is similar to the `SimpleAnimationApp` program. These are the differences between the two programs:

■ In `GraphicAnimationApp` the `frames[]` array was changed from an array of `String` objects to an array of `Image` objects.

■ In `GraphicAnimationApp` the `setup()` method was updated to create a `Toolkit` object and use it to load the stickman images.

These simple changes were all that was needed to convert the program from a simple text-based animation to a graphics-based animation.

Improving Animation Display Qualities

The GraphicAnimationApp program has some serious deficiencies in the way that it displays the animation images. The first and probably the most noticeable problem is that it tries to start displaying the images before they are completely loaded. This is an easy problem to solve using the MediaTracker class.

The MediaTracker class provides the capability to manage the loading of image files. You use the addImage() method to add an image to the list of images being tracked. After adding an image to a MediaTracker object, you can then check on the image or all images managed by the MediaTracker object using the access methods provided by the MediaTracker class.

The other major problem with the animation's display is that the entire screen is repainted with each new frame, which causes a significant amount of flickering. This image flickering can be mitigated by limiting the area of the window that is updated with each new image. The repaint() and update() methods of the component class provide this capability.

You are already familiar with limited screen repainting from using the repaint() method in Chapter 28, "The Canvas." The update()method provides the capability to update a Graphics object without first clearing the current image. This allows successive images to be displayed as marginal increments to the currently displayed image.

Another option to improving an animation's display quality is to change the frame delay. By decreasing the number of frames per second being displayed, you are able to lower the rate at which flickering occurs. However, you do this at the expense of the overall quality of your animation because higher frame display rates tend to smooth out any gaps between successive images.

An Updated Graphics Animation

The GraphicUpdateApp program shows how to use the MediaTracker class, together with limited repainting, and frame delay adjustments to improve the quality of the GraphicAnimationApp program. Its source code is shown in Listing 32.3.

Listing 32.3. The source code of the GraphicUpdateApp program.

```
import java.awt.*;
import java.awt.event.*;
import jdg.ch25.*;

public class GraphicUpdateApp extends Frame implements Runnable {
 Thread animation;
 int frameDelay = 200;
 Image frames[];
 int numFrames;
 int currentFrame = 0;
```

continues

Listing 32.3. continued

```
long lastDisplay = 0;
boolean fullDisplay = false;
MediaTracker tracker;
String menuItems[][] = {{"File","Exit"}};
MenuItemHandler mih = new MenuItemHandler();
MyMenuBar menuBar = new MyMenuBar(menuItems,mih,mih);
int screenWidth = 400;
int screenHeight = 400;
public static void main(String args[]) {
 GraphicUpdateApp app = new GraphicUpdateApp();
}
public GraphicUpdateApp() {
 super("Updated Graphic Animation");
 setup();
 pack();
 setSize(screenWidth,screenHeight);
 addWindowListener(new WindowEventHandler());
 show();
 animation = new Thread(this);
 animation.start();
}
void setup() {
 setMenuBar(menuBar);
 setFont(new Font("default",Font.BOLD,18));
 Toolkit toolkit = getToolkit();
 frames = new Image[4];
 frames[0] = toolkit.getImage("stickman1.gif");
 frames[1] = toolkit.getImage("stickman2.gif");
 frames[2] = toolkit.getImage("stickman3.gif");
 frames[3] = toolkit.getImage("stickman4.gif");
 numFrames = frames.length;
 tracker = new MediaTracker(this);
 for(int i=0;i<numFrames;++i) tracker.addImage(frames[i],i);
}
public void paint(Graphics g) {
 if(allLoaded())
  g.drawImage(frames[currentFrame],125,80,this);
 else{
  String stars = "*";
  for(int i=0;i<currentFrame;++i) stars += "*";
  g.drawString(stars,60,60);
 }
}
boolean allLoaded() {
 for(int i=0;i<numFrames;++i) {
  if(tracker.statusID(i,true) != MediaTracker.COMPLETE) return false;
 }
 return true;
}
public void run() {
 do {
  long time = System.currentTimeMillis();
  if(time - lastDisplay > frameDelay) {
   if(allLoaded()) {
    if(fullDisplay) repaint (115,160,160,90);
    else{
```

```
      fullDisplay = true;
      repaint();
     }
   }else repaint();
   try {
     Thread.sleep(frameDelay);
   }catch(InterruptedException ex){
   }
   ++currentFrame;
   currentFrame %= numFrames;
   lastDisplay = time;
  }
 } while (true);
}
class MenuItemHandler implements ActionListener, ItemListener {
 public void actionPerformed(ActionEvent ev){
  String s=ev.getActionCommand();
  if(s=="Exit"){
   System.exit(0);
  }
 }
 public void itemStateChanged(ItemEvent e){
 }
}
class WindowEventHandler extends WindowAdapter {
 public void windowClosing(WindowEvent e){
  System.exit(0);
 }
 }
}
```

When you run GraphicUpdateApp, it will display an animated string of asterisks while the image files are being loaded. After that, it will immediately display the image animation. This reduces the unsightly flickering caused when an image is displayed while it is being loaded.

Notice how GraphicUpdateApp implements the limited area repainting. You can run your mouse over the image display to determine the boundaries of the repaint area.

You should also notice that GraphicUpdateApp displays images at a slower rate. The frame-delay rate was increased from 100 microseconds to 200 microseconds, decreasing the frame display rate by a factor of 2.

The changes made to GraphicAnimationApp by GraphicUpdateApp consist of the declaration of the fullDisplay and tracker variables and modifications to the setup(), paint(), and run() methods. In addition, the allLoaded() method was created:

■ The fullDisplay variable is used to ensure that a full display of the stickman was accomplished before attempting a limited display using the repaint() method. The tracker variable is used to refer to a MediaTracker object.

■ The setup() method is updated to create the MediaTracker object and to add the images being loaded with this object.

- The paint() method was updated to draw the images after they've been loaded and to draw asterisk strings before the images are loaded.
- The allLoaded() method uses the statusID() method of the MediaTracker class to determine whether all images have been completely loaded.
- The run() method has been modified to use the allLoaded() method and the fullDisplay variable to determine whether it should repaint the entire screen or only a limited portion of it.

Summary

This chapter shows how to include animation sequences in your window programs. It identifies the basic elements of implementing an animation and describes approaches to improving the quality of an animation's display. It shows you how to selectively repaint parts of a window and how to use the MediaTracker class to support the loading of the images used in an animation. Chapter 33, "The Future of AWT," completes Part IV, "Window Programming," by discussing JavaSoft's plans for future enhancements to the AWT.

33

The Future of AWT

You've finally covered all of the chapters focusing on Abstract Window Toolkit (AWT) programming—that's quite a lot of material. In this chapter you'll take a short break and glimpse at the future of the AWT.

The AWT of JDK 1.1 is a significant improvement over that of JDK 1.0. It provides a more efficient event model; support for clipboard operations and printing; additional menu capabilities; and many new classes, interfaces, and methods. Although quite a lot has been added to the AWT, there is still much to be done before it nears completion. Current deficiencies must be corrected, missing capabilities must be added, and the AWT must advance from being a platform-independent clone of current windowing systems to providing the features that will make it the windowing platform of choice by users as well as programmers. The following sections cover the near-term (next version) improvements to the AWT and scheduled developments that will send the AWT on the road to meeting these goals.

Areas for Improvement

Having programmed with and studied most of the classes of the AWT, you probably have some definite opinions on what areas need improvement. My To Do list includes the following:

- Printing—The addition of printing capabilities to JDK 1.1 is a significant accomplishment. However, the Printing API needs to be improved to support platform- and printer-independent printing. The capability to access the actual dimensions of a printed page would be a significant improvement in this area. The capability to work with PostScript printers in a platform-independent manner is also needed.

- Clipboard—The classes and interfaces of the java.awt.datatransfer package provide a solid foundation for supporting platform-independent clipboard operations. However, only a single convenience class is supported: StringSelection. Other convenience classes are needed to support the copying and pasting of MIME types such as HTML, rich text, and common graphics formats.

- Layout—The layout classes provided with the AWT work fine for organizing GUI components into simple layouts. More advanced component organizations require a significant amount of work in the absence of GUI building tools. Additional classes to simplify the absolute and relative positioning of GUI components would be appreciated. Support of multilayered layouts is also desirable.

- HTML Support—Java is a language that's born of the Web. Why doesn't the AWT support HTML rendering? The capability to display HTML to a Graphics object would greatly simplify the development of Web-oriented Java applications.

- Advanced Graphics—JDK 1.1 provides great support for low-level graphics drawing and display. Let's build upon what we have and provide the capability to easily work with advanced 2D and 3D graphics. AWT support of VRML would be especially attractive.

■ Multimedia Support—Although multimedia support can be considered external to the AWT, hooks for multimedia display would certainly contribute to the appeal of Java-based window applications. At a minimum, support for common audio and video formats should be provided.

While the preceding list may seem to be asking for a lot from a language that provides so much already, the addition of these capabilities would increase the AWT's attractiveness for developing advanced window-based applications.

New Developments

Fortunately, JavaSoft is working hard on improving the AWT and will make many of the improvements identified in the previous section. The following subsections summarize some of JavaSoft's current AWT initiatives. This work is discussed in greater detail in JavaSoft's on-line document, "AWT: The Next Generation," available at `http://java.sun.com/products/jdk/1.1/docs/guide/awt/designspec/nextAWT.html`.

> **NOTE**
>
> The AWT home page at `http://java.sun.com/products/jdk/awt/` provides up-to-date information on new AWT plans and developments.

Platform-Independent Look and Feel

The current approach to AWT platform-independence focuses on the use of peer classes that access the native GUI capabilities of the host windowing environment. AWT window components are mapped to native window components via these peer classes. AWT implementations differ from platform to platform in the peer classes used to interface the platform-independent AWT components with the native windowing system components.

The AWT has been remarkably successful in providing a platform-independent AWT across diverse windowing environments. However, there are some glitches with this approach. These glitches arise from the fact that the native windowing components do not function in exactly the same manner across all platforms. In these cases, the AWT must try to resolve these behavioral differences to ensure that the platform-independent AWT components operate in the same manner across all windowing environments. The end result is that the AWT capabilities are the least common denominator of the features provided by the supported windowing systems. In addition, the AWT "look and feel" differs with the appearance and behavioral inconsistencies of the native windowing systems.

JavaSoft is currently developing peerless versions of the platform-independent GUI components based upon a lightweight user interface framework. These components will be implemented entirely in Java and will provide a common look and feel across all native windowing systems. This is a fundamental change in the AWT philosophy. Instead of focusing on how AWT components can be mapped to native GUI components, emphasis will be placed on determining how the native GUI components can be tailored to support the platform-independent AWT look and feel. The end result will be that the AWT will take advantage of the best features of all windowing systems and move away from its current least common denominator component support.

Additional Components

In addition to the development of peerless components, the next generation AWT will expand upon the list of basic components that it supports. Current candidates include tree views, tables, and text enhancements. I hope that HTML-rendering `Graphics` objects are also supported!

Drag-and-Drop

Most windowing environments (Microsoft Windows, Macintosh, OS/2, and others) support drag-and-drop. AWT drag-and-drop was intended for the JDK 1.1 release. However, it wasn't ready in time and had to be put off until the next JDK release. When it becomes available, drag-and-drop will be implemented via additional classes and interfaces in the `java.awt.datatransfer` package. The drag-and-drop support will include the capability to drag-and-drop objects between Java and non-Java applications.

Java 2D

The basic graphics capabilities of the JDK 1.0 and 1.1 are being enhanced through the development of the Java 2D and Java 3D APIs. These APIs will support layering and advanced transformations of geometrical objects. These transformations include dynamic resizing, movement, and rotation. The grouping and ungrouping of displayed objects also will be supported.

The Java 2D API is being developed by JavaSoft and Adobe Systems Incorporated. It will provide a common approach to using graphical objects in a device and resolution-independent manner. Adobe is famous for its Portable Document Format and brings to bear a wealth of experience in developing platform-independent text, graphics, and documents. A rich drawing library, advanced text support, device-independent graphics, and advanced imaging capabilities will be the end result of this effort.

Multimedia Support

The Java Media API will provide comprehensive support for multimedia capabilities. This support consists of the Java 2D API (discussed in the previous section); a Java 3D API; an Animation API; Speech API; and related Telephony, Collaboration, and Media Framework APIs.

The Java 3D API will support interactive 3D imaging and will provide the basis for developing advanced virtual reality simulations. The Animation API will support the transformation and movement of 2D objects. Timing and synchronization support will also be provided. The Speech API will support both speech recognition and text-to-speech generation. The Telephony and Collaboration APIs will provide high-level communication interfaces to the AWT. The Media Framework API will provide complete audio and video playing, capturing, recording, and conferencing capabilities. It will support both streamed and stored media.

Summary

The AWT has come a long way since Java 1.0, but still has a way to go before it becomes the premier windowing system of choice. Several areas of improvement have been identified. JavaSoft is currently working on these improvements and, at the same time, planning and designing additional AWT capabilities and related APIs that will provide the next generation AWT with the best features of all windowing systems.

This chapter ends Part IV, "Window Programming." You've come a long way in your study of Java and the JDK 1.1. In Part V, "Network Programming," you'll learn how to use the JDK's extensive network programming features to develop Internet-based client/server applications.

V

Network Programming

34

Client Programs

In this chapter you'll learn how to write client programs that support networked client/server applications. You'll learn about the typical client programs found on the Internet and how they are structured. You'll develop simple client programs that support remote login and the sending of mail, and that fetch a list of Web pages. This chapter builds on the material presented in Chapter 17, "Network Programming with the `java.net` Package." You might want to review Chapter 17 before continuing with the material presented in this chapter.

Types of Clients

Of the client/server applications that are found on the Internet, only a small group is typically used. These include e-mail, the Web, FTP, Usenet news groups, and telnet. Gopher and WAIS, both precursors of the Web, have declined in popularity, having been subsumed by the Web. Typical Internet client programs include e-mail programs, Web browsers, FTP programs, and telnet clients.

E-mail programs provide an easy-to-use interface by which mail can be created and sent, retrieved and displayed, and managed. Popular Windows-based clients include Eudora and Pegasus. UNIX systems provide a number of popular e-mail clients including Pine, Elm, and mh.

Web browsers provide a window on the World Wide Web and support the display of Web pages, including, of course, Java programs. The Netscape Navigator browser is the most popular browser on the Web and is Java-capable. It is supported on UNIX, Windows, Macintosh, and other systems.

FTP programs provide a convenient way to retrieve files from public Internet file servers or from private file directories. Although a number of user-friendly FTP client programs are available, the simple text-based FTP client is still the most popular and most widely supported.

News reader programs simplify the process of working with messages that are posted to Usenet news groups. A number of netnews client programs are available for Windows, Macintosh, UNIX, and other operating system platforms.

Telnet clients are used to remotely log in to other systems. These systems are usually UNIX or other operating systems that are powerful enough to provide the underlying capabilities needed to implement multiuser support. Windows and Macintosh systems, because of their inherent limitations, do not support telnet server applications.

Client Responsibilities

Client programs perform a service for their users by connecting with their server counterparts, forwarding service requests based on user inputs, and providing the service results back to the user.

In most cases, the client must initiate the connection. Typically, the server listens on a well-known port for a client connection. The client initiates the connection, which is accepted by the server. The client sends a service request to the server, based on user inputs. The server receives the service request, performs the service, and returns the results of the service to the client. The client receives the service results and displays them to the user.

A Simple Telnet Client

A telnet client program provides users with the capability to log in to remote systems. It connects to a telnet server (called a *telnet daemon*) that listens on port 23 for an incoming connection. The telnet client connects to the daemon, which usually runs a login program and, upon successful login, runs a shell program.

The telnet client must be capable of simultaneously exchanging data with both the user and the remote system. The protocol used for communication between the client and the server is specified in RFC 854, the Telnet Protocol Specification. RFC 854 identifies three basic elements of the telnet protocol: the concept of a network virtual terminal, the principle of negotiated options, and the symmetry between terminals and processes.

The Network Virtual Terminal

The *network virtual terminal* (NVT) is a simple device that forms the basis for establishing telnet-based communication. All telnet clients and servers are required to support the NVT as a minimum capability. It is an abstract device that consists of a printer and a keyboard. The user types characters on the keyboard that are forwarded to the server. The server returns data to the user and the NVT displays it on the printer. The NVT provides local character echoing and half-duplex operation, although remote echoing and full-duplex operation can be used as negotiated options. Lines are terminated using a standard carriage-return–line-feed combination.

The NVT also provides for control operations that support process interruption and the discarding of excessive output. These operations are signaled by using the *Interpret as Command* (IAC) code as described in the next section.

The Interpret as Command Code

The IAC code is sent from a client or server to a program on the other end of a telnet connection to send a control code or to negotiate an option, as described in the next section. The IAC is a single byte consisting of the value 255 or hex 0xFF. The IAC may be followed by a single byte to send a control code, or by two or more bytes to negotiate an option. For example, the IAC followed by a byte with the decimal value of 243 is used to send a break command.

Because the IAC is used to indicate a command or option negotiated, a special byte sequence is needed to send the byte value 255 used for the IAC. This is accomplished by sending two IACs in succession.

Negotiated Options

Because all telnet clients and servers are required to implement the NVT, they all have a common, but primitive, basis from which to begin operation. Additional options, such as full-duplex operation and character echoing, can be used based on the principle of negotiated options.

Options are *negotiated* when either the client or server program sends an IAC code to the other. The IAC code is followed by a WILL or DO code and an option code. The WILL code informs the program on the other side of the connection that it intends to use a particular option. The other program may respond with a DO or a DONT response, consisting of the IAC, followed by the DO or DONT code, followed by the option.

A program can also request that the program on the other side of the connection implement an option. This is accomplished by sending the IAC code, the DO code, and the option code. The other program can respond with a WILL or WONT response. A WILL response is indicated by sending the IAC, followed by the WILL code, followed by the option code. A WONT response is sent in the same manner, with the WONT code being used instead of the WILL code.

Symmetry Between Terminals and Processes

As you probably have surmised from reading the previous sections, the communication between client and server is highly symmetrical. Either the client or server can initiate option negotiation. The use of symmetry between client and host simplifies the implementation of the telnet protocol and allows client and host software to be developed from a common base. The TelnetApp program, presented in the next section, makes use of two I/O filters, NVTInputStream and NVTOutputStream, that implement some of the basic elements of the telnet protocol. These streams do not support control characters or additional options. Option negotiation is handled by refusing any additional options other than those provided by the basic NVT.

The TelnetApp Program

The TelnetApp program implements a minimum set of features of the telnet protocol in order to accomplish a remote login to a telnet server. The purpose of the program is not to provide you with a telnet client, but to show you the basics of how these clients work. More sophisticated and powerful telnet client programs can be retrieved from the Internet. In addition, many operating systems supply telnet client programs. The source code of the TelnetApp program is shown in Listing 34.1.

Listing 34.1. The source code for the TelnetApp program.

```
import java.lang.*;
import java.net.*;
```

```
import java.io.*;
import jdg.ch34.NVTInputStream;
import jdg.ch34.NVTOutputStream;
import jdg.ch34.NVTPrinter;

public class TelnetApp {
 public static void main(String args[]){
  PortTalk portTalk = new PortTalk(args);
  portTalk.start();
 }
}

class PortTalk extends Thread {
 Socket connection;
 OutputStream outStream;
 NVTInputStream inStream;
 NVTPrinter printer;
 public PortTalk(String args[]){
  if(args.length!=2) error("Usage: java TelnetApp host port");
  String destination = args[0];
  int port = 0;
  try {
   port = Integer.valueOf(args[1]).intValue();
  }catch (NumberFormatException ex) { error("Invalid port number"); }
  try{
   connection = new Socket(destination,port);
  }catch (UnknownHostException ex) { error("Unknown host"); }
  catch (IOException ex) { error("IO error creating socket"); }
  try{
   outStream = connection.getOutputStream();
   inStream = new NVTInputStream(connection.getInputStream(),outStream);
  }catch (IOException ex) { error("IO error getting streams"); }
  System.out.println("Connected to "+destination+" at port "+port+".");
 }
 public void run() {
  printer = new NVTPrinter(inStream);
  printer.start();
  yield();
  processUserInput();
  shutdown();
 }
 public void processUserInput() {
  try {
   String line;
   boolean finished = false;
   BufferedReader userInputStream = new BufferedReader(
    new InputStreamReader(System.in));
   do {
    line = userInputStream.readLine();
    if(line == null) finished = true;
    else{
     try {
      for(int i=0;i<line.length();++i)
       outStream.write(line.charAt(i));
      outStream.write('\n');
     } catch (IOException ex) {
     }
```

continues

Listing 34.1. continued

```
    }
  } while(!finished);
  } catch(IOException ex) {
   error("Error reading user input");
  }
}
 public void shutdown(){
  try{
   connection.close();
  }catch (IOException ex) { error("IO error closing socket"); }
 }
 public void error(String s){
  System.out.println(s);
  System.exit(1);
 }
}
```

> **NOTE**
>
> The `TelnetApp` class uses the `NVTPrinter`, `NVTInputStream`, and `NVTOutputStream` classes that are supplied in the following sections. You must type in the `NVTPrinter.java`, `NVTInputStream.java`, and `NVTOutputStream.java` files before compiling `TelnetApp.java`. The Java compiler will automatically compile these files when `TelnetApp.java` is compiled. These files must be placed in the `jdg\ch34` directory because they are part of the `jdg.ch34` package.

You use the `TelnetApp` program in the same way as any other telnet program. But bear in mind that it is only a minimal telnet client. Run the program by invoking it with the host name of a computer that supports telnet and the well-known telnet port number, port 23.

In the following example, I use the program to log in to my account at CTS. Note that the program operates in half-duplex mode, so characters are echoed locally. I substituted asterisks (*) for my password. Take caution when using this program because it will display your password characters in the same manner as any other text that you type. In addition, like other telnet client programs, it sends passwords in the clear to the system to which a telnet connection is being made.

Also, notice that commands that I type were echoed by my `cts.com` host:

```
C:\jdk1.1.1\jdg\Ch34>java TelnetApp cts.com 23
Connected to cts.com at port 23.

UNIX System V Release 3.2 (crash.cts.com) (ttyp21)

 login: jaworski
```

```
Password:****

Last    successful login for jaworski: Tue Feb 25 22:19:23 PST 1997 on ttyp4
Last unsuccessful login for jaworski: Fri Feb 14 13:56:05 PST 1997 on ttyp11

                    Welcome to CTSNET!

          Enter 'help' for assistance and information.

TERM = (vt100)
 Terminal type is vt100
1% l
l
total 394
drwx------    2 jaworski guest           272 Sep 08  1995 Mail
drwxr-xr-x    2 jaworski guest           208 Dec 07  1995 News
drwxr-xr-x    2 jaworski guest           224 Sep 08  1995 bin
drwxr-xr-x    2 jaworski guest           384 Apr 04  1996 download
lrwxrwxrwx    1 root     root             15 Mar 15  1996 dropbox -> /ftp/j/jaworski

-rw-rw-r--    1 jaworski guest          6509 Oct 11 09:34 format.zip
drwx------    2 jaworski guest           160 Dec 08  1995 ga
-rwx--x--x    1 jaworski guest          6282 Aug 22  1996 lookup
drwx------    2 jaworski guest           288 Feb 19 10:42 mail
-rw-rw-r--    1 jaworski guest        176717 Feb 04 21:33 ra.zip
drwx------    2 jaworski guest           256 Nov 15 15:01 temp
drwxr-xr-x    3 jaworski guest           112 Dec 01  1995 writing
2% exit
exit
3% logout

Connection broken.

C:\jdk1.1.1\jdg\ch34>
```

The `TelnetApp` program creates an object of class `PortTalk` to perform its processing. This class extends the `Thread` class in order to implement multithreading capabilities. Its constructor uses the parameters passed in the `TelnetApp` command-line invocation to set up the connection to the specified host and port.

The `run()` method creates an object of the `NVTPrinter` class to interface with the destination host and invokes the `processUserInput()` method to interface with the user. The `processUserInput()` method reads a line at a time from the user's console and sends it to the telnet server.

The NVTPrinter Class

The `NVTPrinter` class performs most of the interesting processing because it interfaces with the server. It does this using the `NVTInputStream` class covered in the next section. `NVTPrinter` is also implemented as a subclass of `Thread`. Its source code is shown in Listing 34.2.

Listing 34.2. The source code for the NVTPrinter class.

```
package jdg.ch34;

import java.io.*;

public class NVTPrinter extends Thread {
 NVTInputStream inStream;
 public NVTPrinter(NVTInputStream in) {
  super();
  inStream = in;
 }
 public void run() {
  boolean finished = false;
  try {
   do {
    int i = inStream.read();
    if(i == -1) finished = true;
    else{
     System.out.print((char) i);
     System.out.flush();
     yield();
    }
   } while(!finished);
   System.out.println("\nConnection broken.");
   System.exit(0);
  } catch (IOException ex) {
   System.out.println("NVTPrinter error");
   System.exit(1);
  }
 }
}
```

The NVTInputStream Class

The NVTInputStream class implements the network virtual terminal input interface. Its source code is shown in Listing 34.3.

Listing 34.3. The source code for the NVTInputStream class.

```
package jdg.ch34;

import java.io.*;

public class NVTInputStream extends FilterInputStream {
 byte IAC = (byte) 0xff;
 byte DO = (byte) 0xfd;
 byte WILL = (byte) 0xfb;
 byte CR = 13;
 byte LF = 10;
 int WONT = 252;
 int DONT = 254;
 int BUFFER_SIZE = 1024;
 OutputStream out;
```

```
byte lineBuffer[] = new byte[BUFFER_SIZE];
int numBytes = 0;
public NVTInputStream(InputStream inStream,OutputStream outStream) {
 super(inStream);
 out = outStream;
}
public int read() throws IOException {
 boolean recIAC;
 int i;
 do {
  recIAC = false;
  i = in.read();
  if(i == -1) return i;
  byte b = (byte) i;
  if(b == IAC) {
   recIAC = true;
   int cmd = in.read();
   if(cmd == -1) return cmd;
   byte b2 = (byte) cmd;
   if(b2 == IAC) return 255;
   else if(b2 == DO) {
    int opt = in.read();
    if(opt == -1) return opt;
    out.write(255);
    out.write(WONT);
    out.write(opt);
    out.flush();
   }else if(b2 == WILL) {
    int opt = in.read();
    if(opt == -1) return opt;
    out.write(255);
    out.write(DONT);
    out.write(opt);
    out.flush();
   }
  }
 } while(recIAC);
 return i;
}
public String readLine() throws IOException {
 numBytes = 0;
 boolean finished = false;
 do {
  int i = read();
  if(i == -1) return null;
  byte b = (byte) i;
  if(b == LF) {
   if(numBytes>0) {
    if(lineBuffer[numBytes-1] == 13)
     return new String(lineBuffer,0,numBytes-1);
   }
  }
  lineBuffer[numBytes] = b;
  ++numBytes;
 } while (!finished);
 return null;
}
}
```

NVTInputStream uses the network virtual terminal conventions, covered earlier in this chapter, to filter the input stream associated with the connection. It implements the basic read() method and also a convenient readLine() method.

The NVTOutputStream Class

The NVTOutputStream class provides an output analog to the NVTInputStream class. It implements the basic write() method according to the NVT conventions. It also provides a println() method that uses the carriage return-line feed(CR-LF) end-of-line conventions. Its source code is shown in Listing 34.4.

Listing 34.4. The source code for the NVTOutputStream class.

```
package jdg.ch34;

import java.io.*;

public class NVTOutputStream extends FilterOutputStream {
 int IAC = 255;
 byte CR = 13;
 byte LF = 10;
 public NVTOutputStream(OutputStream outStream) {
  super(outStream);
 }
 public void write(int i) throws IOException {
  if(i == IAC) super.write(i);
  super.write(i);
 }
 public void println(String s) {
  try {
   byte[] sBytes = s.getBytes();
   for(int i=0;i<sBytes.length;++i)
    super.write(sBytes[i]);
   super.write(CR);
   super.write(LF);
   super.flush();
  } catch(IOException ex) {
  }
 }
}
```

A Mail Client

Although mail is sent on the Internet using a variety of protocols, the *Simple Mail Transfer Protocol* (SMTP), described in Request for Comments (RFC) 821, is the basic protocol used to move mail from one host to another. SMTP consists of a mail sender, a mail receiver, and a set of line-oriented commands used to send mail from the sender to the receiver.

RFC 821 describes the complete set of commands used by mail senders and receivers. Here I am using only a minimal subset of these commands to illustrate the development of an SMTP client, the mail sender:

1. An SMTP client connects to an SMTP server by establishing a connection to port 25 of the server's host. The server accepts the connection, sends a one-line ready notification to the client, and awaits client commands.

2. The client sends the HELO command with its host name to introduce itself to the server. The server responds by sending a code that indicates that it is okay to initiate a mail transmission.

3. The client sends the MAIL command to the server to indicate that it has mail from a specific user. The server responds with a notification to proceed.

4. The client sends the RCPT command to identify the recipient of the e-mail. The server responds by telling the client whether the recipient is valid.

5. The client sends the DATA command to indicate that it is ready to send the message. The server responds by telling the client that it is okay to begin sending message data.

6. The client sends the message, a line at a time, terminating the message with a line containing a single period (.). A line of message text beginning with a period is sent by prepending an extra initial period to the message line.

7. The server acknowledges receiving the last line of text by sending an OK command to the client.

8. The client then terminates the connection by sending a QUIT command to the server. The server then responds by notifying the client that it is closing the connection.

The MailClientApp Program

The MailClientApp program illustrates the basic operation of a mail client program. It implements the basic SMTP commands described in the previous section. Its source code is shown in Listing 34.5.

Listing 34.5. The source code for the MailClientApp program.

```
import java.lang.*;
import java.net.*;
import java.io.*;
```

continues

Listing 34.5. continued

```java
import java.util.Vector;
import jdg.ch34.NVTInputStream;
import jdg.ch34.NVTOutputStream;
import jdg.ch34.NVTPrinter;

public class MailClientApp {
 public static void main(String args[]){
  MessageInterface messageInterface = new MessageInterface();
  Message msg = messageInterface.getMsg();
  MailTalk mailTalk = new MailTalk(msg);
  mailTalk.run();
 }
}

class Message {
 String source;
 String destination;
 String subject;
 String text[];
 public Message() {
  super();
 }
 public void setDestination(String dest) {
  destination = dest;
 }
 public String getDestination() {
  return destination;
 }
 public void setSource(String src) {
  source = src;
 }
 public String getSource() {
  return source;
 }
 public String getDestinationHost() {
  return destination.substring(destination.indexOf('@')+1);
 }
 public void setSubject(String subj) {
  subject = subj;
 }
 public String getSubject() {
  return subject;
 }
 public void setText(Vector txt) {
  int n = txt.size();
  text = new String[n];
  for(int i = 0; i< n; ++i) {
   text[i] = (String) txt.elementAt(i);
  }
 }
 public String[] getText() {
  return text;
 }
}

class MessageInterface {
 Message msg;
 public MessageInterface() {
```

```
 msg = new Message();
}
public Message getMsg() {
 try {
 System.out.print("From: ");
 System.out.flush();
 BufferedReader inStream = new BufferedReader(
  new InputStreamReader(System.in));
 msg.setSource(inStream.readLine());
 System.out.print("To: ");
 System.out.flush();
 msg.setDestination(inStream.readLine());
 System.out.print("Subject: ");
 System.out.flush();
 msg.setSubject(inStream.readLine());
 System.out.println("Enter message text.");
 System.out.println("Terminate message text with an initial period.");
 Vector text = new Vector();
 boolean finished = false;
 do {
  String line = inStream.readLine();
  if(endOfText(line)) finished = true;
  else text.addElement(line);
 } while(!finished);
 msg.setText(text);
 System.out.println("End of message read.");
 }catch (IOException ex) {
  System.out.println("IO Exception");
  System.exit(1);
 }
 return msg;
}
 boolean endOfText(String s) {
 if(s.length() == 0) return false;
 if(s.charAt(0) == '.') return true;
 return false;
 }
}

class MailTalk {
 // Communication states
 static final int START = 0;
 static final int HELO = 1;
 static final int MAIL = 2;
 static final int RCPT = 3;
 static final int DATA = 4;
 static final int TEXT = 5;
 static final int QUIT = 6;
 static final int FINISHED = 9;
 Socket connection;
 String localHostName;
 NVTOutputStream outStream;
 NVTInputStream inStream;
 Message msg;
 public MailTalk(Message msg){
  this.msg = msg;
  String destination = msg.getDestinationHost();
  int port = 25;
```

continues

Listing 34.5. continued

```
try{
 connection = new Socket(destination,port);
 localHostName = InetAddress.getLocalHost().getHostName();
}catch (UnknownHostException ex) { error("Unknown host"); }
catch (IOException ex) { error("IO error creating socket"); }
try{
 outStream = new NVTOutputStream(connection.getOutputStream());
 inStream = new NVTInputStream(connection.getInputStream(),outStream);
}catch (IOException ex) { error("IO error getting streams"); }
System.out.println("Connected to "+destination+" at port "+port+".");
}
public void run() {
 sendMail();
 shutdown();
}
public void sendMail() {
 try {
  int state = START;
  String line;
  do {
   line = inStream.readLine();
   if(line == null) state = FINISHED;
   else{
    System.out.println(line);
    switch(state) {
    case START:
     if(gotResponse(220,line)){
      outStream.println("HELO "+localHostName);
      System.out.println(">>>HELO "+localHostName);
      state = HELO;
     }else state=FINISHED;
     break;
    case HELO:
     if(gotResponse(250,line)){
      outStream.println("MAIL FROM:<"+msg.getSource()+">");
      System.out.println(">>>MAIL FROM:<"+msg.getSource()+">");
      state = MAIL;
     }else state=FINISHED;
     break;
    case MAIL:
     if(gotResponse(250,line)){
      outStream.println("RCPT TO:<"+msg.getDestination()+">");
      System.out.println(">>>RCPT TO:<"+msg.getDestination()+">");
      state = RCPT;
     }else state=FINISHED;
     break;
    case RCPT:
     if(gotResponse(250,line)){
      outStream.println("DATA");
      System.out.println(">>>DATA");
      state = DATA;
     }else state=FINISHED;
     break;
    case DATA:
     if(gotResponse(354,line)){
      String text[] = msg.getText();
      int len = text.length;
      outStream.println("Subject: "+msg.getSubject());
```

```
      outStream.println("");
      System.out.println("Subject: "+msg.getSubject());
      System.out.println("");
      for(int i=0;i<len;++i) {
       if(text[i].length() > 0 && text[i].charAt(0) == '.') {
        outStream.println("."+text[i]);
        System.out.println("."+text[i]);
       }else{
        outStream.println(text[i]);
        System.out.println(">>>"+text[i]);
       }
      }
      outStream.println(".");
      System.out.println(">>>.");
      state = TEXT;
     }else state=FINISHED;
     break;
    case TEXT:
     if(gotResponse(250,line)){
      outStream.println("QUIT");
      System.out.println(">>>QUIT");
      state = QUIT;
     }else state=FINISHED;
     break;
    case QUIT:
     state=FINISHED;
     break;
    }
   }
  } while(state != FINISHED);
 } catch(IOException ex) {
  error("IO Exception while sending mail");
 }
}
boolean gotResponse(int n,String s) {
 try {
  int responseCode = Integer.valueOf(s.trim().substring(0,3)).intValue();
  String line = s;
  while(line.charAt(3) == '-') {
   line = inStream.readLine();
   System.out.println(line);
  }
  if(responseCode == n) return true;
 }catch(NumberFormatException ex) {
 }catch(IOException ex){
 }
 return false;
}
public void shutdown(){
 try{
  connection.close();
 }catch (IOException ex) { error("IO error closing socket"); }
}
public void error(String s){
 System.out.println(s);
 System.exit(1);
}
}
```

The `MailClientApp` program prompts you for the `from:` name that you want associated with the sent message. SMTP is inherently insecure and will allow you to send e-mail using the e-mail address of another person as the `from:` `address`. In the example, I send a message using my daughter's e-mail address to myself. The subject of the message is `Test` `Message` and it contains a mere two lines of text. The following output shows a sample dialog with the `MailClientApp` program:

```
C:\jdk1.1.1\jdg\Ch34>java MailClientApp
From: emily@jaworski.com
To: jamie@jaworski.com
Subject: Test Message
Enter message text.
Terminate message text with an initial period.
This is a test.
It is only a test.
.
End of message read.
Connected to jaworski.com at port 25.
220 jaworski.com ESMTP Sendmail 8.7.5/8.7.3; Tue, 25 Feb 1997 23:44:26 -0800
>>>HELO biscuit.jaworski.com
250 jaworski.com Hello [204.212.153.198], pleased to meet you
>>>MAIL FROM:<emily@jaworski.com>
250 <emily@jaworski.com>... Sender ok
>>>RCPT TO:<jamie@jaworski.com>
250 Recipient ok
>>>DATA
354 Enter mail, end with "." on a line by itself
Subject: Test Message

>>>This is a test.
>>>It is only a test.
>>>.
250 XAA09509 Message accepted for delivery
>>>QUIT
221 jaworski.com closing connection

C:\jdk1.1.1\jdg\Ch34>
```

After the message is received by the e-mail client, it connects to my SMTP server and sends the message using the SMTP commands summarized earlier in this chapter.

The >>> arrows indicate commands that were sent by the program.

The Web Fetcher Program

Web *browsers* are the most popular client programs found on the Internet. They allow users to download and display Web pages, usually one at time. The program shown in Listing 34.6 allows the user to specify a list of Web pages to be retrieved, and retrieves these Web pages and stores them on the local file system. This is an example of how custom Web clients can be implemented in Java.

Listing 34.6. The source code for the WebFetchApp program.

```java
import java.util.Vector;
import java.io.*;
import java.net.*;

public class WebFetchApp {
 public static void main(String args[]){
  WebFetch fetch = new WebFetch();
  fetch.run();
 }
}

class WebFetch {
 String urlList = "url-list.txt";
 Vector URLs = new Vector();
 Vector fileNames = new Vector();
 public WebFetch() {
  super();
 }
 public void getURLList() {
  try {
   BufferedReader inStream = new BufferedReader(new FileReader(urlList));
   String inLine;
   while((inLine = inStream.readLine()) != null) {
    inLine = inLine.trim();
    if(!inLine.equals("")) {
     int tabPos = inLine.lastIndexOf('\t');
     String url = inLine.substring(0,tabPos).trim();
     String fileName = inLine.substring(tabPos+1).trim();
     URLs.addElement(url);
     fileNames.addElement(fileName);
    }
   }
  }catch(IOException ex){
   error("Error reading "+urlList);
  }
 }
 public void run() {
  getURLList();
  int numURLs = URLs.size();
  for(int i=0;i<numURLs;++i)
   fetchURL((String) URLs.elementAt(i),(String) fileNames.elementAt(i));
  System.out.println("Done.");
 }
 public void fetchURL(String urlName,String fileName) {
  try{
   URL url = new URL(urlName);
   System.out.println("Getting "+urlName+"...");
   File outFile = new File(fileName);
   PrintWriter outStream = new PrintWriter(new FileWriter(outFile));
   BufferedReader inStream = new BufferedReader(
    new InputStreamReader(url.openStream()));
   String line;
   while ((line = inStream.readLine())!= null) outStream.println(line);
   inStream.close();
   outStream.close();
  }catch (MalformedURLException ex){
```

continues

Listing 34.6. continued

```
   System.out.println("Bad URL");
  }catch (IOException ex){
   System.out.println("IOException occurred.");
  }
 }
 public void error(String s){
  System.out.println(s);
  System.exit(1);
 }
}
```

To use the program, create a file named `url-list.txt` that contains the names of the URLs you want to retrieve and the names of the files in which you want them stored. The following `url-list.txt` file was used to retrieve some pretty famous Web pages; it is included on the CD that comes with this book, in the `\jdg\ch34` directory:

```
http://www.yahoo.com          yahoo.htm
http://www.cnn.com            cnn.htm
http://home.netscape.com      netscape.htm
```

The URL and filename are separated by a tab character in the preceding list.

The output generated for the `WebFetchApp` program was as follows:

```
C:\jdk1.1.1\jdg\ch34>java WebFetchApp
Getting http://www.yahoo.com...
Getting http://www.cnn.com...
Getting http://home.netscape.com...
Done.

C:\jdk1.1.1\jdg\ch34>
```

Note that only the HTML file associated with each Web site is retrieved. Supporting graphics files are not downloaded unless they are identified in `url-list.txt`.

Summary

In this chapter you learned how to write client programs that implement the client end of Internet client/server applications. You learned about the common client programs found on the Internet and how they are structured. You developed a simple telnet client, an e-mail program, and the Web fetcher program. In Chapter 35, "Server Programs," you'll learn how to write simple server applications.

35

Server Programs

In this chapter you'll learn how to write server programs to support Internet client/server applications. You'll also learn about the server programs found on the Internet and how they are written. You'll develop simple server programs that support the sending of mail and the retrieval of Web pages. This chapter builds on the material presented in Chapters 17, "Network Programming with the java.net Package," and 34, "Client Programs." You might want to review these chapters before continuing with the material presented in this chapter.

Types of Servers

Chapter 34 introduced you to the types of client programs found on the Internet. For every client, there must be a server. Typical servers include e-mail, Web, FTP, telnet, netnews, and DNS. Other, less-popular servers such as echo, ping, and finger are also commonly supported.

E-mail servers move mail from client programs through the Internet to their destination hosts and store it until it is retrieved. The *Simple Message Transfer Protocol* (SMTP) is used to move mail. The *Post Office Protocol* (POP) is used to store mail and send it to destination client programs.

Web servers implement the *Hypertext Transfer Protocol* (HTTP) in order to serve Web pages over the Internet. The most popular Web server is the Apache Web server. It is publicly available and may be freely downloaded. Commercial Web servers, such as those provided by Netscape and Microsoft, are only a small percentage of those that are in current operation.

FTP servers implement the File Transfer Protocol to make files available over the Internet. The most popular FTP server is a publicly available server developed by Washington University in St. Louis, Missouri.

The *domain name system* provides the backbone for Internet communication by translating domain names to their IP addresses. The most popular DNS software is the publicly available BIND software developed by the University of California at Berkeley.

Telnet servers are found in UNIX, VMS, and other multiuser operating systems. These servers allow remote login and implement the telnet protocol covered in Chapter 34.

Server Responsibilities

A server program listens for incoming connections on the well-known port associated with its service protocol. When an incoming connection is initiated by a client, the server accepts the connection, and typically spawns a separate thread to service that client. The client sends service requests over the connection. The server performs the service and then returns the results to the client.

An SMTP Server

Chapter 34 introduced the SMTP and developed a client program for generating Internet e-mail and sending it to an SMTP server. This section shows how the other side of the client/server connection is implemented. RFC 821 describes the details of this protocol. Here I will implement only a minimal subset of the available features of SMTP.

An *SMTP server* listens on port 25 for incoming client connections. When a connection request is received, the server accepts the connection and sends a server-ready notification to the client. When the client sends the HELO command, the server responds by sending a 250 code that indicates it is okay to initiate a mail transmission. The server then waits for the client to send the MAIL command. It acknowledges the MAIL command with another 250 code.

Having processed the MAIL command, the server then waits for the RCPT command. The server processes the RCPT command by checking to see if the destination e-mail address is valid for the server. It responds by indicating that the address is valid (using the 250 code) or that the user is not known to the server (using the 550 code).

When the client sends the DATA command, the server sends the 354 code to tell the client to start sending the contents of the mail message. The client then sends the message data one line at a time. The server checks each line to see if it consists of a single period (.), indicating the end of the message data. When this happens, it sends another 250 code to the client, indicating that it has found the end of the message.

The server removes the first period occurring in any message text line that it receives from the client.

After the server receives the end of the message text, it waits for the QUIT command. When it receives the QUIT command, it sends a 221 code, indicating that it is closing the transmission channel. It then closes the socket connection.

The SMTPServerApp Program

The SMTPServerApp program illustrates the basic operation of an SMTP server program. It implements the basic SMTP commands described in the previous section. Its source code is shown in Listing 35.1.

Listing 35.1. The source code for the SMTPServerApp program.

```
import java.net.*;
import java.io.*;
import jdg.ch34.NVTInputStream;
import jdg.ch34.NVTOutputStream;

public class SMTPServerApp {
 public static void main(String args[]){
```

continues

Listing 35.1. continued

```
 SMTPServer server = new SMTPServer();
 server.run();
 }
}
class SMTPServer {
 static final int HELO = 1;
 static final int MAIL = 2;
 static final int RCPT = 3;
 static final int DATA = 4;
 static final int END_DATA = 5;
 static final int QUIT = 6;
 static final int FINISHED = 9;
 NVTOutputStream out;
 NVTInputStream in;
 String hostName;
 public SMTPServer() {
  super();
 }
 public void run() {
  try{
   ServerSocket server = new ServerSocket(25);
   int localPort = server.getLocalPort();
   hostName = InetAddress.getLocalHost().getHostName();
   System.out.println("SMTPServerApp is listening on port "+localPort+".");
   boolean finished = false;
   do {
    Socket client = server.accept();
    String destName = client.getInetAddress().getHostName();
    int destPort = client.getPort();
    System.out.println("Accepted connection to "+destName+" on port "+
     destPort+".");
    out = new NVTOutputStream(client.getOutputStream());
    in = new NVTInputStream(client.getInputStream(),out);
    getMail();
    client.close();
   } while(!finished);
  }catch (UnknownHostException ex) {
   System.out.println("UnknownHostException occurred.");
  }catch (IOException ex){
   System.out.println("IOException occurred.");
  }
 }
 void getMail() {
  out.println("220 "+hostName+" Simple Mail Transport Service Ready");
  int state = HELO;
  do {
   String line = "";
   try {
    line = in.readLine();
    if(line == null) state = FINISHED;
   }catch(IOException ex) {
    System.out.println("IOException occurred.");
    System.exit(1);
   }
   switch(state){
   case HELO:
```

```
 if(commandIs("HELO",line)) {
  out.println("250 Hello");
  System.out.println(line);
  state = MAIL;
 }else{
  out.println("500 ERROR");
  System.out.println(line);
 }
 break;
case MAIL:
 if(commandIs("MAIL",line)) {
  out.println("250 OK");
  System.out.println(line);
  state = RCPT;
 }else{
  out.println("500 ERROR");
  System.out.println(line);
 }
 break;
case RCPT:
 if(commandIs("RCPT",line)) {
  out.println("250 OK");
  System.out.println(line);
  state = DATA;
 }else{
  out.println("500 ERROR");
  System.out.println(line);
 }
 break;
case DATA:
 if(commandIs("DATA",line)) {
  out.println("354 Start mail input; end with <CRLF>.<CRLF>");
  System.out.println(line);
  state = END_DATA;
 }else{
  out.println("500 ERROR");
  System.out.println(line);
 }
 break;
case END_DATA:
 if(endOfData(line)) {
  out.println("250 OK");
  System.out.println("End of Message Received.");
  state = QUIT;
 }else{
  System.out.println(stripFirstPeriod(line));
 }
 break;
case QUIT:
 if(commandIs("QUIT",line)) {
  out.println("221 "+hostName+" Service closing transmission channel");
  System.out.println(line);
  System.out.println("");
  state = FINISHED;
 }else{
  out.println("500 ERROR");
  System.out.println(line);
```

continues

Listing 35.1. continued

```
      }
      break;
    }
  } while(state != FINISHED);
}
boolean commandIs(String s,String line) {
  int n = s.length();
  if(s.equalsIgnoreCase(line.substring(0,n))) return true;
  return false;
}
boolean endOfData(String s) {
  if(s.equals(".")) return true;
  return false;
}
String stripFirstPeriod(String s) {
  try {
    if(s.charAt(0) == '.') return s.substring(1);
  }catch(Exception ex){
  }
  return s;
}
}
```

To run SMTPServerApp, type `java SMTPServer` at the DOS prompt. It will then display the following notice to indicate that it is up and running:

```
C:\jdk1.1.1\jdg\Ch35>java SMTPServerApp
SMTPServerApp is listening on port 25.
```

In order to use SMTPServerApp, you have to send e-mail to your machine's Internet address. You can use any e-mail client program to send e-mail to SMTPServerApp, but I'll use MailClientApp, developed in the previous chapter, to allow you to track both sides of the SMTP connection.

Open a second console window and run MailClientApp as shown in the following text (substitute your host system name as the e-mail's destination). If you don't know your host name, you can use localhost instead:

```
C:\jdk1.1.1\jdg\Ch34>java MailClientApp
From: jamie@jaworski.com
To: jamie@biscuit.jaworski.com
Subject: Test of SMTPServerApp
Enter message text.
Terminate message text with an initial period.
This is a test of SMTPServerApp.
.
End of message read.
Connected to biscuit.jaworski.com at port 25.
220 biscuit.jaworski.com Simple Mail Transport Service Ready
>>>HELO biscuit.jaworski.com
250 Hello
>>>MAIL FROM:<jamie@jaworski.com>
250 OK
```

```
>>>RCPT TO:<jamie@biscuit.jaworski.com>
250 OK
>>>DATA
354 Start mail input; end with <CRLF>.<CRLF>
Subject: Test of SMTPServerApp

>>>This is a test of SMTPServerApp.
>>>.
250 OK
>>>QUIT
221 biscuit.jaworski.com Service closing transmission channel

C:\jdk1.1.1\jdg\Ch34>
```

In this example, I am sending e-mail from a computer at home (jaworski.com) to the computer that I am currently using (biscuit.jaworski.com). You can work the example by sending e-mail to the same computer using separate windows for sender and receiver.

> **NOTE**
>
> If you cannot determine your host name or IP address, you can always use localhost as your host name.

Now look at the data displayed in the SMTPServerApp window:

```
C:\jdk1.1.1\jdg\Ch35>java SMTPServerApp
SMTPServerApp is listening on port 25.
Accepted connection to 204.212.153.198 on port 1162.
HELO biscuit.jaworski.com
MAIL FROM:<jamie@jaworski.com>
RCPT TO:<jamie@biscuit.jaworski.com>
DATA
Subject: Test of SMTPServerApp

This is a test of SMTPServerApp.
End of Message Received.
QUIT
```

> **NOTE**
>
> The SMTPServerApp program is designed to loop forever to receive and process new SMTP connections. When you are finished running the program, use Ctrl+C to terminate its operation.

The data display is not as verbose as that of the mail client, but it shows all of the commands and data received. Compare the display of SMTPServerApp with that of MailClientApp to follow how both sides of the Simple Mail Transport Protocol were implemented.

The `main()` method of `SMTPServerApp` creates an object of the `SMTPServer` class and invokes its `run()` method.

The `SMTPServer` class declares seven constants that are used to maintain the state of the mail protocol as it interacts with a mail client program. It also declares the `NVTInputStream` and `NVTOutputStream` objects that it uses for client communication. The `hostName` variable is used to store the name of the local host running the SMTP server.

The `run()` method creates a `ServerSocket` object on port 25. It retrieves the local host name and stores it using the `hostName` variable. It then identifies on which port it is listening.

The `do` statement is used to service individual mail clients in a sequential manner. It accepts a client socket connection, gets the parameters of the connection, and displays them to the console window. The input and output streams associated with the connection are created and assigned to the `in` and `out` variables. The `getMail()` method is then invoked to receive mail from the client.

The `getMail()` method implements a subset of SMTP in order to receive mail from the client. It does not store the messages it receives, but merely displays the results of the client interaction on the console window.

When `getMail()` is invoked, it sends the `220 Simple Mail Transport Service Ready` line to the mail client along with its host name. It then sets the `state` variable to the `HELO` constant. The `state` variable is used to maintain the state of communication with the client. The `getMail()` method uses a `do` statement to receive and process commands that it receives from the mail client. It reads a line from the client and verifies that the line is not `null`. (A `null` line signals that the connection with the client has been terminated.) The `getMail()` method processes the newly read line in different ways depending on the setting of the `state` variable.

If the current state is `HELO`, it checks to see if the received line contains the `HELO` command. If it does, a `250 OK` response is sent to the client and the state is set to `MAIL`. If it does not, a `500 ERROR` response is sent to the client and the current state remains unchanged.

If the current state is `MAIL`, it checks to see if the received line contains the `MAIL` command. If it does, a `250 OK` response is sent to the client and the state is set to `RCPT`. If it does not, a `500 ERROR` response is sent to the client and the current state remains unchanged.

If the current state is `RCPT`, it checks to see if the received line contains the `RCPT` command. If it does, a `250 OK` response is sent to the client and the state is set to `DATA`. If it does not, a `500 ERROR` response is sent to the client and the current state remains unchanged.

If the current state is `DATA`, it checks to see if the received line contains the `DATA` command. If it does, a `354 Start mail input; end with <CRLF>.<CRLF>` response is sent to the client and the state is set to `END_DATA`. If it does not, a `500 ERROR` response is sent to the client and the current state remains unchanged.

If the current state is END_DATA, it checks to see if the received line contains the end-of-message data command—a line consisting of a single period (.). If it does, a 250 OK response is sent to the client and the state is set to QUIT. If it does not, the first period of the received line (if any) is stripped before the line is displayed to the console window.

If the current state is QUIT, it checks to see if the received line contains the QUIT command. If it does, a 250 OK response is sent to the client and the state is set to FINISHFD. If it does not, a 500 ERROR response is sent to the client and the current state remains unchanged.

When the current state becomes FINISHED, the do statement is terminated.

The commandIs() method is used to determine whether a command received from a mail client matches a specific command string.

The endOfData() method checks a received line to see if it consists of a single period indicating the end of a message transmission.

The stripFirstPeriod()method is used to strip out the first period of a message text line.

A Web Server

Web servers implement the Hypertext Transfer Protocol (HTTP) in order to retrieve Web resources identified by URLs. HTTP is an application-level protocol that is designed to be quick and efficient. It is based on the request-response paradigm. Web browsers initiate connections with Web servers and submit service requests. The servers, upon receiving a request, locate the specified resource and perform the requested operation. Typical Web browser requests are to retrieve a designated file or send data to a CGI program. HTTP supports several request types, referred to as *methods*. These include the GET, HEAD, and POST methods. The Web server developed in the following section only supports the GET request.

The server responds to GET requests by returning the requested resource to the browser. The server's response begins with a header and is followed by the requested data. The *header* consists of a status line and one or more general header lines. The status line identifies the version of HTTP being used and a status code. General header lines include a MIME version identifier, a date/time line, a content type indicator, and a content length identifier. A blank line is inserted between the header and the body of the resource data.

The WebServerApp Program

The WebServerApp program illustrates the basic operation of a Web server. (See Listing 35.2.) It is a single-threaded Web server that supports a subset of the HTTP 1.0 protocol. Many Web servers are multithreaded, allowing them to simultaneously support multiple browser connections. Some Web servers for low-end PC platforms are single threaded to make up for processing deficiencies of slow PCs and slower Internet connections. WebServerApp can easily be converted to a multithreaded server by implementing the interior of the outer do statement as a separate thread.

Listing 35.2. The source code for the WebServerApp program.

```java
import java.net.*;
import java.io.*;
import jdg.ch34.NVTInputStream;
import jdg.ch34.NVTOutputStream;

public class WebServerApp {
 public static void main(String args[]){
  WebServer server = new WebServer();
  server.run();
 }
}
class WebServer {
 public WebServer() {
  super();
 }
 public void run() {
  try{
   ServerSocket server = new ServerSocket(8080);
   int localPort = server.getLocalPort();
   System.out.println("WebServerApp is listening on port "+localPort+".");
   do {
    Socket client = server.accept();
    String destName = client.getInetAddress().getHostName();
    int destPort = client.getPort();
    System.out.println("Accepted connection to "+destName+
     " on port "+destPort+".");
    NVTOutputStream outStream =
     new NVTOutputStream(client.getOutputStream());
    NVTInputStream inStream =
     new NVTInputStream(client.getInputStream(),outStream);
    boolean finished = false;
    String inLine = inStream.readLine();
    System.out.println("Received: "+inLine);
    String otherLines;
    do {
     otherLines = inStream.readLine();
    } while(otherLines.length()>0);
    if(getRequest(inLine)) {
     String fileName = getFileName(inLine);
     File file = new File(fileName);
     if(file.exists()) {
      System.out.println(fileName+" requested.");
      outStream.println("HTTP/1.0 200 OK");
      outStream.println("MIME-Version: 1.0");
      outStream.println("Content-Type: text/html");
      int len = (int) file.length();
      outStream.println("Content-Length: "+len);
      outStream.println("");
      sendFile(outStream,file);
      outStream.flush();
     }else{
```

```
      outStream.println("HTTP/1.0 404 Not Found");
      String notFound =
       "<TITLE>Not Found</TITLE><H1>Error 404 - File Not Found</H1>";
      outStream.println("Content-Type: text/html");
      outStream.println("Content-Length: "+notFound.length()+2);
      outStream.println("");
      outStream.println(notFound);
     }
    }
    client.close();
   } while(true);
  }catch (IOException ex){
   System.out.println("IOException occurred.");
  }
 }
 boolean getRequest(String s) {
  if(s.length() > 0) {
   if(s.substring(0,3).equalsIgnoreCase("GET")) return true;
  }
  return false;
 }
 String getFileName(String s) {
  String f = s.substring(s.indexOf(' ')+1);
  f = f.substring(0,f.indexOf(' '));
  try {
   if(f.charAt(0) == '/') f =  f.substring(1);
  } catch(StringIndexOutOfBoundsException ex) {
  }
  if(f.equals("")) f = "index.htm";
  return f;
 }
 void sendFile(NVTOutputStream out,File file) {
  try {
   DataInputStream in = new DataInputStream(new FileInputStream(file));
   int len = (int) file.length();
   byte buffer[] = new byte[len];
   in.readFully(buffer);
   out.write(buffer,0,len);
   in.close();
  }catch(Exception ex){
   System.out.println("Error retrieving file.");
   System.exit(1);
  }
 }
}
```

Run `WebServerApp` as follows:

```
C:\jdk1.1.1\jdg\Ch35>java WebServerApp
WebServerApp is listening on port 8080.
```

It responds by indicating that it is listening on port 8080. I had it use port 8080 instead of the standard port 80 so as not to interfere with any Web server that you might currently have running on your system.

I have supplied a default Web page, index.htm, that is retrieved by WebServerApp. (See Listing 35.3.) You can also retrieve other Web pages by placing them in the same directory as WebServerApp and referencing them in the URL opened by your Web browser.

Listing 35.3. The contents of the index.htm file.

```
<HTML>
<HEAD><TITLE>Test Document for WebServerApp</TITLE></HEAD>
<BODY>
<H1>This is a test of WebServerApp.</H1>
<H1>Hooray, it works!</H1>
</BODY>
</HTML>
```

> **NOTE**
>
> If the WebServerApp program does not find the index.htm file, it will return an error message.

Because WebServerApp is a server, you need to use a client program in order to interact with it. Launch your favorite Web browser and open the URL of your machine followed by :8080 to have the browser submit its request to port 8080 instead of port 80. For example, if your host name is my.host.name.com, open the URL http://my.host.name.com:8080. WebServerApp responds by identifying the browser connection and sending the index.htm file. You can access other files by appending their names to the URL. For example, to access the test.htm file in the directory where you launched WebServerApp, use the URL http://my.host.name.com:8080/index.htm.

The following output is displayed by WebServerApp on the console window:

```
C:\jdk1.1.1\jdg\Ch35>java WebServerApp
WebServerApp is listening on port 8080.
Accepted connection to 204.212.153.198 on port 1175.
Received: GET / HTTP/1.0
index.htm requested.
```

When you access the URL http://my.host.name.com:8080, WebServerApp is instructed to return the default no name HTML file. It responds by sending index.htm to the Web browser. Your browser's display should contain the message shown in Figure 35.1.

> **NOTE**
>
> If you cannot find your host name, you can use localhost instead. For example, the URL http://localhost:8080 can be used instead of http://my.host.name.com:8080.

FIGURE 35.1.

Web browser display.

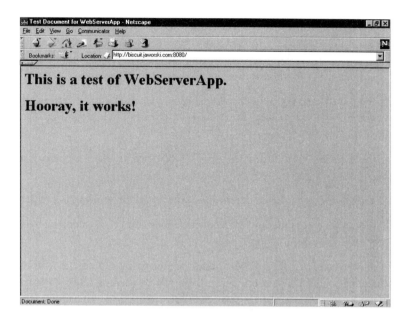

Experiment by creating your own HTML files and using your browser to access them using WebServerApp. Use Ctrl+C to terminate the operation of WebServerApp.

The main() method of WebServerApp creates a WebServer object and invokes its run() method.

The WebServer class implements a single default constructor and three access methods.

The run() method supports Web client retrieval requests and is the heart of the WebServerApp processing. It creates a ServerSocket object using port 8080 and then displays its operational status on the console window.

A do statement is used to accept and process incoming client connections. It retrieves the parameters associated with a connection and displays them to the console window. The input and output streams associated with the connection are created and assigned to the inStream and outStream variables. A line is then read from the input stream and displayed to the console window.

The first line received from the browser client is checked to see if it is a GET request. If it is, the name of the requested HTML file is retrieved from the browser request line. If the file exists within the current directory, a 200 OK status line is sent to the browser, followed by a MIME-version 1.0 header line. This line tells the browser that the server is cognizant of MIME version 1.0 when returning the requested file. It then specifies the MIME type of the requested file as text or html. Real Web servers would send a MIME type that matched the extension of the file returned. See Chapter 36, "Content Handlers," for a discussion of MIME types and their use by Web servers and browsers.

The length of the file to be returned is obtained using the length() method of the File class, and a notification of the file's length is returned to the browser using a Content-Length header line. A blank line follows the Content-Length header line to signal the end of the HTTP header. The sendFile() method is then invoked to send the requested file to the browser.

If the file requested by the browser does not exist, the HTTP status line sent to the browser contains a 404 Not Found error code and a short HTML file indicating that the error is sent to the browser.

If the request received from the browser client is not a GET request, it is ignored and the connection is closed.

The getRequest() method determines whether an incoming client request uses the GET method.

The getFileName() method extracts the requested HTML filename from an incoming browser request line.

The sendFile() method sends the file requested by a Web client using the output stream of the server-client connection. It sends the file by reading all bytes of the file into a byte array and then sending the entire array over the connection. This approach works well with small files, but may break with large files, depending on available memory resources.

Summary

In this chapter you learned how to write programs that implement the server end of Internet client/server applications. You learned about the common server programs found on the Internet and how they are structured. You developed an SMTP server and a primitive Web server. In Chapter 36, you'll learn how to write content handlers that are used with Web client applications.

36

Content Handlers

In this chapter you'll learn how to write content handlers to support the retrieval of objects by Web browsers. You'll also learn about the Multipurpose Internet Mail Extensions (MIME) and how they are used to identify the type of objects that are provided by Web servers. You'll then develop a simple content handler and integrate it with a Web client program. This chapter builds on the material presented in Chapter 17, "Network Programming with the java.net Package."

Using Content Handlers

If you have been extensively involved with using your Web browser, you probably have encountered a number of external viewers or plug-ins that are used to supplement the capabilities provided by your browser. These external viewers are used to display and process files that are not normally supported by browsers.

Java supports additional internal or external viewers through the content handler mechanism. Content handlers are used to retrieve objects via an URLConnection object.

Content handlers are implemented as subclasses of the ContentHandler class. A content handler is only required to implement a single method—the getContent() method that overrides the method provided by the ContentHandler class. This method takes an URLConnection object as a parameter and returns an object of a specific MIME type. You'll learn about MIME types in the following section of this chapter.

The purpose of a content handler is to extract an object of a given MIME type from an URLConnection object's input stream. Content handlers are not directly instantiated or accessed. The getContent() methods of the URL and URLConnection classes cause content handlers to be created and invoked to perform their processing.

A content handler is associated with a specific MIME type through the use of the ContentHandlerFactory interface. A class that implements the ContentHandlerFactory interface must implement the createContentHandler() method. This method returns a ContentHandler object to be used for a specific MIME type. A ContentHandlerFactory object is installed using the static setContentHandlerFactory() method of the URLConnection class.

Multipurpose Internet Mail Extensions (MIME)

Content handlers are associated with specific MIME types. Many Internet programs, including e-mail clients, Web browsers, and Web servers, use the Multipurpose Internet Mail Extensions to associate an object type with a file. These object types include text, multimedia files, and application-specific files. MIME types consist of a type and a subtype. Examples are text/ html, text/plain, image/gif, and image/jpeg, where text and image are the types and html, text, gif, and jpeg are the subtypes. The URL classes provided by Java support the processing of each of these types; however, the number of MIME type/subtype combinations is large and growing. Content handlers are used to support MIME type processing.

Web servers map MIME types to the files they serve using the files' extensions. For example, files with the `.htm` and `.html` extensions are mapped to the text/html MIME type/subtype. Files with the `.gif` and `.jpg` extensions are mapped to image/gif and image/jpeg. The MIME type of a file is sent to Web browsers by Web servers when the server sends the designated files to the browsers in response to browser requests.

Developing a Content Handler

The first step to implementing a content handler is to define the class of the object to be extracted by the content handler. The content handler is then defined as a subclass of the `ContentHandler` class. The `getContent()` method of the content handler performs the extraction of objects of a specific MIME type from the input stream associated with an `URLConnection` object.

A content handler is associated with a specific MIME type through the use of a `ContentHandlerFactory` object. The `createContentHandler()` method of the `ContentHandlerFactory` interface is used to return a content handler for a specific MIME type.

Finally, the `setContentHandlerFactory()` method of the `URLConnection` class is used to set a `ContentHandlerFactory` as the default `ContentHandlerFactory` to be used with all MIME types.

A Simple Content Handler

This section presents an example of implementing a simple content handler. A bogus MIME type, text/cg, is created to implement objects of the character grid type. A *character grid type* is a two-dimensional grid made up of a single character. An example follows:

```
0   0
 0 0
  0
 0 0
0   0
```

This example is a character grid object that is five character positions wide and five character positions high. It uses the 0 character to draw the grid. The grid is specified by a `boolean` array that identifies how the drawing character is to be displayed.

This particular character grid is represented using the following text string:

`5501000101010001000101010001`

The first character (5) represents the grid's height. The second character (also 5) represents the grid's width. The third character is the grid's drawing character. The remaining characters specify whether the draw character should be displayed at a particular grid position. A one (1) signifies that the draw character should be displayed and a zero (0) signifies that it should not be displayed. The array is arranged in row order beginning with the top of the grid.

The definition of the CharGrid class is shown in Listing 36.1.

Listing 36.1. The source code for the CharGrid class.

```
public class CharGrid {
 public int height;
 public int width;
 public char ch;
 public boolean values[][];
 public CharGrid(int h,int w,char c,boolean vals[][]) {
  height = h;
  width = w;
  ch = c;
  values = vals;
 }
}
```

The GridContentHandler Class

The GridContentHandler class is used to extract CharGrid objects from an URLConnection. Its source code is shown in Listing 36.2.

Listing 36.2. The source code for the GridContentHandler class.

```
import java.net.*;
import java.io.*;

public class GridContentHandler extends ContentHandler {
 public Object getContent(URLConnection urlc) throws IOException {
  DataInputStream in = new DataInputStream(urlc.getInputStream());
  int height = (int) in.readByte() - 48;
  int width = (int) in.readByte() - 48;
  char ch = (char) in.readByte();
  boolean values[][] = new boolean[height][width];
  for(int i=0;i<height;++i) {
   for(int j=0;j<width;++j) {
    byte b = in.readByte();
    if(b == 48) values[i][j] = false;
    else values[i][j] = true;
   }
  }
  in.close();
  return new CharGrid(height,width,ch,values);
 }
}
```

The `GridContentHandler` class extends the `ContentHandler` class and provides a single method. The `getContent()` method takes an `URLConnection` object as a parameter and returns an object of the `Object` class. It also throws the `IOException` exception.

The `getContent()` method creates an object of class `DataInputStream` and assigns it to the `in` variable. It uses the `getInputStream()` method of the `URLConnection` class to access the input stream associated with an `URLConnection`.

The height, width, and draw character of the `CharGrid` object are read one byte at a time from the input stream. The `values` array is read and converted to a `boolean` representation. A `CharGrid` object is then created from the extracted values and returned.

The `GetGridApp` Program

The `GetGridApp` program illustrates the use of content handlers. It retrieves an object of the `CharGrid` type from my Web sever. I use the NCSA HTTPD server on a Linux system. I've set up the server's MIME type file to recognize files with the `.cg` extension as text/cg.

The source code of the `GetGridApp` program is shown in Listing 36.3.

Listing 36.3. The source code for the `GetGridApp` program.

```
import java.net.*;
import java.io.*;

public class GetGridApp {
 public static void main(String args[]){
  try{
   GridFactory gridFactory = new GridFactory();
   URLConnection.setContentHandlerFactory(gridFactory);
   if(args.length!=1) error("Usage: java GetGridApp URL");
   System.out.println("Fetching URL: "+args[0]);
   URL url = new URL(args[0]);
   CharGrid cg = (CharGrid) url.getContent();
   System.out.println("height: "+cg.height);
   System.out.println("width: "+cg.width);
   System.out.println("char: "+cg.ch);
   for(int i=0;i<cg.height;++i) {
    for(int j=0;j<cg.width;++j) {
     if(cg.values[i][j]) System.out.print(cg.ch);
     else System.out.print(" ");
    }
    System.out.println();
   }
  }catch (MalformedURLException ex){
   error("Bad URL");
  }catch (IOException ex){
   error("IOException occurred.");
  }
 }
 public static void error(String s){
  System.out.println(s);
```

continues

Listing 36.3. continued

```
  System.exit(1);
 }
}
class GridFactory implements ContentHandlerFactory {
 public GridFactory() {
 }
 public ContentHandler createContentHandler(String mimeType) {
  if(mimeType.equals("text/cg")) {
   System.out.println("Requested mime type: "+mimeType);
   return new GridContentHandler();
  }
  return null;
 }
}
```

Compile CharGrid.java and GridContentHandler.java before compiling GetGridApp.java. When you invoke the GetGridApp program, provide it with the http://www.jaworski.com/java/chargrid.cg URL as a parameter.

The GetGridApp program's output is as follows:

```
C:\jdk1.1.1\jdg\Ch36>java GetGridApp http://www.jaworski.com/java/chargrid.cg
Fetching URL: http://www.jaworski.com/java/chargrid.cg
Requested mime type: text/cg
height: 5
width: 5
char: j
jjjjj
  j
  j
j j
 jj

C:\jdk1.1.1\jdg\Ch36>
```

This connects to my Web server, retrieves the chargrid.cg file, extracts the CharGrid object contained in the file, and displays it on the console window. The character grid object displays a grid of j characters.

The main() method creates an object of the GridFactory class, which implements the ContentHandlerFactory interface. It then sets the object as the default content handler. An URL object is created using the URL string passed as the program's parameter. The getContent() method of the URL class is then used to extract the CharGrid object from the URL. The getContent() method results in the GridFactory object assigned to the gridFactory variable being invoked to retrieve an appropriate content handler. An object of class GridContentHandler is returned and its getContent() method is invoked to extract the CharGrid object. This is performed behind the scene as the result of invoking the URL class's getContent() method. The CharGrid object is then displayed.

The GetGridApp program defines the GridFactory class as a ContentHandlerFactory. It implements the createContentHandler() method and checks to see if the MIME type passed to it is text/cg. If it is not, the null value is returned to signal that the Java-supplied content handler should be used. If the MIME type is text/cg, the requested MIME type is displayed and a GridContentHandler object is returned.

> **NOTE**
>
> Check your Web server's documentation if you want to learn how to set up your Web server to work with a new MIME type. Almost all Web servers provide the capability to define new MIME types. However, there is no common approach to doing this that works across all Web servers.

Summary

In this chapter you learned how to write content handlers to support the retrieval of objects by Web browsers. You learned about the Multipurpose Internet Mail Extensions and how they are used to identify the type of objects that are provided by Web servers. You developed the GridContentHandler class and integrated it with the GetGridApp program. Chapter 37, "Protocol Handlers," shows you how to integrate custom protocol handlers into your Web-based applications.

37

Protocol Handlers

In this chapter you'll learn how to write protocol handlers to support the use of custom protocols by Web browsers. You'll also learn how Web browsers implement protocols other than HTTP and how these protocols are integrated into the browser's operation. You'll develop a simple protocol handler and integrate it with a Web client program. This chapter builds on the material presented in Chapter 17, "Network Programming with the java.net Package."

Using Protocol Handlers

Most popular Web browsers support protocols other than HTTP. These other protocols include FTP, Gopher, e-mail, as well as application-specific protocols. Support for these protocols is usually built into the browser, causing the browsers to become larger and slower to load.

Java supports additional protocols through the use of *protocol handlers,* also referred to as *stream handlers.* These protocol handlers are used to retrieve Web objects using application-specific protocols. These protocols are specified in the URL referencing the object.

Protocol handlers are implemented as subclasses of the URLStreamHandler class. The URLStreamHandler class defines four access methods that can be overridden by its subclasses, but only the openConnection() method is required to be overridden.

The openConnection()method takes an URL with its assigned protocol as a parameter and returns an object of class URLConnection. The URLConnection object can then be used to create input and output streams and to access the resource addressed by the URL.

The parseURL() and setURL() methods are used to implement custom URL syntax parsing. The toExternalForm() method is used to convert an URL of the protocol type to a String object.

The purpose of a protocol handler is to implement a custom protocol needed to access Web objects identified by URLs that require the custom protocol. Protocol handlers, like content handlers, are not directly instantiated or accessed. The methods of the URLConnection object that is returned by a protocol handler are invoked to access the resource referenced by the protocol.

A protocol is identified beginning with the first character of the URL and continuing to the first colon (:) contained in the URL. For example, the protocol of the URL http://www.jaworski.com is http and the protocol of the URL fortune://jaworski.com is fortune.

A protocol handler is associated with a specific protocol through the use of the URLStreamHandlerFactory interface. A class that implements the URLStreamHandlerFactory interface must implement the createURLStreamHandler() method. This method returns an URLStreamHandler object to be used for a specific protocol. An URLStreamHandlerFactory object is installed using the static setURLStreamHandlerFactory() method of the URL class.

Developing a Protocol Handler

The first step to implement a protocol handler is to define the protocol handler as a subclass of the URLStreamHandler class. The openConnection() method of the protocol handler creates an URLConnection object that can be used to access an URL designating the specified protocol.

A protocol handler is associated with a specific protocol type through the use of an URLStreamHandlerFactory object. The createURLStreamHandler() method of the URLStreamHandlerFactory interface is used to return a protocol handler for a specific protocol type.

The setURLStreamHandlerFactory() method of the URL class is used to set an URLStreamHandlerFactory as the default URLStreamHandlerFactory to be used with all protocol types.

A Simple Protocol Handler

This section presents an example of implementing a simple protocol handler. My NCSA server comes with a CGI program, named fortune, that returns a fortune cookie–type message when the program's URL is accessed. This section will define the fortune protocol to access the fortune program on my Web server and on other NCSA Web servers. The fortune protocol is not a real Internet protocol; I contrived it to illustrate the use of protocol handlers. The URL for the fortune protocol consists of fortune:// followed by the host name. For example, fortune:// jaworski.com accesses the fortune protocol on my Web server.

The definition of the URLFortuneHandler class is shown in Listing 37.1.

Listing 37.1. The source code for the URLFortuneHandler class.

```
import java.net.*;
import java.io.*;

public class URLFortuneHandler extends URLStreamHandler {
 public URLConnection openConnection(URL url) throws IOException {
  String host=url.getHost();
  URL newURL = new URL("http://"+host+"/cgi-bin/fortune");
  return newURL.openConnection();
 }
}
```

The URLFortuneHandler class extends the URLStreamHandler class and provides a single method. The openConnection() method takes an URL object as a parameter and returns an object of the URLConnection class. It also throws the IOException exception.

The openConnection() method uses the getHost() method of the URL class to extract the host name contained in the URL. It then uses a new HTTP URL by concatenating http:// with the host name and the location of the fortune CGI program, /cgi-bin/fortune. The openConection() method of the URL class is used to return the URLConnection object associated with the new URL.

The URLFortuneHandler class wraps the fortune CGI program using the fortune protocol. This protocol is implemented through an HTTP connection to the CGI program.

The GetFortuneApp Program

The GetFortuneApp program illustrates the use of protocol handlers. It accesses the fortune CGI program on my Web server using the fortune protocol. The source code of the GetFortuneApp program is shown in Listing 37.2. Be sure to compile URLFortuneHandler.java before compiling GetFortuneApp.java.

Listing 37.2. The source code for the GetFortuneApp program.

```
import java.net.*;
import java.io.*;

public class GetFortuneApp {
 public static void main(String args[]){
  try{
   FortuneFactory fortuneFactory = new FortuneFactory();
   URL.setURLStreamHandlerFactory(fortuneFactory);
   if(args.length!=1) error("Usage: java GetFortuneApp FortuneURL");
   System.out.println("Fetching URL: "+args[0]);
   URL url = new URL(args[0]);
   BufferedReader inStream = new BufferedReader(
    new InputStreamReader(url.openStream()));
   String line = "";
   while((line = inStream.readLine()) != null)
    System.out.println(line);
  }catch (MalformedURLException ex){
   error("Bad URL");
  }catch (IOException ex){
   error("IOException occurred.");
  }
 }
 public static void error(String s){
  System.out.println(s);
  System.exit(1);
 }
}
class FortuneFactory implements URLStreamHandlerFactory {
 public FortuneFactory() {
 }
```

```
public URLStreamHandler createURLStreamHandler(String protocol) {
  if(protocol.equals("fortune")){
   System.out.println("Requested protocol: "+protocol);
   return new URLFortuneHandler();
  }
  return null;
 }
}
```

When you invoke the `GetFortuneApp` program, provide it with the `fortune://jaworski.com` URL as a parameter. The `GetFortuneApp` program's output is as follows (you will get a different fortune each time you execute the program):

```
C:\jdk1.1.1\jdg\ch37>java GetFortuneApp fortune://jaworski.com
Fetching URL: fortune://jaworski.com
Requested protocol: fortune
                    JACK AND THE BEANSTACK
                       by Mark Isaak

        Long ago, in a finite state far away, there lived a JOVIAL
character named Jack.  Jack and his relations were poor.  Often their
hash table was bare.  One day Jack's parent said to him, "Our matrices
are sparse.  You must go to the market to exchange our RAM for some
BASICs."  She compiled a linked list of items to retrieve and passed it
to him.
        So Jack set out.  But as he was walking along a Hamilton path,
he met the traveling salesman.
        "Whither dost thy flow chart take thou?" prompted the salesman
in high-level language.
        "I'm going to the market to exchange this RAM for some chips
and Apples," commented Jack.
        "I have a much better algorithm.  You needn't join a queue
there; I will swap your RAM for these magic kernels now."
        Jack made the trade, then backtracked to his house.  But when
he told his busy-waiting parent of the deal, she became so angry she
started thrashing.
        "Don't you even have any artificial intelligence?  All these
kernels together hardly make up one byte," and she popped them out the
window ...


C:\jdk1.1.1\jdg\ch37>
```

`GetFortuneApp` connects to my Web server, invokes the `fortune` CGI program, and then displays the program's results. The source code of the `fortune` CGI program is available at `http://www.jaworski.com/jdg/`.

The `main()` method creates an object of the `FortuneFactory` class that implements the `URLStreamHandlerFactory` interface. It then sets the object as the default protocol handler. An URL object is created using the URL string passed as the program's parameter. The `openStream()` method of the URL class is then used to open an input stream to extract the information generated by accessing the URL via the fortune protocol. The `openStream()` method results in the

FortuneFactory object assigned to the fortuneFactory variable being invoked to retrieve an appropriate protocol handler. An object of class URLFortuneHandler is returned and its openConnection() method is invoked to extract the URLConnection object. This is performed behind the scenes as the result of invoking the URL class's openStream() method. The information returned from accessing the URL is then displayed.

The GetFortuneApp program defines the FortuneFactory class as implementing the URLStreamHandlerFactory interface. It implements the createURLStreamHandler() method and checks to see if the protocol type passed to it is fortune. If it is not, the null value is returned to signal that the Java-supplied protocol handler should be used. If the protocol type is fortune, the requested protocol is displayed and an URLFortuneHandler object is returned.

Summary

In this chapter you learned how to write protocol handlers to access URLs via custom protocols. You developed the URLFortuneHandler and integrated it with the GetFortuneApp program. In the next chapter you will learn how to use Jeeves, an application server framework developed by Sun.

38

Using Jeeves

In Chapter 35, "Server Programs," you learned how to write server programs in Java. You saw how easy it is to listen for incoming connections, read requests from the connection's input stream, process the requests, and write responses to the connection's output stream. JavaSoft also realizes that it has a winner in Java when it comes to server development and server-side programming. As a result, JavaSoft has developed the Java Server and Server API. The Java Server is a server framework from which other servers can be developed. One of the servers developed from this framework is a Java Web server formerly named Jeeves. Jeeves doesn't stand for anything—it's just a cool name.

One of the key features (among many) of Java Server is its support for Java server-side programming in the form of servlets. *Servlets* are the server-side analog to applets. JavaSoft has developed a Servlet API for servlet programming.

In this chapter, you'll install Java Server and learn how it works. You'll learn about servlets, cover the basics of the Servlet API, and develop a few servlets of your own. When you finish this chapter, you'll be able to use Java Server and servlets to build an advanced Web site.

What Are Java Server and Jeeves?

Java Server is a framework for building Internet and intranet servers. It implements the functions that are common to all servers:

- It listens on a port (or ports) for connection requests.
- It accepts connection requests.
- It creates threads to handle the requests.
- It hands the connections to the threads for processing.
- It manages the threads and connections.

The Java Server is organized into three types of components:

- The connection acceptor that performs the preceding functions
- Connection handlers that implement the connection handling threads
- Servlets that handle specific types of client requests

The Java Server framework was used to develop the Web server formerly known as Jeeves. I'll still call it Jeeves because the alternative, "the Java Web server developed by JavaSoft," is too pedantic.

How Does Jeeves Work?

Because Jeeves is built using the Java Server framework, it follows its basic execution paradigm. An acceptor listens for incoming connection requests on the TCP ports managed by the server.

It hands off accepted connections to connection handlers. The connection handlers receive HTTP requests from Web server clients and load and invoke servlets to process the HTTP requests. Figure 38.1 provides an overview of Jeeves's operation.

FIGURE 38.1.

How Jeeves works.

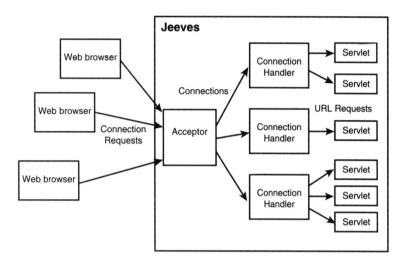

What's unique about Java Server, in general, and Jeeves, in particular, is the use of servlets. Servlets are server extensions that are written in Java. They are associated with particular URLs. When a request for the URL of a servlet is received from a Web browser, Jeeves invokes the servlet to process the request. Jeeves provides the servlet with all the information it needs to process the request; it also provides a mechanism for the servlet to send response information back to the Web browser. The Servlet API (covered later in this chapter in the "Servlet API" section) is used to develop servlets. Servlets can be preloaded by Jeeves or loaded on-the-fly as they are needed.

Installing Jeeves

In order to run the examples of this chapter, you'll need to download and install Jeeves. It is available from JavaSoft at the URL `http://jeeves.javasoft.com/products/java-server/webserver/`. Jeeves for Windows 95 and NT is distributed as a self-extracting executable file. Run the file and follow the installation instructions to install Jeeves on your system.

Once you have installed Jeeves, you will need to edit your AUTOEXEC.BAT file. Include a line to specify the location of your JDK installation. I'm using JDK 1.1.1, which is installed in the c:\jdk1.1.1 directory, so I put the following line in my AUTOEXEC.BAT file:

```
SET JAVA_HOME=C:\jdk1.1.1
```

In order to develop servlets, you'll need to include the Servlet API classes in your `CLASSPATH`. I am using a beta version of Jeeves that is installed in the `c:\Program Files\JavaServerBeta` directory, so I add `C:\PROGRA~1\JAVASE~1\LIB\classes.zip` to my `CLASSPATH`.

After you make the preceding changes, restart your system so that they go into effect. You do not have to restart your system if you are using Windows NT.

NOTE

If you are using Windows NT, use the `System` applet of the Control Panel to set `JAVA_HOME` and to modify your `CLASSPATH`.

Running Jeeves

Jeeves comes with extensive documentation that describes its features (such as secure HTTP) and shows how they work. I'm not going to duplicate the documentation here, but I will give you enough information to get you up and running and to show you how to develop and use servlets.

To start Jeeves, open a DOS window, change to Jeeves's `bin` directory and run `httpd`, as follows:

```
C:\Program Files\JavaServerBeta\bin>httpd
```

Jeeves provides Web service on port 8080 as a default. This lets you use Jeeves without having to stop your current Web server (if any). I've temporarily installed Jeeves on a host named `athome.jaworski.com`. Figure 38.2 shows the server's default Web page located at `http://athome.jaworski.com:8080/`.

The default Web page informs you that you administer your server on port 9090. For example, when I load the default Web page of my server on port 9090 and click on the server administration link, the applet shown in Figure 38.3 is displayed.

You can log in to this applet to administer your server. I won't cover server administration any more than you need to install a servlet. The Jeeves documentation explains all aspects of server administration.

FIGURE 38.2.

The Jeeves default Web page.

FIGURE 38.3.

The Jeeves administration applet.

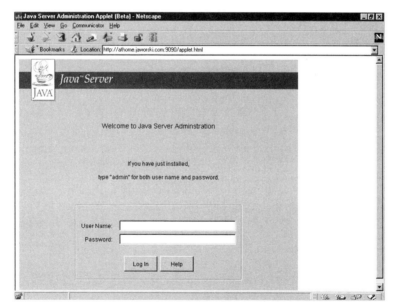

Using Servlets

Before I show you how to develop servlets, I'm going to whet your appetite by taking you on a tour of the servlets that come with Jeeves.

Open your Web server to the default Web page (`http://your.host.name.com:8080`). Here you'll find a list of demo servlets, as shown in Figure 38.4.

FIGURE 38.4.

Links to demo servlets.

Click on the link to the Link Checker servlet. This servlet provides a handy tool to check for broken links in your Web documents, as shown in Figure 38.5.

Go back to the default page and click on the link to the Bulletin Board servlet. This servlet implements a message board using your Web server, as shown in Figure 38.6. You can enter messages in the text area on the bottom of the page and have them posted for all to see.

Go back to the default page and click on the link to the Protection Example servlet. This servlet illustrates the use of the access control features of Jeeves. It prompts you with the login dialog, shown in Figure 38.7. If you fail to log in correctly, it displays the notice shown in Figure 38.8. If you log in correctly (`User Name=admin` and `Password=admin`), it displays the Web page shown in Figure 38.9.

FIGURE 38.5.

The Link Checker servlet.

FIGURE 38.6.

The Bulletin Board servlet.

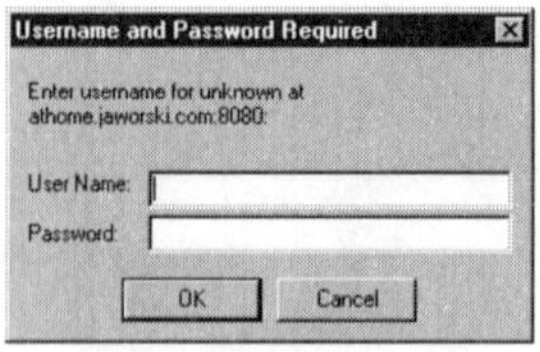

FIGURE 38.7.
The authorization dialog box.

FIGURE 38.8.
Wrong password!

FIGURE 38.9.
The protected Web page.

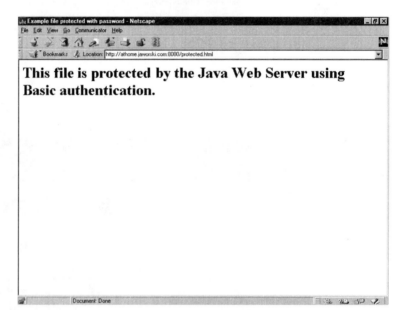

Writing Servlets

Now that you have a taste for servlets, I'll show you how they work and help you to develop a couple of servlets of your own.

Servlets are the server-side analog of applets. They are written to the Servlet API (covered in next section) and are installed on a Web server. Currently only Jeeves supports servlets, but it is expected that other commercial Web servers will support them soon.

Servlets are located in the `servlets` directory of the Web server and can be invoked via the URL `http://your.host.com/servlet/`*ServletName.class*`[?`*arguments*`]` where the name of your

Web server host is substituted for *your.host.com* and the class name of your servlet is substituted for *ServletName.class*. The optional *arguments* are a standard URL-encoded query string.

Jeeves can also be configured to associate servlets with other URLs or to be invoked as the result of processing a particular type of URL. Consult the Jeeves documentation for information on how to do this. Standard servlets that are used by Jeeves include the `FileServlet` and the `CgiServlet`. The `FileServlet` services general HTTP file requests, and the `CgiServlet` provides a Common Gateway Interface (CGI) capability. Most likely, the servlets that you'll develop will be similar to CGI programs in the services they provide. The advantages of servlets over CGI programs are that there is minimal server overhead in invoking servlets, servlets are provided with direct access to server resources, and servlets are written in Java.

The Servlet API

The Servlet API is a Standard Extension API, meaning that it is not a part of the core Java Platform. See Chapter 56, "Java Platform and Extensions," for a description of the Java Platform, the Core API, and the Standard Extension API. The documentation of the Servlet API packages is included with Jeeves. These packages include the `java.servlet` package and the `java.servlet.http` package.

The `java.servlet` Package

The `java.servlet` package defines the following five interfaces and three classes:

■ **`java.servlet` Interfaces**

   ■ `Servlet`—The `Servlet` interface must be implemented by all servlets. The `init()` and `destroy()` methods are invoked by the server to start and stop a servlet. The `getServletConfig()` and `getServletInfo()` methods are overridden to return information about a servlet. The `service()` method is invoked by the server so that a servlet can perform its service. It has two parameters—one of the `ServletRequest` interface and one of the `ServletResponse` interface.

   ■ `ServletRequest`—The `ServletRequest` interface encapsulates a client request for service. It defines a number of methods for obtaining information about the server, requestor, and request. The `getInputStream()` method returns an object of the `ServerInputStream` class that may be used to read request information sent by the client.

   ■ `ServletResponse`—The `ServletResponse` interface is used by a servlet to respond to a request by sending information back to the requestor. The `getOutputStream()` method returns an object of the `ServerOutputStream` class that is used to send response information to the client. The `setContentType()` method sets the MIME type of the response information. The `setContentLength()` method specifies the length of the response in bytes.

- ■ ServletConfig—The ServletConfig interface is used by the server to pass configuration information to a servlet. Its methods are used by the servlet to retrieve this information.
- ■ ServletContext—The ServletContext interface defines the environment in which an applet is executed. It provides methods that are used by applets to access environment information.

■ **java.servlet Classes**

- ■ GenericServlet—The GenericServlet class is a convenience class that implements the Servlet interface. You can subclass this class to define your own servlets.
- ■ ServletInputStream—The ServletInputStream class is used to access request information supplied by a Web client. An object of this class is returned by the getInputStream() method of the ServletRequest interface.
- ■ ServletOutputStream—The ServletOutputStream class is used to send response information to a Web client. An object of this class is returned by the getOutputStream() method of the ServletResponse interface.

The java.servlet.http Package

The java.servlet.http package is used to define HTTP-specific servlets. It defines the following interfaces and classes.

■ **java.servlet.http Interfaces**

- ■ HttpServletRequest—The HttpServletRequest interface extends the ServletRequest interface and adds methods for accessing the details of an HTTP request.
- ■ HttpServletResponse—The HttpServletResponse interface extends the ServletResponse interface and adds constants and methods for returning HTTP-specific responses.

■ **java.servlet.http Classes**

- ■ HttpServlet—The HttpServlet class extends the GenericServlet class to use the HttpServletRequest and HttpServletResponse interfaces.
- ■ HttpUtils—The HttpUtils class provides the parseQueryString() method for parsing a query string contained in an HTTP request.

The TimeServlet Class

The TimeServlet class, shown in Listing 38.1, is a simple servlet that will ease you into servlet programming. Compile the servlet and move the TimeServlet.class file to Jeeves's servlet directory. Don't worry about the deprecation warning. I'll explain it in the next section.

> **NOTE**
>
> It is recommended that you use HotJava 1.0 or Netscape 4.0 to run this example. Internet Explorer 3.0 might not work.

Listing 38.1. The `TimeServlet` servlet.

```
import java.servlet.*;
import java.util.*;
import java.io.*;

public class TimeServlet extends GenericServlet  {
 public String getServletInfo() {
  return "Time Servlet";
 }
 public void service(ServletRequest request, ServletResponse response)
  throws ServletException, IOException {
  String date=new Date().toString();
  PrintStream outputStream = new PrintStream(response.getOutputStream());
  outputStream.println(date);
 }
}
```

Next, you must install the servlet on Jeeves. To do this open the URL `http://your.server. com:9090/applet.html`. Your server's administration applet is loaded and displays the login shown in Figure 38.10. Log in as `admin` with the `admin` password.

FIGURE 38.10.

The server administration applet.

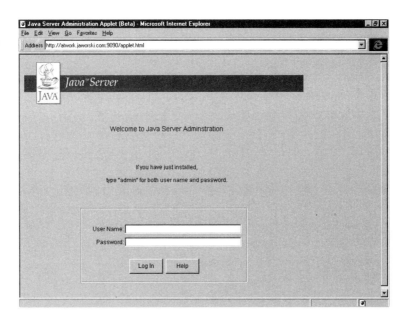

After you log in, the administration main screen is displayed, as shown in Figure 38.11. Highlight the Web service and click on the Manage button to configure the Web service.

The Web service administration screen is displayed, as shown in Figure 38.12. Click the Servlets button to add the TimeServlet.

FIGURE 38.11.

The server administration main screen.

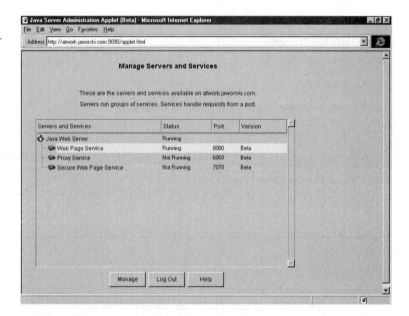

FIGURE 38.12.

The Web service administration applet.

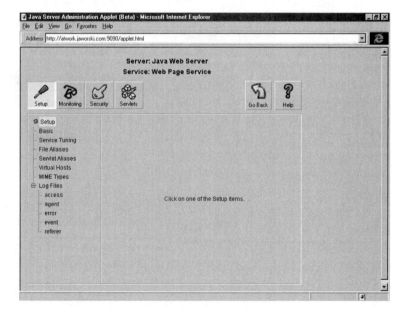

The Servlets configuration screen is displayed, as shown in Figure 38.13. Click on Add in the selection list on the left of the screen to add a servlet to the list of servlets known to Jeeves.

An Add a New Servlet dialog appears, as shown in Figure 38.14. Enter `TimeServlet` for the servlet's name and `TimeServlet.class` for the servlet's class. Then click the Add button to add the servlet.

FIGURE 38.13.

The Servlet administration applet.

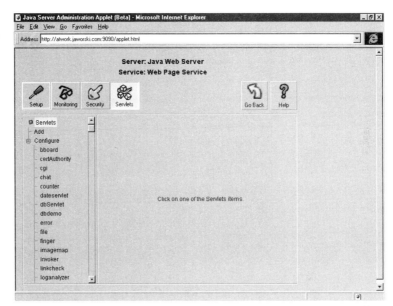

FIGURE 38.14.

The Add a New Servlet dialog.

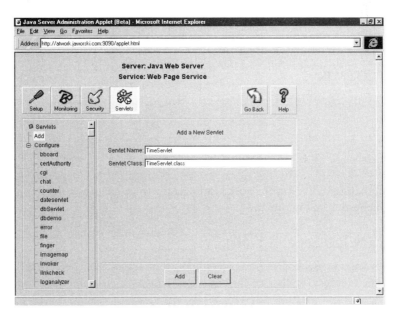

The screen is updated to display information about the servlet. Click the Load at Startup radio button to cause the servlet to be loaded automatically when the server starts. Then click the Save button to save the change. (See Figure 38.15.)

FIGURE 38.15.

Completing the servlet's configuration.

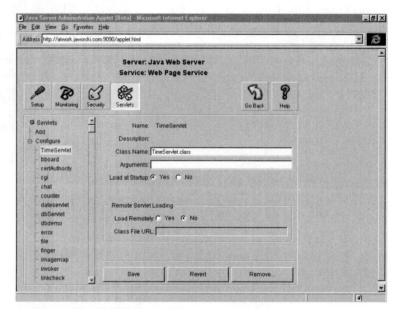

You're finished configuring the servlet. Click the Go Back button and then the Log Out button to log out of the administration applet.

Now you're ready to use the `TimeServlet` servlet. Open the URL `http://your.server.com:8080/servlet/TimeServlet.class` to access the servlet. It displays the output shown in Figure 38.16.

FIGURE 38.16.

The `TimeServlet`'s *output display.*

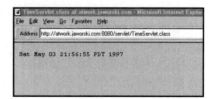

If that seems like a lot of work just to get the time, hang in there; the next servlet will be more interesting and informative.

How `TimeServlet` Works

In order to use servlets, you must import the `java.servlet` package, as shown in Listing 38.1. The `TimeServlet` class extends the `GenericServlet` class and overrides the `getServletInfo()`

and `service()` methods. The `getServletInfo()` method returns a string that provides information about the servlet. The `service()` method implements the actual servlet request handling and response handling. It is invoked by the Web server when the URL of the servlet is requested. The server passes the `ServletRequest` and `ServletResponse` arguments to the servlet.

The `TimeServlet` is pretty simple and does not need any particular information contained in the `ServletRequest` object to perform its processing. It creates a new `Date` object, converts it to a `String`, and stores it using the `date` variable. It uses the `getOutputStream()` method of the `ServletResponse` class to create a `ServletOutputStream` object for sending response information back to the browser client. The `ServletOutputStream` object is filtered as a `PrintStream`.

> **NOTE**
>
> When you compile `TimeServlet`, you get a deprecation warning because you used `PrintStream` instead of its JDK 1.1 `PrintWriter` replacement. `PrintWriter` did not work with Jeeves at the time of this writing.

Finally, you write the date string to the output stream to send it to the browser client.

The `EchoRequest` Servlet

The `EchoRequest` servlet, shown in Listing 38.2, shows how `ServletRequest` parameters are processed. Compile `EchoRequest.java` and copy the `EchoRequest.class` file to the `servlets` directory used by Jeeves. Again, don't worry about the deprecation warning. Configure `EchoRequest` using the administration applet, as discussed for `TimeServlet`. Set its name to `EchoRequest` and its class name to `EchoRequest.class`. (See Figure 38.17.)

Listing 38.2. The `EchoRequest` servlet.

```
import java.servlet.*;
import java.util.*;
import java.io.*;

public class EchoRequest extends GenericServlet  {
 public String getServletInfo() {
  return "Echo Request Servlet";
 }
 public void service(ServletRequest request, ServletResponse response)
  throws ServletException, IOException {
  response.setContentType("text/plain");
  PrintStream outputStream = new PrintStream(response.getOutputStream());
  outputStream.print("Server: "+request.getServerName()+":");
  outputStream.println(request.getServerPort());
  outputStream.print("Client: "+request.getRemoteHost()+" ");
  outputStream.println(request.getRemoteAddr());
  outputStream.println("Protocol: "+request.getProtocol());
  Enumeration params = request.getParameterNames();
```

continues

Listing 38.2. continued

```
if(params != null) {
  while(params.hasMoreElements()){
    String param = (String) params.nextElement();
    String value = request.getParameter(param);
    outputStream.println(param+" = "+value);
  }
 }
}
}
```

FIGURE 38.17.
Configuring the
EchoRequest *servlet.*

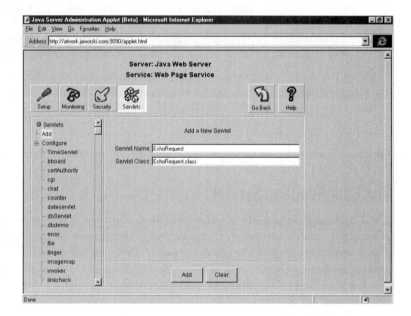

Open the URL http://*your.server.com*/servlet/EchoRequest.class. It displays the IP address and port number of the Jeeves Web server, and the host name and address of the computer on which your browser resides. It also displays the version of the HTTP protocol being used. (See Figure 38.18.)

FIGURE 38.18.
Using the
EchoRequest *servlet.*

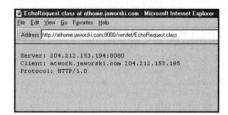

Now open the same URL with the `?n1=v1&n2=v2&n3=v3` query string appended. `EchoRequest` displays the name-value pairs in the query string, as shown in Figure 38.19.

FIGURE 38.19.

Using the
`EchoRequest` *servlet*
with a query string.

You can also use `EchoRequest` with forms. Copy the `formtest.htm` file, shown in Listing 38.3, to the `public_html` directory of your Web server. Open it with the URL `http://`*your.server.com*`:8080/formtest.htm`. The form shown in Figure 38.20 is displayed.

Listing 38.3. The `formtest.htm` file.

```
<HTML>
<HEAD>
<TITLE>Using a form with EchoRequest</TITLE>
</HEAD>
<BODY>
<FORM ACTION="servlet/EchoRequest.class">
Enter text: <INPUT NAME="textField" TYPE="TEXT" SIZE="30"><P>
Check this out: <INPUT NAME="checkbox" TYPE="CHECKBOX"><P>
Select me: <SELECT NAME="mySelection">
<OPTION>Number one
<OPTION>Number two
<OPTION>Number three
</SELECT><P>
<INPUT NAME="Submit" TYPE="SUBMIT">
</FORM>
</BODY>
</HTML>
```

FIGURE 38.20.

Using the
`EchoRequest` *servlet*
with an HTML form.

Enter a value for the text field, check or uncheck the text box, and make a selection from the selection list. Then click the Submit button. The EchoRequest servlet is invoked to process the form. It displays the output shown in Figure 38.21. Note that it correctly identifies the form values that you submitted.

FIGURE 38.21.

EchoRequest *displays the data you entered in the form.*

How EchoRequest **Works**

As you would expect, the overall structure of EchoRequest is the same as TimeServlet. Both servlets extend GenericServlet and override the getServletInfo() and service() methods.

The service() method of EchoRequest begins by setting the content type of the response to the text/plain MIME type. We set the MIME type because we'll be generating more than one line of output and we don't want the browser client to mistake it for HTML.

Next, service() creates an output stream in the same manner as TimeServlet, using the getOutputStream() method of the ServletResponse interface. It then prints information about the server, client, and protocol that it obtains using the getServerName(), getServerPort(), getRemoteHost(), getRemoteAddr(), and getProtocol() methods of the ServletRequest interface.

The service() method invokes the getParameterNames() method of the ServletRequest interface to retrieve an enumeration of the parameter names that are passed in the query string of the HTTP request. It displays each parameter name along with its value. The parameter values are retrieved via the getParameter() method of the ServletRequest interface.

Summary

In this chapter, you installed Java Server and learned how it works. You learned about servlets and covered the basics of the Servlet API. You then developed the TimeServlet and the EchoRequest servlet and learned how servlets can be used to process form data. In the next chapter, you'll learn how to use the Java Management API to manage your enterprise network.

39

Working with the Java Management API

With the growing reliance of companies and other organizations on their enterprise networks, the management of these networks and the systems and services they support has become critical. Network administrators use a wide array of system monitoring and management tools to ensure continuous reliable operation. These tools are designed to detect and respond to potential problems that could affect service continuity. However, with the heterogeneous nature of modern networks, these tools run on a variety of operating system platforms, do not operate well together, and sometimes conflict. The Java Management API (JMAPI) is being developed by JavaSoft to provide an integrated solution to system, network, and service management. Because of Java's platform-independent nature, it eliminates the need to use several nonintegrated, platform-specific system and network management tools to manage the diverse computing resources that are common to medium- to large-sized enterprise networks.

In this chapter, you'll learn about the JMAPI. You'll be given an overview of the typical problems confronting system and network administrators. You'll then be introduced to JMAPI and learn how it can be used to provide a common integrated solution to system, network, and service management. You'll cover the Java management architecture and learn how it allows enterprise resources to be managed from a browser interface. You'll learn about the components of JMAPI and how they are used to support this architecture. When you finish this chapter, you'll have an understanding of how JMAPI works and insight on how you can use it to solve your organization's system, network, and service management problems.

Overview of System, Network, and Service Management

Imagine that you are responsible for the management of a medium- to large-scale enterprise network. Your primary responsibilities are to keep the network up and running, keep its systems operational, make sure that its services are available, and keep its users happy. Your users demand the latest Internet and intranet services from the moment that they read about them on a Web page or in a magazine. Continuous reliable operation is expected 24 hours a day, 7 days a week.

In a typical medium- to large-scale enterprise network, you'll find thousands of users, some quite sophisticated and some not. These users will have workstations, PCs, Macintoshes, X terminals, and dumb terminals. They will use several flavors of UNIX, all versions of Windows and MacOS, NetWare, DOS, and anything else that's available. Your networks will run TCP/IP, IPX, NetBEUI, AppleTalk, and other protocols. Your enterprise will maintain legacy systems that run on DEC VAXes and IBM minicomputers and mainframes. You'll also interface to customers, vendors, and suppliers via the Internet, dedicated lines, and dial-up connections. You'll have one or more firewalls, several routers, a slew of network hubs, and all sorts of system, network, and service management tools.

The tools that you'll use to manage your network will run on a variety of platforms, mostly UNIX and Windows. These tools will be independent. They will not know about or interoperate with each other, and will sometimes conflict when run concurrently.

Some of these tools will be system-specific. They'll let you manage the legacy applications that you have running on DEC and IBM minicomputers and mainframes. They'll tell you that you need to change disk volumes, do a backup, or perform some application-specific maintenance.

Some tools will be protocol- and service-specific. You'll use them to manage specific protocols, such as TCP/IP, IPX, AppleTalk, and SNA. They'll tell you what your network traffic load is like, when you have interruptions in service, and what network components are malfunctioning. You'll also have a sniffer or two to tell you what these other tools can't. Service-specific tools will tell you what types of hits your Web and FTP servers are taking, what your e-mail situation looks like, and how file and print servers are behaving.

Some tools try to be integrated network management solutions, at least from the vendor's viewpoint. You'll run HP OpenView, Microsoft's System Management Server, and possibly one or two other management tools. In the end, you'll use a chair that rolls easily in order to move among the computers that run each of your system management tools.

The JMAPI Solution

Is this scenario far fetched? Not at all. If you are a system or network manager, you are probably working in an environment like this right now—the type of environment that JMAPI is being developed to deal with.

If Java's motto is "Write Once. Run Everywhere," then JMAPI's is "Why can't we just all work together?" The goal of JMAPI is to leverage Java's platform independence to provide a set of system management building blocks that can be used to integrate a diverse set of system and network management tools under a common look and feel.

> **NOTE**
>
> The Java Management home page is located at `http://www.javasoft.com/products/JavaManagement/index.html`.

The look and feel of JMAPI is provided by a Java-enabled browser. All management applications are run from a browser. Not only do you have a common, cross-platform user interface, but the organization of this interface is governed by the recommendations and standards of the JMAPI User Interface Guide. This guide describes a standard approach to developing browser-based interfaces for use with JMAPI.

Not only does JMAPI provide you with a standard browser-based interface, it also provides you with a common architecture for managing systems, networks, and services. This architecture, referred to as the Java management architecture, is shown in Figure 39.1.

Administrators use Java-enabled Web browsers to manage the systems, networks, and services of a network. The browsers interface with managed object servers that manage one or more appliances within their domain. An appliance is any system that is to be managed. It can be a network computer, PC, workstation, or any other type of computer or device that is capable of running the JVM.

FIGURE 39.1.

The Java management architecture.

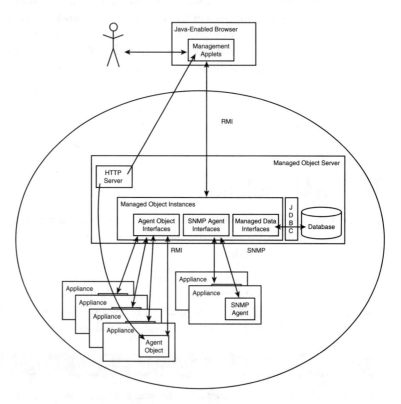

Agents are objects that execute on appliances and communicate with managed object servers. Agent objects maintain information about the configuration and status of the appliances they manage, and they report this information to managed object servers. The agent objects provide methods that allow managed object servers to control and reconfigure their appliances. The agent software can be dynamically updated and is installed on appliances as Java classes that are loaded from Web servers.

Managed object servers are the link between the browser interface and the managed appliances of an enterprise. Managed object servers consist of Java applications that provide the following capabilities:

- Appliance configuration and status reporting—Managed object servers make appliance configuration and status information that was retrieved from agent objects available as managed objects that can be browsed by administrators.

- Control and configuration of appliances—The managed objects provide methods that can be used to control the appliances or modify the appliances' configuration data.

- SNMP agent interfaces—Managed object servers support interfaces to traditional SNMP agents. These interfaces are presented to administrators as browsable managed objects.

- Managed data interfaces—Managed object servers support data interfaces that allow management information to be maintained by relational database servers.

- Database connectivity through JDBC—Managed object servers use JDBC to interface with relational database servers.

- A Web server—Managed object servers use HTTP servers to make management applets available to the browsers used by administrators. These applets provide GUI controls that are used to browse and display managed objects. The HTTP servers are also used to distribute agent objects throughout the domains of the managed object servers.

The Java Management API and architecture help system and network administrators solve the problem of managing multiple heterogeneous components. By leveraging Java's platform independence and the classes and interfaces of JMAPI, agent software can be quickly developed and deployed to any appliance that is capable of running the JVM. New and updated software can be easily distributed via the Web server components of the managed object servers. These same Web servers provide the management applets that are used by administrators to monitor and control network resources as managed objects.

The managed object servers create managed object abstractions that allow resources to be managed without knowing the details of the object's implementation. This separation between management and implementation allows administrators to concentrate on the problem at hand. Resources can be monitored, reconfigured, and controlled independent of the protocols, vendor packages, or hardware and software platforms used to provide these resources.

By using a common browser interface, administrators are able to take advantage of consistent, intuitive GUI controls for managing all system and network resources. By providing access to all managed resources as managed objects, administrators can use the single browser interface for all management functions. Administrators no longer have to move from station to station to use the tools that are independently implemented at each station. In addition, the single browser interface can be accessed via any computer that supports a Java-enabled Web browser. When an administrator is paged in the middle of the night, he can securely access the managed object server by launching his browser from home, a hotel, or a coffee shop.

The Components of JMAPI

JMAPI is distributed as a set of Java classes and interfaces and associated documentation. It can be downloaded from the Java Management home page. It consists of the following components:

- Admin View Module—The Admin View Module is a set of classes and interfaces for developing the GUI components of management applets. It builds on the AWT and is oriented toward applications that run as applets within the context of a Web browser. It can also be used to develop standalone applications.

- Base Object Interfaces—The Base Object Interfaces are Java interfaces that are used to create managed objects. These interfaces allow managed objects to be created quickly, easily, and consistently.

- Managed Container Interfaces—The Managed Container Interfaces are Java interfaces that allow managed objects to be collected and managed as a group.

- Managed Notification Interfaces—The Managed Notification Interfaces are used to support event delivery between the elements of the Java management architecture. These interfaces are also used to support event handling.

- Managed Data Interfaces—The Managed Data Interfaces are used to maintain system management data via a relational database. These interfaces use JDBC to support database connectivity.

- Managed Protocol Interfaces—The Managed Protocol Interfaces support the secure communication of management information. These interfaces use the Security API and remote method invocation.

- SNMP Interfaces—The SNMP Interfaces are used to provide access to existing SNMP agents. These interfaces allow you to incorporate your existing network management agents into the Java management architecture.

- Applet Integration Interfaces—The Applet Integration Interfaces allow developers to integrate their applets within the Java management architecture. Support of applet, page, and link registration is provided.

The Java Management API User Interface Style Guide is also included. The style guide describes a standard approach to developing browser-based interfaces for use with JMAPI.

The JMAPI components previously listed are used to create all elements of the Java management architecture. The Admin View Module and Applet Integration Interfaces simplify the task of creating management applets that conform to the JMAPI User Interface Style Guide. The other interfaces are used to create managed objects, agent objects, and interface with existing SNMP agents, and to provide database connectivity.

Summary

In this chapter, you learned how JMAPI can be used to provide a common integrated solution to system, network, and service management. You covered the Java management architecture and learned how it is deployed within an organization. You were introduced to the components of JMAPI and learned how they are used to support this architecture. You should now have an understanding of how JMAPI works and some insight on how it can be used to solve your organization's system, network, and service management problems.

VI

Web Programming

40

Sample Applets

This chapter is the first of eight chapters that cover Web programming. It introduces you to Java applets by way of several examples that illustrate different aspects of the classes and methods used to implement simple applets. Its purpose is to quickly get you up to speed developing applets. Subsequent chapters fill in the details of the classes and methods that are introduced here. You should approach this chapter by trying to get a good general understanding of what is going on in the sample applets without dwelling on the details. You will learn the details when you study them in later chapters. This chapter assumes that you have covered the window-programming examples in Part IV, "Window Programming."

Hello Web!

The first program that you wrote in Chapter 4, "First Programs: Hello World! to BlackJack," was the HelloWorldApp program. It displayed the traditional Hello World! text to the console window. The main purpose of the program was to show you how to develop a simple Java program that actually produced some noticeable effect. The same rationale applies to the HelloWeb applet that you'll develop shortly. The program shows you how to write a simple applet that displays the text Hello Web! to the browser window. The code for the HelloWeb applet is shown in Listing 40.1. Note that I do not add the App (application) suffix to the names of applets. This is a personal coding style convention.

Listing 40.1. The source code of the HelloWeb applet.

```
import java.applet.*;
import java.awt.*;

public class HelloWeb extends Applet {
 public void paint(Graphics g) {
  g.setFont(new Font("TimesRoman",Font.BOLD+Font.ITALIC,36));
  g.setColor(Color.blue);
  g.drawString("Hello Web!",10,80);
 }
}
```

Create the HelloWeb.java file in the \jdk1.1\jdg\ch40 directory and compile it using javac HelloWeb.java.

In order to run the HelloWeb applet, you need to include it in a Web page. Using a text editor, create the HTML file shown in Listing 40.2 and save it as \jdk1.1\jdg\ch40\helloweb.htm.

Listing 40.2. The helloweb.htm file.

```
<HTML>
<HEAD>
<TITLE>Hello Web!</TITLE>
</HEAD>
```

```
<BODY>
<APPLET CODE="HelloWeb.class" WIDTH=200 HEIGHT=200>
[HelloWeb applet]
</APPLET>
</BODY>
</HTML>
```

Now open the `helloweb.htm` file with your Java-enabled browser. I use Netscape Navigator 4.0; my browser display appears as shown in Figure 40.1.

FIGURE 40.1.

The `helloweb.htm` *file, as displayed by a browser.*

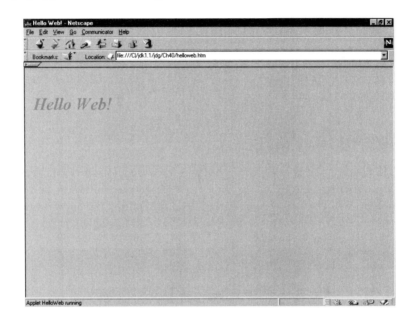

Although this example is rather trivial—you could have created the same results using just HTML—it provides a basic starting point from which to embark on your study of applets. Let's cover the `HelloWeb.java` applet first and then examine the `helloweb.htm` file.

The `HelloWeb` applet, like all Java applets, extends the `Applet` class or one of its subclasses. `HelloWeb` consists of a single method—the `paint()` method, which you encountered several times in Part IV. Because the `Applet` class is a subclass of `Panel`, many of the window-programming techniques that you studied in Part IV come into play. The `paint()` method is passed a `Graphics` object that it uses to paint the screen. In this case, I set the current font to a bold, italic 36-point TimesRoman font and set the drawing color to blue. I then use the `drawString()` method of the `Graphics` class to draw the text `Hello Web!` on the screen at position 10,80.

The `helloweb.htm` file is the Web page that is used to contain the `HelloWeb` applet. Web pages are written in the Hypertext Markup Language (HTML). Learning HTML, in itself, is the subject of many books. Here I'll use a common HTML document to hold the applets and not go off on a tangent of learning HTML.

The `helloweb.htm` file begins and ends with the `<HTML>` and `</HTML>` tags. These tags signify the start and finish of an HTML file. The HTML file consists of a head and a body. The *head* is contained between the `<HEAD>` and `</HEAD>` tags. Within the head is the title, which is displayed at the top of the browser window. The title is contained within the `<TITLE>` and `</TITLE>` tags.

The *body* of an HTML file is where all the Web page descriptions are located. The body is enclosed within the `<BODY>` and `</BODY>` tags. The body of this document, and of those used in the other examples of this chapter, consists of a single applet. The applet is denoted by the `<APPLET>` and `</APPLET>` tags.

Within the opening `<APPLET>` tag are several attributes. The `CODE` attribute has the value `HelloWeb.class`, which identifies the class file for this applet. Its `WIDTH` and `HEIGHT` attributes specify the dimensions of the applet, as displayed on the browser window.

The text `[HelloWeb applet]`, appearing between the `<APPLET>` and `</APPLET>` tags, is displayed by browsers that are not capable of loading Java applets.

An Audio Player

The `Applet` class, as small as it is, provides a few useful features for developing attractive Web pages. Among these are the capability to load and play audio files, and to easily load and display images. The `AudioPlayer` applet, developed in this section, shows off these features. The source code for the `AudioPlayer` applet is shown in Listing 40.3.

> **NOTE**
>
> You need a sound board and speaker(s) to run this applet. You also need to be connected to the Internet.

Listing 40.3. The source code of the `AudioPlayer` applet.

```
import java.applet.*;
import java.awt.*;
import java.awt.event.*;
import java.net.*;

public class AudioPlayer extends Applet {
 AudioClip music;
 Image background;
 public void init() {
  try {
   music = getAudioClip(new URL("http://www.jaworski.com/java/spacemusic.au"));
   background = getImage(new URL("http://www.jaworski.com/java/space.gif"));
  }catch (MalformedURLException ex) {
  }
  setLayout(new BorderLayout());
```

```
   Panel buttons = new Panel();
   Button playButton = new Button("Play");
   Button stopButton = new Button("Stop");
   Button loopButton = new Button("Loop");
   playButton.addActionListener(new ButtonHandler());
   stopButton.addActionListener(new ButtonHandler());
   loopButton.addActionListener(new ButtonHandler());
   buttons.add(playButton);
   buttons.add(stopButton);
   buttons.add(loopButton);
   add("South",buttons);
 }
 public void stop() {
   music.stop();
 }
 public void paint(Graphics g) {
  g.drawImage(background,0,0,this);
 }
 class ButtonHandler implements ActionListener {
  public void actionPerformed(ActionEvent e){
   String s = e.getActionCommand();
   if("Play".equals(s)) music.play();
   else if("Stop".equals(s)) music.stop();
   else if("Loop".equals(s)) music.loop();
  }
 }
}
```

Create and compile AudioPlayer.java in the same manner as you did HelloWeb.java. The HTML file that is used to display the applet is shown in Listing 40.4. Note that the CODE, WIDTH, and HEIGHT attributes of the applet have been changed. You will need two additional files to run the applet—space.gif and spacemusic.au. These files are located on my Web server. They will be automatically loaded when you run the applet. Depending upon the load on my Web server, it may take a minute or two for the files to be loaded.

Listing 40.4. The audio.htm file.

```
<HTML>
<HEAD>
<TITLE>Audio Player</TITLE>
</HEAD>
<BODY>
<APPLET CODE="AudioPlayer.class" WIDTH=300 HEIGHT=350>
[AudioPlayer applet]
</APPLET>
</BODY>
</HTML>
```

Open the audio.htm file with appletviewer using the following command:

```
appletviewer audio.htm
```

The appletviewer will create a window display similar to the one shown in Figure 40.2.

FIGURE 40.2.

The audio.htm *file, as displayed by appletviewer.*

If you have the HotJava browser installed, you can use it to load the applet over the Internet. I have the audio.htm, AppletViewer.class, AppletViewer$ButtonHandler.class, space.gif, and spacemusic.au files located in the \java directory of my Web server. Use HotJava to open the URL http:\\www.jaworski.com\java\audio.htm. It will display the window shown in Figure 40.3.

FIGURE 40.3.

The audio.htm *file, as displayed by HotJava.*

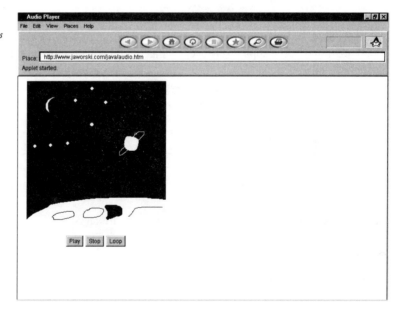

HotJava loads the `audio.htm` file and then the files `AudioPlayer.class` and `AudioPlayer$ButtonHandler.class`. The applet itself loads the background image and an audio file. To play the audio file, click on the Play button. The space music will be played, using your sound board and speakers. When the end of the music file is reached, the sound will end. If you click on the Loop button, the music will be continuously played in a never-ending fashion. Clicking the Stop button causes the music to cease.

The `AudioPlayer` class, for all of its additional capabilities, is only slightly longer than the `HelloWeb` class. It declares two field variables, `music` and `background`, which are used to hold the audio file and background image. The `music` variable is declared as type `AudioClip`, which is an interface defined in the `java.applet` package.

The `AudioPlayer` class contains three access methods: `init()`, `stop()`, and `paint()`. You are already familiar with the use of `paint()` from Part IV.

The `init()` method is invoked by the browser's runtime system when an applet is initially loaded. It performs any initialization required before the main part of the applet is executed. The `stop()` method is invoked when the execution of an applet is terminated as the result of an applet's Web page no longer being displayed by the browser. You never need to invoke `init()` or `stop()` directly. They are invoked by the runtime system.

The `init()` method of `AudioPlayer` begins by loading the audio and image files. The `getAudioClip()` method of the `Applet` class loads an audio file that is referenced by an URL. The `http://www.jaworski.com/java/spacemusic.au` URL is used to load the `spacemusic.au` file from my Web server. The `http:// www.jaworski.com/java /space.gif` URL is used in a similar manner.

After the audio and image files are loaded, the layout of the applet is set to a `BorderLayout` object. A `Panel` object is created and assigned to the `buttons` variable. The Play, Stop, and Loop buttons are created and added to the `buttons` panel. `ButtonHandler` objects are used to handle the events associated with these buttons. The `buttons` panel is then added to the bottom of the applet display area.

The `stop()` method uses the `stop()` method of the `AudioClip` interface to stop the music when the applet is no longer being displayed by the browser.

The `paint()` method draws the `space.gif` image assigned to the background variable on the `Graphics` context of the applet's display area.

The `actionPerformed()` method of the `ButtonHandler` inner class handles the three prominent events associated with the applet. These events are the clicking of the Play, Stop, and Loop buttons. When the Play button is clicked, the `play()` method of the `AudioClip` interface is invoked to play the audio clip. When the Stop button is clicked, the `stop()` method of the `AudioClip` interface is invoked to stop the music. Finally, when the Loop button is clicked, the `loop()` method of the `AudioClip` interface is invoked to cause the music to be played in a never-ending, looping fashion.

BlackJack Revisited

From the previous example, you have probably surmised that it is easy to convert Java window programs to applets. This is possible because of the fact that an applet is nothing more than a souped-up panel. It is also relatively easy to convert console programs to applets.

One of the first Java programs that you wrote, way back in Chapter 4, was the `BlackJackApp` program. This program allows you to play blackjack on the console display. Because you used a class- and object-oriented approach to developing `BlackJackApp` (even before you were formally introduced to classes and objects), this program is relatively easy to convert to a simple applet. The source code of the converted applet is shown in Listing 40.5.

Listing 40.5. The source code of the `Blackjack.java` applet.

```java
import java.applet.*;
import java.awt.*;
import java.awt.event.*;
import java.util.Random;

public class Blackjack extends Applet {
 static final int BET = 0;
 static final int PLAY = 1;
 static final int DEALER = 2;
 int state = BET;
 int money = 1000;
 int bet = 0;
 Deck deck = new Deck();
 Hand playersHand;
 Hand dealersHand;
 Label topLine = new Label("Welcome to Blackjack!",Label.CENTER);
 Label totalLine = new Label("You have $1000.",Label.CENTER);
 Label dealersLabel = new Label("Dealer's Hand",Label.CENTER);
 Label playersLabel = new Label("Your Hand",Label.CENTER);
 TextArea dealerText = new TextArea(9,20);
 TextArea playerText = new TextArea(9,20);
 Button hitButton = new Button("Hit");
 Button stayButton = new Button("Stay");
 Label betLabel = new Label("Enter your bet: ",Label.RIGHT);
 TextField betField = new TextField();
 GridBagLayout gridbag = new GridBagLayout();;
 GridBagConstraints constraints = new GridBagConstraints();
 public void init() {
  hitButton.addActionListener(new ButtonHandler());
  stayButton.addActionListener(new ButtonHandler());
  betField.addActionListener(new TextHandler());
  setLayout(gridbag);
  constraints.fill = GridBagConstraints.BOTH;
  addComponent(topLine,0,0);
  addComponent(totalLine,0,1);
  addComponent(dealersLabel,1,0);
  addComponent(playersLabel,1,1);
  dealerText.setEditable(false);
  playerText.setEditable(false);
```

```
   addComponent(dealerText,2,0);
   addComponent(playerText,2,1);
   addComponent(hitButton,3,0);
   addComponent(stayButton,3,1);
   addComponent(betLabel,4,0);
   addComponent(betField,4,1);
}
void addComponent(Component c,int y,int x) {
 constraints.gridx = x;
 constraints.gridy = y;
 gridbag.setConstraints(c, constraints);
 add(c);
}
public void updateBet() {
 betField.setEditable(false);
 betLabel.setText("Bet: ");
 try {
  Integer i = new Integer(betField.getText());
  bet = i.intValue();
 } catch (NumberFormatException ex) {
  bet = 1;
 }
 betField.setText(String.valueOf(bet));
 initialDeal();
 if(playersHand.blackjack()) playerWins();
 else state = PLAY;
}
void initialDeal() {
 playersHand = new Hand();
 dealersHand = new Hand();
 for(int i = 0;i<2;++i) {
  playersHand.addCard(deck.deal());
  dealersHand.addCard(deck.deal());
 }
 dealersHand.show(dealerText,true);
 playersHand.show(playerText,false);
}
void openBetting() {
 betLabel.setText("Enter your bet: ");
 betField.setText("");
 betField.setEditable(true);
 state = BET;
}
void playerWins() {
 money += bet;
 topLine.setText("Player wins $"+bet+".");
 totalLine.setText("You have $"+money+".");
 openBetting();
}
void dealerWins() {
 money -= bet;
 topLine.setText("Player loses $"+bet+".");
 totalLine.setText("You have $"+money+".");
 openBetting();
}
void tie() {
```

continues

Listing 40.5. continued

```
    topLine.setText("Tie.");
    totalLine.setText("You have $"+money+".");
    openBetting();
  }
  void showResults() {
    if(playersHand.busted() && dealersHand.busted()) tie();
    else if(playersHand.busted()) dealerWins();
    else if(dealersHand.busted()) playerWins();
    else if(playersHand.bestScore() > dealersHand.bestScore()) playerWins();
    else if(playersHand.bestScore() < dealersHand.bestScore()) dealerWins();
    else tie();
  }
  class TextHandler implements ActionListener {
    public void actionPerformed(ActionEvent e){
      if(state == BET) updateBet();
    }
  }
  class ButtonHandler implements ActionListener {
    public void actionPerformed(ActionEvent e){
      String s=e.getActionCommand();
      if(state == PLAY) {
        if("Hit".equals(s)) {
          playersHand.addCard(deck.deal());
          playersHand.show(playerText,false);
          if(!playersHand.under(22)) state = DEALER;
        }else if("Stay".equals(s)) state = DEALER;
        if(state == DEALER) {
          while(dealersHand.mustHit())
            dealersHand.addCard(deck.deal());
          dealersHand.show(dealerText,false);
          showResults();
        }
      }
    }
  }
}

class Deck {
  // Variable declarations
  int cards[];      // Array of 52 cards
  int topCard;      // 0-51 (index of card in deck)
  Random random;

  // Method declarations
  public Deck() { // Constructor
    cards = new int[52];
    for(int i = 0;i<52;++i) cards[i] = i;
    topCard = 0;
    random = new Random();
    shuffle();
  }

  public void shuffle() {
    // Repeat 52 times
    for(int i = 0;i<52;++i) {
      // Randomly exchange two cards in the deck.
```

```
    int j = randomCard();
    int k = randomCard();
    int temp = cards[j];
    cards[j] = cards[k];
    cards[k] = temp;
  }
}

int randomCard() {
 int r = random.nextInt();
 if(r<0) r = 0-r;
 return r%52;
}

Card deal() {
 if(topCard>51) {
  shuffle();
  topCard = 0;
 }
 Card card = new Card(cards[topCard]);
 ++topCard;
 return card;
}
} // End of Deck class

class Hand {
 // Variable declarations
 int numCards;
 Card cards[];
 static int MaxCards = 12;

 //Method declarations
 public Hand() { // Constructor
  numCards = 0;
  cards = new Card[MaxCards];
 }

 void addCard(Card c) {
  cards[numCards] = c;
  ++numCards;
 }

 void show(TextArea t,boolean hideFirstCard) {
  String results = "";
  for(int i = 0;i<numCards;++i) {
   if(i == 0 && hideFirstCard) results += "Hidden\n";
   else results += cards[i].value+" of "+cards[i].suite+"\n";
  }
  t.setText(results);
 }

boolean blackjack() {
 if(numCards == 2) {
  if(cards[0].iValue == 1 && cards[1].iValue == 10) return true;
  if(cards[1].iValue == 1 && cards[0].iValue == 10) return true;
 }
```

continues

Listing 40.5. continued

```
 return false;
}

boolean under(int n) {
 int points = 0;
 for(int i = 0;i<numCards;++i) points += cards[i].iValue;
 if(points<n) return true;
 else return false;
}

int bestScore() {
 int points = 0;
 boolean haveAce = false;
 for(int i = 0;i<numCards;++i) {
  points += cards[i].iValue;
  if(cards[i].iValue == 1) haveAce = true;
 }
 if(haveAce) {
  if(points+10 < 22) points += 10;
 }
 return points;
}

boolean mustHit() {
 if(bestScore()<17) return true;
 else return false;
}

 boolean busted() {
  if(!under(22)) return true;
  else return false;
 }
} // End of Hand class

class Card {
 // Variable declarations
 int iValue;   // Numeric value corresponding to card.
 String value; // "A" "2" through "9" "T" "J" "Q" "K"
 String suite; // "S" "H" "C" "D"

 // Method declarations
 public Card(int n) { // Constructor
  int iSuite = n/13;
  iValue = n%13+1;
  switch(iSuite) {
   case 0:
    suite = "Spades";
    break;
   case 1:
    suite = "Hearts";
    break;
   case 2:
    suite = "Clubs";
    break;
   default:
    suite = "Diamonds";
  }
```

```
  if(iValue == 1) value = "Ace";
  else if(iValue == 10) value = "Ten";
  else if(iValue == 11) value = "Jack";
  else if(iValue == 12) value = "Queen";
  else if(iValue == 13) value = "King";
  else value = Integer.toString(iValue);
  if(iValue>10) iValue = 10;
 }

 int getValue() {
  return iValue;
 }
} // End of Card class
```

Create and compile Blackjack.java in the same manner as the previous examples. The HTML file that is used to display the applet is shown in Listing 40.6. Note that the CODE, WIDTH, and HEIGHT attributes of the applet have been changed.

Listing 40.6. The blackjack.htm file.

```
<HTML>
<HEAD>
<TITLE>Blackjack</TITLE>
</HEAD>
<BODY>
<APPLET CODE="Blackjack.class" WIDTH=400 HEIGHT=400>
[Blackjack applet]
</APPLET>
</BODY>
</HTML>
```

Open the blackjack.htm file with HotJava or the appletviewer. It should display the applet, as shown in Figure 40.4.

The top text line in the applet welcomes you to the game and tells you that you have $1,000 to gamble. The Dealer's Hand and Your Hand text boxes are initially blank. Below them are the Hit and Stay buttons, which are initially disabled. To start the game, enter a bet, as shown in Figure 40.5.

When you enter a bet, the label to the right of the text field changes from Enter your bet: to Bet:. The text field is grayed and can no longer be edited. This prevents you from changing your bet during the play of a hand.

The initial hands for the dealer and the player are displayed after the bet is entered. The first card of the dealer is hidden. You can now use the Hit and Stay buttons to obtain more cards or to stay with what you were dealt and let the dealer draw. Click the Hit button until you are finished drawing cards. If you bust (go over 21), your hand will be finished and the dealer will draw his cards.

FIGURE 40.4.

The BlackJack initial display.

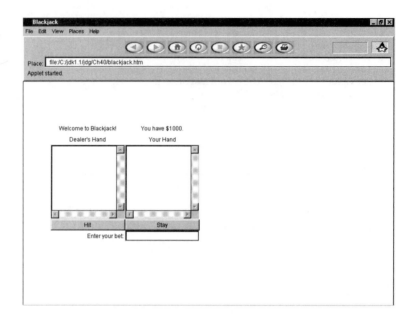

FIGURE 40.5.

Entering a bet.

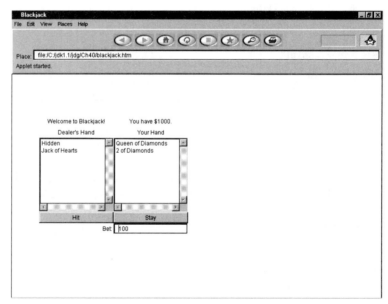

After you click Stay or bust, the dealer draws his hand and a win, loss, or tie results. Your available money is then updated based on your winnings. The Blackjack applet is more forgiving than the BlackJackApp program in Chapter 4: You can continue playing after you've run out of money. You can even bet $0 or negative values.

Go ahead and play the game for a while to become familiar with its operation.

Although the Blackjack applet may appear to be quite large, it reuses all of the classes developed for the original BlackJackApp program, with minor modifications.

The Blackjack program declares several variables. Most of these are used to create its GUI interface. The BET, PLAY, and DEALER constants are used to maintain the state of the user's interaction with the game. The state variable is set to the initial BET state.

The money, bet, deck, playersHand, and dealersHand variables are declared and used in the same manner as in the BlackJackApp program.

Five labels are created and assigned to the topLine, totalLine, dealersLabel, playersLabel, and betLabel variables. The topLine and totalLine variables are displayed at the top of the applet. They display the welcome string and the amount of money that the player has available. The dealersLabel and playersLabel variables are used to label the text areas containing the dealer's and user's hands. The betLabel variable prompts the user to enter his or her bet.

The dealerText and playerText variables are used to refer to the TextArea objects that display the hands of the dealer and player. The betField text field is used to enter and display the user's bet.

The hitButton and stayButton variables are used to draw another card or to turn the draw over to the dealer.

The gridbag and constraints variables refer to the GridBagLayout and GridBagConstraints objects used to lay out the screen's display.

The init() method sets the layout to a GridBagLayout, invoking the addComponent() method to add the GUI components to the applet. The addComponent() method adds a component to an x,y location within the gridbag layout.

The updateBet() method is a new method that is added to support the applet conversion. It disables editing of the text field and changes the Label object referenced by the betLabel variable from Enter your bet: to Bet:. It then checks the bet for a valid value and redisplays it in the disabled text field. The initialDeal() method is invoked to deal an initial hand to the player and dealer. If the user is dealt blackjack, the hand is ended and the user is given his winnings. Otherwise, the state variable is set to PLAY to enable the operation of the Hit and Stay buttons.

The initialDeal() method remains unchanged from the original BlackJackApp program.

The openBetting() method is used to change to the initial BET state. It sets the Enter your bet: prompt and enables the text field to be edited.

The playerWins(), dealerWins(), and tie() methods have been modified to display their results within the applet instead of on the console window. They also invoke the openBetting() method to return to the BET state.

The showResults() method remains unchanged from the original BlackJackApp program.

The TextHandler class handles the event generated when the user enters text in the Bet: text field by invoking the updateBet() method.

The ButtonHandler class handles the clicking of the Hit and Stay buttons by first making sure that the applet is in the PLAY state. This prevents the user from clicking on these buttons at arbitrary times during the applet's execution.

The Hit button is handled by adding a card to the player's hand, using the same approach as in BlackJackApp. The show() method of the Hand class is modified to display the player's hand to the TextArea object referenced by the playerText variable. If the user busts, the state is set to DEALER, preventing the user from drawing another card.

The Stay button is handled by setting the state variable to DEALER.

When the state is set to DEALER, the dealer is dealt additional cards using the same code as in BlackJackApp. The showResults() method is modified to update the applet's display labels and not the console window.

No changes were made to the Deck or Card classes. The show() method of the Hand class was modified to display the dealer's and player's hands to the TextArea objects.

The changes required to convert from the original BlackJackApp program to the Blackjack applet were minimal. This illustrates the power of object-oriented programming and the reusability of the components that are created using this approach.

Summary

This chapter introduces you to applet programming by way of several sample programs that illustrate the classes and methods used to implement simple applets. You should now be comfortable with applets, especially if you have worked through the window programming examples of Part IV. Chapter 41, "Developing Applets," lays the framework for developing applets by expanding on the basics introduced here.

41

Developing Applets

In this chapter you will learn what an applet is, how it relates to HTML, and what some of the possible uses of applet technology are. By the time you finish this chapter, you will have an understanding of what an applet is, how it works, and what it can do.

How Applets Work

Applet technology is the driving force behind the intensity of the Java revolution. Applets enhance Web documents with animation, sound, and other special effects. However, applets are just standard Java programs with a few special hooks into the Web browser's environment. The capability of applets to take advantage of the resources provided by a Web browser's environment is what allows them to be easily and powerfully integrated within Web pages.

Figure 41.1 describes the steps an applet takes to display itself in the browser's window.

FIGURE 41.1.

How a Java applet works.

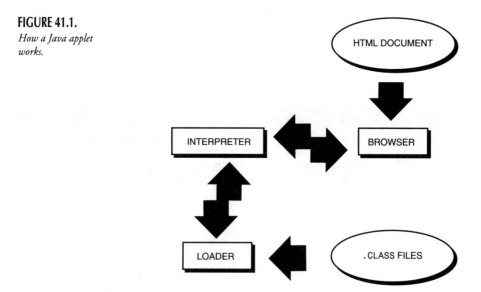

As the figure shows, the browser makes a request to the loader to fetch the applet specified in the document's HTML. After the applet has been fetched, the applet begins to execute. The applet is executed by the Java runtime interpreter attached to the browser. The browser acts as a conduit between the Java virtual machine inside the interpreter and the outside user interface.

The Applet class provides an application framework and tools to access the facilities provided by the browser. Via the browser, the applet has access to graphics, sound, and network capabilities. The Applet class can be viewed as merely a wrapper around the capabilities provided by the browser.

The Relationship Between HTML and Applets

An applet is like a child application of the browser. The browser launches the applet in a predefined environment inside the browser. In turn, the browser obtains the information pertaining to the applet's environment from the current document's HTML. In this sense, the relationship between HTML and an applet is that of a command line executing a program.

From within HTML, the syntax to specify the execution of an applet is provided by the applet and parameter tags as discussed in Chapter 16, "Web Programming with the `java.applet` Package."

The applet tag provides all of the information needed to launch the applet. Everything from the base directory to command-line parameters can be specified from within this tag. Here's an example:

```
<APPLET  CODE = "lights.class" width=400 height=75 align=center >
<PARAM NAME="text" VALUE="Blink">
<BLOCKQUOTE>
<HR>
If you were using a Java(tm)-enabled browser,
you would see blinking lights instead of this paragraph.
<HR>
</BLOCKQUOTE>
</APPLET>
```

From this HTML command line, the browser is told how to launch the `lights.class` file with the parameter `text`. The HTML merely specifies a command line of sorts to the browser.

Applets and Interactive Web Pages

Usually, when the word *applet* is mentioned, the World Wide Web is not far out of mind. There is good reason for this: An applet is a Java program designed to run in the environment provided by a Web browser. The last statement might seem a little simplistic, but take a second to think what that environment provides to an application.

Inside the browser, an application has the capability to display images, play audio files, and access the Internet. The `Applet` class provides methods to tap these resources provided by the Web browser.

Because applets are executed locally on your machine, you are able to interact with the applet as part of the Web page's display. Other Web applications that rely on CGI programs do not provide interactivity at the local level. Instead, your browser must send information processing requests to programs that are located on remote Web servers. Beside performance impacts, this remote processing approach also suffers from the difficulties involved in maintaining information about the state of the applications it supports. The Java model of local execution is capable of supporting a high degree of interactivity. All state information is maintained within the local browser environment and is not distributed between the browser and Web server.

Applets Versus Scripts

As discussed previously, applets are launched from within an HTML command. After an applet is launched, it operates in a well-defined area of the browser window and is restricted from altering the state or content of the current HTML document. Scripts written in the JavaScript language are not placed under these restrictions and have more latitude in modifying the state of the HTML document being displayed.

An applet is treated as a self-contained object by a Web browser and is handled in much the same way as an inline image. On the other hand, scripts are integrated within the document's HTML. Because it is the browser that executes the script and not the Java runtime interpreter, the script has the capability to modify the contents of the entire browser window—a task that an applet cannot perform.

Applets and scripts each serve a different purpose. Scripts provide the capability to dynamically alter the content of an HTML document, whereas applets are separate, interactive applications that execute within the context of the browser and display information in a limited area of the browser window.

The Execution of an Applet

When the browser comes across the applet tag, it begins gathering the information needed to launch the applet. After the HTML document has been completely interpreted and displayed, the Java runtime interpreter is requested to execute the applet.

When the interpreter receives the request to execute the applet, it executes a loader mechanism to fetch the binary file. After the file is successfully transferred onto the local machine, it undergoes a number of tests to verify its security and stability. Chapter 60, "Java Security," covers applet security. If all is well, the interpreter begins execution of the applet.

Execution continues until the applet terminates or the current browser document is dismissed. This can occur in a couple of different ways: The user might jump to another URL or the browser might terminate. In either case, the applet is terminated.

Using Window Components

Window components can be added to the applet to create a friendly user interface. Java provides a number of window components, which can be found in the java.awt library.

All of the window components added to an applet are confined to the applet window area in the current browser document. The applet window contains the entire paintable region; anything that does not fit inside that region is clipped.

Using the provided window components, applets have the capability to contain the same look and feel of other window application programs. Applets can use all GUI components that can be used by `Panel` objects. In addition, applets have access to many of the capabilities provided by the browser.

Adding Content and Protocol Handlers to Applets

Java supplies a set of interfaces that support the development of content and protocol handlers. Chapters 36, "Content Handlers," and 37, "Protocol Handlers," cover the use of these interfaces. Content and protocol handlers may be added to applets to provide the capability to retrieve and display different types of Web objects or to use services provided by new or custom Internet protocols. By using these content and protocol handlers, Java applications become more capable network clients and can be used to support distributed processing applications, as discussed in Part VIII, "Developing Distributed Applications."

Using Applets as Inline Viewers

Applets have the capability to present images, sounds, and other multimedia objects inside an HTML document. Scripts provide the means to dynamically change the content of an HTML document. The combination of the two produces very powerful results, including the capability to use applets as inline viewers.

The interactive Web catalog is a perfect example of the inline viewer concept. A Web page contains a script-enabled order form that contains a selection field. The user uses this selection field to select the product to order. When this happens, the script launches an applet to give a visual presentation of the item selected, providing the user with more information with which to make a purchase decision.

Using an applet as an inline viewer allows for more flexibility than standard HTML facilities. The content to be viewed might contain contextual interactive information rather than being a flat piece of media.

Using Applets as Network Clients

The concept of containing a network client inside an HTML document might seem a little strange to you, and for good reason—embedding a client inside a client seems redundant. However, the browser client can be viewed as a delivery mechanism for the embedded client, allowing Web-based support of other application protocols.

By combining applets with protocol handlers, an applet can quickly become a telnet, FTP, or even an embedded HTTP client. If a custom protocol handler is used, the applet can become the means for users to access custom network applications.

Optimizing Applets

Like most applications on the Internet, applets are constrained by their user's communication bandwidth capabilities. You know it is a good idea to optimize Web pages for optimal low bandwidth performance; the same holds for applets.

Fortunately, graphics usually constitute a much greater physical size than the applet's executable size. I say *fortunately* because it is far easier to optimize the loading of media than worry about code generation.

Applets, being a mechanism for a graphical user interface, usually require the transfer of graphics files. This process may take varied amounts of time depending on the speed of the connection. Taking the approach of loading media in the background, while the user is busy doing something else, limits the annoying delays associated with media transfers.

Hopefully, low bandwidth will not always be a problem for Internet applications. However, for as long as users have to wait for something to display on their screen, optimizing applications for low-bandwidth situations will produce applications that are more likely to satisfy user expectations.

Chapter 42, "Using .jar Files and Signed Applets," discusses other approaches to applet optimization based on the use of .jar files. These files allow applets and their resources to be loaded via a single compressed file. Use of .jar files also reduces the browser and server overhead, eliminating the need for multiple browser/server interactions.

Learning from Online Examples

As technologies advance, the early adopter usually provides examples to promote the technology. So is the case with scripts and applets. A number of companies have jumped on the Java wagon from the get-go and provide examples of their endeavors. The following are a few sites where valuable information can be found:

- `http://www.gamelan.com`
- `http://www.jars.com/`
- `http://www.javasoft.com/applets/`
- `http://www.yahoo.com/Computers_and_Internet/Programming_Languages/Java/Applets/`

Summary

This chapter gives background information on how applets work and how they relate to scripts written in the JavaScript language. You were also given a little taste of what applets and scripts can achieve. The next chapter discusses the use of .jar files for applet compression and signatures to support additional applet security.

42

Using .jar Files and Signed Applets

Now that you are familiar with the basics of creating and using applets, we'll cover some new applet capabilities introduced with JDK 1.1. The capabilities that we'll cover include the use of .jar files to store applet-related files in a single compressed archive file and the use of digital signatures to differentiate between trusted and untrusted applets. In this chapter, you'll learn how to create .jar files using the Java archive tool and how to digitally sign .jar files using the javakey tool. You'll also learn how to use javakey to manage a database of digital identities, their public keys, and signatures that guarantee the authenticity of their public keys. When you finish this chapter, you'll be able to use signed and unsigned .jar files to distribute the applets you develop.

What Is a .jar File?

A .jar file is a compressed archive file that is created using the Java archive tool (jar). The jar tool is similar to the PKZIP program developed by Phil Katz. It combines multiple files into a single archive file that is compressed using the ZLIB compression library. Although jar is a general purpose file archive and compression tool, its main purpose is to combine the files used by an applet into a single compressed file for efficient loading by a Java-enabled Web browser.

> **NOTE**
>
> A description of the ZLIB compression format is available at the URL http://www.cdrom.com/pub/infozip/zlib/.

The use of jar with applets can greatly improve browser performance. By combining all of the files used by an applet into a single file, a browser only needs to establish a single HTTP connection with a Web server. This reduces the communication processing overhead on both the browser and the server. By using file compression, the time required to download an applet may be reduced by 50% or more. This benefits both the applet's user and publisher.

Another feature of .jar files is that they support the capability to sign archived files. This permits the browser to differentiate between untrusted applets and those applets that (because they are signed by a reputable identity) may be trusted to perform sensitive processing in a secure manner.

Using the Java Archive Tool

The jar tool is easy to use. You invoke it using the following command line:

```
jar [options] [manifest] jar-file input-file(s)
```

The *jar-file* is the file that is to be used as an archive. The .jar extension should be supplied in the command line. The *input-file(s)* are written as a space separated list of files to be placed in the archive. Filename wild card characters may be used (for example, *.class).

The *manifest* is a file that contains information about the archived files. It need not be supplied—jar will create one automatically and store it as META-INF\MANIFEST.INF within the archive. Information about the manifest file can be found in the file docs\guide\jar\manifest.html that is included with the JDK 1.1.1 API documentation.

The jar *options* are used to control the input and output of the jar tool. They are described in Table 42.1.

Table 42.1. The jar tool options.

Option	Description
c	Creates a new (empty) archive file.
t	Displays the archive's table of contents.
x [*file(s)*]	Extracts the specified *file(s)*. If no files are specified, all files are extracted.
f	Identifies the file to be created, listed, or extracted.
v	Generates verbose output.
m *manifest*	Uses the supplied manifest file.

NOTE

The syntax of the jar tool is similar to the UNIX tar command.

Examples of using the jar tool are provided in the following sections.

Creating a .jar file

If you have ever used the UNIX tar command or the DOS PKZIP program, you will find the jar tool to be familiar and easy to use. In this section, you'll learn how to create a .jar file for the Blackjack applet that you developed in Chapter 40, "Sample Applets."

We'll use the Blackjack applet because it created several class files, which makes it a good candidate for archival and compression. Start by copying the Blackjack.java file to your Ch42 working directory:

```
C:\jdk1.1.1\jdg\Ch42>copy ..\ch40\Blackjack.java
        1 file(s) copied
```

Now recompile `Blackjack.java`:

```
C:\jdk1.1.1\jdg\Ch42>javac Blackjack.java
```

Blackjack's six class files are re-created in your `Ch42` directory. Let's use `jar` to archive and compress them into a file named `bj.jar`:

```
C:\jdk1.1.1\jdg\Ch42>jar cf bj.jar *.class
```

List your directory to verify that the `.jar` file was created:

```
C:\jdk1.1.1\jdg\Ch42>dir

 Volume in drive C has no label
 Volume Serial Number is 0A5D-1ECD
 Directory of C:\jdk1.1.1\jdg\Ch42

 .              <DIR>         04-13-97  2:45p .
 ..             <DIR>         04-13-97  2:45p ..
 BLACKJ~1 JAV      7,052      03-12-97  4:39p Blackjack.java
 BLACKJ~1 CLA      4,411      04-13-97  5:11p Blackjack.class
 BLACKJ~2 CLA        664      04-13-97  5:11p Blackjack$TextHandler.class
 BLACKJ~3 CLA      1,354      04-13-97  5:11p Blackjack$ButtonHandler.class
 DECK~1   CLA        929      04-13-97  5:11p Deck.class
 HAND~1   CLA      1,759      04-13-97  5:11p Hand.class
 CARD~1   CLA        925      04-13-97  5:11p Card.class
 BJ       JAR      7,101      04-13-97  5:11p bj.jar
          8 file(s)         24,195 bytes
          2 dir(s)      74,481,664 bytes free
```

Note that `bj.jar` is only 7,101 bytes long. Because the six class files are 10,058 bytes, the `jar` tool compressed them to 71% of their original size. Now that the `.class` files are archived, delete them using `del *.class`. If you don't delete these files, you'll get an error when you run the `appletviewer` with `blackjack.htm`.

Listing the Contents of a `.jar` File

Let's use the list option of the `jar` command to see what's inside the `bj.jar` file:

```
C:\jdk1.1.1\jdg\Ch42>jar tf bj.jar
META-INF/MANIFEST.MF
Blackjack$ButtonHandler.class
Blackjack$TextHandler.class
Blackjack.class
Card.class
Deck.class
Hand.class
```

The only thing that looks out of place is the `META-INF/MANIFEST.MF` entry. That's the file used to keep a manifest of the `.jar` file's contents.

Viewing a .jar File

You're probably wondering how you would include the bj.jar file in an applet. The answer is that you simply add the ARCHIVE="bj.jar" attribute to the applet tag. This attribute tells the browser to load the bj.jar archive file in order to find the Blackjack.class file and other related classes. Listing 42.1 shows the file bj.htm that is used to display the Blackjack applet.

Listing 42.1. The bj.htm file.

```
<HTML>
<HEAD>
<TITLE>Blackjack</TITLE>
</HEAD>
<BODY>
<APPLET CODE="Blackjack.class" ARCHIVE="bj.jar" WIDTH=400 HEIGHT=400>
[Blackjack applet]
</APPLET>
</BODY>
</HTML>
```

You can view the Blackjack applet using the appletviewer tool, as follows:

C:\jdk1.1.1\jdg\Ch42>appletviewer bj.htm

This results in the applet being displayed, as shown in Figure 42.1.

FIGURE 42.1.

The Blackjack *applet viewed by appletviewer.*

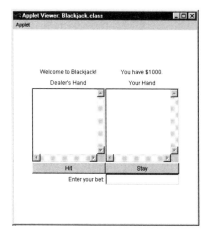

Extracting the Contents of a `.jar` File

The x option of the `jar` tool lets you extract the file's contents. You can use it to re-create the `.class` files that you deleted:

```
C:\jdk1.1.1\jdg\Ch42>jar xvf bj.jar
 extracted: META-INF\MANIFEST.MF
 extracted: Blackjack$ButtonHandler.class
 extracted: Blackjack$TextHandler.class
 extracted: Blackjack.class
 extracted: Card.class
 extracted: Deck.class
 extracted: Hand.class
```

List your directory to see exactly what came back:

```
C:\jdk1.1.1\jdg\Ch42>dir

 Volume in drive C has no label
 Volume Serial Number is 0A5D-1ECD
 Directory of C:\jdk1.1.1\jdg\Ch42

 .              <DIR>        04-13-97  2:45p .
 ..             <DIR>        04-13-97  2:45p ..
 BLACKJ~1 JAV      7,052     03-12-97  4:39p Blackjack.java
 BJ       HTM        179     04-13-97  5:04p bj.htm
 META-INF       <DIR>        04-13-97  5:22p META-INF
 BLACKJ~1 CLA      1,354     04-13-97  5:22p Blackjack$ButtonHandler.class
 BLACKJ~2 CLA        664     04-13-97  5:22p Blackjack$TextHandler.class
 BLACKJ~3 CLA      4,411     04-13-97  5:22p Blackjack.class
 CARD~1   CLA        925     04-13-97  5:22p Card.class
 BJ       JAR      7,101     04-13-97  5:11p bj.jar
 DECK~1   CLA        929     04-13-97  5:22p Deck.class
 HAND~1   CLA      1,759     04-13-97  5:22p Hand.class
        9 file(s)       24,374 bytes
        3 dir(s)    75,350,016 bytes free
```

Note that the META-INF directory was created.

The `javakey` Security Tool

In the previous sections, you learned how the `jar` tool is used to combine all of the files used by an applet into a single compressed archive file. The `javakey` tool is also an important tool for applet development. It allows you to create digital signatures for your archive files. These signatures can be used to verify that an archive file was signed by its purported signer and was not modified since it was signed. A verified signature can be used as the basis for trusting an applet to perform sensitive-processing in a secure manner.

> **NOTE**
>
> As of JDK 1.1.1, `javakey` supports certificate creation but not certificate verification.

The javakey tool helps you to manage a database of identities or potential signers, their public keys, certificates guaranteeing their identity, and the trust placed in these individuals. It can also be used to manage public and private keys.

The objects managed by the javakey tool consist of *identities* and *signers.* These objects correspond to instances of the Identity and Signer classes that you studied in Chapter 20, "Security and the java.security Packages."

An identity is a real-world entity (such as a person, organization, or software process) that has the capability to create a digital signature. The public key of the identity is kept in the javakey database along with any certificates that attest to the fact that the identity's public key is correct. Public keys are used for signature verification.

A signer is an identity that is capable of signing a certificate using your local Java installation. The private keys of signers are also managed by javakey. Private keys are used for signature creation.

Both identities and signers have usernames. The usernames name the identities and signers of the javakey database. Identities and signers are collectively referred to as *users.*

> **NOTE**
>
> The default database file used by javakey is identitydb.obj. It should be protected from disclosure because it may contain the private keys of signers. A different database file can be specified by setting the identity.database property in the jdk1.1.1\lib\security\java.security file.

Using javakey

The javakey tool manages identities and signers, generates and manages keys and certificates, and signs .jar files. The javakey options used to perform these functions are identified in Table 42.2. The following section provides a tutorial on using javakey.

Table 42.2. The javakey tool options.

Option	Description
-c *identity* [true|false]	Add *identity* to the database and specify whether it is trusted. An identity is untrusted by default.
-cs *signer* [true|false]	Add *signer* to the database and specify whether it is trusted. A signer is untrusted by default.
-t *username* [true|false]	Change the trust level of an identity or signer.

continues

Table 42.2. continued

Option	Description
-ld	List and describe the usernames contained in the database.
-l	List the usernames contained in the database.
-li *username*	List information about the specified user.
-r *username*	Remove a user from the database.
-ii *username*	Add information about *username* to the database. Input is terminated by a Ctrl-Z (Windows) or Ctrl-D (UNIX).
-gk *signer algorithm size* [*pubfile*] [*privfile*]	Generate a key pair using the specified *algorithm* and key *size* (in bits) and associate it with *signer*. The keys may be optionally written to *pubfile* and *privfile*. -g may be used as a shortcut for --gk.
-ik *identity keyfile*	Import the X.509-formatted public key contained in *keyfile* and associate it with *identity*.
-ikp *signer pubfile privfile*	Import the X.509-formatted public and private keys contained in *pubfile* and *privfile* and associate them with *signer*.
-gc *directivefile*	Generate a certificate using *directivefile*.
-dc *certfile*	Display the certificate contained in *certfile*.
-ic *username certfile*	Import the certificate contained in *certfile* and associate it with *username*.
-ek *username pubfile* [*privfile*]	Export the public key of *username* to *pubfile*. Optionally, the private key of *username* may be exported to *privfile*.
-ec *username number certfile*	Export the *numbered* certificate of *username* to *certfile*.
-gs *directivefile jarfile*	Sign *jarfile* using the *directivefile*.

Don't worry about learning all of the commands in Table 42.2 now. You'll become familiar with them when you take the tutorial presented in the next section.

A `javakey` Tutorial

In order to use `javakey`, the first thing that you need to do is to add the usernames of identities and signers to the `javakey` database. We'll add the users Emily, Lisa, Jason, and Jamie. Emily and Jason will be trusted signers. Lisa and Jamie will be untrusted identities who aren't signers. Add these users with the following commands:

```
C:\jdk1.1.1\jdg\Ch42>javakey -cs Emily true
Created identity [Signer]Emily[identitydb.obj][trusted]

C:\jdk1.1.1\jdg\Ch42>javakey -cs Jason true
Created identity [Signer]Jason[identitydb.obj][trusted]

C:\jdk1.1.1\jdg\Ch42>javakey -c Lisa
Created identity Lisa[identitydb.obj][not trusted]

C:\jdk1.1.1\jdg\Ch42>javakey -c Jamie
Created identity Jamie[identitydb.obj][not trusted]
```

Now let's display the contents of the database:

```
C:\jdk1.1.1\jdg\Ch42>javakey -ld

Scope: sun.security.IdentityDatabase, source file: C:\JDK1.1.1\BIN\..\identityd
.obj

[Signer]Emily[identitydb.obj][trusted]
        no keys
        no certificates
        No further information available.

Lisa[identitydb.obj][not trusted]
        no public key
        no certificates
        No further information available.

[Signer]Jason[identitydb.obj][trusted]
        no keys
        no certificates
        No further information available.

Jamie[identitydb.obj][not trusted]
        no public key
        no certificates
        No further information available.
```

The output of the database listing alerts us that we need to add key and certificate information to the database. Let's make this process a little simpler by deleting one of the users:

```
C:\jdk1.1.1\jdg\Ch42>javakey -r Jamie
Removed Jamie.
```

Also, let's make Emily untrusted:

```
C:\jdk1.1.1\jdg\Ch42>javakey -t Emily false
Emily is trusted: false
```

```
C:\jdk1.1.1\jdg\Ch42>javakey -ii Jason
Please enter the info for this identity.
[End with ctrl-D on Unix and ctrl-Z on Win32]
Jason is the only individual that is trusted to create signatures.
Set information for Jason
```

Let's check the database to make sure the information was correctly entered:

```
C:\jdk1.1.1\jdg\Ch42>javakey -li Jason
Identity: Jason
[Signer]Jason[identitydb.obj][trusted]
        no keys
        no certificates

Jason is the only individual that is trusted to create signatures.
```

So far, so good. Let's generate a public/private key pair for Jason. This may take a few minutes, depending on the speed of your processor:

```
 C:\jdk1.1.1\jdg\Ch42>javakey -gk Jason DSA 512
Generated DSA keys for Jason (strength: 512).
```

Let's see how the database entry for Jason has changed:

```
C:\jdk1.1.1\jdg\Ch42>javakey -li Jason
Identity: Jason
[Signer]Jason[identitydb.obj][trusted]
        public and private keys initialized
        certificates:


Jason is the only individual that is trusted to create signatures.
```

Note that Jason's public and private keys have been initialized. Let's export Jason's public key to the file pubjason:

```
C:\jdk1.1.1\jdg\Ch42>javakey -ek Jason pubjason
Public key exported to pubjason.
```

The file publisa, created at another host, contains Lisa's public key. This file is installed from the CD-ROM into your CH42 directory. Let's import it into our database:

```
C:\jdk1.1.1\jdg\Ch42>javakey -ik Lisa publisa
Set public key from publisa for Lisa.
```

Now let's check Lisa's database information:

```
C:\jdk1.1.1\jdg\Ch42>javakey -li Lisa
Identity: Lisa
Lisa[identitydb.obj][not trusted]
        public key initialized
        certificates:

        No further information available.
```

Jason needs a certificate to vouch for his identity. Let's create one for him using the certificate directive file named `jasondir`, used in the following and shown in Listing 42.2:

```
C:\jdk1.1.1\jdg\Ch42>javakey -gc jasondir
Generated certificate from directive file jasondir.
```

Listing 42.2. Certificate directive file for Jason (`jasondir`).

```
issuer.name=Jason

subject.name=Jason
subject.real.name=Jason Jaworski
subject.org.unit=4th Grade
subject.org=Clear View
subject.country=USA

start.date=1 Apr 1997
end.date=31 Dec 2010
serial.number=2001
```

The syntax of a certificate directive file is as follows:

- `issuer.name`—The name of the signer signing and issuing the certificate.
- `issuer.cert`—Identifies by number which of the signer's certificates is used to sign the certificate file.
- `subject.name`—The name of the identity whose public key is authenticated by the certificate.
- `subject.real.name`—Full name of the subject being authenticated.
- `subject.org.unit`—Subject's organizational unit.
- `subject.org`—Subject's organization.
- `subject.country`—Subject's country.
- `start.date`—Date when certificate becomes valid.
- `end.date`—Last day of certificate's validity.
- `serial.number`—A unique serial number is assigned to all certificates issued by the signer.
- `signature.algorithm`—The name of the signature algorithm used to create the certificate. Its default value is DSA.
- `out.file`—The optional name of a file to which the certificate is to be saved.

Having created Jason's certificate, let's recheck Jason's database information:

```
C:\jdk1.1.1\jdg\Ch42>javakey -li Jason
Identity: Jason
[Signer]Jason[identitydb.obj][trusted]
        public and private keys initialized
```

```
                certificates:
                certificate 1    for  : CN=Jason Jaworski, OU=4th Grade, O=Clear View, C=
        USA
                                 from : CN=Jason Jaworski, OU=4th Grade, O=Clear View, C=
        USA


        Jason is the only individual that is trusted to create signatures.
```

Note that Jason signed his own certificate. Because he is a signer, he can do that. Let's export Jason's certificate to the file jasoncert:

```
C:\jdk1.1.1\jdg\Ch42>javakey -ec Jason 1 jasoncert
Certificate 1 exported to jasoncert.
```

I wonder what Jason's certificate looks like. Let's take a peek:

```
C:\jdk1.1.1\jdg\Ch42>javakey -dc jasoncert
[
  X.509v1 certificate,
  Subject is CN=Jason Jaworski, OU=4th Grade, O=Clear View, C=USA
  Key:  Sun DSA Public Key
parameters:
p: fca682ce8e12caba26efccf7110e526db078b05edecbcd1eb4a208f3ae1617ae01f35b91a47e6
df63413c5e12ed0899bcd132acd50d99151bdc43ee737592e17
q: 962eddcc369cba8ebb260ee6b6a126d9346e38c5
g: 678471b27a9cf44ee91a49c5147db1a9aaf244f05a434d6486931d2d14271b9e35030b71fd73d
a179069b32e2935630e1c2062354d0da20a6c416e50be794ca4

y: c736c93d02384a884f1a95002e16f2435deffd22afc8f7c8cab9bd7c1aeaffc5b06a45f7beaa5
88db2a8c94be8be03fc6069f493113ae2b62c1f08504032fe8b
  Validity <Mon Mar 31 15:00:00 PST 1997> until <Thu Dec 30 16:00:00 PST 2010>
  Issuer is CN=Jason Jaworski, OU=4th Grade, O=Clear View, C=USA
  Issuer signature used [SHA1withDSA]
  Serial number =      07d1
]
```

Don't worry if the values you display are different from those above.

A certificate for Lisa is available (created on another host) in the file lisacert. Let's import it into the database:

```
C:\jdk1.1.1\jdg\Ch42>javakey -ic Lisa lisacert
Imported certificate from lisacert for Lisa.
```

Now let's check to see how her database information was updated:

```
C:\jdk1.1.1\jdg\Ch42>javakey -li Lisa
Identity: Lisa
Lisa[identitydb.obj][not trusted]
        public key initialized
        certificates:
        certificate 1    for  : CN=Lisa Jaworski, OU=Nutrition, O=Tiffany, C=USA
                         from : CN=Lisa Jaworski, OU=Nutrition, O=Tiffany, C=USA

        No further information available.
```

Looks like she signed her own certificate, too.

Because Jason is a signer he has the ability to sign a `.jar` file. Let's sign the `bj.jar` file that we created earlier in the chapter. In order to do this we need a signature directive file. We'll use the certificate directive file `jasonsigdir`, shown in Listing 42.3. The following output is generated when you use this certificate directive file to sign the `bj.jar` file:

```
C:\jdk1.1.1\jdg\Ch42>javakey -gs jasigdir bj.jar
Adding entry: META-INF/MANIFEST.MF
Creating entry: META-INF\JASIGN.SF
Creating entry: META-INF\JASIGN.DSA
Adding entry: Blackjack$ButtonHandler.class
Adding entry: Blackjack$TextHandler.class
Adding entry: Blackjack.class
Adding entry: Card.class
Adding entry: Deck.class
Adding entry: Hand.class
Signed JAR file bj.jar using directive file jasigdir.
```

Listing 42.3. The signature directive file used to sign `bj.jar`. (`jasigdir`).

```
signer=Jason

cert=1

chain=0

signature.file=jasign

out.file=signedbj.jar
```

The syntax of a signature directive file is as follows:

- `signer`—The name of the signer entity used to sign the certificate.
- `cert`—The number of the signer's certificate as kept by the database.
- `chain`—The length of the chain of certificates to be included. For example, certificates of the signer, the signer's signer, and so on may be included to show the authentication chain from the prime signer (Postal Service; Verisign, Inc.; and so on). Unfortunately, this capability is not supported in JDK 1.1.
- `signature.file`—The name of the generated signature file (eight characters or less).
- `out.file`—The name of the signed `.jar` file.

Note that the `signedbj.jar` file was created as the result of the signing of `bj.jar`:

```
C:\jdk1.1.1\jdg\Ch42>dir *.jar

 Volume in drive C has no label
 Volume Serial Number is 0A5D-1ECD
 Directory of C:\jdk1.1.1\jdg\Ch42
```

```
BJ        JAR        7,101  04-13-97  5:11p bj.jar
SIGNEDBJ  JAR        8,622  04-13-97  9:43p signedbj.jar
          2 file(s)         15,723 bytes
          0 dir(s)      82,558,976 bytes free
```

Working with Signed Applets

The point of creating a signed .jar file is to enable the file to be trusted and to execute using greater privileges. The Blackjack applet from Chapter 40 does not require any extra privileges. So let's create an applet that does. The ReadFile applet, shown in Listing 42.4, reads a file from your local file system. This is a definite security violation as far as applets are concerned.

Listing 42.4. The ReadFile applet.

```java
import java.applet.*;
import java.awt.*;
import java.io.*;

public class ReadFile extends Applet {
 public void init() {
  TextArea text = new TextArea(30,70);
  add(text);
  String s="";
  try {
   FileReader f = new FileReader("c:\\autoexec.bat");
   BufferedReader r = new BufferedReader(f);
   String line;
   while((line=r.readLine())!=null) s+=line+"\n";
  }catch(Exception ex){
   s=ex.toString();
  }
  text.setText(s);
 }
}
```

The ReadFile applet attempts to read the user's c:\autoexec.bat file and display it to a text area. If you do not have a c:\autoexec.bat file, change the filename to the name of a file that is on your local file system. Compile ReadFile.java and create a .jar file using the following commands:

```
C:\jdk1.1.1\jdg\Ch42>javac ReadFile.java
```

```
C:\jdk1.1.1\jdg\Ch42>jar cf rf.jar ReadFile.class
```

The HTML file shown in Listing 42.5 can be used to display the ReadFile applet. Note the use of the ARCHIVE attribute to identify the rf.jar file.

Listing 42.5. The `rf.htm` file.

```
<HTML>
<HEAD>
<TITLE>ReadFile</TITLE>
</HEAD>
<BODY>
<APPLET CODE="ReadFile.class" ARCHIVE="rf.jar" WIDTH=450 HEIGHT=450>
[ReadFile applet]
</APPLET>
</BODY>
</HTML>
```

Try to view `rf.htm` using `appletviewer`. You will get a well-deserved security exception. This exception is also displayed in the applet's text area, as shown in Figure 42.2:

```
C:\jdk1.1.1\jdg\Ch42>appletviewer rf.htm
sun.applet.AppletSecurityException: checkread
        at sun.applet.AppletSecurity.checkRead(AppletSecurity.java:384)
        at sun.applet.AppletSecurity.checkRead(AppletSecurity.java:346)
        at java.io.FileInputStream.<init>(FileInputStream.java:58)
        at java.io.FileReader.<init>(FileReader.java:43)
        at ReadFile.init(ReadFile.java:11)
        at sun.applet.AppletPanel.run(AppletPanel.java:273)
        at java.lang.Thread.run(Thread.java:474)
sun.applet.AppletSecurityException: checkread
        at sun.applet.AppletSecurity.checkRead(AppletSecurity.java:384)
        at sun.applet.AppletSecurity.checkRead(AppletSecurity.java:346)
        at java.io.FileInputStream.<init>(FileInputStream.java:58)
        at java.io.FileReader.<init>(FileReader.java:43)
        at ReadFile.init(ReadFile.java:11)
        at sun.applet.AppletPanel.run(AppletPanel.java:273)
        at java.lang.Thread.run(Thread.java:474)
```

FIGURE 42.2.

A security exception is generated for the untrusted par *file.*

Now that we know that we have an applet that cannot perform its processing without extra privileges, let's sign the applet's jar file to give it those privileges. We'll use the signature directive file jasigdir.2, shown in Listing 42.6, to create the signature.

Listing 42.6. The signature directive file for the rf.jar file.

```
signer=Jason

cert=1

chain=0

signature.file=jasign

out.file=srf.jar
```

The signature directive file uses Jason as the signer and creates the srf.jar signed .jar file. The command for creating the signature follows:

```
C:\jdk1.1.1\jdg\Ch42>javakey -gs jasigdir.2 rf.jar
Adding entry: META-INF/MANIFEST.MF
Creating entry: META-INF\JASIGN.SF
Creating entry: META-INF\JASIGN.DSA
Adding entry: ReadFile.class
Signed JAR file rf.jar using directive file jasigdir.2.
```

We'll need a new HTML file to refer to the signed srf.jar file. The srf.htm file is shown in Listing 42.7.

Listing 42.7. An HTML file for displaying the signed srf.jar file.

```
<HTML>
<HEAD>
<TITLE>ReadFile</TITLE>
</HEAD>
<BODY>
<APPLET CODE="ReadFile.class" ARCHIVE="srf.jar" WIDTH=450 HEIGHT=450>
[ReadFile applet]
</APPLET>
</BODY>
</HTML>
```

View srf.htm with appletviewer. It will display your c:\autoexec.bat file, as shown in Figure 42.3:

```
C:\jdk1.1.1\jdg\Ch42>appletviewer srf.htm
```

FIGURE 42.3.

The trusted ReadFile *applet is capable to read from your local file system.*

```
: Applet Viewer: ReadFile.class                        _ □ X
 Applet

IF EXIST BPCDDRV$ \BPCDROM\MSCDEX /D:BPCDDRV$
PATH=C:\HOTJAVA\BIN;C:\HOTJAVA\RUNTIME\BIN;C:\JDK1.1.1\BIN
CLASSPATH=C:\PROGRA~1\NETSCAPE\COMMUN~1\PROGRAM\JAVA\CLASSES\
CLASSPATH=;C:\JDK1.1.1\LIB\CLASSES.ZIP;C:\jdk1.1.1;%CLASSPATH%
GS_FONTPATH=C:\gstools\gs4.03\fonts
```

Security Warning—Make Sure You Read This!

In this chapter, you've added a few identities to your javakey database. Although the inclusion of these identities does not pose a security threat, it is wise to delete these identities from your database. Suppose a security flaw in Sun's implementation of the DSA key generation algorithm were to be found. Then it may be possible for someone to predict Jason's private key and forge the signature on applets that would be trusted by your system. As you have seen from the ReadFile applet, this could have a significant impact on the security of your system. Use the following commands to delete Jason, Lisa, and Emily:

```
javakey -r Jason
javakey -r Lisa
javakey -r Emily
```

In general, trust as few identities as possible. The more identities that you trust, the higher the likelihood that your trust may be exploited.

Summary

In this chapter, you learned how to create .jar files using the Java archive tool and how to digitally sign .jar files using the javakey tool. You learned how to use javakey to manage a database of digital identities, their public keys, and signatures that guarantee the authenticity of public keys. You developed a trusted Java application that is only permitted to perform security-sensitive operations if it is digitally signed by a trusted signer. In the Chapter 43, "Working with Netscape's LiveConnect," you'll learn how to develop applets that take advantage of the LiveConnect feature of Netscape browsers.

43

Working with Netscape's LiveConnect

Netscape was one of Java's earliest supporters. The capability to execute Java applets was incorporated into Navigator 2.0, 3.0, and the Navigator 4.0 component of Netscape Communicator. Netscape has remained committed to its support of Java, making it an integral part of Navigator. The Navigator LiveConnect feature allows applets to access JavaScript objects and installed plug-ins. In this chapter, you'll learn how to use LiveConnect to build applets that use JavaScript objects. You'll also learn how to use applet methods and variables from within JavaScript. When you finish this chapter, you'll know the ins and outs of LiveConnect programming using Java.

What Is LiveConnect?

LiveConnect is a feature of Netscape browsers that supports communication between Java applets, JavaScript scripts, and plug-ins. Using LiveConnect, you can access plug-ins and JavaScript objects from within applets. You also can develop applets that can be accessed by JavaScript. LiveConnect enables all browser programs to work together in a seamless fashion.

Using LiveConnect to Access JavaScript Objects

JavaScript is Netscape's scripting language for developing client and server-side Web applications. JavaScript is also supported in limited form by Microsoft's Internet Explorer. (The Microsoft subset of JavaScript is referred to as JScript.) JavaScript borrows much of its syntax from Java.

Although JavaScript is a simple, easy-to-use scripting language, it provides a powerful object framework that can be used to manipulate browser windows, handle user events, and perform animation, among other things. As such, it is an ideal language for integrating HTML, applets, and plug-ins into advanced Web applications.

LiveConnect makes JavaScript's object hierarchy available to Java applets. You can access JavaScript objects from within applets to do such things as open and close Navigator windows, display HTML, and work with advanced Navigator features, such as layers.

There are a couple of things that you must do in order to use LiveConnect with your applets:

1. Set your CLASSPATH to include the appropriate LiveConnect classes so that you can reference them when you compile your applet. These classes are contained in the file java_*nn*, where *nn* is the version number of your copy of Navigator. For example, I use Navigator 4.0 of Netscape Communicator and include C:\PROGRA~1\NETSCAPE\ COMMUN~1\PROGRAM\JAVA\CLASSES\java_40 in my CLASSPATH. If I used Navigator 3.0, I would include java_30 in my CLASSPATH.

2. Include the MAYSCRIPT attribute in your <APPLET> tag to tell LiveConnect that you give your applet permission to access JavaScript.

3. Import the `netscape.javascript` package in your applet to make it LiveConnect aware. You should also import the `netscape.plugin` package if you intend to access plug-ins from your applet.

Having completed each of the preceding three steps, you can now use the `netscape.javascript` and `netscape.plugin` packages in your applets.

> **NOTE**
>
> The rest of this chapter assumes a basic familiarity with the JavaScript language. For more information on JavaScript, visit Netscape's documentation library at `http://developer.netscape.com`. You can also check out my new book, *Mastering JavaScript*, published by Sybex, Inc.

The `netscape.javascript` Package

The `netscape.javascript` package declares the `JSObject` class and the `JSException` class. The `JSObject` class allows you to access the JavaScript `window` object of the window in which the applet executes. The methods of this object can then be used to access other JavaScript objects and methods. The static `getWindow()` method of `JSObject` allows you to access a JavaScript `window` object:

```
JSObject win = JSObject.getWindow(this);
```

The `this` argument is used to refer to the window in which the applet executes.

The `getMember(String propertyName)` method is used to retrieve a property of a JavaScript object. The `getSlot(int index)` method is used to retrieve an indexed property (an element of a property array). Both methods return the property as an object of the `Object` class. The `setMember(String propertyName, Object newValue)` and `setSlot(int index, Object newValue)` methods are used to set the properties of a JavaScript object. The `removeMember(String propertyName)` method removes a property from a JavaScript object.

The `call(String methodName, Object args[])` method invokes the *methodName* method of a JavaScript object passing it the specified arguments array. The `eval(String expression)` method evaluates a JavaScript expression. Both methods return an object of the `Object` class.

The `toString()` method returns the `String` representation of a JavaScript object, and the `finalize()` method is used to dereference a `JSObject`.

The `JSException` class is used to define exceptions that are thrown as the result of JavaScript errors.

The `netscape.plugin` Package

The `netscape.plugin` package consists of a single `Plugin` class. This class is subclassed by plugins that provide access to Java via LiveConnect. It contains a single parameterless `Plugin()` constructor and the following methods:

- `destroy()`—The method called by Navigator to destroy a `Plugin` object. You should not call this method.
- `getPeer()`—Returns a reference to the native code implementation of a `Plugin` object.
- `getWindow()`—Returns the JavaScript `window` object in which a `Plugin` object is embedded.
- `init()`—The method called by Navigator to initialize a `Plugin` object. You should not call this method.
- `isActive()`—Returns a `boolean` value indicating whether a `Plugin` object is still active.

Specific plug-ins provide additional methods that you can use to control plug-in behavior.

A Java/JavaScript LiveConnect Example

The `GetText` applet, shown in Listing 43.1, provides an example of how JavaScript objects can be accessed from Java using LiveConnect. The HTML file (`gettext.htm`) used to load the `GetText` applet is shown in Listing 43.2.

> **NOTE**
>
> When you compile the `GetText` applet you will get a deprecation warning. This is because we use the old-style Java 1.02 event handling in the applet to support compatibility with earlier preview versions of Netscape Communicator.

Listing 43.1. The `GetText` applet.

```
import netscape.javascript.JSObject;
import netscape.javascript.JSException;
import java.applet.*;
import java.awt.*;

public class GetText extends Applet {
 Font font = new Font("TimesRoman",Font.BOLD+Font.ITALIC,36);
 Button connect = new Button("LiveConnect");
 JSObject textField;
 public void init() {
  JSObject window = JSObject.getWindow(this);
  JSObject document = (JSObject) window.getMember("document");
  JSObject form = (JSObject) document.getMember("htmlForm");
  textField = (JSObject) form.getMember("htmlTextField");
```

```
  add(connect);
 }
 public void paint(Graphics g) {
  g.setFont(font);
  g.setColor(Color.blue);
  String text = (String) textField.getMember("value");
  g.drawString(text,50,100);
 }
 public boolean handleEvent(Event event) {
  if(event.target instanceof Button &&
   event.id==Event.ACTION_EVENT){
   repaint();
   return true;
  }
  return false;
 }
}
```

Listing 43.2. The `gettext.htm` file loads the `GetText` applet.

```
<HTML>
<HEAD>
<TITLE>Accessing JavaScript from Java</TITLE>
</HEAD>
<BODY>
<FORM NAME="htmlForm">
<P>Enter some text to be read by the applet:
<INPUT NAME="htmlTextField" TYPE="text" SIZE="30"></P>
<P>Click the LiveConnect button to have the applet display
the text.</P>
</FORM>
<APPLET CODE="GetText.class" WIDTH="600" HEIGHT="300"
 MAYSCRIPT>
[The GetText Applet]
</APPLET>
</BODY>
</HTML>
```

When you open `gettext.htm`, it displays the opening window shown in Figure 43.1. Type some text in the text field and click the LiveConnect button. The `GetText` applet reads the value of the text field and displays it on the applet's default canvas, as shown in Figure 43.2.

The `GetText` applet imports the `JSObject` and `JSException` classes of the `netscape.javascript` package. It creates a `Font` object to set the text it displays to a 36-point bold italic Times Roman font. It creates the `connect` button that is used to signal the applet that it is time to read the text field and display its results. The `textField` variable is declared to be of the `JSObject` type. This is because it is used to access a JavaScript text field and not a Java `TextField` object.

The `init()` method uses the static `getWindow()` object to retrieve the JavaScript `window` object associated with the current window. This object is retrieved as a Java object of the `JSObject` class. The `document` property of the `window` object, `htmlForm` property of the `document` object, and `htmlTextField` property of the `htmlForm` object are retrieved using the `getMember()` method of the `JSObject` class. The connect button is then added to the applet container and laid out using the default flow layout.

FIGURE 43.1.

The `gettext.htm` *file opening display.*

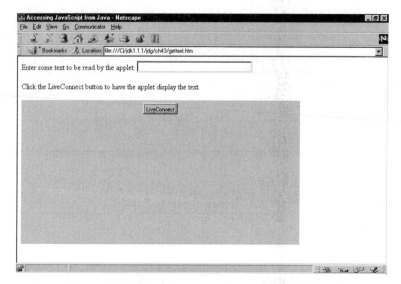

FIGURE 43.2.

The `GetText` *applet displays the text you type.*

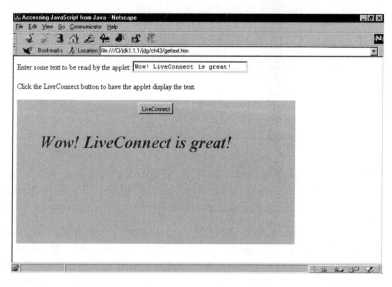

The applet's `paint()` method sets the display font to the `Font` object referred to by the `font` variable and sets the foreground color to blue. The value of the JavaScript text field is retrieved using the `getMember()` method of the `JSObject` class. The text then displays the `drawString()` method of the `Graphics` class.

The handleEvent() method implements the old-style (Java 1.02) event-handling approach. It checks the Event object passed as an argument to determine if it is the action event of a button. In this case, it invokes repaint() to redisplay the applet window and returns true to indicate that the event was handled. If the event is not the action event of a button, it returns false to indicate that the event was not handled.

Making Your Applets Accessible to JavaScript

In addition to providing applets with access to JavaScript objects and plug-ins, LiveConnect also gives you the capability to access applet methods and variables from within JavaScript. In order to access an applet's methods and variables, they must be declared public.

Listing 43.3 shows a Java applet that displays a text string at a specified location within its window. The disptext.htm file, shown in Listing 43.4, is an HTML/JavaScript file that invokes the applet's update method to display "LiveConnect" at random locations, as shown in Figure 43.3.

Listing 43.3. The DispText applet.

```
import java.applet.*;
import java.awt.*;

public class DispText extends Applet {
 public String text = "";
 public int x = 25;
 public int y = 25;
 Font font = new Font("TimesRoman",Font.BOLD+Font.ITALIC,24);
 public void paint(Graphics g) {
  setFont(font);
  g.drawString(text,x,y);
 }
 public void update(String s,int xVal,int yVal){
  text=s;
  x=xVal;
  y=yVal;
  repaint();
 }
}
```

Listing 43.4. The disptext.htm file.

```
<HTML>
<HEAD>
<TITLE>Accessing an Applet from JavaScript</TITLE>
<SCRIPT LANGUAGE="JavaScript">
function displayText(){
 x=200*Math.random()+25
 y=300*Math.random()+25
```

continues

Listing 43.4. continued

```
x=Math.round(x)
y=Math.round(y)
window.document.dispText.update("LiveConnect",x,y)
}
function setup(){
 setInterval("displayText()",2000)
}
</SCRIPT>
</HEAD>
<BODY onLoad="setup()">
<APPLET CODE="DispText.class" WIDTH="400" HEIGHT="400"
 MAYSCRIPT NAME="dispText">
[The DispText Applet]
</APPLET>
</BODY>
</HTML>
```

FIGURE 43.3.

The DispText *applet displays text in random locations.*

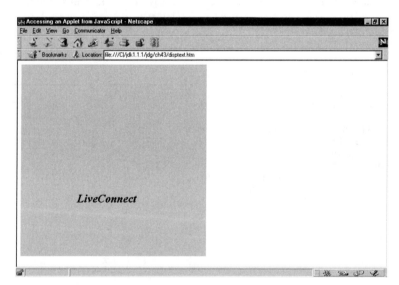

The DispText applet is easy to follow. Most of the interesting code of the application is in the disptext.htm file. DispText uses the text, x, and y variables to determine what text should be displayed and where it should be displayed. The applet initially displays a blank text string at the location (25,25). Because text, x, and y are public, these values can be set directly. However, the update() method provides a simpler interface, allowing all three variables to be specified and the repaint() method to be invoked.

Even if you've never encountered JavaScript before, you should be able to follow the script in the disptext.htm file because JavaScript's syntax is very similar to Java's. The <SCRIPT> tags enclose the declaration of the displayText() and setup() functions.

The `displayText()` function calculates the value of the x and y variables as random integers. The x variable ranges between 25 and 225 and the y variable ranges between 25 and 325. The `random()` method of the `Math` object type (JavaScript object types are the same as Java classes) returns a random floating-point value between 0 and 1. The last line of `displayText()` invokes the `update()` method of the `dispText` applet with the `"LiveConnect"` string and calculated x and y values. The `dispText` applet is a property of the `document` object (current document), which is a property of the `window` object (current window). It is named in the applet tag.

The `setup()` function invokes the `setInterval()` method of the current `window` object to set up a timer to invoke the `displayText()` function every 2,000 microseconds (that is, every two seconds).

The body tag contains the following code:

```
onLoad="setup()"
```

This invokes the `setup()` method when the entire HTML document has been loaded. This is necessary to prevent the `displayText()` method from executing before the applet is loaded.

Summary

In this chapter, you learned how to use LiveConnect to build applets that communicate with JavaScript. You also learned how to access applet variables and methods from JavaScript. In Chapter 44, "Using JavaBeans," you'll learn how to develop and use JavaBeans.

44

Using JavaBeans

Back in Chapter 22, "Building Reusable Components with java.beans," you learned about JavaBeans and the java.beans package. At that time, you did not know how to create GUI-based programs using the Abstract Window Toolkit (AWT). But now that you do, we'll revisit JavaBeans and show how beans are created and used in applets. When you finish this chapter, you'll be able to create your own beans and use them to simplify the development of applets and standalone applications.

Developing Beans

In Chapter 22, you learned about the advantages of component-based software development. You took a tour of the BeanBox and saw how beans can be visually arranged and connected to create a working application. You also covered the JavaBeans API. Now that you know how to work with graphical user interface (GUI) components using the java.awt package, and how to create applets using the java.applet package, you'll learn how to create your own beans and use them in an applet. First, you'll create a simple gauge that can be used as a widget for applets and applications. Next, you'll create a bean that can be used to display text without the use of a TextArea or TextField object. After that, you'll learn how to use these beans in an applet that displays multiple-choice quiz questions.

A Gauge Bean

When you studied all of the classes and interfaces of java.beans in Chapter 22, you might have been left with the impression that beans are complicated and hard to develop. In fact, the opposite is true. You can easily convert existing classes to beans with minimal programming overhead.

Listing 44.1 contains the code for a bean that displays a simple gauge. The gauge is displayed as a 3D-style box that is filled somewhere between its minimum and maximum values. The color of the gauge's border and its fill color are both configurable. So are its dimensions and horizontal/vertical orientation.

Listing 44.1. The Gauge.java bean.

```
import java.io.Serializable;
import java.beans.*;
import java.awt.*;
import java.awt.event.*;

public class Gauge extends Canvas implements Serializable {
 public static final int HORIZONTAL = 1;
 public static final int VERTICAL = 2;
 public static final int WIDTH = 100;
 public static final int HEIGHT = 20;
 public int orientation = HORIZONTAL;
 public int width = WIDTH;
```

```
public int height = HEIGHT;
public double minValue = 0.0;
public double maxValue = 1.0;
public double currentValue = 0.0;
public Color gaugeColor = Color.lightGray;
public Color valueColor = Color.blue;
public Gauge() {
 super();
}
public Dimension getPreferredSize() {
 return new Dimension(width,height);
}
public synchronized void paint(Graphics g) {
 g.setColor(gaugeColor);
 g.fill3DRect(0,0,width-1,height-1,false);
 int border=3;
 int innerHeight=height-2*border;
 int innerWidth=width-2*border;
 double scale=(double)(currentValue-minValue)/
  (double)(maxValue-minValue);
 int gaugeValue;
 g.setColor(valueColor);
 if(orientation==HORIZONTAL){
  gaugeValue=(int)((double)innerWidth*scale);
  g.fillRect(border,border,gaugeValue,innerHeight);
 }else{
  gaugeValue=(int)((double)innerHeight*scale);
  g.fillRect(border,border+(innerHeight-gaugeValue),innerWidth,gaugeValue);
 }
}
public double getCurrentValue(){
 return currentValue;
}
public void setCurrentValue(double newCurrentValue){
 if(newCurrentValue>=minValue && newCurrentValue<=maxValue)
  currentValue=newCurrentValue;
}
public double getMinValue(){
 return minValue;
}
public void setMinValue(double newMinValue){
 if(newMinValue<=currentValue)
  minValue=newMinValue;
}
public double getMaxValue(){
 return maxValue;
}
public void setMaxValue(double newMaxValue){
 if(newMaxValue >= currentValue)
  maxValue=newMaxValue;
}
public int getWidth(){
 return width;
}
public void setWidth(int newWidth){
 if(newWidth > 0){
  width=newWidth;
```

continues

Listing 44.1. continued

```
   updateSize();
  }
 }
 public int getHeight(){
  return height;
 }
 public void setHeight(int newHeight){
  if(newHeight > 0){
   height=newHeight;
   updateSize();
  }
 }
 public Color getGaugeColor(){
  return gaugeColor;
 }
 public void setGaugeColor(Color newGaugeColor){
  gaugeColor=newGaugeColor;
 }
 public Color getValueColor(){
  return valueColor;
 }
 public void setValueColor(Color newValueColor){
  valueColor=newValueColor;
 }
 public boolean isHorizontal(){
  if(orientation==HORIZONTAL) return true;
  else return false;
 }
 public void setHorizontal(boolean newOrientation){
  if(newOrientation){
   if(orientation==VERTICAL) switchDimensions();
  }else{
   if(orientation==HORIZONTAL) switchDimensions();
   orientation=VERTICAL;
  }
  updateSize();
 }
 void switchDimensions(){
  int temp=width;
  width=height;
  height=temp;
 }
 void updateSize(){
  setSize(width,height);
  Container container=getParent();
  if(container!=null){
   container.invalidate();
   container.doLayout();
  }
 }
}
```

To see how the bean works, copy the `Gauge.jar` file from your `ch44` directory to the `\bdk\jars` directory and then start up the BeanBox using the following commands:

```
C:\jdk1.1.1\jdg\ch44>copy Gauge.jar \bdk\jars
        1 file(s) copied

C:\jdk1.1.1\jdg\ch44>cd \bdk\beanbox

C:\BDK\beanbox>run
```

The BeanBox opens and displays the ToolBox, BeanBox, and PropertySheet windows. You will notice a new bean at the bottom of the ToolBox. This is the `Gauge` bean of Listing 44.1. Note that it comes with its own icon, as shown in Figure 44.1.

FIGURE 44.1.

The Gauge *bean has an icon in the ToolBox.*

Click the `Gauge` bean's ToolBox icon and then click in the BeanBox. The bean is displayed as a horizontal 3D box, as shown in Figure 44.2.

FIGURE 44.2.

Adding the Gauge *bean to the BeanBox.*

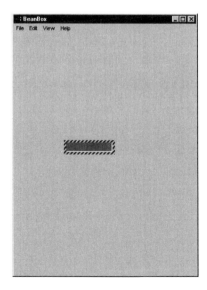

The bean's property sheet displays a number of properties that may be changed to alter the bean's appearance, as shown in Figure 44.3. The foreground, background, and font properties are the default properties of visible beans. These properties reflect the getForeground(), setForeground(), getBackground(), setBackground(), getFont(), and setFont() methods of the Component class.

FIGURE 44.3.

The Gauge *bean's*
PropertySheet.

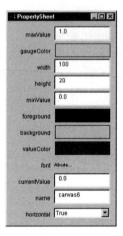

The rest of the properties shown in the style sheet are properties that are defined in Listing 44.1. The minValue and maxValue properties identify the minimum and maximum values associated with the gauge. The currentValue property identifies the current value of the gauge.

The width and height properties control the gauge's dimensions. The horizontal property takes on boolean values. When set to true, the gauge is displayed horizontally. When set to false, the gauge is displayed vertically. When the orientation of a gauge is switched, so are its width and height.

The gaugeColor and valueColor properties identify the color of the gauge's border and the color to be displayed to identify the gauge's current value.

To see how the gauge's properties work, make the following changes:

- Change the currentValue property to .7.
- Change the horizontal property to false.
- Change the height property to 200.
- Change the gaugeColor property to green.
- Change the valueColor property to orange.

Figure 44.4 shows the results of these changes on the bean's display.

FIGURE 44.4.

Changing the Gauge *bean's properties.*

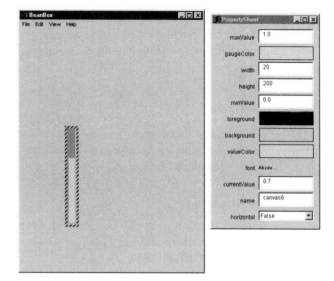

How the Gauge Bean Works

The first thing that you'll notice about the Gauge bean's source code is that it imports java.io.Serializable. All bean classes implement Serializable or Externalizable. These interfaces support bean persistence allowing beans to be read from and written to permanent storage (for example, hard disk). When a bean implements Serializable, serialization of the bean's data is performed automatically by Java, meaning you don't have to figure out how to write objects to streams or read them back in. When a bean implements Externalizable, the bean is responsible for performing all the serialization overhead. Serializable is obviously the easiest to implement of the two interfaces. All you have to do is add Serializable to your class's implements clause and poof!—serialization is automatically supported.

Besides serialization, you won't notice anything bean-specific about the rest of the Gauge class. In fact, it looks just like any other custom AWT class. Gauge extends Canvas so that it can draw to a Graphics object. It defines a few constants for use in initializing its field variables. You should note that these field variables correspond to the Gauge bean's properties.

The getPreferredSize() method is an important method for visible beans to implement. It tells application builder tools how much room is needed to display a bean. All of your visible beans should implement getPreferredSize().

The paint() method draws the bean on a Graphics object. Visible beans need to implement paint() in order to display themselves. The paint() method of Gauge works by drawing a 3D rectangle using the gaugeColor and then drawing an inner rectangle using the valueColor. The dimensions of the inner rectangle are calculated based on the value of currentValue and the orientation variables.

Gauge provides *getter* and *setter* methods for each of its properties. These methods adhere to the naming conventions used for bean properties. The Introspector class of java.beans automatically reports the properties corresponding to these methods to application builder tools, such as the BeanBox.

The switchDimensions() method is used to switch the values of width and height when the bean's orientation is switched.

The updateSize() method is invoked when the bean changes its size. It invokes setSize() to inform a layout manager of its new size. It invokes the invalidate() method of its container to invalidate the container's layout and doLayout() to cause the component to be redisplayed.

The GaugeBeanInfo Class

You may be wondering, "What about all of those other classes and interfaces of java.beans?" For simple beans, you don't really need them. However, we'll create a GaugeBeanInfo class so that the bean's icon can be displayed. The GaugeBeanInfo class is shown in Listing 44.2.

Listing 44.2. The GaugeBeanInfo class.

```
import java.beans.*;
import java.awt.*;

public class GaugeBeanInfo extends SimpleBeanInfo {
 public Image getIcon(int size) {
  switch(size){
  case ICON_COLOR_16x16:
   return loadImage("gauge16c.gif");
  case ICON_COLOR_32x32:
   return loadImage("gauge32c.gif");
  case ICON_MONO_16x16:
   return loadImage("gauge16m.gif");
  case ICON_MONO_32x32:
   return loadImage("gauge32c.gif");
  }
  return null;
 }
}
```

The GaugeBeanInfo class extends the SimpleBeanInfo class and implements one method— getIcon(). The getIcon() method is invoked by application builders to obtain an icon for a bean. It uses the constants defined in the BeanInfo interface to select a color or monochrome icon of size 16×16 or 32×32 bits.

The Gauge.mf Manifest File

The Gauge.mf manifest file, shown in Listing 44.3, is used to build the Gauge.jar file. It identifies the Gauge.class file as a bean. To create the Gauge.jar file, use the following command:

```
C:\jdk1.1.1\jdg\ch44>jar cfm Gauge.jar Gauge.mf Gauge*.class gauge*.gif
```

All the files that you need for this example are installed in your ch44 directory. Remember to copy your beans' .jar files from the ch44 directory to the \bdk\jars directory to have them loaded by the BeanBox.

Listing 44.3. The Gauge.mf manifest file.

```
Manifest-Version: 1.0

Name: Gauge.class
Java-Bean: True
```

A Text Canvas Bean

Did you ever wish that you could draw text on a canvas without having to fiddle around with fonts and font metrics? The bean that you'll develop next will make your wish come true. You can use it in place of the TextArea and TextField classes to display text in applets and window applications.

The name of this bean is TCanv, which is short for Text Canvas. The source code for the TCanv bean is shown in Listing 44.4. Let's start by learning how TCanv works. Copy the TCanv.jar file from the ch44 directory to the \bdk\jars directory using the following command:

```
C:\jdk1.1.1\jdg\ch44>copy TCanv.jar \bdk\jars
```

When you open up your BeanBox, you will notice the TCanv bean at the bottom of your ToolBox, as shown in Figure 44.5.

FIGURE 44.5.

The TCanv bean is in the ToolBox.

Click on the TCanv icon and then in the BeanBox. The TCanv bean is displayed as shown in Figure 44.6. Its property sheet is shown in Figure 44.7. The background, foreground, and font properties are the default properties of visible beans. The leftMargin and topMargin properties are used to insert space between the edges of the bean and the text it displays. The border property is used to display a border around the perimeter of the bean. The width and height properties control the bean's dimensions.

FIGURE 44.6.

The TCanv *bean is in the BeanBox.*

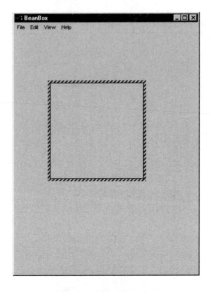

FIGURE 44.7.

The TCanv *bean's PropertySheet.*

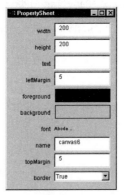

The text property identifies the actual text that is displayed by the bean. Because some application builders, such as the BeanBox, do not let you enter a new line character in a text property, the vertical bar character (¦) is used to indicate a new line. At least one character should be contained on a line for the line to be displayed.

To distinguish it from the rest of the BeanBox and to show how its properties work, make the following changes:

- Change the `text` property to This¦is¦a¦test!.
- Change the `leftMargin` and `topMargin` properties to 20.
- Change the `font` property to a 14-point font.
- Change the `background` property to yellow.

Figure 44.8 shows the effect of these changes on the bean.

FIGURE 44.8.

Changing the TCanv *bean's properties.*

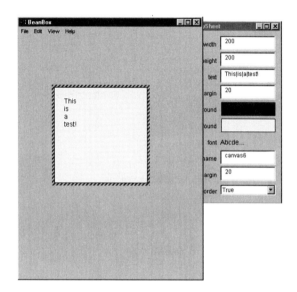

Listing 44.4. The TCanv bean.

```
import java.io.*;
import java.util.*;
import java.beans.*;
import java.awt.*;
import java.awt.event.*;

public class TCanv extends Canvas implements Serializable {
 public static final int WIDTH = 200;
 public static final int HEIGHT = 200;
 public int width = WIDTH;
 public int height = HEIGHT;
 public int leftMargin = 5;
 public int topMargin = 5;
 public String text = "";
```

continues

Listing 44.4. continued

```
public boolean border = true;
public TCanv() {
 super();
}
public Dimension getPreferredSize() {
 return new Dimension(width,height);
}
public synchronized void paint(Graphics g) {
 if(border) g.drawRect(0,0,width-1,height-1);
 Font font = g.getFont();
 FontMetrics fm = g.getFontMetrics(font);
 int lineHeight = fm.getHeight();
 int y=fm.getLeading()+fm.getAscent();
 StringTokenizer tokenizer = new StringTokenizer(text,"¦");
 String line;
 while(tokenizer.hasMoreTokens()){
  line=tokenizer.nextToken();
  if(border) g.drawString(line,leftMargin+1,topMargin+y+1);
  else g.drawString(line,leftMargin,topMargin+y);
  y+=lineHeight;
 }
}
public String getText(){
 return text;
}
public void setText(String newTextValue){
 text=newTextValue;
}
public int getWidth(){
 return width;
}
public void setWidth(int newWidth){
 if(newWidth > 0){
  width=newWidth;
  updateSize();
 }
}
public int getHeight(){
 return height;
}
public void setHeight(int newHeight){
 if(newHeight > 0){
  height=newHeight;
  updateSize();
 }
}
public int getLeftMargin(){
 return leftMargin;
}
public void setLeftMargin(int newLeftMargin){
 if(newLeftMargin >= 0) leftMargin=newLeftMargin;
}
public int getTopMargin(){
 return topMargin;
}
public void setTopMargin(int newTopMargin){
```

```
 if(newTopMargin >= 0) topMargin=newTopMargin;
}
public boolean isBorder(){
 return border;
}
public void setBorder(boolean newBorder){
 border = newBorder;
}
void updateSize(){
 setSize(width,height);
 Container container=getParent();
 if(container!=null){
  container.invalidate();
  container.doLayout();
 }
}
}
```

Inside TCanv

The TCanv class, like the Gauge class, extends Canvas and implements Serializable. It defines the field variables corresponding to its properties and implements getPreferredSize() and paint(). It also implements a few *getter* and *setter* methods. Starting to recognize a pattern?

The paint() method checks the border variable and draws a border around the bean, as required. It then gets the value of the current font and the font's FontMetrics object. It invokes the getHeight() method of the FontMetrics class to get the line height of the current font in pixels. It then uses a StringTokenizer object to parse the String object of the text variable based on the ¦ delimiter. Finally, the text is displayed one line at a time. The hasMoreTokens() and nextToken() methods of StringTokenizer are used to step through the parsed text string and to display them on the Graphics object of the bean's canvas.

Listing 44.5 shows the code of the TCanvBeanInfo. This class is similar to GaugeBeanInfo and is used to provide icons to application builders.

Listing 44.5. The TCanvBeanInfo class.

```
import java.beans.*;
import java.awt.*;

public class TCanvBeanInfo extends SimpleBeanInfo {
 public Image getIcon(int size) {
  switch(size){
  case ICON_COLOR_16x16:
   return loadImage("tcanv16c.gif");
  case ICON_COLOR_32x32:
   return loadImage("tcanv32c.gif");
  case ICON_MONO_16x16:
```

continues

Listing 44.5. continued

```
   return loadImage("tcanv16m.gif");
 case ICON_MONO_32x32:
   return loadImage("tcanv32c.gif");
 }
 return null;
 }
}
```

Listing 44.6 shows the manifest file used to create TCanv.jar. This file is used to identify the TCanv class as a bean. The following command is used to create the TCanv.jar file:

```
C:\jdk1.1.1\jdg\ch44>jar cvfm TCanv.jar TCanv.mf TCanv*.class tcanv*.gif
```

Listing 44.6. The TCanv.mf manifest file.

```
Manifest-Version: 1.0

Name: TCanv.class
Java-Bean: True
```

A Quiz Applet

Now that you have a couple of beans under your belt, let's use them in an applet. The Quiz applet, shown in Listing 44.7, uses both beans. It displays arithmetic multiple-choice quiz questions to the user. These questions are displayed in a TCanv bean. A second TCanv bean displays status information. A Gauge bean displays the user's quiz score in graphical form.

Figure 44.9 shows how the applet is initially displayed by appletviewer. The applet is displayed by opening the quiz.htm file contained in your ch44 directory. The questions are randomized; you won't display the same question, as shown in Figure 44.9. When you click on an answer, the TCanv beans are updated with new questions and status information. The Gauge bean updates the user's quiz score, as shown in Figure 44.10.

FIGURE 44.9.

The Quiz *applet as displayed by* appletviewer.

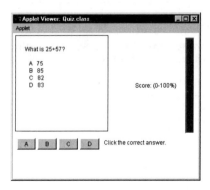

FIGURE 44.10.

Keeping track of the score using the Gauge *bean.*

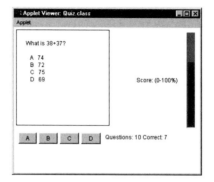

Listing 44.7. The `Quiz` applet.

```
import java.applet.*;
import java.awt.*;
import java.awt.event.*;

public class Quiz extends Applet {
 TCanv question = new TCanv();
 Gauge gauge = new Gauge();
 String labels[]={"   A   "," B   ","   C   ","   D   "};
 Button button[] = new Button[labels.length];
 TCanv status=new TCanv();
 int questions = 0;
 int correctAnswers = 0;
 int currentAnswer;

 public void init() {
  Panel mainPanel = new Panel();
  Panel gaugePanel = new Panel();
  Panel bottomPanel = new Panel();
  Panel buttons = new Panel();
  question.setLeftMargin(20);
  question.setTopMargin(20);
  gauge.setHorizontal(false);
  gauge.setMaxValue(100.0);
  gauge.setCurrentValue(100.0);
  gauge.setHeight(200);
  gauge.setWidth(20);
  status.setHeight(20);
  status.setWidth(200);
  status.setTopMargin(0);
  status.setBorder(false);
  mainPanel.setLayout(new BorderLayout());
  mainPanel.add("Center",question);
  gaugePanel.add(new Label("Score: (0-100%)"));
  gaugePanel.add(gauge);
  mainPanel.add("East",gaugePanel);
  bottomPanel.setLayout(new BorderLayout());
  for(int i=0;i<labels.length;++i){
   button[i] = new Button(labels[i]);
```

continues

Listing 44.7. continued

```
   button[i].addActionListener(new ButtonHandler());
   buttons.add(button[i]);
  }
  buttons.add(status);
  bottomPanel.add("Center",buttons);
  mainPanel.add("South",bottomPanel);
  add(mainPanel);
 }

 public void start(){
  displayQuestion();
 }

 void displayQuestion() {
  question.setText(nextQuestion());
  if(questions==0) status.setText("Click the correct answer.");
  else{
   String s="Questions: "+String.valueOf(questions);
   s+=" Correct: "+String.valueOf(correctAnswers);
   status.setText(s);
  }
 }

 String nextQuestion() {
  String q = "What is ";
  String operand[] = {"+","-","*"};
  int op1 = randomInt(100);
  int op2 = randomInt(100);
  int op = randomInt(3);
  String operator = operand[op];
  int ans=0;
  switch(op){
  case 0:
   ans=op1+op2;
   break;
  case 1:
   ans=op1-op2;
   break;
  case 2:
   ans=op1*op2;
   break;
  }
  currentAnswer=randomInt(labels.length);
  q+=String.valueOf(op1)+operator+String.valueOf(op2)+"?¦ ";
  for(int i=0;i<labels.length;++i){
   q+="¦"+labels[i];
   if(i==currentAnswer) q+=String.valueOf(ans);
   else{
    int delta = randomInt(10);
    if(delta==0) delta=1;
    int add = randomInt(2);
    if(add==1) q+=String.valueOf(ans+delta);
    else q+=String.valueOf(ans-delta);
   }
  }
  return q;
 }
```

```
int randomInt(int max){
 int r = (int) (max*Math.random());
 r %= max;
 return r;
}

void answer(int i){
 ++questions;
 if(i==currentAnswer){
  ++correctAnswers;
  displayQuestion();
 }else{
  status.setText("Try again!");
 }
 double score = (double) correctAnswers/(double) questions;
 gauge.setCurrentValue(score*100.0);
 gauge.repaint();
 question.repaint();
 status.repaint();
}

class ButtonHandler implements ActionListener {
 public void actionPerformed(ActionEvent e){
  String s = e.getActionCommand();
  for(int i=0;i<labels.length;++i){
   if(labels[i].equals(s)){
    answer(i);
    break;
   }
  }
 }
}
}
```

Inside the Quiz Applet

The Quiz applet provides a crude example of using beans in an applet. Normally, if you were using beans, you would slap together an applet using a visual programming tool. In this case, you could avoid having to do most of the applet programming.

The Quiz applet is valuable in that it shows you how beans can be used in the same manner as other GUI components. A second purpose of the applet is to make you appreciate the use of serialization. You'll learn about beans, serialization, and applets when you study a serialized clone of Quiz, named Quiz2, later in this chapter.

The Quiz applet creates two TCanv beans and assigns them to the question and status variables. A Gauge bean is created and assigned to the gauge variable. The bean assigned to the question variable displays the text of a question. The bean assigned to the status variable displays the status information to the right of the answer buttons.

The applet's init() method lays out the applet and sets the properties of the beans. The left and top margins of the question bean are set to 20. The Gauge bean is changed to vertical and its maximum value is set to 100. Its current value is also set to 100, giving the user a vote of confidence. The gauge's width and height dimensions are also modified. The dimensions of the status bean are adjusted. Its top margin is set to 0 and its border is turned off.

The applet's start() method simply invokes the displayQuestion() method to display a quiz question to the user. The displayQuestion() method invokes the question bean's setText() method to display the text of the question. The setText() method of the status bean is invoked to display status information to the user.

Questions are created by the nextQuestion() method. This method generates an arithmetic question based on the addition, subtraction, and multiplication of integers between 0 and 100. It displays the answer along with three other incorrect answers. These answers are displayed in random order.

The randomInt() method generates a random integer from 0 to one less than a specified maximum.

The answer() method supports the handling of the answer buttons by checking to see if the user answered correctly and then updating and displaying the score accordingly. The repaint() methods of the beans are invoked to cause the beans to update their respective displays.

The ButtonHandler class supports the handling of the events associated with clicking the answer buttons.

The quiz.htm file, shown in Listing 44.8, is used to display the Quiz applet.

Listing 44.8. The quiz.htm file.

```
<HTML>
<HEAD>
<TITLE>Quiz</TITLE>
</HEAD>
<BODY>
<APPLET CODE="Quiz.class" WIDTH=400 HEIGHT=300>
[Quiz applet]
</APPLET>
</BODY>
</HTML>
```

Using Serialization

While reading through the source code of the Quiz applet, you probably were wondering what benefit, if any, was derived from using beans. That's a legitimate concern. The answer is that in the absence of an application builder tool, beans are just a little easier to work with than other classes. The one feature of beans that is apparent, whether you are using beans as part of an application builder, or by hand, is their support for persistence.

The Quiz applet did not make use of persistence. Instead of customizing beans using the BeanBox, the Quiz applet included special code in the init() method to accomplish bean editing and customization. The Quiz2 applet, shown in Listing 44.9, which is a takeoff on the Quiz applet, does show how persistence is used. Listing 44.10 shows the quiz2.htm file used to display the applet. Go ahead and display quiz2.htm using the appletviewer. You should notice that the Quiz2 applet behaves in the same way as Quiz.

Listing 44.9. The Quiz2 applet.

```
import java.applet.*;
import java.awt.*;
import java.awt.event.*;
import java.beans.*;

public class Quiz2 extends Applet {
 TCanv question, status;
 Gauge gauge;
 String labels[]={"   A   "," B   "," C   "," D   "};
 Button button[] = new Button[labels.length];
 int questions = 0;
 int correctAnswers = 0;
 int currentAnswer;

 public void init() {
  Panel mainPanel = new Panel();
  Panel gaugePanel = new Panel();
  Panel bottomPanel = new Panel();
  Panel buttons = new Panel();
  try{
   question = (TCanv) Beans.instantiate(null,"qcanv");
   gauge = (Gauge) Beans.instantiate(null,"vgauge");
   status = (TCanv) Beans.instantiate(null,"scanv");
  }catch(Exception ex){
  }
  mainPanel.setLayout(new BorderLayout());
  mainPanel.add("Center",question);
  gaugePanel.add(new Label("Score: (0-100%)"));
  gaugePanel.add(gauge);
  mainPanel.add("East",gaugePanel);
  bottomPanel.setLayout(new BorderLayout());
  for(int i=0;i<labels.length;++i){
   button[i] = new Button(labels[i]);
   button[i].addActionListener(new ButtonHandler());
   buttons.add(button[i]);
  }
  buttons.add(status);
  bottomPanel.add("Center",buttons);
  mainPanel.add("South",bottomPanel);
  add(mainPanel);
 }
```

continues

Listing 44.9. continued

```
public void start(){
 displayQuestion();
}

void displayQuestion() {
 question.setText(nextQuestion());
 if(questions==0) status.setText("Click the correct answer.");
 else{
  String s="Questions: "+String.valueOf(questions);
  s+=" Correct: "+String.valueOf(correctAnswers);
  status.setText(s);
 }
}

String nextQuestion() {
 String q = "What is ";
 String operand[] = {"+","-","*"};
 int op1 = randomInt(100);
 int op2 = randomInt(100);
 int op = randomInt(3);
 String operator = operand[op];
 int ans=0;
 switch(op){
 case 0:
  ans=op1+op2;
  break;
 case 1:
  ans=op1-op2;
  break;
 case 2:
  ans=op1*op2;
  break;
 }
 currentAnswer=randomInt(labels.length);
 q+=String.valueOf(op1)+operator+String.valueOf(op2)+"?¦ ";
 for(int i=0;i<labels.length;++i){
  q+="¦"+labels[i];
  if(i==currentAnswer) q+=String.valueOf(ans);
  else{
   int delta = randomInt(10);
   if(delta==0) delta=1;
   int add = randomInt(2);
   if(add==1) q+=String.valueOf(ans+delta);
   else q+=String.valueOf(ans-delta);
  }
 }
 return q;
}

int randomInt(int max){
 int r = (int) (max*Math.random());
 r %= max;
 return r;
}

void answer(int i){
 ++questions;
```

```
 if(i==currentAnswer){
  ++correctAnswers;
  displayQuestion();
 }else{
  status.setText("Try again!");
 }
 double score = (double) correctAnswers/(double) questions;
 gauge.setCurrentValue(score*100.0);
 gauge.repaint();
 question.repaint();
 status.repaint();
}

class ButtonHandler implements ActionListener {
 public void actionPerformed(ActionEvent e){
  String s = e.getActionCommand();
  for(int i=0;i<labels.length;++i){
   if(labels[i].equals(s)){
    answer(i);
    break;
   }
  }
 }
}
}
```

Quiz2 works in the same manner as Quiz. The only difference is in how the properties of its beans are initialized. In Quiz, these properties are initialized through Java code in the init() method. In Quiz2, the question, status, and gauge beans were customized in the BeanBox and written to the qcanv.ser, scanv.ser, and vgauge.ser files. These files contain not only class information but also the values of the beans' customized properties. The instantiate() method of the Beans class is used to read the beans from serialized storage in the .ser files.

Listing 44.10. The quiz2.htm file.

```
<HTML>
<HEAD>
<TITLE>Quiz</TITLE>
</HEAD>
<BODY>
<APPLET CODE="Quiz2.class" WIDTH=400 HEIGHT=300>
[Quiz applet]
</APPLET>
</BODY>
</HTML>
```

Creating the .ser Files

You probably want to know how the .ser files were created in the first place. I used the BeanBox to customize each of the beans used by Quiz2 and saved them to .ser files using the

SerializeComponent command of the BeanBox File menu. (See Figure 44.11.) I could have written a program to create the .ser file, but working with the BeanBox is much easier.

FIGURE 44.11.

Using the
SerializeComponent
command.

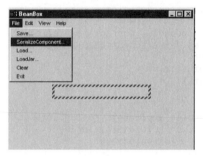

Let's change the font used to display the text of the status bean. Run the BeanBox and move a TCanv object into the box, as shown in Figure 44.12. Now edit the properties of the TCanv object as follows:

- ■ Set the height property to 20.
- ■ Set the width property to 200.
- ■ Set the topMargin property to 0.
- ■ Set the border property to false.
- ■ Change the font property to a 12-point, italic TimesRoman font.

When you have finished making these property changes, save the customized bean to a file using the SerializeComponent command under the File menu. Save the new file over the scanv.ser file that's in your Ch44\ directory.

Now open quiz2.htm with appletviewer, as shown in Figure 44.12. Note how the status text is displayed in the new font you just selected.

FIGURE 44.12.

Displaying the changed
properties.

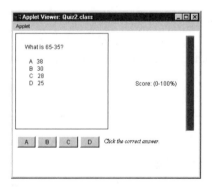

Summary

In this chapter, you revisited JavaBeans and learned how to create the Gauge and TCanv beans. You then learned how to use these beans in the Quiz applet. You also learned how serialization simplifies the process of configuring beans and saving the properties of preconfigured beans. In the next chapter, you'll cover Java's capability to support electronic commerce.

45

Java Commerce

Not only is the Web changing the way that we share information, it is also changing the way that we do business. Since the earliest days of the Web, businesses arrived in droves to advertise their wares and set up electronic store fronts. With the omnipresence of business activity throughout the Web, approaches to implementing electronic commerce were eagerly sought. JavaSoft answers the call for a practical approach to electronic commerce with its Java Electronic Commerce Framework (JECF).

In this chapter, you'll be introduced to the JECF and learn about its key components. You'll cover the JECF architecture and learn how it supports a multiplicity of electronic commerce protocols. You'll cover the Commerce API and learn about the services it provides. You'll also cover the Java Commerce Toolkit and Java Wallet. Finally, you'll learn how the Java Card API is being developed to take electronic commerce to smart cards. When you finish this chapter, you'll be familiar with the various ways in which Java is being used to support electronic commerce applications.

Java Electronic Commerce Framework

The JECF is a framework for developing products and applications that are used in electronic commerce. This framework was developed by JavaSoft to leverage Java's platform-independence to create secure and reliable software components for carrying out financial transactions.

> **NOTE**
>
> The Java Commerce home page is located at the URL http://www.javasoft.com/products/commerce/.

The JECF consists on an architecture and a set of APIs for implementing electronic commerce solutions. Its architecture consists of the following four layers:

■ The Java Environment Layer—This layer provides the foundation for the other layers. It consists of the Java virtual machine and other elements of the Java runtime environment. It may be implemented in the context of a browser, as part of the normal JDK distribution, or in hardware such as a Java microprocessor.

■ The Java Commerce Package Layer—This layer consists of those classes and interfaces that provide the foundation for developing electronic commerce applications. These classes consist of the Java Commerce API and supporting APIs, such as the Security API, JDBC, the AWT, and others. The Java Commerce Package Layer is built on top of the Java Environment Layer and supports the other layers of the JECF architecture.

■ The Cassette Layer—The Cassette Layer consists of cassettes that implement specific electronic commerce transaction protocols. Cassettes store sensitive and valuable information related to electronic financial transactions, such as account numbers, digital certificates, and payment information. They make extensive use of the encryption capabilities supported by the Java API. Unique cassettes are developed for different payment protocols, such as Secure Electronic Transaction (SET), electronic money, and online banking. The Cassette Layer is built on top of the Java Commerce Package and Java Environment Layers.

NOTE

Java Commerce cassettes are *logical* objects, not *physical* objects.

■ The Merchant Applet Layer—The Merchant Applet Layer consists of Java applets that are designed to provide an interface to financial transactions. Examples are shopping applets, banking applets, and financial investment applets. The Merchant Applet Layer is built on top of the other three layers of the JECF architecture.

Figure 45.1 provides an overview of the JECF architecture. The Java Environment and Java Commerce Layers provide the foundation for implementing electronic commerce. These layers consist of the classes and interfaces from which cassettes are built.

FIGURE 45.1.
The JECF architecture.

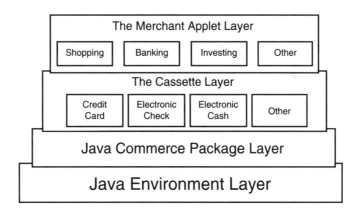

The JECF provides a flexible framework for the development of electronic commerce applications. Instead of limiting itself to a particular payment protocol, the JECF allows standard and custom payment protocols to be implemented in terms of cassettes.

Cassettes are used as the building blocks for developing electronic commerce services. Some, but not all, of these services may be presented to consumers, businesses, and other organizations in the form of Java applets. These applets will provide attractive, easy-to-use interfaces to their customers and will use cassettes to carry out commerce transactions. For example, a shopping applet may use a number of alternative cassettes to support credit card payments, electronic checks, or electronic cash.

The Java Commerce API

The Java Commerce API provides the classes and interfaces for building commerce applications within the JECF. These APIs are implemented within the Java Commerce Package Layer of the JECF architecture. These APIs support a number of capabilities including the following:

■ The downloading, installation, operation, and management of cassettes

■ The secure storage of sensitive and valuable information such as account numbers, transaction details, and encryption keys

■ A database interface

■ Special GUI controls

At the time this chapter was written, the Java Commerce API was in the Alpha 0.5 release and consisted of the following packages:

■ `java.commerce.base`—Provides base classes and interfaces that are used by other packages of the Commerce API

■ `java.commerce.cassette`—Provides classes and interfaces for the installation and operation of cassettes

■ `java.commerce.database`—Provides classes and interfaces that support database access

■ `java.commerce.example.post`—Provides two classes that are used to post credit card information and drive cassette installation

■ `java.commerce.gencc`—Provides classes and an interface for the handling of credit cards

■ `java.commerce.gui`—Provides a number of classes that implement custom GUI controls

■ `java.commerce.purchase`—Is an empty package intended to support electronic purchasing

■ `java.commerce.security`—Implements encryption and other security controls

■ `java.commerce.util`—Provides classes that encapsulate money

These packages make use of other packages of the Java Commerce Package Layer, such as those of the Security API.

The Java Commerce Toolkit

The Java Commerce Toolkit is a set of tools for developing electronic commerce applications using the Java Commerce API. You can use it to quickly get a commerce application off the ground. It includes the Java Wallet, sample Java cassettes, and a sample shopping cart applet.

The cassettes implement common electronic commerce protocols. The shopping cart applet is used by customers to hold items to be purchased while browsing through an electronic store. The Java Wallet is covered in the next section.

Java Wallet

The Java Wallet provides GUI controls that are used to carry out financial transactions. These GUI controls are designed to provide a graphical representation of a traditional wallet. Figure 45.2 provides a screen capture of the Java Wallet interface.

FIGURE 45.2.
The Java Wallet.

The purpose of the Java Wallet is to make users comfortable using electronic commerce applications. The Java Wallet interfaces with cassettes that carry out electronic commerce protocols. The wallet is extensible and can support a number of different cassettes. It was also designed with financial institutions in mind. It provides institutions with the capability to tailor the wallet to display institution-specific information, such as logos and address information, in a manner similar to credit cards, such as MasterCard and Visa.

The Java Wallet is not tied to any particular implementation. It is written in pure Java and will run on all platforms that support the Commerce API.

The Java Card API

The Java Card API is an API for creating specialized applications that run on smart cards. Smart cards are plastic cards that are the size, shape, and appearance of normal credit cards. They differ from credit cards in that they have a small programmable computer embedded within them. The card contains memory and is capable of storing a limited amount of information. The availability and use of smart cards are expected to grow tremendously toward the end of the century.

The Java Card API was developed to program smart cards. It is a specialized API in that it is designed to run on a limited version of the JVM—a JVM that runs within the tight constraints of a smart card.

The Java Card API is ISO 7816-4 compliant. This means that it will run on any standard smart card. The Java Card API can be used to program smart cards for a variety of applications, such as identification and authentication, storage of medical information, and, of course, electronic commerce. It is intended that the Java Card API be used to provide a smart card implementation of the Java Wallet.

The Java Card API consists of a single `java.iso7816` package that is based on the ISO 7816-4 standard (`http://www.iso.ch`). This package provides very low-level methods for controlling smart card operation.

Summary

In this chapter, you were introduced to the JECF and learned about its key components. You covered the JECF architecture and learned how it uses cassettes to support a range of electronic commerce protocols. You covered the Commerce API and learned about the services it provides. You also covered the Java Commerce Toolkit and Java Wallet. Finally, you learned about how the Java Card API is being used to implement electronic commerce with smart cards. In the next chapter, you'll learn how Java is used to perform server-side Web programming.

46

Server-Side Web Programming with Java

In Chapter 38, "Using Jeeves," you learned about Jeeves and the server-side Java programming capabilities that it supports through servlets. Jeeves is an example of the server-side programming capabilities that will be provided in next-generation Web servers. But what about Web servers that are currently in use? Can they be programmed in Java? The answer is a qualified yes. Currently available Web servers can be programmed in Java, but unlike Jeeves, Java is not the primary server-side programming language of these servers.

In this chapter, you'll take a look at server-side programming using Java. You'll cover the Common Gateway Interface (CGI) and learn why the CGI is not conducive to server-side Java programming. You'll learn about a CGI to Java bridge developed for Linux platforms and the server-side Java programming capabilities provided by Netscape and Microsoft Web servers. When you finish this chapter, you'll have a better understanding of the Java server-side programming options that are available to you.

Java and the Common Gateway Interface

The Common Gateway Interface was adopted early on as a standard for interfacing external programs to Web servers. The CGI allows these external programs, referred to as CGI programs or CGI scripts, to be written in such a way that they are not dependent on the particular Web server being used. The CGI specification describes a standard interface for a Web server to send browser requests to the CGI program and for the CGI program to return response data to the browser, via the Web server. These interfaces are summarized as follows.

> **NOTE**
>
> A variation of the CGI, known as WinCGI, has been popularized by some early Windows-based Web servers.

Web Server to CGI Program Communication

Web servers communicate with CGI programs using environment variables, command line arguments, and the standard input stream. These three communication methods are used as follows:

■ Environment variables—Environment variables are the most common way that a Web server passes information to a CGI program. Environment variables are variables that are defined outside of a program, but in the program's execution context, or environment. The CGI defines a number of environment variables for communicating with a CGI program. These variables are described in Table 46.1. Unfortunately, the capability for a program to read environment variables is important for CGI programming and the Java API does not support this capability well.

■ Command line arguments—Certain types of browser requests, such as HTTP ISINDEX queries, cause the Web server to pass information to CGI programs using the command line arguments of the CGI program. For example, in the following Java program invocation v1, v2, and v3 would be command line arguments:

```
java ProgramName v1 v2 v3
```

A Java program reads the command line variables via the `args` parameter of its `main()` function.

■ Standard input—Browser requests that are submitted using the POST method are sent to the CGI program via its standard input stream. This allows the CGI program to read the data using its standard I/O capabilities. Java programs use the methods of the `java.io` package to read data via an input stream.

CGI Program to Web Server Communication

While there are three ways that information is provided to a CGI program, there is only one way that the CGI program returns information to the Web server (and on to the browser). CGI program output is simply written to the standard output stream. Java programs use the methods of the `java.io` package to write data to an output stream.

There are some additions to the CGI, such as the use of non-parsed header programs, but these additions are not significant for Java programming.

Table 46.1. Environment variables used with the CGI.

Variable	Description
AUTH_TYPE	The authentication scheme used with the request
CONTENT_LENGTH	The length of standard input in bytes
CONTENT_TYPE	The MIME type of the standard input
GATEWAY_INTERFACE	The version of the CGI in use by the server
PATH_INFO	Extra path information added to the URL of the CGI program
PATH_TRANSLATED	The full path name of the CGI program
QUERY_STRING	The query string appended to the request URL
REMOTE_ADDR	The IP address of the requestor
REMOTE_HOST	The host name of the requestor
REMOTE_IDENT	The verified host name of the requestor
REMOTE_USER	The name of the user making the request
REQUEST_METHOD	The HTTP method used to make the request
SCRIPT_NAME	The name of the CGI program

continues

Table 46.1. continued

Variable	Description
SERVER_NAME	The host name of the server
SERVER_PORT	The TCP port used by the Web server
SERVER_PROTOCOL	The protocol used to submit the request
SERVER_SOFTWARE	The name and version of the Web server software

Most CGI programs are written in scripting languages. Perl and UNIX shell languages are the most popular scripting languages. CGI programs can also be written in compiled languages, such as C and C++. Some Windows-based CGI programs are written in Visual Basic, Delphi, and other Windows-specific programming languages.

Java is not a good programming language for writing CGI programs, for two reasons: It doesn't support environment variables well and the loading of the Java interpreter adds quite a bit of overhead to CGI processing.

Java's inability to read environment variables is an API problem. The pre-JDK 1.0 API was used to support the getenv() method of the System class for obtaining access to environment variables. However, this method has been deprecated and is no longer supported. Instead, the preferred solution is to use the getProperties() and getProperty() methods of the System class to access environmental properties of the Java program. When the Java interpreter is loaded and executed by a Web server, the server sets the CGI-standard environment variables in the interpreter's environment. However, the Java interpreter does not pass these variables on to the Java program as properties. This fundamental flaw makes Java incompatible with the CGI.

Even if Java programs could read the environment variables of the Java interpreter, the overhead of loading the Java interpreter for every Java CGI program is prohibitive. This is not a showstopper as far as Java CGI programming is concerned, but it is a serious limiting factor.

Because Java is a popular programming language and many people want to develop server-side programs in Java, there have been a number of approaches to making Java suited for server-side programming. In Chapter 38, you saw how Jeeves supports server-side Java programming using servlets. This is an optimal approach to server-side Java programming and will undoubtedly be the way of the future. The following sections cover some of the other approaches to server-side Java programming.

NOTE

Additional information on the Common Gateway Interface can be obtained at the URL http://hoohoo.ncsa.uiuc.edu/cgi/interface.html.

A CGI to Java Bridge

David Silber of Stellar Orbits Technology Services (http://www.orbits.com) has developed an approach and API for Java CGI programming for Web servers running on Linux systems. This approach is also portable to other UNIX implementations. David has published a How-To document concerning this approach at http://www.orbits.com/software/Java_CGI.html. His approach makes use of the Java CGI package. Links to the latest version of this package are included in the How-To document.

The Java CGI package makes use of a shell script named java.cgi that provides a bridge between the Web server and Java interpreter. This script is invoked by the Web server (as a CGI script) to process browser requests. It gathers up all of the CGI environment variables passed by the server and puts them in a temporary file. Then it starts up the Java interpreter and passes the interpreter the name of the Java class to be executed and the name of the temporary file. The name of the Java class is provided as extra path information in the URL is being requested. For example, the following URL could be used to run the YourJava program implemented by the class YourJava.class:

```
http://your.server.com/cgi-bin/java.cgi/YourClass
```

Additional information could be appended to the URL as a query string.

To further simplify the process of accessing the request data passed via the Web server and java.cgi script, David developed the Orbits.net package. This package consists of the following classes:

- CGI—Provides access to the request data as a Properties object
- Email—Creates and sends e-mail messages
- HTML—Dynamically creates an HTML document to be returned by the CGI program
- Text—The parent class of Email and HTML
- CGI_Test—Used to test the CGI class to verify that it is working correctly
- Email_Test—Used to test the Email class to verify that it is working correctly
- HTML_Test—Used to test the HTML class to verify that it is working correctly

By using java.cgi and the Orbits.net package, you can bring server-side Java programming to your UNIX Web server. However, you'll still have the overhead of invoking the Java interpreter with every CGI program instance.

Server-Side Java Programming with Netscape Servers

As you would expect, Netscape and Microsoft, being major Web server vendors, have created their own solutions to Java Web server programming. However, neither of these solutions is as elegant as Jeeves. We'll discuss Netscape's approach in this section and Microsoft's in the next.

Netscape solved the processing overhead problem of loading the Java interpreter with each CGI request by building the Java interpreter inside its FastTrack and Enterprise Web servers. The Java interpreter is loaded and started with the Web server and remains in memory throughout the server's operation. Server-side Java programs (referred to as server-side applets by Netscape) are placed in a special applets directory and installed with the Web server. The server is also configured to map specific URLs to the server-side applets.

When a browser requests the URL of an applet, the server invokes the applet and passes the request information to the applet via special classes defined in the netscape.server.applet package. These classes are as follows:

- ServerApplet—The top-level class implemented by server applets. It is similar to the Servlet interface of Jeeves's Servlet API. It provides methods for accessing browser request information and for obtaining an output stream to be used to return information to the browser.
- HttpApplet—Extends ServerApplet to support HTTP-specific requests. ServerApplet can also be extended for other types of requests, such as Gopher and FTP. Your server applets are written by subclassing HttpApplet and overriding its run() method.
- Server—Contains methods that provide information about the Web server.
- URIUtil—Contains methods used to process the URL requested by the browser.

Developing server applets using the netscape.server.applet package is a snap. You simply subclass HttpApplet with your applet and override its run() method to implement the applet's processing. Use the various methods of HttpApplet to access request information and the getOutputStream() method of HttpApplet to obtain a stream that you can use to send response information back to the browser. The netscape.server.applet package is the next best thing to Jeeves's servlets for server-side Java programming.

Server-Side Java Programming with Microsoft Servers

Microsoft's Internet Information Server provides the capability to develop server-side programs in Java. This capability, however, is buried inside of its Active Server Pages (ASP) scripting environment.

ASP is an environment for developing dynamic Web applications, primarily using VBScript and JScript (Microsoft's clone of JavaScript). ASP is developed as a substitute for the CGI. It supports the embedding of scripts within HTML files. The Web server executes these scripts when browsers request the HTML files. The results of the scripts' execution are embedded in the files before they are sent to the browsers.

Scripts may use objects to access request information provided by Web browsers and to send response information back to the browsers. The five primary objects supported by ASP are as follows:

- `Request`—Encapsulates a browser request
- `Response`—Provides the capability to send response information back to the browser
- `Server`—Provides access to the server environment
- `Application`—Provides the capability to communicate with other users of the same Web application
- `Session`—Stores information about the current browser session

The preceding objects are referred to as built-in objects. You use the properties and methods of these objects in scripts in a similar manner to the way that you would use a Java object's variables and methods.

ActiveX server components are server-side components (think of them as server-side JavaBeans) that can be used by scripts. These components can be used to provide interfaces with databases, legacy applications, or just about anything that you would use a CGI program for. You can create server-side components using a variety of languages, one of which is Java.

To build an ActiveX server component using Java, you use the object interfaces that are provided in the `asp` package. These interfaces are as follows:

- `IScriptingContext`—Used to access the five built-in ASP objects
- `IRequest`—Used to access the `Request` object
- `IResponse`—Used to access the `Response` object
- `IServer`—Used to access the `Server` object
- `IApplicationObject`—Used to access the `Application` object
- `ISessionObject`—Used to access the `Session` object
- `IReadCookie`—Allows cookies to be read
- `IWriteCookie`—Supports writing of cookies
- `IRequestDictionary`—Used to access client certificates
- `IStringList`—Used to access the individual values of a browser request

The ASP approach to Web applications wasn't exactly developed with Java in mind. You can develop ActiveX server components in Java, but you're probably better off using the ASP scripting languages. If you have the urge to develop server-side programs in Java, get Jeeves or a Netscape server. The server-side programming capabilities they offer are both elegant and easy to use.

Summary

In this chapter, you delved into the issues involved with server-side programming using Java. You covered the Common Gateway Interface and learned why the CGI is not conducive to server-side Java programming. You learned about a CGI to Java bridge developed for Linux platforms and the server-side Java programming capabilities provided by Netscape and Microsoft Web servers. In the next chapter, you'll learn about a new way to distribute information over the Internet using the Castanet transmitter and tuner.

47

Java Broadcasting and Castanet

One of the new and interesting technologies developed using Java is the Castanet product for automating the distribution of Web applications and software. Castanet, developed by Marimba, Inc., consists of a client/server publishing system that automatically updates users' computers with Web applications and software that are made available over specific distribution channels. In this chapter, you'll be introduced to Castanet and learn how the Castanet Transmitter and Tuner are used to publish applets and other executable content. When you finish this chapter, you'll be able to use Castanet to publish your own Java applets.

What Is Castanet?

Castanet is a new paradigm for distributing Web applications and software that was developed by Marimba, Inc. (http://www.marimba.com), a company that was started by four of the original members of the Java team. Marimba provides three main products that are used to implement Castanet:

- Castanet Tuner—Castanet Tuner is a freely distributed client for accessing Castanet channels. It is similar to a TV or radio tuner. It allows users to select channels over which specific Web applications are distributed. Castanet Tuner receives applications that are published on a channel and stores them on users' computers. It also provides a GUI front end for managing and executing these applications.

- Castanet Transmitter—Castanet Transmitter is the server component of Castanet. It is used to publish Web applications over specific channels that are received, installed, and executed by the Castanet Tuner client.

- Bongo—Bongo is a visual development environment that is used to create applications, called *presentations*, that are published using Castanet. Bongo greatly speeds up the process of application development. However, it is not needed to develop Castanet applications. Castanet applications can be developed just using HTML and Java.

All three of these Marimba products were developed in Java. They are available for Windows 95, Windows NT, and Solaris platforms. Ports of these products are also available for Linux and other operating system platforms.

> **NOTE**
>
> Version 1.0 of Castanet and Bongo only support the Java Development Kit 1.02. Applications written using the newer JDK 1.1 API do not work with Castanet.
>
> Castanet also provides repeater and proxy products. Repeaters are used to add supplementary transmission capabilities. Proxies are used to support transmission through a firewall.

How Castanet Works

Castanet uses the analogy of radio and television broadcasting. Web applications are published using Castanet Publish, a component of Castanet Transmitter. These applications may consist of simple HTML files, Java applets, presentations developed using Bongo, or Java applications. The applications are published to a Castanet Transmitter and are associated with a named channel. The Castanet Transmitter is analogous to a Web server. A channel is analogous to a Web site. For example, Marimba provides a transmitter on the host `trans.marimba.com`. This transmitter provides access to a number of channels ranging from Castanet documentation to a couple of interesting games.

The Castanet Tuner is a client that is run by users in order to access Castanet channels. The tuner allows users to subscribe to a particular Castanet Transmitter and channel. When a user subscribes to a channel, the tuner contacts the transmitter responsible for that channel and downloads all of the files published on that channel to a directory on the user's computer. It then allows the user to execute these applications locally. The tuner also periodically checks back with the transmitter to see if the application files have been updated, and if so, downloads any changes to the user's computer. In this way, the user is ensured of having the latest information that is published on a channel available locally on his computer.

Figure 47.1 summarizes how Castanet works. A content developer creates HTML files, Java applets and applications, and Bongo presentations that he wants to publish. He organizes these files into three channels: A, B, and C. For example, A could be news and weather, B could be art and literature, and C could be games. He uses Castanet Publisher to publish these files to a transmitter. Different users subscribe to these channels using their tuner clients. The tuners download the files for the subscribed channels and store them on the users' hard drives. The users execute the application files locally using the tuner. The tuner also periodically checks back with the transmitter and updates the locally stored application files after they have been updated and republished by the content developer.

What's So Good About Castanet?

As you can see in Figure 47.1, Castanet uses a much different approach than most other Internet client/server systems. In most client/server systems, the interaction between a client and server is limited to a single transaction or a single group of transactions. For example, when a Web browser fetches a Web page from a Web server, the interaction between the browser and the server is complete. The user may never go back to that Web page again. In Castanet, once you subscribe to a channel, your tuner periodically checks back with the transmitter to make sure that you have the latest content published on the channel. If new information is published on the channel, the tuner automatically downloads it to the user's hard drive. This is a great benefit to the user, allowing him to keep abreast of the latest information of interest without having to continually check back with the server. The tuner does all the leg work for him.

FIGURE 47.1.
How Castanet works.

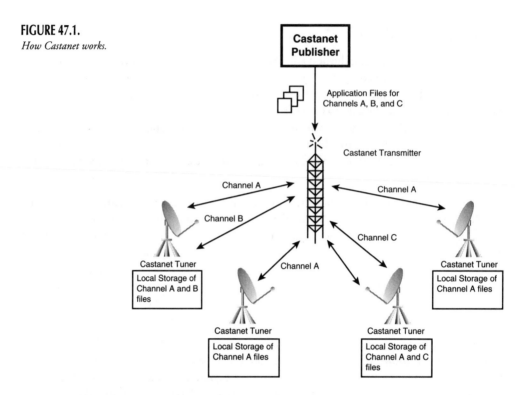

Another advantage of the Castanet approach is that the tuner maintains the information that is published on a channel, locally on the user's hard disk. This means that the user does not have to be connected to the Internet to access this information. For example, suppose you were using a notebook computer. You could dial into your Internet service provider and use your tuner to subscribe to a channel. Your tuner would download the channel's content and store it on your hard drive. You could then take your notebook computer on a plane and access the channel's content while you were flying away to a distant location. When you arrived at your destination, you could call into your ISP and get an update of any new content that was added to the channel.

Castanet is especially helpful to users that have low-bandwidth Internet connections. Because the tuner works in the background to update your channels, it can be checking on your favorite channels while you are running other applications or doing other things. You can leave your computer running overnight and when you wake up the next day, it will be automatically updated with the latest channel content.

As mentioned earlier, Castanet channels support HTML, Java applets and applications, and Bongo presentations. Bongo presentations are a scripted hybrid of applets and applications. Think of them as Java applets or applications that are implemented using scripts rather than byte code.

When HTML files are published over a channel, the tuner executes them by invoking your default browser. You must configure your browser to use Castanet as a local proxy for accessing the Web. Castanet works with both Netscape Navigator and Microsoft Internet Explorer, as well as other popular browsers. The main advantage of Castanet, when used for HTML publishing, is that it maintains the HTML files on your system. When you need to access them, they're there. You don't have to worry about accessing the Internet or whether the destination Web server is down.

When Java applets are published over a channel, the tuner executes the applet in much the same way as the appletviewer tool of the JDK. The tuner provides the applet with all of the capabilities that it would have if it were executed via a browser. For example, an applet can retrieve and display images and play audio files. Castanet is an advantage for applet developers and users. Because Castanet maintains the applet and the files used by the applet on users' computers, the applet developer can use more bandwidth-consuming audio, image, and video files. When users access the applet, they don't have to wait for the multimedia files to be downloaded. They're waiting for them on their hard disks. Most applets can be used with Castanet without modification.

When Java applications are published over a channel, the tuner executes the application locally on your machine. However, the tuner implements a security manager that prevents the application from causing any damage to your system. The security manager confines all application disk I/O to a specific directory on your hard disk, prevents applications from making network connections to any host other than the transmitter, and keeps applications from executing local programs or dynamic link libraries. Castanet facilitates the installation and execution of Java applications, while limiting the exposure of users to accidental or deliberate damage.

The Castanet Tuner

The Castanet Tuner is freely available for download from Marimba's Web site. It is supported on Windows 95, Windows NT, and Solaris platforms. It has also been ported to Linux and other operating systems. The Linux version is available from the Java Linux Web site at `http://www.blackdown.org/java-linux/Products.html`. The Windows 95 version of Castanet Tuner is distributed as a self-extracting executable file that installs quickly and easily on your system. Go ahead and download and install Castanet Tuner. When you have finished, select Castanet Tuner from the Start menu to run it.

NOTE

When you first run the tuner, it will connect to Marimba's transmitter and update itself with the latest version of the tuner software. This may take a few minutes.

Figure 47.2 shows how the tuner appears when you execute it. It provides five tabs that are used to access various parts of the application. The Marimba tab displays the Marimba logo and copyright information.

FIGURE 47.2.

The Castanet Tuner.

The Channels tab lists the channels that you are currently subscribed to and allows you to execute these channels by double-clicking on them. (See Figure 47.3.)

FIGURE 47.3.

The Channels tab lists the channels to which you've subscribed.

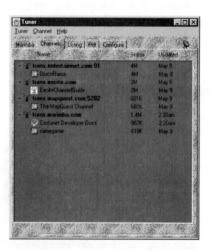

The Listing tab allows you to list all of the channels that are available from a particular transmitter, as shown in Figure 47.4. Just enter the host name of the transmitter and click on the List button. You can subscribe to a channel by double-clicking on it.

FIGURE 47.4.

The Listings tab lists the channels of a transmitter.

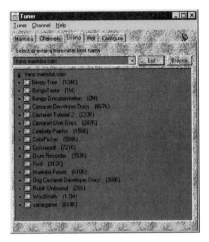

The Hot tab displays those channels that are new and interesting, as shown in Figure 47.5.

FIGURE 47.5.

The Hot tab identifies channels of interest.

The Configure tab, shown in Figure 47.5, allows you to configure your tuner. It contains the Updates, User, Network, and Options subtabs. The Updates subtab lets you control how frequently the tuner contacts transmitters. The User subtab allows you to enter name and address information. The Network subtab is used to configure a firewall proxy. The Options subtab is used to configure your network connection.

FIGURE 47.6.

The Configure tab lets you configure your tuner.

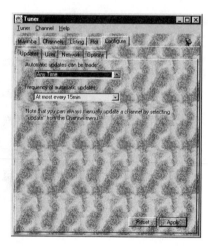

Subscribing to a Channel

We'll subscribe to a transmitter and channel to show you how it works. Click on the Listing tab, enter trans.marimba.com in the pull-down text field, and click on the List button. A listing of the Marimba channels is displayed, as shown in Figure 47.4. Double-click on the SameGame channel. This subscribes you to the SameGame Channel. The SameGame application is downloaded and then executed, as shown in Figure 47.7. You can play the game by clicking twice on groups of two or more squares of the same color. The objective is to remove all of the squares.

FIGURE 47.7.

The SameGame channel.

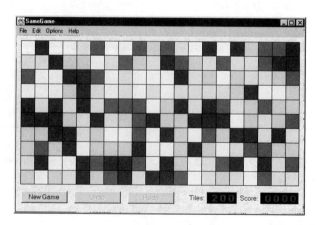

When you are finished with the SameGame channel, close it and return to the Listing tab. Enter gday.bloke.com:81 and click the List button. The channels for the gday.bloke.com transmitter are listed. Double-click on the What's New channel to subscribe to it. This channel provides a great starting place to learn about other channels. Its application window is shown in Figure 47.8.

FIGURE 47.8.
The What's New channel.

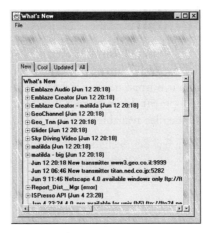

When using Castanet Tuner to access transmitter channels, remember that it stores all channel content locally on your hard disk. If you are not vigilant about your channel usage, you'll find yourself running out of hard disk storage space.

The Castanet Transmitter

The Castanet Transmitter is a product of Marimba, Inc. It is not freeware or shareware. However, Marimba makes evaluation copies available for download from its Web site. Castanet Transmitter also comes in Windows 95, Windows NT, and Solaris versions. The Windows 95 version is distributed as a self-extracting executable installation program.

To run the examples later in this chapter, you'll need to download and install Castanet Transmitter.

Castanet Transmitter allows you to create your own channels for distributing executable content and HTML files over the Internet. It consists of two products: the transmitter itself and Castanet Publish. The transmitter is self-installing and provides excellent help support. Castanet Publish is covered in the next section.

Castanet Publish

You use Castanet Publish to publish your executable content to a transmitter. Castanet Publish doesn't provide any Web content development capabilities. You develop your Java and HTML files using your normal development tools. All Castanet Publish does is move your files from your development directory to a directory on the transmitter and configure your transmitter to make the files available over a particular channel.

Castanet comes with a few demo channels. These channels are contained in the `C:\Marimba\ Castanet Transmitter\channels` directory. I'll show you how to publish one so that you'll learn how Castanet Publish works. If you do not have your transmitter running, now is a good time to start it.

> **WARNING**
>
> You cannot circumvent Castanet Publish by copying files directly to your transmitter. Castanet Publish must copy your files so that it can properly configure them on a channel.

Open Castanet Publish from the Start menu. It displays the window shown in Figure 47.9.

FIGURE 47.9.
The Castanet Publish opening window.

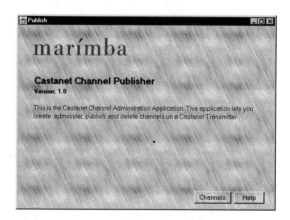

Click on the Channels button to go to the Channels under Development window, shown in Figure 47.10.

Click the Add button to go to the Add/Create a Channel window, shown in Figure 47.11.

FIGURE 47.10.

The Channels under Development window.

FIGURE 47.11.

The Add/Create a Channel window.

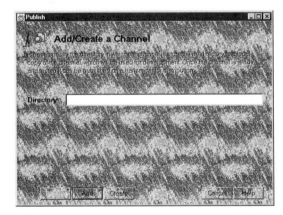

Enter `C:\Marimba\Castanet Transmitter\channels\Crossword` and click the Add button. The channel is added to the Channels under Development window, as shown in Figure 47.12.

FIGURE 47.12.

The channel is added to the Channels under Development window.

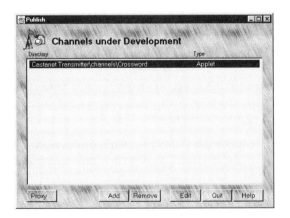

Now click the Edit button. The seven-tabbed window, shown in Figure 47.13, is displayed.

FIGURE 47.13.
The channel configura-
tion tabs.

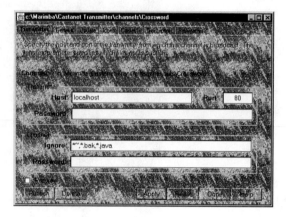

You can use these tabs to configure your channel before publishing it. These tabs are described in the following paragraphs:

■ The Transmitter tab is used to identify the host name and port of the transmitter. Use `localhost` if you are publishing to a transmitter on the same host as Castanet Publish. You can enter a password for your transmitter or the channel you are publishing. You can also specify file types that are excluded from being published. Never exclude `*.txt` files because they are used by the transmitter to store channel configuration information.

■ The General tab allows you to name your channel and to identify the type of channel that you are publishing. Four different types of channels can be published: HTML, Java Applet, Java Application, and Bongo Presentation. When you select one of these types, configuration fields for that type are displayed.

■ The Update tab lets you specify the frequency at which tuners should check back with the transmitter for channel updates. The Inactive parameters refer to when your channel application is not executing. The Active parameters refer to when your channel application is executing. The Data Available Action field tells the tuner what to do with new channel updates.

■ The Icons tab allows you to specify icons to be used with your channel.

■ The Contacts tab allows you to specify information that channel users can use to contact you.

■ The Description tab allows you to specify descriptive information about your channel.

■ The Parameters tab is used to specify applet parameters.

Now that you've taken a brief tour through publisher, click the Publish button to publish the Crossword channel.

Click the Done button twice and then the Quit button to exit Castanet Publish.

FIGURE 47.14.

Publishing the Crossword channel.

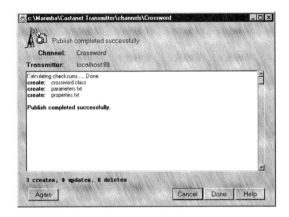

Running the Crossword Application

Now that you've published the Crossword channel to your transmitter, you can use your tuner to execute it. Open your tuner and turn to the Listing tab. Enter the host name of your transmitter and click the List button. The Crossword channel is displayed under your transmitter, as shown in Figure 47.15. Double-click on the Crossword channel to execute it.

FIGURE 47.15.

Listing the Crossword channel on your transmitter.

Figure 47.16 shows the Crossword channel. It displays a crossword puzzle that you can complete.

FIGURE 47.16.

*Executing the
Crossword channel.*

Creating an Applet and Publishing It with Castanet

Although we haven't covered all of Castanet's features or capabilities, you now know enough to develop an applet and publish it using Castanet. Listing 47.1 shows the Gallery applet. The Gallery applet is contained in the ch47\publish directory. It is written using the old-style Java 1.02 event handling. Remember Castanet 1.0 does not support the JDK 1.1. When you compile the applet, you will get a deprecation warning. You can ignore this warning.

After you compile the Gallery applet, the ch47\publish directory contains the following files:

- Gallery.java
- Gallery.class
- MyCanvas.class
- image.jpg
- audio.au

The image.jpg file contains a photographic image. The audio.au file contains an audio description of the photo.

Now use Castanet Publish to distribute the applet and its supporting files via a channel. When you open Castanet Publish, click the Channels button to go to the Channels under Development window. Then click the Add button. Type c:\jdk1.1.1\jdg\ch47\publish in the Directory text field (as shown in Figure 47.17) and then click the Add button.

FIGURE 47.17.

Specifying the channel's source directory.

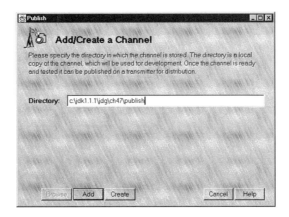

The channel configuration window is displayed. Click on the General tab. Set the Name field to `Daily Photo Gallery`. Set the Type field to `Applet`. Set the Code field to `Gallery`. Set the Width field to `500` and the Height field to `450`, as shown in Figure 47.18.

FIGURE 47.18.

Specifying the channel's name and type.

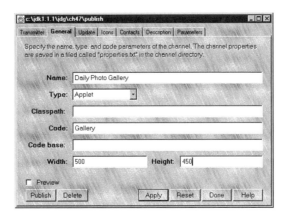

Click on the Update tab and then set the Update Frequency for an Inactive application to Daily. Then click the Publish button. The `Gallery` channel is published to your transmitter. Castanet Publish displays a confirmation, as shown in Figure 47.19. Go ahead and exit Castanet Publish.

Start your tuner and click on the Listing tab. Enter the host name of your transmitter and click the List button. The name of the new channel is displayed, as shown in Figure 47.20.

Double-click on the Daily Photo Gallery channel and the `Gallery` applet is executed, as shown in Figure 47.21. You can click the Audio Description button to find out information about the photograph that is displayed. Close the applet and the tuner.

FIGURE 47.19.
Confirming the channel's publication.

FIGURE 47.20.
Listing the new channel under your transmitter.

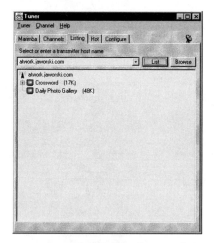

FIGURE 47.21.
The Daily Photo Gallery channel.

Updating the Information Displayed By the Applet

The previous example shows how easy it is to publish an applet using Castanet. In this section, I'll show you how easy it is to update the information displayed by the applet. In your `ch47` directory are files named `image2.jpg` and `audio2.au`. These files contain a new image and audio description. Copy these files over the `image.jpg` and `audio.au` files contained in the `publish` subdirectory as follows:

```
C:\jdk1.1.1\jdg\ch47>copy image2.jpg publish\image.jpg
Overwrite publish\image.jpg (Yes/No/All)?y
        1 file(s) copied

C:\jdk1.1.1\jdg\ch47>copy audio2.au publish\audio.au
Overwrite publish\audio.au (Yes/No/All)?y
        1 file(s) copied
```

You've just updated the Daily Photo Gallery's source directory. Now let's publish the new information to the transmitter. Open Castanet Publish and click the Channels button. Select the channel and click the Edit button. Now click the Publish button to republish the channel. That's all you need to do to update your channel. You can exit from Castanet Publish.

Because your channel specified a daily update frequency, all channel tuners will check back with your transmitter in about a day to get the updated channel information. Let's check out the new information that you published. Open your tuner and click on the Channels tab. Now double-click on the Daily Photo Gallery channel. The same photo that was displayed in Figure 47.21 is displayed. That's because your tuner didn't check in with your transmitter yet.

Close the Daily Photo Gallery channel, but keep it selected in the Channels tab of your tuner. Select Update from the Channel pull-down menu to force your tuner to check back with the transmitter. Now double-click on the Daily Photo Gallery channel again. This time it displays the photo shown in Figure 47.22.

FIGURE 47.22.

The Daily Photo Gallery channel.

How the Gallery Applet Works

Up to this point, we've been focusing on how Castanet works. In this section we'll describe how the Gallery applet works. It creates two field variables named image and audio to refer to the image that is displayed and its associated audio description. The init() method invokes the getCodeBase() method of the Applet class to retrieve the URL associated with the applet's code base. This URL is used to read the image and audio files that are located in the same directory as the applet. Even though the applet, image file, and audio file are executed by a tuner from the user's hard disk, we can still use getCodeBase() to refer to their location. The getImage() and getAudioClip() methods retrieve the image and audio files. The rest of init() consists of applet layout.

The stop() method simply stops the playing of the audio file.

The handleEvent() method is used to perform old-style JDK 1.02 event handling. (Remember Castanet 1.0 doesn't work with JDK 1.1.) The handleEvent() method checks an event to see if a button was clicked and, if so, plays the audio file.

The MyCanvas class is used to display the image in the middle of the applet window. The paint() method calculates the difference between the canvas size and the image size and adjusts the image to the center of the canvas. Note that the deprecated JDK 1.02 size() method is used instead of the JDK 1.1 getSize() method.

Listing 47.1. The Gallery applet.

```
import java.applet.*;
import java.awt.*;
import java.net.*;

public class Gallery extends Applet {
 AudioClip audio;
 Image image;
 public void init() {
  try {
   URL base = getCodeBase();
   image = getImage(base,"image.jpg");
   audio = getAudioClip(base,"audio.au");
   setLayout(new BorderLayout());
   add("Center",new MyCanvas(image));
   add("South",new Button("Audio Description"));
  }catch (Exception ex) {
  }
 }
 public void stop() {
   audio.stop();
 }
 public boolean handleEvent(Event event) {
  if(event.target instanceof Button){
   audio.play();
   return true;
  }
```

```
  return false;
 }
}
class MyCanvas extends Canvas {
 Image image;
 public MyCanvas(Image image) {
  this.image = image;
 }
 public void paint(Graphics g) {
  Dimension canvasSize = size();
  int imageHeight = image.getHeight(this);
  int imageWidth = image.getWidth(this);
  int x = (canvasSize.width - imageWidth)/2;
  int y = (canvasSize.height - imageHeight)/2;
  if(x<0) x=0;
  if(y<0) y=0;
  g.drawImage(image,x,y,this);
 }
}
```

Other Castanet Publishing Capabilities

So far, you have seen how easy it is to publish applets with Castanet. However, Castanet provides many more capabilities than we've covered here. Some of these capabilities are as follows:

- Java applications can be published using Castanet. Marimba provides special classes that can be used to implement applications as channels.

- Java applications can be updated while they are executing to take advantage of information that is dynamically published.

- Java applications can maintain information locally on the user's hard disk.

- Java applications can send information back to transmitters that can be used to keep track of user preferences.

- Bongo presentations can be published using Castanet. Bongo presentations are easy to develop using Bongo's visual development environment and Java-based scripting language.

The use of these capabilities in channels is a book in itself. For more information, I suggest that you subscribe to the Castanet Developer Docs channel that is published by trans.marimba.com.

Summary

In this chapter, you were introduced to Castanet and you learned how the Castanet Transmitter and Tuner are used to automatically distribute Java applets and other executable content.

You created an applet, published it using Castanet publisher, and then updated the information displayed by the applet. This chapter concludes Part VI, "Web Programming." In Part VII, "Database Programming," you'll learn all about Java's database programming capabilities.

VII

Database Programming

48

Database Fundamentals

Back in Chapter 19, "Connecting to Databases with the `java.sql` Package," you studied the `java.sql` package and learned how to use its classes and interfaces to connect to databases and to execute SQL statements that add data to and retrieve data from databases. Chapter 19 is oriented toward describing the JDBC API. Depending upon your prior experience with database programming, the material presented in Chapter 19 might have ranged from illuminating to confusing. This chapter provides background information on database programming. You'll learn how relational databases work and how SQL is used to update and retrieve data from relational databases. You'll learn how databases are accessed and about the different types of drivers that can be used. When you finish this chapter, you'll have the background you need to begin Java database programming. If you made your way through Chapter 19 without difficulty, you can probably skip over this chapter.

What Is a Database?

A *database* is a collection of data that is organized so that it may be easily searched and updated. The important feature of a database is its organization. A database's organization supports both ease of use and efficient data retrieval. Consider an office that is organized with numbered file cabinets containing carefully labeled folders. Office information is stored by subject in specific folders that are kept in designated file cabinets. In such a system, every folder has its place, and it is easy to find a particular folder. Now consider a different environment where information is stored in folders but the folders are haphazardly stored in boxes that are placed at seemingly random locations throughout an office building. How do you find a particular folder in such an environment? Where do you store a folder when you're finished with it?

The well-organized environment is analogous to a database. Information that is entered into a database is stored in specific locations within the database. Because of the database's structure and organization, information can be easily retrieved. The database can be accessed remotely and is shared among many users.

The unorganized environment is analogous to a situation where information is stored in files on various user's computers. In such an environment, it is very hard to locate information. What file contains the information you need? Whose computer contains that file? Where is the computer located? Where is the file located in the user's file system?

A *database server* is a software program that manages databases, keeps them organized, and provides shared access to its databases. Database servers manage and organize databases at both a physical level and at a logical level. At a *physical level*, database servers store database information in specific locations within the particular files, directories, and disk volumes used by the server. The server keeps track of what information goes where so that you don't have to know or care how the information is physically stored. The server is like a trusty office assistant that you can turn to and say, "Get me the file on..." and the assistant immediately retrieves the information you need and places it on your desk.

As previously mentioned, database servers also manage and organize information at a *logical level*. This logical level corresponds to the type of information that you store in a database. For example, you may have a database that stores the names, companies, e-mail addresses, and phone numbers of your business contacts. The logical organization of the database could consist of a `Contacts` table with five columns: `LastName`, `FirstName`, `Company`, `Email`, and `Phone`. Specific contacts would be identified by rows of the table, as shown in Table 48.1.

Table 48.1. A business contact table.

LastName	FirstName	Company	Email	Phone
Smith	Joe	XYZ, Corp.	joe@xyz.com	(123) 456-7890
Jones	Sally	UVW, Corp.	sally@uvw.com	(234) 567-8901
Woods	Al	RST, Corp.	al@rst.com	(345) 678-9012

Relational Databases

While there a number of different ways that databases can be logically organized, one particular organization, called the *relational model*, is the predominant method by which modern databases are organized. The relational model was developed by E.F. Codd, a mathematician at IBM, during the late 1960s. Databases that adhere to the relational model are referred to as *relational databases*.

Relational databases are organized into tables that consist of rows and columns. As shown in Table 48.1, the columns of the table identify what type of information is contained in each row. The rows of the table contain specific records that have been entered in the database. The first row of Table 48.1 indicates that Joe Smith works for XYZ, Corp., and has e-mail address joe@xyz.com and phone number (123) 456-7890. (The table column headings are not counted as rows within the table.)

Organizing Tables

A relational database can have one table or 1,000 tables. The number of tables is only limited by the relational database server software and the amount of available physical storage. Some relational database servers, also referred to as *relational database management systems* (RDBMs), organize tables into schemas. A *schema* is a collection of tables where the tables of a database belong to exactly one schema. In a similar fashion, schemas are organized into *catalogs*. Each schema belongs to exactly one catalog, as shown in Figure 48.1. The purpose of schemas and catalogs is to organize tables into related groups and to control access to the information contained in a database according to these groups.

FIGURE 48.1.
*Tables are organized
into schemas and
catalogs.*

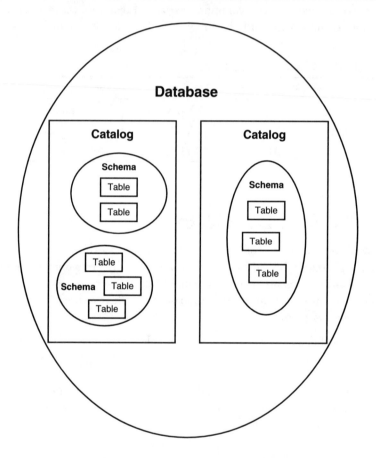

Working with Keys

Access to information contained within tables is organized by keys. A *key* is a column or group of columns that uniquely identifies a row of a table. Keys are used to find a particular row within a table and to determine whether a new row is to be added to a table or to replace an existing row. Suppose that the business contacts table of Table 48.1 was updated to include everybody in the world with an e-mail address. What columns should we use as a key? At first glance we may choose the LastName column. However, many people have the same last names. After further consideration, even if we chose the LastName, FirstName, and Company columns as our key, we would still run into problems with companies that had more than one Joe Smith working for them. However, the `Email` column would make a good key. If two people in the same company have the same name, they are still given unique e-mail addresses, such as joe@xyz.com and joe.smith@xyz.com. (For the purpose of the example, we'll ignore the cases where people share the same e-mail address or a person has more than one e-mail address.)

Using `Email` as our key, we can easily manage our business contacts table. When we update the table, we can check to see whether the `Email` column of the new row is already in the table. In this case, we can overwrite the existing row with new information. If the `Email` column of the new row is not in the table, we can add a new row to the table.

Normalizing Tables

When we design the tables of a database, how do we decide what information to put in which tables? Is it better to use one big table or lots of little tables?

The answer to these questions was provided by Codd in his paper on the relational data model. He described a process called *normalization*, which could be used to optimize the way that data is organized into tables. The purpose of normalization is to minimize the number of columns in database tables and promote data consistency. More tables with fewer columns are the result of normalization. Five levels of normalization are recognized. A database that is normalized to a particular level is said to be in *normal form* for that level (that is, first normal form through fifth normal form). The purpose of normalization is to remove redundant information from the database to simplify database update and maintenance.

First normal form is the simplest and easiest to achieve. In first normal form, duplicate columns of a table are eliminated. For example, consider Table 48.2. This table keeps track of how much taxes an individual paid in the years 1995 through 1997. The first column is the person's social security number and is the key for the table. The second through fourth columns represent the amount of tax an individual paid.

Table 48.2. Individual taxes paid table.

SSN	Tax95	Tax96	Tax97	
123-45-6789	10,000	11,000	11,500	
234-56-7890	4,500	5,000	5,250	

Because the second through fourth columns contain the same type of information, the table can be put into first normal form by organizing it as shown in Table 48.3.

Table 48.3. First normal form of individual taxes paid table.

SSN	Year	Tax
123-45-6789	95	10,000
123-45-6789	96	11,000
123-45-6789	97	11,500
234-56-7890	95	4,500
234-56-7890	96	5,000
234-56-7890	97	5,250

Subsequent normal forms are more complicated and harder to achieve. In most cases, achieving high levels of normalization are neither necessary nor desired. For example, databases that are put in fifth normal form have a high degree of consistency because redundant database columns are eliminated. However, this consistency comes at the expense of requiring more tables. The additional number of tables increases the storage space required by the database as a whole and also increases the time to perform a database search. In general, database design is a trade-off between data consistency, database size, and database performance.

Structured Query Language

The Structured Query Language, or SQL (pronounced *sequel*), is a language for interacting with relational databases. It was developed by IBM during the 1970s and 1980s and standardized in the late 1980s. The SQL standard has been updated over the years and several versions currently exist. In addition, several database vendors have added product-specific extensions and variations to the language. The JDBC requires JDBC-compliant drivers to support the American National Standards Institute (ANSI) SQL-92 Entry Level version of the standard that was adopted in 1992. The SQL Standards Home Page (http://www.jcc.com/sql_stnd.html) contains information about SQL standardization.

SQL has many uses. When SQL is used to create or design a database, it is used as a *data definition language*. When SQL is used to update the data contained in a database, it is used as a *data maintenance language*. When SQL is used to retrieve information from a database, it is used as a *data query language*. We'll cover each of these uses in the following subsections.

> **NOTE**
>
> The following sections present enough SQL to get you started in database programming. For a complete description of SQL, check out the SQL Standards home page for links to standards and books on SQL. More sophisticated versions of the described

SQL statements may be available. Consult the ANSI SQL standard for a complete description of each statement.

Using SQL as a Data Definition Language

You can use SQL to define a database. For example, there are SQL statements to create a database, create tables and add them to a database, update the design of existing tables, and remove tables from a database. However, most database systems provide GUI tools for database definition, and these tools are far easier to work with than SQL in designing a database. For example, Microsoft Access 97 provides wizards that guide you through the entire process of creating a database and the tables that it contains. If you have access to a GUI-based database design tool, then use it. It will save you time in creating your database and make it much easier to update. For those of you who do not have a GUI database design tool, I'll describe some of the basic SQL statements.

The CREATE DATABASE Statement

The CREATE DATABASE statement can be used to create a database:

```
CREATE DATABASE databaseName
```

Substitute the name of the table to be created for *databaseName*. For example, the following statement creates a database named MyDB:

```
CREATE DATABASE MyDB
```

NOTE

The CREATE DATABASE statement is not supported by all SQL implementations.

The CREATE TABLE Statement

The CREATE TABLE statement creates a table and adds it to the database:

```
CREATE TABLE tableName (columnDefinition, ... ,columnDefinition)
```

Each *columnDefinition* is of the form

```
columnName columnType
```

The *columnName* is unique to a particular column in the table. The *columnType* identifies the type of data that may be contained in the table. Common data types are

- char(*n*)—An *n* character text string
- int—An integer value
- float—A floating point value
- bit—A boolean (1 or 0) value
- date—A date value
- time—A time value

The Types class of java.sql identifies the SQL data types supported by Java. The get methods of the ResultSet interface are used to convert SQL data types into Java data types. The set methods of the PreparedStatement interface are used to convert Java types into SQL data types.

The following is an example of a CREATE TABLE statement:

```
CREATE TABLE Contacts (
LastName char(30),
FirstName char(20),
Company char(50),
Email char(40),
Phone char(20)
)
```

The preceding statement creates a Contacts table with the following columns:

- LastName—A 30-character wide text field
- FirstName—A 20-character wide text field
- Company—A 50-character wide text field
- Email—A 40-character wide text field
- Phone—A 20-character wide text field

The ALTER TABLE Statement

The ALTER TABLE statement adds a row to an existing table:

```
ALTER TABLE tableName ADD (columnDefinition ... columnDefinition)
```

The row values of the newly added columns are set to NULL. Columns are defined as described in the previous section.

The following is an example of the ALTER TABLE statement that adds a column named Fax to the Contacts table:

```
ALTER TABLE Contacts ADD (Fax char(20))
```

The DROP TABLE Statement

The DROP TABLE statement deletes a table from the database:

```
DROP TABLE tableName
```

The dropped table is permanently removed from the database. The following is an example of the DROP TABLE statement:

```
DROP TABLE Contacts
```

The preceding statement removes the Contacts table from the database.

Using SQL as a Data Maintenance Language

One of the primary uses of SQL is to update the data contained in a database. There are SQL statements to insert new rows into a database, delete rows from a database, and to update existing rows.

The INSERT Statement

The INSERT statement inserts a row into a table:

```
INSERT INTO tableName VALUES ('value1', ..., 'valuen')
```

In the preceding form of the INSERT statement *value1* through *valuen* identify all column values of a row. Values should be surrounded by single quotes.

The following is an example of the preceding form of the INSERT statement:

```
INSERT INTO Contacts VALUES (
 'Zepernick',
 'Ken',
 'SAIZ, Inc.',
 'kenz@cts.com',
 '619-555-5555'
)
```

The preceding statement adds Ken Zepernick to the Contacts table. All columns of Ken's row are filled in.

An alternative form of the INSERT statement may be used to insert a partial row into a table. The following is an example of this alternative form of the INSERT statement:

```
INSERT INTO tableName (columnName1, ..., columnNamem) VALUES ('value1', ..., 'valuem')
```

The values of *columnName1* through *columnNamem* are set to *value1* through *valuem*. The values of the other columns of a row are set to NULL.

An example of this form of the INSERT statement follows:

```
INSERT INTO Contacts (LastName, Email) VALUES (
 'Deloach',
'timdel@ix.netcom.com'
)
```

The preceding statement adds a person with the last name of Deloach and the e-mail address timdel@ix.netcom.com to the Contacts table. The person's FirstName, Company, and Phone fields are set to NULL.

The DELETE Statement

The DELETE statement deletes a row from a table:

```
DELETE FROM tableName [WHERE condition]
```

All rows of the table that meet the condition of the WHERE clause are deleted from the table. The WHERE clause is covered in a subsequent section of this chapter.

> **WARNING**
>
> If the WHERE clause is omitted, then all rows of the table are deleted.

The following is an example of the DELETE statement:

```
DELETE FROM Contacts WHERE LastName = 'Zepernick'
```

The preceding statement deletes all contacts with the last name of Zepernick from the Contacts table.

The UPDATE Statement

The UPDATE statement is used to update an existing row of a table:

```
UPDATE tableName SET columnName1 = 'value1', ... ,columnNamen = 'valuen' [WHERE
➥condition]
```

All the rows of the table that satisfy the condition of the WHERE clause are updated by setting the value of the columns to the specified values. If the WHERE clause is omitted, all rows of the table are updated.

An example of the UPDATE statement follows:

```
UPDATE Contacts SET FirstName = 'Tim' WHERE LastName = 'Deloach'
```

The preceding statement changes the FirstName of all contacts with the LastName of Deloach to Tim.

Using SQL as a Data Query Language

The most important use of SQL for many users is to retrieve data contained in a database. The SELECT statement specifies a database query:

```
SELECT columnList1 FROM table1, ..., tablem [WHERE condition] [ORDER BY
➥columnList2]
```

In the preceding syntax description, *columnList1* and *columnList2* are comma-separated lists of column names from the tables *table1* through *tablen*. The SELECT statement returns a result set consisting of the specified columns of the *table1* through *tablem* such that the rows of these tables meet the condition of the WHERE clause. If the WHERE clause is omitted, all rows are returned.

> **NOTE**
>
> An asterisk (*) may replace *columList1* to indicate that all columns of the table(s) are to be returned.

The ORDER BY clause is used to order the result set by the columns of *columnSet2*. Each of the column names in the column list may be followed by the ASC or DESC keywords. If DESC is specified, the result set is ordered in descending order. Otherwise, the result set is ordered in ascending order.

An example of the SELECT statement follows:

```
SELECT * FROM Contacts
```

This statement returns all rows and columns of the Contact table.

The WHERE Clause

The WHERE clause is a boolean expression consisting of column names, column values, relational operators, and logical operators. For example, suppose you have columns Department, Salary, and Bonus. You could use the following WHERE clause to match all employees in the engineering department that have a salary over $100,000 and a bonus less than $5,000:

```
WHERE Department = 'Engineering' AND Salary > '100000' AND Bonus < '5000'
```

Relational operators are =, !=, <, >, <=, and >=. Logical operators are AND, OR, and NOT.

> **NOTE**
>
> The ANSI SQL standard provides additional operators besides those listed in this section.

Remote Database Access

Most useful databases are accessed remotely. In this way, shared access to the database can be provided to multiple users at the same time. For example, you can have a single database server that is used by all employees in the accounting department.

In order to access databases remotely, users need a *database client*. A database client communicates to the database server on the user's behalf. It provides the user with the capability to update the database with new information or to retrieve information from the database. In this book, you learn to write Java applications and applets that serve as database clients. Your database clients talk to database servers using SQL statements. (See Figure 48.2.)

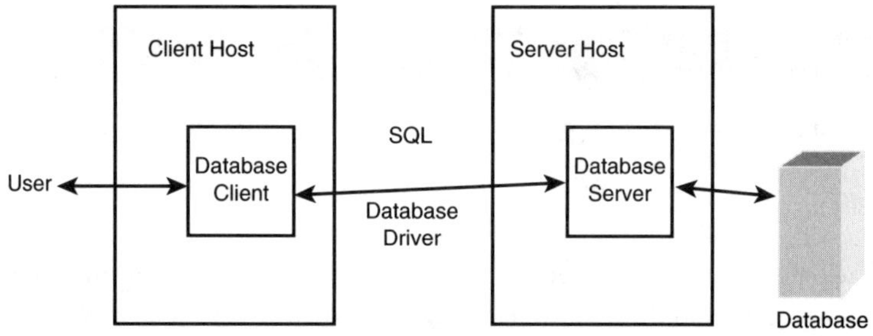

FIGURE 48.2.

A database client talks to a database server on the user's behalf.

ODBC and JDBC Drivers

Database clients use database drivers to send SQL statements to database servers and to receive result sets and other responses from the servers. JDBC drivers are used by Java applications and applets to communicate with database servers.

Microsoft's ODBC

Many database servers use vendor-specific protocols. This means that a database client has to learn a new language to talk to a different database server. However, Microsoft established a common standard for communicating with databases called Open Database Connectivity (ODBC). Until ODBC, most database clients were server specific. ODBC drivers abstract away vendor-specific protocols providing a common API to database clients. By writing your database clients to the ODBC API, you enable your programs to access more database servers. (See Figure 48.3.)

FIGURE 48.3.
A database client can talk to many database servers via ODBC drivers.

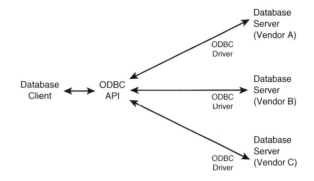

Enter JDBC

So where does JDBC fit into this picture? JDBC is not a competitor to ODBC yet, but it soon will be. JDBC provides a common database programming API for Java programs. However, JDBC drivers do not yet directly communicate with as many database products as ODBC drivers. Instead, many JDBC drivers communicate with databases using ODBC. In fact, one of the first JDBC drivers was the JDBC-ODBC bridge driver developed by JavaSoft and Intersolv.

Why did JavaSoft create JDBC? What was wrong with ODBC? There are a number of reasons why JDBC was needed. These answers boil down to the simple fact that JDBC is a better solution for Java applications and applets:

- ODBC is a C language API, not a Java API. Java is object-oriented and C is not. C uses pointers and other "dangerous" programming constructs that Java does not support. A Java version of ODBC would require a significant rewrite of the ODBC API.

- ODBC drivers must be installed on client machines. This would mean that applet access to databases would be constrained by the requirement to download and install a JDBC driver. A pure Java solution allows JDBC drivers to be automatically downloaded and installed along with the applet. This greatly simplifies database access for applet users.

JavaSoft created the Java-ODBC bridge driver as a temporary solution to database connectivity until suitable JDBC drivers were developed. The JDBC-ODBC bridge driver translates the JDBC API into the ODBC API and is used with an ODBC driver. The JDBC-ODBC bridge driver is not an elegant solution, but it allows Java developers to use existing ODBC drivers. (See Figure 48.4.)

FIGURE 48.4.

The JDBC-ODBC bridge lets Java database clients talk to databases via ODBC drivers.

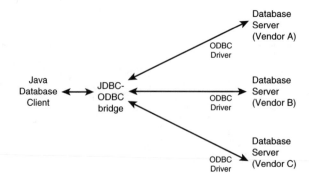

Since the release of the JDBC API, a number of JDBC drivers have been developed. These drivers provide varying levels of capability. As a service to Java developers, JavaSoft has classified JDBC drivers into the following four driver types:

■ JDBC-ODBC bridge plus ODBC driver—This driver category refers to the original JDBC-ODBC bridge driver. The JDBC-ODBC bridge driver uses Microsoft's ODBC driver to communicate with database servers. It is implemented in both binary code and Java and must be pre-installed on a client computer before it can be used.

■ Native-API partly Java driver—This driver category consists of drivers that talk to database servers in the server's native protocol. For example, an Oracle driver would speak SQLNet, while a DB2 driver would use an IBM database protocol. These drivers are implemented in a combination of binary code and Java, and they must be installed on client machines. (See Figure 48.5.)

FIGURE 48.5.

A Type 2 JDBC driver uses a vendor-specific protocol and must be installed on client machines.

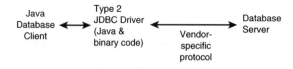

■ JDBC-Net pure Java driver—This driver category consists of pure Java drivers that speak a standard network protocol (such as HTTP) to a database access server. The database access server then translates the network protocol into a vendor-specific database protocol (possibly using an ODBC driver). (See Figure 48.6.)

FIGURE 48.6.

A Type 3 JDBC driver is a pure Java driver that uses a database access server to talk to database servers.

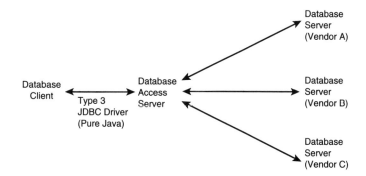

■ Native-protocol pure Java driver—This driver category consists of a pure Java driver that speaks the vendor-specific database protocol of the database server that it is designed to interface with. (See Figure 48.7.)

FIGURE 48.7.

A Type 4 JDBC driver is a pure Java driver that uses a vendor-specific protocol to talk to database servers.

Of the four types of drivers, only the Type 3 and Type 4 drivers are pure Java drivers. This is important to support zero installation for applets as you'll learn in Chapter 50, "Integrating Database Support into Web Applications." The Type 4 driver communicates with the database server using a vendor-specific protocol, such as SQLNet. The Type 3 driver makes use of a separate database access server. It communicates with the database access server using a standard network protocol, such as HTTP. The database access server communicates with database servers using vendor-specific protocols or ODBC drivers. The IDS JDBC driver that I used in Chapter 19, "Connecting to Databases with the java.sql Package," (and also in Chapters 49, "Using JDBC," and 50, "Integrating Database Support into Web Applications") is an example of a Type 3 driver. In Chapter 50, you'll learn why Type 3 drivers are an ideal solution for use with applets.

NOTE

Chapter 50 discusses the suitability of the preceding driver types for use with applets.

Summary

In this chapter, you covered the basics of database programming. You learned how relational databases work and how SQL is used to update and retrieve data from relational databases. You also learned how databases are accessed and about the different types of drivers that can be used to access databases. In the following chapter, you'll learn how to use JDBC to connect to databases, execute SQL statements, and manage database transactions.

49

Using JDBC

Chapter 48, "Database Fundamentals," covered the essential concepts of database programming that you need in order to get started. This chapter continues your introduction to database programming by showing you how to work with vendor-specific JDBC drivers and database servers. You'll get hands-on experience using SQL and you'll learn how to work with the results of SQL queries. You'll also cover transaction processing and database security. When you finish this chapter, you'll be able to write your own Java database applications.

Using Alternate JDBC Drivers and Databases

In Chapter 48, you learned about the four different types of JDBC drivers:

■ JDBC-ODBC bridge plus ODBC driver

■ Native-API partly Java driver

■ JDBC-Net pure Java driver

■ Native-protocol pure Java driver

In this section, you'll work with three of the four driver types. You'll learn how to access a Microsoft Access 97 database using the JDBC-ODBC bridge driver and the IDS JDBC driver. You'll also learn how to access an mSQL database using a Type 4 JDBC driver. When you finish this section, you'll have enough experience working with database drivers to figure out how to use other vendor-specific JDBC drivers.

Setting Up ODBC Drivers to Work with Microsoft Access Databases

I've provided a small Microsoft Access 97 database named action.mdb in the ch49 directory. In order to use this database you'll have to set it up as an ODBC data set. You do this using the 32-bit ODBC applet found in the Control Panel.

> **NOTE**
>
> If you have Microsoft Access 97 and want to use it to run the examples of this chapter, install it before setting up the action.mdb database.

After you open the applet, click the System DSN tab and then the Add button to add a new data source. Enter Actions as the name for the data source in the Data Source Name field. Click the Select button to set the path to the database to the location of the ch49 directory. (See Figure 49.1.)

NOTE

A System DSN is accessible to more than one user, while a User DSN is limited to a single user. It is important to set up your database as a System DSN, rather than a User DSN, in order to make it accessible to other users.

FIGURE 49.1.

Setting up the Actions *data source.*

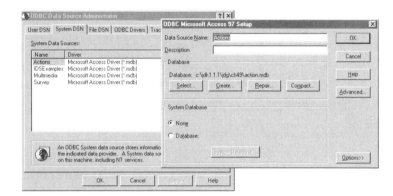

If you do not have Microsoft Access 97, you'll still be able to follow the example. In a later section of this chapter, "Setting Up the mSQL Server," I'll show you how to download and install the mSQL database server.

Setting Up the IDS Server and IDS JDBC Driver

As mentioned in Chapter 19, "Connecting to Databases with the java.sql Package," I highly recommend using the IDS JDBC driver, provided by IDS Software. It is a Type 3 JDBC driver that works with the IDS Server—a database access server that connects the IDS JDBC driver with your database. You can download an evaluation copy of the IDS Server and JDBC driver from the IDS Software Web site at http://www.idssoftware.com. The IDS software is distributed as a self-extracting executable file. Open this file and follow the installation instructions.

After installing the IDS software, read through the User's Guide. In particular, Section 1 describes how to set up the IDS Server, and Section 4 describes how to set up the IDS JDBC driver. Don't worry. You probably won't have to make many changes to configure the server and driver for your particular needs. I installed the software in the default c:\IDSServer directory on the same machine as Microsoft Access. Be sure to include the IDS JDBC driver in your CLASSPATH. I added C:\IDSServer\classes to my CLASSPATH.

> **NOTE**
>
> If your organization intends on pursuing Java database programming, you should seriously consider obtaining a production version of the IDS Server and JDBC driver. They are an excellent solution to providing database connectivity to Java applications and applets.

Setting Up the mSQL Server

Whether you have Microsoft Access or not, it will be worth your time to download and install the mSQL database server. If you don't have Microsoft Access 97, you can use mSQL to work some of the examples in this book. If you do have Microsoft Access 97, then using mSQL will broaden your base of experience. You can obtain a copy of the Windows version of mSQL from `ftp://bond.edu.au/pub/Minerva/msql/Contrib/Win-mSQL/`.

The Windows version of mSQL is a zipped file that you must unzip before installing mSQL. After unzipping the file, read the `Readme` and `Readme.w32` files for installation instructions. The mSQL server is easy to install and use if you follow these instructions. The `mSQL.htm` file located in the `\DOC` directory of the unzipped files provides you with all the information you need to run mSQL.

Make sure that you read the license that comes with mSQL. It is distributed as shareware and must be registered as specified in the license.

Setting Up the mSQL JDBC Driver

In order to connect to an mSQL server from Java, you need an appropriate JDBC driver. Luckily, an mSQL JDBC driver was developed by George Reese. You can download the latest version from `http://www.imaginary.com/Java/`.

The driver is distributed as a tarred, gzipped file. You can extract the contents of this file using an unarchiving tool such as WinZip. After extracting the file, copy the `classes` subdirectory to somewhere in your `CLASSPATH`. I copied it to my `c:\msql` directory and added `c:\msql\classes` to my `CLASSPATH`.

Setting Up the `ActmSQL` Database

An mSQL database is provided in the `ch49\ActmSQL` directory. To use this database with mSQL, move the entire `ActmSQL` directory under `c:\msql\msqldb`. The `c:\msql\msqldb` directory is where mSQL keeps its database files. The `c:\msql\msqldb\ActmSQL` directory is the directory used for the `ActmSQL` database.

Using the AccessApp Program

Now that you've gone through all the trouble of installing and configuring the IDS Server, the IDS JDBC driver, the mSQL server, and the mSQL JDBC driver, you can reap the fruits of your labor. The AccessApp program, shown in Listing 49.1, allows you to use a variety of JDBC drivers to access the Microsoft Access 97 database (action.mdb) and the mSQL database (ActmSQL).

Listing 49.1. The AccessApp program.

```
import java.awt.*;
import java.awt.event.*;
import java.sql.*;
import jdg.ch25.*;

public class AccessApp extends Frame {
 Object menuItems[][] = {
  {"File","Exit"}
 };
 MenuItemHandler mih = new MenuItemHandler();
 MyMenuBar menuBar = new MyMenuBar(menuItems,mih,mih);
 TextField driver = new TextField(60);
 TextField url = new TextField(60);
 TextField sql = new TextField(60);
 Button doIt = new Button("Do it!");
 TextArea resultArea = new TextArea(10,60);
 public static void main(String args[]){
  AccessApp app = new AccessApp();
 }
 public AccessApp() {
  super("AccessApp");
  setup();
  pack();
  addWindowListener(new WindowEventHandler());
  show();
 }
 void setup() {
  setMenuBar(menuBar);
  setLayout(new GridLayout(2,1));
  Panel topPanel = new Panel();
  topPanel.setLayout(new GridLayout(4,1));
  Panel panels[]=new Panel[4];
  for(int i=0;i<panels.length;++i){
   panels[i]=new Panel();
   panels[i].setLayout(new FlowLayout(FlowLayout.LEFT));
  }
  panels[0].add(new Label("Driver:"));
  panels[0].add(driver);
  panels[1].add(new Label("URL: "));
  panels[1].add(url);
  panels[2].add(new Label("SQL: "));
  panels[2].add(sql);
```

continues

Listing 49.1. continued

```
   doIt.addActionListener(new ButtonHandler());
   panels[3].add(doIt);
   for(int i=0;i<panels.length;++i)
    topPanel.add(panels[i]);
   add(topPanel);
   add(resultArea);
  }
  void accessDB() {
   try{
    Class.forName(driver.getText());
    Connection connection=DriverManager.getConnection(url.getText());
    Statement statement = connection.createStatement();
    boolean hasResults = statement.execute(sql.getText());
    if(hasResults){
     ResultSet result = statement.getResultSet();
     if(result!=null) displayResults(result);
    }else resultArea.setText("");
    connection.close();
   }catch(Exception ex){
    resultArea.setText(ex.toString());
   }
  }
  void displayResults(ResultSet r) throws SQLException {
   ResultSetMetaData rmeta = r.getMetaData();
   int numColumns=rmeta.getColumnCount();
   String text="";
   for(int i=1;i<=numColumns;++i) {
    if(i<numColumns)
     text+=rmeta.getColumnName(i)+" ¦ ";
    else
     text+=rmeta.getColumnName(i);
   }
   text+="\n";
   while(r.next()){
    for(int i=1;i<=numColumns;++i) {
     if(i<numColumns)
      text+=r.getString(i)+" ¦ ";
     else
      text+=r.getString(i).trim();
    }
    text+="\n";
   }
   resultArea.setText(text);
  }
  class ButtonHandler implements ActionListener {
   public void actionPerformed(ActionEvent ev){
    String s=ev.getActionCommand();
    if(s=="Do it!") accessDB();
   }
  }
  class MenuItemHandler implements ActionListener, ItemListener {
   public void actionPerformed(ActionEvent ev){
    String s=ev.getActionCommand();
    if(s=="Exit"){
     System.exit(0);
    }
   }
```

```
 public void itemStateChanged(ItemEvent e){
 }
}
class WindowEventHandler extends WindowAdapter {
 public void windowClosing(WindowEvent e){
   System.exit(0);
 }
 }
}
```

Before you run the AccessApp program, start the IDS Server by selecting IDS Server from the Start menu. Also, open an MS-DOS window and change directories to the c:\msql directory. Start up the mSQL server by running the msqld.bat file.

When you run AccessApp, it displays the opening window shown in Figure 49.2. The Driver text field allows you to enter the name of a JDBC driver. The URL field allows you to enter the URL of a database to be accessed by the driver. The SQL field allows you to enter an SQL command to update the database or retrieve information from it. You can use this program to access the Access 97 database and the mSQL database using the JDBC-ODBC bridge, IDS JDBC driver, and mSQL JDBC driver.

FIGURE 49.2.

Opening window for AccessApp.

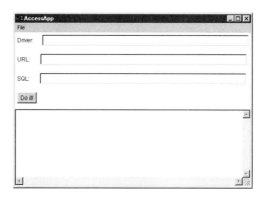

Let's start with the JDBC-ODBC bridge. This driver comes with the JDK 1.1. Enter sun.jdbc.odbc.JdbcOdbcDriver into the Driver field to load the JDBC-ODBC bridge driver. Enter jdbc:odbc:Actions in the URL field to tell the driver to access the Actions data set that you set up earlier in this chapter. Now enter SELECT * FROM ActionItem in the SQL field to dump the contents of the ActionItem table. Click the Do it! button to execute the SQL statement. The program displays the contents of the ActionItem table, as shown in Figure 49.3.

FIGURE 49.3.

Using the JDBC-ODBC bridge driver.

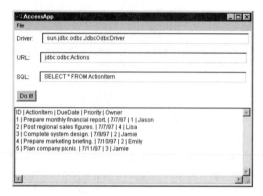

Now let's execute the same command using the IDS JDBC driver. The IDS driver will access the same Actions data set, but it will access it through the IDS Server. Enter `ids.sql.IDSDriver` in the Driver field to load the IDS driver. Enter `jdbc:ids://your.host.com:port/conn?dbtype=odbc&dsn='Actions'` in the URL field. Substitute the name of the host where you installed the IDS Server for *your.host.com* and your IDS Server's port number for *port*. (The default port is 12.) Now click the Do it! button. Figure 49.4 shows the results of the query.

FIGURE 49.4.

Using the IDS JDBC driver.

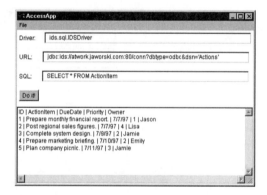

What, no change? Don't worry—the results should stay the same. You just executed the same command using a different driver. Try executing some other SQL commands. It really works!

So far, we've accessed the Actions data set using the JDBC-ODBC bridge driver and the IDS JDBC driver. Now we'll access the ActmSQL database using the mSQL database server and the mSQL JDBC driver.

Enter `COM.imaginary.sql.msql.MsqlDriver` in the Driver field. Enter `jdbc:ids://your.host.com:port/ActmSQL` in the URL field. Substitute the name of the host where you installed the mSQL server for *your.host.com* and your server's port number for *port*. (The default port is 1112.) Enter `SELECT * from Action` in the SQL field and then click the Do it! button.

Voilà! You have done it again, as shown in Figure 49.5.

FIGURE 49.5.

*Using the mSQL JDBC
bridge driver.*

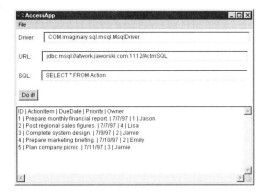

How AccessApp **Works**

AccessApp begins by creating and laying out the three text fields, the Do it! button, and the text area. The ButtonHandler class handles the clicking of the Do it! button by invoking the accessDB() method.

> **NOTE**
>
> If you haven't read Chapter 19 yet, now would be a good time. It covers the classes and interfaces of the java.sql package.

The accessDB() method invokes the forName() method of the Class class to load the JDBC driver identified by the driver variable. It then invokes the getConnection() method of the DriverManager class to establish a connection to the database at the specified URL. The createStatement() method of the Connection class is invoked to create a Statement object. The execute() method of this object is invoked to execute the SQL statement entered in the text field referenced by the sql variable.

If the execute() method returns a true value, indicating that it has produced a ResultSet object, the getResultSet() method is invoked to retrieve this object. The displayResults() method is then invoked to display the returned results in the text area.

If no results were returned by the execute() method, the text area is emptied. The close() method of the Connection interface is invoked to close the database connection.

The displayResults() method takes a ResultSet object as an argument. It invokes the getMetaData() method of the ResultSet class to retrieve a ResultSetMetaData object that describes the ResultSet object. It invokes the getColumnCount() method to determine the number of columns in the result set. It then retrieves each column name using the `getColumnName()` method of the `ResultSetMetaData` class. It builds a column header using these names. Each column is separated using a vertical bar (|).

After building the column header, `displayResults()` executes a `while` loop that reads each row of the `ResultSet` object. It uses the `next()` method to move between rows of the result set. It reads the column values of the row using the `getString()` method of the `ResultSet` class. The rows of the result set are formatted in the same manner as the column header. The columns of each row are separated by vertical bars. The resulting text string is then displayed in the `TextArea` object referenced by the `resultArea` variable.

Executing SQL

Now that you know how to use JDBC drivers to connect to databases, you are on your way to becoming a JDBC programmer. Once you connect to a database, the bulk of your programming involves executing SQL statements and displaying the results of those statements.

The `AccessApp` program provides you with a good opportunity to practice the SQL that you learned in Chapter 48. You'll be executing SQL statements directly. If you were writing a Java program to act as an SQL client, you would write a GUI front end to the SQL. The GUI front end would shield your users from having to learn SQL.

Open `AccessApp` and enter the name of a JDBC driver in the Driver field and the URL of the `Actions` data set in the URL field, as shown in Figure 49.6. I'll be using the JDBC-ODBC driver this time. You can use the IDS driver or any other driver that works with ODBC.

FIGURE 49.6.

Specifying the JDBC driver and database URL.

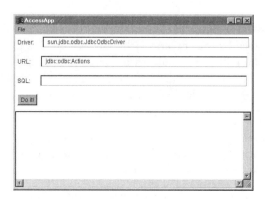

Enter the following SQL statement in the SQL field, as shown in Figure 49.7. Click Do it! to execute the statement:

```
CREATE TABLE Test (Col1 char(20), Col2 int, Col3 float)
```

This statement creates a new table named Test in the Actions data set (Microsoft Access 97 action.mdb database). The table has columns named Col1, Col2, and Col3. Col1 is a 20-character wide text column. Col2 stores integer values, and Col3 stores floating point values.

FIGURE 49.7.

Using the CREATE
TABLE *statement to*
create the Test *table.*

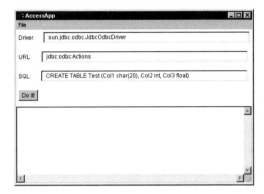

Enter the following SQL statement and click the Do It! button (see Figure 49.8):

```
INSERT INTO Test VALUES ('Java', 1, 10.0)
```

This statement inserts a new row into the database with the value of Col1 set to 'Java', Col2 set to 1, and Col3 set to 10.0.

FIGURE 49.8.

Using the INSERT
statement to add new
rows to the Test *table.*

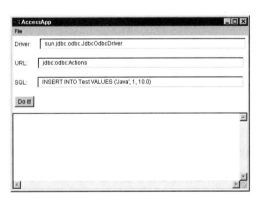

Enter the following two rows in the same manner:

```
INSERT INTO Test VALUES ('JDBC', 10, 1.0)
INSERT INTO Test VALUES ('ODBC', 100, 0.1)
```

Now let's see what our database looks like. Enter the following and click the Do it! button:

```
SELECT * FROM Test
```

The text area displays the contents of the Test table, as shown in Figure 49.9.

FIGURE 49.9.

Checking the results of the INSERT statements.

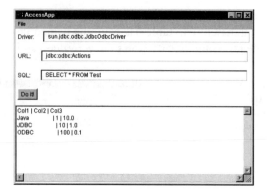

Enter the following statement to delete all rows where the value of Col2 is 100 (see Figure 49.10):

```
DELETE FROM Test WHERE Col2 = 100
```

Click the Do it! button to execute the DELETE statement.

FIGURE 49.10.

Using the DELETE statement to delete the last row.

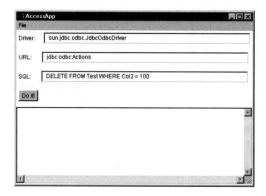

Let's replace the deleted row using the following INSERT statement:

```
INSERT INTO Test VALUES ('SQL', 50, 2.5)
```

Now execute the UPDATE statement, shown in Figure 49.11:

```
UPDATE Test SET Col2 = 99 WHERE Col3 < 10.0
```

Are you curious to see what the Test table looks like? Execute the following statement to dump all rows of test:

```
SELECT * FROM Test
```

Figure 49.12 shows the results of the query.

FIGURE 49.11.

Using the UPDATE
*statement to change
selected rows.*

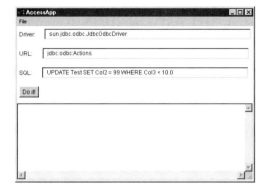

FIGURE 49.12.

Checking the updated
Test *table.*

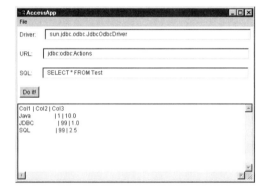

Let's rearrange the first and second columns and sort by the third column by executing the following SELECT statement:

```
SELECT Col2, Col1, Col3 FROM TEST ORDER BY Col3
```

Figure 49.13 shows the modified output.

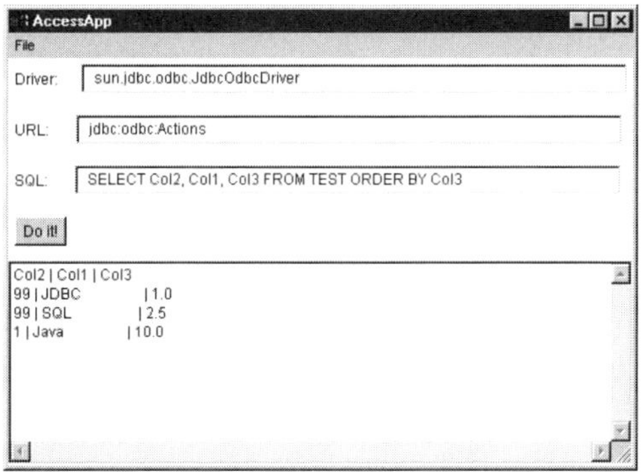

FIGURE 49.13.

*Sorting the results of a
query.*

Working with Result Sets

As you saw in the previous section, working with SQL is pretty easy. There are only a handful of important SQL statements. Once you learn their syntax, you can accomplish quite a bit.

Connecting to databases and executing SQL statements enables you to add information to the databases and retrieve information in the form of ResultSet objects. You can think of ResultSet objects as custom tables that are generated by the database as the result of processing a SELECT statement. The SELECT statement identifies the columns to be selected and the way the results should be ordered.

Accessing the data contained in a ResultSet object is pretty straightforward. However, like laying out a GUI, it can be somewhat tedious. A ResultSet object can be thought of as a window on the custom table returned as the result of processing a SELECT statement. This window lets you view only one row of the table at a time. You can move the window forward to the next row (using the next() method), but you can never move it back. This means that you have to store the information of interest in a particular row before moving on to the next row. The get methods of the ResultSet interface allow you to retrieve the information contained in a particular column of the current row. These methods convert the column data from its SQL type to a Java type. In most cases, you will use the getString() method to retrieve information as a Java String object. However, there are methods that work with all primitive types and objects. The getAsciiStream(), getUnicodeStream(), and getBinaryStream() methods that are used to retrieve large column values are Java streams. You can use the read() methods of the particular stream class to access the contents of the stream in manageable amounts.

The ResultSet interface does not provide any methods to find out how many columns are in a particular row. Instead, it provides the getMetaData() method to return a ResultSetMetaData object.

A ResultSetMetaData object provides quite a bit of information about its corresponding ResultSet object. There are several methods that return information about the columns of the ResultSet object, the table from which the columns originated, as well as other helpful information. While you probably won't use most of these methods, you will find yourself using some methods, such as the getColumnCount() and getColumnName() methods, in almost all of your Java database applications.

Transaction Processing

So far, whenever we've executed an SQL statement, the statement automatically updated the contents of the database. This approach to database updating works fine for some database applications but not well for others.

Consider the case where several database tables need to be updated to input a new customer order into a database that supports an online ordering application. For example, a `Customers` table may need to be updated with information about the new customer, an `Orders` table may need to be updated with information about the order, and a `ProductAvailability` table may need to be updated to mark a product as sold. What happens if a database connection is broken before all three tables are updated? The database is left in a corrupted state.

Transaction processing was invented as a solution to this database update problem. A *transaction* consists of a group of related database operations. The SQL statements comprising a transaction update the database at the same time. Even though the statements are executed in sequence, they do not permanently update the database until they are *committed*. If an error occurs during the processing of a transaction, the SQL statements comprising the transaction can be *rolled back*.

The `setAutoCommit()`, `commit()`, and `rollback()` methods of the `Connection` interface are used to implement transaction processing. The `setAutoCommit()` method is used to turn off automatic committing of SQL statements. When autocommit is turned off, SQL statements are organized into a single transaction until a `commit()` or `rollback()` method is invoked. The `commit()` method completes a transaction by committing all SQL statements that were executed since the last commit or rollback. The `rollback()` method reverses a transaction that is in progress by erasing the effects of all SQL statements that were executed since the last commit or rollback.

Transaction Isolation

Transaction processing helps to eliminate many problems associated with multiple database updates. However, it creates some problems of its own. Consider the case where two separate transactions occur simultaneously. An SQL statement of the first transaction changes a row in a table, and an SQL statement of the second transaction performs a query that reads the changed row. If the first transaction has not yet been committed, what row value should be reported in the query?

Transaction isolation levels are used to specify how potential conflicts between transactions should be resolved. Higher levels of transaction isolation prevent conflicts from occurring between concurrent transactions. However, this isolation comes at the expense of reduced database performance. At the highest level of transaction isolation, transactions are required to occur in a serial fashion, eliminating concurrent database transactions completely.

The `Connection` interface defines constants that can be used to specify transaction isolation levels. The `getTransactionIsolation()` and `setTransactionIsolation()` methods of the `Connection` interface are used to access transaction isolation levels. The `supportsTransactionIsolation()` method of the `DatabaseMetaData` interface can be used to determine what levels of transaction isolation are supported by a particular database.

The CommitApp Program

The CommitApp program, shown in Listing 49.2, illustrates the use of transaction processing. I use the IDS JDBC driver in CommitApp. You can use a different driver; however, you'll have to change the first couple lines of the setupDB() method to reflect your driver and database URL. If you decide to stick with the IDS driver, make sure that you start the IDS Server before running CommitApp.

Listing 49.2. The CommitApp program.

```
import java.awt.*;
import java.awt.event.*;
import java.sql.*;
import jdg.ch25.*;

public class CommitApp extends Frame {
 Object menuItems[][] = {
  {"File","Exit"}
 };
 MenuItemHandler mih = new MenuItemHandler();
 MyMenuBar menuBar = new MyMenuBar(menuItems,mih,mih);
 TextField sql = new TextField(60);
 Button commit = new Button("Commit");
 Button execute = new Button("Execute");
 TextArea resultArea = new TextArea(10,60);
 Connection connection;
 public static void main(String args[]){
  CommitApp app = new CommitApp();
 }
 public CommitApp() {
  super("CommitApp");
  setup();
  setupDB();
  pack();
  addWindowListener(new WindowEventHandler());
  show();
 }
 void setup() {
  setMenuBar(menuBar);
  setLayout(new GridLayout(2,1));
  Panel topPanel = new Panel();
  topPanel.setLayout(new GridLayout(2,1));
  Panel panels[]=new Panel[2];
  for(int i=0;i<panels.length;++i){
   panels[i]=new Panel();
   panels[i].setLayout(new FlowLayout(FlowLayout.LEFT));
  }
  panels[0].add(new Label("SQL: "));
  panels[0].add(sql);
  commit.addActionListener(new ButtonHandler());
  execute.addActionListener(new ButtonHandler());
  panels[1].add(commit);
  panels[1].add(execute);
  for(int i=0;i<panels.length;++i)
   topPanel.add(panels[i]);
```

```
 add(topPanel);
 add(resultArea);
}
void setupDB() {
 try{
  Class.forName("ids.sql.IDSDriver");
  String url = "jdbc:ids://atwork.jaworski.com:80/";
  url+="conn?dbtype=odbc&dsn='Actions'";
  connection=DriverManager.getConnection(url);
  DatabaseMetaData meta=connection.getMetaData();
  if(meta.supportsTransactions())
   connection.setAutoCommit(false);
  else{
   String err="Your database server/driver does not support transactions.";
   System.out.println(err);
   System.exit(0);
  }
 }catch(Exception ex){
  resultArea.setText(ex.toString());
 }
}
void commitTransactions() {
 try{
  connection.commit();
 }catch(Exception ex){
  resultArea.setText(ex.toString());
 }
}
void executeTransaction() {
 try{
  Statement statement = connection.createStatement();
  boolean hasResults = statement.execute(sql.getText());
  if(hasResults){
   ResultSet result = statement.getResultSet();
   if(result!=null) displayResults(result);
  }else resultArea.setText("");
 }catch(Exception ex){
  resultArea.setText(ex.toString());
 }
}
void displayResults(ResultSet r) throws SQLException {
 ResultSetMetaData rmeta = r.getMetaData();
 int numColumns=rmeta.getColumnCount();
 String text="";
 for(int i=1;i<=numColumns;++i) {
  if(i<numColumns)
   text+=rmeta.getColumnName(i)+" ¦ ";
  else
   text+=rmeta.getColumnName(i);
 }
 text+="\n";
 while(r.next()){
  for(int i=1;i<=numColumns;++i) {
   if(i<numColumns)
    text+=r.getString(i)+" ¦ ";
```

continues

Listing 49.2. continued

```
      else
        text+=r.getString(i).trim();
    }
    text+="\n";
  }
  resultArea.setText(text);
}
void closeConnection(){
  try {
    connection.close();
  }catch(Exception ex){
  }
}
class ButtonHandler implements ActionListener {
  public void actionPerformed(ActionEvent ev){
    String s=ev.getActionCommand();
    if(s=="Commit") commitTransactions();
    else if(s=="Execute") executeTransaction();
  }
}
class MenuItemHandler implements ActionListener, ItemListener {
  public void actionPerformed(ActionEvent ev){
    String s=ev.getActionCommand();
    if(s=="Exit"){
      closeConnection();
      System.exit(0);
    }
  }
  public void itemStateChanged(ItemEvent e){
  }
}
class WindowEventHandler extends WindowAdapter {
  public void windowClosing(WindowEvent e){
    closeConnection();
    System.exit(0);
  }
}
}
```

Open `CommitApp` and list the current content of the `ActionItem` table using the `SELECT * FROM ActionItem` SQL statement. See Figure 49.14. (Click the Execute button to execute an SQL statement.)

Now insert a new row into the `ActionItem` table by executing the following SQL statement, as shown in Figure 49.15. (Make sure that you **don't** click the Commit button.)

```
INSERT INTO ActionItem VALUES('6', 'Close out quarter.', '7/15/97', 1, 'Jason')
```

When you redisplay the `ActionItem` table, the newly added row is shown, as in Figure 49.16.

FIGURE 49.14.

Displaying the original ActionItem *table.*

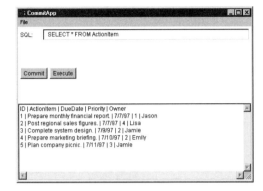

FIGURE 49.15.

Inserting a new row into the ActionItem *table.*

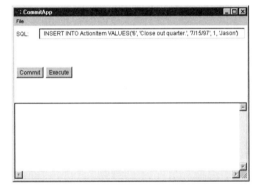

FIGURE 49.16.

Displaying the updated table.

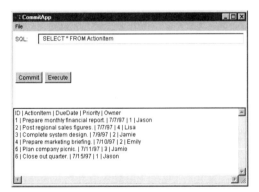

Exit the CommitApp program and then open CommitApp a second time. When you redisplay the ActionItem table this time, the newly added row is not displayed, as shown in Figure 49.17. That's because you terminated the database connection before committing the new row.

FIGURE 49.17.

The transaction was not committed.

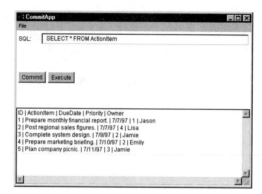

Reinsert the row by executing the following statement again:

```
INSERT INTO ActionItem VALUES('6', 'Close out quarter.', '7/15/97', 1, 'Jason')
```

Now click the Commit button to commit the transaction. Exit `CommitApp` and then open it a third time. When you list the `ActionItem` table, the newly inserted row is displayed because you committed the new transaction before exiting the `CommitApp` program.

FIGURE 49.18.

This time the transaction was committed.

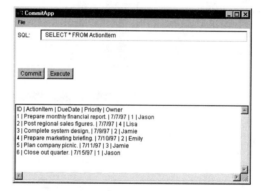

How `CommitApp` Works

`CommitApp` is similar to `AccessApp` in that it allows you to enter SQL commands directly into a database. It differs in that it uses the IDS JDBC driver (and IDS Server) and works with the `action.mdb` Microsoft Access 97 database that you used earlier in the chapter.

The `setupDB()` method is invoked during the program's initialization. It establishes a connection to the `Actions` data set via the IDS JDBC driver and IDS server. The `getMetaData()` method is invoked to retrieve the `DatabaseMetaData` object that describes the database to which the connection was established. The `supportsTransactions()` method is invoked to determine whether the database supports transaction processing. If the database does support transaction processing, the `setAutoCommit()` method is invoked to turn off the automatic committing of database transactions. Note that the database connection is left open.

When a user clicks the Commit or Execute button, the `ButtonHandler` object associated with the button checks to see what button was clicked and invokes the `commitTransactions()` or `executeTransactions()` methods.

The `commitTransactions()` method invokes the `commit()` method of the `Connection` interface to close the database connection.

The `executeTransactions()` method invokes the `execute()` method of the `Statement` class to execute the SQL statement entered by the user. If the SQL statement returns a `ResultSet` object, it invokes `getResultSet()` to retrieve the `ResultSet` object and `displayResults()` to display it.

The `displayResults()` method is the same method used in the `AccessApp` program.

Note that the `MenuItemHandler` and `WindowEventHandler` classes invoke the `closeConnection()` method to terminate the database connection before exiting the program.

Database Security

Until now, we have left the issue of database security unaddressed. Database security is a serious concern for most organizations. Because databases may contain sensitive information about a company's operation, it is often imperative that such information be restricted to those who are trusted to handle the information in a secure manner.

The integrity of database information is also paramount. Unauthorized changes to critical database information could have an adverse impact on a company's capability to carry out business operations.

Finally, data availability is important. Users must be able to get access to database information when they need it. This access often needs to be provided 24 hours a day and seven days a week.

How does the JDBC support database security? The answer is not very comforting. The JDBC currently relies on the database server to provide security protection. You probably noticed that we didn't even need to use a password to access the databases used as examples for this chapter. That's because we were working with personal database products (Microsoft Access and mSQL). Enterprise-wide database servers, such as Microsoft SQL Server, do require a user ID and password in order to establish a database connection. However, even password protection is not very secure. If passwords are not encrypted between client and server, they can easily be intercepted and compromised.

Fortunately, many vendors are working on solutions to Java database security. Approaches to securing JDBC driver to database server communication are in the making. The most promising approaches involve the use of encrypted communication between drivers and servers.

Summary

In this chapter you learned how to work with vendor-specific JDBC drivers and database servers. You used type 1 and 3 drivers with Microsoft Access, and a type 4 driver with mSQL. You then gained some hands-on experience working with SQL and the results of SQL queries. You also covered transaction processing and database security. In the next chapter, you'll learn how to access databases with applets.

50

Integrating Database Support into Web Applications

The Web is a global medium from which you can find information on any topic. Because of the Web's capability to distribute information to a worldwide audience, different approaches to integrating databases with the Web have been explored. Early Web pioneers relied on the Common Gateway Interface (CGI) as a way to marry Web and database technologies. The complexities, inefficiencies, and security problems associated with CGI programs resulted in second generation approaches to database integration. Major Web software vendors, such as Netscape, have devised solutions, such as LiveWire Pro, to connect databases to Web applications.

In this chapter, you'll learn how to use the JDBC to connect applets with online databases. You'll learn what kind of JDBC drivers to use to support zero installation database connectivity. You'll develop an applet that inserts form data directly into an online database. You'll create a general SQL statement processing applet for searching online databases and for testing other database-enabled applets. You'll then explore approaches to integrating multimedia and databases and develop a multimedia photo album. When you finish this chapter, I think that you'll find the JDBC to be a superior conduit for connecting the Web to online databases.

Using `java.sql` with Applets

Although applets can communicate with databases using any type of JDBC driver, the elegance or crudeness of the solution depends on which type of driver you use. The following is a list of the available drivers:

■ JDBC-ODBC bridge plus ODBC driver—This is the crudest possible solution. Applets access your database using a combination of the JDBC-ODBC bridge and an ODBC driver. This requires both drivers to be installed on the user's computer—a very cumbersome solution for both Internet and intranet users.

■ Native-API partly Java driver—This solution is also cumbersome. Applets use a hybrid Java-native API driver that also must be installed on the client machine. Its only benefit is that its installation is easier than installing both the JDBC-ODBC bridge **and** an ODBC driver.

■ JDBC-Net pure Java driver—This is an ideal solution for both intranets and the Internet. Applets use pure Java drivers that are served from Web servers along with the applets. The Java drivers are automatically installed on the user's machine in a transparent manner. The pure Java drivers communicate with a database access server using a protocol such as HTTP or Secure HTTP that can be proxied by a firewall. The database access server translates database requests into a vendor-specific protocol. The IDS JDBC driver and IDS server fit into this category.

■ Native-protocol pure Java driver—This solution is also useful because it uses a pure Java driver. However, instead of communicating with a database server using a proxiable protocol, the JDBC driver uses a database vendor–specific protocol. This approach is efficient for intranet applications but suffers from the drawback that the vendor's protocol may not be supported by a firewall. Lack of firewall support may rule out some potential Internet applications for security reasons.

NOTE

Chapter 48, "Database Fundamentals," introduces and describes each of the preceding JDBC driver types.

As you can tell by now, I am sold on the JDBC-Net pure Java driver—that's why I use the IDS driver. The first two approaches are just too cumbersome for Web applications. Users should not have to install database drivers on their machines to use an applet.

Security and standardization are important considerations for Internet use. When I am not writing books, I am involved in Internet security, sometimes in the area of Internet firewalls. Because of the significant lack of firewall proxies for vendor-specific database protocols, any database-enhanced Web application should consider the availability of a standard protocol for database access (like HTTP and SHTTP). The JDBC-Net pure Java driver solution allows you to use a standard protocol. This is important so that both your firewall *and* the user's firewall can support applet-to-database communication.

NOTE

Proxies are programs that run on a firewall to support secure use of a protocol through the firewall. In order for a firewall to support a protocol in a secure manner, it needs a proxy for that protocol.

The third and fourth types of drivers support zero installation applets. Because the JDBC drivers are written entirely in Java, they are downloaded from the Web server along with the applet. In order to support zero installation, the drivers must be placed on the Web server in the same directory as the applet. In this chapter, I'll be placing the applets in the /ch50 directory off of my Web server root. You should also create a /ch50 directory off of your Web server's root if you intend to run the examples in this chapter. Copy the C:\IDSServer\classes\ids directory and all of its subdirectories to your Web server so that it is accessible as /ch50/ids. By doing so you're making the IDS JDBC driver accessible to applets so that zero installation can be accomplished. If you are not using the IDS driver, you will need to consult your driver's documentation to determine how to make that driver available for installation for applet users.

Trusted Versus Untrusted Applets

Another important consideration for setting up a database-enabled Web application using applets is the location of your database server and database access server. Untrusted applets can communicate only with the host from which they are served. This means that they can talk back only to the Web server from which they are loaded. The purpose of this restriction is to prevent applets from obtaining sensitive information (such as that entered into a form) and disclosing that information to other hosts on the Internet.

If you are using type 1, 2, or 4 JDBC drivers, you have to put your database server on the same host as your Web server. This can lead to a performance problem for a busy Web site that supports a high level of database accesses. Your alternative is to require users to trust your applets to talk to other Internet hosts in a secure manner. This is an imposition on the user for two reasons: 1) technically, there is no reason why he should have to reconfigure his browser to run your applet, other than your inability to come up with a workable solution, and 2) any trust that the user extends creates a potential security vulnerability.

If you use a type 3 driver, you can place the database access server on the same host as your Web server (enabling the use of untrusted applets) and the actual database server on a separate machine. This can greatly reduce any potential performance problems with running the database server and the Web server on the same host. Several of the database access servers are integrated with a Web server and share the HTTP protocol port. This supports greater combined performance of the Web server and database access server. In addition, a separate database access server allows you to use multiple database servers that are located on independent hosts. Overall, type 3 drivers provide the most flexible and easy-to-use solution.

Form Handling and Database Access

Now that we've explored the virtues of different JDBC driver types as they relate to applets, we'll develop an applet that displays a survey form to a user and updates a database with the data entered by the user.

I'll be running this application under Windows 95. I've put together a small Microsoft Access 97 database (survey.mdb) that you can use to run the application on your computer. Use the 32-bit ODBC applet of Control Panel to set up the survey.mdb database as a System DSN. (DSN stands for data set name.) To do this, click the System DSN tab, click Survey as the Data Source Name, and use the Select button to select C:\jdk1.1.1\jdg\ch50\survey.mdb as the database. (See Figure 50.1.)

I've installed the System DSN on a host named atwork.jaworski.com. It's the notebook computer that I'm using to write this book. I've also installed an evaluation copy of the IDS server (database access server) on this machine. The IDS server also duals as a Web server. Feel free to use your own Web server. However, if you use a type 3 JDBC driver and a database access server, you'll have far fewer installation hassles.

FIGURE 50.1.

Setting up the System DSN.

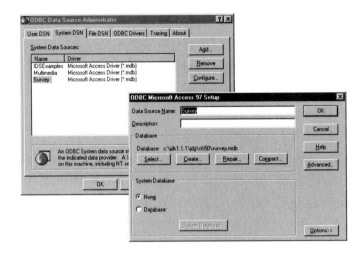

The `Survey` applet is shown in Listing 50.1. To run it, you'll have to tailor the first few lines of the `updateDatabase()` method for your JDBC driver and host name:

```
void updateDatabase(){
  try{
  Class.forName("ids.sql.IDSDriver");
  String url="jdbc:ids://atwork.jaworski.com:80/";
  url+="conn?dbtype=odbc&dsn='Survey'";
  Connection connection=DriverManager.getConnection(url);
```

As a minimum, you'll have to change `atwork.jaworski.com:80` to your database server's (or database access server's) host name. If you use a driver other than the IDS driver, you'll need to consult your driver's documentation for information on how to do this.

When you're finished with these changes, compile `Survey.java` and then copy the `survey.htm` (see Listing 50.2), `Survey.class`, and `Survey$ButtonHandler.class` files to the `/ch50` directory off of your Web server's root.

Now you're ready for action. Use a JDK 1.1–compatible browser, such as HotJava 1.0 or Netscape Communicator 4.0, to access the applet, as shown in Figure 50.2.

Use your Web server's host name instead of `atwork.jaworski.com` to access the applet. You can run your browser from the same host or a different host. If you've used a type 3 or 4 driver and copied the driver to the `/ch50` directory, you'll be able to easily access the applet from any host. Otherwise, you'll have to install your JDBC drivers on the host from which you run your browser.

FIGURE 50.2.

The Survey *applet opening display.*

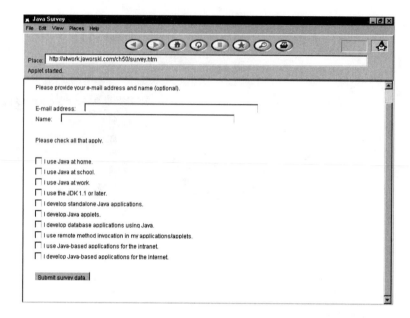

Fill out the Survey form as you wish and click the Submit survey data button. Your survey results are added to your database. The applet then displays a Thank you! message, as shown in Figure 50.3.

FIGURE 50.3.

The applet completes the survey by thanking the user.

To verify that the survey information was added to the database, start up Microsoft Access 97, open the survey.mdb database, and view the contents of the RawData table. Your alternative to verifying the database is to wait until we create a general-purpose database search applet in the next section.

Listing 50.1. The Survey applet.

```java
import java.applet.*;
import java.awt.*;
import java.awt.event.*;
import java.sql.*;

public class Survey extends Applet {
 Label blankLine = new Label(" ");
 TextField email = new TextField(50);
 TextField name = new TextField(50);
 Checkbox home = new Checkbox("I use Java at home.");
 Checkbox school = new Checkbox("I use Java at school.");
 Checkbox work = new Checkbox("I use Java at work.");
 Checkbox jdk11 = new Checkbox("I use the JDK 1.1 or later.");
 Checkbox standalone = new Checkbox("I develop standalone Java applications.");
 Checkbox applets = new Checkbox("I develop Java applets.");
 Checkbox database = new Checkbox("I develop database applications using Java.");
 Checkbox rmi = new Checkbox("I use remote method invocation in my applications/
⮑applets.");
 Checkbox intranet = new Checkbox("I use Java-based applications for the
⮑intranet.");
 Checkbox internet = new Checkbox("I develop Java-based applications for the
⮑Internet.");
 Button submitButton = new Button("Submit survey data.");
 public void init() {
  setLayout(new GridLayout(21,1));
  Panel panels[]=new Panel[21];
  for(int i=0;i<panels.length;++i){
   panels[i]=new Panel();
   panels[i].setLayout(new FlowLayout(FlowLayout.LEFT));
  }
  submitButton.addActionListener(new ButtonHandler());
  panels[0].add(blankLine);
  panels[1].add(new Label("Please provide your e-mail address and name
⮑(optional)."));
  panels[2].add(blankLine);
  panels[3].add(new Label("E-mail address:"));
  panels[3].add(email);
  panels[4].add(new Label("Name:"));
  panels[4].add(name);
  panels[5].add(blankLine);
  panels[6].add(new Label("Please check all that apply."));
  panels[7].add(blankLine);
  panels[8].add(home);
  panels[9].add(school);
  panels[10].add(work);
  panels[11].add(jdk11);
```

continues

Listing 50.1. continued

```
 panels[12].add(standalone);
 panels[13].add(applets);
 panels[14].add(database);
 panels[15].add(rmi);
 panels[16].add(intranet);
 panels[17].add(internet);
 panels[18].add(blankLine);
 panels[19].add(submitButton);
 panels[20].add(blankLine);
 for(int i=0;i<panels.length;++i) add(panels[i]);
}
void updateDatabase(){
 try{
  Class.forName("ids.sql.IDSDriver");
  String url="jdbc:ids://atwork.jaworski.com:80/";
  url+="conn?dbtype=odbc&dsn='Survey'";
  Connection connection=DriverManager.getConnection(url);
  Statement statement = connection.createStatement();
  String sql="INSERT INTO RawData VALUES ('"+email.getText()+"'";
  sql+=",'"+name.getText()+"'";
  sql+=toDigit(home);
  sql+=toDigit(school);
  sql+=toDigit(work);
  sql+=toDigit(jdk11);
  sql+=toDigit(standalone);
  sql+=toDigit(applets);
  sql+=toDigit(database);
  sql+=toDigit(rmi);
  sql+=toDigit(intranet);
  sql+=toDigit(internet);
  sql+=")";
  statement.executeUpdate(sql);
  connection.close();
  displayPanel("Thank you!");
 }catch(Exception ex){
  displayPanel(ex.toString());
 }
}
String toDigit(Checkbox ch){
 boolean state = ch.getState();
 if(state) return ",'1'";
 else return ",'0'";
}
void displayPanel(String s){
 removeAll();
 setLayout(new BorderLayout());
 Font currentFont = getFont();
 setFont(new Font(currentFont.getName(),Font.ITALIC+Font.BOLD,18));
 add("Center",new Label(s,Label.CENTER));
 invalidate();
 doLayout();
}
class ButtonHandler implements ActionListener {
 public void actionPerformed(ActionEvent e){
```

```
      String s = e.getActionCommand();
      if("Submit survey data.".equals(s)){
       updateDatabase();
      }
     }
    }
 }
}
```

Listing 50.2. The `survey.htm` file.

```
<HTML>
<HEAD>
<TITLE>Java Survey</TITLE>
</HEAD>
<BODY>
<APPLET CODE="Survey.class" WIDTH=550 HEIGHT=475>
[Survey applet]
</APPLET>
</BODY>
</HTML>
```

How the Survey Applet Works

Most of the code of the `Survey` applet is used to present the survey form to the user. This involves the creation and layout of the text fields and checkbox buttons that you see in Figure 50.2.

The clicking of the Submit survey data button is handled by the `ButtonHandler` class. The `updateDatabase()` method is invoked to update the database with the information collected in the form.

The `updateDatabase()` method loads the JDBC driver and establishes a connection to the database specified in the database URL. It executes the `"INSERT INTO RawData VALUE (...)"` SQL statement with the values of the form fields inserted into the statement at the appropriate column positions. The `toDigit()` method is invoked to convert the values of the checkbox fields into strings of 1 or 0 so that they are in the correct format for Microsoft Access.

> **NOTE**
>
> You can open the `survey.mbd` database with Microsoft Access 97 to see how the `RawData` table is structured.

Performing Database Searches

The Survey applet shows how form data can be collected and stored in a database. You typically would not let a user search a database that collected data from users via forms (mainly because of privacy considerations). In this case, you would use your database management system's reporting features to view the stored form data.

However, there are some cases where you'll want to provide users with the capability to search your databases. The SQL applet shown in Listing 50.3 provides a general capability to search (and update) selected databases. While you most likely won't want to provide your users with this much flexibility, you can use the processing performed by this applet and tailor it to your specific search and update needs.

Because the SQL applet is a general-purpose applet, you'll need to tailor only the first couple of lines of processQuery() to work with your JDBC driver:

```
void processQuery(){
  try{
    Class.forName("ids.sql.IDSDriver");
    String url="jdbc:ids://"+hostPort.getText()+"/";
    url+="conn?dbtype=odbc&dsn='"+dsn.getText()+"'";
    Connection connection=DriverManager.getConnection(url);
```

Compile SQL.java and then copy SQL.class, SQL$ButtonHandler.class, and sql.htm (see Listing 50.4) to the /ch50 directory of your Web server.

Open sql.htm with your JDK 1.1–capable browser, as shown in Figure 50.4.

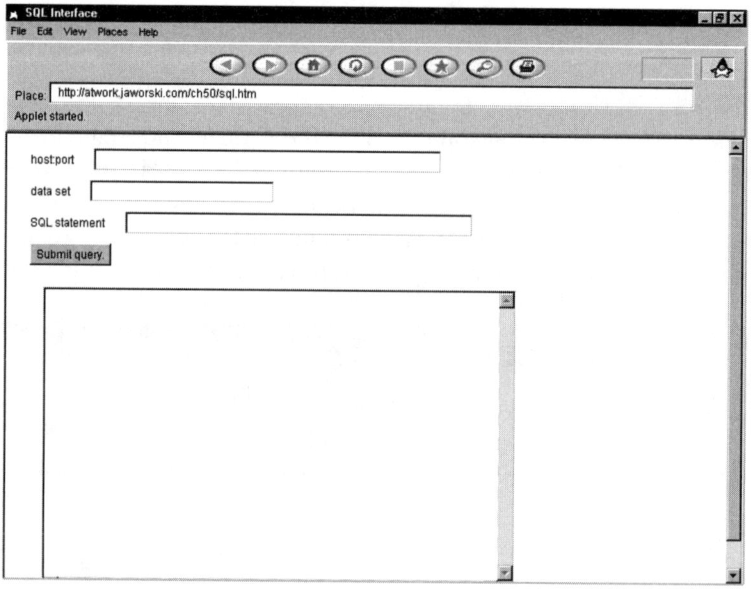

FIGURE 50.4.

The SQL applet can query or update a variety of databases.

The SQL applet provides a great deal of flexibility for accessing different databases. You can use it to maintain your databases and test other database-enabled applets. The SQL applet allows you to specify the host name and port of the database access server, the data set name, and an SQL statement. Click the Submit query button to send an SQL statement to the database server for execution. If the SQL statement returns a result, the results of the query are displayed in the text area.

Let's use the SQL applet to view the contents of the Survey data set. First, enter your database access server's host name and port number. Then enter the data set that you want to access. Finally, enter the SQL statement that you want to execute and click the Submit query button. The results of the query are displayed in the text area. Figure 50.5 shows a query that displays the contents of the RawData table of the Survey data set.

FIGURE 50.5.

Using the SQL *applet to view the Survey database.*

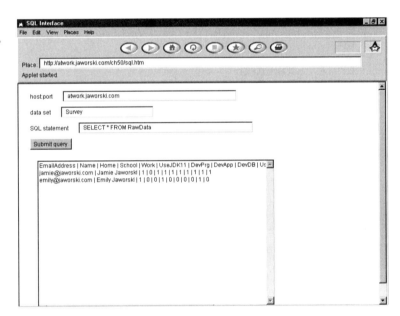

Listing 50.3. The SQL applet.

```
import java.applet.*;
import java.awt.*;
import java.awt.event.*;
import java.sql.*;

public class SQL extends Applet {
  Label blankLine = new Label(" ");
  TextField hostPort = new TextField(50);
  TextField dsn = new TextField(25);
  TextField sqlStatement = new TextField(50);
  TextArea results = new TextArea(20,70);
```

continues

Listing 50.3. continued

```
Button submitButton = new Button("Submit query.");
public void init() {
 Panel topPanel = new Panel();
 Panel bottomPanel = new Panel();
 Panel topPanels[] = new Panel[4];
 for(int i=0;i<topPanels.length;++i){
  topPanels[i]=new Panel();
  topPanels[i].setLayout(new FlowLayout(FlowLayout.LEFT));
 }
 topPanel.setLayout(new GridLayout(4,1));
 topPanels[0].add(new Label("host:port "));
 topPanels[0].add(hostPort);
 topPanels[1].add(new Label("data set "));
 topPanels[1].add(dsn);
 topPanels[2].add(new Label("SQL statement "));
 topPanels[2].add(sqlStatement);
 submitButton.addActionListener(new ButtonHandler());
 topPanels[3].add(submitButton);
 for(int i=0;i<topPanels.length;++i)
  topPanel.add(topPanels[i]);
 bottomPanel.add(results);
 setLayout(new BorderLayout());
 add("North",topPanel);
 add("South",bottomPanel);
}
void processQuery(){
 try{
  Class.forName("ids.sql.IDSDriver");
  String url="jdbc:ids://"+hostPort.getText()+"/";
  url+="conn?dbtype=odbc&dsn='"+dsn.getText()+"'";
  Connection connection=DriverManager.getConnection(url);
  Statement statement = connection.createStatement();
  String sql=sqlStatement.getText();
  boolean hasResults = statement.execute(sql);
  if(hasResults){
   ResultSet result = statement.getResultSet();
   if(result!=null) displayResults(result);
  }else results.setText("");
  connection.close();
 }catch(Exception ex){
  results.setText(ex.toString());
 }
}
void displayResults(ResultSet r) throws SQLException {
 ResultSetMetaData rmeta = r.getMetaData();
 int numColumns=rmeta.getColumnCount();
 String text="";
 for(int i=1;i<=numColumns;++i) {
  if(i<numColumns)
   text+=rmeta.getColumnName(i)+" ¦ ";
  else
   text+=rmeta.getColumnName(i);
 }
 text+="\n";
 while(r.next()){
  for(int i=1;i<=numColumns;++i) {
```

```
    if(i<numColumns)
      text+=r.getString(i)+" ¦ ";
    else
      text+=r.getString(i).trim();
    }
    text+="\n";
  }
  results.setText(text);
}
class ButtonHandler implements ActionListener {
  public void actionPerformed(ActionEvent e){
    String s = e.getActionCommand();
    if("Submit query.".equals(s)){
      processQuery();
    }
  }
 }
}
```

Listing 50.4. The `sql.htm` file.

```
<HTML>
<HEAD>
<TITLE>SQL Interface</TITLE>
</HEAD>
<BODY>
<APPLET CODE="SQL.class" WIDTH=550 HEIGHT=475>
[SQL applet]
</APPLET>
</BODY>
</HTML>
```

How the SQL Applet Works

The main bulk of the SQL applet involves creating and laying out the form fields. The ButtonHandler class handles the clicking of the Submit query button by invoking the processQuery() method. The processQuery() method loads the JDBC driver and connects to the database access server specified in the hostPort text field and the data set specified in the dsn text field. The execute() method of the Statement class is invoked to execute the SQL statement specified in the sql text field.

If the execute() method returns a value of true, the getResultSet() method is invoked to retrieve a ResultSet object and the displayResults() method is invoked to display the ResultSet object in the text area.

The displayResults() method displays the column names separated by the vertical bar character (¦). It then displays each row of the result table, also separating columns using the vertical bar.

Accessing Multimedia Databases

So far the database results that we've been displaying have consisted of boring text. Most databases allow you to store images, audio files, and other multimedia. The JDBC provides the capability to read arbitrary objects from the columns of a `ResultSet` object. However, in many cases, it is inconvenient to do so. To work with multimedia objects from a database, you must put the objects in the database in the first place. Your database server has to retrieve the objects and forward them to your applet. Then your applet has to convert the object to a format that is suitable to display. While each of these steps is technically feasible, there is an easier way. Instead of putting all of your multimedia files in your database, just put their names or URLs in the database. Move the actual multimedia files to your Web server. This will speed up your database access and let you use the applet methods for loading multimedia files.

The `Multimedia` applet of Listing 50.5 shows how easy it is to combine applets, databases, and multimedia. I've provided a `multimed.mdb` database with the descriptions of image and audio files and a `\ch50\multimedia` directory containing multimedia files. These multimedia files include circus photographs and audio files that comment on the photographs. The photographs were taken by a Kodak DC-20 digital camera and converted to JPEG format. The audio files were recorded by the Windows 95 sound recorder and converted to Sun audio (`.au`) format. Copy the `\ch50\multimedia` directory to your Web server so that it is `/ch50/multimedia` under your server's root. Use the Windows 95 Control Panel's 32-bit ODBC applet to set up the `multimed.mdb` file as a system data set, as shown in Figure 50.6.

FIGURE 50.6.

Setting up the system data set for the Multimedia database.

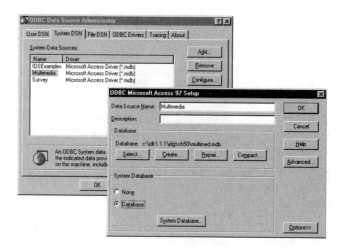

In order to run the `Multimedia` applet you need to tailor `Multimedia.java` to your host name and JDBC driver. First, modify the `init()` method to change `atwork.jaworski.com` to your host name:

```
public void init() {
  try{
   baseURL = new
    URL("http://atwork.jaworski.com/ch50/multimedia/");
  }catch(Exception ex){
  }
```

Second, change the first few lines of `getQueryResults()` to use your JDBC driver and substitute your host name for `atwork.jaworski.com`:

```
String[][] getQueryResults(String sql){
  try{
   Class.forName("ids.sql.IDSDriver");
   String url="jdbc:ids://atwork.jaworski.com:80/";
   url+="conn?dbtype=odbc&dsn='Multimedia'";
   Connection connection=DriverManager.getConnection(url);
```

Finally, compile `Multimedia.java` and copy the `Multimedia$ChoiceHandler.class`, `Multimedia.class`, `Multimedia$MyCanvas.class`, and `multimedia.htm` (see Listing 50.6) files to your Web server.

Open `multimedia.htm` with your JDK 1.1–capable browser, as shown in Figure 50.7. Be sure to substitute your Web server's host name for `atwork.jaworski.com`.

FIGURE 50.7.

The Multimedia *applet's opening screen.*

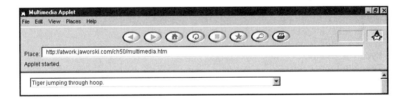

Select an item from the choice list. A photograph is displayed and an audio file is played, as shown in Figure 50.8.

You can step through the circus photos for amusement. This applet is very simple; it was designed that way. However, it is a good example of how applets, databases, and multimedia files can be combined into an easy-to-use (and easy-to-develop) Web application.

FIGURE 50.8.

Combining applets, databases, and multimedia.

Listing 50.5. The `Multimedia` applet.

```java
import java.applet.*;
import java.awt.*;
import java.awt.event.*;
import java.sql.*;
import java.util.*;
import java.net.*;

public class Multimedia extends Applet {
 Choice choice = new Choice();
 MyCanvas canvas = new MyCanvas();
 Image photo = null;
 AudioClip audio = null;
 String imageName="";
 String audioName="";
 URL baseURL;
 public void init() {
  try{
   baseURL = new
    URL("http://atwork.jaworski.com/ch50/multimedia/");
  }catch(Exception ex){
  }
  String choices[]=getChoices();
  if(choices!=null){
   try{
    for(int i=0;i<choices.length;++i)
     choice.add(choices[i]);
   }catch(Exception ex){
    choice.add(ex.toString());
   }
  }
```

```
 setLayout(new BorderLayout());
 choice.addItemListener(new ChoiceHandler());
 add("North",choice);
 add("Center",canvas);
}
String[] getChoices(){
 String results[][] =
  getQueryResults("SELECT Description FROM Photographs");
 if(results == null){
  String err[]= {"No choices returned from database."};
  return err;
 }
 String column[] = new String[results.length];
 for(int i=0;i<results.length;++i)
  column[i]=results[i][0];
 return column;
}
String[][] getQueryResults(String sql){
 try{
  Class.forName("ids.sql.IDSDriver");
  String url="jdbc:ids://atwork.jaworski.com:80/";
  url+="conn?dbtype=odbc&dsn='Multimedia'";
  Connection connection=DriverManager.getConnection(url);
  Statement statement = connection.createStatement();
  ResultSet results = statement.executeQuery(sql);
  ResultSetMetaData rmeta = results.getMetaData();
  int numColumns=rmeta.getColumnCount();
  Vector v = new Vector();
  while(results.next()){
   String row[] = new String[numColumns];
   for(int i=0;i<numColumns;++i)
    row[i]=results.getString(i+1);
   v.addElement(row);
  }
  int numRows=v.size();
  String resultTable[][] = new String[numRows][];
  for(int i=0;i<numRows;++i)
   resultTable[i]=(String[]) v.elementAt(i);
  connection.close();
  return resultTable;
 }catch(Exception ex){
  return null;
 }
}
void loadMedia(String s){
 String sql = "SELECT Image, Audio FROM Photographs";
 sql += "WHERE Description = '"+s+"'";
 String results[][] = getQueryResults(sql);
 if(results!=null){
  imageName = results[0][0];
  audioName = results[0][1];
  if(imageName != "TBD") photo=getImage(baseURL,imageName);
  if(audioName != "TBD") audio=getAudioClip(baseURL,audioName);
 }
 canvas.repaint();
}
class ChoiceHandler implements ItemListener {
```

continues

Listing 50.5. continued

```
public void itemStateChanged(ItemEvent e){
 String s = choice.getSelectedItem();
 imageName="";
 audioName="";
 photo=null;
 if(audio!=null){
  audio.stop();
  audio=null;
 }
 loadMedia(s);
 }
}
class MyCanvas extends Canvas {
 public void paint(Graphics g){
  if(photo!=null) g.drawImage(photo,20,20,this);
  else g.drawString(imageName,10,20);
  if(audio!=null) audio.play();
  else g.drawString(audioName,10,40);
 }
 }
}
```

Listing 50.6. The `multimedia.htm` file.

```
<HTML>
<HEAD>
<TITLE>Multimedia Applet</TITLE>
</HEAD>
<BODY>
<APPLET CODE="Multimedia.class" WIDTH=540 HEIGHT=450>
[Multimedia applet]
</APPLET>
</BODY>
</HTML>
```

How the `Multimedia` Applet Works

The `Multimedia` applet displays a `Choice` object referenced by the `choice` variable and a `MyCanvas` object referenced by the `canvas` variable. The values of the `Choice` object are retrieved from the `Photographs` table of the `Multimedia` data set. The `photo` and `audio` variables are used to reference the `Image` object that is displayed on the `MyCanvas` object and the `AudioClip` object that is played. The `baseURL` variable is used to identify the URL of the directory where the image and audio files are located.

The `init()` method initializes the `baseURL` variable. (Be sure to substitute your server's URL.) It then invokes the `getChoices()` method to retrieve the list of photograph descriptions from the `Multimedia` data set. It then adds this list of descriptions to the `Choice` object referenced by the `choice` variable. The `Choice` object and `MyCanvas` objects are then laid out for display.

The `getChoices()` method invokes the `getQueryResults()` method with the `"SELECT Description FROM Photographs"` SQL statement. It then converts the results (if not null) from a two-dimensional `String` array to a one-dimensional `String` array. The `String` array is then returned to the caller.

The `getQueryResults()` method executes an SQL statement and returns the tabular results as a two-dimensional array. It begins by loading the JDBC driver and connecting to the `Multimedia` data set. It executes the SQL query and converts the result set to a `Vector` object containing a one-dimensional array for each row of the result set. A vector is used because there is no way to determine the size of the result set without stepping through it. The `Vector` object is then converted to a two-dimensional `String` array.

The `ChoiceHandler` class handles the `ItemEvent` associated with selecting an item from the choice list. It resets the values of the `imageName`, `audioName`, `photo`, and `audio` variables and then invokes `loadMedia()` with the value of the selected choice.

The `loadMedia()` method invokes `getQueryResults()` with the `"SELECT Image, Audio FROM Photographs WHERE Description = 'description'"` SQL statement where the selected choice (as identified by the s variable) is substituted for *description*. This statement returns the values of the `Image` and `Audio` columns for the row with the `Description` column set to *description*. The `imageName` and `audioName` variables are updated based on the results returned. If the `imageName` is not `"TBD"`, the `getImage()` method of the `Applet` class is used to load the image from the Web server and assign it to the `photo` variable. If the `audioName` is not `"TBD"`, the `getAudioClip()` method of the `Applet` class is used to load the audio file from the Web server and assign it to the `audio` variable. Using `getImage()` and `getAudioClip()` is much easier than retrieving an image or audio file from the database. The `repaint()` method of the `MyCanvas` class is invoked to cause the image to be displayed and the audio file to be played.

The `paint()` method of the `MyCanvas` class checks to see if the `photo` variable references a valid image. If it does, the image is drawn on the canvas. Otherwise, the image name is displayed. Similarly, the audio file is played if it is valid. Otherwise, its name is displayed.

Summary

In this chapter, you learned how to use the JDBC to connect applets with online databases. You learned what kind of JDBC drivers you should use to support zero installation database connectivity. You developed an applet that inserts form data directly into an online database. You then created a general SQL statement processing applet for searching databases and for testing other database-enabled applets. Finally, you developed a multimedia photo album that explored approaches to integrating multimedia and databases.

This chapter concludes Part VII, "Database Programming." In Part VIII, "Developing Distributed Applications," you'll learn how to develop distributed applications using Java's remote method invocation capabilities.

VIII

Developing Distributed Applications

51

Distributed Applications Architecture

This chapter provides background information on Java's distributed programming capabilities. It discusses the various approaches to designing and implementing distributed applications and shows how Java's distributed object model compares to these approaches. It describes how Java's RMI capabilities are implemented using a three-tiered protocol set and finishes with a discussion of the security issues involved with using RMI. When you finish this chapter, you'll have the background information you need to understand how RMI works and how it is used to develop distributed applications. This chapter expands on the information presented in Chapter 18, "Building Distributed Applications with the java.rmi Packages."

Distributed Application Design Approaches

A *distributed application* is an application whose processing is distributed across multiple networked computers. Distributed applications are able to concurrently serve multiple users and, depending on their design, make more optimal use of processing resources.

Distributed applications are typically implemented as client/server systems that are organized according to the user interface, information processing, and information storage layers, shown in Figure 51.1.

FIGURE 51.1.

Distributed systems are organized according to user interface, information processing, and information storage layers.

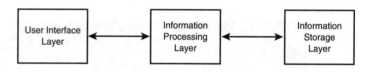

The user interface layer is implemented by an application client. E-mail programs and Web browsers are examples of the user-interface component of distributed applications.

The information processing layer is implemented by an application client, an application server, or an application support server. For example, a database application may utilize a database client to convert user selections into SQL statements, a database access server may be used to support communication between the client and a database server, and the database server may use reporting software to process the information requested by a client.

The information storage layer is implemented by database servers, Web servers, FTP servers, file servers, and any other servers whose purpose is to store and retrieve information.

Distributed Applications on the Internet

The popularity of the Internet and Web has resulted in an almost fully networked world. Computers on opposite ends of the world are directly accessible to each other via the TCP/IP protocol suite. This worldwide connectivity has given rise to distributed applications that run within the Internet's client/server framework. These first generation applications support client/server communication using application-specific protocols such as HTTP, FTP, and SQL*NET. Figure 51.2 illustrates a typical Internet application.

FIGURE 51.2.

A distributed Internet application.

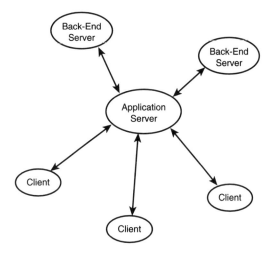

Typically, a client program is executed on multiple host computers. The client uses TCP to connect to a server that listens on a well-known port. The client makes one or more requests of the server. The server processes the client's requests, possibly using gateway programs or back-end servers, and forwards the response to the client.

Applets on the Intranet

In an intranet environment, corporate information systems support services that are tailored to the organizational needs of the company. These services consist of applications that support business areas such as management, accounting, marketing, manufacturing, customer support, vendor interface, shipping and receiving, and so on. These intranet services can be implemented using client/server services, such as a company-internal Web. Java applets provide the capability to run the client interface layer and part of the information processing layer of business applications within the context of a Web browser. Figure 51.3 shows an approach to implementing corporate information services using the applet paradigm.

The approach shown in Figure 51.3 is essentially the Internet client/server approach shown in Figure 51.2 applied to the intranet, using Java applets to program client information system interfaces. This approach is popular for developing distributed intranet applications and can also be used with Internet applications as well. It allows business applications to be distributed among browsers, Web servers, and other back-end servers.

FIGURE 51.3.
Implementing intranet services using applets.

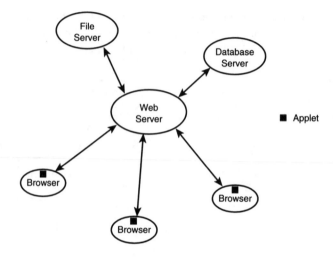

The Distributed Computing Environment

The Distributed Computing Environment (DCE) is another approach to building distributed applications. DCE was developed by the Open Software Foundation, now referred to as the Open Group. DCE integrates a variety of fundamental services and technologies to build distributed applications. Distributed systems are organized into *cells*, which are groups of processing resources, services, and users that support a common function and share a common set of DCE services. For example, cells can be organized according to company functions. In this case, you may have separate cells for your finance, manufacturing, and marketing departments.

The DCE services of a cell are used to implement distributed applications that serve the users of the cell and interface with the applications implemented by other cells. The services and technologies used within a DCE cell consist of the following:

■ Directory services—DCE directory services store the names of resources that are available within the distributed environment. The Cell Directory Service (CDS) supports naming within a cell, and the Global Directory Service (GDS) supports naming across all cells within an enterprise. GDS implements the X.500 directory service standard.

■ Distributed File Service (DFS)—DFS is an optional DCE service that provides a seamless file system that operates across all computers contained within a cell.

■ Distributed Time Service (DTS)—DTS is used to synchronize time across all computers within a cell.

- Security service—The security service is used to authenticate cell users and control access to the resources that are available within a cell.

- Remote Procedure Calls (RPCs)—RPCs replace TCP sockets as the basic mechanism for client/server communication. They are implemented as a layer that is built on top of the TCP/IP transport layer and abstracts away connection management and protocol-specific concerns.

- DCE threads—DCE threads are similar to Java threads. They are lightweight processes that simplify the design of client/server applications.

DCE is referred to as middleware because it is not a standalone product, but rather a bundle of services that are integrated into an operating system or operating environment. These services are used as an alternative approach to constructing distributed applications. They are used to build the same kinds of applications as the Web-based example covered in the previous section. They just go about it in a different manner.

The Common Object Request Broker Architecture

The Common Object Request Broker Architecture (CORBA) provides another approach to building distributed systems. CORBA, unlike DCE, is object-oriented. It allows objects on one computer to invoke the methods of objects on other computers. Because of this, CORBA is a great choice for building distributed object-oriented applications.

CORBA makes use of objects that are accessible via Object Request Brokers (ORBs). ORBs are used to connect objects to one another across a network. An object on one computer (client object) invokes the methods of an object on another computer (server object) via an ORB.

The client's interface to the ORB is a stub that is written in the Interface Definition Language (IDL). The stub is a local proxy for a remote object. The IDL provides a programming-language independent mechanism for describing the methods of an object.

The ORB's interface to the server is through an IDL skeleton. The skeleton provides the ORB with a language-independent mechanism for accessing the remote object.

Remote method invocation under CORBA takes place as follows. The client object invokes the methods of the IDL stub corresponding to a remote object. The IDL stub communicates the method invocations to the ORB. The ORB invokes the corresponding methods of the IDL skeleton. The IDL skeleton invokes the methods of the remote server object implementation. The server object returns the result of the method invocation via the IDL skeleton, which passes the result back to the ORB. The ORB passes the result back to the IDL stub, and the IDL stub returns the result back to the client object. Figure 51.4 summarizes this process.

FIGURE 51.4.
How CORBA works.

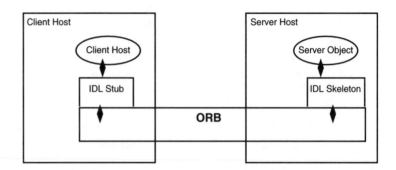

Figure 51.4 shows the ORB as being a single layer across the client and server hosts. This is the standard way in which the ORB is viewed. A number of possible ORB implementations are possible. For example, peer ORBs could be implemented on the client and server hosts or a central system ORB could be implemented on a local server. Other ORB implementations are also possible.

Now that you know how CORBA works, you may be wondering how it is used to develop distributed applications. The answer is that CORBA provides a flexible approach to distributed application development. It provides a finer level of granularity in the implementation of client/server systems. Instead of relying on monolithic clients and servers (as is the case of the browsers and servers of the Web), both clients and servers can be distributed over several hosts.

The advantages of CORBA over other distributed application integration approaches are significant:

■ CORBA provides a true object-oriented approach to developing distributed applications.

■ CORBA is language independent. It can be used to connect objects that are developed in any programming language, as long as an IDL stub for the objects can be furnished.

■ CORBA is recognized as an international standard and is supported by nearly all major software vendors.

We'll cover CORBA more in Chapter 54, "Java IDL and ORBs," where you'll learn how to use Java objects with CORBA.

Java Remote Method Invocation

Given the various approaches to distributed application development discussed in the previous sections, you may be wondering why Java just doesn't pick the best approach and go with it instead of using RMI. There are a number of reasons for this:

■ TCP sockets—Java does support TCP sockets, as you learned in Part V, "Network Programming." You can build traditional socket-based client/server applications using Java for the intranet and Internet. Java applets and servlets can be used to distribute the application's information processing layer between the client and server. Even though Java supports TCP sockets, JavaSoft decided that a more fine-grain, low overhead approach to distributed application development, such as that provided by CORBA, would be needed to develop advanced distributed applications using Java.

■ DCE—DCE is based on RPC, which is a procedure-oriented approach to developing distributed applications. RPC does not mesh well with distributed object-oriented applications. The remote method invocation approach supported by CORBA is much better able to suit the Java object model.

■ CORBA—CORBA provides an excellent approach to building distributed object-oriented applications, and Java does support CORBA, as you'll learn in Chapter 54. However, CORBA is designed to support a language-independent object model. Java RMI has all the benefits of CORBA, but is specifically tailored to the Java object model. This makes Java RMI far more efficient and easier to use than CORBA for pure Java applications.

Chapter 18, "Building Distributed Applications with the `java.rmi` Packages," provides an introduction to Java RMI and covers the RMI API. It also shows you how to develop a simple distributed application using RMI. In the next section, I'll describe the Java distributed object model and explain why it is a natural extension of the Java object model used within a single JVM.

The Java Distributed Object Model

The distributed object model used by Java allows objects that execute in one JVM to invoke the methods of objects that execute in other JVMs. These other JVMs may be JVMs that execute as a separate process on the same computer or on other remote computers. The object making the method invocation is referred to as the *client object*. The object whose methods are being invoked is referred to as the *server object*. The client object is also referred to as the *local object* and is said to execute locally. The server object is referred to as the *remote object* and is said to execute remotely.

In the Java distributed object model, a client object never references a remote object directly. Instead, it references a remote interface that is implemented by the remote object. The use of remote interfaces allows server objects to differentiate between their local and remote interfaces. For example, an object could provide methods to objects that execute within the same JVM that are in addition to those that it provides via its remote interface. The use of remote interfaces also allows server objects to present different remote access modes. For example, a server object can provide both a remote administration interface and a remote user interface. Finally, the use of remote interfaces allows the server object's position within its class hierarchy to be abstracted away from the manner in which it is used. This allows client objects to be compiled using the remote interface alone, eliminating the need for server class files to be locally present during the compilation process.

The Three-Tiered Layering of the Java RMI

In addition to remote interfaces, the model makes use of stub and skeleton classes in much the same way as CORBA. Stub classes serve as local proxies for the remote objects. Skeleton classes act as remote proxies. Both stub and skeleton classes implement the remote interface of the server object. The client interface invokes the methods of the local stub object. The local stub communicates these method invocations to the remote skeleton, and the remote skeleton invokes the methods of the server object. The server object returns a value to the skeleton object. The skeleton object returns the value to the stub object, and the stub object returns the value to the client. Figure 51.5 summarizes the use of stubs and skeletons.

FIGURE 51.5.

The use of stubs and skeletons in the Java distributed object model.

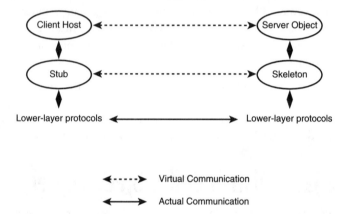

If you are a CORBA programmer, you'll notice the conspicuous absence of IDL and ORBs in Figure 51.5. The stub and skeleton classes are automatically generated by the rmic compiler from the server object. These classes are true Java classes and do not rely on an external IDL. No ORB is required because the Java RMI is a pure Java solution. The client object and stub communicate using normal Java method invocations. So do the skeleton and the server object. The stub and the skeleton communicate via a remote reference layer.

The remote reference layer supports communication between the stub and the skeleton. In the case that the stub communicates with more than one skeleton instance (not currently supported), the stub object communicates with the multiple skeletons in a multicast fashion. The RMI API currently only defines classes that support unicast communication between a stub and a single skeleton. The remote reference layer may also be used to activate server objects when they are invoked remotely. However, this capability is not currently implemented.

The remote reference layer on the local host communicates with the remote reference layer on the remote host via the RMI transport layer. The transport layer sets up and manages connections between the address spaces of the local and remote hosts, keeps track of objects that can be accessed remotely, and determines when connections have timed out and become inoperable. The transport layer uses TCP sockets, by default, to communicate between the local and remote hosts. However, other transport layer protocols, such as UDP, may also be used.

Figure 51.6 illustrates the three-tier layering used to implement Java RMI. In this expanded view of the model, the client object invokes the methods of the local stub of the server object. The local stub uses the remote reference layer to communicate with the server skeleton. The remote reference layer uses the transport layer to set up a connection between the local and remote address spaces and to obtain a reference to the skeleton object.

FIGURE 51.6.

The three-tier layering of Java RMI.

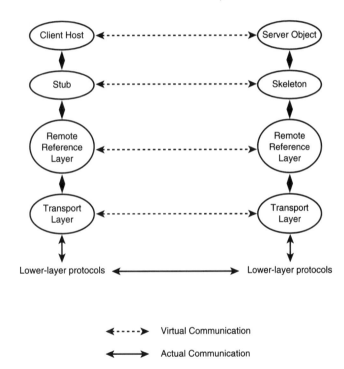

In order for a server object to be accessed remotely, it must register itself with the remote registry. It does this by associating its object instance with a name. The remote registry is a process that runs on the server host. This process is created by running the `rmiregistry` program.

The remote registry maintains a database of server objects and the names by which these objects can be referenced. When a client creates an instance of a server object's interface (that is, its local stub), the transport layer on the local host communicates with the transport layer on the remote host to determine if the referenced object does, in fact, exist and the type of interface the referenced object implements. The server-side transport layer uses the remote registry to access this information.

Passing Arguments and Returning Values

In order for a client object to pass an argument as part of a remote method invocation, the type of the argument must be *serializable*. A serializable type is a primitive or reference type that can be written to and read from a stream. In practice, all Java primitive types are serializable and so are all classes and interfaces that implement or extend the `Serializable` interface. The `Serializable` interface is defined in the `java.io` package. See Chapter 53, "Using Object Serialization," for more information.

Object references are used within the JVM that contains the object. When a local object is passed as an argument to a remote method invocation, the local object is copied from the local JVM to the remote JVM. Only non-static and non-transient field variables are copied.

When a remote object is passed via a remote method invocation within the same JVM, the reference to the remote object is passed. This is because the remote JVM already contains the object being referenced.

When an object is returned by a server object as the result of a remote method invocation, the object is copied from the remote JVM to the local JVM.

Objects and Remote Method Invocation

The Java distributed object model is a natural extension of the Java object model used within a single JVM. It implements RMI in an easy-to-use fashion and places minimal requirements on objects in order for them to be accessed remotely. These requirements are as follows:

- The object's class must implement an interface that extends the `Remote` interface. This interface must define the methods that the object will allow to be remotely invoked. These methods must throw `RemoteException`.

- The object's class must extend the `RemoteServer` class. This is typically done by extending the `UnicastRemoteObject` subclass of `RemoteServer`.

- The stub and skeleton classes of the object's class must be created using the `rmic` compiler. The stub must be distributed to the client host.

- The remote object's class, interface, and skeleton class must be in the `CLASSPATH` of the remote host.

- The remote registry must be started.

■ A remote object instance must be created and registered with the remote registry. The `bind()` and `rebind()` methods of the `Naming` class are used to register an object with its associated name. The remote object should install a security manager to enable loading of RMI classes.

Chapter 18 builds a simple distributed application that shows how each of these requirements are accomplished. Chapter 52, "Remote Method Invocation," provides more advanced examples of implementing remote objects.

Distributed Application Security

The Java distributed object model implements security through the use of class loaders and security managers in the same way that it does for applications and applets. The class loader trusts classes that are loaded from the local host. Classes are not allowed to be loaded from the network unless a security manager is in place that permits remote class loading.

An applet security manager is automatically put into place for applets as they are loaded. The security manager used in distributed Java applications is the `RMISecurityManager` class. An instance of this class should be set via the `setSecurityManager()` method of the `System` class at the beginning of execution of a client or server object. Less restrictive security managers can be developed by subclassing `RMISecurityManager` and overriding its methods.

Authentication and Access Control

Authentication is the process of verifying the identity of an individual or an object that acts on the individual's behalf. *Access control* is the process of restricting access to resources or services based on an object or individual's identity. Authentication and access control work hand in hand. Without strong authentication, unscrupulous individuals may be able to masquerade as trusted individuals. Without access control, authentication has no teeth.

Authorization and access control are important in distributed applications. For example, you may want to limit the objects that are able to remotely invoke the methods of a particular server object to those objects that execute on a specific host or set of hosts or that act on behalf of a particular individual.

The RMI API does not provide classes and interfaces that directly support authentication and access control. However, these capabilities may be built on top of the classes that are provided by the RMI API. For example, the `getClientHost()` method of the `RemoteServer` class can be used by a server object to determine the name of the host from which a remote method invocation is initiated. This may be used to limit RMI access to a specified list of hosts. This approach is not foolproof. There are demonstrated ways for malicious hosts to masquerade as trusted hosts. However, it may be used to provide a limited degree of protection. More advanced authentication and access control can be implemented through the use of digital certificates in the overall distributed application supported by RMI.

Firewalls may be used to protect distributed applications that run on an intranet. They are typically used to restrict access to the distributed application to those hosts that are on the corporate intranet or on a selected segment of the intranet. However, firewalls introduce problems of their own. If a firewall exists in the communication path between client and server objects, the firewall may prevent remote method invocations from occurring. Fortunately, JavaSoft recognized this problem; the RMISocketFactory class provides the capability for RMI to be used with a firewall. This class uses alternative approaches to client/server communication that can be used to circumvent the security restrictions imposed by many firewalls.

Summary

In this chapter you covered background information about approaches to designing and implementing digital applications and learned how Java's distributed object model compares to these approaches. You delved into the details of Java's distributed object model and learned how RMI is implemented using a three-layered protocol set. You then investigated the security issues involved with using RMI. In the next chapter, you'll cover RMI in more detail and use it to develop sample distributed applications.

52

Remote Method Invocation

In Chapters 18, "Building Distributed Applications with the java.rmi Packages," and 51, "Distributed Applications Architecture," you covered the RMI API and learned how it is used to develop distributed applications. In this chapter, you'll develop a few distributed applications of your own to get some practical experience using RMI. You'll create an applet that uses RMI to connect to a server object, retrieve information, and display the information in a text area. You'll create a random number server and a client that accesses the server. You'll learn how to use class loaders and security managers to bootstrap the client from a remote host. You'll also develop a program that contacts the remote registry of a host and obtains a list of the remote objects that it services. When you finish this chapter, you'll have enough experience using RMI to build your own distributed applications.

Using Remote Objects

In Chapter 18, you learned how to use RMI to develop simple client and server objects. The server object contained a main() method that set a security manager. It also registered the server object with the remote registry. The client performed a remote lookup of the server object in order to gain access to a local stub. It then used the stub to access the server object. The approach used in this example is common to most distributed applications that use RMI.

In order to use the client object, you copied its class file, the stub's class file, and the class file of the remote interface to a client host. While this may not have seemed to be an inconvenience at the time, one of the features of Java is the capability to automatically distribute software to client hosts. In this section, you'll learn how to use applets as clients for distributed applications. In the following section, you'll learn how to bootstrap clients from a remote host.

The InfoClient Applet

Listing 52.1 presents an applet that is used as a local client to access a remote server. The server generates news flashes that the client displays in a text area. The InfoClient.java file is stored in the ch52\info\client directory and is implemented as part of the jdg.ch52.info.client package. Note that it imports the jdg.ch52.info.server package. This package contains the classes and interfaces of the remote server.

Listing 52.1. The InfoClient applet.

```
package jdg.ch52.info.client;

import jdg.ch52.info.server.*;
import java.applet.*;
import java.awt.*;
```

```
import java.awt.event.*;
import java.net.*;
import java.rmi.*;

public class InfoClient extends Applet {
 String text = "Click Update for an InfoServer update.";
 TextArea textArea = new TextArea(15,50);
 Button update = new Button("Update");
 InfoServer server;
 public void init() {
  setLayout(new BorderLayout());
  add("Center",textArea);
  update.addActionListener(new ButtonHandler());
  add("South",update);
  try {
   URL hostURL = getCodeBase();
   String host = hostURL.getHost();
   server = (InfoServer) Naming.lookup("//"+host+"/InfoServer");
   textArea.setText(text);
  } catch (Exception ex) {
   textArea.setText(ex.toString());
  }
 }
 class ButtonHandler implements ActionListener {
  public void actionPerformed(ActionEvent ev){
   String s=ev.getActionCommand();
   if("Update".equals(s)){
    try {
     String newText=server.getInfo();
     text=newText+"\n"+text;
     textArea.setText(text);
    } catch (Exception ex){
     textArea.setText(ex.toString());
    }
   }
  }
 }
}
```

You won't get to run the applet until a little later in this chapter. I have to show you how to compile, run, and install it first. However, I'll give you a preview of its operation so that you'll be able to more easily follow the discussion.

The InfoClient applet displays a text area and an Update button to a user, as shown in Figure 52.1. When you click the Update button, the applet invokes a method of an object that executes remotely on a Web server. The remote object returns a news update to the applet, and the applet displays this news update in the text area. See Figure 52.2.

FIGURE 52.1.

The initial display of the InfoClient *applet.*

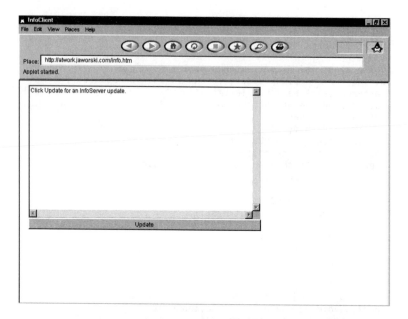

FIGURE 52.2.

The applet's display is updated with news flashes from a remote server.

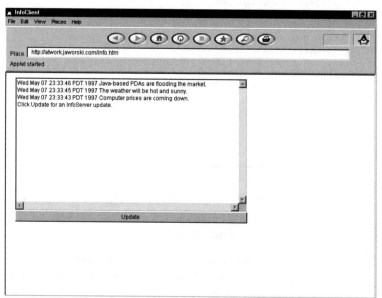

The processing performed by InfoClient consists of creating and laying out the applet's GUI, establishing access to the remote server object, and processing the event associated with the clicking of the Update button.

The server object implements the InfoServer interface. The server field variable is declared as the InfoServer type and is used to refer to the server object via a local stub. The init() method sets up the GUI and accesses the server object. The getCodebase() method retrieves the applet's URL, and the getHost() method retrieves the name of the host from which the applet was served. The lookup() method of the Naming class returns a local stub for the remote object named InfoServer. The InfoServer object executes on the Web server from which the applet was served. The local stub of the remote InfoServer object is referenced by the server variable.

The ButtonHandler class handles the clicking of the Update button by invoking the getInfo() method of the server object. This causes the server object to return a news flash in the form of a String. The returned String is then prepended to the text displayed in the text area.

Listing 52.2 contains the info.htm file that is used to display the applet. Note that it sets the CODEBASE attribute to the URL from which the applet's class file is retrieved. You must set this URL to the URL of your Web server. The actual applet is loaded from the following URL:

```
http://your.host.com/codebase/jdg/ch52/info/client/InfoClient.class
```

You'll need to create a codebase directory off of your Web server's root directory. You'll also store the compiled applet in the path /codebase/jdg/ch52/info/client/. See the section, "Compiling and Installing the InfoServer Application," later in this chapter, for information on how to compile both the client and server parts of the InfoServer application.

Listing 52.2. The info.htm file used to display the InfoClient applet.

```
<HTML>
<HEAD>
<TITLE>InfoClient</TITLE>
</HEAD>
<BODY>
<APPLET CODEBASE="http://atwork.jaworski.com/codebase/"
CODE="jdg.ch52.info.client.InfoClient.class"
WIDTH=500 HEIGHT=300>
[InfoClient Applet]
</APPLET>
</BODY>
</HTML>
```

NOTE

Make sure that you substitute your server's host name for atwork.jaworski.com in the InfoClient applet's CODEBASE attribute.

The `InfoServer` Interface

Listing 52.3 contains the `InfoServer` interface that is implemented by the server object and referenced by the `InfoClient` applet. It is contained in the `jdg.ch52.info.server` package and defines the `getInfo()` method.

Listing 52.3. The `InfoServer` interface.

```
package jdg.ch52.info.server;

import java.rmi.*;

public interface InfoServer extends Remote {
 String getInfo() throws RemoteException;
}
```

The `InfoServerImpl` Class

Listing 52.4 shows the `InfoServerImpl` class that implements the `InfoServer` interface. It declares and initializes the `info` array to a list of five news flashes. The `getInfo()` method retrieves the current date/time as a `Date` object and then randomly selects one of the elements of the `info` array. It converts the `Date` to a `String`, appends the `info` element, and returns the `String` to the invoking object.

The `main()` method sets the default security manager and creates an instance of the `InfoServerImpl` object. It invokes the `rebind()` method of the `Naming` class to register the new object with the remote registry under the name `InfoServer`. It then displays a message to the console window notifying you that the server object was successfully registered.

Listing 52.4. The `InfoServerImpl` class.

```
package jdg.ch52.info.server;

import java.rmi.*;
import java.rmi.server.*;
import java.util.*;

public class InfoServerImpl extends UnicastRemoteObject
 implements InfoServer {
 String info[] = {"Gold is up to $500 per ounce.",
  "The Chargers beat the Raiders 41-0.",
  "The weather will be hot and sunny.",
  "Computer prices are coming down.",
  "Java-based PDAs are flooding the market."};
 public InfoServerImpl() throws RemoteException {
  super();
 }
 public String getInfo() throws RemoteException {
  String newInfo;
```

```
 Date date=new Date();
 int n = new Double(100.0*Math.random()).intValue();
 n %= info.length;
 newInfo=date.toString()+" "+info[n];
 return newInfo;
}
public static void main(String args[]){
 System.setSecurityManager(new RMISecurityManager());
 try {
  InfoServerImpl instance = new InfoServerImpl();
  Naming.rebind("///InfoServer", instance);
  System.out.println("InfoServer is registered.");
 } catch (Exception ex) {
  System.out.println(ex.toString());
 }
}
}
```

Compiling and Installing the `InfoServer` Application

Now that you've covered each of the four source files, let's compile and install them on the server.

The `InfoServer.java` and `InfoServerImpl.java` files are in your `ch52\info\server` directory. Compile them as follows:

`C:\jdk1.1.1\jdg\ch52\info\server>javac InfoServer.java`

`C:\jdk1.1.1\jdg\ch52\info\server>javac InfoServerImpl.java`

Use the `rmic` compiler to create a stub and skeleton for the `InfoServerImpl` class:

`C:\jdk1.1.1\jdg\ch52\info\server>rmic jdg.ch52.info.server.InfoServerImpl`

Now switch over to the client directory and compile `InfoClient.java`:

`C:\jdk1.1.1\jdg\ch52\info\client>javac InfoClient.java`

Your class files are already to go. All you need to do is to move them to your Web server. Create the following `codebase\jdg\ch52\info\client` and `codebase\jdg\ch52\info\server` paths off of your Web server's root directory. Move the `InfoClient.class` and `InfoClient$ButtonHandler.class` classes to the `codebase\jdg\ch52\info\client` directory and the `InfoServer.class`, `InfoServerImpl.class`, `InfoServerImpl_Stub.class`, and `InfoServerImpl_Skel.class` classes to the `codebase\jdg\ch52\info\server` directory. Also copy the `info.htm` file to your Web server's root directory.

In order to execute the `InfoServerImpl` class, you'll need to include the `codebase` directory in the CLASSPATH of the computer that's hosting your Web server. Go ahead and do this before going on to the next section. If you are running Windows 95, you'll have to restart your system for the new CLASSPATH to go into effect.

Running the `InfoServer` Application

Hang on. We're almost there. Just a few more things to do and we can run the `InfoServer` application.

At this time, you should start your Web server if it isn't already up and running. I'm using Jeeves as my Web server for this example. I configured it so that it listens for HTTP requests on port 80 instead of the default port 8080.

Start the remote registry program, as follows:

```
C:\jdk1.1.1\jdg\ch52\info>start rmiregistry
```

On Windows 95 systems the preceding command will create and open a blank DOS window. Just minimize the window and go on.

Now start up the server object, as follows:

```
C:\jdk1.1.1\jdg\ch52\info>java jdg.ch52.info.server.InfoServerImpl
InfoServer is registered.
```

The server object will inform you that it has successfully registered itself with the remote registry program. That completes the server setup.

To run the application, you will need a Web browser that supports the JDK 1.1. I'll use HotJava. If you do not have HotJava, you can use appletviewer. From the same host or a different host, launch HotJava and open up the URL `http://your.server.com/info.htm`, where `your.server.com` is the URL of the Web server where you installed the HTML and class files and ran the server object. If you are running the client and server on the same host, you can use `localhost` for your host name. Figure 52.1 shows the initial browser window. Now click the Update button a few times to receive news flashes from the remote object. (Refer to Figure 52.2.)

Working with Class Loaders and Security Managers

The previous example showed how easy it is to use applets as the clients of distributed applications. After creating and compiling the required classes and starting the remote object, you just load the appropriate classes on your Web server. Users download the client applet as part of a Web page. No client installation is required.

The applet-based approach that you learned in the previous section works great for many distributed applications. However, there may be times when you want to run the client as an application and not as an applet. In this section, I'll show you an approach to distributing application clients that is almost as easy to use as the applet approach. This approach makes use of class loaders and security managers and provides a practical introduction to these topics.

A Random Number Server

In many numerical applications (such as simulations, applied genetic algorithms, and cryptography), it is important to have a good random number generator. All software-based random number generators are pseudorandom and create repeating patterns after a time. Hardware-based random number generators, such as noisy diodes, have been developed that overcome the problems with software random number generators. Unfortunately, not everyone has immediate access to high-grade random number generators. That's where random number servers come in. You ask the server for a random number and it gives you one.

The distributed application that you'll develop is a random number server. You'll be using the `Math.random()` function to generate random numbers. However, you can use this application as a basis for developing more advanced random number generators if you wish. The distributed application makes use of a random number client that is a window application program, as opposed to an applet. The client is maintained on a Web server, along with the random number server. A bootstrap program is developed that allows clients to remotely load the client. This bootstrap program is generic in nature and may be used with other distributed applications. The bootstrap program illustrates the use of class loaders and security managers within the context of distributed applications.

The `RandomServer` Interface

Listing 52.5 shows the `RandomServer` interface. This interface defines the `getRandom()` function that returns a double value between 0 and 1. Note that the interface is contained in the `jdg.ch52.random.server` package.

Listing 52.5. The `RandomServer` interface.

```
package jdg.ch52.random.server;

import java.rmi.*;

public interface RandomServer extends Remote {
 double getRandom() throws RemoteException;
}
```

The `RandomServerImpl` Class

The `RandomServerImpl` class, shown in Listing 52.6, implements the `RandomServer` interface. The `getRandom()` method just returns a random number generated by the standard `Math.random()` method. To implement a high-grade random number server, you would replace this method with one that obtains its data from an external random number source. You would probably use a native method (see Chapter 59, "Creating Native Methods") to accomplish this.

The `main()` method installs a default `RMISecurityManager` object as the security manager and registers an instance of the `RandomServerImpl` class with the remote registry. It then displays a message to the console window informing you of its success.

Listing 52.6. The `RandomServerImpl` class.

```
package jdg.ch52.random.server;

import java.rmi.*;
import java.rmi.server.*;

public class RandomServerImpl extends UnicastRemoteObject
 implements RandomServer {
 public RandomServerImpl() throws RemoteException {
  super();
 }
 public double getRandom() throws RemoteException {
  return Math.random();
 }
 public static void main(String args[]){
  System.setSecurityManager(new RMISecurityManager());
  try {
   RandomServerImpl instance = new RandomServerImpl();
   Naming.rebind("///RandomServer", instance);
   System.out.println("RandomServer is registered.");
  } catch (Exception ex) {
   System.out.println(ex.toString());
  }
 }
}
```

The `RandomClient` Class

The client application used with the random number server is shown in Listing 52.7. This application has an interesting twist. There's no `main()` method because the client's class file remains on the Web server and is loaded remotely (and executed) by a second bootstrap program. The bootstrap program is a generic program that can be used to remotely load distributed application clients. We'll cover the bootstrap program in the following section.

As a point of reference, Figure 52.3 shows the initial display of the `RandomClient` program. You click the New Random button and a new random number is displayed, as shown in Figure 52.4.

FIGURE 52.3.

The initial display of
`RandomClient`.

FIGURE 52.4.

The random number returned by RandomServer.

Note that the host variable is assigned the host name atwork.jaworski.com. You'll need to change this to your Web server's host name in order to run it with your Web server.

RandomClient implements the Runnable interface. This is so that it can be executed as a separate thread by the bootstrap program. It implements an empty run() method in order to satisfy the Runnable interface. The main processing performed by RandomClient is in the creation of the application window and the handling of the clicking of the New Random button.

During the creation of the application window, the connectToServer() method is invoked to obtain a reference to the RandomServer object. This reference is stored in the server variable.

The ButtonHandler class handles the clicking of the New Random button by invoking the getRandom() method of the RandomServer object and displaying the returned value as a text string.

Listing 52.7. The RandomClient class.

```
package jdg.ch52.random.client;

import jdg.ch52.random.server.*;
import java.awt.*;
import java.awt.event.*;
import java.net.*;
import java.rmi.*;
import java.rmi.server.*;

public class RandomClient extends Frame implements Runnable {
 String host="atwork.jaworski.com";
 TextField text = new TextField(50);
 Button newRandom = new Button("New Random");
 RandomServer server;
 int screenWidth = 500;
 int screenHeight = 100;
 public void run(){
 }
 public RandomClient() {
  super("RandomClient");
  setup();
  setSize(screenWidth,screenHeight);
  addWindowListener(new WindowEventHandler());
  show();
 }
 void setup() {
  setLayout(new FlowLayout(FlowLayout.LEFT));
  newRandom.addActionListener(new ButtonHandler());
```

continues

Listing 52.7. continued

```
   add(newRandom);
   add(text);
   connectToServer();
  }
  void connectToServer() {
   try {
    server = (RandomServer) Naming.lookup("//"+host+"/RandomServer");
   } catch (Exception ex) {
    text.setText(ex.toString());
   }
  }
  class ButtonHandler implements ActionListener {
   public void actionPerformed(ActionEvent ev){
    String s=ev.getActionCommand();
    if("New Random".equals(s)){
     try {
      double rand=server.getRandom();
      text.setText(new Double(rand).toString());
     } catch (Exception ex){
      text.setText(ex.toString());
     }
    }
   }
  }
  class WindowEventHandler extends WindowAdapter {
   public void windowClosing(WindowEvent e){
    System.exit(0);
   }
  }
}
```

The Bootstrap Class

We finally get to the Bootstrap class, shown in Listing 52.8. This class implements the most interesting processing of the RandomServer application. However, before I get into the details of this processing, let me summarize its operation. You run the Bootstrap program on a client host and specify the URL and name of a client application (that is, RandomClient). Bootstrap retrieves the client application from a remote Web server and executes it locally. The client application (running locally) uses RMI to invoke the methods of server objects (that is, RandomServer) executing on the Web server. The Bootstrap program solves the problem of maintaining and distributing client programs. The clients are maintained and stored on a central Web server. They can be upgraded and modified without having to be installed on users' computers. You only need to distribute the Bootstrap program. It is a small program that can be used to load and execute clients from any host.

The `Bootstrap` program is invoked with the `-D` option to set the `java.rmi.server.codebase` property to the URL where all classes should be loaded. The name of the class of the client program is also identified. The following is an example of the program's invocation:

```
java -Djava.rmi.server.codebase=http://host.com/codebase/ Bootstrap Client
```

The preceding command runs `Bootstrap` and sets the `java.rmi.server.codebase` property to `http://host.com/codebase/`. All classes are loaded from this URL. In particular, the `Client` class is loaded remotely and executed locally. Any classes that are loaded by `Client` are also loaded from the identified URL. If you can't picture how `Bootstrap` works, hang in there. When you actually run `Bootstrap`, its function will be obvious.

`Bootstrap` is a simple console program. Its first few lines just display directions on how it is to be used. It is important to note that in the first line, it sets the security manager to an object of the `BootstrapSecurityManager` class. This class overrides `RMISecurityManager` and supports a more liberal policy for remotely loaded clients. `BootstrapSecurityManager` is covered in the next section.

The main processing performed by `Bootstrap` takes place within the `try` statement. It invokes the static `loadClass()` method of the `RMIClassLoader` class to load the class named as a command line argument. This class is the name of the client application. The class is loaded from the URL specified by the `java.rmi.server.codebase` property.

The loaded class is assigned to the `clientClass` variable. An instance of the loaded class is then created and cast as a `Runnable` object. This creates a separate thread of execution. (That's why we implemented `RandomClient` as `Runnable`.) The `run()` method of the newly created thread is then invoked to cause the thread to be executed.

The three lines of code within the `try` statement accomplish quite a bit. They load a user-selected client application from a specified URL and execute it locally.

Listing 52.8. The `Bootstrap` class.

```
import java.rmi.*;
import java.rmi.server.*;

public class Bootstrap {
 public static void main(String args[]) {
  System.setSecurityManager(new BootstrapSecurityManager());
  if(args.length!=1){
   System.out.print("Usage: java -Djava.rmi.server.codebase=URL ");
   System.out.println("Bootstrap clientName");
   System.out.println("\n  Notes:");
   System.out.print("    Use a URL of the form: ");
   System.out.println("http://host.com/codebase/");
```

continues

Listing 52.8. continued

```
System.out.print("    Substitute the name of the client's ");
System.out.println("class for clientName");
System.out.println("\n  Example:");
System.out.print("     java -Djava.rmi.server.codebase=");
System.out.println("http://host.com/codebase/ Bootstrap Client");
System.exit(0);
}
System.out.println("Loading "+args[0]+" ...");
try {
 Class clientClass = RMIClassLoader.loadClass(args[0]);
 Runnable clientInstance = (Runnable) clientClass.newInstance();
 clientInstance.run();
} catch (Exception ex) {
 System.out.println(ex.toString());
 }
 }
}
```

The BootstrapSecurityManager Class

The BootstrapSecurityManager class is needed to let Bootstrap run without any security exceptions. The default RMISecurityManager is somewhat restrictive in the capabilities that it permits for remotely loaded applications. It is similar to the security manager used with applets in this regard. How do we overcome these restrictions? By simply extending RMISecurityManager and overriding the methods that perform certain security checks.

Listing 15.9 shows the methods of RMISecurityManager that are overridden by BootstrapSecurityManager. These methods check a variety of operations to determine whether they are permissible under the RMI security policy. The RMISecurityManager methods with a void return value raise a SecurityException when an operation that violates the RMI security policy is detected. By overriding them in BootstrapSecurityManager, you prevent the SecurityException from occurring. The checkTopLevelWindow() method returns a boolean value indicating whether it is permissible for a remotely loaded class to open a top level application window. By always returning a true value, you ensure that a top level window can be created and opened by the remotely loaded client.

The methods that have been overridden by BootstrapSecurityManager are described in the RMISecurityManager class. You can override other methods in addition to these. The methods that were overridden were selected to allow clients, like RandomClient, to execute without a SecurityException.

Listing 52.9. The BootstrapSecurityManager class.

```
import java.rmi.*;
import java.io.*;
```

```
public class BootstrapSecurityManager extends RMISecurityManager {
 public synchronized void checkAccess(Thread t){}
 public synchronized void checkAccess(ThreadGroup g){}
 public synchronized void checkExit(int status){}
 public synchronized void checkPropertiesAccess(){}
 public synchronized void checkAccept(String host,int port){}
 public synchronized void checkConnect(String host,int port){}
 public synchronized boolean checkTopLevelWindow(Object window){
  return true;
 }
 public synchronized void checkPackageAccess(String pkg){}
 public void checkAwtEventQueueAccess(){}
 public synchronized void checkRead(FileDescriptor fd){}
 public synchronized void checkRead(String file){}
}
```

Compiling and Installing the RandomServer Application

You compile and install the RandomServer application using the following steps:

1. Compile RandomServer.java, RandomServerImpl.java, and RandomClient.java.

2. Run rmic on RandomServerImpl to create RandomServerImpl_Stub.class and RandomServerImpl_Skel.class. Remember to run rmic using the full package name of RandomServerImpl (that is, rmic jdg.ch52.random.server.RandomServerImpl).

3. Move RandomServer.class, RandomServerImpl.class, RandomServerImpl_Stub.class, and RandomServerImpl_Skel.class to the /codebase/jdg/ch52/random/server directory off of your Web server's root.

4. Move RandomClient.class, RandomClient$WindowEventHandler.class, and RandomClient$ButtonHandler.class to the /codebase/jdg/ch52/random/client directory off of your Web server's root.

5. Make sure that the codebase directory is in your CLASSPATH.

6. Compile BootstrapSecurityManager.java and Bootstrap.java.

7. Copy Bootstrap.class and BootstrapSecurityManager.class to a client host.

This may seem like a lot of work, but you'll only have to do all but the last step once. You'll need to copy the Bootstrap classes to any clients that want to remotely load a client application.

Running the RandomServer Application

To run the distribute RandomServer application, do the following:

1. Make sure that your Web server is running.

2. Start rmiregistry on your Web server host.

3. Run `java jdg.ch52.random.server.RandomServerImpl` on your Web server host.
4. Run the `Bootstrap` program on a client host.

The last step is performed as follows:

```
java -Djava.rmi.server.codebase=http://atwork.jaworski.com/codebase/
➥Bootstrap jdg.ch52.random.client.RandomClient
```

Substitute your Web server's host name for `atwork.jaworski.com`.

> **NOTE**
>
> If you intend to use the `Bootstrap` program, you may want to consider putting the long command line in a batch file.

When you run `Bootstrap`, it loads `RandomClient` from your Web server and executes it locally. Figure 52.3 shows its opening display. When you click the New Random button, `RandomClient` invokes the `getRandom()` method of the `RandomServer` object (executing on your Web server) and displays the value returned by `getRandom()`.

Locating Remote Objects

In a large network running a multitude of server objects, it is sometimes difficult to keep track of which objects are running on which hosts. In this section, we'll develop a client application, named `Browser`, that enables you to browse a host's registry to see what remote objects it supports.

Listing 52.10 shows the `Browser` program. You compile it using `javac Browser.java` and run it using `java Browser`. Before you run `Browser`, start `rmiregistry` and run `RandomServerImpl` and `InfoServerImpl`. This will put two object names in your remote registry.

The `Browser` application's opening window is shown in Figure 52.5. Enter the name of the host running the remote registry and click on the Browse host button. The text area in the center of the program window displays the objects that are maintained in the local registry. (See Figure 52.6.) You can also use this program to browse the remote registries of other hosts.

`Browser`'s `ButtonEventHandler` uses the static `getRegistry()` method of the `LocateRegistry` class to return a `Registry` object for a specified host. The `list()` method of the `Registry` interface returns an array that contains the names of all objects that are currently registered in the registry. These objects are displayed to the text area in the middle of the `Browser` window.

FIGURE 52.5.

The Browser *opening display.*

FIGURE 52.6.

The Browser *displays the remote objects maintained by the remote registry on the specified host.*

Listing 52.10. The Browser **program.**

```
import java.awt.*;
import java.awt.event.*;
import java.rmi.registry.*;

public class Browser extends Frame {
 TextField host = new TextField(30);
 TextArea objectNames = new TextArea(15,50);
 Button browse = new Button("Browse host");
 int screenWidth = 500;
 int screenHeight = 400;
 public static void main(String args[]){
  Browser app = new Browser();
 }
 public Browser() {
  super("Browser");
  setup();
```

continues

Listing 52.10. continued

```
  setSize(screenWidth,screenHeight);
  addWindowListener(new WindowEventHandler());
  show();
 }
 void setup() {
  browse.addActionListener(new ButtonHandler());
  Panel panel = new Panel();
  panel.add(new Label("Host name: "));
  panel.add(host);
  panel.add(browse);
  add("North",panel);
  add("Center",objectNames);
 }
 class ButtonHandler implements ActionListener {
  public void actionPerformed(ActionEvent ev){
   String s=ev.getActionCommand();
   if("Browse host".equals(s)){
    try {
     Registry registry = LocateRegistry.getRegistry(host.getText());
     String objectList[] = registry.list();
     String objects="";
     for(int i=0;i<objectList.length;++i){
      objects+=objectList[i]+"\n";
     }
     objectNames.setText(objects);
    } catch (Exception ex){
     objectNames.setText(ex.toString());
    }
   }
  }
 }
 class WindowEventHandler extends WindowAdapter {
  public void windowClosing(WindowEvent e){
   System.exit(0);
  }
 }
}
```

Summary

In this chapter, you developed a few distributed applications that gave you some practical experience using RMI. You created an applet that uses RMI to connect to a server object, retrieve information, and display the information in a text area. You created a random number server and a client that accesses the server. You also learned how to use class loaders and security managers to bootstrap the client from a remote host. Finally, you developed a program that contacts the remote registry of a host and obtains a list of the remote objects that it services. In the next chapter, you'll learn about object serialization, an important topic for RMI and JavaBeans, as well.

53

Using Object Serialization

Most meaningful Java applications provide a way to save the Java objects they create and to restore these objects at a later point in time. For example, in Chapter 44, "Using JavaBeans," you saw how the BeanBox lets you change the properties of a component and then save the component's state. The BeanBox also lets you restore the state of a saved component.

The capability for an object to exist beyond the execution of the program that created it is known as *persistence*. Serialization is the key to implementing persistence. *Serialization* provides the capability to write an object to a stream and to read the object back in at a later time.

Serialization allows you to store objects in files, to communicate them across networks, and to use them in distributed applications. In this chapter, you'll be introduced to object serialization. You'll learn how it works and how it is used in both distributed and non-distributed applications. You'll cover the Serializable and Externalizable interfaces and the security issues related to object serialization. When you finish this chapter, you'll be better able to use serialization in your programs.

Storing Objects to Streams

On the surface, the process of storing an object to a stream may seem trivial. But, it is, in fact, quite involved. When an object is written to a stream, information about its class must be stored along with the object. Without class information, there is no way to reconstruct an object that is read from a stream. In addition to class information, all objects that are referenced by that object must also be stored. If the referenced objects are not stored along with the object, the references of the stored object become meaningless.

The Serializable Interface

The JDK 1.1 provides the Serializable and Externalizable interfaces of the java.io package to support object serialization. We'll cover the Serializable interface in this section and the Externalizable interface in the next. The Serializable interface is easy to use. It contains no methods. You just declare your class as being Serializable and use the ObjectOutputStream filter to write objects to a stream. The writeObject() method of ObjectOutputStream automatically takes care of storing the correct information when objects of the class are written to a stream. Objects are read back in using the readObject() method of the ObjectInputStream class. The objects that are read back in are cast to their original types.

Listing 53.1 provides an example of using the Serializable interface. The SerialApp program creates an instance of ObjectOutputStream on the temp file and assigns it to the outputStream variable. The SerialApp program invokes the getProperties() method of the System class to obtain the current system properties. It invokes the writeObject() method of ObjectOutputStream to write the Properties object to the output stream. Note that the Properties class is Serializable. It then closes the output stream and creates an instance of ObjectInputStream on the temp file. It reads an object from the input stream using the readObject() method of the

ObjectInputStream class. The object is cast into an object of the Properties class and assigned to the newProp variable. The list() method of the Properties class displays the object as follows:

```
-- listing properties --
user.language=en
java.home=C:\jdk1.1.1
awt.toolkit=sun.awt.windows.WToolkit
file.encoding.pkg-sun.io
java.version=1.1.1
file.separator=\
line.separator=

user.region=US
file.encoding=8859_1
java.vendor=Sun Microsystems Inc.
user.timezone=PST
user.name=Jamie
os.arch=x86
os.name=Windows 95
java.vendor.url=http://www.sun.com/
user.dir=C:\jdk1.1.1\jdg\ch53
java.class.path=.;C:\JDK1.1.1\LIB\CLASSES.ZIP;C:\jdk1...
java.class.version=45.3
os.version=4.0
path.separator=;
user.home=C:\jdk1.1.1
```

The properties that are displayed on your computer will differ depending on your operating system and how you have set up the JDK.

Java's object serialization capabilities make it easy to read and write objects from a file. Without these capabilities, you would be forced to read and write each primitive value of each property.

Listing 53.1. The SerialApp program.

```
import java.io.*;
import java.util.*;

public class SerialApp {
 public static void main(String args[]) {
  try {
   ObjectOutputStream outputStream = new ObjectOutputStream(
    new FileOutputStream("temp"));
   Properties prop = System.getProperties();
   outputStream.writeObject(prop);
   outputStream.close();
   ObjectInputStream inputStream = new ObjectInputStream(
    new FileInputStream("temp"));
   Properties newProp = (Properties) inputStream.readObject();
   inputStream.close();
   newProp.list(System.out);
  } catch(Exception ex) {
   System.out.println(ex.toString());
  }
 }
}
```

Special Requirements for Using Serializable

Only objects that are Serializable can be stored to a stream using the ObjectOuputStream class. This includes all objects that are referenced by the object being written. If the object being written to a stream refers to an object that is not Serializable, the NotSerializableException is thrown.

When a serialized object is written to a stream, the class of the object, the class's signature, and the values of all non-transient and non-static field variables are written to the stream. If an object references other objects (except in transient or static fields), those objects are also written to the stream.

> **NOTE**
>
> Static and transient field variables are not saved when a Serializable object is written to a stream using the writeObject(). These field variables are ignored by readObject() when a Serializable object is read from a stream.

In order for a class to be Serializable, its parent class must either be Serializable or have a default constructor that does not take any arguments. The no-argument constructor is used to initialize an object's parent class when the object is read from a stream. If a parent class is not Serializable, it is the responsibility of the Serializable subclass to save and restore the state of its parent beyond the default initialization. A Serializable class can tailor the way that it is serialized by declaring readObject() and writeObject() methods of the following form:

```
private void writeObject(ObjectOutputStream stream) throws IOException {
}
private void readObject(ObjectInputStream stream) throws IOException,
ClassNotFoundException {
}
```

In general, because all primitive types and most classes are Serializable, you don't need to mess around with tailoring the way that your classes are serialized.

The serialver Tool

You can determine if a class is Serializable by looking up its API description or writing a program to see if its objects are instances of the Serializable interface. In some cases, the first alternative may not be possible—you may be using a class that is not documented. The second alternative is somewhat an inconvenience. The serialver tool that is included with the JDK 1.1 provides a quick and easy way to determine whether a class is Serializable. It also returns the serialVersionUID of the class. The serialVersionUID is used to uniquely identify the class of an object that is written to a stream. The serialver tool can be run from the command line by identifying the fully qualified name of a class as an argument. Examples of its use follow:

```
C:\WINDOWS>serialver java.lang.Object
Class java.lang.Object is not Serializable.

C:\WINDOWS>serialver java.lang.String
java.lang.String:    static final long serialVersionUID = -6849794470754667710L;
```

You can also run `serialver` as a window application by invoking it with the `-show` option. For example, `serialver -show` creates the application window shown in Figure 53.1. You can then enter the name of the class you want to check and click the Show button. The program displays the results of the query, as shown in Figures 53.2 and 53.3.

FIGURE 53.1.

The window version of serialver.

FIGURE 53.2.

The serialver *program identifies the* serialVersionUID *of a class.*

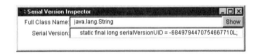

FIGURE 53.3.

The serialver *program identifies a class as not being* Serializable.

The Externalizable Interface

The `Serializable` interface and the `writeObject()` and `readObject()` methods of `ObjectOutputStream` and `ObjectInputStream` provide the most convenient way to save objects to a stream and restore them at a later time. This convenience comes at the expense of relinquishing control of how the objects are stored in and read from streams.

The `Externalizable` interface extends the `Serializable` interface to provide you with additional control in the way that objects are written to and read from streams. Because the `Externalizable` interface extends the `Serializable` interface, you can use `Externalizable` objects with `ObjectOutputStream` and `ObjectInputStream` in the same manner that you could use `Serializable` objects. The only difference is that the class of an `Externalizable` object must implement the `writeExternal()` and `readExternal()` methods defined by the `Externalizable` interfaces. These methods are of the following form:

```
public void writeExternal(ObjectOutput out) throws IOException {
}

public void readExternal(ObjectInput in) throws IOException, ClassNotFoundException {
}
```

The writeExternal() method is implemented by an Externalizable object to write itself to an output stream represented by an ObjectOutput interface. The ObjectOutput interface provides methods for writing objects to an output stream. The ObjectOutput interface extends the DataOutput interface, which provides methods for writing primitive types to an output stream.

The readExternal() method is the input analog of the writeExternal() method. It is implemented by an Externalizable object to read its values from an input stream represented by an ObjectInput interface. The ObjectInput interface provides methods for reading objects from an input stream. It extends the DataInput interface, which provides methods for reading primitive data types from an input stream. When an Externalizable object is read from an input stream, an instance of the object is created using its default no-argument constructor. The object's readExternal() method is then invoked.

The Externalizable interface gives you complete control over the way that objects are written to and read from streams. This control comes at the expense of having to implement your own methods for reading and writing the objects. The Exteralizable objects are responsible for storing and retrieving the state of their parent class as well as any objects that they reference.

Listing 53.2 provides an example of using the Externalizable interface. The main() method of ExternalApp is similar to the main() method of SerialApp. The only difference is that you are writing and reading an object of MyClass.

The MyClass class implements the Externalizable interface. It declares three variables that are of the GregorianCalendar and String types. Its no-argument constructor creates a default GregorianCalendar object and two strings that are set to uninitialized. Its other constructor takes a Date parameter. It invokes the setFieldValues() method to set the cal, timeVal, and dateVal variables based on the value of the Date object that is passed as a parameter.

The writeExternal() method saves a MyClass object to a stream as a Date object. The Date object is created using the getTime() method of the Calendar class. The readExternal() method reads a MyClass object as a Date object and invokes the setFieldValues() method to initialize the fields of the MyClass object.

The toString() method returns a String value of a MyClass object. The setFieldValues() method initializes the field variables of a MyClass object based on the value of a Date parameter.

The ExternalApp program shows how the Externalizable interface is used to control the manner in which objects are serialized. The writeExternal() and readExternal() methods serialize MyClass objects as Date objects. This allows these objects to be stored in a more compact form.

The program displays the current date and time as shown:

```
C:\jdk1.1.1\jdg\ch53>java ExternalApp
5/8/1997 4:52:20
```

Listing 53.2. The ExternalApp program.

```
import java.io.*;
import java.util.*;

public class ExternalApp {
 public static void main(String args[]) {
  try {
   ObjectOutputStream outputStream = new ObjectOutputStream(
    new FileOutputStream("temp"));
   MyClass obj = new MyClass(new Date());
   outputStream.writeObject(obj);
   outputStream.close();
   ObjectInputStream inputStream = new ObjectInputStream(
    new FileInputStream("temp"));
   MyClass newObj = (MyClass) inputStream.readObject();
   inputStream.close();
   System.out.println(newObj);
  } catch(Exception ex) {
   System.out.println(ex.toString());
  }
 }
}

class MyClass implements Externalizable {
 GregorianCalendar cal;
 String timeVal;
 String dateVal;
 public MyClass() {
  cal = new GregorianCalendar();
  timeVal="uninitialized";
  dateVal="uninitialized";
 }
 public MyClass(Date d){
  cal = new GregorianCalendar();
  setFieldValues(d);
 }
 public void writeExternal(ObjectOutput out) throws IOException {
  out.writeObject(cal.getTime());
 }
 public void readExternal(ObjectInput in) throws IOException,
  ClassNotFoundException {
  Date date = (Date) in.readObject();
  setFieldValues(date);
 }
 public String toString() {
  if(timeVal=="uninitialized") return timeVal;
  return dateVal+" "+timeVal;
 }
 void setFieldValues(Date d){
  cal.setTime(d);
  timeVal = String.valueOf(cal.get(cal.HOUR))+":";
  timeVal += String.valueOf(cal.get(cal.MINUTE))+":";
  timeVal += String.valueOf(cal.get(cal.SECOND));
  dateVal = String.valueOf(cal.get(cal.MONTH)+1)+"/";
  dateVal += String.valueOf(cal.get(cal.DATE))+"/";
  dateVal += String.valueOf(cal.get(cal.YEAR));
 }
}
```

Object Serialization and RMI

Object serialization is used extensively in remote method invocation (RMI). It is used to send the arguments of a method invocation from the client object to the remote object, and to send return values from the server object back to the client object. As a consequence, all arguments to a remote method invocation must be `Serializable`. Similarly, any values returned by a remote object must also be `Serializable`.

The serialization used by RMI is transparent to the client and server objects. It is performed by the stubs and skeletons, remote reference layer, and transport layer. This is a great convenience and a major benefit of RMI. Applications that use TCP sockets for client/server communication are responsible for serializing and deserializing objects via input and output streams. With RMI, you only need to ensure that your arguments and return values are `Serializable`; RMI takes care of serialization and deserialization.

Security Considerations

Because object serialization is used as the primary mechanism to store and retrieve Java objects and to send them over a network, it is of considerable importance for the security of Java objects and programs. While a Java object is stored in a file or is being transmitted over a network, it is outside of the Java Virtual Machine (JVM) and is vulnerable to deliberate or accidental modification. In addition, any sensitive data contained in the object can be read.

Whenever an object is read from a stream, the object cannot be trusted to be a faithful representation of the object that was written to the stream. The validity of an object must be determined when it is read. This can be accomplished by implementing the `readObject()` and `writeObject()` or `readExternal()` and `writeExternal()` methods. A digital signature of the object can be created, using the methods of the Security API, and stored with the object. The object's signature can be verified when the object is read from the stream.

When sensitive information contained in an object is written to a stream, that information is subject to disclosure. One solution to this problem is to encrypt objects when they are serialized. This can be readily accomplished using the Security API by creating output and input streams that act as filters for the `ObjectOutputStream` and `ObjectInputStream` classes.

Another solution involves the judicious use of static and transient variables. Because static and transient variables are never serialized, the information contained in these variables is never exposed. The drawback to this approach is that the sensitive information is not persistent and expires at the termination of the program that created it. An even harsher solution would be to ensure that sensitive objects do not implement the `Serializable` or `Externalizable` interfaces.

Summary

In this chapter, you were introduced to object serialization. You learned how it works and how it is used in both distributed and non-distributed applications. You covered the `Serializable` and `Externalizable` interfaces and learned about security issues related to object serialization. In the next chapter, you'll extend your distributed application programming capabilities by learning how Java fits into the Common Object Request Broker Architecture (CORBA).

54

Java IDL and ORBs

In Chapter 51, "Distributed Applications Architecture," you learned about different approaches to developing distributed applications. One of the approaches that you covered was Common Object Request Broker Architecture (CORBA). You learned about the similarities and differences between Java RMI and CORBA and how RMI provides a pure Java implementation of the distributed object model used by CORBA. While RMI is much easier to use for developing distributed applications in Java, it is limited to pure Java applications. CORBA, on the other hand, is language-neutral and allows you to interface Java objects with objects written in other programming languages.

In this chapter, you'll learn about the current work that is underway at JavaSoft to connect Java objects to objects written in other languages. You'll learn how Object Request Brokers (ORBs) are used to connect distributed objects, how the Interface Definition Language (IDL) is used to define object interfaces, and how the `idlgen` compiler is used to create Java stub and skeleton classes. You'll also learn about JavaSoft's portable ORB core and its plans to develop protocols to connect the portable ORB core to other ORBs. When you finish this chapter, you'll have a good understanding of how Java objects will be able to connect with other objects through CORBA.

The Object Management Group and CORBA

The Object Management Group (OMG), which can be reached at `http://www.omg.org`, is a consortium of companies and other organizations that were founded in 1989 to promote the development of component-based software through the establishment of object-oriented software standards and guidelines. The OMG currently has over 700 members.

Since its creation the OMG has focused on standards for implementing distributed objects. CORBA is a result of this effort. It provides a standard architecture for developing distributed object-oriented systems. This architecture specifies how a client object, written in one language, is able to invoke the methods of a remote server object, developed in a different language.

> **NOTE**
>
> An overview of CORBA is provided in Chapter 51.

CORBA makes use of stubs and skeletons in much the same way as Java RMI. A stub is a local proxy for a remote object. It presents the same interface as the server object but runs on the same computer as the client. A skeleton is a remote interface to the server object's implementation. It runs on the same computer as the server object and provides an interface between the server object's implementation and other objects.

The stub and skeleton are connected via an ORB. The ORB forwards method invocations from the stub to the skeleton and makes use of a special object called an Object Adapter (OA), which runs on the same computers as the server object. The OA activates the server object, if required, and helps to manage its operation. You can think of the ORB as analogous to the remote reference and transport layers of Java RMI and the OA as being like the remote registry.

Figure 54.1 provides an overview of how client and server objects communicate using CORBA. When a client object invokes the methods of a server object, it does so via the local stub of the server object. The stub presents two interfaces. Its interface to the client object is in a form that is recognized by the client object's implementation. Its interface to the ORB is in a form that is common to the ORB.

The local stub communicates with an ORB and provides it with the name of the object, the method being invoked, and any arguments to the method invocation. The ORB finds the referenced object in its network domain and contacts the OA running on the same computer as the server object. The ORB passes the method invocation and argument information to the OA.

The OA will do a number of things based on the way that it manages objects on the server's computer. Its basic responsibility, however, is to activate the server object's implementation and then pass the method invocation and arguments to the server object's implementation via the skeleton. The server object processes the method invocation and returns any results to the skeleton, which forwards them to the ORB.

The skeleton, like the stub, presents two interfaces. Its interface to the OA and ORB is a standard interface that each expect. Its interface with the server object is in a form that is known to the server object. Later in this chapter you'll learn how stubs and skeletons are specified in the Interface Definition Language and automatically generated.

When the skeleton returns a value to the ORB, the ORB forwards the return value to the stub, and the stub returns the value to the client object.

FIGURE 54.1.
How client and server objects communicate using CORBA.

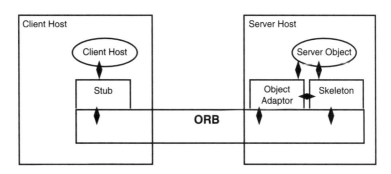

Object Request Brokers

The ORB is the key to making CORBA work. It is the essential glue that ties together stubs, skeletons, and OAs. It is responsible for communicating with the stub, finding the server object, and communicating with the OA and skeleton. It provides a language-neutral interface to the stub and skeleton and helps them to abstract away the fact that the client and server objects are implemented on different computers and in different languages. To the client there must be no difference between invoking the methods of a local and remote object. To the server, the fact that its methods are being invoked remotely is transparent. The transparency that the ORB, stub, and skeleton provide to the client and server objects is the greatest feature of CORBA.

In Figure 54.1, the ORB is shown as a single entity between the client and server. This is a logical representation of the ORB. The actual implementation of an ORB may vary depending upon the ORB. The ORB may be implemented as peer components that are installed on both the client and server's computers. It may be implemented as an ORB server that resides on a separate computer. Other ORB implementations are also possible.

> **NOTE**
>
> The part of the ORB that provides the basic representation of objects and communication of requests is referred to as the *ORB core*.

Interoperability Between ORBs

There may be multiple ORB implementations from different vendors within the same network that are used in the same distributed application. A client may simultaneously use two different ORBs to access multiple objects. A client may also use one ORB to access an object that is serviced by another ORB. Because multiple ORBs may exist within the same application, it is necessary that the ORBs be able to communicate with each other.

The General Inter-ORB Protocol (GIOP) is the common interface that is used to support communication between ORBs. The GIOP specifies a syntax and set of message formats for inter-ORB communication. Because ORBs may be implemented on networks that use a variety of transport protocols, such as TCP/IP, IPX, or SNA, the protocol used to transport information between ORBs is not specified in GIOP.

The Internet Inter-ORB Protocol (IIOP) is used to map the GIOP to the TCP/IP protocol suite. Different ORBs are able to communicate with each other, using GIOP and IIOP, across TCP/IP networks, as shown in Figure 54.2.

FIGURE 54.2.
*Different ORBs
communicate using
GIOP and IIOP across
TCP/IP networks.*

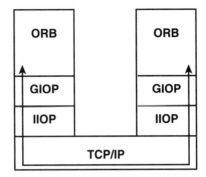

In addition to GIOP and IIOP, CORBA also provides Environment-Specific Inter-ORB Protocols (ESIOPs). ESIOPs are used to connect legacy applications to distributed applications that are CORBA-compliant. Legacy systems use ESIOPs to communicate with ORBs. ESIOPs, like the GIOP, need to be tailored to their networking environment. The DCE Common Inter-ORB Protocol (DCE-CIOP) is used with ESIOP to integrate DCE applications with CORBA applications.

The Interface Definition Language

Now that you have the big picture of what CORBA is all about, we'll cover one more important element of CORBA before we go on and look at Java IDL. Because one of CORBA's main goals is to provide a distributed object-oriented framework for which objects created in a variety of programming languages can interact, it needs a way to bridge the gap between multiple programming language interfaces and the ORB. IDL is the key to achieving this goal.

IDL provides a language-neutral way of describing the interfaces of objects. IDL describes an interface in the same manner that Java interfaces do. IDL defines the methods contained in an interface, their arguments, and their return values. IDL does not specify how the interfaces are implemented.

A server object's interface is specified in IDL, and the IDL specification is compiled to produce the stub and skeleton to be used for that object. For example, you could specify the interface of a server in IDL and then compile the IDL to create the C++ source code for the server's skeleton. You could also compile the same IDL to create a Java stub.

IDL compilers are available for C, C++, SmallTalk, and of course, Java. These compilers translate IDL into stubs and skeletons in the source code of these languages. You then use a language-specific compiler to compile the stubs and skeletons to binary code or byte code.

In order to develop an IDL compiler for a particular language, a language mapping must be developed that shows how the data types and method invocation semantics of IDL map to the language. The Java language mapping has been completed and is available at `http://splash.javasoft.com/JavaIDL/pages/IDLtoJava.html`.

Java IDL

The capability to use Java objects within CORBA is currently being developed by JavaSoft and other software vendors. The JavaSoft project is referred to as Java IDL. The home page of this project is `http://splash.javasoft.com/JavaIDL/pages/index.html`. At the time of this writing, Java IDL is in the Alpha stage and the API has not been published. However, a number of important milestones have been completed:

■ The Java mapping has been published.

■ An IDL compiler has been developed for Java.

■ A portable Java ORB core is available.

■ An ORB, referred to as the Door ORB, is available with the Alpha version of the Java IDL distribution.

■ A Java implementation of IIOP is being developed.

■ A transport module for connecting the portable Java ORB core to Sun's NEO ORB is being developed.

The Java mapping takes each element of the IDL and maps it to Java language elements. Because you know Java pretty well, the mapping provides a great way to learn IDL. The following section introduces the Java IDL compiler and shows how to translate IDL definitions into Java stubs and skeletons.

The portable Java ORB core implements an ORB as a set of Java classes. The ORB core uses the Door ORB as its default ORB protocol, but supports multiple ORB protocols, as shown in Figure 54.3.

FIGURE 54.3.

The Java portable ORB core.

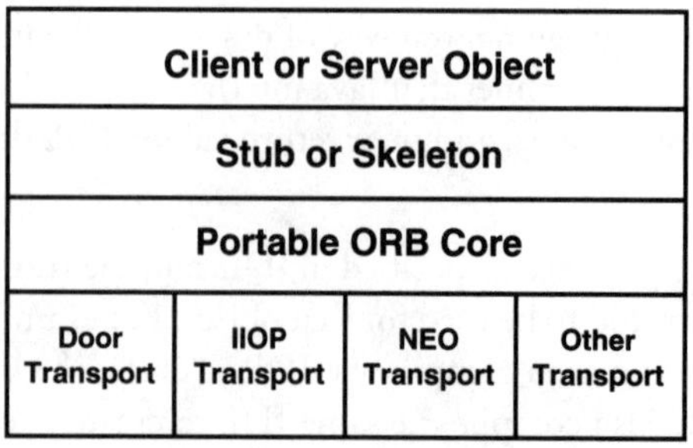

Client or Server Object			
Stub or Skeleton			
Portable ORB Core			
Door Transport	IIOP Transport	NEO Transport	Other Transport

The Door ORB protocol is implemented using TCP/IP and uses *door handles* to identify server objects. Door handles are remote object references. The Door ORB keeps track of which door handles are available to which clients and controls access to server objects based on this information.

The Java IIOP will provide the primary means of connecting the Java ORB to other vendors' ORBs. A separate transport module is being developed to connect the Java ORB with Sun's NEO ORB. NEO (http://www.sun.com/sunsoft/neo/index.html) is Sun's CORBA-based distributed object environment. It provides its own ORB as well as connectivity to legacy Windows applications.

Using `idlgen`

The `idlgen` program translates IDL files to Java stubs and skeletons. The program comes with the Java IDL distribution, which is available from the Java IDL home page. It is located in the `bin` directory of the distribution.

The `idlgen` program is easy to use and comes with a number of options. Check the documentation that comes with the Java IDL distribution for a complete description of these options. There are only a few options that you'll need in most cases:

- `-fclient`—Generates code for a client-side stub
- `-fserver`—Generates code for a server-side skeleton
- `-fcpp`—Runs the IDL source through your C++ compiler's preprocessor
- `-fno-cpp`—Doesn't run the IDL source through your C++ compiler's preprocessor

You must specify either `-fclient` or `-fserver` when you run `idlgen`.

Listing 54.1 provides a small sample IDL description. It defines the `MyServer` interface that is contained in the sample module. An IDL interface corresponds to a Java interface. An IDL module corresponds to a Java package. The `getServerData()` method takes the `string` input argument identified by the `dataID` variable and returns an IDL `string` value.

You can create a Java stub for this interface using the following command:

```
C:\jdk1.1.1\jdg\ch54>idlgen -fclient -fno-cpp MyServer.idl
```

This command generates four Java files in the `example` directory of your `ch54` directory. These files implement the Java client. The `MyServerOperations.java` file is generated by `idlgen` and is shown in Listing 54.2. Note how the `example` IDL module was translated into the `example` Java package and the `MyServer` IDL interface was translated into the `MyServerOperations` Java interface. Also note how the `getServerData()` method was created. You can look through the rest of the Java files that were generated. These files are used to implement the stub of the `MyServer` interface.

Listing 54.1. An IDL description of the MyServer interface.

```
module example {
 interface MyServer {
  string getServerData(in string dataID);
 };
};
```

Listing 54.2. The MyServerOperations.java file generated by idlgen.

```
// ./example/MyServerOperations.java
// from MyServer.idl dated Fri May 09 02:42:22 1997
// by C:\JDK11~1.1\BIN\IDLGEN.EXE (alpha2-961209) dated Mon Dec 16 09:46:25 1996

package example;
public interface MyServerOperations {
    String getServerData(String dataID)
        throws sunw.corba.SystemException;
}
```

Summary

In this chapter, you learned about the current work that is underway at JavaSoft to connect Java objects to objects written in other languages. You learned how ORBs are used to connect distributed objects, how the IDL is used to define object interfaces, and how the idlgen compiler is used to create Java stub and skeleton classes. You also learned about JavaSoft's portable ORB core and its plans to develop protocols to connect the portable ORB core to other ORBs. In the next chapter you'll learn about network computers and how Sun's JavaStation provides a pure Java solution to network computing.

55

Network Computers and JavaStation

Of all the available technologies for implementing a distributed intranet, network computers (NCs) have received the most attention. Network computers have been brought to market by computer giants such as Sun, IBM, Oracle, and others. Even Microsoft and Intel are trying to jump on the network computer bandwagon. Can you guess what programming language is the language of choice for network computer software? I hope you guessed Java.

In this chapter, you'll be introduced to network computers and learn about their advantages and disadvantages. You'll cover the NC-1 specification and review the network computers that are currently in the market. You'll then focus on the architecture and operation of one particular network computer—Sun's JavaStation. You'll learn how the JavaStation works and how it supports both intranet and Internet applications. When you finish this chapter, you'll understand what network computers are all about and how they may be deployed within your organization.

Network Computers

A network computer is a computer that is designed to operate as an integral component of a network rather than as a desktop computer with network connectivity. This difference is subtle, yet significant.

In a desktop PC computer environment, each desktop computer is its own separate domain. Each PC boots locally, maintains its own local file storage, and locally installs most of its applications. These applications are typically compiled into the machine code language that is native to the computer's microprocessor.

The desktop computer's resources consist mainly of application (word processing, graphics, spreadsheet, database, and so on) files that are developed by the desktop user. These resources are "owned" by the user and may be shared over the network. The desktop utilizes the network for file and printer sharing, access to client/server intranet applications, and access to Internet/Web services.

The desktop user is responsible for maintaining his computer using the help provided by his PC support group. The user is also responsible for backing up his files. If the user's computer fails, the user's productivity comes to a halt until his files are recovered and made available on a desktop of a similar configuration.

Contrast the network computer environment with that of the desktop computer. In a network computer environment, the network is a single common shared resource in which all corporate information resides. Network computers extend this resource to employees. Business applications are installed on the network and execute in a distributed fashion across NCs and network servers.

NCs are clients that provide access to the information and applications served by the network. They boot from distributed network servers, load their application programs from these servers, and access files that are stored on the servers. Network applications execute as Java programs on NCs, but their current state is maintained on NC servers. This enables a high level of fault tolerance. If an NC craps out, you can toss it away and plug in a new one and bring up your network application right where you left off.

Maintenance of network applications and the backing up of user files is periodically performed by server administrators.

Advantages of Network Computers

The advantages of NCs are tremendous. First and foremost, deployment of NCs causes an important shift in the way computers are perceived and used within an organization. Instead of being the personal information repositories of individual users, NCs are the conduits by which corporate resources are accessed. This shift in perspective from the individual to the organization affects the way that information is created, stored, and disseminated. The end result is greater online collaboration, coordination, and communication. In a desktop environment, employees must leave their computers to attend meetings in order to collaborate, share information, reach consensus, and make decisions. In an NC environment, the enterprise network replaces unproductive meetings with dynamic, online information exchanges that solve critical problems in a timely manner.

NC applications are tailored to organizational and user needs. Instead of purchasing and installing mass market software applications that try to be all things to all people, network applications are developed around NC software products that are tailored to the needs of the enterprise as well as specific users.

The capability to tailor NC applications makes them easier to use. Instead of being locked into a windowed desktop metaphor, NC applications can be designed using whatever works best for the user. For example, the HotJava Views user environment eschews multiple overlapping windows for an easy-to-use pushbutton interface.

Network applications also are able to balance flexibility and ease of use with standardization. Users are free to tailor network applications to their needs, but they all use the same application. Gone are the problems associated with trying to disseminate files to users running PCs, Macs, and UNIX workstations that run incompatible versions of word processing, graphics, spreadsheet, and other desktop software. Once a new or upgraded network application is installed, it is immediately available throughout the enterprise. Because network applications are configured at the server, the days of scurrying around to each and every user's computer to install new software are gone for good.

Because software is installed centrally on network servers, the organization has more control over the software being run by users. This may mean that users will spend less time playing Free Cell and more time using work-related software.

In addition to the benefits described in the previous paragraphs, NCs are cheaper to purchase than PCs; they are less than half the price of a PC. They are also much cheaper to maintain. Because all software is installed and maintained on network servers, large organizations do not require the huge support staffs needed by those that deploy PCs.

The NC environment is based on the use of open standards. This means that proprietary bottle-necks are eliminated, lowering overall enterprise computing costs. This lower total cost of ownership of NCs is a primary consideration for organizations that deploy NCs.

Finally, NCs are based around the use of the Java Virtual Machine and Java Runtime Environment, greatly enhancing application security. In addition, network server security controls can be used to limit the accesses of individual users.

Disadvantages of Network Computers

While there are a number of advantages to using network computers, there are also some disadvantages. The most significant shortcoming is the current lack of software applications. This disadvantage, however, is quickly diminishing. Major software houses, such as Corel, are porting complete office suites to Java. Given the current interest in Java, it is expected that additional vendors will develop Java application software.

Another short term disadvantage of NCs is that they are new. Some individuals do not like change, and the transition to network computing is a significant one. In any organization there will be individuals who whine, "I liked it better when we used Windows."

A common problem for any organization that moves to a network computing environment is figuring out what to do with legacy hardware and systems. Until legacy applications are ported to the network computing environment, the most prudent solution is to let the legacy systems peacefully coexist. After porting, the system hardware can be converted to network computing resources. (Sun is working on a product that will let low-end PCs run JavaOS and NC applications.) PCs, UNIX, and Macintosh systems can be used to run NC applications by running Java client software on browsers or local JDK installations.

Some individuals fear a lack of control when they change to network computing. Because network applications are configured on network servers, users no longer need to tinker with their systems to install, uninstall, and reinstall software. This is a blessing in disguise. By removing the capability to install and configure applications, you are freeing users to perform their jobs instead of playing with their computers. On the other hand, any sizable NC environment will require a suitable stable of wizards to maintain the network servers.

Because NC applications are distributed across the enterprise network, continuous and reliable network service is essential to business operation. Any significant network failure can bring an organization to its knees. The potential for network failure can be offset by the use of redundant servers, and network topologies and routing strategies that minimize failure impacts.

The Network Computer Standard

Now that we've summarized the advantages and disadvantages of network computers, you're probably wondering exactly what an NC consists of. In order to standardize network computers, Sun, IBM, Oracle, Netscape, and Apple created the Network Computer-1 (NC-1) specification. This specification identifies the following minimum hardware and software capabilities:

- VGA monitor
- Keyboard
- Mouse
- Network interface card
- Sound card and speakers
- JVM
- Java runtime environment
- Java API class libraries
- TCP/IP networking support
- Web browser
- E-mail support
- Multimedia support

From the preceding list, you can see that NCs are reasonably well-stocked. What's missing from the preceding list is hard or floppy disk support. Instead, the specification encourages the use of the BOOTP protocol to boot the NC from a network server.

NOTE

Most companies provide additional features besides those identified in NC-1.

Network Computer Products

A number of vendors have released network computer products that meet the NC-1 standard (or at least come close). These products are summarized in the following subsections. The Sun JavaStation is covered later in this chapter in the "JavaStation" section.

IBM Network Station

The IBM Network Station (`http://www.ibm.com`) meets the NC-1 specification and runs on a PowerPC microprocessor. It comes with 8MB of RAM and is expandable to 64MB. The Network Station also provides extensive terminal emulation capabilities, including X Window, IBM 3270, and IBM 5250 terminal support.

Network Computing Devices HMX

The Network Computing Devices HMX network computer (`http://www.ncd.com`) runs on a high performance R4000 processor. It offers a 1600×1200 pixel monitor and an array of advanced multimedia options. It also provides options for accessing UNIX and Windows applications.

HDS @workstation

The HDS @workstation (`http://www.hds.com`) is an NC that is comprised of an X terminal with the JVM and Netscape Navigator. It runs on the Intel i960 processor using the HDS netOS operating system. It comes with 8MB RAM and is expandable to 128MB. A number of other expansion options, such as hard and floppy disk drives and PCMCIA slots, are available.

NCI NC Software

Network Computer, Inc. (`http://www.nc.com`) is a wholly owned subsidiary of Oracle that provides the NC Desktop, NC Server, and NC Card products. NC Desktop is a software product that provides an HTML- and Java-enabled interface for network computers as well as Web browsing, e-mail, and other applications. The NC Server product provides the software needed to manage a network of NCs. The NC Card is used to authenticate NC users to the network.

JavaStation

The Sun JavaStation was the first computer to meet the NC-1 specification and is the premier network computer on the market. It provides a 100MHz microSPARC II microprocessor and

8MB of RAM that is expandable to 64MB. It supports 10-BaseT or 100-BaseT Ethernet cards and a single RS-232C serial port. It adds 16-bit audio and a speaker.

The graphics card supports 8- or 16-bit color and screen resolutions up to 1024×768 pixels. Both 14- and 17-inch monitors are available in .28 millimeter dot pitch. It comes with a PS-2 keyboard and a two-button mouse.

The best feature of the JavaStation isn't in hardware. The JavaStation runs JavaSoft's JavaOS operating system, which is designed from the ground up to support Java applications in a networked environment. The JavaOS is a fast, small memory footprint operating system for NCs, PDAs, and consumer electronic devices. The JavaOS optimizes the JavaStation for distributed Java applications. (See Chapter 58, "The JavaOS.")

The JavaStation also comes with the HotJava browser and the HotJava Views user interface environment. These applications provide Web browsing, e-mail, distributed calendar, and other capabilities to NC users.

Requirements for Using JavaStation

What makes the JavaStation so special is that it is a true NC in the sense that it boots from a network server, loads applications from the server, and uses the server's file system. Furthermore, the JavaStation is stateless in the sense that it maintains all information about the current state of an application on the server.

The fact that JavaStation relies so heavily on the server is a distinct advantage. It enables all client administration to be performed on the server. Support personnel never have to visit a JavaStation. Users never have to install or configure software. This provides a significant cost savings in terms of reduced maintenance costs and millions of man hours spent by users tinkering with their computers.

The stateless nature of the JavaStation provides other advantages. The user never has to worry about losing data. If his JavaStation fails, he can replace it with a new one, even in the middle of an application. The user never has to back up his data. Because it resides on the server, periodic backup is performed by the server administrator.

NC—Network Server Interaction

JavaStations depend heavily on the network server for their operation. A JavaStation, upon power up, boots the JavaOS from the server using the boot protocol (BOOTP).

After initializing JavaOS, the NC responds to user inputs by loading the client part of network applications from the server and executing this software on the NC. The NC maintains state information on the server and stores application information using the file systems of the network server and other dedicated file servers. The NC makes use of services provided by Web, FTP, mail, and other servers and utilizes Java remote method invocation and database capabilities to interact with enterprise-wide applications and information repositories.

Netra j Server

The Netra j server is the server used by Sun to support network computer applications that use the JavaStation. The Netra j server enables network booting of JavaStations using the BOOTP protocol. It also supports the centralized management of applications used by the JavaStations. The Netra j server provides connectivity to legacy systems and databases via the OpenConnect and OpenVista software packages.

Netra j runs the Solaris operating system on UltraSPARC computers. It comes with the Netscape Enterprise Server, JavaStation management and support software, Java software development tools, and Java applications written for the JavaStation. These tools make it easy to set up a JavaStation network. It takes about an hour to install the Netra server and a JavaStation network.

Developing Java Software Applications for JavaStation

Software for the JavaStation and other NC-1–compliant network computers is written as Java applets and applications. Applets are the preferred solution because they can be executed from the HotJava browser or other Java-enabled browsers that run on the NC. Use of applets is encouraged because applets can also run on non-NC hosts via a browser interface.

NC software can be written as Java application programs. The advantages of applications over applets are that they do not run in the context of a browser window and the security restrictions associated with applets are removed. The disadvantages of applications are that they are less portable and are more difficult to distribute to non-NC hosts.

In general, any Java applet or application that runs on a browser or via the JDK will run on an NC. The advantage of using NCs stems from the low cost of the NC hardware and the even lower costs of maintaining the network application software.

What kind of applications are being targeted to NCs? While it is technically possible to run any application written in Java, some applications are more suited to the NC environment. Sun recommends that NC networks be used to initially support a single mission-critical business function (such as customer support, manufacturing, or shipping) and provide general office productivity software (such as Corel Office for Java).

The reason for focusing on a single business function is to make the NC network and its applications more focused and easier to deploy. It's much easier to deploy an NC network to replace a legacy inventory management system than it is to replace all corporate information systems. By biting off a single function at a time, your support staff will be able to incorporate valuable lessons learned into subsequent NC deployments.

The most well-suited applications for NCs are those that require information dissemination and access to databases, and are limited to a few process-oriented software applications. A good example is patient reception and registration in the medical field. A receptionist would use a JavaStation to enter patient information into a database and schedule a room, nurse, and doctor to treat the patient. NCs would be provided to nurses, doctors, pharmacists, and cashiers for updating the patient's record, entering diagnosis and treatment notes, prescribing/ dispensing medication, and billing.

Applications that are ill-suited to NCs are those that require extensive processing and memory support, such as modeling and simulation, event prediction, and software development. However, even these applications could be supported by NC clients as long as the bulk of the computation is performed on application-specific servers.

JavaStation and the Intranet

The focus of the JavaStation is the intranet, and the JavaStation works well in this environment. A typical intranet deployment of the JavaStation is shown in Figure 55.1. JavaStation *thin clients* are managed by Netra j servers that provide boot up, application loading, and data storage capabilities. The JavaStations also make use of other network file, print, mail, and directory servers. The Netra j servers support connectivity to legacy applications hosted on mainframes and high-end workstations. They also provide bridges to legacy database applications. New network applications are developed using open standards and make use of Web, database, multimedia, VRML, and other technologies. These applications are implemented on Web, database, and application-specific servers and are accessed via Java-based client software that executes on the JavaStations. The simplicity of JavaStation software maintenance makes it possible to deploy new network applications throughout an enterprise within a single day.

The JavaStation also supports Internet applications. The integrated HotJava browser and e-mail capabilities, combined with Telnet and FTP support, provides JavaStation users with the typical Internet client software used on PCs. The multimedia features of the JavaStation support the audio, video, and graphics capabilities expected by desktop PC users.

FIGURE 55.1.

The integration of JavaStations within a company's intranet.

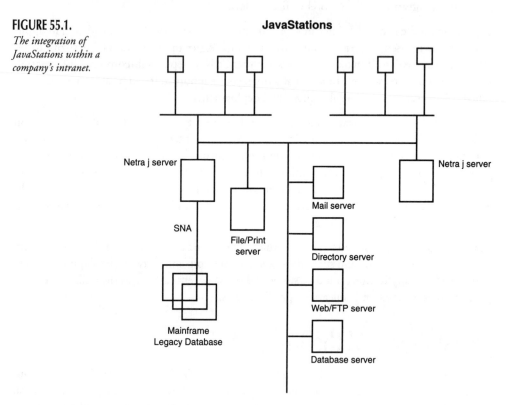

JavaStations

Netra j server

Netra j server

SNA

Mail server

File/Print server

Directory server

Web/FTP server

Mainframe Legacy Database

Database server

Summary

In this chapter, you learned how network computers work and how they are deployed within an organization's intranet. You covered a few of the popular network computer products, but focused on Sun's JavaStation. This chapter completes Part VIII, "Developing Distributed Applications." In Part IX, "Extending Java," you'll learn how to extend the capabilities provided by the JDK.

IX

Extending Java

56

Java Platform and Extensions

Java's immense popularity has resulted in its being implemented on a variety of operating system platforms including Solaris, Windows NT, Windows 95, Linux, Macintosh, and others. Java's omnipresence has made it a platform within a platform. In this chapter, you'll cover the Java Platform and examine each of its parts. You'll also look at the most popular extensions to the Java Platform. You'll revisit Netscape's Internet Foundation Classes and the next generation Java Foundation Classes. You'll also learn about Microsoft's Application Foundation Classes, ObjectSpace's JGL, and Dimension X's Liquid Reality classes. When you finish this chapter, you'll be familiar with the Java Platform and the capabilities provided by its popular extensions.

Operating System Platforms Supporting Java

Java's service mark is "Write Once, Run Anywhere." This is not an overstatement—Java runs on every major operating system platform. Sun's platform of choice is its own Solaris. Java runs on both the SPARC and Intel x86 versions of Solaris. Next in line is Microsoft Windows. Java runs on Windows NT, Windows 95, and with the help of IBM's Applet Development Kit (ADK), it also runs on Windows 3.1. Of course, IBM didn't stop with Windows 3.1. It has ported Java to its AIX, OS/2 Warp, OS/390, and OS/400 operating systems.

Java runs on the Macintosh and on every major brand of UNIX, including the enormously popular Linux. Java also runs on NetWare.

As you would expect, Java runs on the JavaOS. This means that Java will soon be running on hand-held computers and consumer electronic devices. Who knows? It might be in your next TV or toaster!

By definition, Java runs on all network computers.

The Java Platform

Because Java is ubiquitous, it is an operating platform in its own right. But what exactly is the Java Platform? JavaSoft has taken special care to define what it calls the Java Platform.

The Java Platform is the Java virtual machine and a portion of the Java API, referred to as the *Core API*. The Core API is the minimum subset of the Java API that must be supported by the Java Platform. All other Java API classes and interfaces that are not in the Core API are in the *Standard Extension API*. A special API, referred to as the *Embedded API*, is a subset of the Core API that is being defined for consumer electronic devices.

Core API

Because the Core API must be supported by all Java Platforms, it is the API to which most Java applications will be written. The Core API is quite extensive. It includes all of the packages of the JDK 1.1.1, plus other packages that will be added to the next JDK release. These packages include the following:

- Java 2D—Java 2D is an imaging model that includes line art, image processing, and image transformations/composition.
- Java IDL—Java IDL is the Interface Definition Language used to support Java-to-CORBA connectivity.
- Java Commerce API—Part of the Commerce API will be Core and the rest will be Standard Extension. The Commerce API provides the capability to perform electronic financial transactions. The part of the Java API to be included in the Core is referred to as *Java Wallet.* Java Wallet supports the client-side functions of electronic commerce.

Other APIs that are part of the Standard Extension will be added to the Core after they are widely supported.

Standard Extensions

The Standard Extension API includes all packages that are not part of the Core API. The Standard Extension API is not supported on all Java platforms, but it contains the most exciting new API developments. The following Standard Extension API packages are being developed:

- Java Naming and Directory Interface (JNDI)—JNDI provides access to common naming and directory services, such as the Lightweight Directory Access Protocol (LDAP).
- Java Server and Servlet APIs—The Server API facilitates the development of Internet servers, such as Web servers. The Servlet API supports the development of server-side applications.
- Java Commerce API—The Standard Extension part of the Commerce API includes classes and interfaces for implementing the server-side components of electronic financial transactions.
- Java Media Framework (JMF)—The JMF provides a common API for multimedia players, multimedia capture, and multimedia conferencing.
- Java Collaboration API—The Collaboration API supports the development and sharing of multiuser applications over a network.
- Java Telephony API—The Java Telephony API provides access to telephonic communication and supports call control.
- Java Speech API—The Speech API supports speech recognition and synthesis.
- Java Animation API—The Animation API supports 2D animation.
- Java 3D API—The 3D API provides a 3D library that supports VRML.
- Java Management API—The Management API supports network and system management functions.

JavaSoft is continually adding to its list of new APIs that are being developed. If the preceding list does not quench your thirst for Java, check the Java API Overview and Schedule Web page (`http://www.javasoft.com/products/api-overview/index.html`) for new developments.

Netscape's Internet Foundation Classes

Netscape has added its own extensions to the Java Platform for use within the Netscape Navigator. These extensions are referred to as Internet Foundation Classes (IFCs). The IFC is an API for developing Web applications that execute within the context of the Netscape browser. The API includes additional graphical user interface (GUI) controls, besides those included with the AWT; a multifont text object for developing word processor-like applications; drag-and-drop support; animation support; and other capabilities. The IFC can be downloaded from Netscape using the URL `http://developer.netscape.com/library/ifc/index.html`.

JavaSoft, IBM, and Netscape are working on a replacement for IFC referred to as the Java Foundation Class (JFC). The JFC will incorporate the IFC into the Java API and develop a common set of GUI interface controls implemented as JavaBeans.

Microsoft's Application Foundation Classes

Not to be left out, Microsoft has developed its own Java API extensions, referred to as the Application Foundation Classes (AFCs). The AFC consists of a set of class libraries that implements GUI controls and multimedia capabilities. The AFC is written entirely in Java and is built on top of the AWT. It runs on all Java platforms.

ObjectSpace JGL

ObjectSpace, Inc. has made its Generic Collection Library for Java (JGL) free for commercial use by Java Developers from its Web site (`http://www.objectspace.com`). The JGL contains 11 collection objects (such as lists) used to organize other objects and 65 algorithms (such as sorting) used to manipulate groups of objects. The JGL is licensed and provided by most major Java tool vendors.

Dimension X Liquid Reality Classes

Dimension X, the maker of Liquid Motion and Liquid Reality, offers the Liquid Reality Software Developer's Kit (SDK) (`http://www.dimensionx.com/products/lr`), which provides, among other things, over 450 Java classes for developing 3D applications with 3D sound. If you're interested in developing VRML applications for the Web, the Liquid Reality SDK is the place to start.

Native Methods

All the Java API extensions we've mentioned so far have been pure Java extensions. While it is technically possible to extend Java using native methods, this approach is not recommended. By using native extensions, you lose the platform-independent capability of Java.

There are some special circumstances when native methods may be an appropriate solution for Java software development. For example, when interfacing Java to legacy systems, it may be necessary to create a Java wrapper around the API of the legacy system that you're attempting to salvage. In this case, you would use native methods to provide the interface with your legacy code. Other reasons to use native methods are based on the absence of appropriate features within the Java API. For example, you may need to access the native NetBEUI or IPX protocols of your operating system. Native methods can be used to wrap a Java interface on these protocols. Chapter 59, "Creating Native Methods," shows you how to extend the Java Platform using native methods.

Summary

In this chapter, you covered the Java Platform and examined each of its parts. You looked at the most popular extensions to the Java Platform including Netscape's Internet Foundation Classes, Microsoft's Application Foundation Classes, ObjectSpace's JGL, and Dimension X's Liquid Reality classes. In the next chapter, you'll investigate popular Java development tools and learn how they can be used to simplify Java programming.

57

Java Development Tools

The purpose of this book is to teach you to program in Java. As such, I have avoided visual development tools and instead have concentrated on programming examples that are built from scratch. By taking this learning approach, you'll be better prepared to understand the code that is generated by visual development tools.

There is certainly a place for Java development tools. These tools help you to develop Java applications and applets more quickly and effectively. They make you a better organized programmer and help you to build a more maintainable, higher quality product.

In this chapter, you'll examine some of the popular Java development tools and learn how they can be used to simplify the process of Java application and applet development.

Visual Development Tools

Visual development tools simplify the software development process by letting you create the graphical user interface of applets and applications by dragging and dropping user interface components to their desired locations. These tools provide hooks for event handling associated with GUI components, typically letting you create and maintain event handling code by clicking on the GUI components.

Visual development tools commonly provide a class browser for viewing and traversing the application class hierarchy. They also include a source code editor that highlights Java syntax elements using special colors. Most tools support automatic code generation and a just-in-time compiler.

Second generation Java development tools provide JavaBeans support, team programming capabilities, JDBC drivers for popular database products, CORBA compatibility, and tools that simplify connectivity with legacy applications.

Java Workshop

Java Workshop from Sun Microsystems (http://www.sun.com/workshop/java/WSjava_tech.html) is an integrated development environment (IDE) for developing Web pages and Internet applications. It provides a Web browser interface and uses Sun's Visual Java for developing applets and standalone applications. It includes a graphical interface for software development, Java debugging tools, and intranet and Internet publishing capabilities.

Java Workshop runs on Solaris, Windows NT, and Windows 95.

JavaPlan

JavaPlan from Lighthouse Design, Limited (http://www.lighthouse.com/Product.html) is an enterprise-wide visual development tool for Java applets and applications. JavaPlan consists of an integrated set of tools that is aimed at the development of reusable Java components, such as JavaBeans.

JavaPlan supports graphical modeling of applications via an electronic whiteboard. The *whiteboard* is a tool that enables multiuser collaboration over a network. It provides a reverse engineering capability for analyzing compiled byte code files and supports the porting of C and C++ legacy applications. JavaPlan also provides extensive documentation generation capabilities.

JavaPlan runs on Solaris and Windows NT 4.0.

Visual Café

Visual Café from Symantec (`http://www.symantec.com/vcafe/fs_vcafe.html`) provides a top of the line integrated visual development environment for the development of Java applets and applications. It supports drag-and-drop visual application development and comes with an extensive prebuilt component library.

Visual Café supports a sophisticated automated code generation capability that lets users interact with and edit the generated code. It comes with a just-in-time compiler that speeds up the software development process, a class browser/editor, a color-based source code editor that highlights Java syntax, and a graphical source code debugger.

Visual Café Professional provides connectivity to popular database products. Visual Café runs on Windows NT and Windows 95.

VisualAge for Java

VisualAge for Java (`http://www.software.ibm.com/ad/vajava/body.htm`) is IBM's solution for Java software development. VisualAge for Java uses the same technology as other VisualAge products. It is an enterprise-wide Java software development environment that focuses on the development of Java applications that connect to existing server data, transactions, and applications. VisualAge for Java also makes extensive use of JavaBean components via the VisualAge WebRunner toolkit and tools that provide the capability to convert ActiveX components into JavaBeans.

VisualAge for Java includes a source code editor, debugger, class browser, and extensive class library. These tools are provided in a team programming environment. The Enterprise Access Builder tool facilitates the connection of Java code with legacy applications and data.

The BeanMachine tool for developing JavaBeans is being integrated into VisualAge for Java. This tool will simplify the creation and integration of JavaBeans components.

VisualAge for Java runs on Windows NT, Windows 95, and OS/2.

Visual J++

Visual J++ (`http://www.microsoft.com/visualj/indexpgs/start.htm`) is Microsoft's answer to Java development. It includes wizards for applet development, a class browser, an advanced color syntax highlighted source code editor, a visual debugger, and a just-in-time compiler. Besides providing all of the traditional integrated visual development capabilities, Visual J++ Professional includes database support for a plethora of popular database products.

Visual J++ runs on Windows NT and Windows 95.

JBuilder Client/Server Suite

JBuilder Client/Server Suite by Borland (`http://www.borland.com/jbuilder/jfact/jfact.html`) is a component-oriented visual development environment for developing enterprise-wide Java applications. It provides connectivity to SQL databases, supporting both JDBC and ODBC. It supports team programming and provides distributed object support through CORBA connectivity.

The JBuilder Client/Server Suite runs on Windows NT and Windows 95.

Mojo

Mojo by Penumbra Software, Inc. (`http://www.penumbrasoftware.com/`) uses a component-oriented approach to developing Java software. It consists of a GUI Designer and a Coder. The GUI Designer provides drag-and-drop development of an applet or application's graphical user interface. The Coder organizes objects in a way that facilitates code development. An integrated class and method browser lets users view code that is automatically generated.

Mojo is written in Java and runs on all platforms that support Java.

JFactory

The JFactory by Rogue Wave Software (`http://www.roguewave.com/products/jfactory/jfactory.html`) is a Java interface builder and application generator. It supports the visual design of applets and applications, software testing, and code generation. It includes a Project Manager that lets you manage the components comprising an application and an Object Library for maintaining reusable Java components.

JFactory runs on Windows NT, Windows 95, Solaris, HP-UX, and OS/2.

JDesignerPro

JDesignerPro by the BulletProof Corporation (`http://www.bulletproof.com`) consists of an application development environment and application middleware. The application development environment provides traditional visual development tools. The middleware consists of the JAGGServer, which provides JDBC/ODBC database connectivity. BulletProof plans to enhance the JAGGServer to handle IIOP and CORBA connectivity.

JDesignerPro is written in Java and runs on Windows NT, Windows 95, and UNIX platforms.

Summary

In this chapter, you've examined some of the popular Java development tools and learned how they can be used to simplify the process of Java application and applet development. In the following chapter, you'll be introduced to the JavaOS, study its architecture, and learn how it can be used to support networked applications.

58

The JavaOS

One of the most exciting new products released by JavaSoft is the JavaOS version 1.0. JavaOS promises to be the operating system of choice for network computers (NCs), Personal Digital Assistants (PDAs), and commercial electronics devices. This chapter looks at the JavaOS, describes its architecture, and examines its features.

Why JavaOS?

With Java supported on Windows, Macintosh, Linux, and UNIX platforms, why would JavaSoft create JavaOS? It was developed as a means to take Java to future hardware platforms such as PDAs, NCs, and consumer electronics products. Rather than porting an existing operating system to new hardware and running Java on top of that operating system, the engineers at JavaSoft and Sun decided to create JavaOS as a small, memory-efficient, fast, and highly portable operating system (OS) that provides direct support for the Java runtime environment, windowing system, networking capabilities, and other features of the Java API. The goal of the JavaOS is to make Java available on low-powered and low memory devices, such as NCs and PDAs.

JavaOS 1.0 is currently available for the Intel X86, Sun SPARC, and StrongARM hardware platforms. Of course, JavaOS will also run on the JavaChip family of processors (picoJava, microJava, and UltraJava).

JavaOS Features

Besides providing native Java support, the JavaOS has a number of features that make it an ideal operating system for intranet applications. Its small memory footprint and efficient use of processing resources make it an ideal OS for running thin-client applications on network computers. Four megabytes of RAM are sufficient to run JavaOS, HotJava, and other common applications. The JavaOS is being ported to low-end x86 machines, extending their lives as network computers. The JavaOS can be burnt into ROM, allowing it to run on PDAs, handheld PCs, and consumer electronics devices.

The integrated networking support of JavaOS provides the TCP/IP communication capabilities required in an intranet environment. Its remote boot and network login capabilities enable Java applications and support files to be installed on and managed from a central server. This allows system administrators to automatically upgrade client software across the enterprise and to back up client data at periodic intervals. The central management of JavaOS clients enables zero client administration and facilitates enterprise-wide software distribution and management.

The JavaOS windowing system supports the HotJava and HotJava Views user environments providing users with a full graphical user interface and the capability to browse Web pages, run Java applets, and exchange e-mail.

Finally, because Java supports the complete Java API, any pure Java application will run on the JavaOS. This means that new Java applications, such as Corel Office for Java, will run, as is, on the JavaOS. It also means that even small Java platforms, such as PDAs, will be able to take advantage of the mulithreading, memory management, graphics, and networking capabilities of the Java API.

The JavaOS Architecture

The JavaOS is organized into platform-dependent and platform-independent code. The platform-dependent code is referred to as the *kernel* and consists of the *microkernel* and Java virtual machine (JVM). The microkernel provides memory management, interrupt and trap handling, multithreading, DMA, and other low-level operating system functions. The JVM interprets and executes Java byte codes. The purpose of the kernel is to abstract hardware-specific details and provide a platform-neutral interface for the rest of the JavaOS.

The platform-independent code of the JavaOS is referred to as the Java *runtime*. The runtime is written in Java, enabling it to be easily ported and upgraded. The runtime consists of device drivers, networking support, a graphics system, windowing system, and other elements of the Java API. The device drivers support communication with a display monitor, keyboard, mouse, and network interface card. The networking support classes implement the TCP/IP protocol suite using the network device driver. The graphics and windowing systems provide and implement the Abstract Windowing Toolkit (AWT). Other layers support stream I/O and the remaining elements of the Java API.

Figure 58.1 provides an overview of the JavaOS architecture. The JavaOS is a layered operating system that may be tailored for a particular application environment. The layers are functionally independent and may be added or omitted to support the needs of the operating environment. For example, a network computer would utilize all layers of the JavaOS and add the HotJava browser and HotJava Views application environments. A consumer electronics device, on the other hand, may only require a limited number of JavaOS layers to run custom application software.

FIGURE 58.1.
The JavaOS architecture.

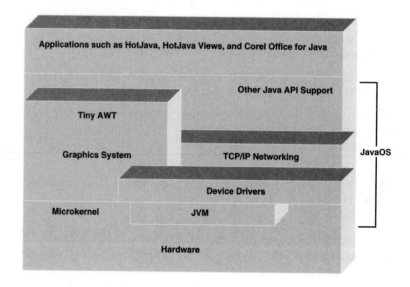

The JavaOS Kernel

Because the JavaOS runtime provides many operating system elements, such as device drivers, file I/O, and windowing and networking support, the JavaOS kernel needs only to provide an interface with the underlying hardware and implement the JVM. This enables the kernel to be small, fast, and portable. The following sections cover the functions performed by the kernel.

System Booting

The JavaOS is intended for a number of different hardware platforms ranging from computer electronic devices to network computers. As such, it must be capable of booting from a variety of sources including disks, CD-ROMs, and network devices. The kernel booting software need not provide all booting capabilities on all hardware platforms, but may be individually tailored for a specific hardware implementation.

Memory Management

Different microprocessors provide varying levels of memory management features to allow memory to be allocated and made available to executing programs. Some microprocessors convert real memory addresses into virtual addresses in order to simplify memory access. Others implement memory access controls that prevent conflicts between programs and enhance system security and integrity. The objective of the memory management function of the JavaOS kernel is to remove these hardware details from the concern of the runtime software by providing a common interface for the allocation and deallocation of memory resources. It uses the underlying hardware memory management capabilities to translate physical memory addresses into virtual addresses and manage the allocation of virtual memory units. The kernel memory management software does not require physical-to-virtual address translation hardware. Instead, it utilizes whatever capabilities are provided by the hardware platform and makes up for any shortcomings using software translation.

The JavaOS operates in a single virtual address space that it shares with the runtime and application programs. This address space is never seen outside of the JVM because the Java memory model does not provide access to memory pointers.

Interrupt and Exception Handling

External devices, such as keyboards, mice, disks, and I/O cards, communicate with an operating system by generating interrupts that are handled and processed by the operating system. Software interrupts, referred to as *traps*, are used in a similar manner by application programs to request services of the OS. Exceptions consist of traps and other OS calls that are used to signal the occurrence of an error or anomalous condition. The interrupt, trap, and exception processing component of the JavaOS kernel utilizes the underlying hardware's interrupt vectoring capabilities to assign interrupts, traps, and exceptions to the appropriate handling routines and device drivers.

Timer Management

The system clock and timer devices generate periodic interrupts to the operating system that are used to keep track of the current time, perform thread scheduling, control the operation of device drivers, and provide API timer support. The JavaOS timer management software utilizes the platform-dependent clock and timer hardware to provide these functions.

Direct Memory Access Control

Direct memory access (DMA) is used by high-speed devices, such as disks, to quickly move information in and out of RAM. The DMA support software of the kernel uses the hardware DMA capabilities to communicate with system devices that use DMA. This software provides a hardware-independent DMA interface to device drivers.

Multithreading Support

The multithreading support function of the kernel manages the memory used by executable threads, saves the current context of a thread, schedules the next thread to be executed, and performs context-switching. The multithreading support function interfaces with the memory management, timer management, and other kernel functions in order to implement multithreading capabilities.

File System Access

Low-level kernel file system support is required in environments, such as a network boot environment, where the kernel must interface with foreign file systems prior to the loading of the device drivers of the runtime system.

Native Code Interface

The kernel may provide the capability to interface with native machine code when that code is required to implement OS functions. An example would be an interface to native code that would drive an advanced video card.

Debugging Support

Certain types of software debugging require the capability to step between machine or byte code instructions under hardware control. Many microprocessors support a special debugging mode of execution. The kernel debugging support software utilizes native debugging facilities to accommodate application-level debugging requirements.

The Java Virtual Machine

The previously discussed kernel components focus on the utilization of the underlying hardware capabilities to support the needs of the JavaOS runtime. The JVM takes `.class` files in the Java byte code format and executes them using the machine code instructions of the underlying microprocessor. In order to do this, the JVM must synchronize and control the operation of the rest of the kernel functions. It utilizes the memory management function to control the allocation of memory resources in the form of Java objects, the interrupt handling, DMA, and timer management functions to support Java device drivers, the multithreading and timer management functions to support Java threads, and so on. The JVM is the nucleus of the Java kernel. The other kernel functions provide support to the JavaOS runtime under the direction and control of the JVM.

JavaOS Runtime Components

The JavaOS runtime consists of operating system–specific functions that are written in Java. While the purpose of the JavaOS kernel is to abstract away hardware-specific characteristics to implement the platform-independent JVM interface, the purpose of the runtime is to provide the platform-independent resources of the Java API to application programs. The components of the Java runtime are covered in the following sections.

Device Drivers

Device drivers are used to enable communication between the operating system and external devices such as display monitors, keyboards, mice, and network interface cards. The availability of device drivers is a critical factor in determining the success or failure of an operating system. How many times have you heard someone say things such as, "I couldn't get Windows NT to work with my sound card" or "The Macintosh doesn't have a driver for that scanner"? The popularity of an operating system and the availability of device drivers are so closely related that it's hard to determine which one causes the other. Operating systems are popular because they support a variety of devices. Device drivers were written for popular operating systems long before they were written for less popular operating systems.

In JavaOS, all device drivers are written in Java (with two minor exceptions, as discussed in the following note). This has advantages and disadvantages. The primary advantage is that device drivers are highly portable. Once a device driver is written for JavaOS, it is highly likely that the device driver will run across all JavaOS hardware implementations.

> **NOTE**
>
> Device drivers require the capability to directly address specific physical memory addresses and the capability to handle device interrupts. The software to implement these capabilities is implemented in C language code and made available via the Memory and Interrupt classes. The Memory class provides direct access to memory addresses. The Interrupt class supports interrupt handling. These classes can only be accessed by registered device drivers.

The disadvantage of using only Java device drivers is that no existing device drivers will work with JavaOS. All device drivers have to be written from scratch. Fortunately, the JavaOS is so popular that many device drivers are being written by hardware vendors and third-party software developers.

TCP/IP Networking

One of the strongest features of the JavaOS is its support for TCP/IP networking. In fact, the JavaOS provides more comprehensive TCP/IP networking support than Windows NT. JavaOS supports the basic IP, TCP, and UDP protocols you learned about in Part V, "Network Programming." It also supports the Internet Control Message Protocol used by the Ping command and network management functions, the Dynamic Host Configuration Protocol (DHCP) used to dynamically assign IP addresses, the Reverse Address Resolution Protocol (RARP) used to determine a host's address, the Domain Name Service (DNS) for hostname-to-IP address translation, and the Network Information Service (NIS) to support network login. It also supports the Network File System (NFS) protocol to share files across a network and the Simple Network Management Protocol (SNMP) to manage network clients and servers. Such extensive networking support is reason alone to dump your old desktop OS and install the JavaOS.

Graphics System

The graphics system of the JavaOS runtime consists of the basic graphics functions required to manage a display monitor and provide the foundation for an AWT implementation. These functions provide the capability to draw and fill geometric objects, render fonts, and control and display cursors. For performance reasons, some of these functions require direct access to physical memory locations and are implemented as native C language methods.

Windowing System

The windowing system of the JavaOS runtime is none other than the AWT. A special Tiny AWT library is used to implement GUI components. The Tiny AWT does not rely on platform-dependent peer classes of the GUI components.

Other API Classes

The Java runtime provides full support of all classes and interfaces of the Java API. This includes stream input and output, applets, math functions, and all of the other goodies found in the core Java API classes.

HotJava and HotJava Views

Although HotJava and HotJava Views are not part of the JavaOS, they are a welcome addition to any Java system, and they provide the graphical desktop environment for running user applications. HotJava is a full-featured Web browser, written entirely in Java. It supports HTML 3.2, FTP downloading, e-mail, and, of course, the execution of Java applets. HotJava Views is a user interface environment referred to by JavaSoft as a *webtop*. It provides pushbutton access to e-mail, calendaring, Web browsing, and other networked applications. HotJava Views was developed to provide a user interface for network computer users.

Summary

In this chapter, you examined the software architecture of the JavaOS and looked at its main features. You also learned about the HotJava browser and the HotJava Views user environment. In the next chapter, you'll get back to Java programming and learn how to extend the Java API through native methods.

59

Creating Native Methods

The power of Java is its portability. Once you write a pure Java applet or program, it can run on any hardware and operating system that supports the Java Platform. That's fine for applications that are written entirely in Java, but what happens if you need to access some non-Java code from your Java program? Java will let you do this, but it comes at the expense of portability. Once you use non-Java code in an application or applet, it can only run on those platforms to which the non-Java code is also ported.

The Java Native Interface (JNI) is the link between your Java application and native code. It allows you to invoke native methods from an application or applet, pass arguments to these methods, and use the results returned by the methods. In this chapter, you'll learn how to write a Java application that invokes a native method to perform a specialized calculation. You'll use the javah header generation tool to generate a C header file for the native method and implement the native method in the C programming language. You'll also cover important information about the conversion of Java types to and from C types. When you finish this chapter, you'll be able to use native methods in your Java applications.

The Java Native Interface

Java's motto is "Write Once, Run Anywhere." In order to accomplish this, Java is designed to provide all that you would need to write a platform-independent program. However, there may be a time when you need to access a platform-dependent function or method. These platform-dependent functions or methods are written in a non-Java language (typically C or C++) and are referred to as *native methods*. Reasons for using native methods include interfacing with a legacy application and accessing capabilities that aren't present (yet) in the Java API.

The Java Native Interface (JNI) provides the capability to access native methods through shared dynamic link libraries, referred to as DLLs on Windows systems. The JNI allows Java programs to invoke the native method, pass arguments to the native method, and receive the results returned by the native method. The JNI also provides programmers with the capability to include the JVM in non-Java applications.

Accessing Native Methods

In order to access a native method from a Java program, you need to create a class for the native method and invoke the native method using the normal Java method invocation syntax.

Listing 59.1 contains the NativeApp program that is used to calculate and display Fibonacci numbers. The Fibonacci numbers are an important sequence of numbers in mathematics. They were developed by Leonardo of Pisa, who was also called Fibonacci, meaning "son of good fortune" in Italian. The first Fibonacci number is 0 and the second Fibonacci number is 1. Subsequent Fibonacci numbers are the sum of the previous two Fibonacci numbers. For example, the first 10 Fibonacci numbers are 0, 1, 1, 2, 3, 5, 8, 13, 21, and 34.

> **NOTE**
>
> For more information on Fibonacci numbers check out the Web page `http://` `www.ee.surrey.ac.uk/Personal/R.Knott/Fibonacci/fib.html`.

Anyway, back to the `NativeApp` program. It takes an integer command-line parameter and assigns it to the variable n. It then creates a new instance of the `Native` class and invokes the instance's `fibonacci()` method, passing it the value of n. The result returned by the method is assigned to the `answer` variable and then displayed to the console window.

> **NOTE**
>
> The names, `NativeApp` and `Native`, are my own. These names are not required to use native methods.

The `NativeApp` program looks pretty simple, as shown in Listing 59.1. You are probably wondering where the native methods are declared and used. The `fibonacci()` method is a native method that is declared in the `Native` class. To find out how this is done, you must move along to the next section.

Listing 59.1. The `NativeApp` program.

```
class NativeApp {
 public static void main(String[] args) {
  if(args.length!=1) {
   System.out.println("Usage: java NativeApp n");
   System.exit(0);
  }
  int n=new Integer(args[0]).intValue();
  int answer = new Native().fibonacci(n);
  System.out.println(answer);
 }
}
```

Creating a Class for Native Methods

In order to simplify the use of native methods, it is always a good idea to put them in their own class. The `Native` class is the class used to declare the `fibonacci()` method, as shown in Listing 59.2. Note that the `fibonacci()` method is declared just like Java methods, except that it is preceded by the `native` keyword and its body is replaced by a semicolon (;). In addition, the `loadLibrary()` method of the `System` class is invoked to load the shared library specified by native. In Windows 95 and Windows NT, this causes the `native.dll` dynamic link library to be loaded. The `loadLibary()` method is invoked as part of a static initializer of the `Native` class. A static initializer is used so that the library is loaded only once, when the `Native` class itself is loaded.

Go ahead and compile `Native.java` and `NativeApp.java` before proceeding to the next section.

Listing 59.2. The `Native` class.

```
class Native {
 public native int fibonacci(int n);
 static {
  System.loadLibrary("native");
 }
}
```

Using `javah`

The `javah` tool is part of the JDK. It is used to create C language header files that specify the interface between C language native methods and Java. It provides a number of options, which you can read about by invoking the `-help` option:

```
C:\jdk1.1.1\jdg\ch59>javah -help
Usage: JAVAH.EXE [-v] [-options] classes...

where options include:
    -help       print out this message
    -o          specify the output file name
    -d          specify the output directory
    -jni        create a JNI-style header file
    -td         specify the temporary directory
    -stubs      create a stubs file
    -trace      adding tracing information to stubs file
    -v          verbose operation
    -classpath  <directories separated by colons>
    -version    print out the build version
```

In practice, the only option that you'll ever need is `-jni`, which creates a JNI-style header file as opposed to the old style header files used with the JDK 1.02.

Create a header for the `Native` class as follows:

```
C:\jdk1.1.1\jdg\ch59>javah -jni Native
```

This causes the `Native.h` file, shown in Listing 59.3, to be created. It is a C language header file. Heed the warning of the first line of the file:

```
/* DO NOT EDIT THIS FILE - it is machine generated */
```

The second line of the file includes the jni.h file that defines the types used in Native.h. The jni.h file contains a number of type and function definitions. If you are a C programmer, you may want to scan this file to see what's in it. The jni.h file is located in the \jdk1.1.1\include directory. It is accessed using the following:

```
#include <jni.h>
```

After that, several conditional compilation directives and a comment are included:

```
#ifndef _Included_Native
#define _Included_Native
#ifdef __cplusplus
extern "C" {
#endif
/*
 * Class:     Native
 * Method:    fibonacci
 * Signature: (I)I
 */
```

The preceding lines beginning with (#) are of no consequence and are included in all header files generated by javah. They are used to determine whether Native.h was previously included in the current compilation.

The comment identifies the Native class, the fibonacci() method, and the method's signature.

The heart of the Native.h file is the declaration of the Java_Native-fibonacci() method. This is the method that you'll need to implement. It specifies that it has three parameters of the types, JNIEnv *, jobject, and jint. The JNIEnv * and jobject parameters are passed to all native methods and usually can be ignored. The JNIEnv * parameter is a pointer to the environment in which the method is invoked. The jobject parameter is a reference to the object or class in which the method is defined (for example, Native). The jint parameter corresponds to the int parameter of the fibonacci() method, shown in Listing 59.2. You'll use this parameter to calculate a Fibonacci number.

The return value of the Java_Native_fibonacci() method looks pretty complicated, but it's not:

```
JNIEXPORT jint JNICALL Java_Native_fibonacci
  (JNIEnv *, jobject, jint);
```

JNIEXPORT and JNICALL surround the actual jint return value. This jint return value is the type of value that you'll actually return from the native method. JNIEXPORT and JNICALL are used to define the function calling sequence and are defined in the jni_md.h file, which is located in the \jdk1.1.1\include\win32 directory on Windows 95 and NT implementations.

The remainder of the file ends the conditional compilation directives.

Listing 59.3. The `Native.h` file.

```
/* DO NOT EDIT THIS FILE - it is machine generated */
#include <jni.h>
/* Header for class Native */

#ifndef _Included_Native
#define _Included_Native
#ifdef __cplusplus
extern "C" {
#endif
/*
 * Class:     Native
 * Method:    fibonacci
 * Signature: (I)I
 */
JNIEXPORT jint JNICALL Java_Native_fibonacci
  (JNIEnv *, jobject, jint);

#ifdef __cplusplus
}
#endif
#endif
```

Implementing Native Methods

The `Native.h` header file tells you what the C implementation of the `fibonacci()` method must look like. In order to implement this method you must create a C language file with the implementation of `Java_Native_fibonacci()`, as shown in Listing 59.4.

The file begins with the following two `include` statements:

```
#include <jni.h>
#include "Native.h"
```

The first line includes the `jni.h` header file that was mentioned earlier. The second line includes the `Native.h` header file that you generated in the previous section.

Following the `include` statements is the C language `fibo()` function which calculates the nth Fibonacci number:

```
int fibo(int n){
 if(n<=1) return 0;
 if(n==2) return 1;
 return fibo(n-1)+fibo(n-2);
}
```

And finally, we include an implementation for `Java_Native_fibonacci()`:

```
JNIEXPORT jint JNICALL
Java_Native_fibonacci(JNIEnv *env, jobject obj, jint n) {
 return fibo(n);
}
```

This method is defined in the same manner as in the `Native.h` header file. All it does is retrieve the n parameter, pass it to `fibo()`, and return the result. The complete code of the `NativeImp.c` file is shown in Listing 59.4.

Listing 59.4. The `NativeImp.c` file.

```
#include <jni.h>
#include "Native.h"

int fibo(int n){
 if(n<=1) return 0;
 if(n==2) return 1;
 return fibo(n-1)+fibo(n-2);
}

JNIEXPORT jint JNICALL
Java_Native_fibonacci(JNIEnv *env, jobject obj, jint n) {
 return fibo(n);
}
```

Creating a Shared Library

At this point, all of our coding is done. All we need to do is compile `NativeImp.c` in such a way that it produces a shared library (that is, a DLL on Windows systems). I use an old version 2.0 of the Microsoft C++ compiler. After Java came out as an alpha version on Windows NT in 1995, I stopped using C++. This is how I compile `NativeImp.c` using the Microsoft C++ compiler:

```
cl -Ic:\jdk1.1.1\include -Ic:\jdk1.1.1\include\win32 -Ic:\msvc20\include -LD
NativeImp.c
➥ c:\msvc20\lib\*.lib -Fenative.dll
```

The same command line works with subsequent versions of Microsoft C++. If you use a different compiler, you'll have to check with its documentation to see how to build a DLL. Note that I include the `c:\jdk1.1.1\include` and `c:\jdk1.1.1\include\win32` directories. These directories are where the `jni.h` and `jni_md.h` files are located.

Your compiler should produce the `native.dll` file, which is the shared library loaded to implement the native method. This file is contained in the `ch55` directory.

Putting It All Together

Now that you've gone through the trouble of implementing the `fibonacci()` native method, you can enjoy your reward. Use the program to generate as many Fibonacci numbers as you desire. For example, you can generate the 13th Fibonacci number as follows:

```
C:\jdk1.1.1\jdg\ch59>java NativeApp 13
144
```

You could have easily implemented `fibonacci()` in Java, but the point of the example was to show you how to create and invoke a native method, pass an argument to the method, and receive the value returned by the method.

Converting Between Java Types and C Types

The one thing that we haven't talked about up to this point is the use of the `jint` type. The JNI defines a list of C language types that correspond to Java types. These types are defined in `jni.h`. The primitive Java `boolean`, `byte`, `char`, `short`, `int`, `long`, `float`, and `double` types are represented by the C `jboolean`, `jbyte`, `jchar`, `jshort`, `jint`, `jlong`, `jfloat`, and `jdouble` types. See a pattern here?

Java objects are represented by the `jobject` type, arrays by the `jarray` type, and `String` objects by the `jstring` type. In addition, the `jni.h` file defines other C types for other kinds of Java objects.

The Java `void` type is implemented by the C `void` type. (They must have run out of Js.)

The Java primitive types are converted to C types in a natural fashion and can be used without problem. However, nonprimitive types, including the `String` type, are not converted to C types in a natural, easy-to-use manner. For example, Java `String` objects are 16-bit Unicode strings where C strings are 8-bit ASCII strings. The `jni.h` file defines a number of conversion functions that can be used to access the converted types. These conversion functions are provided as a convenience. You can use DLLs that are compiled without `jni.h`.

Summary

In this chapter, you learned how to write a Java application that invokes a native method to calculate a Fibonacci number. You used the `javah` header generation tool to generate a C header file for the native method and implemented the native method in the C programming language. You also covered important information about the conversion of Java types to and from C types. In the next chapter, you'll learn all about Java security.

60

Java Security

In this chapter you'll study the security of Java applets and programs. You'll learn about the threats faced by those who use Java applets and programs and the security restrictions placed on Java applets. You'll cover the security features of the Java language, compiler, and runtime environment. You'll also explore the security mechanisms implemented by Java-enabled browsers. When you finish this chapter, you'll be aware of the security issues associated with Java applets and programs, and of the ways Java and Java-enabled browsers resolve these issues.

Threats to Java Security

Those who use Java applets and programs face significant security threats. Information on their computers may be selectively altered, destroyed, or disclosed by those who develop Java applets and programs and those who have the capability to modify them. Damage may result from deliberately planned attacks on your system or from errors that are introduced into Java source or compiled code. Although the threat associated with inadvertent errors is far less than with malicious actions, it cannot be discounted. The damage resulting from instances of Murphy's Law sometimes exceeds that of the most cunning hackers. However, this chapter examines all security threats as if they are the result of deliberate hostile actions.

The Threat Posed by Running Java Programs

The threat posed by a standalone Java program is the same as any other program that you run on your computer. When a program runs on your behalf, it has access to your files, system capabilities, and system resources, and can use this access to modify, delete, or compromise sensitive data or misuse these capabilities and resources. The program's access is limited only by the access controls enforced by your operating system or other security software. In most cases, these access controls are nonexistent or minimally effective. The danger of running a standalone Java program is the same as running any other program that you do not develop yourself. Unless you can verify the security of the program through rigorous analysis and testing, you are forced to trust that the programs will not cause deliberate or inadvertent damage.

The level of trust that you place in a program is usually based on the source from which you obtained the program. You generally place more trust in programs that you receive from well-established software vendors than those that you download from obscure, publicly accessible file archives. Standalone Java programs provide no more or less security than any other programs you may encounter. They may be written to cause the same level of damage to your system as a program that is written in another programming language. Because of this unfortunate fact, the security of standalone Java programs is not explicitly considered in the remainder of this chapter. However, certain applet security countermeasures, such as digital signatures, apply equally as well to standalone programs as they do to applets.

The Threat Posed by Applets

The threat posed by Java applets expands the threat posed by standalone programs to the Web as a whole. Because Web pages may contain applets, scripts, and other types of embedded programming, clicking on a Web page is equivalent to executing a program. The increased danger associated with applets is the lack of control that you have over the programs you execute. Any Web page may bring an insidious intruder into your system. You may, of course, disable the execution of applets by your browser, but doing so eliminates all the potential benefits of Java.

Java Security Features

To counter the threat posed by those who would bring harm to your computer and to mitigate the risk associated with running applets, the developers of Java and Java-enabled browsers have included a powerful set of security features in the Java language, compiler, runtime system, and Web browsers. These security features include security mechanisms that have been specifically designed to eliminate potential security vulnerabilities and other mechanisms. The following sections describe these security features.

> **NOTE**
>
> This section and its subsections address the security issues associated with running applets that are loaded over a network. The same issues apply to applets that are loaded from a local file system, but the potential risks are somewhat lower. The intent is to deal with the worst-case scenario.

Language Security Features

A number of features have been incorporated into the Java language to make it more reliable and capable. Although these features may not have been driven by security concerns, they still help to minimize security risks. The most important of these features is the removal of all pointer-based operations from the Java language. The absence of pointers eliminates entire classes of security vulnerabilities related to memory browsing, the modification of memory-resident code, and illegal access to security-related objects.

Java's use of strong typing also contributes to security. All objects are associated with a well-defined type and cannot be freely converted from one type to another. Methods cannot be used with classes to which they do not apply. Methods cannot return objects of a type that is incompatible with their return type. Strong typing enforces the Java object-oriented approach and prevents numerous kinds of errors that could lead to security-related malfunctions.

Compiler Security Features

The Java compiler also provides features that support security. These features are implemented in the form of compiler checks that prevent errors and undesired actions.

The compiler enforces Java's strong typing by generating compilation errors for statements that violate the language's strong typing rules. It ensures that all methods are appropriate for the objects for which they are invoked.

The compiler checks array operations to make sure that they are valid for the array objects being acted upon and that memory overrun errors do not occur. These checks are duplicated and extended by the runtime system.

The compiler checks all class, interface, variable, and method accesses to ensure that the accesses are consistent with the access modifiers used in their declaration. This prevents classes, interfaces, variables, and methods from being used in unintended ways and enforces the information hiding capabilities provided by the access modifiers.

The compiler generates code that treats `String` objects as constants and supports `String` operations through the `StringBuffer` class. This eliminates overrun errors that could cause in-memory modification of data or code.

The compiler also prevents uninitialized variables from being read and constants from being modified. These checks eliminate errors resulting from incorrect variable reading and writing.

Runtime Security Mechanisms

The Java runtime system is designed to prevent applets from modifying, deleting, or disclosing your files, accessing in-memory programs and data, and misusing network resources. This is accomplished through a *sandbox* approach to security. In this approach, Java applets are given unlimited access to a limited area of the browser window and a limited set of operating system resources. However, all applet access to resources outside of its sandbox is prevented. These restrictions prevent the applet from modifying other areas of the browser window; accessing files on your computer; using services that affect other programs, applet-external data, or the host operating system; and establishing network connections to computers other than the host from which an applet is loaded. The specific security mechanisms that implement these controls are discussed in the following subsections.

> **NOTE**
>
> The JDK 1.1 supports applets that can be digitally signed by their creators. The digital signature of an applet can be used to verify that an applet was signed by a particular person or organization and was not modified by a third party. Because of the traceability and integrity verification features of signed applets, JDK 1.1 provides the capability

to allow signed applets to have a bigger sandbox—that is, it allows signed applets to be trusted to perform specific security-sensitive actions in a secure manner. Signed applets are covered later in this chapter.

Class Loader Security Checks

Applets are loaded over a network using a class loader. The class loader prevents classes that are loaded from the network from masquerading as or conflicting with classes that are resident on the local file system. This ensures that the security-critical classes of the Java API are not replaced by less trustworthy classes that are loaded over a network.

The class loader separates local and network-loaded classes by placing classes that are loaded from a particular network host into a name space that is unique to that host. This approach also keeps network-loaded classes from different hosts from conflicting with each other.

The Byte Code Verifier

The security of classes that are loaded over a network is verified using the byte code verifier. The byte code verifier checks that the loaded classes are correctly formed and that they do not have the capability to violate type and name space restrictions.

The verifier uses a mini-theorem prover to prove that a class file initially satisfies certain security constraints and that when it is executed it will always transition into states in which these security constraints are satisfied. This proof by induction verifies that basic security rules will be enforced throughout the execution of the class file. The verifier proves that no illegal conversion between types can occur, that parameters are correct for the methods and instructions to which they apply, that stack operations do not cause overflows or underflows, that access modifiers are enforced, that no forged pointers can be created, and that register operations do not lead to errors.

Memory Management and Control

The memory locations of Java classes and objects are determined at runtime based on the platform hosting the runtime system and the current memory allocation maintained by the operating system. By performing memory layout decisions at runtime, the potential for inducing errors that cause memory overruns and lead to security malfunctions is greatly reduced. This is because it is very difficult to predict the memory locations at which objects will be stored during code execution. Without this knowledge, complex memory overrun attacks are thwarted.

The Java garbage collector reduces the likelihood that an applet or program may make mistakes in its management of memory resources. Because memory deallocation is automatically handled through the garbage collection process, errors resulting from multiple deallocation of the same memory area or failure to deallocate memory are avoided.

Runtime array bounds checking also reduces the likelihood that errors resulting in illegal memory accesses can occur. By confining array operations to valid array locations, these potential security-related errors are prevented.

Security Manager Checks

The Java security manager provides a central decision point for implementing Java security rules. This ensures that security access controls are implemented in a manageable and consistent manner. The SecurityManager class of the java.lang package may be overridden to implement a custom security policy for standalone Java programs such as those that load applets. A SecurityManager object cannot, however, be created, invoked, or accessed by a network-loaded applet. This prevents applets from modifying the security policy implemented by the runtime system's SecurityManager object.

The applet security policy implemented by the default SecurityManager object varies from one browser to another. Netscape Navigator 3.0 implements a security policy that enforces the following rules for applets that are loaded over a network:

- Applets cannot create or install a class loader or security manager.
- Applets cannot create classes in the local class name space.
- Applets cannot access local packages outside the standard packages of the Java API.
- Applets cannot access files and directories on the local system in any manner.
- Applets may only establish network connections to the host system from which they were loaded.
- Applets cannot create or install a content handler, protocol handler, or socket implementation.
- Applets cannot read system properties that provide information about a user.
- Applets cannot modify system properties.
- Applets cannot run other programs or load dynamic link libraries on the local system.
- Applets cannot terminate other programs or the runtime system.
- Applets cannot access threads or thread groups that are outside of their thread group.
- All windows created by an applet are clearly labeled as being untrusted.

Netscape Communicator and HotJava implement a more flexible applet security policy. These JDK 1.1–capable browsers support the execution of signed applets that can be trusted to perform a limited set of security-sensitive actions in a safe, reliable, and secure manner. The following section discusses the use of applet signatures to extend the bounds of the applet sandbox.

Extending the Sandbox for Signed Applets

The Security API of JDK 1.1 provides the capability to digitally sign an applet and then verify that signature by a browser before an applet is loaded and executed. This capability enables browsers to authenticate an applet to show that it was indeed signed by the source from which it is assumed and that it has not been modified since the time of its signature. Given this additional level of security assurance, signed applets may be considered to be as trustworthy (or more) than shrink-wrapped software that is purchased through retail channels.

For example, when you purchase a software program from a reputable vendor, such as Microsoft, you trust Microsoft not to distribute a program that could compromise the security of your computer. What if you could load an applet that was digitally signed by Microsoft and you could verify Microsoft's digital signature? Wouldn't that applet be as trustworthy as the software that you purchased through retail channels? And if so, wouldn't it seem reasonable to let the signed applet run with the same privileges as the shrink-wrapped software?

This is the rationale for extending the sandbox for signed applets. Certain signed applets are trusted because you trust the organization that signs them. You are free to determine who you trust, be it Microsoft, your company's software support department, or Wiley Bill's Trick Software Shop. You are also given the flexibility to determine what sandbox extensions, if any, you will allow, based on the level of trust that you place in the applet. You could allow some applets to print information, others to read files from your hard drive, and still others to write to your local file system. The important point is that you are in control of determining what applet security policy is in effect on your computer.

> **NOTE**
>
> Chapter 20, "Security and the `java.security` Packages," describes the features provided by the Security API introduced with JDK 1.1. This API supports application-level security by providing classes and interfaces that support message digests, digital signatures, data encryption, key generation and management, and access controls. These additional security capabilities may be used to implement secure, high-integrity communication between applets and Web servers, among the various elements of distributed systems, and within distributed database applications.

The HotJava browser allows the security manager to be configured to support a flexible security policy for signed applets. This policy tailors an applet's capabilities to access local resources (files, printers, programs, and so on) and network resources based upon the signer of the applet. Figure 60.1 shows a screen shot of the HotJava form for customizing applet security.

FIGURE 60.1.

Configuring the HotJava Applet Security Policy.

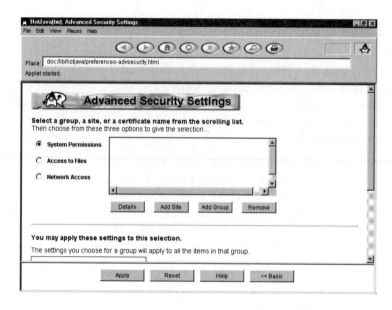

Netscape Communicator also supports signed applets. It allows applet access to local system and network resources to be configured in a similar manner. Figure 60.2 shows the Navigator 4.0 window for applet security configuration. Note that Navigator 2.0 and 3.0 do not support signed applets. The restrictions placed on applets by these pre-JDK 1.1 browsers are discussed earlier in this chapter in the section, "Security Manager Checks."

FIGURE 60.2.

Configuring the Navigator 4.0 Applet Security Policy.

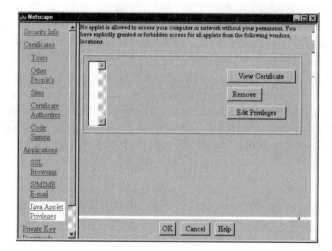

> **NOTE**
>
> Chapter 42, "Using `.jar` Files and Signed Applets," covers the steps involved in creating JAR files and generating and attaching digital signatures to these files.

Staying Current with Java Security Issues

Keeping Java secure is an ongoing process. Several security flaws have been identified to date, and it is reasonable to expect that new Java security flaws will continue to be found. Sun and Netscape have responded quickly to newly discovered security flaws, often releasing fixes within days. As new versions of Java are released and the Java API is expanded, new security flaws will most likely be introduced. To stay current with Java security issues, you should periodically review the FAQ on applet security maintained by JavaSoft. This FAQ contains the status of all known security-related bugs in Java and Java-enabled browsers. The FAQ is located at the URL `http://java.sun.com/sfaq/`. A source of information on general Java bugs in the JDK 1.1 release can be found at `http://www.javasoft.com/products/jdk/1.1/knownbugs/index.html`. The Java security home page, located at `http://java.sun.com/security/`, provides a great place to learn about new security features being incorporated into the JDK.

Summary

In this chapter you learned about the security of Java applets and programs. You were exposed to the threats faced by those who use Java applets and programs, and the security restrictions placed on Java applets. You have covered the security features of the Java language, compiler, and runtime environment and explored the security mechanisms implemented by Java-enabled browsers. You also learned about signed applets and reviewed the security features of the Security API.

Staying Current with Java Security Issues

Summary

X

Appendixes

A

Differences Between Java and C++

The Java language is similar to the C and C++ languages, from which it is derived. These similarities make Java an easy language to learn for those who have previously programmed in C++. These similarities, however, also mask some of the important differences between Java and C++. This appendix summarizes these differences.

Program Structure

The following sections identify the differences between the way Java and C++ programs are structured.

The `main()` Method

Every Java program contains a public class with a `main()` method that serves as the entry point for that program. A typical Java program often references other Java classes included within the same package as the program's class or in other compiled packages.

C++ programs also make use of a `main()` entry point. The C++ analog of Java methods is referred to as a *member function*, or just as *function*. The C++ `main()` function takes two parameters: the int argc variable, which identifies the number of arguments passed to the invoked program, and the argv[][] character array, which contains the program arguments. The Java `main()` method takes a single args[] parameter of the String class. The number of arguments passed via the `main()` method invocation is determined by args.length.

The first value passed as the argument to a C++ program is the name of the program. Subsequent arguments are used to pass other values. Java programs do not pass the program name as the first argument to the program and are therefore off by one position with respect to the arguments passed to C++ programs.

The `main()` function of a C++ program has an int return type by default. This is used to return an exit code. The Java `main()` method has a void return type. The exit() method of the java.lang.System class can be used to return an exit code.

Packages

All Java classes are defined relative to a package, even if it is the default noname package. C++ programs do not support a package approach.

Importing Classes

Java programs reference classes that are defined in other packages using the import statement. C++ classes that are declared outside of a compilation unit are referenced using #include compiler directives.

Functions and Variables Declared Outside of Classes

C++ allows functions and variables to be defined outside the scope of a class. In fact, C++ does not require any classes to be defined.

Java strictly adheres to a class-oriented approach to program design. It is impossible to define a method or variable outside the scope of a class. At least one public class must be defined within a Java program to support the main() method.

Program Development

The following sections identify differences between the way Java and C++ programs are developed.

Compilation and Execution

C++ programs are generally compiled into native machine object code and executed directly as a process running under the local operating system.

Java programs are compiled into the byte code instructions of the Java virtual machine and are executed using the Java interpreter or a Java-compatible browser.

The Preprocessor and Compiler Directives

C++ source code files are processed by a preprocessor before they are submitted to the compiler. Java does not use a preprocessor.

C++ provides the capability to communicate with the C++ compiler using compiler directives. Java does not provide any similar capability.

Java API Versus C++ Libraries

The Java API provides a rich set of classes that can be used to support program development. These classes are largely incompatible with standard C and C++ libraries. Existing C and C++ code can be made available to Java programs using native methods.

Using CLASSPATH

Java uses the CLASSPATH environment variable to identify Java classes. Other environment variables are used by C and C++ programs.

Language Syntax

The following sections identify significant distinctions between the syntax of Java and C++.

Comments

Java and C++ both use the same style of comments. Java also provides the capability to insert doc comments, which are processed by the `javadoc` program to support automated program documentation.

Constants

C++ defines constants using the `#DEFINE` compiler directive and the `const` keyword. Java constants are identified using the `final` keyword.

Primitive Data Types

Java provides the `boolean`, `byte`, `short`, `char`, `int`, `long`, `float`, and `double` primitive data types. C++ supports the same data types but does not use exactly the same type names as Java. Java's `char` data type uses a 16-bit character value to represent Unicode characters. C++ uses 8-bit ASCII `char` values.

Keywords

Java and C++ each identify different sets of reserved keywords, although some keywords are reserved by both Java and C++.

Java Classes Versus C++ Classes

Java classes are declared using a similar, but different, syntax than C++ classes.

C++ allows functions to be separately prototyped from their actual implementation. Java does not allow separate function prototyping.

C++ allows class definitions to be nested. Java does not.

C++ classes support multiple inheritance. Java classes support only single inheritance. Java uses interfaces to implement certain features of multiple inheritance. C++ does not support an analog to the Java interface.

C++ supports templates. Java does not.

Public, Private, and Protected Keywords

The access keywords used by Java and C++ have the same names, but they are used slightly differently. Java access keywords are defined relative to the package in which a class, interface, variable, or method is defined. C++ access keywords are defined relative to the class, data member, and member functions to which they apply.

Variables

A Java *variable* either contains the value of a primitive data type or refers to a Java object. Java *objects* are instances of classes or arrays.

C++ variables are not restricted in the same manner as Java variables. They may refer to primitive data types, instances of classes, arrays, structs, unions, and other data structures.

Types

The types supported by Java are the primitive data types, classes, interfaces, and arrays. C++ supports a variety of types, including primitive types, classes, structs, unions, and defined types. The C++ typedef construct does not have an analog in Java. C++ also supports enumerated data types and Java does not. C++ is much more flexible in providing implicit casting between types. Java supports C++-style casting operators, but does not support implicit casting to the same extent as C++.

Pointers

C++ allows pointers to other objects to be defined. Java does not support pointers. All variables that do not contain the values of primitive data types are references to an object. This reference value may only be changed as the result of an assignment to a new object. The reference value may not be directly tampered with or manipulated as is possible with C++ pointers.

Objects

Java objects are instances of classes or arrays. C++ objects do not include arrays.

Java objects are created using the new operator and are deallocated automatically via the Java garbage collector. C++ objects can be statically or dynamically allocated. Static allocation is accomplished using a type declaration. Dynamic allocation is accomplished using the new operator. C++ variables must be explicitly deallocated using a destructor or the delete operator.

Arrays

Java arrays are similar to C++ arrays; however, there are some significant differences between the two languages.

C++ supports true multidimensional arrays. Java supports single-dimensional arrays; it simulates multidimensional arrays as arrays of arrays. The approach used by Java is actually more flexible than that of C++. Java arrays can consist of arrays of different dimensions.

Java arrays are objects and inherit the methods of the Object class. C++ arrays are not objects in their own right.

Java arrays are allocated using the new operator and are deallocated when they are garbage-collected. Java arrays are separately declared and allocated, although both steps may occur in the same statement. Java arrays may be statically initialized using the same syntax as C++ arrays. However, C++ requires static initializers to be constant expressions, but Java does not.

Java arrays are declared with a more flexible syntax than C++ arrays. In particular, the brackets used in Java array declarations may be associated with the name or type of the array being declared.

Strings

The String and StringBuffer classes are used to implement text strings. These classes allow strings to be treated as objects. C++ implements strings as null-terminated arrays of characters.

null Versus NULL

The Java null keyword is used to identify a variable as not referencing any object. The null keyword cannot be assigned to a variable that is declared with a primitive data type. The C++ NULL value is a constant that is defined as 0.

Statements

The syntax of Java statements is nearly identical to that of C++. However, Java does not support a goto statement, whereas C++ does. Java does, however, reserve the goto keyword.

The Java if, while, and do statements require that the conditional expression used to determine the flow of control results in a boolean value. C++ does not place this restriction on these statements.

Java supports labeled break and continue statements to break out of and continue executing complex switch and loop constructs.

Java provides the synchronized statement to support multithreading operations on critical sections. C++ does not support a synchronized statement.

Java implements exception handling using the try statement and the catch and finally clauses. C++ implements exception handling in a similar manner. C++ does not support a finally clause.

Methods Versus Functions

The C++ analog of the Java method is the member function. C++ functions are more powerful and flexible than Java methods. C++ functions allow variable-length argument lists and optional arguments. Java does not support these capabilities.

C++ allows inline functions to be specified; Java does not. C++ implements friend functions to circumvent the normal class access restrictions. Java does not support friend functions.

Operators

The set of operators supported by Java is based on those provided by C++, although not all C++ operators are supported. In addition, Java provides operators that are not supported by C++. These include the instanceof operator and the + operator used with String objects.

C++ supports operator overloading and Java does not.

B

Moving C/C++ Legacy Code to Java

Java is a new and powerful language that provides many useful features to the software developer. However, if your software organization is typical of most, you will have to trade-off moving to Java with the constraints imposed by dependencies on in-place legacy code. This appendix summarizes the pros and cons of moving existing legacy code to Java. It identifies a spectrum of approaches for accomplishing software transition and discusses the issues involved with each approach. It also covers approaches to translating C and C++ code to Java. This appendix assumes that the transition of C/C++ code to Java is being performed by a moderately large software organization. Some of the software porting issues become insignificant if only a few small programs are translated into Java.

Why Move to Java?

When deciding whether to move existing applications to Java, a trade-off between the advantages and disadvantages of such a move must be considered. This section identifies many of the advantages of Java programs over C- and C++-based applications. The following section considers some disadvantages of using Java and identifies roadblocks to any software transition effort.

Platform Independence

One of the most compelling reasons to move to Java is its platform independence. Java runs on most major hardware and software platforms including Windows 95 and NT, Macintosh, and several varieties of UNIX. Java applets are supported by Java-compatible browsers, such as Netscape Navigator and Internet Explorer. By moving existing software to Java, you are able to make it instantly compatible with these software platforms. Your programs become more portable. Any hardware and operating-system dependencies are removed.

Although C and C++ are supported on all platforms that support Java, these languages are not supported in a platform-independent manner. C and C++ applications that are implemented on one operating system platform are usually severely intertwined with the native windowing system and OS-specific networking capabilities. Moving between OS platforms requires recompilation, as a minimum, and significant redesign, in most cases.

Object Orientation

Java is a true object-oriented language. It does not merely provide the capability to implement object-oriented principles; it enforces these principles. You can develop object-oriented programs in C++, but you are not required to do so; you can use C++ to write C programs as well. Java does not allow you to slip outside the object-oriented framework. You either adhere to Java's object-oriented development approach or you do not program in Java.

Security

Java is one of the first programming languages to consider security as part of its design. The Java language, compiler, interpreter, and runtime environment were each developed with security in mind. The compiler, interpreter, API, and Java-compatible browsers all contain several levels of security measures that are designed to reduce the risk of security compromise, loss of data and program integrity, and damage to system users. Considering the enormous security problems associated with executing potentially untrusted code in a secure manner and across multiple execution environments, Java's security measures are far ahead of even those developed to secure military systems. C and C++ do not have any intrinsic security capabilities. Can you download an arbitrary untrusted C or C++ program and execute it in a secure manner?

Reliability

Security and reliability go hand in hand. Security measures cannot be implemented with any degree of assurance without a reliable framework for program execution. Java provides multiple levels of reliability measures, beginning with the Java language itself. Many of the features of C and C++ that are detrimental to program reliability, such as pointers and automatic type conversion, are avoided in Java. The Java compiler provides several levels of additional checks to identify type mismatches and other inconsistencies. The Java runtime system duplicates many of the checks performed by the compiler and performs additional checks to verify that the executable byte codes form a valid Java program.

Simplicity

The Java language was designed to be a simple language to learn, building on the syntax and many of the features of C++. However, in order to promote security, reliability, and simplicity, Java has left out those elements of C and C++ that contribute to errors and program complexity. In addition, Java provides automated garbage collection, freeing you from having to manage memory deallocation in your programs. The end result of Java's focus on simplicity is that it is easy to get up to speed writing Java programs for those who have programmed in C or C++. Java programs are also less complex than C and C++ programs due to the fact that many of the language elements that lead to program complexity have been removed.

Language Features

The Java language provides many language features that make it preferable to C or C++ for modern software development. On the top of this list is Java's intrinsic support for multithreading, which is lacking in both C and C++. Other features are its exception handling capabilities, which were recently introduced into C++; its strict adherence to class and object-oriented software development; and its automated garbage-collection support. In addition to these features, Java enforces a common programming style by removing the capability to slip outside of the class- and object-oriented programming paradigm to develop C-style function-oriented programs.

Standardization

Although C and C++ have been standardized by the American National Standards Institute (ANSI), many C and C++ compilers provide custom enhancements to the language, usually through additional preprocessor directives. Because these enhancements usually make their way into source code programs, a general lack of standardization results. Java does not yet suffer from any standardization problems because its syntax and semantics are controlled by a single organization.

The Java API

The predefined classes of the Java API provide a comprehensive platform-independent foundation for program development. These classes provide the capability to develop window and network programs that execute on a wide range of hosts. The Java API's support of remote method invocation, database connectivity, and security are unmatched by the API of any other language. In addition, no other language provides as much platform-independent power as Java's API.

Transition to Distributed Computing

Sun has taken important steps to support fully distributed computing with its support of RMI and JDBC. These APIs provide the capability to develop and integrate remote objects into standalone programs and applet-based Web applications.

Rapid Code Generation

Because Java is an interpreted language, it can be used to rapidly prototype applications that would require considerably more base software support in languages such as C or C++. The Java API also contributes to the capability to support rapid code generation. The classes of the Java API provide an integrated, easy-to-use repository for the development of application-specific software. Because the Java API provides high-level windows, networking, and database support, custom application prototypes can be constructed more quickly using these classes as a foundation.

Ease of Documentation and Maintenance

Java software is essentially self-documenting when doc comments and the `javadoc` tool are used to generate software documentation. The excellent Java API documentation is an example of the superior documentation capabilities provided by Java. Because Java software is inherently better structured and documented than C or C++ software, it is generally easier to maintain. In addition, the package orientation of Java software affords considerable modularity in software design, development, documentation, and maintenance.

Reasons Against Moving to Java

Java provides many benefits that make it an attractive language to use in developing new applications and porting existing legacy code. The previous section discussed some of the advantages of porting existing code to Java. This section identifies some of the disadvantages of any C or C++ to Java migration effort.

Compatibility

Although Java is supported on many platforms, it is not supported on all of them. If your target hardware or software platform does not support Java, you are out of luck. Your alternatives are to switch to a different platform or to wait for Java to be ported to your existing software platform.

Compatibility may also be a problem at a design level. Suppose that your target software platform does, in fact, support Java. If your legacy code is designed in such a manner that it is unstructured and incompatible with a class- and object-oriented model, the effort required to migrate the software may be prohibitive.

Performance

Java is interpreted, and although its execution is efficient, it might not meet the performance demands of those applications in which execution speed is of paramount importance. Examples of these types of applications include numerical "number crunching" programs, real-time control processes, language compilers, and modeling and simulation software. Just because your application fits into one of these categories does not necessarily rule out Java, however. For example, the Java compiler is written in Java and performs admirably for small programs. However, its performance is greatly enhanced when it is compiled into native machine code instructions. Java-to-C translators allow programs to be developed in Java and translated into C for native machine code compilation. The translation process generally improves the performance of Java programs.

Retraining

Although Java is simple, easy to learn, and based on C++, some training may be required to get programmers up and running writing Java code. This is especially true if the programmers have been using C++ in a nonstructured, non–object-oriented fashion. I never really appreciated the object-oriented programming features provided by C++ before I began programming in Java. Until I had adopted the Java program-development mindset, I was trying to apply my outdated and inefficient C++ programming techniques to Java software development. After I had made the mental transition to the Java object-oriented programming model, I became much more comfortable and efficient in writing Java programs.

Impact on Existing Operations

Moving legacy code to Java may result in adverse affects on company operations that are supported with legacy software. This is especially true when the legacy code is implemented in a poorly structured, convoluted manner that typically evolves from extensive software patches and upgrades. In the case when existing system software is tightly coupled and fragile, a transition to Java (or any other language) may break the software application to the point where a complete software redevelopment is required.

Cost, Schedule, and Level of Effort

Any software transition effort is subject to cost and schedule constraints. Moving current legacy software to Java might not be cost effective given the current software investment and its expected operational life. The software transition may also have a significant impact on system availability and prior scheduled activities. Transition from C or C++ to Java might also require a significant level of effort that would exceed the expected budget for the maintenance of the legacy code.

Transition Approaches and Issues

There are many ways to integrate Java into existing software applications. This section identifies some of these approaches and explores the issues involved in transitioning to a Java-based software environment.

Interfacing with Existing Legacy Code

One of the easiest ways to introduce Java to an operational environment is to use it to add functionality to existing legacy code. Java programs do not replace existing legacy software; they merely enhance it to support new applications. This approach involves minimal impact to existing software, but does introduce a potentially thorny maintenance issue with Java being added to the current list of languages that must be used to maintain the system.

Incremental Reimplementation of Legacy Code

An incremental approach to reimplementing legacy code in Java can be used to cut over to a Java-based software-development approach while minimizing the impact on existing legacy software. This approach assumes that the legacy software is developed in a modular fashion and can be replaced in an incremental manner. If this is the case, legacy software can be migrated to Java on a module-by-module basis with the legacy code ultimately replaced by new Java software.

Off-Boarding Access to Legacy Objects

If in-place legacy code can be upgraded using Java software that is implemented on separate hardware platforms, Java can be used to "off board" many of the functions performed by the legacy code. The use of off-board server software allows the investment in legacy code to be preserved while expanding the services provided by the system as a whole.

Full-Scale Redevelopment

In some cases, it is more cost effective to keep legacy code in place while completely redeveloping system software from scratch. This is typically the case when the system is subject to large-scale reengineering or when it is so fragile that it breaks as the result of the simplest upgrades. The case where full-scale system redevelopment is necessary is actually an advantage to Java software development because the developed software is under no legacy compatibility constraints and can take full advantage of Java's capabilities.

Translation Approaches and Issues

Translation of existing C and C++ code into Java can be performed in several different ways, depending upon the compatibility of the existing software with Java. This section describes some of the different approaches to software translation.

Automated Translation

Tools and utilities have been developed that allow Java source and byte code to be translated into C to support native machine code compilation. Future Java-integrated software-development environments are planned where either Java or C++ code may be generated based on the configuration of the development software. These development tools will allow easy movement between C++ and Java. These tools require a common set of libraries that can be used by either Java or C++ programs. Automated translation between these two languages will be supported to some extent.

The degree to which C++ programs may be automatically translated into Java will depend on the planning and effort put into the code's design to develop it in a way that makes it more amenable to automated translation. Factors to be considered include the use of compatible libraries, the use of single inheritance, the use of object-oriented programming capabilities, and minimization of the use of incompatible language features.

Manual Translation

Manual translation of C and C++ to Java will probably be the most common approach to moving C and C++ legacy programs to Java. This approach requires you to use two editor windows— one for the legacy C++ code being translated and the other for the Java program being created. Some of the translation is accomplished by cutting and pasting C++ statements into the Java window, making the corrections necessary to adjust for language differences. Other parts of the translation require that new Java classes, interfaces, variables, and methods be developed to implement C++ functions and data structures that cannot be directly translated from C++ to Java. The effectiveness of the manual translation process will be determined by the degree to which the C++ legacy code meets the compatibility considerations identified at the end of the previous section.

Source-Level Redesign

In many cases, manual translation may be hampered by the fact that the C++ legacy code might be written in a style that renders it impossible to migrate using cut-and-paste–based translation methods. In these cases, a class- and object-oriented design of the legacy code needs to be extracted from the legacy code and used as the basis for the Java source code development. A two-level approach to software translation is followed. The legacy code is reverse-engineered to an object-oriented design, and the recovered design information is used to develop a Java software design which is, in turn, translated into Java source code. Code is not translated from one language to another. Instead, legacy code is translated into general design information that is used to drive the Java design and implementation.

I

Index

MACMILLAN COMPUTER PUBLISHING USA

A VIACOM COMPANY

Support:

If you need assistance with the information in this book or with a CD/Disk accompanying the book, please access the Knowledge Base on our Web site at **http://www.superlibrary.com/general/support**. Our most Frequently Asked Questions are answered there. If you do not find the answer to your questions on our Web site, you may contact Macmillan Technical Support **(317) 581-3833** or e-mail us at **support@mcp.com**.

Teach Yourself Java 1.1 in 21 Days, Second Edition

—Laura Lemay & Charles Perkins

This updated bestseller is the definitive guide to learning Java 1.1. *Teach Yourself Java 1.1 in 21 Days, Second Edition* carefully steps you through the fundamental concepts of the Java language, as well as the basics of applet design and integration with Web presentations. Learn the basics of object-oriented programming and Java development. Create standalone cross-platform applications. Add interactivity and animation to your Web sites with Java applets.

CD-ROM includes Sun's JDK 1.1, JDK 1.02 for Macintosh, and Sun's Bean Development Kit for Windows 95, Windows NT, and Solaris.

Price: $39.99 USA/$56.95 CAN   *User Level: New–Casual*
ISBN: 1-57521-142-4   *775 pp.*

Web Publishing Unleashed, Professional Reference Edition

—William Stanek, et al.

Web Publishing Unleashed, Professional Reference Edition is a completely new version of the first edition, combining coverage of all Web development technologies in one volume. It now includes entire sections on JavaScript, Java, VBScript and ActiveX, plus expanded coverage of multimedia Web development, adding animation, developing intranet sites, Web design, and much more! Includes a 200-page reference section. CD-ROM includes scripting tools and Sams.net Web Publishing Library.

Price: $69.99 USA/$98.95 CAN   *Intermediate–Advanced*
ISBN: 1-57521-198-X   *1,501 pp.*

Teach Yourself Internet Game Programming with Java in 21 Days

—Michael Morrison

Game developers will turn to this book for the latest information on game-programming technology. It shows in detail how to use Java to program games for interactive use on the Internet and Web. Because the Net represents the next evolutionary step for game programming, this book is sure to be a hit. Details information on the Java Developer's Kit, class libraries, and multiplayer gaming.

CD-ROM includes the source code from the book, sample applications, and demo software from the leading Internet game-development companies.

Price: $39.99 USA/$56.95 CAN   *User Level: Accomplished–Expert*
ISBN: 1-57521-148-3   *456 pp.*

Java Developer's Reference

—Mike Cohn, et al.

This is the information-packed development package for professional developers. It explains the components of the Java Development Kit (JDK) and the Java programming language. Everything needed to program Java is included within this comprehensive reference, making it the tool developers will turn to over and over again for timely and accurate information on Java and the JDK. CD-ROM contains source code from the book and powerful utilities.

Price: $59.99 USA/$84.95 CAN   *User Level: Accomplished–Expert*
ISBN: 1-57521-129-7   *1,296 pp.*

Add to Your Sams.net Library Today
with the Best Books for Internet Technologies

ISBN	Quantity	Description of Item	Unit Cost	Total Cost
1-57521-142-4		Teach Yourself Java 1.1 in 21 Days (Book/CD-ROM)	$39.99	
1-57521-198-x		Web Publishing Unleashed, Professional Reference Edition (Book/CD-ROM)	$69.99	
1-57521-148-3		Teach Yourself Internet Game Programming with Java in 21 Days (Book/CD-ROM)	$39.99	
1-57521-129-7		Java Developer's Reference (Book/CD-ROM)	$59.99	
		Shipping and Handling: See information below.		
		TOTAL		

Shipping and Handling: $4.00 for the first book, and $1.75 for each additional book. If you need to have it NOW, we can ship product to you in 24 hours for an additional charge of approximately $18.00, and you will receive your item overnight or in two days. Overseas shipping and handling adds $2.00. Prices subject to change. Call between 9:00 a.m. and 5:00 p.m. EST for availability and pricing information on latest editions.

201 W. 103rd Street, Indianapolis, Indiana 46290

1-800-428-5331 — Orders   1-800-835-3202 — FAX   1-800-858-7674 — Customer Service

Book ISBN 1-57521-283-8

Installation Instructions

Windows 95/NT 4

1. Insert the CD-ROM into your CD-ROM drive.
2. From the Windows desktop, double-click on the My Computer icon.
3. Double-click on the icon representing your CD-ROM drive.
4. To run the installation program, double-click on the icon titled SETUP.EXE.
5. Installation creates a program group titled Java Dev Guide. This group will contain icons to browse the CD-ROM.

NOTE

If Windows 95/NT 4.0 is installed on your computer, and you have the AutoPlay feature enabled, the SETUP.EXE program starts automatically whenever you insert the CD into your CD-ROM drive.

UNIX/Linux

Look in the individual directories for software and associated documentation. A README file in standard text format is available in the root directory of the CD-ROM for program descriptions.

Macintosh

1. Insert the CD-ROM into your CD-ROM drive.
2. When an icon for the CD appears on your desktop, open the CD by double-clicking on its icon.
3. Double-click on the icon titled Guide to the CD-ROM and follow the directions that appear.